Poems of
Ossian

The
Poems of
Ossian

and related works

James Macpherson

Edited by Howard Gaskill
with an introduction by
Fiona Stafford

EDINBURGH UNIVERSITY PRESS

Reprinted 1996, 2002, 2003
Transferred to digital printing 2006

Edinburgh University Press
22 George Square, Edinburgh

CIP Data for this publication is available
from the British Library

ISBN-10 0 7486 0707 2 (paperback)
ISBN-13 978 0 7486 07075 (paperback)

The Publisher acknowledges
subsidy from the Scottish Arts Council
towards the publication of
this volume

CONTENTS

INTRODUCTION:
The Ossianic Poems of James Macpherson

Fiona Stafford

During November 1854, Lady Jane Wilde wrote to friends to announce the birth of her second son: "He is to be called Oscar Fingal Wilde. Is not that grand, misty, and Ossianic?"[1] The choice of names reflects her passionate nationalism, since "Oscar" and "Fingal" were meant to evoke the great figures of early Irish legend, but the subsequent comment also shows her debt to the Scottish incarnations of the ancient Celtic heroes, famous throughout the Western world since the 1760s, when James Macpherson had startled the reading public with his Ossianic poetry. For although Macpherson's *Ossian* is often regarded as a curious phenomenon of the later eighteenth century, its enduring appeal is clear from the steady stream of reprints, selections and new editions that continued to appear for the next hundred-and-fifty years. By 1923 the Ossianic characters were still sufficiently recognisable to be featured in an advertising campaign for Bulloch Lade Scotch whisky, while even today there are hotels in the Highlands whose names derive from Macpherson's work. The impact of *Ossian* was immediate and permanent, even if the individual poems eventually fell out of fashion. It is one of those rare texts that generates a life beyond its own pages, not only by providing direct inspiration for numerous poems, paintings and pieces of music, but also through its much more nebulous influence on Western culture, and the popular image of the Celtic.

For Lady Wilde, "Ossianic" was synonymous with grandeur and mistiness, but this distinctive combination of qualities had already enthralled generations of readers. The strange Celtic past created by Macpherson's *Fragments of Ancient Poetry*, *Fingal* and *Temora*, which appeared in rapid succession between 1760 and 1763, prompted astonished eulogies on Ossian's "infinite beauty" and "noble wild imagination" while even doubts over the authenticity of the translations did little to diminish their imaginative power.[2] Thomas Gray, the leading English poet and antiquarian of the day admitted to having "gone mad about them", but it was more the other-worldly atmosphere than the scholarly significance of the poetry that seems to have struck him so forcefully:

> Ghosts ride on the tempest to-night:
> Sweet is their voice between the gusts of wind;
> *Their songs are of other worlds!*

Did you never observe (*while rocking winds are piping loud*) that pause, as the gust is recollecting itself, and rising upon the ear in a shrill and plaintive note, like the swell of an Aeolian harp? I do assure you there is nothing in the world so like the noise of a spirit.[3]

Gray's response anticipates the rapid convergence of the Ossianic and the Gothic, and the way in which writers such as Ann Radcliffe, Sydney Owenson, Charles Maturin and Walter Scott would draw on Macpherson's image of Celtic Scotland to create their own romantic fictions.[4] Nor was the influence merely literary, as more and more visitors travelled North to see wild Morven, take a boat to Fingal's Cave, or like Dorothy Wordsworth, to celebrate the great mountains where "old Ossian's friends, sunbeams and mists, as like as ghosts in the mid-afternoon could be, were keeping company with them".[5]

The extraordinary inspiration of Macpherson's texts can still be seen at Malmaison, where the Ossianic paintings commissioned by Napoleon are kept. For the great French commander, *The Poems of Ossian* represented a military ideal, ("they contain the purest and most animating principles and examples of true honour, courage and discipline, and all the heroic virtues that can possibly exist"),[6] an attitude realised in Girodet's *The Apotheosis of Napoleon's Generals* which shows Ossian and the Fiana embracing the Imperial Army. Rather more Gothic in atmosphere is Gerard's dramatic picture of *Ossian evoking Spirits on the Banks of the Lora*, with its dark silhouettes against a Highland landscape, while in Ingres' *The Dream of Ossian*, the Celtic heroes are frozen in the background of a composition dominated by the figure of the old bard, slumped over his harp.[7]

For English critics, however, the melancholy spirit of Macpherson's work has generally seemed more important than the martial; and it was as the great poet of loss and isolation that the William Hazlitt remembered Ossian, in his selection of the world's principal works of poetry (the others being Homer, the Bible and Dante): "Ossian is the decay and old age of poetry. He lives only in the recollection and regret of the past. There is one impression that he conveys more entirely than all other poets, namely the sense of privation, the loss of all things, of friends, of good name, of country - he is even without God in the world".[8] But even as he emphasised the "decay", Hazlitt recognised the power of Ossian, as a "feeling and a name that can never be destroyed in the minds of his readers".

Some fifty years later, when Matthew Arnold addressed undergraduates at the University of Oxford on *The Study of Celtic Literature*, he too tapped into this Ossianic "feeling" to create his image of the Celt. Like the original readers, Arnold admired the "passion" and "extravagance" of Ossian, but his perception of vanishing genius has a more obvious political dimension than Hazlitt's "old age of poetry". For even as Arnold celebrated the "passion", "sensibility" and "natural magic" of the "Celtic spirit", he asserted that this "colossal, impetuous, adventurous wanderer, the Titan of the early world ... dwindles and dwindles as history goes on, and at last is shrunk to what we now see him ...'They went forth to the war', says Ossian most truly, *'but they always fell'*."[9] In the context of nineteenth-century Irish politics, Arnold's apparently wistful emphasis on the Celts as a once heroic, but now defeated, race is somewhat double-edged.

The political implications of the Ossianic melancholy may also have contributed, albeit subliminally, to the hostility that Macpherson has often attracted from Celtic scholars, even as they have focused their displeasure on his "falsification" of traditional sources. *Fingal* and *Temora* were greeted by a barrage of objections from Dublin, as scholars such as Charles O'Connor and Sylvester O'Halloran criticised Macpherson's free-handling of Gaelic poetry, and particularly the way in which stories from the Fionn and Ulster Cycles had been confused.[10] Even more aggravating was his appropriation of Irish heroes, and the refusal to accept that the Scots were originally inhabitants of Ireland. A further problem, however, may well have been an instinctive rejection of Macpherson's mistiness: his rendering of Fionn and Cuchullain as dim figures living only in the memories of old men and widows and whose power was thus emasculated by time. For the response of those Celtic scholars who have reacted against Macpherson has often been to emphasise the vitality of "true" Gaelic poetry, just as Kenneth Jackson countered what he saw as the spurious "Ossianic" image of the Celtic mind as "something mysterious, magical, filled with dark broodings over a mighty past", with a collection of accurately translated verse where the emphasis is on "vivid imagination", "freshness" and "humour".[11]

Jackson's very charge, however, is evidence of the extraordinary power of *Ossian*; and even if Macpherson's work did constitute a transformation of old Gaelic verse into something quite new, he nevertheless deserves credit from Celtic scholars for saving Gaelic manuscripts that might otherwise have been lost. At the time that Macpherson made his journeys through the Scottish Highlands and Islands in search of Ossian's poetry, little value was placed on the few surviving manuscript collections of early verse and, had it not been for Macpherson, even *The Book of the Dean of Lismore* might have met the same fate as the legendary Douay manuscript, which ended up being used as a firelighter.[12] His very translations, too, by provoking questions over their authenticity, stimulated enormous research into early Gaelic literature and its transmission, which is still being carried out today.[13]

Readers unfamiliar with the heroic verse of the Scottish Highlands or the Ulster and Fionn cycles of early Gaelic literature do not have to overcome the linguist's resistance to a translation that fails to adhere strictly to an original text. The more general association between Macpherson and forgery, however, seems to prove even more of an obstacle. Although the relationship between *The Poems of Ossian* and traditional Gaelic verse has been the subject of major scholarly investigations since the 1760s, and it has long been established that Macpherson drew on traditional sources to produce imaginative texts not modelled closely on any single identifiable original, the idea that he was the author of an elaborate hoax persists (in April 1995, for example, the BBC World Service produced a series of programmes under the title *Fake*, and featured Macpherson in the company of the Hitler Diaries and Piltdown Man). In academic discussions of eighteenth-century literature, James Macpherson is frequently mentioned alongside Thomas Chatterton, even though the Rowley poems and their manuscripts were entirely created by Chatterton. This widespread misconception has made twentieth-century readers especially uneasy about approaching *The Poems of Ossian*. Their ancestors, in an "age of sensibility", were more ready to enjoy the poetry, even as they acknowledged problems of provenance, flying like Goethe's young Werther or Lady Morgan's Wild Irish Girl, to the pleasing melancholy of Macpherson.[14]

Contemporary readers are perhaps less likely to find this kind of emotional solace in *Ossian*, but the revival of critical interest in James Macpherson during the late 1980s and the 1990s suggests that his work is once again attracting serious attention. As literary studies have diversified and texts traditionally marginalised have begun to demand academic attention, Macpherson's *Ossian* has re-emerged from the mist. It is, after all, pre-eminently a text of the margins - not in the sense that it is peripheral to serious literary study, but because it inhabits the margins of contrasting, oppositional cultures. For Macpherson's "translations" involved acts of interpretation not only between Gaelic and English, but also between the oral culture of the depressed rural communities of the Scottish Highlands, and the prosperous urban centres of Lowland Britain, where the printed word was increasingly dominant. Once seen in the context of eighteenth-century Scottish history, *The Poems of Ossian* seem less the work of an inexpert linguist, or an unscrupulous "Scotsman on the make" than a sophisticated attempt to mediate between two apparently irreconcilable cultures.

Although James Macpherson was a Highlander by birth, and grew up in a Gaelic-speaking area of rural Badenoch, he was exposed, from childhood, to influences quite alien to the local environment. Within half a mile of the farm at Invertromie near Kingussie, where he was born in October 1736, stands the imposing fortress erected by the British army in the 1720s as part of the campaign to bring order to the Highlands after the 1715 Rising.[15] Ruthven Barracks, with its commanding view of the Spey valley, formed one of the strategic centres in the great network of roads and bridges built under the command of General Wade to reduce the possibility of further insurrection, and to enable the troops to move swiftly through the mountainous areas. From his earliest days, then, Macpherson's idea of home must have included the presence of soldiers, whose purpose was to check movement among his own extended family.

At the same time, however, he imbibed the traditional culture of his community, growing up in the heart of the clan and listening to the local legends and folklore that had been passed down through generations of

Macphersons. The common Gaelic inheritance of North West Scotland and Ireland meant that ballads and tales relating to Fionn, Oscar and Oisin were current throughout Inverness-shire, and it is easy to imagine James Macpherson as a child sitting at the hearth of his neighbour, the well-known story-teller, Finlay Macpherson of Lyneberack. In the long winter nights, story-telling and recitations of poetry were popular social events, and the eminent nineteenth-century folklorist, J.F. Campbell of Islay included an account of these gatherings in his *Popular Tales of the West Highlands*:

> During the recitation of these tales, the emotions of the reciters are occasionally very strongly excited, and so also are those of the listeners, almost shedding tears at one time, and giving way to loud laughter at another. A good many of them firmly believe in the extravagance of these stories.
>
> They speak of the Ossianic heroes with as much feeling, sympathy, and belief in their existence and reality as the readers of the newspapers do of the exploits of the British army in the Crimea or India; and whatever be the extravagance of the legends they recite respecting them, it is exceedingly remarkable that the same character is always ascribed to the same hero in almost every story and by almost every reciter.[16]

Knowledge of Highland folk mythology was part of Macpherson's upbringing, and he lived in a country where mountains, streams and caves were named after the Celtic heroes.

Life in Badenoch, however, was to change dramatically in 1745, and in the years following the disastrous campaign of Charles Edward Stuart. Though too young to take up arms, James would have seen his uncle, the Clan Chief, Ewan Macpherson of Cluny, join forces with the Jacobite army on the march south. A few months later, they returned, seizing Ruthven Barracks and leaving it to blaze on their way to Inverness. Soon afterwards, those who survived Culloden rallied briefly at Ruthven, before going into hiding as Government troops reclaimed the Highlands. With defeat came disgrace for Clan Macpherson, as Cluny Castle was razed and much of the local community destroyed by the violence of the victorious army. During the summer of 1746, Charles Edward Stuart himself was concealed in Badenoch, together with Cluny, Cameron of Lochiel and a handful of supporters, in a hidden shelter in the woods on the high reaches of Ben Alder. By September, the Prince had escaped to France, but Cluny was to remain a fugitive in his own territory for nine years, while the British army maintained its intensive search for the rebel leader.

Between the ages of ten and eighteen, James Macpherson thus lived through scenes of appalling violence, and saw his home and family under the constant threat of further oppression. During this period, a series of measures were implemented to crush the distinctive Highland way of life, and render the region safe for ever. After 1746, the tartan plaid was banned,

and no Highlander allowed to carry arms or play the bagpipes. The estates
of prominent rebel chiefs (including Cluny) were forfeited to the Crown,
while the ancient systems of ward-holding and heritable jurisdiction were
abolished. Such measures were a more Draconian development from the
earlier, relatively peaceful, attempts to open communications and transport
networks in the Highlands, and to encourage the use of English rather than
Gaelic. But it is in the context of systematic cultural destruction that
Macpherson's efforts to collect old heroic poetry can be seen; they were, at
least in part, an attempt to repair some of the damage to the Highlands sus-
tained in the wake of the Jacobite Risings.[17]

If the period following the Forty Five opened Macpherson's eyes to the
vulnerability of his culture, however, it also made him aware of the limita-
tions being imposed on the local area, and therefore on the inhabitants, ir-
respective of their individual talents. The extravagance of his later life
reveals a great zest not only for material possessions, but also for impress-
ing people on a grand scale - and post-Culloden Badenoch could hardly
offer the opportunity to fulfil such ambitions.[18] Macpherson's intellectual
abilities, however, secured him a place at the University of Aberdeen, and
an academic education which was to prove as important to his subsequent
literary work as his early years in the Highlands.

Macpherson arrived in Aberdeen in the autumn of 1752, when both the
city and the University were undergoing a period of transition. The growth
of trade and industry had stimulated a large building programme and, as
Old Aberdeen declined, the new town with its elegant houses and streets
was expanding rapidly. In the University, too, the traditional Arts curricu-
lum, with its emphasis on Logic, was being replaced by a new course which
began with more empirical subjects, such as History and Natural Philoso-
phy. The progressive atmosphere generated by the lively circle of intellec-
tuals (which included such thinkers as Thomas Reid, Thomas Blackwell,
Alexander Gerard and George Campbell) must have contrasted strongly
with the shattered community Macpherson had left behind, and provided a
very different sort of inspiration to the Highland student. At the same time,
however, Macpherson appears to have found surprising reminders of home
in the texts he studied, and in the approach of his tutors to their research.

The energies of the formidable classical scholar Thomas Blackwell were
directed towards not only the education of his students, but also the societies
of the Ancient World. For Blackwell, Homer's genius was directly related to
the environment in which he lived: the unsettled state of early Greece had
all the variety to inspire the great creative mind, while the language was
still fluid enough to capture his ideas in the most imaginative verse.[19]
Similar admiration for the freedom and energy of early society informs
William Duncan's preface to his translation of *Caesar's Commentaries*
which was published in 1753, the year before he became Macpherson's
tutor. Although apparently presented as a threat to Rome, the German

tribes, with their strength, physical courage and austere lifestyle, had great appeal to Scottish intellectuals of the mid eighteenth century, when anxieties about the corrupting effects of luxury and refinement on civilised states were already developing.[20]

These were strange ideas for a student from the Highlands, who had witnessed at first hand the suppression of a culture deemed "uncivilised" by the ruling powers. Many of the characteristics of the societies admired by Blackwell and Duncan had been part of Macpherson's upbringing: the existence of a popular folk mythology from which poets could draw inspiration, the transmission of verse through an oral tradition, and the role of the bard were all part of traditional Highland culture, while even the violence that Blackwell deemed essential to the creation of an epic was only too familiar. The discovery that, in academic circles, "primitive" might be associated with not only creativity, but even virtue may well have effected the transformation of Macpherson's view of his own culture.[21] Rather than feeling defensive, or merely indifferent to the stories he had known since birth, there were apparently good reasons for regarding them with serious, and even scholarly interest. The emphasis on antiquity too, would have corroborated the Highland veneration for age and tradition, and indeed, the very antiquarian spirit of the classicists, who sought to reconstruct lost societies through careful scholarship, showed Macpherson the value of a culture that had survived apparently unbroken for centuries. When, after his career as an undergraduate, he returned to Ruthven school as a teacher then, it is not surprising that he should have begun to collect the local ballads and tales from oral recitation - that most fragile medium.

Nor was Macpherson alone in his interests. As early as 1512, the Dean of Lismore, James MacGregor, and his brother Duncan, had begun to collect a miscellany of Gaelic poetry, while further collections from Ardchonaill, and Rea, in Caithness, date from 1690 and 1739 respectively. By the 1750s, the desire to record oral poetry had become more urgent and both Donald MacNicol, the Minister of Lismore, and Jerome Stone, a schoolteacher in Dunkeld began collections, while Archibald Fletcher is known to have learned poetry from various people in Argyllshire and dictated it to scribes.[22] It was Stone who first made the heroic poetry accessible to a wider audience, by translating one of the ballads in his collection, *Bas Fhraoch*, and submitting it to *The Scot's Magazine* where it appeared in January 1756 as 'Albin and the Daughter of Mey'. Had it not been for Stone's early death in the same year, he might well have gone on to publish large collections of imaginative translations of Highland verse, since his accompanying letter reveals a desire to promote Gaelic poetry as the work of "simple and unassisted genius", in accordance with the growing aesthetic demand for "Original Genius".[23] Interest in Gaelic poetry was thus spreading beyond the Highland line, and so when James Macpherson, by now a private tutor, met one of Edinburgh's best known literary figures, John Home, on the bowling green at Moffat in October 1759, the scene was set for the production of the first *Fragments* of the English *Ossian*.

John Home's interest in Scottish folklore was already well-established. On his return to Scotland from London early in 1750, he had received the 'Ode on the Popular Superstitions of the Highlands of Scotland' from his friend William Collins, which urged him to seek inspiration in "Fancy's land" and, when he came to write *Douglas*, he drew on Border legend for his plot.[24] To discover a young man from the Highlands, who was not only "a good classical scholar", but who also a collector of Gaelic tales thus seemed a wonderful opportunity for gaining access to the traditional poetry of Northern Scotland.[25] Home asked Macpherson to translate a piece for him. Macpherson was initially very reluctant, but eventually complied, producing 'The Death of Oscur', which appeared a few months later as one of the *Fragments of Ancient Poetry, collected in the Highlands of Scotland*.

The speed with which Macpherson found himself in print, and indeed, at the centre of a great literary controversy, is indicative of the excitement felt by John Home when he read the first translations. Within days, he had shown Macpherson's work to his friends, Alexander Carlyle and George Laurie, and then travelled to see Hugh Blair and other members of the literary society in Edinburgh. Macpherson was duly invited to dinner and, by the following summer, found himself on a journey through the Highlands and Islands in search of more heroic poetry, and in particular the lost epic of ancient Scotland.

Fragments of Ancient Poetry had been published in June 1760, and immediately caught the attention of the press. Extracts were reprinted in the July issues of *The Scots Magazine* and *The Gentleman's Magazine*, while reviewers raved over the new discovery. Although the thin pamphlet contained only 15 short pieces, each apparently lamenting lost warriors, the rhythmic prose, simple diction and striking natural imagery was different in every respect from the poetry that generally appeared in contemporary magazines and miscellanies. Modern readers seemed to be hearing the very voices of a vanished heroic age, and their excitement was overwhelming. But if the *Fragments* seemed the tantalising remains of a lost body of poetry, they also carried the promise of a more substantial work, still waiting to be recovered, as the Preface made clear:

> It is believed that, by a careful inquiry, many more remains of ancient genius, no less valuable than those now given to the world, might be found in the same country where these have been collected. In particular there is reason to hope that one work of considerable length, and which deserves to be styled an heroic poem, might be recovered and translated.[26]

The idea of the Scottish epic also had particular appeal to the Edinburgh literati. Conversations with Macpherson suggested that there were still old men living in the Highlands who could repeat the lost epic from memory and thus, if the translator could be sent out to record any suitable recitations, and to gather up any available manuscripts of verse, the ancient poetry of Scotland might be rescued from oblivion.[27] Nationalistic considerations fuelled the interest of men such as Adam Ferguson, David Hume, Hugh Blair and Lord Elibank, who were conscious of the absence not only of a distinguished literary heritage but also, since the outbreak of the war with France in 1756, of a Scottish militia.[28] Macpherson's enthusiastic talk of a Celtic Homer - a blind bard of the third century, whose great epic described the successful defeat of an invading army by Fingal and his band of heroes - thus seemed to offer a perfect, and timely, boost to the national morale. At the same time, the emphasis on fragmentation seemed to diffuse any threatening Jacobite potential, since the power of the ancient Celts was sufficiently broken to require a Lowland subscription for its recovery, and could thus be purchased for the creation of a new, unified Scottish mythology.

When Macpherson set off for the Northwest in August 1760, he was equipped with a clear agenda: the recovery of Scotland's ancient epic. As he journeyed through the Highlands and across to Skye and the Outer Hebrides, he was helped by a vast number of people. Some recited verse for him directly, some transcribed the tales of elderly local storytellers, some supplied manuscripts and many offered friendship and hospitality. In a matter of weeks, Macpherson had collected bags full of poetry and stories and, with the help of his kinsman, Lachlan Macpherson of Strathmashie, and his friend Andrew Gallie, he set to work on retrieving the commissioned epic.

Exactly what Macpherson did with his Gaelic materials has been the subject of scholarly debate ever since.[29] The results of his researches (including a further tour in the summer of 1761, to Argyllshire and Mull) quickly acquired international fame in the form of *Fingal: An Ancient Epic Poem in Six Books. Together with several Other Poems composed by Ossian the Son of Fingal*, and *Temora: An Ancient Epic Poem in Eight Books. Together with several Other Poems composed by Ossian the Son of Fingal*, and the two volumes were published together in 1765 as *The Works of Ossian*. But the extent to which they were literal translations of original Gaelic poems provoked the most famous controversy of a period marked by debates and disagreements. In the years following Macpherson's death in 1796, the Highland Society of Scotland set up a Committee of investigation which concluded that, although Macpherson had not produced close translations of individual poems, he had nevertheless drawn on the traditional tales collected in his tours, using certain recognisable characters, plots and episodes. He also developed his own very distinctive measured prose as the medium for presenting the Gaelic material in English, and while this was indebted to the prose tales of Gaelic Scotland,[30] it also reflected Macpherson's academically influenced preconceptions about the nature of early

poetry. For while he undoubtedly came across a large number of heroic
ballads in the Highlands, he seems to have regarded his sources somewhat
dismissively as the broken remains of great Celtic epics, and to have seen
the task of recovery in the light of sympathetic restoration, rather than as a
painstaking translation of the miscellaneous mass. As his friend Andrew
Gallie later explained:

> I remember Mr Macpherson reading the MSS. found in Clanronald's,
> execrating the bard himself who dictated to the amanuensis, saying,
> "D--n the scoundrel, it is he himself that now speaks, and not Ossian."
> This took place in my house, in two or three instances: I thence conjec-
> ture that the MSS. were kept up, lest they should fall under the view of
> such as would be more ready to publish their deformities than to point
> out their beauties.
>
> It was, and I believe still is well known, that the broken poems of
> Ossian, handed down from one generation to another, got corrupted. In
> the state of the Highlands and its language, this evil, I apprehend, could
> not be avoided; and I think great credit is due ... to him who restores a
> work of great merit to its original purity.[31]

Macpherson's editorial decisions resulted in an impressive quarto volume
which, with its scholarly page layout and footnote references to classical
authors, seemed more than equal to the original promise of a Scottish epic.

The title poem, 'Fingal', begins *in medias res*, with the arrival of the ships
of Lochlin (Scandinavia), and the rallying of Cuchullin and his men in
defence. Despite warnings from the ghost of Crugal, Cuchullin engages
with the invading force but suffers a humiliating defeat; victory is neverthe-
less secured by the arrival of Fingal, who beats the enemy leader in single
combat. Far from being a straightforward military narrative, however, the
action is interwoven with tales of broken love and premature death, and
rather than sounding triumphantly jingoistic, the tone is generally wistful
and elegiac. The same atmosphere of drifting melancholy pervades the
"Other Poems" which, like their immediate predecessors, *Fragments of
Ancient Poetry*, dwell on loss, isolation and transience:

> His thin ghost appeared, on a rock, like the watry beam of the moon,
> when it rushes from between two clouds, and the midnight shower is on
> the field.—She followed the empty form over the heath, for she knew
> that her hero fell.—I heard her approaching cries on the wind, like the
> mournful voice of the breeze, when it sighs on the grass of the cave.[32]

That *The Poems of Ossian* pleased Macpherson's literary patrons is under-
standable because, irrespective of the political dimension, he had succeeded
in bringing together apparently contradictory aesthetic ideals with remark-
able harmony. The traditional neo-classical view of the epic as the highest
form of poetry had been combined, through the development of the bard
figure and his personal memories, with the newer demands for originality,
individuality and spontaneous composition, while Macpherson's Celts

seemed to satisfy not only the modern admiration for the primitive virtues of courage, action and austerity, but also the fine feelings of an audience tuned to appreciate the melancholy of Gray's *Elegy*, or the gentlemanly behaviour of *Sir Charles Grandison*.

To take Dr Johnson's line on *Ossian*, then, and see it as the concoction of a charlatan is to ignore the complexities of Macpherson's achievement, and indeed the circumstances under which he worked.[33] *Fingal* may not be a direct translation of Gaelic poems that had survived intact since the third century, but neither is it a "fake" or "forgery", because of Macpherson's peculiar situation at the confluence of very different cultures. As a Highlander, he was at liberty to draw on the common pool of stories and characters, whose chronologies had become mixed in the oral tradition centuries before he began to listen to them, and to recreate his own versions of the old tales (it was also common in the Highlands to attribute poems to Ossian, without worrying greatly about questions of transmission and appropriation). As a gentleman with a university education, he was inclined to view the oral tradition as the unreliable medium of a people yet to experience "civilisation", and to share his patrons' hopes that the early poetry of Scotland should have resembled that of Homeric Greece, surviving along with the ancient Gaelic language, as a result of the local geography. Macpherson's *Ossian* is thus a text belonging exclusively to neither Gaelic nor English culture, and can only be understood sympathetically as an attempt to mediate between the two.

The degree of controversy generated by Macpherson's work indicates its resistance to any fixed interpretation since, from its first appearance, it has prompted angrily diverse responses. The very confusion over its authorship has always placed the burden of meaning on the reader, for even those who accepted Macpherson's claim to have translated the works of Ossian were then faced with a text whose author was a mysterious figure from an unknown society, and whose very words had been transformed into a foreign language. Those who insisted that the poetry was modern were perhaps adopting the easier line, because if the "translations" were fake, there was no need to tackle them at all. And yet, even among those who refused to believe that Macpherson was translating Gaelic verse, the degree of moral indignation and desire to expose his supposed fraudulence is still indicative of a surprisingly passionate response.

Readers prepared to enjoy *Ossian*, too, have exhibited an unusual degree of emotion, partly perhaps in response to the hostile criticism, but largely, it seems, in response to the texts themselves. And this is the aspect of the *"Ossian* phenomenon" that has most puzzled twentieth-century readers. For neither the nationalistic dimensions of the dispute, nor the intrinsic antiquarian interest of Macpherson's claims, can entirely account for the way in which *The Poems of Ossian* were read, reprinted and translated into Italian, French, German, Polish, Russian, Danish, Spanish, Dutch, Bohemian and

Hungarian.[34] Nor is it particularly enlightening to reconstruct a "Critical Heritage", since early readers of *Ossian* tended either to fall into eulogistic abstraction, or to sit down and compose their own Ossianic poetry. This very inspirational quality, however, may hold the clue to understanding Macpherson's success, since his work evidently offers readers the opportunity to enter the text and begin creating their own imaginative worlds.

Many of the peculiarities of *The Poems of Ossian* can, indeed, be seen to function as creative catalysts for the reader. The difficulties of following the plot, for example, which led Lord Kames to suggest that Macpherson should add head notes, and rearrange the order of the poems into a more comprehensible, chronological sequence,[35] are also opportunities for readers to make their own connections, and to fill out the narrative gaps with their own stories. The sudden juxtapositions from the main narrative to the tales enclosed within are disorienting, but since so much of the text is constituted from episodes or "digressions", the reader seems to be invited to move further and further into the Ossianic world, leaving behind any critical apparatus. The repetitious nature of the language, imagery, metre and even the plots, has an almost mesmeric quality, while at the same time evoking a landscape and cast of characters sufficiently imprecise to allow the reader's full participation in the creative experience. Just as Macpherson seems to have responded to what he saw as the fragments of a heroic culture with an act of creative reconstruction, so his audience is forced to share the work of restoration, and produce an imaginative experience that is unique to each reader.

The curiously insubstantial nature of Macpherson's texts may also account for the way in which they were so rapidly harnessed by contemporary theorists. Taking their lead, perhaps, from the Dissertations prefacing the Ossianic poetry, aestheticians such as Lord Kames, Hugh Blair and William Duff seized on Macpherson's work as evidence of the creative genius of early societies, and evaluated the text according to their own ideals.[36] *Ossian* seemed to fulfil their expectations of what early poetry was like, and in doing so, confirmed the historicist approach that associated epic grandeur with the earliest periods of society. As a consequence, Macpherson also helped to define the nebulous concept of Sublimity, which Blair saw as one of the "great characteristics" of his texts (the other being "tenderness").[37] If Burke had stressed the importance of fear and obscurity in the sublime elevation of the mind, Blair's emphasis was on simple diction and moral perfection: ideas which he developed in his *Critical Dissertation on The Poems of Ossian* and went on to espouse in his influential *Lectures on Rhetoric and Belles Lettres*.

The creation of *The Poems of Ossian* owed much to the aesthetic ideas of Aberdeen University, and its publication influenced further theory; so too its recent revival has coincided with the explosion of interest in different approaches to literature, many of which may offer further ways in to

Macpherson's enigmatic text. For although the "rehabilitation" of *Ossian* has come about partly as a result of further research into the Gaelic tradition, notably by Donald Meek, it has also derived energy from the newer critical approaches that have sought to set the text in its context, and seen it differently as a result of examining the peculiar circumstances of its composition. With the continuing development of political criticism, and in particular the great interest in colonialism, cultural imperialism and post-colonial theory, *The Poems of Ossian* look less and less like the quaint hoax of a few decades ago.[38]

Nor is *Ossian* accessible only to cultural materialist and historicist readings. Ever since Paul Van Tieghem published his mammoth studies of *Ossian en France* and *Le Préromantisme*, the importance of Macpherson's work in the evolution of European Romanticism has been acknowledged.[39] The full impact of Macpherson's introduction of a largely unknown mythology to a generation of creative talents for whom so much of the classical inheritance had become stale, and who sought in different ways to develop a new artistic identity, has still to be charted adequately, however, as indeed have the more problematic issues of influence (and the anxieties thus engendered) which are both articulated in the text and generated by its own success.

Feminist critics have yet to turn their attention to the Ossianic poetry, but recent studies of sensibility have important implications for Macpherson's texts. The pre-eminence of feeling or "tenderness", for example, could be seen as an early and very influential example of what Anne Mellor regards as the appropriation of the traditionally feminine by male poets of the Romantic period, which in turn looks forward to the feminisation of the Celt by Matthew Arnold and other writers of the later nineteenth century.[40] The plots, too, allow the blurring of gender distinctions; although Malvina plays the traditional muse to the male poet, and many of the female figures are represented as grieving widows, there are also instances of female voices within Ossian's tales, such as that of Colma in 'The Songs of Selma', while some of the women characters are as much viragoes as victims. Indeed it was a characteristic scene of cross-dressing that inspired Angelika Kauffmann in her painting of *Trenmor and Inibaca*, which represents the two figures as remarkably similar and androgynous.

From a formal perspective, too, *The Poems of Ossian* offer numerous avenues for exploration. The peculiar status of Macpherson's work has often diverted critics from seeing it in relation to contemporary English or Scottish literature, except generally as a text of "sensibility" or "Preromanticism". Once placed in the company of the great novels of the period, however, the experimental nature of Macpherson's engagement with epic, his interest in the narrator, and the creation of a complex prose narrative built up from stories within stories, begins to seem exciting and ground-breaking, rather than merely false to a pure original.

Macpherson was at once an innovator and a traditionalist, his texts a curious synthesis of the ancient and the modern. Rather than seeking to judge him according to his supposed intentions, which now seems a somewhat hazardous enterprise in relation to any author, it is perhaps more fruitful simply to read the poems as they appeared in the 1760s, and enjoy them, even if the pleasure of the text now derives from sources rather different from those that inspired Macpherson's original readers.

Fiona Stafford, Somerville College, Oxford

Notes

1. Richard Ellmann, *Oscar Wilde* (London, 1987), 16.
2. See Thomas Gray's letters of June 1760 to Wharton and Stonehewer, *The Correspondence of Thomas Gray*, ed. Paget Toynbee and L. Whibley, rev. edn., H.W. Starr, 3 vols (Oxford, 1935), 2:672-685.
3. ibid, 2:685.
4. Ann Radcliffe, *The Castles of Athlin and Dunblayne* (1789), Sydney Owenson, Lady Morgan, *The Wild Irish Girl* (1806), Charles Maturin, *The Wild Irish Boy* (1808). Scott's debt to Macpherson is complicated by his scepticism concerning the authenticity of *Ossian*, but is nevertheless obvious, particularly in his poetry and in *Waverley* (1814). See his review of the *Report of the Highland Society* in the *Edinburgh Review* 6 (1805), 429-62, and discussions by Robert Crawford, *Devolving English Literature* (Oxford, 1992), 113-32 and Colin Kidd, *Subverting Scotland's Past* (Cambridge, 1993), 256-9.
5. *Recollections of a Tour made in Scotland (AD 1803)* (1805), in *The Journals of Dorothy Wordsworth*, ed. E. De Selincourt, 2 vols (London, 1941), 1:320.
6. Anon, *Ossian's Poems and Mr Hugh Campbell* (London, 1826).
7. See H. Okun, 'Ossian in Painting', *Journal of the Warburg and Courtauld Institutes*, 30 (1967), 327-56; *Ossian*, Catalogue of the Hamburg Exhibition (Paris, 1974).
8. 'On Poetry in General', *Lectures on the English Poets* (1818), *The Complete Works of William Hazlitt*, ed. P. P. Howe, 21 vols (London, 1930-34), 5:18.
9. 'On the Study of Celtic Literature', *The Complete Prose Works of Matthew Arnold*, ed. R. H. Super, 11 vols (Michigan, 1962), 3:370. See also Seamus Deane, *Celtic Revivals* (London, 1985); W. G. McCormack, *From Burke to Beckett*, rev. edn. (Cork, 1994), 226-31.
10. On the Irish response to Macpherson, see Clare O'Halloran, 'Irish Recreations of the Gaelic Past; The Challenge of Macpherson's *Ossian*', *Past and Present*, 124 (1989), 69-95.
11. *A Celtic Miscellany*, ed. K. Jackson, 1951, rev. edn. (Harmondsworth, 1971), 19-20.
12. National Library of Scotland, ADV MS 73. 2. 12/66. See also John Sinclair's edition of *The Poems of Ossian in the Original Gaelic, with a literal translation into Latin, by the late Robert Macfarlan, AM*, 3 vols (London, 1807), 1:40.
13. See for example H. Mackenzie (ed.) *The Report of the Committee of the Highland Society of Scotland, appointed to Inquire into the Nature and Authenticity of The Poems of Ossian* (Edinburgh, 1805); J. F. Campbell, *Leabhar na Féinne* (London, 1872); D. S. Thomson, *The Gaelic Sources of Macpherson's Ossian* (Edinburgh, 1952) and 'Macpherson's *Ossian*: Ballads to Epics', in *The Heroic Process*, ed. B. Almqvist, S. O'Cathan and P. O'Healain (Dublin, 1987); D. Meek, 'The Gaelic Ballads of Scotland: Creativity and Adaptation', in *Ossian Revisited*, ed. H. Gaskill (Edinburgh, 1991).
14. F. Stafford, ' "Dangerous Success": *Ossian*, Wordsworth and English Romantic Literature', *Ossian Revisited*, 49-72. See also J. J. Dunn, 'The Role of Macpherson's *Ossian* in the Development of British Romanticism' unpublished doctoral

dissertation (Duke, 1966); N. Frye, 'Towards Defining an Age of Sensibility', *E.L.H.*, 23 (1956), 144-52.

15.   For biographical information concerning Macpherson, see B. Saunders, *The Life and Letters of James Macpherson* (London, 1894); F. Stafford, *The Sublime Savage: James Macpherson and The Poems of Ossian* (Edinburgh, 1988); P. deGategno, *James Macpherson*, (Boston, Mass., 1989).

16.   From the account given by Hector Maclean, the schoolmaster of Ballygrant in Islay, to J. F. Campbell, *Popular Tales of the West Highlands*, 1860-2, 2nd edn., 4 vols (London, 1890), 1:iv-v.

17.   For the Jacobite context of Macpherson's work, see M. G. H. Pittock, *Poetry and Jacobite Politics in Eighteenth-Century Britain and Ireland* (Cambridge, 1984).

18.   By the time of his death in 1796, Macpherson owned a villa in Putney and an estate in Badenoch, complete with the mansion Robert Adam had designed for him. He was renowned for his extravagant lifestyle.

19.   T. Blackwell, *An Enquiry into the Life and Writings of Homer* (London, 1735).

20.   See for example, Adam Ferguson, *An Essay on the History of Civil Society* (London, 1767); J. Brown, *An Estimate of the Manners and Principles of the Times* (London, 1757).

21.   On the "primitivism" current in Aberdeen, see for example, D. Foerster, 'Scottish Primitivism and the Historical Approach', *P. Q.*, 29 (1950), 307-23; l. Whitney, *Primitivism and the Idea of Progress* (Baltimore, 1934).

22.   Descriptions of these collections, and texts of many of the original poems, are published in J. F. Campbell, *Leabhar na Féinne*.

23.   *The Scots Magazine*, 18 (1756), 15-16; *Report of the ... Highland Society*, Appendix, 99-117. Stone died at the age of 29. The idea of "Original Genius" was publicised by E. Young, *Conjectures on Original Composition* (London, 1759); W. Duff, *An Essay on Original Genius* (London, 1767); but see also K. Simonsuuri, *Homer's Original Genius*, (Cambridge, 1979).

24.   *Douglas* was written c 1754, and performed in 1757. Home was later inspired by Macpherson's work to write an Ossianic tragedy, *The Fatal Discovery*, 1769.

25.   Home's account is recorded in the *Report of the Highland Society*, Appendix, 68-9.

26.   *Fragments of Ancient Poetry, collected in the Highlands of Scotland* (Edinburgh, 1760), Preface, vii (see below, p. 6). The preface was written by Hugh Blair, inspired by discussions with Macpherson.

27.   David Hume's interest in Macpherson's accounts of Highland epic is evident in his letters of August 1760, see *The Letters of David Hume*, ed. J. Y. T. Grieg, 2 vols (Oxford, 1932), 1:329-31. But see also D. Raynor, 'Ossian and Hume', *Ossian Revisited*, 147-63.

28.   R. B. Sher, '"Those Scotch Impostors and their Cabal": *Ossian* and the Scottish Enlightenment', *Man and Nature: Proceedings of the Canadian Society for Eighteenth Century Studies*, 1 (London and Ontario, 1982); R. B. Sher, *Church and University in the Scottish Enlightenment* (Edinburgh, 1985); J. Robertson, *The Scottish Enlightenment and the Militia Issue* (Edinburgh, 1985).

29.   Some important contributions are listed in Note 13 above. But for further examples see: W. Shaw, *An Enquiry into the Authenticity of the Poems ascribed to*

Ossian, 2nd edn (with *An Answer from Mr Clark on the Subject of Ossian's Poems*) (London, 1782); M. Laing (ed) *The Poems of Ossian*, 2 vols (Edinburgh, 1805); P. Graham, *An Essay on the Authenticity of Ossian's Poems* (Edinburgh, 1807); P. H. Waddell, 'The state of the Ossianic Controversy', *Celtic Magazine*, 1 (1876); H. Trevor-Roper, 'The Invention of Tradition: The Highland Tradition of Scotland', *The Invention of Tradition*, ed. E. Hobsbawm and T. Ranger (Cambridge, 1983), 15-41; H. Gaskill, ' "Ossian" Macpherson: Towards a Rehabilitation', *Comparative Criticism*, 8 (1986), 113-46.

30. D. Meek, 'The Gaelic Ballads of Scotland'.

31. A. Gallie to Dr Kemp, 4 March, 1801, *Report of the Highland Society*, 44.

32. 'The Battle of Lora', *Fingal*, 119 (see below, p. 123).

33. Johnson's unsympathetic view of Macpherson's work was published in his *A Journey to the Western Islands of Scotland* (London, 1775). For Macpherson's response, see James Boswell, *Boswell's Life of Johnson*, ed. G. B. Hill, rev. L. F. Powell, 6 vols (Oxford, 1934-50), 2:297-8; F. Stafford, 'Dr Johnson and the Ruffian: New Evidence in the Dispute between Samuel Johnson and James Macpherson', *Notes and Queries*, n.s., 36 (1989), 70-7.

34. G. F. Black, *Macpherson's Ossian and the Ossianic Controversy* (New York, 1926); J. J. Dunn, 'Macpherson's *Ossian*: A Supplementary Bibliography', *Bulletin of the New York Public Library*, 75 (1971), 467-73.

35. A. Tytler, *Memoirs of the Life and Writings of Lord Kames*, 2 vols (Edinburgh, 1807), 2:90.

36. Henry Home, Lord Kames, *Elements of Criticism*, 3 vols (London, 1762), *Sketches of the History of Man*, 2 vols (Edinburgh, 1774); H. Blair, *A Critical Dissertation on the Poems of Ossian* (London, 1763); W. Duff, *An Essay on Original Genius*.

37. Blair, *Critical Dissertation*, below, p. 356.

38. See for example, R. Crawford, *Devolving English Literature*; P. Womack, *Improvement and Romance; Constructing the Myth of the Highlands* (London, 1989).

39. P. Van Tieghem, *Ossian en France*, 2 vols (Paris, 1917); 'Ossian et l'ossianisme', in *Le Préromantisme*, 3 vols (Paris, 1924), 1:195-285. For a more recent survey, see H. Gaskill, '*Ossian* in Europe', *Canadian Review of Comparative Literature*, 21 (1994), 643-78.

40. A. K. Mellor, *Romanticism and Gender* (London, 1993), 23-4. Perhaps the most interesting "feminised" Celt of the late nineteenth century was William Sharp/Fiona Macleod, who edited *The Poems of Ossian* in 1896.

ABOUT THIS EDITION

One may argue about the intrinsic merits of the poetry, and there are no doubt those who would deny that it has any. Yet Macpherson's *Ossian* is one of the most important and influential works ever to have emerged from these islands. Its historical significance is fact, whether we like it or not. That the fact has proved to be a somewhat uncomfortable one, best ignored or suppressed, is suggested by the experience of anyone in the last generation or so who has actually tried to locate a copy of the poems in order to read them. This has not been an impossible task, but the obstacles have been quite formidable. Unless one was lucky enough to pick up the reprint of Laing (1805), published by James Thin in a limited edition in 1971, the only practical option was usually to resort to antiquarian booksellers or university libraries, the result in either case as likely as not being some dusty Victorian tome with an unreliable text and a pious introduction. There has, it is true, been one outstanding modern edition of *Ossian*: Otto Jiriczek's facsimile reprint which appeared in Heidelberg in 1940. The third volume, with its meticulous apparatus of introductory articles, comprehensive variants, copious genealogies, descriptive register of Ossianic names and more, makes Jiriczek's the closest approximation to a historical-critical edition which we are ever likely to see. Unfortunately, it is not much used, even by scholars, unless they happen to have easy library access to it and can read German. I freely admit that my debt to Jiriczek is massive. If the present edition were to do no more than to make his work (or at least a significant part of it) available to the English-speaking world in a usable form, that would seem to me to be sufficient justification. Its ambitions do, however, go a little further.

Here for the first time, as far as I am aware, the entire corpus of Macpherson's Ossianic writing is embraced within a single edition. That is to say, it presents versions of all the poetry contained in the *Fragments*, *Fingal* and *Temora*, together with the expository material in the form of notes and dissertations. In addition, it includes Hugh Blair's *Critical Dissertation*—this was appended to most editions of *Ossian* from 1765 onwards and thus constituted a vital element in the work's reception. As the basis for the text of the *Fragments* I have chosen the second edition which appeared in the same year as the first (1760) and includes an extra poem and some emendations; all differences from the first edition have been duly signalled in the notes. (I have departed from the source only in shifting the 'Advertisement' from the end to the beginning where it seemed to me to be more usefully positioned.) In contrast, the choice of source for the main body of the Ossianic texts was not an easy one to make, and certainly requires some explanation.

The publication history of *Ossian* is perhaps not inordinately complex, but neither it is as simple as those who talk about the work as if it constituted a single fixed entity would have us believe. *Fingal* made its first appearance in December 1761 (dated 1762). The success was such that it was reissued the following month. This so-called "second edition" is thus identical with the first. *Fingal* was followed in March 1763 by *Temora*. Both were published as handsome (and expensive) quarto volumes. It is these that are reproduced by Jiriczek. It was not until the second half of 1765 that a "popular" edition in more affordable octavo format was published. This was the two-volume combined *Works of Ossian* which styles itself the "third edition", but is effectively only the second. It does, however, represent a genuinely new edition in that it contains some 400 textual revisions. These are admittedly mostly of a minor nature, but not always—for instance, many of the notes are rewritten, a few are excised or truncated, and others expanded or added. The *Works* also offered the bonus of Blair's authoritative *Critical Dissertation*, complete with authenticating 'Appendix'. Though it was to be officially superseded in 1773, it is in fact this edition which proved most influential on the Continent. It is from the text of 1765 that Goethe translates in *Werther*; and the only significant French translations—widely read in other countries—are based on it. Given the enormous impact of *Ossian* in Europe, this seems as good a reason as any for making the *Works* text available again. Another is the nature of the "carefully corrected, and greatly improved" two-volume *Poems of Ossian* of 1773. It is neither. According to Macpherson himself, "one of the chief improvements, on this edition, is the care taken, in arranging the poems in the order of time; so as to form a kind of regular history of the age to which they relate" (see below, p. 412). And perhaps a case could be made for arguing that the new order does indeed make for a more pleasant reading experience, since some of the best work, in the form of shorter, more purely lyrical pieces, now comes first and the reader is not immediately plunged into bulky dissertations and even bulkier epics. However, the text has been mutilated. It undergoes an extensive stylistic revision: the staccato effect of the insistently paratactic prose is unbearably intensified by the ruthless pruning of conjunctions, and the jettisoning of commas in favour of full stops and full stops in favour of exclamation marks; the variable-length dashes which are such a distinctive feature of the earlier editions and which are an extremely effective form of rhythmic punctuation, particularly if the poetry is to be read aloud, are abandoned *en masse*. Past tenses are altered to the present, presumably in order to suggest spontaneous utterance, though the effect on the reader is confusing and ultimately wearying. Other changes, for instance the more consistent use of quotation marks for direct speech, might seem unobjectionable, if not particularly necessary. And perhaps some of the altered images have not sustained much harm. Yet whatever one makes of such revisions—and some contemporaries clearly did approve—it is difficult to find any defence for Macpherson's procedure with his notes. In itself the fact that he omitted and abbreviated so many might not be held against him, had he made a proper job of it which he certainly did not (the many resulting incongruities are pointed out in my own notes)—and were it not for his motives. The removal from *Fingal* of all the parallel passages drawn from Homer, Virgil, Milton *et al.* was perhaps only to be expected, since they had no longer featured in *Temora*. But by making these and other changes Macpherson was now not so much helping to emphasize Ossian's authenticity as underlining his own originality. It is authorial vanity which is really behind so many of these revisions. Macpherson is tired of being an epigone and is evidently no longer willing to be upstaged by a figure he regards in large part (and in larger part than is warranted) as his own creation. He is jealous of Ossian. Hence the attempt to downplay the blind bard's role as creator of—rather than character in—the poetry. That this goes hand in hand with vehement reassertion of its authentic status is not in itself such a paradox. The poems did after all owe their existence to a genuine and ancient literary tradition, and who was it who had taken the trouble to drag this out of obscurity and mediate it to an astonished world? And was it not this very tradition which sanctioned the attribution of one's own poetry to the legendary bard? The latter was not, however, expected to reach down from his airy hall and snatch all the glory. It seems that Macpherson could not bear, either to be disbelieved or to be taken at his word. Be that as it may, all this leaves the 1773 text as something of a mess. It is a mess which has been bequeathed to us in edition after edition ever since. In the Preface Macpherson tells us that he has now resigned the poems for ever to their fate (p. 412). There is no evidence of his involvement in the three further English editions which appeared before his death in 1796 (though in his later years he was occupied with the production of a Gaelic Ossian which was eventually published in 1807). He definitely would not have given his imprimatur to Malcolm Laing's debunking edition of 1805. This is a major achievement and it is good to have it, if only for the annotations which are often rather funny (mostly intentionally so). But it has to be said that it is a unique hybrid which bears only a rather distant relationship to anything ever published as the "genuine" article. Laing uses the revised text of 1773, but reproduces the poems in the order of the first two editions. He does not include the dissertations, either Macpherson's or Blair's. When it suits his purposes he quotes from the original notes, though these are often arbitrarily truncated, as indeed are some from the 1773 edition, that is, if they are not omitted altogether. In this he anticipates the practice of his successors. For the process of pruning down Macpherson's notes, and indeed (according to Jiriczek) making adjustments to the actual text, was to continue in edition after edition throughout the nineteenth century.

If the reader is to gain an adequate impression of what it was that caused such a sensation when it first appeared, the 1773 *Ossian*, or any of its offspring, would seem to me to represent the worst possible choice. As the basis for a new edition the 1765 text suggested itself for a number of reasons, most of which have already been given. In terms of the poetic text it does not really constitute a half-way house, since it is much closer to the original editions of 1762 and 1763 which are in any case apparently those later used by Macpherson as the starting-point for his radical stylistic overhaul. The notes and dissertations are a different matter, and there it is possible to gain fascinating glimpses into the evolution of Macpherson's attitudes. For any such development to be visible it was necessary that everything written by Macpherson about Ossian be reproduced, in the form of earlier and later prefaces, and most obviously in that of comprehensive variant readings. Variants are also offered for the poetic text, but the extensive nature of the later revisions meant that these had of necessity to be selective. In the main only significant differences are noted, these consisting for the most part of variations in imagery. One criterion for deciding which variants to include was whether or not I considered that the difference would show in a (German) translation—unlikely, for instance, in the case of close synonyms. Changes in syntax and punctuation have generally not been noted, unless they significantly affect the meaning or appear to throw light on which text Macpherson had in front of him for his revisions in 1773. The convention adopted for the listing of variants is, I hope, reasonably transparent: initial expression from text (in whole or ellipsis), followed by], followed by variant, followed by year of edition. With regard to Macpherson's notes: these are flagged with an [M] at the end; there follow any variants, and then editorial annotations (signalled by the use of italics). It was clearly not feasible to reproduce them in the form of foot-rather than endnotes. The reader therefore finds himself confronted with pages of poetic text, many or most of which are littered with note numbers, and having no way of knowing which of these refer to Macpherson's notes, editorial notes or textual variants. One strategy which might be recommended is simply to ignore them all and attempt to savour the text without distraction. That is not an option which was realistically open to Macpherson's contemporaries who often had to contend with pages containing minimal Ossian, and maximal Macpherson, not to mention Homer and Virgil. With respect to the latter I have to admit to a reluctant compromise. In order not to add further to an already unwieldy critical apparatus, I have dispensed with the reproduction of Latin or Greek quotations in those cases (the overwhelming majority) where Macpherson offers translations. Such omissions are indicated by [gr.q.] for "Greek quoted", [l.q.] for "Latin quoted", followed by the original reference, where given, and then the translation (usually Pope or Dryden).

Macpherson's spelling tends to be somewhat idiosyncratic and inconsistent, but no attempt has been made to standardize or correct it, except in the case of obvious misprints. All three editions show variations in the spelling of names, for instance in the use of accents and hyphens. They are here reproduced as given.

Finally, I should like to express my heartfelt thanks to Jutta Gaskill for the many hundreds of hours spent typing and tirelessly checking the text. Macpherson can rarely have had a more patient reader. Thanks are also due to my parents for their constant help and encouragement. Anything that is good about this edition is dedicated to the memory of Peter Gaskill.

Howard Gaskill, Edinburgh, August 1995

FRAGMENTS

OF

ANCIENT POETRY,

Collected in the HIGHLANDS of SCOTLAND,

AND

Translated from the GALIC or ERSE Language.

The SECOND EDITION.

Vos quoque qui fortes animas, belloque peremtas
Laudibus in longum vates dimittitis ævum,
Plurima securi fudistis carmina Bardi.[1]

LUCAN.

Advertisement.

In this edition some passages will be found altered from the former. The alterations are drawn from more compleat copies the translator had obtained of the originals, since the former publication. One entire poem is also added; which stands N° XIII. in this edition. It may be proper to inform the public, that measures are now taken for making a more full collection of the remaining works of the ancient Scottish Bards; in particular for recovering and translating the heroic poem mentioned in the preface.

P R E F A C E [2].

The public may depend on the following fragments as genuine remains of ancient Scottish poetry. The date of their composition cannot be exactly ascertained. Tradition, in the country where they were written, refers them to an æra of the most remote antiquity: and this tradition is supported by the spirit and strain of the poems themselves; which abound with those ideas, and paint those manners, that belong to the most early state of society. The diction too, in the original, is very obsolete; and differs widely from the style of such poems as have been written in the same language two or three centuries ago. They were certainly composed before the establishment of clanship in the northern part of Scotland, which is itself very ancient; for had clans been then formed and known, they must have made a considerable figure in the work of a Highland Bard; whereas there is not the least mention of them in these poems. It is remarkable that there are found in them no allusions to the Christian religion or worship; indeed, few traces of religion of any kind. One circumstance seems to prove them to be coeval with the very infancy of Christianity in Scotland. In a fragment of the same poems, which the translator has seen,[3] a Culdee or Monk is represented as desirous to take down in writing from the mouth of Oscian, who is the principal personage in several of the following fragments, his warlike atchievements and those of his family. But Oscian treats the Monk and his religion with disdain, telling him, that the deeds of such great men were subjects too high to be recorded by him, or by any of his religion: A full proof that Christianity was not as yet established in the country.

Though the poems now published appear as detached pieces in this collection, there is ground to believe that most of them were originally episodes of a greater work which related to the wars of Fingal. Concerning this hero innumerable traditions remain, to this day, in the Highlands of Scotland. The story of Oscian, his son, is so generally known, that to describe one in whom the race of a great family ends, it has passed into a proverb; "Oscian the last of the heroes."

There can be no doubt that these poems are to be ascribed to the Bards; a race of men well known to have continued throughout many ages in Ireland and the north of Scotland. Every chief or great man had in his family a Bard or poet, whose office it was to record in verse, the illustrious actions of that family. By the succession of these Bards, such poems were handed down from race to race; some in manuscript, but more by oral tradition. And tradition, in a country so free of intermixture with foreigners, and among a people so strongly attached to the memory of their ancestors, has preserved many of them in a great measure incorrupted to this day.

They are not set to music, nor sung. The versification in the original is simple; and to such as understand the language, very smooth and beautiful. Rhyme is seldom used: but the cadence, and the length of the line varied, so as to suit the sense. The translation is extremely literal. Even the arrangement of the words in the original has been imitated; to which must be imputed some inversions in the style, that otherwise would not have been chosen.

Of the poetical merit of these fragments nothing shall here be said. Let the public judge, and pronounce.[4] It is believed, that, by a careful inquiry, many more remains of ancient genius, no less valuable than those now given to the world, might be found in the same country where these have been collected. In particular there is reason to hope that one work of considerable length, and which deserves to be styled an heroic poem, might be recovered and translated, if encouragement were given to such an undertaking. The subject is, an invasion of Ireland by Swarthan King of Lochlyn; which is the name of Denmark in the Erse language. Cuchulaid, the General or Chief of the Irish tribes, upon intelligence of the invasion, assembles his forces; councils are held; and battles fought. But after several unsuccessful engagements, the Irish are forced to submit. At length, Fingal King of Scotland, called in this poem, "The Desert of the hills," arrives with his ships to assist Cuchulaid. He expels the Danes from the country; and returns home victorious. This poem is held to be of greater antiquity than any of the rest that are preserved: And the author speaks of himself as present in the expedition of Fingal. The three last poems in the collection are fragments which the translator obtained of this Epic poem; and tho' very imperfect, they were judged not unworthy of being inserted. If the whole were recovered, it might serve to throw considerable light upon the Scottish and Irish antiquities.

FRAGMENT

I.[5]

SHILRIC, VINVELA.

VINVELA.

My love is a son of the hill. He pursues the flying deer. His gray dogs are panting around him; his bow-string sounds in the wind. Whether by the fount of the rock, or by the stream of the mountain thou liest; when the rushes are nodding with the wind, and the mist is flying over thee, let me approach my love unperceived, and see him from the rock. Lovely I saw thee first by the aged oak of Branno;[6] thou wert returning tall from the chace; the fairest among thy friends.

SHILRIC.

What voice is that I hear? that voice like the summer-wind.——I sit not by the nodding rushes; I hear not the fount of the rock. Afar, Vinvela, afar I go to the wars of Fingal. My dogs attend me no more. No more I tread the hill. No more from on high I see thee, fair-moving by the stream of the plain; bright as the bow of heaven; as the moon on the western wave.

VINVELA.

Then thou art gone, O Shilric! and I am alone on the hill. The deer are seen on the brow; void of fear they graze along. No more they dread the wind; no more the rustling tree. The hunter is far removed; he is in the field of graves. Strangers! sons of the waves! spare my lovely Shilric.

SHILRIC.

If fall I must in the field, raise high my grave, Vinvela. Grey stones, and heaped-up earth, shall mark me to future times. When the hunter shall sit by the mound, and produce his food at noon, "Some warrior rests here," he will say; and my fame shall live in his praise. Remember me, Vinvela, when low on earth I lie!

VINVELA.

Yes!—I will remember thee—indeed my Shilric will fall. What shall I do, my love! when thou art gone for ever? Through these hills I will go at noon: I will go through the silent heath. There I will see the place of thy rest,[7] returning from the chace. Indeed, my Shilric will fall; but I will remember him.

II.[8]

I sit by the mossy fountain; on the top of the hill of winds. One tree is rustling above me. Dark waves roll over the heath. The lake is troubled below. The deer descend from the hill. No hunter at a distance is seen; no whistling cow-herd is nigh. It is mid-day: but all is silent. Sad are my thoughts alone.[9] Didst thou but appear, O my love, a wanderer on the heath! thy hair floating on the wind behind thee; thy bosom heaving on the sight; thine eyes full of tears for thy friends, whom the mist of the hill had concealed! Thee I would comfort, my love, and bring thee to thy father's house.

But is it she that there appears, like a beam of light on the heath? bright as the moon in autumn, as the sun in a summer-storm,[10] comest thou lovely maid over rocks, over mountains to me?[11]—She speaks: but how weak her voice! like the breeze in the reeds of the pool. Hark!

Returnest thou safe from the war? Where are thy friends, my love? I heard of thy death on the hill; I heard and mourned thee, Shilric!

Yes, my fair, I return; but I alone of my race. Thou shalt see them no more: their graves I raised on the plain. But why art thou on the desert hill? why on the heath, alone?

Alone I am, O Shilric! alone in the winter-house. With grief for thee I expired. Shilric, I am pale in the tomb.

She fleets, she sails away; as grey mist before the wind!—and, wilt thou not stay, my love? Stay and behold my tears? fair thou appearest, my love! fair thou wast, when alive!

By the mossy fountain I will sit; on the top of the hill of winds. When mid-day is silent around, converse, O my love, with me! come on the wings of the gale! on the blast of the mountain, come! Let me hear thy voice, as thou passest, when mid-day is silent around.

III.

Evening is grey on the hills. The north wind resounds through the woods. White clouds rise on the sky: the thin-wavering[12] snow descends. The river howls afar, along its winding course. Sad, by a hollow rock, the grey-hair'd Carryl sat. Dry fern waves over his head; his seat is in an aged birch. Clear to the roaring winds he lifts his voice of woe.

Tossed on the wavy ocean is He, the hope of the isles; Malcolm, the support of the poor; foe to the proud in arms! Why hast thou left us behind? why live we to mourn thy fate? We might have heard, with thee, the voice of the deep; have seen the oozy rock.

Sad on the sea-beat shore thy spouse looketh for thy return. The time of thy promise is come; the night is gathering around. But no white sail is on the sea; no voice but[13] the blustering winds. Low is the soul of the war! Wet are the locks of youth! By the foot of some rock thou liest; washed by the waves as they come. Why, ye winds, did ye bear him on the desert rock? Why, ye waves, did ye roll over him?

But, Oh! what voice is that? Who rides on that meteor of fire! Green are his airy limbs. It is he! it is the ghost of Malcolm!—Rest, lovely soul, rest on the rock; and let me hear thy voice[14]—He is gone, like a dream of the night. I see him through the trees. Daughter of Reynold! he is gone. Thy spouse shall return no more. No more shall his hounds come from the hill, forerunners of their master. No more from the distant rock shall his voice greet thine ear. Silent is he in the deep, unhappy daughter of Reynold!

I will sit by the stream of the plain. Ye rocks! hang over my head. Hear my voice, ye trees! as ye bend on the shaggy hill. My voice shall preserve the praise of him, the hope of the isles.

IV.[15]

CONNAL, CRIMORA.

CRIMORA.

Who cometh from the hill, like a cloud tinged with the beam of the west? Whose voice is that, loud as the wind, but pleasant as the harp of Carryl? It is my love in the light of steel; but sad is his darkened brow. Live the mighty race of Fingal? or what disturbs my Connal?

CONNAL.

They live. I saw them return from the chace, like a stream of light. The sun was on their shields: Like a ridge of fire they descended the hill.[16] Loud is the voice of the youth; the war, my love, is near. To-morrow the enormous Dargo comes to try the force of our race. The race of Fingal he defies; the race of battle and wounds.

CRIMORA.

Connal, I saw his sails like grey mist on the sable wave. They slowly came to land.[17] Connal, many are the warriors of Dargo!

CONNAL.

Bring me thy father's shield; the iron shield of Rinval; that shield like the full moon when it is darkened in the sky.

CRIMORA.

That shield I bring, O Connal; but it did not defend my father. By the spear of Gauror he fell. Thou mayst fall, O Connal!

CONNAL.

Fall indeed I may: But raise my tomb, Crimora. Some stones, a mound of earth, shall keep my memory. Bend thy red eye over my tomb, and beat thy breast of sighs.[18] Though fair thou art, my love, as the light; more pleasant than the gale of the hill; yet I will not stay. Raise my tomb, Crimora.

CRIMORA.

Then give me those arms of light; that sword, and that spear of steel. I shall meet Dargo with thee, and aid my lovely Connal. Farewell, ye rocks of Ardven! ye deer! and ye streams of the hill!—We shall return no more. Our tombs are distant far.

V.[19]

Autumn is dark on the mountains; grey mist rests on the hills. The whirl-wind is heard on the heath. Dark rolls the river thro'[20] the narrow plain. A tree stands alone on the hill, and marks the grave of Connal. The leaves whirl round with the wind, and strew the grave of the dead. At times are seen here the ghosts of the deceased, when the musing hunter alone stalks slowly over the heath. Appear in thy armour of light, thou ghost of the mighty Connal! Shine, near thy tomb, Crimora! like a moon-beam from a cloud.[21]

Who can reach the source of thy race, O Connal? and who recount thy Fathers? Thy family grew like an oak on the mountain, which meeteth the wind with its lofty head. But now it is torn from the earth. Who shall supply the place of Connal?

Here was the din of arms; and here the groans of the dying. Mournful are the wars of Fingal! O Connal! it was here thou didst fall. Thine arm was like a storm; thy sword, a beam of the sky; thy height, a rock on the plain; thine eyes, a furnace of fire. Louder than a storm was thy voice, when thou confoundedst the field. Warriors fell by thy sword, as the thistle by the staff of a boy.

Dargo the mighty came on, like a cloud of thunder. His brows were contracted and dark. His eyes like two caves in a rock. Bright rose their swords on each side; dire was the clang of their steel.

The daughter of Rinval was near; Crimora, bright in the armour of man; her hair loose behind, her bow in her hand. She followed the youth to the war, Connal her much-beloved. She drew the string on Dargo; but erring pierced her Connal. He falls like an oak on the plain; like a rock from the shaggy hill. What shall she do, hapless maid!—He bleeds; her Connal dies. All the night long she cries, and all the day, O Connal, my love, and my friend! With grief the sad mourner died.

Earth here incloseth the loveliest pair on the hill. The grass grows between the stones of their tomb; I sit in the mournful shade. The wind sighs through the grass; and their memory rushes on my mind. Undisturbed you now sleep together; in the tomb of the mountain you rest alone.

VI.[22]

Son of the noble Fingal, Oscian, Prince of men! what tears run down the cheeks of age? what shades thy mighty soul?

Memory, son of Alpin, memory wounds the aged. Of former times are my thoughts; my thoughts are of the noble Fingal. The race of the king return into my mind, and wound me with remembrance.

One day, returned from the sport of the mountains, from pursuing the sons of the hill[23], we covered this heath with our youth. Fingal the mighty was here, and Oscur, my son, great in war. Fair on our sight from the sea, at once, a virgin came. Her breast was like the snow of one night. Her cheek like the bud of the rose. Mild was her blue rolling eye: but sorrow was big in her heart.

Fingal renowned in war! she cries, sons of the king, preserve me! Speak secure, replies the king, daughter of beauty, speak: our ear is open to all: our swords redress the injured. I fly from Ullin, she cries, from Ullin famous in war. I fly from the embrace of him who would debase my blood. Cremor, the friend of men, was my father; Cremor the Prince of Inverne.

Fingal's younger sons arose; Carryl expert in the bow; Fillan beloved of the fair; and Fergus first in the race.—Who from the farthest Lochlyn? who to the seas of Molochasquir? who dares hurt the maid whom the sons of Fingal guard? Daughter of beauty, rest secure; rest in peace, thou fairest of women.

Far in the blue distance of the deep, some spot appeared like the back of the ridge-wave. But soon the ship increased on our sight. The hand of Ullin drew her to land. The mountains trembled as he moved. The hills shook at his steps. Dire rattled his armour around him. Death and destruction were in his eyes. His stature like the oak[24] of Morven. He moved in the lightning of steel.

Our warriors fell before him, like the field before the reapers. Fingal's three sons he bound. He plunged his sword into the fair-one's breast. She fell as a wreath of snow before the sun in spring. Her bosom heaved in death; her soul came forth in blood.

Oscur my son came down; the mighty in battle descended. His armour rattled as thunder; and the lightning of his eyes was terrible. There, was the clashing of swords; there, was the voice of steel. They struck and they thrust; they digged for death with their swords. But death was distant far, and delayed to come. The sun began to decline; and the cow-herd thought of home. Then Oscur's keen steel found the heart of Ullin. He fell like a mountain-oak covered over with glistering frost: He shone like a rock on the plain.——Here the daughter of beauty lieth; and here the bravest of men. Here one day ended the fair and the valiant. Here rest the pursuer and the pursued.

Son of Alpin! the woes of the aged are many: their tears are for the past. This raised my sorrow, warrior; memory awaked my grief. Oscur my son was brave; but Oscur is now no more. Thou hast heard my grief, O son of Alpin; forgive the tears of the aged.

VII.[25]

Why openest thou afresh the spring of my grief, O son of Alpin, inquiring how Oscur fell? My eyes are blind with tears; but memory beams on my heart. How can I relate the mournful death of the head of the people! Prince of the warriors, Oscur, my son, shall I see thee no more!

He fell as the moon in a storm; as the sun from the midst of his course, when clouds rise from the waste of the waves, when the blackness of the storm inwraps the rocks of Ardannider. I, like an ancient oak on Morven, I moulder alone in my place. The blast hath lopped my branches away; and I tremble at the wings of the north. Prince of the warriors, Oscur, my son! shall I see thee no more![26]

Dermid and Oscur were one: They reaped the battle together. Their friendship was strong as their steel; and death walked between them to the field. They came on the foe like two rocks falling from the brows of Ardven. Their swords were stained with the blood of the valiant: warriors fainted at their names. Who was a match for Oscur, but Dermid? and who for Dermid, but Oscur!

They killed mighty Dargo in the field; Dargo before invincible. His daughter was fair as the morn; mild as the beam of night. Her eyes, like two stars in a shower: her breath, the gale of spring: her breasts, as the new-fallen snow floating on the moving heath. The warriors saw her, and loved; their souls were fixed on the maid. Each loved her, as his fame; each must possess her or die. But her soul was fixed on Oscur; my son was the youth of her love. She forgot the blood of her father; and loved the hand that slew him.

Son of Oscian, said Dermid, I love; O Oscur, I love this maid. But her soul cleaveth unto thee; and nothing can heal Dermid. Here, pierce this bosom, Oscur; relieve me, my friend, with thy sword.

My sword, son of Morny, shall never be stained with the blood of Dermid.

Who then is worthy to slay me, O Oscur son of Oscian? Let not my life pass away unknown. Let none but Oscur slay me. Send me with honour to the grave, and let my death be renowned.

Dermid, make use of thy sword; son of Morny, wield thy steel. Would that I fell with thee! that my death came from the hand of Dermid!

They fought by the brook of the mountain, by the streams of Branno. Blood tinged the silvery stream, and crudled[27] round the mossy stones. Dermid the graceful fell; fell, and smiled in death.

And fallest thou, son of Morny; fallest thou by Oscur's hand! Dermid invincible in war, thus do I see thee fall!—He went, and returned to the maid whom he loved; returned, but she perceived his grief.

Why that gloom, son of Oscian? what shades thy mighty soul?

Though once renowned for the bow, O maid, I have lost my fame. Fixed on a tree by the brook of the hill, is the shield of Gormur the brave, whom in battle I slew. I have wasted the day in vain, nor could my arrow pierce it.

Let me try, son of Oscian, the skill of Dargo's daughter. My hands were taught the bow: my father delighted in my skill.

She went. He stood behind the shield. Her arrow flew and pierced his breast[28].

Blessed be that hand of snow; and blessed thy bow of yew! I fall resolved on death: and who but the daughter of Dargo was worthy to slay me? Lay me in the earth, my fair-one; lay me by the side of Dermid.

Oscur! I have the blood, the soul of the mighty Dargo. Well pleased I can meet death. My sorrow I can end thus.——She pierced her white bosom with steel. She fell; she trembled; and died.

By the brook of the hill their graves are laid; a birch's unequal shade covers their tomb. Often on their green earthen tombs the branchy sons of the mountain feed, when mid-day is all in flames, and silence is over all the hills.

VIII.

By the side of a rock on the hill, beneath the aged trees, old Oscian sat on the moss; the last of the race of Fingal. Sightless are his aged eyes; his beard is waving in the wind. Dull through the leafless trees he heard the voice of the north. Sorrow revived in his soul: he began and lamented the dead.

How hast thou fallen like an oak, with all thy branches round thee! Where is Fingal the King? where is Oscur my son? where are all my race? Alas! in the earth they lie. I feel their tombs with my hands. I hear the river below murmuring hoarsely over the stones. What dost thou, O river, to me? Thou bringest back the memory of the past.

The race of Fingal stood on thy banks, like a wood in a fertile soil. Keen were their spears of steel. Hardy was he who dared to encounter their rage. Fillan the great was there. Thou Oscur wert there, my son! Fingal himself was there, strong in the grey locks of years. Full rose his sinewy limbs; and wide his shoulders spread. The unhappy met with his arm, when the pride of his wrath arose.

The son of Morny came; Gaul, the tallest of men. He stood on the hill like an oak; his voice was like the streams of the hill. Why reigneth alone, he cries, the son of the mighty Corval? Fingal is not strong to save: he is no support for the people. I am strong as a storm in the ocean; as a whirlwind on the hill. Yield, son of Corval; Fingal, yield to me. He came like a rock from the hill, resounding in his arms.[29]

Oscur stood forth to meet him; my son would meet the foe. But Fingal came in his strength, and smiled at the vaunter's boast. They threw their arms round each other; they struggled on the plain. The earth is ploughed with their heels. Their bones crack as the boat on the ocean, when it leaps from wave to wave. Long did they toil; with night, they fell on the sounding plain; as two oaks, with their branches mingled, fall crashing from the hill. The tall son of Morny is bound; the aged overcame.

Fair with her locks of gold, her smooth neck, and her breasts of snow; fair, as the spirits of the hill when at silent noon they glide along the heath; fair, as the rain-bow of heaven; came Minvane the maid. Fingal! she softly saith, loose me my brother Gaul. Loose me the hope of my race, the terror of all but Fingal. Can I, replies the King, can I deny the lovely daughter of the hill? Take thy brother, O Minvane, thou fairer than the snow of the north!

Such, Fingal! were thy words; but thy words I hear no more. Sightless I sit by thy tomb. I hear the wind in the wood; but no more I hear my friends. The cry of the hunter is over. The voice of war is ceased.

IX.[30]

Thou askest, fair daughter of the isles! whose memory is preserved in these tombs? The memory of Ronnan the bold, and Connan the chief of men; and of her, the fairest of maids, Rivine the lovely and the good. The wing of time is laden with care. Every moment hath woes of its own. Why seek we our grief from afar? or give our tears to those of other times? But thou commandest, and I obey, O fair daughter of the isles!

Conar was mighty in war. Caul was the friend of strangers. His gates were open to all; midnight darkened not on his barred door. Both lived upon the sons of the mountains. Their bow was the support of the poor.

Connan was the image of Conar's soul. Caul was renewed in Ronnan his son. Rivine the daughter of Conar was the love of Ronnan; her brother Connan was his friend. She was fair as the harvest-moon setting in the seas of Molochasquir. Her soul was settled on Ronnan; the youth was the dream of her nights.

Rivine, my love! says Ronnan, I go to my king in Norway[31]. A year and a day shall bring me back. Wilt thou be true to Ronnan?

Ronnan! a year and a day I will spend in sorrow. Ronnan, behave like a man, and my soul shall exult in thy valour. Connan my friend, says Ronnan, wilt thou preserve Rivine thy sister? Durstan is in love with the maid; and soon shall the sea bring the stranger to our coast.

Ronnan, I will defend: Do thou securely go.——He went. He returned on his day. But Durstan returned before him.

Give me thy daughter, Conar, says Durstan; or fear and feel my power.

He who dares attempt my sister, says Connan, must meet this edge of steel. Unerring in battle is my arm: my sword, as the lightning of heaven.

Ronnan the warrior came; and much he threatened Durstan.

But, saith Euran the servant of gold, Ronnan! by the gate of the north shall Durstan this night carry thy fair-one away. Accursed, answers Ronnan, be this arm if death meet him not there.

Connan! saith Euran, this night shall the stranger carry thy sister away. My sword shall meet him, replies Connan, and he shall lie low on earth.

The friends met by night, and they fought. Blood and sweat ran down their limbs as water on the mossy rock. Connan falls; and cries, O Durstan, be favourable to Rivine!—And is it my friend, cries Ronnan, I have slain? O Connan! I knew thee not.

He went, and he fought with Durstan. Day began to rise on the combat, when fainting they fell, and expired. Rivine came out with the morn; and ——O what detains my Ronnan!—She saw him lying pale in his blood; and her brother lying pale by his side. What could she say? what could she do? her complaints were many and vain. She opened this grave for the warriors; and fell into it herself, before it was closed; like the sun snatched away in a storm.

Thou hast heard this tale of grief, O fair daughter of the isles! Rivine was fair as thyself: shed on her grave a tear.

X.[32]

It is night; and I am alone, forlorn on the hill of storms. The wind is heard in the mountain. The torrent shrieks down the rock. No hut receives me from the rain; forlorn on the hill of winds.

Rise, moon! from behind thy clouds; stars of the night, appear! Lead me, some light, to the place where my love rests from the toil of the chace! his bow near him, unstrung; his dogs panting around him. But here I must sit alone, by the rock of the mossy stream. The stream and the wind roar; nor can I hear the voice of my love.

Why delayeth my Shalgar, why the son of the hill, his promise? Here is the rock, and the tree; and here the roaring stream. Thou promisedst with night to be here. Ah! whither is my Shalgar gone? With thee I would fly my father; with thee, my brother of pride. Our race have long been foes; but we are not foes, O Shalgar!

Cease a little while, O wind! stream, be thou silent a while! let my voice be heard over the heath; let my wanderer hear me. Shalgar! it is I who call. Here is the tree, and the rock. Shalgar, my love! I am here. Why delayest thou thy coming? Alas! no answer.

Lo! the moon appeareth. The flood is bright in the vale. The rocks are grey on the face of the hill. But I see him not on the brow; his dogs before him tell not that he is coming. Here I must sit alone.

But who are these that lie beyond me on the heath? Are they my love and my brother?—Speak to me O my friends! they answer not. My soul is tormented with fears.——Ah! they are dead. Their swords are red from the fight. O my brother! my brother! why hast thou slain my Shalgar? why, O Shalgar! hast thou slain my brother? Dear were ye both to me! what shall I say in your praise? Thou wert fair on the hill among thousands; he was terrible in fight.[33] Speak to me; hear my voice, sons of my love! But alas! they are silent; silent for ever! Cold are their breasts of clay!

Oh! from the rock of the hill; from the top of the mountain of winds, speak ye ghosts of the dead! speak, and I will not be afraid.——Whither are ye gone to rest? In what cave of the hill shall I find you? No feeble voice is on the wind: no answer half-drowned in the storms of the hill.[34]

I sit in my grief. I wait for morning in my tears. Rear the tomb, ye friends of the dead; but close it not till I come. My life flieth away like a dream: why should I stay behind? Here shall I rest with my friends by the stream of the sounding rock. When night comes on the hill; when the wind is upon the heath; my ghost shall stand in the wind, and mourn the death of my friends. The hunter shall hear from his booth. He shall fear, but love my voice. For sweet shall my voice be for my friends; for pleasant were they both to me.

XI.[35]

Sad! I am sad indeed: nor small my cause of woe!—Kirmor, thou hast lost no son; thou hast lost no daughter of beauty. Connar the valiant lives; and Annir the fairest of maids. The boughs of thy family flourish, O Kirmor! but Armyn is the last of his race. Dark is thy bed, O Daura! and deep thy sleep in the tomb.—When shalt thou awake with thy songs? with all thy voice of music?[36]

Rise, winds of autumn, rise; blow upon the dark heath! streams of the mountains, roar! howl, ye tempests, in the top of the oak![37] walk through broken clouds, O moon! show by intervals thy pale face! bring to my mind that sad night, when all my children fell; when Arindel the mighty fell; when Daura the lovely failed; when all my children died.[38]

Daura, my daughter! thou wert fair; fair as the moon on the hills of Jura; white as the driven snow; sweet as the breathing gale. Arindel, thy bow was strong, thy spear was swift in the field: thy look was like mist on the wave, thy shield, a red cloud in a storm.[39] Armor renowned in war, came, and sought Daura's love; he was not long denied; fair was the hope of their friends.

Earch, son of Odgal, repined; for his brother was slain by Armor. He came disguised like a son of the sea: fair was his skiff on the wave; white his locks of age; calm his serious brow. Fairest of women, he said, lovely daughter of Armyn! a rock not distant in the sea, bears a tree on its side; red shines the fruit afar. There Armor waiteth for Daura. I came to fetch his love. Come, fair daughter of Armyn!

She went; and she called on Armor. Nought answered, but the son of the rock. Armor, my love! my love! why tormentest thou me with fear? hear, son of Ardnart, hear:[40] it is Daura who calleth thee!—Earch the traitor fled laughing to the land. She lifted up her voice, and cried for her brother and her father. Arindel! Armyn! none to relieve your Daura!

Her voice came over the sea. Arindel my son descended from the hill; rough in the spoils of the chace. His arrows rattled by his side; his bow was in his hand; five dark[41] gray dogs attended his steps. He saw fierce Earch on the shore; he seized and bound him to an oak. Thick fly the thongs of the hide around his limbs; he loads the wind with his groans.

Arindel ascends the surgy deep in his boat, to bring Daura to the land. Armor came in his wrath, and let fly the grey-feathered shaft. It sung; it sunk in thy heart, O Arindel my son! for Earch the traitor thou diedst. The oar is stopped at once; he panted on the rock and expired.[42] What is thy grief, O Daura, when round thy feet is poured thy brother's blood!

The boat is broken in twain by the waves. Armor plunges into the sea, to rescue his Daura or die. Sudden a blast from the hill comes over the waves. He sunk, and he rose no more.

Alone, on the sea-beat rock, my daughter was heard to complain. Frequent and loud were her cries; nor could her father relieve her. All night I stood on the shore. I saw her by the faint beam of the moon.[43] All night I heard her cries. Loud was the wind; and the rain beat hard on the side of the mountain. Before morning appeared, her voice was weak. It died away, like the evening-breeze among the grass of the rocks. Spent with grief she expired. And left thee Armyn alone: gone is my strength in the war, and fallen my pride among women.[44]

When the storms of the mountain come; when the north lifts the waves on high; I sit by the sounding shore, and look on the fatal rock. Often by the setting moon I see the ghosts of my children. Half-viewless,[45] they walk in mournful conference together. Will none of you speak in pity? They[46] do not regard their father.

XII.[47]

RYNO, ALPIN.

RYNO.

The wind and the rain are over: calm is the noon of day. The clouds are divided in heaven. Over the green hills flies the inconstant sun. Red through the stony vale comes down the stream of the hill. Sweet are thy murmurs, O stream! but more sweet is the voice I hear. It is the voice of Alpin the son of the song, mourning for the dead. Bent is his head of age, and red his tearful eye. Alpin, thou son of the song, why alone on the silent hill? why complainest thou, as a blast in the wood; as a wave on the lonely shore?

ALPIN.

My tears, O Ryno! are for the dead; my voice, for the inhabitants of the grave. Tall thou art on the hill; fair among the sons of the plain. But thou shalt fall like Morar; and the mourner shall[48] sit on thy tomb. The hills shall know thee no more; thy bow shall lie in the hall, unstrung.

Thou wert swift, O Morar! as a roe on the hill; terrible as a meteor of fire. Thy wrath was as the storm of December. Thy sword in battle, as lightning in the field. Thy voice was like a stream after rain; like thunder on distant hills. Many fell by thy arm; they were consumed in the flames of thy wrath.

But when thou returnedst from war, how peaceful was thy brow! Thy face was like the sun after rain; like the moon in the silence of night; calm as the breast of the lake when the loud wind is laid.

Narrow is thy dwelling now; dark the place of thine abode. With three steps I compass thy grave, O thou who wast so great before! Four stones with their heads of moss are the only memorial of thee. A tree with scarce a leaf, long grass which whistles in the wind, mark to the hunter's eye the grave of the mighty Morar. Morar! thou art low indeed. Thou hast no mother to mourn thee; no maid with her tears of love. Dead is she that brought thee forth. Fallen is the daughter of Morglan.

Who on his staff is this? who is this, whose head is white with age, whose eyes are red with tears, who quakes at every step?—It is thy father, O Morar! the father of none but thee. He heard of thy fame in battle; he heard of foes dispersed. He heard of Morar's fame; why did he not hear of his wound? Weep, thou father of Morar! weep; but thy son heareth thee not. Deep is the sleep of the dead; low their pillow of dust. No more shall he hear thy voice; no more shall he awake at thy call. When shall it be morn in the grave, to bid the slumberer awake?

Farewell, thou bravest of men! thou conqueror in the field! but the field shall see thee no more; nor the dark wood be lightened with the splendor of thy steel. Thou hast left no son. But the song shall preserve thy name. Future times shall hear of thee; they shall hear of the fallen Morar.

XIII.[49]

Raise high the stones; collect the earth: preserve the name of Fear-comhraic. Blow winds, from all your hills; sigh on the grave of Muirnin.

The dark rock hangs, with all its wood, above the calm dwelling of the heroes.

The sea with its foam-headed billows murmurs at their side.

Why sigh the woods, why roar the waves? They have no cause to mourn.

But Thou hast cause, O Diorma! thou maid of the breast of snow! Spread thou thy hair to the wind; send thy sighs on the blasts of the hills.

They vanished like two beams of light, which fly from the heath in a storm: They sunk like two stars in a cloud when the winds of north arise.

For Thee weep the maids, Fear-comhraic, along the echoing hills. For Thee the women weep, O Muirnin; chief of the wars of Erin. I see not Fear-comhraic on the hill; I see not Muirnin in the storms of ocean. Raise, raise the song, relate the tale. Descend ye tears of other times.

Diorma was the daughter of Connaid the chief of a thousand shields.

Diorma was among the maids, as the white flower among the heath.

Her breast was like a white cloud in heaven. Her bosom like the top of a wave in a storm. Her hair was like smoke in the sun: her eye like the star of morn. Not fairer looks the moon from between two clouds, than the face of Diorma from between her locks.

A thousand heroes loved the maid; the maid loved none but Fear-comhraic. He loved the maid, and well he might; fair among women was the daughter of Connaid. She was the light of his soul in danger; the strength of his arm in battle.

Who shall deny me the maid, said Fear-comhraic, who, the fairest of women, Diorma? Hard must be his helm of steel, and strong his shield of iron.

I deny her, said Muirnin son of the chief of generous shells. My sword is keen, my spear is strong; the valiant yield to Muirnin.

Come then, thou son of Cormac, O mighty Muirnin, come! leave the hills of Erin, come on the foamy wave. Let thy ship, like a cloud, come over the storms of ocean.

He came along the sea: his sails were like grey mist on the heath: long was his spear of ash; his shield like the bloody moon.—Aodan son of Armclach came; the youth of the gloomy brow.

Rise, Fear-comhraic, rise thou love of the soft Diorma! fight, or yield the maid, son of the great Comhfeadan!

He rose like a cloud on the hill, when the winds of Autumn blow.

Tall art thou, said Fear-comhraic, son of mighty Cormac; fair are thy cheeks of youth, and strong thy arm of war. Prepare the feast, and slay the deer; send round the shell of joy: three days we feast together; we fight on the fourth, son of Cormac.

Why should I sheath my sword, son of the noble Comhfeadan? Yield to me, son of battle, and raise my fame in Erin.

Raise Thou my tomb, O Muirnin! If Fear-comhraic fall by thy steel, place my bright sword by my side, in the tomb of the lonely hill.

We fight by the noise of the stream, Muirnin! wield thy steel.

Swords sound on helmets, sound on shields; brass clashes, clatters, rings. Sparkles buzz; shivers fly; death bounds from mail to mail. As leaps a stone from rock to rock, so blow succeeds to blow. Their eyes dart fire; their nostrils blow: they leap, they thrust, they wound.

Slowly, slowly falls the blade of Muirnin son of war. He sinks, his armour rings, he cries, I die, Fear-comhraic, I die.

And falls the bravest of men the chief of Innisfhallin! Stretch wide the sail; ascend the wave, and bring the youth to Erin. Deep on the hills of Erin is the sigh of maids. For thee, my foe, I mourn: thou art the grief of Fear-comhraic.

Rise ye winds of the sounding hill; sigh over the fall of Muirnin! Weep Diorma, for the hero; weep, maid of the arms of snow; appear like the sun in rain; move in tears along the shore!

Aodan saw the fall of Muirnin, and drew the sounding bow: The grey-winged arrow flew, and pierced the breast of Fear-comhraic. Aodan, said Fear-comhraic, where was the sword of war? where was the spear of thy strength, when thus thou hast slain Fear-comhraic? Raise, gloomy youth, raise thou our tombs! I will rest with the chief of Innisfhallin.

Who is that on the hill like a sun-beam in a storm? Who is that with the heaving breasts, which are like two wreaths of snow? Thy blue eyes roll in tears, thou daughter of mighty Connaid! Thy hair flies round thy temples, as the mist on the rocks of Ardven. Thy robe flows on the heath, daughter of grief, Diorma! He is fallen on the hill like a stream of light in a cloud. No more shall he hear thy voice like the sound of the string of music. The strength of the war is gone; the cheek of youth is pale.

XIV.[50]

Cuchulaid sat by the wall; by the tree of the rustling leaf[51]. His spear leaned against the mossy rock. His shield lay by him on the grass. Whilst he thought on the mighty Carbre whom he slew in battle, the scout of the ocean came, Moran the son of Fithil.

Rise, Cuchulaid, rise! I see the ships of Garve. Many are the foe, Cuchulaid; many the sons of Lochlyn.

Moran! thou ever tremblest; thy fears increase the foe. They are the ships of the Desert of hills arrived to assist Cuchulaid.

I saw their chief, says Moran, tall as a rock of ice. His spear is like that fir; his shield like the rising moon. He sat upon a rock on the shore, as a grey cloud upon the hill. Many, mighty man! I said, many are our heroes; Garve, well art thou named[52], many are the sons of our king.

He answered like a wave on the rock; who is like me here? The valiant live not with me; they go to the earth from my hand. The king of the Desert of hills alone can fight with Garve. Once we wrestled on the hill. Our heels overturned the wood. Rocks fell from their place, and rivulets changed their course. Three days we strove together; heroes stood at a distance, and feared. On the fourth, the King saith that I fell; but Garve saith, he stood. Let Cuchulaid yield to him that is strong as a storm.

No. I will never yield to man. Cuchulaid will conquer or die. Go, Moran, take my spear; strike the shield of Caithbait which hangs before the gate. It never rings in peace. My heroes shall hear on the hill.——

XV.[53]

DUCHOMMAR, MORNA.

DUCHOMMAR.

[54]Morna, thou fairest of women, daughter of Cormac-Carbre? why in the circle of stones, in the cave of the rock, alone? The stream murmureth hoarsely. The blast groaneth in the aged tree. The lake is troubled before thee. Dark are the clouds of the sky. But thou art like snow on the heath. Thy hair like a thin cloud of gold on the top of Cromleach. Thy breasts like two smooth rocks on the hill which is seen from the stream of Brannuin. Thy arms, as two white pillars in the hall of Fingal.

MORNA.

Whence the son of Mugruch, Duchommar the most gloomy of men? Dark are thy brows of terror. Red thy rolling eyes. Does Garve appear on the sea? What of the foe, Duchommar?

DUCHOMMAR.

From the hill I return, O Morna, from the hill of the flying deer. Three have I slain with my bow; three with my panting dogs. Daughter of Cormac-Carbre, I love thee as my soul. I have slain a deer for thee. High was his branchy head; and fleet his feet of wind.

MORNA.

Gloomy son of Mugruch, Duchommar! I love thee not: hard is thy heart of rock; dark thy terrible brow. But Cadmor the son of Tarman, thou art the love of Morna! thou art like a sun-beam on the hill, in the day of the gloomy storm. Sawest thou the son of Tarman, lovely on the hill of the chace? Here the daughter of Cormac-Carbre waiteth the coming of Cadmor.

DUCHOMMAR.

And long shall Morna wait. His blood is on my sword. I met him by the mossy stone, by the oak of the noisy stream. He fought; but I slew him; his blood is on my sword. High on the hill I will raise his tomb, daughter of Cormac-Carbre. But love thou the son of Mugruch; his arm is strong as a storm.

MORNA.

And is the son of Tarman fallen; the youth with the breast of snow! the first in the chace of the hill; the foe of the sons of the ocean!—Duchommar, thou art gloomy indeed; cruel is thy arm to me.——But give me that sword, son of Mugruch; I love the blood of Cadmor!

[He gives her the sword, with which she instantly stabs him.]

DUCHOMMAR.

Daughter of Cormac-Carbre, thou hast pierced Duchommar! the sword is cold in my breast; thou hast killed the son of Mugruch. Give me to Moinie the maid; for much she loved Duchommar. My tomb she will raise on the hill; the hunter shall see it, and praise me.——But draw the sword from my side, Morna; I feel it cold.——

[Upon her coming near him, he stabs her. As she fell, she plucked a stone from the side of the cave, and placed it betwixt them, that his blood might not be mingled with hers.]

XVI.[55]

[56]Where is Gealchossa my love, the daughter of Tuathal-Teachvar? I left her in the hall of the plain, when I fought with the hairy Ulfadha. Return soon, she said, O Lamderg! for here I wait in sorrow. Her white breast rose with sighs; her cheek was wet with tears. But she cometh not to meet Lamderg; or sooth his soul after battle. Silent is the hall of joy; I hear not the voice of the singer. Brann does not shake his chains at the gate, glad at the coming of his master. Where is Gealchossa my love, the daughter of Tuathal-Teachvar?

Lamderg! says Firchios son of Aydon, Gealchossa may be on the hill; she and her chosen maids pursuing the flying deer.

Firchios! no noise I hear. No sound in the wood of the hill. No deer fly in my sight; no panting dog pursueth. I see not Gealchossa my love; fair as the full moon setting on the hills of Cromleach. Go, Firchios! go to Allad[57], the grey-haired son of the rock. He liveth in the circle of stones; he may tell of Gealchossa.

Allad! saith Firchios, thou who dwellest in the rock; thou who tremblest alone; what saw thine eyes of age?

I saw, answered Allad the old, Ullin the son of Carbre: He came like a cloud from the hill; he hummed a surly song as he came, like a storm in leafless wood. He entered the hall of the plain. Lamderg, he cried, most dreadful of men! fight, or yield to Ullin. Lamderg, replied Gealchossa, Lamderg is not here: he fights the hairy Ulfadha; mighty man, he is not here. But Lamderg never yields; he will fight the son of Carbre. Lovely art thou, O daughter of Tuathal-Teachvar! said Ullin. I carry thee to the house of Carbre; the valiant shall have Gealchossa. Three days from the top of Cromleach will I call Lamderg to fight. The fourth, you belong to Ullin, if Lamderg die, or fly my sword.

Allad! peace to thy dreams!—sound the horn, Firchios!—Ullin may hear, and meet me on the top of Cromleach.

Lamderg rushed on like a storm. On his spear he leaped over rivers. Few were his strides up the hill. The rocks fly back from his heels; loud crashing they bound to the plain. His armour, his buckler rung. He hummed a surly song like the noise of the falling stream. Dark as a cloud he stood above; his arms, like meteors, shone. From the summit of the hill, he rolled a rock. Ullin heard in the hall of Carbre.——

FINIS.

ADVERTISEMENT
(preceding 1st edition of *Fingal*, 1761/62)

The translator thinks it necessary to make the public acquainted with the motives which induced him to depart from his proposals concerning the Originals. Some men of genius, whom he has the honour to number among his friends, advised him to publish proposals for printing by subscription the whole Originals, as a better way of satisfying the public concerning the authenticity of the poems, than depositing manuscript copies in any public library. This he did; but no subscribers appearing, he takes it for the judgment of the public that neither the one or the other is necessary. However, there is a design on foot to print the Originals, as soon as the translator shall have time to transcribe them for the press; and if this publication shall not take place, copies will then be deposited in one of the public libraries, to prevent so ancient a monument of genius from being lost.

The translator thanks the public for the more than ordinary encouragement given him, for executing this work. The number of his subscribers does him honour. He could have presented to the public the first names in the nation; but, though more have come to his hands, than have appeared before the works of authors of established reputation, yet many more have subscribed; and he chuses to print none at all rather than an imperfect list. Deeply sensible of the generosity of a certain noble person, the translator yet avoids to name him, as his exalted station as well as merit has raised him above the panegyric of one so little known.[1]

PREFACE
(to 1st edition of *Fingal* 1761/62)

The love of novelty, which, in some degree, is common to all mankind, is more particularly the characteristic of that mediocrity of parts, which distinguishes more than one half of the human species. This inconstant disposition is never more conspicuous, than in what regards the article of amusement. We change our sentiments concerning it every moment, and the distance between our admiration and extreme contempt, is so very small, that the one is almost a sure presage of the other. The poets, whose business it is to please, if they want to preserve the fame they have once acquired, must very often forfeit their own judgments to this variable temper of the bulk of their readers, and accommodate their writings to this unsettled taste. A fame so fluctuating deserves not to be much valued.

Poetry, like virtue, receives its reward after death. The fame which men pursued in vain, when living, is often bestowed upon them when they are not sensible of it. This neglect of living authors is not altogether to be attributed to that reluctance which men shew in praising and rewarding genius. It often happens, that the man who writes differs greatly from the same man in common life. His foibles, however, are obliterated by death, and his better part, his writings, remain: his character is formed from them, and he that was no extraordinary man in his own time, becomes the wonder of succeeding ages.—From this source proceeds our veneration for the dead. Their virtues remain, but the vices, which were once blended with their virtues, have died with themselves.

This consideration might induce a man, diffident of his abilities, to ascribe his own compositions to a person, whose remote antiquity and whose situation, when alive, might well answer for faults which would be inexcusable in a writer of this age. An ingenious gentleman made this observation, before he knew any thing but the name of the epic poem, which is printed in the following collection. When he had read it, his sentiments were changed. He found it abounded too much with those ideas, that only belong to the most early state of society, to be the work of a modern poet. Of this, I am persuaded, the public will be as thoroughly convinced, as this gentleman was, when they shall see the poems; and that some will think, notwithstanding the disadvantages with which the works ascribed to Ossian appear, it would be a very uncommon instance of self-denial in me to disown them, were they really of my composition.

I would not have dwelt so long upon this subject, especially as I have answered all reasonable objections to the genuineness of the poems in the Dissertation, were it not on account of the prejudices of the present age against the ancient inhabitants of Britain, who are thought to have been incapable of the generous sentiments to be met with in the poems of Ossian.—If we err in praising too much the times of our forefathers, it is also as repugnant to good sense, to be altogether blind to the imperfections of our own. If our fathers had not so much wealth, they had certainly fewer vices than the present age. Their tables, it is true, were not so well provided, neither were their beds so soft as those of modern times; and this, in the eyes of men who place their ultimate happiness in those conveniences of life, gives us a great advantage over them. I shall not enter farther into this subject, but only observe, that the general poverty of a nation has not the same influence, that the indigence of individuals, in an opulent country, has, upon the manners of the community. The idea of meanness, which is now connected with a narrow fortune, had its rise after commerce had thrown too much property into the hands of a few; for the poorer sort, imitating the vices of the rich, were obliged to have recourse to roguery and circumvention, in order to supply their extravagance, so that they were, not without reason, reckoned, in more than one sense, the worst of the people.

It is now two years since the first translations from the Galic language were handed about among people of taste in Scotland. They became at last so much corrupted, through the carelessness of transcribers, that, for my own sake, I was obliged to print the genuine copies. Some other pieces were added, to swell the publication into a pamphlet, which was entitled, Fragments of Ancient Poetry.—The Fragments, upon their first appearance, were so much approved of, that several people of rank, as well as taste, prevailed with me to make a journey into the Highlands and western isles, in order to recover what remained of the works of the old bards, especially those of Ossian, the son of Fingal, who was the best, as well as most ancient, of those who are celebrated in tradition for their poetical genius. ——I undertook this journey, more from a desire of complying with the request of my friends, than from any hopes I had of answering their expectations. I was not unsuccessful, considering how much the compositions of ancient times have been neglected, for some time past, in the north of Scotland. Several gentlemen in the Highlands and isles generously gave me all the assistance in their power; and it was by their means I was enabled to compleat the epic poem. How far it comes up to the rules of the epopæa, is the province of criticism to examine. It is only my business to lay it before the reader, as I have found it. As it is one of the chief beauties of composition, to be well understood, I shall here give the story of the poem, to prevent that obscurity which the introduction of characters utterly unknown might occasion.

Artho, supreme king of Ireland, dying at Temora the royal palace of the Irish kings, was succeeded by Cormac, his son, a minor. Cuchullin, the son of Semo, lord of the *Isle of Mist*, one of the Hebrides, being at that time in Ulster, and very famous for his great exploits, was, in a convention of the petty kings and heads of tribes assembled for that purpose at Temora, unanimously chosen guardian to the young king.—He had not managed the affairs of Cormac long, when news was brought, that Swaran, the son of Starno, king of Lochlin, or Scandinavia, intended to invade Ireland. Cuchullin immediately dispatched Munan, the son of Stirmal, an Irish chief, to Fingal, king of those Caledonians who inhabited the western coast of Scotland, to implore his aid. Fingal, as well from a principle of generosity, as from his connection with the royal family of Ireland, resolved on an expedition into that country; but before his arrival, the enemy had landed in Ulster.——Cuchullin in the mean time had gathered the flower of the Irish tribes to Tura, a castle of Ulster, and dispatched scouts along the coast, to give the most early intelligence of the enemy.——Such is the situation of affairs, when the poem opens.[1]

The story of this poem is so little interlarded with fable, that one cannot help thinking it the genuine history of Fingal's expedition, embellished by poetry. In that case, the compositions of Ossian are not less valuable for the light they throw on the ancient state of Scotland and Ireland than they are for their poetical merit. Succeeding generations founded on them all their traditions concerning that period; and they magnified or varied them, in proportion as they were swayed by credulity or design. The bards of Ireland, by ascribing to Ossian compositions which are evidently their own, have occasioned a general belief, in that country, that Fingal was of Irish extraction, and not of the ancient Caledonians, as is said in the genuine poems of Ossian. The inconsistencies between those spurious pieces prove the ignorance of their authors. In one of them Ossian is made to mention himself as baptised by St. Patrick, in another he speaks of the famous crusade, which was not begun in Europe for many centuries after.

Though this anachronism quite destroys the authority of the bards with respect to Fingal; yet their desire to make him their countryman shews how famous he was in Ireland as well as in the north of Scotland.

Had the Senachies of Ireland been as well acquainted with the antiquities of their nation as they pretended, they might derive as much honour from Fingal's being a Caledonian, as if he had been an Irishman; for both nations were almost the same people in the days of that hero. The Celtæ, who inhabited Britain and Ireland before the invasion of the Romans, though they were divided into numerous tribes, yet, as the same language and customs, and the memory of their common origin remained among them, they considered themselves as one nation. After South Britain became a province of Rome, and its inhabitants begun to adopt the language and customs of their conquerors, the Celtæ beyond the pale of the empire, considered them as a distinct people, and consequently treated them as enemies. On the other hand, the strictest amity subsisted between the Irish and Scots Celtæ for many ages, and the customs and ancient language of both still remaining, leave no room to doubt that they were of old one and the same nation.

It was at first intended to prefix to Ossian's poems a discourse concerning the ancient inhabitants of Britain; but as a gentleman, in the north of Scotland, who has thoroughly examined the antiquities of this island, and is perfectly acquainted with all the branches of the Celtic tongue, is just now preparing for the press a work on that subject, the curious are referred to it.[2]

THE

W O R K S

OF

O S S I A N ,

THE

S O N of F I N G A L .

IN TWO VOLUMES .

Translated from the GALIC LANGUAGE

By JAMES MACPHERSON.

VOL. I. containing

FINGAL, an Ancient EPIC POEM,

IN SIX BOOKS;

AND

SEVERAL OTHER POEMS

Fortia facta patrum. VIRG.

THE THIRD EDITION.

LONDON:

MDCCLXV.

TO THE

EARL of BUTE,

Knight of the most Noble Order of the Garter, &c. &c.

MY LORD,

I presume to present to your lordship a compleat edition of the Works of Ossian. They have already been honored with your approbation, and have been received with applause by men of taste throughout Europe. This address therefore is not an endeavor to secure the continuance of the public favor through the sanction of your name. Little solicitous myself about the reputation of an author, I permit, with no concern, the Old Bard to take his chance with the world: It proceeds, my Lord, from another cause; the ambition of being hereafter known to have met with your favor and protection in the execution of this work; an honor which will be envied me, perhaps, more some time hence than at present. I throw no reflexions on this age, but there is a great debt of fame owing to the EARL OF BUTE, which hereafter will be amply paid: there is also some share of reputation with-held from Ossian, which less prejudiced times may bestow. This similarity between the Statesman and the Poet, gives propriety to this dedication; though your Lordship's avowed patronage of literature requires no adventitious aid to direct to you the addresses of authors. It is with pleasure I embrace this opportunity of testifying in public with what perfect attachment,

I am,

my Lord,

your Lordship's most humble,

most obliged,

and most obedient servant,

JAMES MACPHERSON.

A

DISSERTATION

CONCERNING THE

ANTIQUITY, &c. of the POEMS

OF

OSSIAN the Son of FINGAL[1]

Inquiries into the antiquities of nations afford more pleasure than any real advantage to mankind. The ingenious may form systems of history on probabilities and a few facts; but at a great distance of time, their accounts must be vague and uncertain. The infancy of states and kingdoms is as destitute of great events, as of the means of transmitting them to posterity. The arts of polished life, by which alone facts can be preserved with certainty, are the production of a well-formed community. It is then historians begin to write, and public transactions to be worthy remembrance. The actions of former times are left in obscurity, or magnified by uncertain traditions. Hence it is that we find so much of the marvellous in the origin of every nation; posterity being always ready to believe any thing, however fabulous, that reflects honour on their ancestors. The Greeks and Romans were remarkable for this weakness. They swallowed the most absurd fables concerning the high antiquities of their respective nations. Good historians, however, rose very early amongst them, and transmitted, with lustre, their great actions to posterity. It is to them that they owe that unrivalled fame they now enjoy, while the great actions of other nations are involved in fables, or lost in obscurity. The Celtic nations afford a striking instance of this kind. They, though once the masters of Europe from the mouth of the river Oby[2], in Russia, to Cape Finisterre, the western point of Gallicia in Spain, are very little mentioned in history. They trusted their fame to tradition and the songs of their bards, which, by the vicissitude of human affairs, are long since lost. Their ancient language is the only monument that remains of them; and the traces of it being found in places so widely distant from each other, serves only to shew the extent of their ancient power, but throws very little light on their history.

Of all the Celtic nations, that which possessed old Gaul is the most renowned; not perhaps on account of worth superior to the rest, but for their wars with a people who had historians to transmit the fame of their enemies, as well as their own, to posterity. Britain was first peopled by them, according to the testimony of the best authors[3]; its situation in respect to Gaul makes the opinion probable; but what puts it beyond all dispute, is that the same customs and language prevailed among the inhabitants of both in the days of Julius Cæsar[4].

The colony from Gaul possessed themselves, at first, of that part of Britain which was next to their own country; and spreading northward, by degrees, as they increased in numbers, peopled the whole island. Some adventurers passing over from those parts of Britain that are within sight of Ireland, were the founders of the Irish nation: which is a more probable story than the idle fables of Milesian and Gallician colonies. Diodorus Siculus[5] mentions it as a thing well known in his time, that the inhabitants of Ireland were originally Britons; and his testimony is unquestionable, when we consider that, for many ages, the language and customs of both nations were the same.

Tacitus was of opinion that the ancient Caledonians were of German extract.[6] By the language and customs which always prevailed in the North of Scotland, and which are undoubtedly Celtic, one would be tempted to differ in opinion from that celebrated writer.[7] The Germans,[8] properly so called, were not the same with the ancient Celtæ. The manners and customs of the two nations were similar; but their language different. The Germans[9] are the genuine descendants of the ancient Daæ, afterwards well known by the name of Daci, and passed originally into Europe by the way of the northern countries, and settled beyond the Danube, towards the vast regions of Transilvania, Wallachia, and Moldavia; and from thence advanced by degrees into Germany.[10] The Celtæ[11], it is certain,[12] sent many colonies into that country, all of whom retained their own laws, language, and customs;[13] and it is of them, if any colonies came from Germany into Scotland, that the ancient Caledonians were descended.

But whether the Caledonians were a colony of the Celtic Germans, or the same with the Gauls that first possessed themselves of Britain, is a matter of no moment at this distance of time. Whatever their origin was, we find them very numerous in the time of Julius Agricola, which is a presumption that they were long before settled in the country. The form of their government was a mixture of aristocracy and monarchy, as it was in all the countries where the Druids bore the chief sway. This order of men seems to have been formed on the same system with the Dactyli Idæi and Curetes of the ancients. Their pretended intercourse with heaven, their magic and divination were the same. The knowledge of the Druids in natural causes, and the properties of certain things, the fruit of the experiments of ages, gained them a mighty reputation among the people. The esteem of the populace soon increased into a veneration for the order; which a cunning and ambitious tribe of men[14] took care to improve, to such a degree, that they, in a manner, ingrossed the management of civil, as well as religious, matters. It is generally allowed that they did not abuse this extraordinary power; the preserving their character of sanctity was so essential to their influence, that they never broke out into violence or oppression. The chiefs were allowed to execute the laws, but the legislative power was entirely in the hands of the Druids[15]. It was by their authority that the tribes were united, in times of the greatest danger, under one head. This temporary king, or Vergobretus[16], was chosen by them, and generally laid down his office at the end of the war. These priests enjoyed long this extraordinary privilege among the Celtic nations who lay beyond the pale of the Roman empire. It was in the beginning of the second century that their power among the Caledonians begun to decline. The poems that celebrate Trathal and Cormac, ancestors to Fingal, are full of particulars concerning the fall of the Druids, which account for the total silence concerning their religion in the poems that are now given to the public.[17]

The continual wars of the Caledonians against the Romans hindered the nobility[18] from initiating themselves, as the custom formerly was, into the order of the Druids. The precepts of their religion were confined to a few, and were not much attended to by a people inured to war. The Vergobretus, or chief magistrate, was chosen without the concurrence of the hierarchy, or continued in his office against their will. Continual power strengthened his interest among the tribes, and enabled him to send down, as hereditary to his posterity, the office he had only received himself by election.

On occasion of a new war against the *King of the World*, as the poems emphatically call[19] the Roman emperor, the Druids, to vindicate the honour of the order, began to resume their ancient privilege of chusing the Vergobretus. Garmal, the son of Tarno, being deputed by them, came to the grandfather of the celebrated Fingal, who was then Vergobretus, and commanded him, in the name of the whole order, to lay down his office. Upon his refusal, a civil war commenced, which soon ended in almost the total extinction of the religious order of the Druids. A few that remained, retired to the dark recesses of their groves, and the caves they had formerly used for their meditations. It is then we find them in *the circle of stones*, and unheeded by the world. A total disregard for the order, and utter abhorrence of the Druidical rites ensued. Under this cloud of public hate, all that had any knowledge of the religion of the Druids became extinct, and the nation fell into the last degree of ignorance of their rites and ceremonies.

It is no matter of wonder then, that Fingal and his son Ossian make so little, if any, mention of the Druids,[20] who were the declared enemies to their succession in the supreme magistracy. It is a singular case, it must be allowed, that there are no traces of religion in the poems ascribed to Ossian; as the poetical compositions of other nations are so closely connected with their mythology.[21] It is hard to account for it to those who are not made acquainted with the manner of the old Scottish bards. That race of men carried their notions of martial honour to an extravagant pitch. Any aid given their heroes in battle, was thought to derogate from their fame; and the bards immediately transferred the glory of the action to him who had given that aid.

Had Ossian brought down gods, as often as Homer hath done, to assist his heroes, this poem had not consisted of eulogiums on his friends, but of hymns to these superior beings.[22] To this day, those that write[23] in the Galic language seldom mention religion in their profane poetry; and when they professedly write of religion, they never interlard with their compositions, the actions of their heroes. This custom alone, even though the religion of the Druids had not been previously extinguished, may, in some measure, account for Ossian's silence concerning the religion of his own times.[24]

To say, that a nation is void of all religion, is the same thing as to say, that it does not consist of people endued with reason.[25] The traditions of their fathers, and their own observations on the works of nature, together with that superstition which is inherent in the human frame, have, in all ages, raised in the minds of men some idea of a superior being.—Hence it is, that in the darkest times, and amongst the most barbarous nations, the very populace themselves had some faint notion, at least, of a divinity.[26] It would be doing injustice to Ossian, who, upon no occasion, shews a narrow mind,[27] to think, that he had not opened his conceptions to that primitive and greatest of all truths. But let Ossian's[28] religion be what it will, it is certain he had no knowledge of Christianity, as there is not the least allusion to it, or any of its rites, in his poems; which absolutely fixes him to an æra prior to the introduction of that religion.[29] The persecution begun by Dioclesian, in the year 303, is the most probable time in which the first dawning of Christianity in the north of Britain can be fixed.—The humane and mild character of Constantius Chlorus, who commanded then in Britain, induced the persecuted Christians to take refuge under him. Some of them, through a zeal to propagate their tenets, or through fear, went beyond the pale of the Roman empire, and settled among the Caledonians; who were the more ready to hearken to their doctrines, as the religion of the Druids had been exploded so long before.[30]

These missionaries, either through choice, or to give more weight to the doctrine they advanced, took possession of the cells and groves of the Druids; and it was from this retired life they had the name of *Culdees*[31], which in the language of the country signified *sequestered persons*. It was with one of the *Culdees* that Ossian, in his extreme old age, is said to have disputed concerning the Christian religion. This dispute is still extant,[32] and is couched in verse, according to the custom of the times. The extreme ignorance on the part of Ossian, of the Christian tenets, shews, that that religion had only been lately introduced, as it is not easy to conceive, how one of the first rank could be totally unacquainted with a religion that had been known for any time in the country. The dispute bears the genuine marks of antiquity. The obsolete phrases and expressions peculiar to the times, prove it to be no forgery. If Ossian then lived at the introduction of Christianity, as by all appearance he did, his epoch will be the latter end of the third, and beginning of the fourth century. What puts this point beyond dispute, is the allusion in his poems to the history of the times.[33]

The exploits of Fingal against Caracul[34], the son of the *King of the World*, are among the first brave actions of his youth. A complete poem, which relates to this subject, is printed in this collection.

In the year 210 the emperor Severus, after returning from his expeditions against the Caledonians, at York fell into the tedious illness of which he afterwards died. The Caledonians and Maiatæ, resuming courage from his indisposition, took arms in order to recover the possessions they had lost. The enraged emperor commanded his army to march into their country, and to destroy it with fire and sword. His orders were but ill executed, for his son, Caracalla, was at the head of the army, and his thoughts were entirely taken up with the hopes of his father's death, and with schemes to supplant his brother Geta.—He scarcely had entered the enemy's country, when news was brought him that Severus was dead.—A sudden peace is patched up with the Caledonians, and, as it appears from Dion Cassius, the country they had lost to Severus was restored to them.

The Caracul of Fingal is no other than Caracalla, who, as the son of Severus, the Emperor of Rome, whose dominions were extended almost over the known world, was not without reason called in the poems of Ossian,[35] *the Son of the King of the World*. The space of time between 211, the year Severus died, and the beginning of the fourth century, is not so great, but Ossian the son of Fingal, might have seen the Christians whom the persecution under Dioclesian had driven beyond the pale of the Roman empire.

Ossian, in one of his many lamentations on the death of his beloved son Oscar, mentions among his great actions, a battle which he fought against Caros, king of ships, on the banks of the winding Carun[36].[37] It is more than probable, that the Caros mentioned here, is the same with the noted usurper Carausius, who assumed the purple in the year 287, and seizing on Britain, defeated the emperor Maximian Herculius, in several naval engagements, which gives propriety to his being called in Ossian's poems,[38] *the King of Ships*. The *winding Carun* is that small river retaining still the name of Carron, and runs in the neighbourhood of Agricola's wall, which Carausius repaired to obstruct the incursions of the Caledonians. Several other passages in the poems[39] allude to the wars of the Romans; but the two just mentioned clearly fix the epoch of Fingal to the third century; and this account agrees exactly with the Irish histories, which place the death of Fingal, the son of Comhal, in the year 283, and that of Oscar and their own celebrated Cairbre, in the year 296.

Some people may imagine, that the allusions to the Roman history might have been industriously inserted into the poems, to give them the appearance of antiquity. This fraud must then have been committed at least three ages ago, as the passages in which the allusions are made, are alluded to often in the compositions of those times.[40]

Every one knows what a cloud of ignorance and barbarism overspread the north of Europe three hundred years ago. The minds of men, addicted to superstition, contracted a narrowness that destroyed genius. Accordingly we find the compositions of those times trivial and puerile to the last degree. But let it be allowed, that, amidst all the untoward circumstances of the age, a genius might arise, it is not easy to determine what could induce him to give the honour of his compositions to an age so remote.[41] We find no fact that he has advanced,[42] to favour any designs which could be entertained by any man who lived in the fifteenth century. But should we suppose a poet, through humour, or for reasons which cannot be seen at this distance of time, would ascribe his own compositions to Ossian, it is next to impossible, that he could impose upon his countrymen, when all of them were so well acquainted with the traditional poems of their ancestors.[43]

The strongest objection to the authenticity[44] of the poems now given to the public under the name of Ossian, is the improbability of their being handed down by tradition through so many centuries. Ages of barbarism some will say, could not produce poems abounding with the disinterested and generous sentiments so conspicuous in the compositions of Ossian; and could these ages produce them, it is impossible but they must be lost, or altogether corrupted in a long succession of barbarous generations.

These objections naturally suggest themselves to men unacquainted with the ancient state of the northern parts of Britain. The bards, who were an inferior order of the Druids, did not share their bad fortune. They were spared by the victorious king, as it was through their means only he could hope for immortality to his fame. They attended him in the camp, and contributed to establish his power by their songs. His great actions were magnified, and the populace, who had no ability to examine into his character narrowly, were dazzled with his fame in the rhimes of the bards. In the mean time, men assumed sentiments that are rarely to be met with in an age of barbarism. The bards who were originally the disciples of the Druids, had their minds opened, and their ideas enlarged, by being initiated in the learning of that celebrated order. They could form a perfect hero in their own minds, and ascribe that character to their prince. The inferior chiefs made this ideal character the model of their conduct, and by degrees brought their minds to that generous spirit which breathes in all the poetry of the times. The prince, flattered by his bards, and rivalled by his own heroes, who imitated his character as described in the eulogies of his poets, endeavoured to excel his people in merit, as he was above them in station. This emulation continuing, formed at last the general character of the nation, happily compounded of what is noble in barbarity, and virtuous and generous in a polished people.

When virtue in peace, and bravery in war, are the characteristics of a nation, their actions become interesting, and their fame worthy of immortality. A generous spirit is warmed with noble actions, and becomes ambitious of perpetuating them. This is the true source of that divine inspiration, to which the poets of all ages pretended. When they found their themes inadequate to the warmth of their imaginations, they varnished them over with fables, supplied by their own fancy, or furnished by absurd traditions. These fables, however ridiculous, had their abettors; posterity either implicitly believed them, or through a vanity natural to mankind, pretended that they did. They loved to place the founders of their families in the days of fable, when poetry, without the fear of contradiction, could give what characters she pleased of her heroes. It is to this vanity that we owe the preservation of what remain of the works of Ossian.[45] His poetical merit made his[46] heroes famous in a country where heroism was much esteemed and admired. The posterity of these heroes, or those who pretended to be descended from them, heard with pleasure the eulogiums of their ancestors; bards were employed to repeat the poems, and to record the connection of their patrons with chiefs so renowned. Every chief in process of time had a bard in his family, and the office became at last hereditary. By the succession of these bards, the poems concerning the ancestors of the family were handed down from generation to generation; they were repeated to the whole clan on solemn occasions, and always alluded to in the new compositions of the bards. This custom came down near to our own times; and after the bards were discontinued, a great number in a clan retained by memory, or committed to writing, their compositions, and founded the antiquity of their families on the authority of their poems.

The use of letters was not known in the north of Europe till long after the institution of the bards: the records of the families of their patrons, their own, and more ancient poems were handed down by tradition. Their poetical compositions were admirably contrived for that purpose. They were adapted to music; and the most perfect harmony was observed. Each verse was so connected with those which preceded or followed it, that if one line had been remembered in a stanza, it was almost impossible to forget the rest. The cadences followed in so natural a gradation, and the words were so adapted to the common turn of the voice, after it is raised to a certain key, that it was almost impossible, from a similarity of sound, to substitute one word for another. This excellence is peculiar to the Celtic tongue, and is perhaps to be met with in no other language. Nor does this choice of words clog the sense or weaken the expression. The numerous flections of consonants, and variation in declension, make the language very copious.

The descendants of the Celtæ, who inhabited Britain and its isles, were not singular in this method of preserving the most precious monuments of their nation. The ancient laws of the Greeks were couched in verse, and handed down by tradition. The Spartans, through a long habit, became so fond of this custom, that they would never allow their laws to be committed to writing. The actions of great men, and the eulogiums of kings and heroes, were preserved in the same manner. All the historical monuments of the old Germans were comprehended in their ancient songs[47]; which were either hymns to their gods, or elegies in praise of their heroes, and were intended to perpetuate the great events in their nation which were carefully interwoven with them. This species of composition was not committed to writing, but delivered by oral tradition[48]. The care they took to have the poems taught to their children, the uninterrupted custom of repeating them upon certain occasions, and the happy measure of the verse, served to preserve them for a long time uncorrupted. This oral chronicle of the Germans was not forgot in the eighth century, and it probably would have remained to this day, had not learning, which thinks every thing, that is not committed to writing, fabulous, been introduced. It was from poetical traditions that Garcillasso composed his account of the Yncas of Peru. The Peruvians had lost all other monuments of their history, and it was from ancient poems which his mother, a princess of the blood of the Yncas, taught him in his youth, that he collected the materials of his history. If other nations then, that had been often overrun by enemies, and had sent abroad and received colonies, could, for many ages, preserve, by oral tradition, their laws and histories uncorrupted, it is much more probable that the ancient Scots, a people so free of intermixture with foreigners, and so strongly attached to the memory of their ancestors, had the works of their bards handed down with great purity.[49]

It will seem strange to some, that poems admired for many centuries in one part of this kingdom should be hitherto unknown in the other; and that the British, who have carefully traced out the works of genius in other nations, should so long remain strangers to their own. This, in a great measure, is to be imputed to those who understood both languages and never attempted a translation. They, from being acquainted but with detached pieces, or from a modesty, which perhaps the present translator ought, in prudence, to have followed, despaired of making the compositions of their bards agreeable to an English reader. The manner of those compositions is so different from other poems, and the ideas so confined to the most early state of society, that it was thought they had not enough of variety to please a polished age.

This was long the opinion of the translator of the following collection; and though he admired the poems, in the original, very early, and gathered part of them from tradition for his own amusement, yet he never had the smallest hopes of seeing them in an English dress. He was sensible that the strength and manner of both languages were very different, and that it was next to impossible to translate the Galic poetry into any thing of tolerable English verse; a prose translation he could never think of, as it must necessarily fall short of the majesty of an original.[50]

It is therefore highly probable, that the compositions of Ossian would have still remained in the obscurity of a lost language, had not a gentleman, who has himself made a figure in the poetical world, insisted with the present editor for a literal prose translation of some detached piece. He approved of the specimen, and, through him, copies came to the hands of several people of taste in Scotland.

Frequent transcription and the corrections of those, who thought they mended the poems by modernizing the ideas, corrupted them to such a degree, that the translator was induced to hearken to the solicitations of a gentleman deservedly esteemed in Scotland, for his taste and knowledge in polite literature, and published the genuine copies under the title of *Fragments of Ancient Poetry*. The fragments, upon their first appearance, were so much approved of, that several people of rank, as well as taste, prevailed with the translator to make a journey to the Highlands and western isles, in order to recover what remained of the works of Ossian the son of Fingal, the best, as well as most ancient of those who are celebrated in tradition for their poetical genius. A detail of this journey would be both tedious and unentertaining; let it suffice therefore that, after a peregrination of six months, the translator collected from tradition, and some manuscripts, all the poems in the following collection, and some more still in his hands, though rendered less complete by the ravages of time.

The action of the poem that stands the first, was not the greatest or most celebrated of the exploits of Fingal. His wars were very numerous, and each of them afforded a theme which employed the genius of his son. But, excepting the present poem, those pieces are in a great measure[51] lost, and there only remain a few fragments of them[52] in the hands of the translator. Tradition has still preserved, in many places, the story of the poems, and many now living have heard them, in their youth, repeated.

The complete work, now printed, would, in a short time, have shared the fate of the rest. The genius of the highlanders has suffered a great change within these few years. The communication with the rest of the island is open, and the introduction of trade and manufactures has destroyed that leisure which was formerly dedicated to hearing and repeating the poems of ancient times. Many have now learned to leave their mountains, and seek their fortunes in a milder climate; and though a certain *amor patriæ* may sometimes bring them back, they have, during their absence, imbibed enough of foreign manners to despise the customs of their ancestors. Bards have been long disused, and the spirit of genealogy has greatly subsided. Men begin to be less devoted to their chiefs, and consanguinity is not so much regarded. When property is established, the human mind confines its views to the pleasure it procures. It does not go back to antiquity, or look forward to succeeding ages. The cares of life increase, and the actions of other times no longer amuse. Hence it is, that the taste for their ancient poetry is at a low ebb among the highlanders. They have not, however, thrown off the good qualities of their ancestors. Hospitality still subsists, and an uncommon civility to strangers. Friendship is inviolable, and revenge less blindly followed than formerly.

To speak of the poetical merit of the poems, would be an anticipation on the judgment of the public: And all[53] that can be said of the translation, is, that it is literal, and that simplicity is studied. The arrangement of the words in the original is imitated, and the inversions of the style observed. As the translator claims no merit from his version, he hopes for the indulgence of the public where he fails. He wishes that the imperfect semblance he draws, may not prejudice the world against an original, which contains what is beautiful in simplicity, and grand in the sublime.

F I N G A L,

AN ANCIENT

EPIC POEM.

In SIX BOOKS.

ARGUMENT to BOOK I.

Cuchullin[1], *(general of the Irish tribes, in the minority of Cormac, king of Ireland) sitting alone beneath a tree, at the gate of Tura, a castle of Ulster, (the other chiefs having gone on a hunting party to Cromla, a neighbouring hill) is informed of the landing of Swaran, king of Lochlin, by Moran, the son of Fithil, one of his scouts. He convenes the chiefs; a council is held, and disputes run high about giving battle to the enemy. Connal, the petty king of Togorma, and an intimate friend of Cuchullin, was for retreating till Fingal, king of those Caledonians who inhabited the north-west coast of Scotland, whose aid had been previously sollicited, should arrive; but Calmar, the son of Matha, lord of Lara, a country in Connaught, was for engaging the enemy immediately.—Cuchullin, of himself willing to fight, went into the opinion of Calmar. Marching towards the enemy, he missed three of his bravest heroes, Fergus, Duchomar, and Caithbat. Fergus arriving, tells Cuchullin of the death of the two other chiefs; which introduces the affecting episode of Morna, the daughter of Cormac.—The army of Cuchullin is descried at a distance by Swaran, who sent the son of Arno to observe the motions of the enemy, while he himself ranged his forces in order of battle.——The son of Arno returning to Swaran, describes to him Cuchullin's chariot, and the terrible appearance of that hero. The armies engage, but night coming on, leaves the victory undecided. Cuchullin, according to the hospitality of the times, sends to Swaran a formal invitation to a feast, by his bard Carril, the son of Kinfena.—Swaran refuses to come. Carril relates to Cuchullin the story of Grudar and Brassolis. A party, by Connal's advice, is sent to observe the enemy; which closes the action of the first day.*[2]

FINGAL BOOK I.

Cuchullin[3] sat by Tura's wall; by the tree of the rustling leaf.[4]——His spear leaned against the mossy rock. His shield lay by him on the grass. As he thought of mighty Carbar[5], a hero whom he slew in war; the scout[6] of the ocean came, Moran[7] the son of Fithil.

Rise, said the youth, Cuchullin, rise; I see the ships of Swaran. Cuchullin, many are the foe: many the heroes of the dark-rolling sea.

Moran! replied the blue-eyed chief, thou ever tremblest, son of Fithil: Thy fears have much increased the foe. Perhaps it is the king[8] of the lonely hills[9] coming to aid me on green Ullin's plains.[10]

I saw their chief, says Moran, tall as a rock of ice.[11] His spear is like that blasted fir. His shield like the rising moon.[12] He sat on a rock on the shore: his dark host rolled, like clouds, around him.[13]——Many, chief of men! I said, many are our hands of war.—Well art thou named, the Mighty Man,[14] but many mighty men are seen from Tura's windy walls.[15]——He answered, like a wave on a rock, who in this land appears like me? Heroes stand not in my presence: they fall to earth beneath my hand. None can meet Swaran in the fight but Fingal, king of stormy hills.[16] Once we wrestled on the heath of Malmor[17], and our heels overturned the wood. Rocks fell from their place; and rivulets, changing their course, fled murmuring from our strife.[18] Three days we renewed our strife, and heroes stood at a distance and trembled. On the fourth, Fingal says, that the king of the ocean fell; but Swaran says, he stood. Let dark Cuchullin yield to him that is strong as the storms of Malmor.[19]

No: replied the blue-eyed chief, I will never yield to man. Dark Cuchullin will be great or dead. Go, Fithil's son, and take my spear: strike the sounding shield of Cabait[20]. It hangs at Tura's rustling gate; the sound of peace is not its voice. My heroes shall hear on the hill.

He went and struck the bossy shield. The hills and their rocks replied. The sound spread along the wood: deer start by the lake of roes. Curach[21] leapt from the sounding rock; and Connal of the bloody spear. Crugal's[22] breast of snow beats high. The son of Favi leaves the dark-brown hind. It is the shield of war, said Ronnar, the spear of Cuchullin, said Lugar.——Son of the sea, put on thy arms! Calmar lift thy sounding steel! Puno! horrid hero, rise: Cairbar from thy red tree of Cromla. Bend thy white knee, O Eth; and descend from the streams of Lena.——Ca-olt stretch thy white side as thou movest along the whistling heath of Mora: thy side that is white as the foam of the troubled sea, when the dark winds pour it on the murmuring rocks of Cuthon[23].

Now I behold the chiefs in the pride of their former deeds; their souls are kindled at the battles of old, and the actions of other times. Their eyes are like[24] flames of fire, and roll in search of the foes of the land.——Their mighty hands are on their swords; and lightning pours from their sides of steel.——They came like streams from the mountains; each rushed roaring from his hill. Bright are the chiefs of battle in the armour of their fathers. ——Gloomy and dark their heroes followed, like the gathering of the rainy clouds behind the red meteors of heaven.——The sounds of crashing arms ascend. The grey dogs howl between. Unequally bursts the song of battle; and rocking Cromla[25] echoes round. On Lena's dusky heath they stood, like mist[26] that shades the hills of autumn: when broken and dark it settles high, and lifts its head to heaven.

Hail, said Cuchullin, sons of the narrow vales, hail ye hunters of the deer. Another sport is drawing near: it is like the dark rolling of that wave on the coast. Shall[27] we fight, ye sons of war! or yield green Innisfail[28] to Lochlin?——O Connal[29] speak, thou first of men! thou breaker of the shields! thou hast often fought with Lochlin; wilt thou lift[30] thy father's spear?

Cuchullin! calm the chief replied, the spear of Connal is keen. It delights to shine in battle, and to mix with the blood of thousands. But tho' my hand is bent on war, my heart is for the peace of Erin[31]. Behold, thou first in Cormac's war, the sable fleet of Swaran. His masts are as numerous on our coast as reeds in the lake of Lego. His ships are like[32] forests cloathed with mist, when the trees yield by turns to the squally wind. Many are his chiefs in battle. Connal is for peace.——Fingal would shun his arm the first of mortal men: Fingal that scatters the mighty, as stormy winds the heath; when the streams roar thro' echoing Cona: and night settles with all her clouds on the hill.

Fly, thou chief of peace, said Calmar[33] the son of Matha; fly, Connal, to thy silent hills, where the spear of battle never shone; pursue the dark-brown deer of Cromla: and stop with thine arrows the bounding roes of Lena. But, blue-eyed son of Semo, Cuchullin, ruler of the war, scatter thou the sons of Lochlin[34], and roar thro' the ranks of their pride. Let no vessel of the kingdom of Snow bound on the dark-rolling waves of Inis-tore[35]. O ye dark winds of Erin rise! roar ye whirlwinds of the heath![36] Amidst the tempest let me die, torn in a cloud by angry ghosts of men; amidst the tempest let Calmar die, if ever chace was sport to him so much as the battle of shields.

Calmar! slow replied the chief, I never fled, O Matha's son. I was swift with my friends in battle, but small is the fame of Connal. The battle was won in my presence, and the valiant overcame. But, son of Semo, hear my voice, regard the ancient throne of Cormac. Give wealth and half the land for peace, till Fingal come with battle. Or, if war be thy choice, I lift the sword and spear. My joy shall be in the midst of thousands, and my soul brighten in the gloom of the fight.

To me, Cuchullin replies, pleasant is the noise of arms: pleasant as the thunder of heaven before the shower of Spring. But gather all the shining tribes that I may view the sons of war. Let them move along the heath, bright as the sun-shine before a storm; when the west wind collects the clouds, and the oaks of Morven echo along the shore.[37]

But where are my friends in battle? The companions of my arm in danger? Where art thou, white-bosom'd Cathbat[38]? Where is that cloud in war, Duchomar[39]? and hast thou left me, O Fergus[40]! in the day of the storm? Fergus, first in our joy at the feast! son of Rossa! arm of death! comest thou like a roe[41] from Malmor? Like a hart from the echoing hills?——Hail thou son of Rossa! what shades the soul of war?

Four stones[42], replied the chief, rise on the grave of Cathbat.——These hands have laid in earth Duchomar, that cloud in war. Cathbat, thou son of Torman, thou wert a sun-beam on the hill.[43]——And thou, O valiant Duchomar, like[44] the mist of marshy Lano; when it sails over the plains of autumn and brings death to the people.[45] Morna, thou fairest of maids! calm is thy sleep in the cave of the rock. Thou hast fallen in darkness like a star, that shoots athwart the desart, when the traveller is alone, and mourns the transient beam.

Say, said Semo's blue-eyed son, say how fell the chiefs of Erin? Fell they by the sons of Lochlin, striving in the battle of heroes? Or what confines the chiefs of Cromla[46] to the dark and narrow house[47]?

Cathbat, replied the hero, fell by the sword of Duchomar at the oak of the noisy streams. Duchomar came to Tura's cave, and spoke to the lovely Morna.

Morna[48], fairest among women, lovely daughter of Cormac-cairbar.[49] Why in the circle of stones; in the cave of the rock alone? The stream murmurs hoarsely. The old tree's groan is in the wind. The lake is troubled before thee, and dark are the clouds of the sky. But thou art like snow on the heath; and thy hair like the mist of Cromla;[50] when it curls on the rocks, and shines to the beam of the west.——Thy breasts are like[51] two smooth rocks seen from Branno of the streams. Thy arms like two white pillars in the halls of the mighty Fingal.

From whence, the white-armed[52] maid replied, from whence, Duchomar the most gloomy of men? Dark are thy brows and terrible. Red are thy rolling eyes. Does Swaran appear on the sea? What of the foe, Duchomar?

From the hill I return, O Morna, from the hill of the dark-brown hinds. Three have I slain with my bended yew. Three with my long bounding dogs of the chace.——Lovely daughter of Cormac, I love thee as my soul.——I have slain one stately deer for thee.——High was his branchy head; and fleet his feet of wind.

Duchomar! calm the maid replied, I love thee not, thou gloomy man.—— Hard is thy heart of rock, and dark thy terrible brow. But Cathbat, thou son of Torman[53], thou art the love of Morna. Thou art like a sun-beam on the hill in the day of the gloomy storm. Sawest thou the son of Torman, lovely on the hill of his hinds? Here the daughter of Cormac waits the coming of Cathbat.

And long shall Morna wait, Duchomar said, his blood is on my sword.[54] ——Long shall Morna wait for him. He fell at Branno's stream. High on Cromla I will raise his tomb, daughter of Cormac-cairbar; but fix thy love on Duchomar, his arm is strong as a storm.——

And is the son of Torman fallen? said the maid of the tearful eye.[55] Is he fallen on his echoing heath;[56] the youth with the breast of snow? he that was first in the chace of the hill; the foe of the strangers of the ocean.—— Duchomar thou art dark[57] indeed, and cruel is thy arm to Morna. But give me that sword, my foe; I love the blood[58] of Caithbat.

He gave the sword to her tears; but she pierced his manly breast. He fell, like the bank of a mountain-stream; stretched out his arm and said;

Daughter of Cormac-cairbar, thou hast slain Duchomar.[59] The sword is cold in my breast: Morna, I feel it cold. Give me to Moina[60] the maid; Duchomar was the dream of her night. She will raise my tomb; and the hunter shall see it and praise me. But draw the sword from my breast; Morna, the steel is cold.

She came, in all her tears, she came, and drew it from his breast. He pierced her white side with steel; and spread her fair locks on the ground. Her bursting blood sounds from her side: and her white arm is stained with red. Rolling in death she lay, and Tura's cave answered to her groans.[61]——

Peace, said Cuchullin, to the souls of the heroes; their deeds were great in danger. Let them ride around[62] me on clouds; and shew their features of war: that my soul may be strong in danger; my arm like the thunder of heaven.——But be thou on a moon-beam, O Morna, near the window of my rest; when my thoughts are of peace; and the din of arms is over.—— Gather the strength of the tribes, and move to the wars of Erin.——Attend the car of my battles; rejoice in the noise of my course.——Place three spears by my side; follow the bounding of my steeds; that my soul may be strong in my friends, when the battle darkens round the beams of my steel.

As rushes a stream[63] of foam from the dark shady steep[64] of Cromla; when the thunder is rolling above, and dark-brown night on half the hill.[65] So fierce, so vast, so terrible rushed on the sons of Erin. The chief like a whale of ocean, whom all his billows follow, poured valour forth as a stream, rolling his might along the shore.

The sons of Lochlin heard the noise as the sound of a winter-stream.[66] Swaran struck his bossy shield, and called the son of Arno. What murmur rolls along the hill like the gathered flies of evening? The sons of Innis-fail descend, or rustling winds[67] roar in the distant wood. Such is the noise of Gormal before the white tops of my waves arise. O son of Arno, ascend the hill and view the dark face of the heath.

He went, and trembling, swift returned. His eyes rolled wildly round. His heart beat high against his side. His words were faultering, broken, slow.

Rise, son of ocean, rise chief of the dark-brown shields. I see the dark, the mountain-stream of the battle: the deep-moving strength of the sons of Erin.——The car, the car of battle comes, like the flame of death; the rapid car of Cuchullin, the noble son of Semo.[68] It bends behind like a wave near a rock; like the golden[69] mist of the heath. Its sides are embossed with stones, and sparkle like the sea round the boat of night. Of polished yew is its beam, and its seat of the smoothest bone. The sides are replenished with spears; and the bottom is the footstool of heroes. Before the right side of the car is seen the snorting horse. The high-maned, broad-breasted, proud, high-leaping,[70] strong steed of the hill. Loud and resounding is his hoof; the spreading of his mane above is like that stream of smoke on the heath.[71] Bright are the sides of the steed, and his name is Sulin-Sifadda.

Before the left side of the car is seen the snorting horse. The dark-maned,[72] high-headed, strong-hooffed, fleet, bounding son of the hill: his name is Dusronnal among the stormy sons of the sword.——A thousand thongs bind the car on high. Hard polished bits shine in a wreath of foam. Thin thongs bright-studded with gems, bend on the stately necks of the steeds.——The steeds that like wreaths of mist fly over the streamy vales. The wildness of deer is in their course, the strength of the eagle descending on her prey. Their noise is like the blast of winter on the sides of the snow-headed Gormal[73].

Within the car is seen the chief; the strong stormy son[74] of the sword; the hero's name is Cuchullin, son of Semo king of shells. His red cheek is like my polished yew. The look of his blue-rolling eye is wide beneath the dark arch of his brow. His hair flies from his head like a flame, as bending forward he wields the spear. Fly, king of ocean, fly; he comes, like a storm, along the streamy vale.

When did I fly, replied the king, from the battle of many spears? When did I fly, son of Arno,[75] chief of the little soul? I met the storm of Gormal when the foam of my waves was high; I met the storm of the clouds and shall I fly from a hero? Were it Fingal himself my soul should not darken before him.——Rise to the battle, my thousands; pour round me like the echoing main. Gather round the bright steel of your king; strong as the rocks of my land; that meet the storm with joy, and stretch their dark woods[76] to the wind.

As autumn's[77] dark storms pour from two echoing hills, towards each other approached the heroes.——As two dark[78] streams from high rocks meet, and mix and roar on the plain; loud, rough and dark in battle meet Lochlin and Innis-fail. Chief mixed his strokes with chief, and man with man; steel, clanging, sounded on steel, helmets are cleft on high. Blood bursts and smoaks around.——Strings twang[79] on the polished yews. Darts rush along the sky. Spears fall like the circles of light that gild the stormy face of night.

As the troubled noise of the ocean when roll the waves on high; as the last peal of the thunder of heaven, such is the noise of battle. Though Cormac's hundred bards were there to give the war to song; feeble were the voices of a hundred bards to send the deaths to future times. For many were the falls of the heroes; and wide poured the blood of the valiant.

Mourn, ye sons of song, the death of the noble Sithallin[80].——Let the sighs of Fiöna rise on the dark heaths of her lovely Ardan.——They fell, like two hinds of the desart, by the hands of the mighty Swaran; when, in the midst of thousands he roared; like the shrill spirit of a storm, that sits dim, on the clouds of Gormal, and enjoys the death of the mariner.

Nor slept thy hand by thy side, chief of the isle of mist[81]; many were the deaths of thine arm, Cuchullin, thou son of Semo. His sword was like the beam of heaven when it pierces the sons of the vale; when the people are blasted and fall, and all the hills are burning around.——Dusronnal[82] snorted over the bodies of heroes; and Sifadda[83] bathed his hoof in blood. The battle lay behind them as groves overturned on the desart of Cromla; when the blast has passed the heath laden with the spirits of night.

Weep on the rocks of roaring winds, O maid of Inistore[84], bend thy fair head over the waves, thou fairer than the spirit[85] of the hills; when it moves in a sun-beam at noon over the silence of Morven. He is fallen! thy youth is low; pale beneath the sword of Cuchullin. No more shall valour raise the youth[86] to match the blood of kings.——Trenar, lovely Trenar died, thou maid of Inistore. His gray dogs are howling at home, and see his passing ghost. His bow is in the hall unstrung. No sound is in the heath[87] of his hinds.

As roll a thousand waves to the rocks, so Swaran's host came on; as meets a rock a thousand waves, so Innis-fail met Swaran.[88] Death raises all his voices around, and mixes with the sound of shields.——Each hero is a pillar of darkness, and the sword a beam of fire in his hand. The field echoes from wing to wing, as a hundred hammers that rise by turns on the red son of the furnace.

Who are these on Lena's heath that are so gloomy and dark? Who are these like two clouds[89], and their swords like lightning above them? The little hills are troubled around, and the rocks tremble with all their moss.——Who is it but Ocean's son and the car-borne chief of Erin? Many are the anxious eyes of their friends, as they see them dim on the heath. Now night conceals the chiefs in her clouds, and ends the terrible fight.

It was on Cromla's shaggy side that Dorglas placed the deer[90]; the early fortune of the chace, before the heroes left the hill.——A hundred youths collect the heath; ten heroes blow the fire; three hundred chuse the polish'd stones. The feast is smoking wide.

Cuchullin, chief of Erin's war, resumed his mighty soul. He stood upon his beamy spear, and spoke to the son of songs; to Carril of other times, the gray-haired son of Kinfena[91]. Is this feast spread for me alone and the king of Lochlin on Ullin's[92] shore, far from the deer of his hills, and sounding halls of his feasts? Rise, Carril of other times, and carry my words to Swaran; tell him that came from[93] the roaring of waters, that Cuchullin gives his feast. Here let him listen to the sound of my groves amidst the clouds of night.——For cold and bleak the blustering winds rush over the foam of his seas. Here let him praise the trembling harp, and hear the songs of heroes.

Old Carril went, with softest voice, and called the king of dark-brown shields. Rise from the skins of thy chace, rise, Swaran king of groves.—— Cuchullin gives the joy of shells; partake the feast of Erin's blue-eyed chief.

He answered like the sullen sound of Cromla before a storm. Though all thy daughters, Innis-fail! should extend their arms of snow; raise high the heavings of their breasts, and softly roll their eyes of love; yet, fixed as Lochlin's thousand rocks, here Swaran shall remain; till morn, with the young beams of my east, shall light me to the death of Cuchullin. Pleasant to my ear is Lochlin's wind. It rushes over my seas. It speaks aloft in all my shrowds, and brings my green forests to my mind; the green forests of Gormal that often echoed to my winds, when my spear was red in the chace of the boar. Let dark Cuchullin yield to me the ancient throne of Cormac, or Erin's torrents shall shew from their hills the red foam of the blood of his pride.

Sad is the sound of Swaran's voice, said Carril of other times:——

Sad to himself alone, said the blue-eyed son of Semo. But, Carril, raise thy voice on high, and tell the deeds of other times. Send thou the night away in song; and give the joy of grief. For many heroes and maids of love have moved on Innis-fail. And lovely are the songs of woe that are heard on Albion's rocks; when the noise of the chace is over, and the streams of Cona answer to the voice of Ossian[94].

In other days[95], Carril replies, came the sons of Ocean to Erin. A thousand vessels bounded over the waves to Ullin's lovely plains. The sons of Innis-fail arose to meet the race of dark-brown shields. Cairbar, first of men, was there, and Grudar, stately youth. Long had they strove for the spotted bull, that lowed on Golbun's[96] echoing heath. Each claimed him as his own; and death was often at the point of their steel.

Side by side the heroes fought, and the strangers of Ocean fled. Whose name was fairer on the hill than the name of Cairbar and Grudar!——But ah! why ever lowed the bull on Golbun's echoing heath? They saw him leaping like the snow. The wrath of the chiefs returned.

On Lubar's[97] grassy banks they fought, and Grudar like a sun-beam,[98] fell. Fierce Cairbar came to the vale of the echoing Tura, where Brassolis[99], fairest of his sisters, all alone, raised the song of grief. She sung of the actions of Grudar, the youth of her secret soul.——She mourned him in the field of blood; but still she hoped for his return. Her white bosom is seen from her robe, as the moon from the clouds of night.[100] Her voice was softer than the harp to raise the song of grief. Her soul was fixed on Grudar; the secret look of her eye was his.——When shalt thou come in thine arms, thou mighty in the war?——

Take, Brassolis, Cairbar came and said, take, Brassolis, this shield of blood. Fix it on high within my hall, the armour of my foe. Her soft heart beat against her side. Distracted, pale, she flew. She found her youth in all his blood; she died on Cromla's heath. Here rests their dust, Cuchullin; and these two lonely yews, sprung from their tombs, wish to meet on high.[101] Fair was Brassolis on the plain, and Grudar on the hill. The bard shall preserve their names, and repeat them to future times.

Pleasant is thy voice, O Carril, said the blue-eyed chief of Erin; and lovely are the words of other times. They are like the calm shower[102] of spring, when the sun looks on the field, and the light cloud flies over the hills. O strike the harp in praise of my love, the lonely sun-beam of Dunscaich.[103] Strike the harp in the praise of Bragéla[104], of her that I left in the Isle of Mist, the spouse of Semo's son. Dost thou raise thy fair face from the rock to find the sails of Cuchullin?——The sea is rolling far distant, and its white foam shall deceive thee for my sails. Retire, for it is night, my love, and the dark winds sigh[105] in thy hair. Retire to the halls of my feasts, and think of the times that are past: for I will not return till the storm of war is ceased. O Connal, speak of wars and arms, and send her from my mind, for lovely with her raven-hair[106] is the white-bosomed daughter of Sorglan.

Connal, slow to speak, replied, Guard against the race of Ocean. Send thy troop of night abroad, and watch the strength of Swaran.——Cuchullin! I am for peace till the race of the desart[107] come; till Fingal come, the first of men, and beam, like the sun, on our fields.

The hero struck the shield of his alarms——the warriors of the night moved on. The rest lay in the heath of the deer, and slept amidst the dusky wind.——The ghosts[108] of the lately dead were near, and swam on gloomy clouds. And far distant, in the dark silence of Lena, the feeble voices of death were heard.

FINGAL,

AN ANCIENT

EPIC POEM.

BOOK II.

ARGUMENT to BOOK II.

*The ghost of Crugal, one of the Irish heroes who was killed in battle,
appearing to Connal, foretels the defeat of Cuchullin in the next battle;
and earnestly advises him to make peace with Swaran. Connal communi-
cates the vision; but Cuchullin is inflexible; from a principle of honour he
would not be the first to sue for peace, and he resolved to continue the
war. Morning comes; Swaran proposes dishonourable terms to Cuchullin,
which are rejected. The battle begins, and is obstinately fought for some
time, until, upon the flight of Grumal, the whole Irish army gave way.
Cuchullin and Connal cover their retreat: Carril leads them to a neigh-
bouring hill, whither they are soon followed by Cuchullin himself, who
descries the fleet of Fingal making towards the coast; but, night coming
on, he lost sight of it again. Cuchullin, dejected after his defeat, attributes
his ill success to the death of Ferda his friend, whom he had killed some
time before. Carril, to shew that ill success did not always attend those
who innocently killed their friends, introduces the episode of Comal and
Galvina.*

Connal[1] lay by the sound of the mountain stream, beneath the aged tree. A stone, with its moss, supported his head. Shrill thro' the heath of Lena, he heard the voice of night. At distance from the heroes he lay, for the son of the sword feared no foe.

My hero saw in his rest a dark-red stream of fire coming[2] down from the hill. Crugal sat upon the beam, a chief that lately fell. He fell by the hand of Swaran, striving in the battle of heroes. His face is like the beam of the setting moon; his robes are of the clouds of the hill: his eyes are like[3] two decaying flames. Dark is the wound of his breast.

Crugal, said the mighty Connal, son of Dedgal famed on the hill of deer. Why so pale and sad, thou breaker of the shields? Thou hast never been pale for fear.——What disturbs the son of the hill?[4]

Dim, and in tears, he stood and stretched his pale hand over the hero.—— Faintly he raised his feeble voice, like the gale of the reedy Lego.

My ghost,[5] O Connal, is on my native hills; but my corse is on the sands of Ullin.[6] Thou shalt never talk with Crugal, or find his lone steps in the heath. I am light as the blast of Cromla, and I move like the shadow of mist. Connal, son of Colgar[7], I see the dark cloud of death: it hovers over the plains of Lena. The sons of green Erin shall fall. Remove from the field of ghosts.——Like the darkened moon[8] he retired, in the midst of the whistling blast.

Stay, said the mighty Connal, stay my dark-red friend. Lay by that beam of heaven, son of the windy Cromla. What cave of the hill is thy lonely house? What green-headed hill is the place of thy rest? Shall we not hear thee in the storm? In the noise of the mountain-stream? When the feeble sons of the wind come forth, and ride on the blast of the desart.[9]

The soft-voiced Connal rose in the midst of his sounding arms. He struck his shield above Cuchullin. The son of battle waked.

Why, said the ruler of the car, comes Connal through the night? My spear might turn against the sound; and Cuchullin mourn the death of his friend. Speak, Connal, son of Colgar, speak, thy counsel is like the son of heaven.[10]

Son of Semo, replied the chief, the ghost of Crugal came from the cave of his hill.——The stars dim-twinkled through his form; and his voice was like the sound of a distant stream.——He is a messenger of death.——He speaks of the dark and narrow house. Sue for peace, O chief of Dunscaich;[11] or fly over the heath of Lena.

He spoke to Connal, replied the hero, though stars dim-twinkled through his form. Son of Colgar, it was the wind that murmured in the caves of

Lena.[12]——Or if it was the form[13] of Crugal, why didst thou not force him to my sight. Hast thou enquired where is his cave? The house of the son of the wind? My sword might find that voice, and force his knowledge from him. And small is his knowledge, Connal, for he was here to day. He could not have gone beyond our hills, and who could tell him there of our death?

Ghosts fly on clouds and ride on winds, said Connal's voice of wisdom. They rest together in their caves, and talk of mortal men.

Then let them talk of mortal men; of every man but Erin's chief. Let me be forgot in their cave; for I will not fly from Swaran.——If I must fall, my tomb shall rise amidst the fame of future times. The hunter shall shed a tear on my stone; and sorrow dwell round the high-bosomed Bragéla. I fear not death, but I fear to fly, for Fingal saw me often victorious. Thou dim phantom of the hill, shew thyself to me! come on thy beam of heaven, and shew me my death in thine hand; yet will I not[14] fly, thou feeble son of the wind. Go, son of Colgar, strike the shield of Caithbat, it[15] hangs between the spears. Let my heroes rise to the sound in the midst of the battles of Erin. Though Fingal delays his coming with the race of the stormy hills;[16] we shall fight, O Colgar's son, and die in the battle of heroes.

The sound spreads wide; the heroes rise, like the breaking of a blue-rolling wave. They stood on the heath, like oaks with all their branches round them[17]; when they eccho to the stream of frost, and their withered leaves rustle to the wind.

High Cromla's head of clouds is gray; the morning trembles on the half-enlightened ocean. The blue, gray mist[18] swims slowly by, and hides the sons of Innis-fail.

Rise ye, said the king of the dark-brown shields, ye that came from Lochlin's waves. The sons of Erin have fled from our arms——pursue them over the plains of Lena.——And, Morla, go to Cormac's hall and bid them yield to Swaran; before the people shall fall into the tomb; and the hills of Ullin be silent.[19]——They rose[20] like a flock of sea-fowl when the waves expel them from the shore. Their sound was like a thousand streams that meet in Cona's vale, when after a stormy night, they turn their dark eddies beneath the pale light of the morning.

As the dark shades of autumn fly over the hills of grass; so gloomy, dark, successive came the chiefs of Lochlin's echoing woods. Tall as the stag of Morven moved on the king of groves.[21] His shining shield is on his side like a flame on the heath at night, when the world is silent and dark, and the traveller sees some ghost sporting in the beam.[22]

A blast from the troubled ocean removed the settled mist. The sons of Innis-fail[23] appear like a ridge of rocks on the shore.[24]

Go, Morla, go, said Lochlin's king, and offer peace to these. Offer the terms we give to kings when nations bow before us. When the valiant are dead in war, and the virgins weeping on the field.

Great Morla came, the son of Swart,[25] and stately strode the king of shields.[26] He spoke to Erin's blue-eyed son,[27] among the lesser heroes.

Take Swaran's peace, the warrior spoke, the peace he gives to kings, when the nations bow before him. Leave Ullin's lovely[28] plains to us, and give thy spouse and dog. Thy spouse high-bosom'd heaving fair. Thy dog that overtakes the wind. Give these to prove the weakness of thine arm, and live beneath our power.

Tell Swaran, tell that heart of pride, that Cuchullin never yields.——I give him the dark-blue rolling of ocean, or I give his people graves in Erin! Never shall a stranger have the lovely sun-beam of Dunscaich;[29] nor ever deer fly on Lochlin's hills before the nimble-footed Luäth.

Vain ruler of the car, said Morla, wilt thou fight the king; that king whose ships of many groves could carry off thine Isle? So little is thy green-hilled Ullin[30] to the king of stormy waves.

In words I yield to many, Morla; but this sword shall yield to none. Erin shall own the sway of Cormac, while Connal and Cuchullin live. O Connal, first of mighty men, thou hast heard the words of Morla; shall thy thoughts then be of peace, thou breaker of the shields? Spirit of fallen Crugal! why didst thou threaten us with death? The narrow house shall receive me in the midst of the light of renown.——Exalt, ye sons of Innis-fail,[31] exalt the spear and bend the bow; rush on the foe in darkness, as the spirits of stormy nights.

Then dismal, roaring, fierce, and deep the gloom of battle rolled along; as mist[32] that is poured on the valley,[33] when storms invade the silent sunshine of heaven. The chief[34] moves before in arms, like an angry ghost before a cloud; when meteors inclose him with fire; and the dark winds are in his hand.——Carril, far on the heath, bids the horn of battle sound. He raises the voice of the song, and pours his soul into the minds of heroes.

Where, said the mouth of the song, where is the fallen Crugal? He lies forgot on earth, and the hall of shells[35] is silent.——Sad is the spouse of Crugal, for she is a stranger[36] in the hall of her sorrow. But who is she, that, like a sun-beam, flies before the ranks of the foe? It is Degrena[37], lovely fair, the spouse of fallen Crugal. Her hair is on the wind behind. Her eye is red; her voice is shrill. Green,[38] empty is thy Crugal now, his form is in the cave of the hill. He comes to the ear of rest, and raises his feeble voice; like the humming of the mountain-bee, or collected flies of evening. But Degrena falls like a cloud of the morn; the sword of Lochlin is in her side. Cairbar, she is fallen, the rising thought of thy youth. She is fallen, O Cairbar, the thought of thy youthful hours.

Fierce Cairbar heard the mournful sound, and rushed on like ocean's whale; he saw the death of his daughter; and roared in the midst of thousands[39]. His spear met a son of Lochlin, and battle spread from wing to wing. As a hundred winds in Lochlin's groves, as fire in the firs[40] of a hundred hills; so loud, so ruinous and vast the ranks of men are hewn down.——Cuchullin cut off heroes like thistles, and Swaran wasted Erin. Curach fell by his hand, and Cairbar of the bossy shield. Morglan lies in lasting rest; and Ca-olt quivers as he dies. His white breast is stained with his blood; and his yellow hair stretched in the dust of his native land. He often had spread the feast where he fell; and often raised the voice of the harp: when his dogs leapt around for joy; and the youths of the chace prepared the bow.

Still Swaran advanced, as a stream that bursts from the desert. The little hills are rolled in its course; and the rocks half-sunk by its side. But Cuchullin stood before him like a hill[41], that catches the clouds of heaven.——The winds contend on its head of pines; and the hail rattles on its rocks. But, firm in its strength, it stands and shades the silent vale of Cona.

So Cuchullin shaded the sons of Erin, and stood in the midst of thousands. Blood rises like the fount of a rock, from panting heroes around him. But Erin falls on either wing like snow in the day of the sun.

O sons of Innis-fail,[42] said Grumal, Lochlin conquers on the field. Why strive we as reeds against the wind? Fly to the hill of dark-brown hinds. He fled like the stag of Morven, and his spear is a trembling beam of light behind him. Few fled with Grumal, the chief of the little soul: they fell in the battle of heroes on Lena's echoing heath.

High on his car, of many gems, the chief of Erin stood; he slew a mighty son of Lochlin, and spoke, in haste, to Connal. O Connal, first of mortal men, thou hast taught this arm of death! Though Erin's sons have fled, shall we not fight the foe? O Carril, son of other times, carry my living friends to that bushy hill.——Here, Connal, let us stand like rocks, and save our flying friends.

Connal mounts the car of light.[43] They stretch their shields like the darkened moon, the daughter of the starry skies, when she moves, a dun circle, through heaven.[44] Sithfadda panted up the hill, and Dusronnal[45] haughty steed. Like waves behind a whale behind them rushed the foe.

Now on the rising side of Cromla stood Erin's few sad sons; like a grove through which the flame had rushed hurried on by the winds of the stormy night.[46]——Cuchullin stood beside an oak. He rolled his red eye in silence, and heard the wind in his bushy hair; when the scout of ocean came, Moran the son of Fithil.——The ships, he cried, the ships of the lonely isle! There Fingal comes, the first of men, the breaker of the shields. The waves foam before his black prows. His masts with sails are like groves in clouds.

Blow, said Cuchullin, all ye winds that rush over my isle of lovely[47] mist. Come to the death of thousands, O chief of the hills of hinds.[48] Thy sails, my friend, are to me like[49] the clouds of the morning; and thy ships like[49] the light of heaven; and thou thyself like[49] a pillar of fire that giveth light in the night. O Connal, first of men, how pleasant[50] are our friends! But the night is gathering around; where now are the ships of Fingal? Here let us pass the hours of darkness, and wish for the moon of heaven.

The winds came down on the woods. The torrents rushed from the rocks. Rain gathered round the head of Cromla. And the red stars trembled between the flying clouds. Sad, by the side of a stream whose sound was echoed by a tree, sad by the side of a stream the chief of Erin sat. Connal son of Colgar was there, and Carril of other times.

Unhappy is the hand of Cuchullin, said the son of Semo, unhappy is the hand of Cuchullin since he slew his friend.——Ferda, thou son of Damman, I loved thee as myself.

How, Cuchullin, son of Semo, fell the breaker of the shields? Well I remember, said Connal, the noble son of Damman.[51] Tall and fair he was like the rain-bow of the hill.[52]

Ferda from Albion came, the chief of a hundred hills. In Muri's[53] hall he learned the sword, and won the friendship of Cuchullin. We moved to the chace together; and one was our bed in the heath.

Deugala was the spouse of Cairbar, chief of the plains of Ullin. She was covered with the light of beauty, but her heart was the house of pride. She loved that sun-beam of youth, the noble son of Damman.[54] Cairbar, said the white-armed woman, give me half of the herd. No more I will remain in your halls. Divide the herd, dark Cairbar.

Let Cuchullin, said Cairbar, divide my herd on the hill. His breast is the seat of justice. Depart, thou light of beauty.——I went and divided the herd. One snow-white bull[55] remained. I gave that bull to Cairbar. The wrath of Deugala rose.

Son of Damman, begun the fair, Cuchullin pains my soul. I must hear of his death, or Lubar's stream shall roll over me. My pale ghost shall wander near thee, and mourn the wound of my pride. Pour out the blood of Cuchullin or pierce this heaving breast.

Deugala, said the fair-haired youth, how shall I slay the son of Semo? He is the friend of my secret thoughts, and shall I lift the sword? She wept three days before him,[56] on the fourth he consented to fight.

I will fight my friend, Deugala! but may I fall by his sword. Could I wander on the hill and behold the grave of Cuchullin? We fought on the hills[57] of Muri. Our swords avoid a wound. They slide on the helmets of steel; and sound on the slippery shields. Deugala was near with a smile, and said to the son of Damman, thine arm is feeble, thou sun-beam[58] of youth. Thy years are not strong for steel.——Yield to the son of Semo. He is like the rock of Malmor.[59]

The tear is in the eye of youth. He faultering said to me, Cuchullin, raise thy bossy shield. Defend thee from the hand of thy friend. My soul is laden with grief: for I must slay the chief of men.

I sighed as the wind in the chink of a rock. I lifted high the edge of my steel. The sun-beam of the battle fell; the first of Cuchullin's friends.——

Unhappy is the hand of Cuchullin since the hero fell.

Mournful is thy tale, son of the car, said Carril of other times. It sends my soul back to the ages of old, and to the days of other years.——Often have I heard of Comal who slew the friend he loved; yet victory attended his steel; and the battle was consumed in his presence.

Comal was a son of Albion; the chief of an hundred hills. His deer drunk of a thousand streams. A thousand rocks replied to the voice of his dogs. His face was the mildness of youth. His hand the death of heroes. One was his love, and fair was she! the daughter of mighty Conloch. She appeared like a sun-beam among women. And her hair was like[60] the wing of the raven. Her dogs were taught to the chace. Her bow-string sounded on the winds of the forest. Her soul was fixed on Comal. Often met their eyes of love. Their course in the chace was one, and happy were their words in secret.——But Grumal[61] loved the maid, the dark chief of the gloomy Ard-ven. He watched her lone steps in the heath; the foe of unhappy Comal.

One day, tired of the chace, when the mist had concealed their friends, Comal and the daughter of Conloch met in the cave of Ronan[62]. It was the wonted haunt of Comal. Its sides were hung with his arms. A hundred shields of thongs were there; a hundred helms of sounding steel.

Rest here, he said, my love Galvina[63]; thou light of the cave of Ronan. A deer appears on Mora's brow. I go; but I will soon return. I fear, she said, dark Grumal my foe; he haunts the cave of Ronan. I will rest among the arms; but soon return, my love.

He went to the deer of Mora. The daughter of Conloch would try his love. She cloathed her white[64] sides with his armour, and strode from the cave of Ronan. He thought it was his foe. His heart beat high. His colour changed, and darkness dimmed his eyes. He drew the bow. The arrow flew. Galvina fell in blood. He run with wildness in his steps and called the daughter of Conloch. No answer in the lonely rock. Where art thou, O my love! He saw, at length, her heaving heart beating around the feathered dart.[65] O Con-loch's daughter, is it thou? He sunk upon her breast.

The hunters found the hapless pair; he afterwards walked the hill. But many and silent were his steps round the dark dwelling of his love. The fleet of the ocean came. He fought; the strangers fled. He searched for his death over the field. But who could kill the mighty Comal! He threw away his dark-brown shield. An arrow found his manly breast. He sleeps with his loved Galvina at the noise of the sounding surge. Their green tombs are seen by the mariner, when he bounds on the waves of the north.

FINGAL,

AN ANCIENT

EPIC POEM.

BOOK III.

ARGUMENT to BOOK III.

Cuchullin, pleased with the story of Carril, insists with that bard for more of his songs. He relates the actions of Fingal in Lochlin, and death of Agandecca the beautiful sister of Swaran. He had scarce finished when Calmar the son of Matha, who had advised the first battle, came wounded from the field, and told them of Swaran's design to surprise the remains of the Irish army. He himself proposes to withstand singly the whole force of the enemy, in a narrow pass, till the Irish should make good their retreat. Cuchullin, touched with the gallant proposal of Calmar, resolves to accompany him, and orders Carril to carry off the few that remained of the Irish. Morning comes, Calmar dies of his wounds; and, the ships of the Caledonians appearing, Swaran gives over the pursuit of the Irish, and returns to oppose Fingal's landing. Cuchullin ashamed, after his defeat, to appear before Fingal, retires to the cave of Tura. Fingal engages the enemy, puts them to flight; but the coming on of night makes the victory not decisive. The king, who had observed the gallant behaviour of his grandson Oscar, gives him advices concerning his conduct in peace and war. He recommends to him to place the example of his fathers before his eyes, as the best model for his conduct; which introduces the episode concerning Fainasóllis, the daughter of the king of Craca, whom Fingal had taken under his protection, in his youth. Fillan and Oscar are dispatched to observe the motions of the enemy by night; Gaul the son of Morni desires the command of the army, in the next battle; which Fingal promises to give him. Some general reflections of the poet close the third day.

FINGAL BOOK III [1].

Pleasant are the words of the song, said Cuchullin, and lovely are the tales of other times. They are like the calm dew of the morning on the hill of roes, when the sun is faint on its side, and the lake is settled and blue in the vale. O Carril, raise again thy voice, and let me hear the song of Tura:[2] which was sung in my halls of joy, when Fingal king of shields was there, and glowed at the deeds of his fathers.

Fingal! thou man[3] of battle, said Carril, early were thy deeds in arms. Lochlin was consumed in thy wrath, when thy youth strove with the beauty of maids. They smiled at the fair-blooming face of the hero; but death was in his hands. He was strong as the waters of Lora. His followers were like[4] the roar of a thousand streams. They took the king of Lochlin in battle, but restored him to his ships. His big heart swelled with pride; and the death of the youth was dark in his soul.——For none ever, but Fingal, overcame the strength of the mighty Starno.[5]

He sat in the hall[6] of his shells in Lochlin's woody land. He called the grey-haired Snivan, that often sung round the circle[7] of Loda: when the stone of power heard his cry, and the battle turned in the field of the valiant.

Go; gray-haired Snivan, Starno said, to Ardven's sea-surrounded rocks. Tell to Fingal king of the desart;[8] he that is the fairest among his thousands, tell him I give him my daughter, the loveliest maid that ever heaved a breast of snow. Her arms are white as the foam of my waves. Her soul is generous and mild. Let him come with his bravest heroes to the daughter of the secret hall.

Snivan came to Albion's windy hills:[9] and fair-haired Fingal went.[10] His kindled soul flew before him[11] as he bounded on the waves of the north.

Welcome, said the dark-brown Starno, welcome, king of rocky Morven; and ye his heroes of might; sons of the lonely[12] isle! Three days within my halls shall ye feast; and three days pursue my boars, that your fame may reach the maid that dwells in the secret hall.

The king of snow[13] designed their death, and gave the feast of shells. Fingal, who doubted the foe, kept on his arms of steel. The sons of death were afraid, and fled from the eyes of the hero.[14] The voice of sprightly mirth arose. The trembling harps of joy are strung. Bards sing the battle of heroes; or the heaving breast of love.——Ullin, Fingal's bard, was there; the sweet voice of the hill of Cona.[15] He praised the daughter of snow;[16] and Morven's[17] high-descended chief.——The daughter of snow overheard, and left the hall of her secret sigh. She came in all her beauty, like the moon from the cloud of the east.——Loveliness was around her as light. Her steps were like[18] the music of songs. She saw the youth and loved him. He was the stolen sigh of her soul. Her blue eye rolled on him in secret: and she blest the chief of Morven.[19]

The third day, with all its beams, shone bright on the wood of boars. Forth moved the dark-browed Starno; and Fingal, king of shields. Half the day they spent in the chace; and the spear of Fingal was red in the blood of Gormal.[20]

It was then the daughter of Starno, with blue eyes rolling in tears, came with her voice of love and spoke to the king of Morven.

Fingal, high-descended chief, trust not Starno's heart of pride. Within that wood he has placed his chiefs; beware of the wood of death. But, remember, son of the hill, remember Agandecca: save me from the wrath of my father, king of the windy Morven!

The youth, with unconcern, went on; his heroes by his side. The sons of death fell by his hand; and Gormal echoed around.

Before the halls of Starno the sons of the chace convened. The king's dark brows were like clouds. His eyes like meteors of night. Bring hither, he cries, Agandecca to her lovely king of Morven. His hand is stained with the blood of my people; and her words have not been in vain.——

She came with the red eye of tears. She came with her loose raven locks.[21] Her white breast heaved with sighs,[22] like the foam of the streamy Lubar. Starno pierced her side with steel. She fell like a wreath of snow that slides from the rocks of Ronan; when the woods are still, and the echo deepens in the vale.

Then Fingal eyed his valiant chiefs, his valiant chiefs took arms. The gloom of the battle roared, and Lochlin fled or died.——Pale, in his bounding ship he closed the maid of the raven hair.[23] Her tomb ascends on Ardven, and the sea roars round the dark dwelling of Agandecca.[24]

Blessed be her soul, said Cuchullin, and blessed be the mouth of the song.——Strong was the youth of Fingal, and strong is his arm of age. Lochlin shall fall again before the king of echoing Morven. Shew thy face from a cloud, O moon; light his white sails on the wave of the night. And if any strong spirit[25] of heaven sits on that low-hung cloud; turn his dark ships from the rock, thou rider of the storm!

Such were the words of Cuchullin at the sound of the mountain-stream, when Calmar ascended the hill, the wounded son of Matha. From the field he came in his blood. He leaned on his bending spear. Feeble is the arm of battle! but strong the soul of the hero!

Welcome! O son of Matha, said Connal, welcome art thou to thy friends! Why bursts that broken sigh from the breast of him that never feared before?

And never, Connal, will he fear, chief of the pointed steel. My soul brightens in danger, and exults in the noise of battle. I am of the race of steel; my fathers never feared.

Cormar was the first of my race. He sported through the storms of the waves. His black skiff bounded on ocean, and travelled on the wings of the blast. A spirit once embroiled the night. Seas swell and rocks resound. Winds drive along the clouds. The lightning flies on wings of fire. He feared and came to land: then blushed that he feared at all. He rushed again among the waves to find the son of the wind. Three youths guide the bounding bark; he stood with the sword unsheathed. When the low-hung vapour passed, he took it by the curling head, and searched its dark womb with his steel. The son of the wind forsook the air. The moon and stars returned.

Such was the boldness of my race; and Calmar is like his fathers. Danger flies from the uplifted sword. They best succeed who dare.

But now, ye sons of green-vallyed Erin, retire from Lena's bloody heath. Collect the sad remnant of our friends, and join the sword of Fingal. I heard the sound of Lochlin's advancing arms; but Calmar will remain and fight. My voice shall be such, my friends, as if thousands were behind me. But, son of Semo, remember me. Remember Calmar's lifeless corse. After Fingal has wasted the field, place me by some stone of remembrance, that future times may hear my fame; and the mother[26] of Calmar rejoice over the stone of my renown.

No: son of Matha, said Cuchullin, I will never leave thee. My joy is in the unequal field: my soul increases in danger. Connal, and Carril of other times, carry off the sad sons of Erin; and when the battle is over, search for our pale corses in this narrow way. For near this oak we shall stand in the stream of the battle of thousands.——O Fithil's son, with feet of wind, fly over the heath of Lena. Tell to Fingal that Erin is inthralled, and bid the king of Morven hasten. O let him come like the sun in a storm, when he shines on the hills of grass.[27]

Morning is gray on Cromla; the sons of the sea ascend. Calmar stood forth to meet them in the pride of his kindling soul. But pale was the face of the warrior;[28] he leaned on his father's spear. That spear which he brought from Lara's hall,[29] when the soul of his mother was sad.[30] ——But slowly now the hero falls like a tree on the plains of Cona.[31] Dark Cuchullin stands alone like a rock[32] in a sandy vale. The sea comes with its waves, and roars on its hardened sides. Its head is covered with foam, and the hills are echoing around.——Now from the gray mist of the ocean, the white-sailed ships of Fingal appear. High is the grove of their masts as they nod, by turns, on the rolling wave.

Swaran saw them from the hill, and returned from the sons of Erin. As ebbs the resounding sea through the hundred isles of Inis-tore; so loud, so vast, so immense returned the sons of Lochlin against the king of the desart hill.[33] But bending, weeping, sad, and slow, and dragging his long spear behind, Cuchullin sunk in Cromla's wood, and mourned his fallen friends.

He feared the face of Fingal, who was wont to greet him from the fields of renown.

How many lie there of my heroes! the chiefs of Innis-fail![34] they that were chearful in the hall when the sound of the shells arose. No more shall I find their steps in the heath, or hear their voice in the chace of the hinds. Pale, silent, low on bloody beds are they who were my friends! O spirits of the lately-dead, meet Cuchullin on his heath. Converse with him on the wind, when the rustling tree of Tura's cave resounds. There, far remote, I shall lie unknown. No bard shall hear of me. No gray stone shall rise to my renown. Mourn me with the dead, O Bragéla! departed is my fame.

Such were the words of Cuchullin when he sunk in the woods of Cromla.

Fingal, tall in his ship, stretched his bright lance before him. Terrible was the gleam of the steel: it was like the green meteor of death, setting in the heath of Malmor, when the traveller is alone, and the broad moon is darkened in heaven.

The battle is over, said the king, and I behold the blood of my friends. Sad is the heath of Lena; and mournful the oaks of Cromla: the hunters have fallen there in their strength; and the son of Semo is no more.——Ryno and Fillan, my sons, sound the horn of Fingal's war. Ascend that hill on the shore, and call the children of the foe. Call them from the grave of Lamdarg, the chief of other times.——Be your voice like that of your father, when he enters the battles of his strength. I wait for the dark mighty man;[35] I wait on Lena's shore for Swaran. And let him come with all his race; for strong in battle are the friends of the dead.

Fair Ryno flew like lightning;[36] dark Fillan as the shade of autumn. On Lena's heath their voice is heard; the sons of ocean heard the horn of Fingal's war. As the roaring eddy of ocean returning from the kingdom of snows; so strong, so dark, so sudden came down the sons of Lochlin. The king in their front appears in the dismal pride of his arms. Wrath burns in his dark-brown face: and his eyes roll in the fire of his valour.

Fingal beheld the son of Starno; and he remembered Agandecca.——For Swaran with the tears of youth had mourned his white-bosomed sister. He sent Ullin of the songs to bid him to the feast of shells. For pleasant on Fingal's soul returned the remembrance of the first of his loves.

Ullin came with aged steps, and spoke to Starno's son. O thou that dwellest afar, surrounded, like a rock, with thy waves, come to the feast of the king, and pass the day in rest. To-morrow let us fight, O Swaran, and break the echoing shields.

To-day, said Starno's wrathful son, we break the echoing shields: to-morrow my feast will be spread; and Fingal lie on earth.

And to-morrow let his feast be spread, said Fingal with a smile; for to-day, O my sons, we shall break the echoing shields.——Ossian, stand thou near my arm. Gaul, lift thy terrible sword. Fergus, bend thy crooked yew. Throw, Fillan, thy lance through heaven.——Lift your shields like the darkened moon. Be your spears the meteors of death. Follow me in the path of my fame; and equal my deeds in battle.

As a hundred winds on Morven; as the streams of a hundred hills; as clouds fly successive over heaven; or, as the dark ocean assaults the shore of the desart: so roaring, so vast, so terrible the armies mixed on Lena's echoing heath.——The groan of the people spread over the hills; it was like the thunder of night, when the cloud bursts on Cona; and a thousand ghosts shriek at once on the hollow wind.

Fingal rushed on in his strength, terrible as the spirit of Trenmor; when, in a whirlwind, he comes to Morven to see the children of his pride. The oaks resound on their hills, and the rocks fall down before him.[37]—— Bloody was the hand of my father when he whirled the lightning of his sword. He remembers the battles of his youth, and the field is wasted in his course.

Ryno went on like a pillar of fire.——Dark is the brow of Gaul. Fergus rushed forward with feet of wind; and Fillan like the mist of the hill.—— Myself,[38] like a rock, came down, I exulted in the strength of the king. Many were the deaths of my arm; and dismal was the gleam of my sword. My locks were not then so gray; nor trembled my hands of age. My eyes were not closed in darkness; nor failed my feet in the race.

Who can relate the deaths of the people; or the deeds of mighty heroes; when Fingal, burning in his wrath, consumed the sons of Lochlin? Groans swelled on groans from hill to hill, till night had covered all. Pale, staring like a herd of deer, the sons of Lochlin convene on Lena.

We sat and heard the sprightly harp at Lubar's gentle stream. Fingal himself was next to the foe; and listened to the tales of bards. His godlike race were in the song, the chiefs of other times. Attentive, leaning on his shield, the king of Morven sat. The wind whistled through his aged locks, and his[39] thoughts are of the days of other years. Near him on his bending spear, my young, my lovely[40] Oscar stood. He admired the king of Morven: and his actions were swelling in his soul.

Son of my son, begun the king, O Oscar, pride of youth, I saw the shining of thy sword and gloried in my race. Pursue the glory of our fathers, and be what they have been; when Trenmor lived, the first of men, and Trathal the father of heroes. They fought the battle in their youth, and are the song of bards.——O Oscar! bend the strong in arms:[41] but spare the feeble hand. Be thou a stream of many tides against the foes of thy people; but like the gale that moves the grass to those who ask thine aid.——So Trenmor lived; such Trathal was; and such has Fingal been. My arm was the support of the injured; and the weak rested behind the lightning of my steel.

Oscar! I was young like thee, when lovely Fainasóllis came: that sunbeam! that mild light of love! the daughter of Craca's[42] king! I then returned from Cona's heath, and few were in my train. A white-sailed boat appeared far off; we saw it like a mist that rode on ocean's blast. It soon approached; we saw the fair. Her white breast heaved with sighs. The wind was in her loose dark hair; her rosy cheek had tears.——Daughter of beauty, calm I said, what sigh is in that breast? Can I, young as I am, defend thee, daughter of the sea? My sword is not unmatched in war, but dauntless is my heart.

To thee I fly, with sighs she replied, O chief[43] of mighty men! To thee I fly, chief of shells,[44] supporter of the feeble hand! The king of Craca's echoing isle owned me the sun-beam of his race. And often did the hills of Cromala reply to the sighs of love for the unhappy Fainasóllis. Sora's chief beheld me fair; and loved the daughter of Craca. His sword is like[45] a beam of light upon the warrior's side. But dark is his brow; and tempests are in his soul. I shun him on the rolling[46] sea; but Sora's chief pursues.

Rest thou, I said, behind my shield; rest in peace, thou beam of light! The gloomy chief of Sora will fly, if Fingal's arm is like his soul. In some lone cave I might conceal thee, daughter of the sea! But Fingal never flies; for where the danger threatens, I rejoice in the storm of spears.——I saw the tears upon her cheek. I pitied Craca's fair.

Now, like a dreadful wave afar, appeared the ship of stormy Borbar. His masts high-bended over the sea behind their sheets of snow. White roll the waters on either side. The strength of ocean sounds. Come thou, I said, from the roar of ocean, thou rider of the storm. Partake the feast within my hall. It is the house of strangers.——The maid stood trembling by my side; he drew the bow: she fell. Unerring is thy hand, I said, but feeble was the foe.——We fought, nor weak was the strife of death: He sunk beneath my sword. We laid them in two tombs of stones; the unhappy children[47] of youth.

Such have I been in my youth, O Oscar; be thou like the age of Fingal. Never seek the battle, nor shun it when it comes.——Fillan and Oscar of the dark-brown hair; ye children of the race;[48] fly over the heath of roaring winds;[49] and view the sons of Lochlin. Far off I hear the noise of their fear, like the storms of echoing Cona.[50] Go: that they may not fly my sword along the waves of the north.——For many chiefs of Erin's race lie here on the dark bed of death. The children of the storm[51] are low; the sons of echoing Cromla.

The heroes flew like two dark clouds; two dark clouds that are the chariots of ghosts; when air's dark children come to frighten hapless men.

It was then that Gaul[52], the son of Morni, stood like a rock in the night. His spear is glittering to the stars; his voice like many streams.——Son of battle, cried the chief, O Fingal, king of shells! let the bards of many songs sooth Erin's friends to rest. And, Fingal, sheath thy sword of death; and let thy people fight. We wither away without our fame; for our king is the only breaker of shields. When morning rises on our hills, behold at a distance our deeds. Let Lochlin feel the sword of Morni's son, that bards may sing of me. Such was the custom heretofore of Fingal's noble race. Such was thine own, thou king of swords, in battles of the spear.

O son of Morni, Fingal replied, I glory in thy fame.——Fight; but my spear shall be near to aid thee in the midst of danger. Raise, raise the voice, sons of the song, and lull me into rest. Here will Fingal lie amidst the wind of night.——And if thou, Agandecca, art near, among the children of thy land; if thou fittest on a blast of wind among the high-shrowded masts of Lochlin; come to my dreams[53] , my fair one, and shew thy bright face to my soul.

Many a voice and many a harp in tuneful sounds arose. Of Fingal's noble deeds they sung, and of the noble race of the hero. And sometimes on the lovely sound was heard the name of the now mournful[54] Ossian.

Often have I fought, and often won in battles of the spear. But blind, and tearful, and forlorn I now walk with little men. O Fingal, with thy race of battle I now behold thee not. The wild roes feed upon the green tomb of the mighty king of Morven.——Blest be thy soul, thou king of swords, thou most renowned on the hills of Cona!

F I N G A L,

AN ANCIENT

EPIC POEM.

BOOK IV.

ARGUMENT to BOOK IV.

The action of the poem being suspended by night, Ossian takes that oppor-
tunity to relate his own actions at the lake of Lego, and his courtship of
Evirallin, who was the mother of Oscar, and had died some time before
the expedition of Fingal into Ireland. Her ghost appears to him, and tells
him that Oscar, who had been sent, the beginning of the night, to observe
the enemy, was engaged with an advanced party, and almost overpow-
ered. Ossian relieves his son; and an alarm is given to Fingal of the
approach of Swaran. The king rises, calls his army together, and, as he
had promised the preceding night, devolves the command on Gaul the son
of Morni, while he himself, after charging his sons to behave gallantly
and defend his people, retires to a hill, from whence he could have a view
of the battle. The battle joins; the poet relates Oscar's great actions. But
when Oscar, in conjunction with his father, conquered in one wing, Gaul,
who was attacked by Swaran in person, was on the point of retreating in
the other. Fingal sends Ullin his bard to encourage him with a war song,
but notwithstanding Swaran prevails; and Gaul and his army are obliged
to give way. Fingal, descending from the hill, rallies them again: Swaran
desists from the pursuit, possesses himself of a rising ground, restores the
ranks, and waits the approach of Fingal. The king, having encouraged his
men, gives the necessary orders, and renews the battle. Cuchullin, who,
with his friend Connal, and Carril his bard, had retired to the cave of
Tura, hearing the noise, came to the brow of the hill, which overlooked
the field of battle, where he saw Fingal engaged with the enemy. He,
being hindered by Connal from joining Fingal, who was himself upon the
point of obtaining a complete victory, sends Carril to congratulate that
hero on his success.

Who comes with her songs from the mountain, like the bow of the showery Lena? It is the maid of the voice of love. The white-armed daughter of Toscar. Often hast thou heard my song, and given the tear of beauty. Dost thou come to the battles of thy people, and to hear the actions of Oscar? When shall I cease to mourn by the streams of the echoing Cona? My years have passed away in battle, and my age is darkened with sorrow.[2]

Daughter of the hand of snow! I was not so mournful and blind; I was not so dark and forlorn when Everallin loved me. Everallin with the dark-brown hair, the white-bosomed love of Cormac.[3] A thousand heroes sought the maid, she denied her love to a thousand; the sons of the sword were despised; for graceful in her eyes was Ossian.

I went in suit of the maid to Lego's sable surge; twelve of my people were there, the sons of the streamy Morven. We came to Branno friend of strangers: Branno of the sounding mail.——From whence, he said, are the arms of steel? Not easy to win is the maid that has denied the blue-eyed sons of Erin. But blest be thou, O son of Fingal, happy is the maid that waits thee. Tho' twelve daughters of beauty were mine, thine were the choice, thou son of fame!——Then he opened the hall of the maid, the dark-haired Everallin. Joy kindled in our breasts of steel and blest the maid of Branno.

Above us on the hill appeared the people of stately Cormac. Eight were the heroes of the chief; and the heath flamed with their arms. There Colla, Durra of the wounds, there mighty Toscar, and Tago, there Frestal the victorious stood; Dairo of the happy deeds, and Dala the battle's bulwark in the narrow way.——The sword flamed in the hand of Cormac, and graceful was the look of the hero.

Eight were the heroes of Ossian; Ullin stormy son of war; Mullo of the generous deeds; the noble, the graceful Scelacha; Oglan, and Cerdal the wrathful, and Duma-riccan's[4] brows of death. And why should Ogar be the last; so wide renowned on the hills of Ardven?

Ogar met Dala the strong, face to face, on the field of heroes. The battle of the chiefs was like the wind on ocean's foamy waves. The dagger is remembered by Ogar; the weapon which he loved; nine times he drowned it in Dala's side. The stormy battle turned. Three times I pierced[5] Cormac's shield: three times he broke his spear. But, unhappy youth of love! I cut his head away.——Five times I shook it by the lock. The friends of Cormac fled.

Whoever would have told me, lovely maid[6], when then I strove in battle; that blind, forsaken, and forlorn I now should pass the night; firm ought his mail to have been, and unmatched his arm in battle.

Now[7] on Lena's gloomy heath the voice of music died away. The unconstant blast blew hard, and the high oak shook its leaves around me; of Everallin were my thoughts, when she, in all the light of beauty, and her blue eyes rolling in tears, stood on a cloud before my sight, and spoke with feeble voice.

O Ossian, rise and save my son; save Oscar chief[8] of men, near the red oak of Lubar's stream, he fights with Lochlin's sons.——She sunk into her cloud again. I clothed me with my steel. My spear supported my steps, and my rattling armour rung. I hummed, as I was wont in danger, the songs of heroes of old. Like distant thunder[9] Lochlin heard; they fled; my son pursued.

I called him like a distant stream. My son return over Lena. No further pursue the foe, though Ossian is behind thee.——He came; and lovely in[10] my ear was Oscar's sounding steel. Why didst thou stop my hand, he said, till death had covered all? For dark and dreadful by the stream they met thy son and Fillan. They watched the terrors of the night. Our swords have conquered some. But as the winds of night pour the ocean over the white sands of Mora, so dark advance the sons of Lochlin over Lena's rustling heath. The ghosts of night shriek afar; and I have seen the meteors of death. Let me awake the king of Morven, he that smiles in danger; for he is like the son[11] of heaven that rises in a storm.

Fingal had started from a dream, and leaned on Trenmor's shield; the dark-brown shield of his fathers; which they had lifted of old in the battles of their race.——The hero had seen in his rest the mournful form of Agandecca; she came from the way of the ocean, and slowly, lonely, moved over Lena. Her face was pale like the mist of Cromla; and dark were the tears of her cheek. She often raised her dim hand from her robe; her robe which was of the clouds of the desert: she raised her dim hand over Fingal, and turned away her silent eyes.

Why weeps the daughter of Starno, said Fingal, with a sigh? Why is thy face so pale, thou daughter[12] of the clouds?——She departed on the wind of Lena; and left him in the midst of the night.——She mourned the sons of her people that were to fall by Fingal's hand.

The hero started from rest, and still beheld her in his soul.——The sound of Oscar's steps approached. The king saw the grey shield on his side. For the faint beam of the morning came over the waters of Ullin.

What do the foes in their fear? said the rising king of Morven. Or fly they through ocean's foam, or wait they the battle of steel? But why should Fingal ask? I hear their voice on the early wind.—Fly over Lena's heath, O Oscar, and awake our friends to battle.

The king stood by the stone of Lubar; and thrice raised his terrible voice. The deer started from the fountains of Cromla; and all the rocks shook on their hills. Like the noise of a hundred mountain-streams, that burst, and roar, and foam: like the clouds that gather to a tempest on the blue face of the sky; so met the sons of the desert, round the terrible voice of Fingal. For pleasant was the voice of the king of Morven to the warriors of his land: often had he led them to battle, and returned with the spoils of the foe.

Come to battle, said the king, ye children of the storm.[13] Come to the death of thousands. Comhal's son will see the fight.——My sword shall wave on that hill, and be the shield of my people. But never may you need it, warriors; while the son of Morni fights, the chief of mighty men.——He shall lead my battle; that his fame may rise in the song.——O ye ghosts of heroes dead! ye riders of the storm of Cromla! receive my falling people with joy, and bring them to your hills.—And may the blast of Lena carry them over my seas, that they may come to my silent dreams, and delight my soul in rest.

Fillan and Oscar, of the dark-brown hair! fair Ryno, with the pointed steel! advance with valour to the fight; and behold the son of Morni. Let your swords be like his in the strife: and behold the deeds of his hands. Protect the friends of your father: and remember the chiefs of old. My children, I shall see you yet, though here ye should fall in Erin. Soon shall our cold, pale ghosts meet in a cloud, and fly over the hills of Cona.[14]

Now like a dark and stormy cloud, edged round with the red lightning of heaven, and flying westward from the morning's beam, the king of hills[15] removed. Terrible is the light of his armour, and two spears are in his hand.——His gray hair falls on the wind.——He often looks back on the war. Three bards attend the son of fame, to carry his words to the heroes.— High on Cromla's side he sat, waving the lightning of his sword, and as he waved we moved.

Joy rose in Oscar's face. His cheek is red. His eye sheds tears. The sword is a beam of fire in his hand. He came, and smiling, spoke to Ossian.——O ruler of the fight of steel! my father, hear thy son. Retire with Morven's mighty chief; and give me Ossian's fame. And if here I fall; my king, remember that breast of snow, that lonely sun-beam of my love, the white-handed daughter of Toscar. For with red cheek from the rock, and bending over the stream, her soft hair flies about her bosom as she pours the sigh for Oscar. Tell her I am on my hills a lightly-bounding son of the wind; that hereafter, in a cloud, I may meet the lovely maid of Toscar.

Raise, Oscar, rather raise my tomb. I will not yield the fight to thee. For first and bloodiest in the war my arm shall teach thee how to fight. But, remember, my son, to place this sword, this bow, and the horn of my deer, within that dark and narrow house, whose mark is one gray stone. Oscar, I have no love to leave to the care of my son; for graceful[16] Evirallin is no more, the lovely daughter of Branno.

Such were our words, when Gaul's loud voice came growing on the wind. He waved on high the sword of his father, and rushed to death and wounds.

As waves white-bubbling over the deep come swelling, roaring on; as rocks of ooze meet roaring waves: so foes attacked and fought. Man met with man, and steel with steel. Shields sound; men fall. As a hundred hammers on the son[17] of the furnace, so rose, so rung their swords.

Gaul rushed on like a whirlwind in Ardven. The destruction of heroes is on his sword. Swaran was like the fire of the desert in the echoing heath of Gormal. How can I give to the song the death of many spears? My sword rose high, and flamed in the strife of blood. And, Oscar, terrible wert thou, my best, my greatest son! I rejoiced in my secret soul, when his sword flamed over the slain. They fled amain through Lena's heath: and we pursued and slew. As stones that bound from rock to rock; as axes in echoing woods; as thunder rolls from hill to hill in dismal broken peals; so blow succeeded to blow, and death to death, from the hand of Oscar[18] and mine.

But Swaran closed round Morni's son, as the strength of the tide of Inistore. The king half-rose from his hill at the sight, and half-assumed the spear. Go, Ullin, go, my aged bard, begun the king of Morven. Remind the mighty Gaul of battle; remind him of his fathers. Support the yielding fight with song; for song enlivens war. Tall Ullin went, with steps of age, and spoke to the king of swords.

Son[19] of the chief of generous steeds! high-bounding king of spears. Strong arm in every perilous toil. Hard heart that never yields. Chief of the pointed arms of death. Cut down the foe; let no white sail bound round dark Inistore. Be thine arm like thunder. Thine eyes like fire, thy heart of solid rock. Whirl round thy sword as a meteor at night, and lift thy shield like the flame of death. Son of the chief of generous steeds, cut down the foe; destroy.——The hero's heart beat high. But Swaran came with battle. He cleft the shield of Gaul in twain; and the sons of the desert[20] fled.

Now Fingal arose in his might, and thrice he reared his voice. Cromla answered around, and the sons of the desert stood still.——They bent their red faces to earth, ashamed at the presence of Fingal. He came like a cloud of rain in the days of the sun, when slow it rolls on the hill, and fields expect the shower.[21] Swaran beheld the terrible king of Morven, and stopped in the midst of his course. Dark he leaned on his spear, rolling his red eyes around. Silent and tall he seemed as an oak on the banks of Lubar, which had its branches blasted of old by the lightning of heaven. It bends over the stream, and the gray moss whistles in the wind: so stood the king. Then slowly he retired to the rising heath of Lena. His thousands pour around the hero, and the darkness of battle gathers on the hill.

Fingal, like a beam from heaven, shone in the midst of his people. His heroes gather around him, and he sends forth the voice of his power. Raise my standards[22] on high,—spread them on Lena's wind, like the flames of an hundred hills. Let them sound on the winds of Erin, and remind us of the fight. Ye sons of the roaring streams, that pour from a thousand hills, be near the king of Morven: attend to the words of his power. Gaul strongest arm of death! O Oscar, of the future fights; Connal, son of the blue steel[23] of Sora; Dermid of the dark-brown hair, and Ossian king of many songs, be near your father's arm.

We reared the sun-beam[24] of battle; the standard of the king. Each hero's soul exulted with joy, as, waving, it flew on the wind. It was studded with gold above, as the blue wide shell of the nightly sky. Each hero had his standard too; and each his gloomy men.

Behold, said the king of generous shells, how Lochlin divides on Lena.——They stand like broken clouds on the hill, or an half consumed grove of oaks; when we see the sky through its branches, and the meteor passing behind. Let every chief among the friends of Fingal take a dark troop of those that frown so high; nor let a son of the echoing groves bound on the waves of Inistore.

Mine, said Gaul, be the seven chiefs that came from Lano's lake.——Let Inistore's dark king, said Oscar, come to the sword of Ossian's son.——To mine the king of Iniscon, said Connal, heart of steel! Or Mudan's chief or I, said brown-haired Dermid, shall sleep on clay-cold earth. My choice, though now so weak and dark, was Terman's battling king; I promised with my hand to win the hero's dark-brown shield.——Blest and victorious be my chiefs, said Fingal of the mildest look; Swaran, king of roaring waves, thou art the choice of Fingal.

Now, like an hundred different winds that pour through many vales; divided, dark, the sons of the hill[25] advanced, and Cromla echoed around.

How can I relate the deaths when we closed in the strife of our steel? O daughter of Toscar! bloody were our hands! The gloomy ranks of Lochlin fell like the banks of the roaring Cona.——Our arms were victorious on Lena; each chief fulfilled his promise. Beside the murmur of Branno thou didst often sit, O maid; when thy white bosom rose frequent, like the down of the swan when slow she sails the lake, and sidelong winds are blowing.[26]——Thou hast seen the sun[27] retire red and slow behind his cloud; night gathering round on the mountain, while the unfrequent blast[28] roared in narrow vales. At length the rain beats hard; and thunder rolls in peals. Lightning glances on the rocks. Spirits ride on beams of fire. And the strength of the mountain-streams[29] comes roaring down the hills. Such was the noise of battle, maid of the arms of snow. Why, daughter of the hill,[30] that tear? the maids of Lochlin have cause to weep. The people of their country fell, for bloody was the blue steel[31] of the race of my heroes. But I am sad, forlorn, and blind; and no more the companion of heroes. Give, lovely maid, to me thy tears, for I have seen the tombs of all my friends.

It was then by Fingal's hand a hero fell, to his grief.——Gray-haired he rolled in the dust, and lifted his faint eyes to the king. And is it by me thou hast fallen, said the son of Comhal, thou friend of Agandecca! I saw thy tears for the maid of my love in the halls of the bloody Starno. Thou hast been the foe of the foes of my love, and hast thou fallen by my hand? Raise, Ullin, raise the grave of the son of Mathon;[32] and give his name to the song of Agandecca; for dear to my soul hast thou been, thou darkly-dwelling maid of Ardven.

Cuchullin, from the cave of Cromla, heard the noise of the troubled war. He called to Connal chief of swords, and Carril of other times. The gray-haired heroes heard his voice, and took their aspen[33] spears. They came, and saw the tide of battle, like the crowded waves of the ocean; when the dark wind blows from the deep, and rolls the billows through the sandy vale.

Cuchullin kindled at the sight, and darkness gathered on his brow. His hand is on the sword of his fathers: his red-rolling eyes on the foe. He thrice attempted to rush to battle, and thrice did Connal stop him. Chief of the isle of mist, he said, Fingal subdues the foe. Seek not a part of the fame of the king; himself is like a storm.

Then, Carril, go, replied the chief, and greet the king of Morven. When Lochlin falls away like a stream after rain, and the noise of the battle is over, then be thy voice sweet in his ear to praise the king of swords.[34] Give him the sword of Caithbat; for Cuchullin is worthy no more to lift the arms of his fathers.

But, O ye ghosts of the lonely Cromla! ye souls of chiefs that are no more! be ye the companions of Cuchullin, and talk to him in the cave of his sorrow.[35] For never more shall I be renowned among the mighty in the land. I am like a beam that has shone; like a mist[36] that fled away, when the blast of the morning came, and brightened the shaggy side of the hill. Connal, talk of arms no more: departed is my fame.—My sighs shall be on Cromla's wind, till my footsteps cease to be seen.——And thou, white-bosom'd Bragéla, mourn over the fall of my fame; for, vanquished, I will never return to thee, thou sun-beam of Dunscaich.[37]

F I N G A L,

AN ANCIENT

EPIC POEM.

BOOK V.

ARGUMENT to BOOK V.

Cuchullin and Connal still remain on the hill. Fingal and Swaran meet; the combat is described. Swaran is overcome, bound and delivered over as a prisoner to the care of Ossian and Gaul the son of Morni; Fingal, his younger sons, and Oscar, still pursue the enemy. The episode of Orla a chief of Lochlin, who was mortally wounded in the battle, is introduced. Fingal, touched with the death of Orla, orders the pursuit to be discontinued; and calling his sons together, he is informed that Ryno, the youngest of them, was killed. He laments his death, hears the story of Lamderg[1] and Gelchossa, and returns towards the place where he had left Swaran. Carril, who had been sent by Cuchullin to congratulate Fingal on his victory, comes in the mean time to Ossian. The conversation of the two poets closes the action of the fourth day.

****
FINGAL BOOK V[2].
****

Now Connal, on Cromla's windy side, spoke[3] to the chief of the noble car. Why that gloom, son of Semo? Our friends are the mighty in battle. And renowned art thou, O warrior! many were the deaths of thy steel. Often has Bragéla met with blue-rolling eyes of joy, often has she met her hero, returning in the midst of the valiant; when his sword was red with slaughter, and his foes silent in the fields of the tomb. Pleasant to her ears were thy bards, when thine actions rose in the song.

But behold the king of Morven; he moves below like a pillar of fire. His strength is like the stream of Lubar, or the wind of the echoing Cromla; when the branchy forests of night are overturned.[4]

Happy are thy people, O Fingal, thine arm shall fight their battles: thou art the first in their dangers; the wisest in the days of their peace. Thou speakest and thy thousands obey; and armies tremble at the sound of thy steel. Happy are thy people, Fingal, chief of the lonely hills.[5]

Who is that so dark and terrible, coming in the thunder of his course? who is it but Starno's son to meet the king of Morven? Behold the battle of the chiefs: it is like[6] the storm of the ocean, when two spirits meet far distant, and contend for the rolling of the wave. The hunter hears the noise on his hill; and sees the high billows advancing to Ardven's shore.

Such were the words of Connal, when the heroes met in the midst of their falling people.[7] There was the clang of arms! there every blow, like the hundred hammers of the furnace! Terrible is the battle of the kings, and horrid the look of their eyes. Their dark-brown shields are cleft in twain; and their steel flies, broken, from their helmets. They fling their weapons down. Each rushes[8] to the grasp of his foe.[9] Their sinewy arms bend round each other: they turn from side to side, and strain and stretch their large spreading limbs below. But when the pride of their strength arose, they shook the hill with their heels; rocks tumble from their places on high; the green-headed bushes are overturned. At length the strength of Swaran fell; and the king of the groves is bound.

Thus have I seen on Cona; (but Cona I behold no more) thus have I seen two dark hills removed from their place by the strength of the bursting stream. They turn from side to side, and their tall oaks meet one another on high. Then they fall together with all their rocks and trees. The streams are turned by their sides, and the red ruin is seen afar.

Sons of the king of Morven, said the noble Fingal,[10] guard the king of Lochlin; for he is strong as his thousand waves. His hand is taught to the battle, and his race of the times of old. Gaul, thou first of my heroes, and

Ossian king of songs, attend the friend of Agandecca, and raise to joy his grief.——But, Oscar, Fillan, and Ryno, ye children of the race! pursue the rest of Lochlin over the heath of Lena;[11] that no vessel may hereafter bound on the dark-rolling waves of Inistore.

They flew like lightning over[12] the heath. He slowly moved as a cloud of thunder when the sultry plain of summer is silent. His sword is before him as a sun-beam, terrible as the streaming meteor of night. He came toward a chief of Lochlin, and spoke to the son of the wave.

Who is that like a cloud[13] at the rock of the roaring stream? He cannot bound over its course; yet stately is the chief! his bossy shield is on his side; and his spear like the tree of the desart. Youth of the dark-brown[14] hair, art thou of Fingal's foes?

I am a son of Lochlin, he cries, and strong is my arm in war. My spouse is weeping at home, but Orla[15] will never return.

Or fights or yields the hero, said Fingal of the noble deeds? foes do not conquer in my presence: but my friends are renowned in the hall. Son of the wave, follow me, partake the feast of my shells, and pursue the deer of my desart.[16]

No: said the hero, I assist the feeble: my strength shall remain with the weak in arms. My sword has been always unmatched, O warrior: let the king of Morven yield.

I never yielded, Orla, Fingal never yielded to man. Draw thy sword and chuse thy foe. Many are my heroes.

And does the king refuse the combat, said Orla of the dark-brown hair?[17] Fingal is a match for Orla: and he alone of all his race.——But, king of Morven, if I shall fall; (as one time the warrior must die;) raise my tomb in the midst, and let it be the greatest on Lena. And send, over the dark-blue wave, the sword of Orla to the spouse of his love; that she may shew it to her son, with tears, to kindle his soul to war.

Son of the mournful tale, said Fingal, why dost thou awaken my tears? One day the warriors must die, and the children see their useless arms in the hall. But, Orla, thy tomb shall rise, and thy white-bosomed spouse weep over thy sword.

They fought on the heath of Lena, but feeble was the arm of Orla. The sword of Fingal descended, and cleft his shield in twain. It fell and glittered on the ground, as the moon on the stream of night.[18]

King of Morven, said the hero, lift thy sword, and pierce my breast. Wounded and faint from battle my friends have left me here. The mournful tale shall come to my love on the banks of the streamy Loda[19]; when she is alone in the wood; and the rustling blast in the leaves.

No; said the king of Morven, I will never wound thee, Orla. On the banks of Loda let her see thee escaped from the hands of war. Let thy gray-haired father, who, perhaps, is blind with age, hear the sound of thy voice in his hall.[20] ——With joy let the hero rise, and search for his son with his hands.

But never will he find him, Fingal; said the youth of the streamy Loda.
——On Lena's heath I shall die; and foreign bards will talk of me. My broad belt covers my wound of death. And now I give it to the wind.

The dark blood poured from his side, he fell pale on the heath of Lena. Fingal bends over him as he dies, and calls his younger heroes.[21]

Oscar and Fillan, my sons, raise high the memory of Orla. Here let the dark-haired hero rest far from the spouse of his love. Here let him rest in his narrow house far from the sound of Loda. The sons of the feeble[22] will find his bow at home, but will not be able to bend it. His faithful dogs howl on his hills, and his boars, which he used to pursue, rejoice. Fallen is the arm of battle; the mighty among the valiant is low!

Exalt the voice, and blow the horn, ye sons of the king of Morven: let us go back to Swaran, and send the night away on song. Fillan, Oscar, and Ryno, fly over the heath of Lena. Where, Ryno, art thou, young son of fame? Thou art not wont to be the last to answer thy father.

Ryno, said Ullin first of bards, is with the awful forms of his fathers. With Trathal king of shields, and Trenmor of the mighty deeds. The youth is low,—the youth is pale,—he lies on Lena's heath.

And fell the swiftest in the race, said the king, the first to bend the bow? Thou scarce hast been known to me: why did young Ryno fall? But sleep thou softly on Lena, Fingal shall soon behold thee. Soon shall my voice be heard no more, and my footsteps cease to be seen. The bards will tell of Fingal's name; the stones will talk of me. But, Ryno, thou art low indeed, ——thou hast not received thy fame. Ullin, strike the harp for Ryno; tell what the chief would have been. Farewel, thou first in every field. No more shall I direct thy dart. Thou that hast been so fair; I behold thee not— Farewel.

The tear is on the cheek of the king; for terrible was his son in war. His son! that was like a beam of fire by night on the hill; when the forests sink down in its course, and the traveller trembles at the sound.[23]

Whose fame is in that dark-green tomb, begun the king of generous shells? four stones with their heads of moss stand there; and mark the narrow house of death. Near it let my Ryno rest, and be the neighbour of the valiant.[24] Perhaps some[25] chief of fame is here to fly with my son on clouds. O Ullin, raise the songs of other times. Bring to memory the dark dwellers of the tomb. If in the field of the valiant they never fled from danger, my son shall rest with them, far from his friends, on the heath of Lena.[26]

Here, said the mouth of the song,[27] here rest the first of heroes. Silent is Lamderg[28] in this tomb, and Ullin[29] king of swords. And who, soft smiling from her cloud, shews me her face of love? Why, daughter, why so pale art thou, first of the maids of Cromla? Dost thou sleep with the foes in battle, Gelchossa,[30] white-bosomed daughter of Tuathal?——Thou hast been the love of thousands, but Lamderg was thy love. He came to Selma's[31] mossy towers, and, striking his dark buckler, spoke:

Where is Gelchossa, my love, the daughter of the noble Tuathal? I left her in the hall of Selma,[32] when I fought with the gloomy Ulfadda.[33] Return soon, O Lamderg, she said, for here I am in the midst of sorrow.[34] Her white breast rose with sighs. Her cheek was wet with tears. But I see her not coming to meet me; and to sooth my soul after battle. Silent is the hall of my joy; I hear not the voice of the bard.—Bran[35] does not shake his chains at the gate, glad at the coming of Lamderg. Where is Gelchossa, my love, the mild daughter of the generous Tuathal?

Lamderg! says Ferchios the son of Aidon, Gelchossa may be[36] on Cromla; she and the maids of the bow pursuing the flying deer.

Ferchios! replied the chief of Cromla, no noise meets the ear of Lamderg. No sound is in the woods of Lena. No deer fly in my sight. No panting dog pursues. I see not Gelchossa my love, fair as the full moon setting on the hills of Cromla. Go, Ferchios, go to Allad[37] the gray-haired son of the rock. His dwelling is in the circle of stones. He may know of Gelchossa.[38]

The son of Aidon went; and spoke to the ear of age. Allad! thou that dwellest in the rock, thou that tremblest alone, what saw thine eyes of age?

I saw, answered Allad the old, Ullin the son of Cairbar. He came like a cloud[39] from Cromla; and he hummed a surly song like a blast in a leafless wood. He entered the hall of Selma.[40]——Lamderg, he said, most dreadful of men, fight or yield to Ullin. Lamderg, replied Gelchossa, the son of battle, is not here. He fights Ulfadda mighty chief. He is not here, thou first of men. But Lamderg never yielded. He will fight the son of Cairbar.

Lovely art thou, said terrible Ullin, daughter of the generous Tuathal. I carry thee to Cairbar's halls. The valiant shall have Gelchossa. Three days I remain on Cromla, to wait that son of battle, Lamderg. On the fourth Gelchossa is mine, if the mighty Lamderg flies.

Allad! said the chief of Cromla, peace to thy dreams in the cave. Ferchios, sound the horn of Lamderg that Ullin may hear on Cromla.[41] Lamderg[42], like a roaring storm, ascended the hill from Selma.[43] He hummed a surly song as he went, like the noise of a falling stream. He stood like a cloud on the hill, that varies its form to the wind. He rolled a stone, the sign of war. Ullin heard in Cairbar's hall. The hero heard, with joy, his foe, and took his father's spear. A smile brightens his dark-brown cheek, as he places his sword by his side. The dagger glittered in his hand. He whistled as he went.

Gelchossa saw the silent chief, as a wreath of mist ascending the hill.—— She struck her white and heaving breast; and silent, tearful, feared for Lamderg.

Cairbar, hoary chief of shells, said the maid of the tender hand; I must bend the bow on Cromla; for I see the dark-brown hinds.

She hasted up the hill. In vain! the gloomy heroes fought.——Why should I tell the king of Morven[44] how wrathful heroes fight!——Fierce Ullin fell. Young Lamderg came all pale to the daughter of generous Tuathal.

What blood, my love, the soft-haired woman said,[45] what blood runs down my warrior's side?——It is Ullin's blood, the chief replied, thou fairer than the snow of Cromla![46] Gelchossa, let me rest here a little while. The mighty Lamderg died.

And sleepest thou so soon on earth, O chief of shady Cromla?[47] three days she mourned beside her love.——The hunters found her dead.[48] They raised this tomb above the three. Thy son, O king of Morven, may rest here with heroes.

And here my son shall rest, said Fingal, the noise of their fame has reached my ears. Fillan and Fergus! bring hither Orla; the pale youth of the stream of Loda.[49] Not unequalled shall Ryno lie in earth when Orla is by his side. Weep, ye daughters of Morven; and ye maids of the streamy Loda.[50] Like a tree they grew on the hills; and they have fallen like the oak[51] of the desart; when it lies across a stream, and withers in the wind of the mountain.

Oscar! chief of every youth! thou seest how they have fallen. Be thou, like them, on earth renowned. Like them the song of bards. Terrible were their forms in battle; but calm was Ryno in the days of peace. He was like the bow[52] of the shower seen far distant on the stream; when the sun is setting on Mora, and silence on the hill of deer. Rest, youngest of my sons, rest, O Ryno, on Lena. We too shall be no more; for the warrior one day must fall.

Such was thy grief, thou king of hills,[53] when Ryno lay on earth. What must the grief of Ossian be, for thou thyself art gone. I hear not thy distant voice on Cona. My eyes perceive thee not. Often forlorn and dark I sit at thy tomb; and feel it with my hands. When I think I hear thy voice; it is but the blast of the desart.[54]——Fingal has long since fallen asleep, the ruler of the war.

Then Gaul and Ossian sat with Swaran on the soft green banks of Lubar. I touched the harp to please the king. But gloomy was his brow. He rolled his red eyes towards Lena. The hero mourned his people.

I lifted my eyes to Cromla, and I saw the son of generous Semo.——Sad and slow he retired from his hill towards the lonely cave of Tura. He saw Fingal victorious, and mixed his joy with grief. The sun is bright on his armour, and Connal slowly followed. They sunk behind the hill like two pillars of the fire of night: when winds pursue them over the mountain, and the flaming heath resounds. Beside a stream of roaring foam his cave is in a rock. One tree bends above it; and the rushing winds echo against its sides. Here rests the chief of Dunscaich,[55] the son of generous Semo. His thoughts are on the battle[56] he lost; and the tear is on his cheek. He mourned the departure of his fame that fled like the mist of Cona. O Bragéla, thou art too far remote to cheer the soul of the hero. But let him see thy bright form in his soul;[57] that his thoughts may return to the lonely sun-beam of Dunscaich.[58]

Who comes with the locks of age? It is the son of songs. Hail, Carril of other times, thy voice is like the harp in the halls of Tura. Thy words are pleasant as the shower that falls on the fields of the sun. Carril of the times of old, why comest thou from the son of the generous Semo?

Ossian king of swords, replied the bard, thou best raisest the song. Long hast thou been known to Carril, thou ruler of battles. Often have I touched the harp to lovely Evirallin. Thou too hast often accompanied my voice in Branno's hall of generous shells. And often, amidst our voices, was heard the mildest Evirallin. One day she sung of Cormac's fall, the youth that died for her love. I saw the tears on her cheek, and on thine, thou chief of men. Her soul was touched for the unhappy, though she loved him not. How fair among a thousand maids was the daughter of the generous Branno!

Bring not, Carril, I replied, bring not her memory to my mind. My soul must melt at the remembrance. My eyes must have their tears. Pale in the earth is she the softly-blushing fair of my love. But sit thou on the heath, O Bard, and let us hear thy voice. It is pleasant as the gale of spring that sighs on the hunter's ear; when he wakens from dreams of joy, and has heard the music of the spirits[59] of the hill.

FINGAL,

AN ANCIENT

EPIC POEM.

BOOK VI.

ARGUMENT to BOOK VI.

Night comes on. Fingal gives a feast to his army, at which Swaran is present. The king commands Ullin his bard to give the song of peace; a custom always observed at the end of a war. Ullin relates the actions of Trenmor great grandfather to Fingal, in Scandinavia, and his marriage with Inibaca, the daughter of a king of Lochlin who was ancestor to Swaran; which consideration, together with his being brother to Agandecca, with whom Fingal was in love in his youth, induced the king to release him, and permit him to return, with the remains of his army, into Lochlin, upon his promise of never returning to Ireland, in a hostile manner. The night is spent in settling Swaran's departure, in songs of bards, and in a conversation in which the story of Grumal is introduced by Fingal. Morning comes. Swaran departs; Fingal goes on a hunting party, and finding Cuchullin in the cave of Tura, comforts him, and sets sail, the next day, for Scotland; which concludes the poem.

The clouds of night come[2] rolling down and rest on Cromla's dark-brown steep.[3] The stars of the north arise over the rolling of the waves of Ullin;[4] they shew their heads of fire through the flying mist of heaven. A distant wind roars in the wood; but silent and dark is the plain of death.

Still on the darkening Lena arose in my ears the tuneful[5] voice of Carril. He sung of the companions of our youth, and the days of former years; when we met on the banks of Lego, and sent round the joy of the shell. Cromla, with its cloudy steeps,[6] answered to his voice. The ghosts of those he sung came in their rustling blasts.[7] They were seen to bend with joy towards the sound of their praise.

Be thy soul blest, O Carril, in the midst of thy eddying winds. O that thou wouldst come to my hall when I am alone by night!—And thou dost come, my friend, I hear often thy light hand on my harp; when it hangs on the distant wall, and the feeble sound touches my ear. Why dost thou not speak to me in my grief, and tell when I shall behold my friends? But thou passest away in thy murmuring blast; and thy wind whistles through the gray hair of Ossian.

Now on the side of Mora the heroes gathered to the feast. A thousand aged oaks are burning to the wind.——The strength[8] of the shells goes round. And the souls of warriors brighten with joy. But the king of Lochlin is silent, and sorrow reddens in the eyes of his pride. He often turned toward Lena and remembered that he fell.

Fingal leaned on the shield of his fathers. His gray locks slowly waved on the wind, and glittered to the beam of night. He saw the grief of Swaran, and spoke to the first of Bards.

Raise, Ullin, raise the song of peace, and sooth my soul after battle, that my ear may forget the noise[9] of arms. And let a hundred harps be near to gladden the king of Lochlin. He must depart from us with joy.——None ever went sad from Fingal. Oscar! the lightning of my sword is against the strong in battle; but peaceful it lies by my side when warriors yield in war.

Trenmor[10], said the mouth of the songs, lived in the days of other years. He bounded over the waves of the north: companion of the storm. The high rocks of the land of Lochlin, and its groves of murmuring sounds appeared to the hero through the mist;—he bound his white-bosomed sails.—— Trenmor pursued the boar that roared along the woods of Gormal. Many had fled from its presence; but the spear of Trenmor slew it.[11]

Three chiefs, that beheld the deed, told of the mighty stranger. They told that he stood like a pillar of fire in the bright arms of his valour. The king of Lochlin prepared the feast, and called the blooming Trenmor. Three days he feasted at Gormal's windy towers; and got his choice in the combat.

The land of Lochlin had no hero that yielded not to Trenmor. The shell of joy went round with songs in praise of the king of Morven; he that came over the waves, the first of mighty men.

Now when the fourth gray morn arose, the hero launched his ship; and walking along the silent shore waited for the rushing wind. For loud and distant he heard the blast murmuring in the grove.[12]

Covered over with arms of steel a son of the woody Gormal appeared. Red was his cheek and fair his hair. His skin like the snow of Morven. Mild rolled his blue and smiling eye when he spoke to the king of swords.

Stay, Trenmor, stay thou first of men, thou hast not conquered Lonval's son. My sword has often met the brave. And the wise shun the strength of my bow.

Thou fair-haired youth, Trenmor replied, I will not fight with Lonval's son. Thine arm is feeble, sun-beam of beauty.[13] Retire to Gormal's dark-brown hinds.

But I will retire, replied the youth, with the sword of Trenmor; and exult in the sound of my fame. The virgins shall gather with smiles around him who conquered Trenmor.[14] They shall sigh with the sighs of love, and admire the length of thy spear; when I shall carry it among thousands, and lift the glittering point to the sun.

Thou shalt never carry my spear, said the angry king of Morven.——Thy mother shall find thee pale on the shore of the echoing Gormal;[15] and, looking over the dark-blue deep, see the sails of him that slew her son.

I will not lift the spear, replied the youth, my arm is not strong with years. But with the feathered dart I have learned to pierce a distant foe. Throw down that heavy mail of steel; for Trenmor is covered all over.[16]——I first will lay my mail on earth.——Throw now thy dart, thou king of Morven.

He saw the heaving of her breast. It was the sister of the king.—She had seen him in the halls of Gormal;[17] and loved his face of youth.——The spear dropt from the hand of Trenmor: he bent his red cheek to the ground, for he had seen her like a beam[18] of light that meets the sons of the cave, when they revisit the fields of the sun, and bend their aching eyes.

Chief of the windy Morven, begun the maid of the arms of snow; let me rest in thy bounding ship, far from the love of Corlo. For he, like the thunder of the desart, is terrible to Inibaca. He loves me in the gloom of his pride, and shakes ten thousand spears.

Rest thou in peace, said the mighty Trenmor, behind the shield of my fathers. I will not fly from the chief, though he shakes ten thousand spears.

Three days he waited on the shore; and sent his horn abroad. He called Corlo to battle from all his echoing hills. But Corlo came not to battle. The king of Lochlin descended. He feasted on the roaring shore; and gave the maid to Trenmor.

King of Lochlin, said Fingal, thy blood flows in the veins of thy foe. Our families[19] met in battle, because they loved the strife of spears. But often did they feast in the hall; and send round the joy of the shell.——Let thy face brighten with gladness, and thine ear delight in the harp. Dreadful as the storm of thine ocean thou hast poured thy valour forth; thy voice has been like the voice of thousands when they engage in battle. Raise, to-morrow, thy white sails to the wind, thou brother of Agandecca. Bright as the beam of noon she comes on my mournful soul. I saw thy tears for the fair one, and spared thee in the halls of Starno; when my sword was red with slaughter, and my eye full of tears for the maid.——Or dost thou chuse the fight? The combat which thy fathers gave to Trenmor is thine: that thou mayest depart renowned like the sun setting in the west.

King of the race of Morven, said the chief of the waves of Lochlin;[20] never will Swaran fight with thee, first of a thousand heroes! I saw thee in the halls of Starno, and few were thy years beyond my own.——When shall I, said I to my soul, lift the spear like the noble Fingal? We have fought here-tofore, O warrior, on the side of the shaggy Malmor; after my waves had carried me to thy halls, and the feast of a thousand shells was spread. Let the bards send him who overcame to future years, for noble was the strife of heathy[21] Malmor.

But many of the ships of Lochlin have lost their youths on Lena. Take these, thou king of Morven, and be the friend of Swaran. And when thy sons shall come to the mossy towers of[22] Gormal, the feast of shells shall be spread, and the combat offered on the vale.

Nor ship, replied the king, shall Fingal take, nor land of many hills; The desart is enough to me with all its deer and woods. Rise on thy waves again, thou noble friend of Agandecca. Spread thy white sails to the beam of the morning, and return to the echoing hills of Gormal.

Blest be thy soul, thou king of shells, said Swaran of the dark-brown shield. In peace thou art the gale of spring. In war the mountain-storm. Take now my hand in friendship, thou noble king of Morven.[23] Let thy bards mourn those who fell. Let Erin give the sons of Lochlin to earth; and raise the mossy stones of their fame. That the children of the north hereafter may behold the place where their fathers fought. And some hunter may say, when he leans on a mossy tomb, here Fingal and Swaran fought, the heroes of other years. Thus hereafter shall he say, and our fame shall last for ever.

Swaran, said the king of the hills, to-day our fame is greatest. We shall pass away like a dream. No sound will be in the fields of our battles. Our tombs will be lost in the heath. The hunter shall not know the place of our rest. Our names may be heard in song, but the strength of our arms will cease.[24] O Ossian, Carril, and Ullin, you know of heroes that are no more. Give us the song of other years. Let the night pass away on the sound, and morning return with joy.

We gave the song to the kings, and a hundred harps accompanied our voice. The face of Swaran brightened like the full moon of heaven, when the clouds vanish away, and leave her calm and broad in the midst of the sky.

It was then that Fingal spoke to Carril the chief of other times.[25] Where is the son of Semo; the king of the isle of mist? has he retired, like the meteor of death, to the dreary cave of Tura?

Cuchullin, said Carril of other times, lies in the dreary cave of Tura. His hand is on the sword of his strength. His thoughts on the battle[26] which he lost. Mournful is the king of spears; for he has often been victorious.[27] He sends the sword of his war to rest on the side of Fingal. For, like the storm of the desert, thou hast scattered all his foes. Take, O Fingal, the sword of the hero; for his fame is departed like mist when it flies before the rustling wind of the vale.[28]

No: replied the king, Fingal shall never take his sword. His arm is mighty in war; and tell him his fame shall never fail. Many have been overcome in battle, that have shone afterwards like the sun of heaven.[29]

O Swaran, king of the resounding woods, give all thy grief away.——The vanquished, if brave, are renowned; they are like the sun in a cloud when he hides his face in the south, but looks again on the hills of grass.

Grumal was a chief of Cona. He sought the battle on every coast. His soul rejoiced in blood; his ear in the din of arms. He poured his warriors on the sounding[30] Craca; and Craca's king met him from his grove; for then within the circle of Brumo[31] he spoke to the stone of power.

Fierce was the battle of the heroes, for the maid of the breast of snow. The fame of the daughter of Craca had reached Grumal at the streams of Cona; he vowed to have the white-bosomed maid, or die on the echoing Craca. Three days they strove together, and Grumal on the fourth was bound.

Far from his friends they placed him in the horrid circle of Brumo; where often, they said, the ghosts of the dead howled round the stone of their fear. But afterwards he shone like a pillar of the light of heaven. They fell by his mighty hand, and Grumal had his fame.

Raise, ye bards of other times,[32] raise high the praise of heroes; that my soul may settle on their fame; and the mind of Swaran cease to be sad.

They lay in the heath of Mora; the dark winds rustled over the heroes.[33] ——A hundred voices at once arose, a hundred harps were strung; they sung of other times, and the mighty chiefs of former years.

When now shall I hear the bard; or rejoice at the fame of my fathers? The harp is not strung on Morven; nor the voice of music raised on Cona. Dead with the mighty is the bard; and fame is in the desert no more.

Morning trembles with the beam of the east, and glimmers on gray-headed Cromla.[34] Over Lena is heard the horn of Swaran, and the sons of the ocean gather around.——Silent and sad they mount the wave, and the blast of Ullin[35] is behind their sails. White, as the mist of Morven, they float along the sea.

Call, said Fingal, call my dogs, the long-bounding sons of the chace. Call white-breasted Bran; and the surly strength of Luath.——Fillan, and Ryno—but he is not here; my son rests on the bed of death. Fillan and Fergus, blow my horn, that the joy of the chace may arise; that the deer of Cromla may hear and start at the lake of roes.

The shrill sound spreads along the wood. The sons of heathy Cromla arise.——A thousand dogs fly off at once, gray-bounding through the heath.[36] A deer fell by every dog, and three by the white-breasted Bran. He brought them, in their flight, to Fingal, that the joy of the king might be great.

One deer fell at the tomb of Ryno; and the grief of Fingal returned. He saw how peaceful lay the stone of him who was the first at the chace.—— No more shalt thou rise, O my son, to partake of the feast of Cromla. Soon will thy tomb be hid, and the grass grow rank on thy grave. The sons of the feeble shall pass over it, and shall not know that the mighty lie there.

Ossian and Fillan, sons of my strength, and Gaul king[37] of the blue swords[38] of war, let us ascend the hill to the cave of Tura, and find the chief of the battles of Erin.——Are these the walls of Tura? gray and lonely they rise on the heath. The king[39] of shells is sad, and the halls are desolate.[40] Come let us find the king of swords, and give him all our joy.——But is that Cuchullin, O Fillan, or a pillar of smoke on the heath? The wind of Cromla is on my eyes, and I distinguish not my friend.

Fingal! replied the youth, it is the son of Semo. Gloomy and sad is the hero; his hand is on his sword. Hail to the son of battle, breaker of the shields!

Hail to thee, replied Cuchullin, hail to all the sons of Morven. Delightful is thy presence, O Fingal, it is like[41] the sun on Cromla; when the hunter mourns his absence for a season, and sees him between the clouds. Thy sons are like stars that attend thy course, and give light in the night. It is not thus thou hast seen me, O Fingal, returning from the wars of the desart;[42] when the kings of the world[43] had fled, and joy returned to the hill of hinds.

Many are thy words, Cuchullin, said Connan[44] of small renown. Thy words are many, son of Semo, but where are thy deeds in arms? Why did we come over the ocean to aid thy feeble sword? Thou flyest to thy cave of sorrow,[45] and Connan fights thy battles: Resign to me these arms of light; yield them, thou son of Erin.[46]

No hero, replied the chief, ever sought the arms of Cuchullin; and had a thousand heroes sought them it were in vain, thou gloomy youth. I fled not to the cave of sorrow, as long as Erin's warriors lived.[47]

Youth of the feeble arm, said Fingal, Connan, say no more. Cuchullin is renowned in battle, and terrible over the desart.[48] Often have I heard thy fame, thou stormy chief of Innis-fail. Spread now thy white sails for the isle of mist, and see Bragéla leaning on her rock. Her tender eye is in tears, and the winds lift her long hair from her heaving breast. She listens to the winds of night[49] to hear the voice of thy rowers[50]; to hear the song of the sea, and the sound of thy distant harp.

And long shall she listen in vain; Cuchullin shall never return. How can I behold Bragéla to raise the sigh of her breast? Fingal, I was always victorious in the battles of other spears!

And hereafter thou shalt be victorious, said Fingal king of shells.[51] The fame of Cuchullin shall grow like the branchy tree of Cromla. Many battles await thee, O chief, and many shall be the wounds of thy hand. Bring hither, Oscar, the deer, and prepare the feast of shells; that our souls may rejoice after danger, and our friends delight in our presence.

We sat, we feasted, and we sung. The soul of Cuchullin rose. The strength of his arm returned; and gladness brightened on his face. Ullin gave the song, and Carril raised the voice. I, often, joined the bards, and sung of battles of the spear.——Battles! where I often fought; but now I fight no more. The fame of my former actions is ceased; and I sit forlorn at the tombs of my friends.

Thus they passed the night in the song; and brought back the morning with joy. Fingal arose on the heath, and shook his glittering spear in his hand.——He moved first toward the plains of Lena, and we followed like a ridge of fire.[52] Spread the sail, said the king of Morven,[53] and catch the winds that pour from Lena.——We rose on the wave with songs, and rushed, with joy, through the foam of the ocean.[54]

COMÁLA:

A

DRAMATIC POEM[1].

****

The PERSONS.

FINGAL.	MELILCOMA,) daughters
HIDALLAN.	DERSAGRENA,) of Morni.
COMALA.	BARDS.

DERSAGRENA.

The chace is over.—No noise on Ardven but the torrent's roar!——
Daughter of Morni, come from Crona's banks. Lay down the bow and take
the harp. Let the night come on with songs, and our joy be great on Ardven.

MELILCOMA[2].

And night comes on,[3] thou blue-eyed maid, gray night grows dim along
the plain. I saw a deer at Crona's stream; a mossy bank he seemed through
the gloom, but soon he bounded away. A meteor played round his branchy
horns; and the awful faces[4] of other times looked from the clouds of Crona.

DERSAGRENA[5].

These are the signs of Fingal's death.——The king of shields is fallen!—
and Caracul prevails. Rise, Comala[6], from thy rocks; daughter of Sarno, rise
in tears. The youth of thy love is low, and his ghost is already on our hills.

MELILCOMA.

There Comala sits forlorn! two gray dogs near shake their rough ears, and
catch the flying breeze. Her red cheek rests on her arm, and the mountain
wind is in her hair. She turns her blue-rolling[7] eyes towards the fields of his
promise.——Where art thou, O Fingal, for the night is gathering around?

COMALA.

O Carun[8] of the streams! why do I behold thy waters rolling in blood? Has the noise of the battle been heard on thy banks;[9] and sleeps the king of Morven?——Rise, moon, thou daughter of the sky! look from between thy clouds, that I may behold the light[10] of his steel, on the field of his promise.—Or rather let the meteor, that lights our departed[11] fathers through the night, come, with its red light,[12] to shew me the way to my fallen hero. Who will defend me from sorrow? Who from the love of Hidallan? Long shall Comala look before she can behold Fingal in the midst of his host; bright as the beam[13] of the morning in the cloud of an early shower.

HIDALLAN[14].

Roll, thou mist of gloomy Crona, roll[15] on the path of the hunter.[16] Hide his steps from mine eyes, and let me remember my friend no more. The bands of battle are scattered, and no crowding steps are round the noise of his steel. O Carun, roll thy streams of blood, for the chief of the people fell.

COMALA.

Who fell on Carun's grassy[17] banks, son of the cloudy night? Was he white as the snow of Ardven? Blooming as the bow of the shower? Was his hair like the mist of the hill, soft and curling in the day of the sun? Was he like the thunder of heaven in battle? Fleet as the roe of the desart?

HIDALLAN.

O that I might behold his love, fair-leaning from her rock! Her red eye dim in tears, and her blushing cheek half hid in her locks! Blow, thou gentle breeze, and lift the heavy locks of the maid, that I may behold her white arm, and lovely cheek of her sorrow![18]

COMALA.

And is the son of Comhal fallen, chief of the mournful tale? The thunder rolls on the hill!——The lightening[19] flies on wings of fire! But they frighten not Comala; for her Fingal fell. Say, chief of the mournful tale, fell the breaker of shields?

HIDALLAN.

The nations are scattered on their hills; for they shall hear the voice of the chief[20] no more.

COMALA.

Confusion pursue thee over thy plains; and destruction overtake thee, thou king of the world. Few be thy steps to thy grave; and let one virgin mourn thee. Let her be, like Comala, tearful in the days of her youth.——Why hast thou told me, Hidallan, that my hero fell? I might have hoped a little while his return, and have thought I saw him on the distant rock; a tree might have deceived me with his appearance; and the wind of the hill been the sound of his horn in mine ear. O that I were on the banks of Carun! that my tears might be warm on his cheek!

HIDALLAN.

He lies not on the banks of Carun: on Ardven heroes raise his tomb. Look on them, O moon, from thy clouds; be thy beam bright on his breast, that Comala may behold him in the light of his armour.

COMALA.

Stop, ye sons of the grave, till I behold my love. He left me at the chace alone. I knew not that he went to war. He said he would return with the night; and the king of Morven is returned. Why didst thou not tell me that he would fall, O trembling son of the rock[21] ! Thou hast seen him in the blood of his youth, but thou didst not tell Comala!

MELILCOMA.

What sound is that on Ardven? Who is that bright in the vale? Who comes like the strength of rivers, when their crowded waters glitter to the moon?

COMALA.

Who is it but the foe of Comala, the son of the king of the world! Ghost of Fingal! do thou, from thy cloud, direct Comala's bow. Let him fall like the hart of the desert.——It is Fingal in the crowd of his ghosts.—Why dost thou come, my love, to frighten and please my soul?

FINGAL.

Raise, ye bards of the song, the wars of the streamy Carun. Caracul has fled from my arms along the fields of his pride. He sets far distant like a meteor that incloses a spirit of night, when the winds drive it over the heath, and the dark woods are gleaming around.

I heard a voice like the breeze of my hills.[22] Is it the huntress of Galmal,[23] the white-handed daughter of Sarno? Look from thy rocks[24], my love; and let me hear the voice of Comala.

COMALA.

Take me to the cave of thy rest, O lovely son of death!——

FINGAL.

Come to the cave of my rest.——The storm is over,[25] and the sun is on our fields. Come to the cave of my rest, huntress of echoing Cona.[26]

COMALA.

He is returned with his fame; I feel the right hand of his battles.——But I must rest beside the rock till my soul settle from fear.—Let the harp be near; and raise the song, ye daughters of Morni.

DERSAGRENA.

Comala has slain three deer on Ardven, and the fire ascends on the rock; go to the feast of Comala, king of the woody Morven!

FINGAL.

Raise, ye sons of song, the wars of the streamy Carun; that my white-handed maid may rejoice: while I behold the feast of my love.

BARDS.

Roll, streamy Carun, roll in joy, the sons of battle fled. The steed is not seen on our fields; and the wings[27] of their pride spread in other lands. The sun will now rise in peace, and the shadows descend in joy. The voice of the chace will be heard; and the shields hang in the hall. Our delight will be in the war of the ocean, and our hands be red in the blood of Lochlin. Roll, streamy Carun, roll in joy, the sons of battle fled.

MELILCOMA.

Descend, ye light mists from high; ye moon-beams, lift her soul.——Pale lies the maid at the rock! Comala is no more!

FINGAL.

Is the daughter of Sarno dead; the white-bosomed maid of my love? Meet me, Comala, on my heaths, when I sit alone at the streams of my hills.

HIDALLAN.

Ceased the voice of the huntress of Galmal?[28] Why did I trouble the soul of the maid? When shall I see thee, with joy, in the chace of the dark-brown hinds?

FINGAL.

Youth of the gloomy brow! no more shalt thou feast in my halls. Thou shalt not pursue my chace, and my foes shall not fall by thy sword[29].——Lead me to the place of her rest that I may behold her beauty.——Pale she lies at the rock, and the cold winds lift her hair. Her bow-string sounds in the blast, and her arrow was broken in her fall. Raise the praise of the daughter of Sarno, and give her name to the wind of the hills.[30]

BARDS.

See! meteors roll[31] around the maid; and moon-beams lift her soul! Around her, from their clouds, bend the awful faces of her fathers; Sarno[32] of the gloomy brow; and the red-rolling eyes of Fidallan. When shall thy white hand arise, and thy voice be heard on our rocks? The maids shall seek thee on the heath, but they will not find thee. Thou shalt come, at times, to their dreams, and settle peace in their soul. Thy voice shall remain in their ears[33], and they shall think with joy on the dreams of their rest. Meteors roll[34] around the maid, and moon-beams lift her soul!

THE

WAR of CAROS[1]:

A POEM.

Bring, daughter of Toscar, bring the harp; the light of the song rises in Ossian's soul. It is like the field, when darkness covers the hills around, and the shadow grows slowly on the plain of the sun.

I behold my son, O Malvina, near the mossy rock of Crona[2]; but it is the mist[3] of the desert tinged with the beam of the west: Lovely is the mist that assumes the form of Oscar! turn from it, ye winds, when ye roar on the side of Ardven.

Who comes towards my son, with the murmur of a song? His staff is in his hand, his gray hair loose on the wind. Surly joy lightens his face; and he often looks back to Caros. It is Ryno[4] of the song, he that went to view the foe.

What does Caros king of ships, said the son of the now mournful Ossian? spreads he the wings[5] of his pride, bard of the times of old?

He spreads them, Oscar, replied the bard, but it is behind his gathered heap[6]. He looks over his stones with fear, and beholds thee terrible, as the ghost of night that rolls the wave to his ships.

Go, thou first of my bards, says Oscar, and take the spear of Fingal. Fix a flame on its point, and shake it to the winds of heaven. Bid him, in songs, to advance, and leave the rolling of his wave. Tell to Caros that I long for battle; and that my bow is weary of the chace of Cona. Tell him the mighty are not here; and that my arm is young.

He went with the sound of his song.[7] Oscar reared his voice on high. It reached his heroes on Ardven, like the noise of a cave[8]; when the sea of Togorma rolls before it; and its trees meet the roaring winds.——They gather round my son like the streams of the hill; when, after rain, they roll in the pride of their course.

Ryno came to the mighty Caros, and struck his flaming spear. Come to the battle of Oscar, O thou that sittest on the rolling of waters.[9] Fingal is distant far; he hears the songs of his bards in Morven: and the wind of his hall is in his hair. His terrible spear is at his side; and his shield that is like that darkened moon. Come to the battle of Oscar; the hero is alone.

He came not over the streamy Carun[10]; the bard returned with his song. Gray night grows dim on Crona. The feast of shells is spread. A hundred oaks burn to the wind, and faint light gleams over the heath. The ghosts of Ardven pass through the beam, and shew their dim and distant forms. Comala[11] is half unseen on her meteor; and Hidallan is sullen and dim, like the darkened moon behind the mist of night.

Why art thou sad? said Ryno; for he alone beheld the chief. Why art thou sad, Hidallan, hast thou not received thy fame? The songs of Ossian have been heard, and thy ghost has brightened in the wind, when thou didst bend from thy cloud to hear the song of Morven's bard.

And do thine eyes behold the hero,[12] said Oscar, like the dim meteor of night? Say, Ryno, say, how fell the chief[13] that was so renowned in the days of our fathers?——His name remains on the rocks of Cona; and I have often seen the streams of his hills.

Fingal, replied the bard, had driven Hidallan from his wars. The king's soul was sad for Comala, and his eyes could not behold Hidallan.[14]

Lonely, sad, along the heath, he slowly moved with silent steps. His arms hang disordered on his side. His hair flies loose from his helmet.[15] The tear is in his down-cast eyes; and the sigh half-silent in his breast.

Three days he strayed unseen, alone, before he came to Lamor's halls: the mossy halls of his fathers, at the stream of Balva[16].——There Lamor sat alone beneath a tree; for he had sent his people with Hidallan to war. The stream ran at his feet, and his gray head rested on his staff. Sightless are his aged eyes. He hums the song of other times.——The noise of Hidallan's feet came to his ear: he knew the tread of his son.

Is the son of Lamor returned; or is it the sound of his ghost? Hast thou fallen on the banks of Carun, son of the aged Lamor? Or, if I hear the sound of Hidallan's feet; where are the mighty in war? where are my people, Hidallan, that were wont to return with their echoing shields?——Have they fallen on the banks of Carun?

No: replied the sighing youth, the people of Lamor live. They are renowned in battle, my father; but Hidallan is renowned no more. I must sit alone on the banks of Balva, when the roar of the battle grows.

But thy fathers never sat alone, replied the rising pride of Lamor; they never sat alone on the banks of Balva, when the roar of battle rose.——Dost thou not behold that tomb? Mine eyes discern it not: there rests the noble Garmállon who never fled from war.——Come, thou renowned in battle, he says, come to thy father's tomb.——How am I renowned, Garmállon, for my son has fled from war?

King of the streamy Balva! said Hidallan with a sigh, why dost thou torment my soul? Lamor, I never feared.[17]——Fingal was sad for Comala, and denied his wars to Hidallan: Go to the gray streams of thy land, he said, and moulder like a leafless oak, which the winds have bent over Balva, never more to grow.

And must I hear, Lamor replied, the lonely tread of Hidallan's feet? When thousands are renowned in battle, shall he bend over my gray streams? Spirit of the noble Garmállon! carry Lamor to his place; his eyes are dark; his soul is sad: and his son has lost his fame.

Where, said the youth, shall I search for fame to gladden the soul of Lamor? From whence shall I return with renown, that the sound of my arms may be pleasant in his ear?——If I go to the chace of hinds, my name will not be heard.—Lamor will not feel my dogs, with his hands, glad at my arrival from the hill. He will not enquire of his mountains, or of the dark-brown deer of his desarts.

I must fall, said Lamor, like a leafless oak: it grew on a rock, but the winds have overturned it.——My ghost will be seen on my hills, mournful for my young Hidallan. Will not ye, ye mists, as ye rise, hide him from my sight?——My son!—go to Lamor's hall: there the arms of our fathers hang.—Bring the sword of Garmállon;—he took it from a foe.

He went and brought the sword with all its studded thongs.——He gave it to his father. The gray-haired hero felt the point with his hand.——

My son!—lead me to Garmállon's tomb: it rises beside that rustling tree. The long grass is withered;—I heard the breeze whistling there.—A little fountain murmurs near, and sends its water to Balva. There let me rest; it is noon: and the sun is on our fields.

He led him to Garmállon's tomb. Lamor pierced the side of his son.—— They sleep together; and their ancient halls moulder on Balva's banks.[18]— Ghosts are seen there at noon: the valley is silent, and the people shun the place of Lamor.

Mournful is thy tale, said Oscar, son of the times of old!—My soul sighs for Hidallan; he fell in the days of his youth. He flies on the blast of the desart, and his wandering is in a foreign land.——

Sons of the echoing Morven! draw near to the foes of Fingal. Send the night away in songs; and watch the strength of Caros. Oscar goes to the people of other times; to the shades of silent Ardven; where his fathers sit dim in their clouds, and behold the future war.—And art thou there, Hidal-lan, like a half-extinguished meteor? Come to my sight, in thy sorrow, chief of the roaring[19] Balva!

The heroes move with their songs.—Oscar slowly ascends the hill.—The meteors of night are setting on the heath before him. A distant torrent faintly roars.—Unfrequent blasts rush through aged oaks. The half-enlightened moon sinks dim and red behind her hill.—Feeble voices are heard on the heath.——Oscar drew his sword.

Come, said the hero, O ye ghosts of my fathers! ye that fought against the kings of the world!—Tell me the deeds of future times; and your discourse[20] in your caves; when you talk together and behold your sons in the fields of the valiant.

Trenmor came, from his hill, at the voice of his mighty son.—A cloud, like the steed of the stranger, supported his airy limbs. His robe is of the mist of Lano, that brings death to the people. His sword is a meteor[21] half-extinguished. His face is without form, and dark. He sighed thrice over the hero: and thrice the winds of the night roared around. Many were his words to Oscar: but they only came by halves to our ears: they were dark as the tales of other times, before the light of the song arose. He slowly vanished, like a mist that melts on the sunny hill.

It was then, O daughter of Toscar, my son begun first to be sad. He foresaw the fall of his race; and, at times, he was thoughtful and dark; like the sun[22] when he carries a cloud on his face; but he looks afterwards on the hills of Cona.[23]

Oscar passed the night among his fathers, gray morning met him on the banks of Carun.

A green vale surrounded a tomb which arose in the times of old. Little hills lift their head at a distance; and stretch their old trees to the wind. The warriors of Caros sat there, for they had passed the stream by night. They appeared, like the trunks of aged pines, to the pale light of the morning.

Oscar stood at the tomb, and raised thrice his terrible voice. The rocking hills echoed around: the starting roes bounded away. And the trembling ghosts of the dead fled, shrieking on their clouds. So terrible was the voice of my son, when he called his friends.

A thousand spears rose around; the people of Caros rose.—Why daughter of Toscar, why that tear? My son, though alone, is brave. Oscar is like a beam of the sky; he turns around and the people fall. His hand is like[24] the arm of a ghost, when he stretches it from a cloud: the rest of his thin form is unseen: but the people die in the vale.

My son beheld the approach of the foe; and he stood in the silent darkness of his strength.——"Am I alone, said Oscar, in the midst of a thousand foes?—Many a spear is there!—many a darkly-rolling eye!—Shall I fly to Ardven?—But did my fathers ever fly!——The mark of their arm is in a thousand battles.—Oscar too will be renowned.——Come, ye dim ghosts of my fathers, and behold my deeds in war!—I may fall; but I will be renowned like the race of the echoing Morven[25]."

He stood dilated[26] in his place, like a flood swelling in a narrow vale.[27] The battle came, but they fell: bloody was the sword of Oscar.——The noise reached his people at Crona; they came like a hundred streams. The warriors of Caros fled, and Oscar remained like a rock left by the ebbing sea.

Now dark and deep, with all his steeds, Caros rolled his might along: the little streams are lost in his course; and the earth is rocking round.—— Battle spreads from wing to wing: ten thousand swords gleam at once in the sky.——But why should Ossian sing of battles?—For never more shall my steel shine in war. I remember the days of my youth with sorrow;[28] when I feel the weakness of my arm. Happy are they who fell in their youth, in the midst of their renown!—They have not beheld the tombs of their friends:[29] or failed to bend the bow of their strength.——Happy art thou, O Oscar, in the midst of thy rushing blast. Thou often goest to the fields of thy fame, where Caros fled from thy lifted sword.

Darkness comes on my soul, O fair daughter of Toscar, I behold not the form of my son at Carun; nor the figure of Oscar on Crona. The rustling winds have carried him far away; and the heart of his father is sad.

But lead me, O Malvina, to the sound of my woods, and the roar of my mountain streams. Let the chace be heard on Cona; that I may think on the days of other years.—And bring me the harp, O maid, that I may touch it when the light of my soul shall arise.——Be thou near, to learn the song; and future times shall hear of Ossian.[30]

The sons of the feeble hereafter will lift the voice on Cona; and, looking up to the rocks, say, "Here Ossian dwelt." They shall admire the chiefs of old, and the race that are no more: while we ride on our clouds, Malvina, on the wings of the roaring winds. Our voices shall be heard, at times, in the desart; and we shall sing on the winds[31] of the rock.

THE

WAR of INIS-THONA [1]:

A POEM.

Our youth is like the dream of the hunter on the hill of heath. He sleeps in the mild beams of the sun; but he awakes amidst a storm; the red lightning flies around: and the trees shake their heads to the wind. He looks back with joy on the day of the sun, and the pleasant dreams of his rest!

When shall Ossian's youth return, or his ear delight in the sound of arms? When shall I, like Oscar, travel[2] in the light of my steel?—Come, with your streams, ye hills of Cona, and listen to the voice of Ossian! The song rises, like the sun, in my soul; and my heart feels[3] the joys of other times.

I behold thy towers, O Selma! and the oaks of thy shaded wall:—thy streams sound in my ear; thy heroes gather round. Fingal sits in the midst; and leans on the shield of Trenmor:—his spear stands against the wall; he listens to the song of his bards.—The deeds of his arm are heard; and the actions of the king in his youth.

Oscar had returned from the chace, and heard the hero's praise.—He took the shield of Branno[4] from the wall; his eyes were filled with tears. Red was the cheek of youth. His voice was trembling, low. My spear shook its bright head in his hand: he spoke to Morven's king.

Fingal! thou king of heroes! Ossian, next to him in war! ye have fought the battle in your youth; your names are renowned in song.—Oscar is like the mist of Cona: I appear and vanish.—The bard will not know my name.—The hunter will not search in the heath for my tomb. Let me fight, O heroes, in the battles of Inis-thona. Distant is the land of my war!—ye shall not hear of Oscar's fall.——Some bard may find me there, and give my name to the song.—The daughter of the stranger shall see my tomb, and weep over the youth that came from afar. The bard shall say, at the feast, hear the song of Oscar from the distant land.

Oscar, replied the king of Morven; thou shalt fight, son of my fame!—Prepare my dark-bosomed ship to carry my hero to Inis-thona. Son of my son, regard our fame;—for thou art of the race of renown. Let not the children of strangers say, feeble are the sons of Morven!——Be thou, in battle, like the[5] roaring storm: mild as the evening sun in peace.—Tell, Oscar, to Inis-thona's king, that Fingal remembers his youth; when we strove in the combat together in the days of Agandecca.

They lifted up the sounding sail; the wind whistled through the thongs[6] of their masts. Waves lashed the oozy rocks: the strength of ocean roared.——

My son beheld, from the wave, the land of groves. He rushed into the echoing bay of Runa; and sent his sword to Annir king[7] of spears.

The gray-haired hero rose, when he saw the sword of Fingal. His eyes were full of tears, and he remembered the battles of their youth. Twice they lifted the spear before the lovely Agandecca: heroes stood far distant, as if two ghosts contended.[8]

But now, begun the king, I am old; the sword lies useless in my hall. Thou who art of Morven's race! Annir has been in the strife of spears; but he is pale and withered now, like the oak of Lano. I have no son to meet thee with joy, or to carry thee to the halls of his fathers. Argon is pale in the tomb, and Ruro is no more.—My daughter is in the hall of strangers, and longs to behold my tomb.——Her spouse shakes ten thousand spears; and comes[9] like a cloud[10] of death from Lano.—Come thou, to share the feast of Annir, son of echoing Morven.

Three days they feasted together; on the fourth Annir heard the name of Oscar[11].—They rejoiced in the shell[12]; and pursued the boars of Runa.

Beside the fount of mossy stones, the weary heroes rest. The tear steals in secret from Annir: and he broke the rising sigh.——Here darkly rest, the hero said, the children of my youth.—This stone is the tomb of Ruro: that tree sounds over the grave of Argon. Do ye hear my voice, O my sons, within your narrow house? Or do ye speak in these rustling leaves, when the winds of the desart rise?

King of Inis-thona, said Oscar, how fell the children of youth? The wild boar often rushes over their tombs, but he does not disturb the hunters.[13] They pursue deer[14] formed of clouds, and bend their airy bow.—They still love the sport of their youth; and mount the wind with joy.

Cormalo, replied the king, is chief of ten thousand spears; he dwells at the dark-rolling[15] waters of Lano[16]; which send forth the cloud of death. He came to Runa's echoing halls, and sought the honour of the spear[17]. The youth was lovely as the first beam of the sun; and few were they who could meet him in fight!—My heroes yielded to Cormalo: and my daughter loved the son of Lano.[18]

Argon and Ruro returned from the chace; the tears of their pride descended:—They rolled their silent eyes on Runa's heroes, because they yielded to a stranger: three days they feasted with Cormalo: on the fourth my Argon fought.—But who could fight with Argon!—Lano's chief[19] was overcome. His heart swelled with the grief of pride, and he resolved, in secret, to behold the death of my sons.

They went to the hills of Runa, and pursued the dark-brown hinds. The arrow of Cormalo flew in secret; and my children fell.[20] He came to the maid of his love; to Inis-thona's dark-haired[21] maid.——They fled over the desart—and Annir remained alone.

Night came on and day appeared; nor Argon's voice, nor Ruro's came. At length their much-loved dog is seen; the fleet and bounding Runar. He came into the hall and howled; and seemed to look towards the place of their fall.——We followed him: we found them here: and laid them by this mossy stream. This is the haunt of Annir, when the chace of the hinds is over. I bend like the trunk of an aged oak above them: and my tears for ever flow.

O Ronnan! said the rising Oscar, Ogar king of spears! call my heroes to my side, the sons of streamy Morven. To-day we go to Lano's water, that sends forth the cloud of death. Cormalo will not long rejoice: death is often at the point of our swords.

They came over the desart like stormy clouds, when the winds roll them over the heath: their edges are tinged with lightning: and the echoing groves foresee the storm. The horn of Oscar's battle was heard; and Lano shook in all its waves. The children of the lake convened around the sounding shield of Cormalo.

Oscar fought, as he was wont in battle. Cormalo fell beneath his sword: and the sons of the dismal Lano fled to their secret vales.——Oscar brought the daughter of Inis-thona to Annir's echoing halls. The face of age was bright with joy; he blest the king of swords.

How great was the joy of Ossian, when he beheld the distant sail of his son! it was like a cloud of light that rises in the east, when the traveller is sad in a land unknown; and dismal night, with her ghosts, is sitting around him.[22]

We brought him, with songs, to Selma's halls. Fingal ordered the feast of shells to be spread. A thousand bards raised the name of Oscar: and Morven answered to the noise. The daughter of Toscar was there, and her voice was like the harp; when the distant sound comes, in the evening, on the soft-rustling breeze of the vale.

O lay me, ye that see the light, near some rock of my hills: let the thick hazels be around, let the rustling oak be near. Green be the place of my rest; and let the sound of the distant torrent be heard. Daughter of Toscar, take the harp, and raise the lovely song of Selma; that sleep may overtake my soul in the midst of joy; that the dreams of my youth may return, and the days of the mighty Fingal.

Selma! I behold thy towers, thy trees, and shaded wall. I see the heroes of Morven; and hear the song of bards. Oscar lifts the sword of Cormalo; and a thousand youths admire its studded thongs. They look with wonder on my son; and admire the strength of his arm. They mark the joy of his father's eyes; they long for an equal fame.

And ye shall have your fame, O sons of streamy Morven.—My soul is often brightened with the song; and I remember the companions of my youth.——But sleep descends with the sound of the harp; and pleasant dreams begin to rise. Ye sons of the chace stand far distant, nor disturb my rest[23]. The bard of other times converses now with his fathers, the chiefs of the days of old.—Sons of the chace, stand far distant; disturb not the dreams of Ossian.

THE

BATTLE of LORA:

A POEM[1].

Son of the distant land, who dwellest in the secret cell! do I hear the sounds of thy grove? or is it the voice of thy songs?[2] The torrent was loud in my ear, but I heard a tuneful voice; dost thou praise the chiefs of thy land; or the spirits[3] of the wind?—But, lonely dweller of the rock! look over that heathy plain: thou seest green tombs, with their rank, whistling grass, with their stones of mossy heads: thou seest them, son of the rock, but Ossian's eyes have failed.

A mountain-stream comes roaring down and sends its waters round a green hill: four mossy stones, in the midst of withered grass, rear their heads on the top: two trees, which the storms have bent, spread their whistling branches around.——This is thy dwelling, Erragon[4]; this thy narrow house: the sound of thy shells has[5] been long forgot in Sora: and thy shield is become dark in thy hall.——Erragon, king of ships! chief of distant Sora! how hast thou fallen on our mountains[6]! How is the mighty low!

Son of the secret cell! dost thou delight in songs? Hear the battle of Lora; the sound of its steel is long since past. So thunder on the darkened hill roars and is no more. The sun returns with his silent beams: the glittering rocks, and green heads of the mountains smile.

The bay of Cona received our ships[7], from Ullin's[8] rolling waves: our white sheets hung loose to the masts: and the boisterous winds roared behind the groves of Morven.——The horn of the king is sounded, and the deer start from their rocks. Our arrows flew in the woods; the feast of the hill was spread. Our joy was great on our rocks, for the fall of the terrible Swaran.

Two heroes were forgot at our feast; and the rage of their bosoms burned. They rolled their red eyes in secret: the sigh burst from their breasts. They were seen to talk together, and to throw their spears on earth. They were two dark clouds, in the midst of our joy; like pillars of mist on the settled sea: it glitters to the sun, but the mariners fear a storm.

Raise my white sails, said Ma-ronnan, raise them to the winds of the west; let us rush, O Aldo, through the foam of the northern wave. We are forgot at the feast: but our arms have been red in blood. Let us leave the hills of Fingal, and serve the king of Sora.——His countenance is fierce, and the war darkens round his spear. Let us be renowned, O Aldo, in the battles of echoing Sora.[9]

They took their swords and shields of thongs; and rushed to Lumar's sounding bay. They came to Sora's haughty king, the chief of bounding steeds.——Erragon had returned from the chace: his spear was red in blood. He bent his dark face to the ground: and whistled as he went.——He took the strangers to his feasts: they fought and conquered in his wars.

Aldo returned with his fame towards Sora's lofty walls.—From her tower looked the spouse of Erragon, the humid, rolling eyes of Lorma.——Her dark-brown[10] hair flies on the wind of ocean: her white breast heaves, like snow on the heath; when the gentle winds arise, and slowly move it in the light. She saw young Aldo, like the beam of Sora's setting sun. Her soft heart sighed: tears filled her eyes; and her white arm supported her head.

Three days she sat within the hall, and covered grief with joy.—On the fourth she fled with the hero, along the rolling[11] sea.——They came to Cona's mossy towers, to Fingal king of spears.

Aldo of the heart of pride! said the rising king of Morven,[12] shall I defend thee from the wrath[13] of Sora's injured king? who will now receive my people into their halls, or give the feast of strangers, since Aldo, of the little soul, has carried away the fair of Sora?[14] Go to thy hills, thou feeble hand, and hide thee in thy caves; mournful is the battle we must fight, with Sora's gloomy king.——Spirit of the noble Trenmor! when will Fingal cease to fight? I was born in the midst of battles[15], and my steps must move in blood to my tomb. But my hand did not injure the weak, my steel did not touch the feeble in arms.—I behold thy tempests, O Morven, which will overturn my halls; when my children are dead in battle, and none remains to dwell in Selma. Then will the feeble come, but they will not know my tomb: my renown is in the song:[16] and my actions shall be as a dream to future times.

His people gathered around Erragon, as the storms round the ghost of night; when he calls them from the top of Morven, and prepares to pour them on the land of the stranger.——He came to the shore of Cona, and sent his bard to the king; to demand the combat of thousands; or the land of many hills.

Fingal sat in his hall with the companions of his youth around him. The young heroes were at the chace, and far distant in the desert. The gray-haired chiefs talked of other times, and of the actions of their youth; when the aged Narthmor[17] came, the king[18] of streamy Lora.

This is no time, begun the chief,[19] to hear the songs of other years: Erragon frowns on the coast, and lifts ten thousand swords. Gloomy is the king among his chiefs! he is like the darkened moon, amidst the meteors of night.[20]

Come, said Fingal, from thy hall, thou daughter of my love; come from thy hall, Bosmina[21], maid of streamy Morven! Narthmor, take the steeds[22] of the strangers, and attend the daughter of Fingal: let her bid the king of Sora to our feast, to Selma's shaded wall.——Offer him, O Bosmina, the peace of heroes, and the wealth of generous Aldo: our youths are far distant, and age is on our trembling hands.

She came to the host of Erragon, like a beam of light to a cloud.——In her right hand shone an arrow of gold; and in her left a sparkling shell, the sign of Morven's peace.[23]——Erragon brightened in her presence as a rock, before the sudden beams of the sun; when they issue from a broken cloud, divided by the roaring wind.

Son of the distant Sora, begun the mildly blushing maid, come to the feast of Morven's king, to Selma's shaded walls. Take the peace of heroes, O warrior, and let the dark sword rest by thy side.—And if thou chusest the wealth of kings, hear the words of the generous Aldo.——He gives to Erragon an hundred steeds, the children of the rein; an hundred maids from distant lands; an hundred hawks with fluttering wing, that fly across the sky. An hundred girdles[24] shall also be thine, to bind high-bosomed women;[25] the friends of the births of heroes, and the cure of the sons of toil.—Ten shells studded with gems shall shine in Sora's towers: the blue[26] water trembles on their stars, and seems to be sparkling wine.——They gladdened once the kings of the world[27], in the midst of their echoing halls. These, O hero, shall be thine; or thy white-bosomed spouse.——Lorma shall roll her bright eyes in thy halls; though Fingal loves the generous Aldo:—Fingal!—who never injured a hero, though his arm is strong.

Soft voice of Cona! replied the king, tell him, that he spreads his feast in vain.——Let Fingal pour his spoils around me; and bend beneath my power. Let him give me the swords of his fathers, and the shields of other times; that my children may behold them in my halls, and say, "These are the arms of Fingal."

Never shall they behold them in thy halls, said the rising pride of the maid; they are in the mighty[28] hands of heroes who never yielded in war.— King of the echoing Sora! the storm is gathering on our hills. Dost thou not foresee the fall of thy people, son of the distant land?

She came to Selma's silent halls; the king beheld her down-cast eyes. He rose from his place, in his strength, and shook his aged locks.——He took the sounding mail of Trenmor, and the dark-brown shield of his fathers. Darkness filled Selma's hall, when he stretched his hand to his spear:—the ghosts of thousands were near, and foresaw the death of the people. Terrible joy rose in the face of the aged heroes: they rushed to meet the foe; their thoughts are on the actions[29] of other years: and on the fame of the tomb.[30]

Now the dogs of the chace appeared at Trathal's tomb: Fingal knew that his young heroes followed them, and he stopt in the midst of his course. ——Oscar appeared the first;—then Morni's son, and Nemi's race:— Fercuth[31] shewed his gloomy form: Dermid spread his dark hair on the wind. Ossian came the last. O son of the rock[32], I hummed the song of other times: my spear supported my steps over the little streams, and my thoughts were of mighty men. Fingal struck his bossy shield; and gave the dismal sign of war; a thousand swords[33], at once unsheathed, gleam on the waving heath. Three gray-haired sons of song raise the tuneful, mournful voice. ——Deep and dark with sounding steps, we rush, a gloomy ridge, along: like the shower of a storm when it pours on the narrow vale.

The king of Morven sat on his hill: the sun-beam[34] of battle flew on the wind: the companions of his youth are near, with all their waving locks of age.——Joy rose in the hero's eyes when he beheld his sons in war; when he saw them amidst the lightning of swords, and mindful of the deeds of their fathers.——Erragon came on, in his strength, like the roar of a winter stream: the battle falls in his course, and death is at his side.[35]

Who comes, said Fingal, like the bounding roe, like the hart of echoing Cona? His shield glitters on his side; and the clang of his armour is mournful.——He meets with Erragon in the strife!—Behold the battle of the chiefs!—it is like the contending of ghosts in a gloomy storm.——But fallest thou, son of the hill, and is thy white bosom stained with blood? Weep, unhappy Lorma, Aldo is no more.

The king took the spear of his strength; for he was sad for the fall of Aldo: he bent his deathful eyes on the foe; but Gaul met the king of Sora.—— Who can relate the fight of the chiefs?—The mighty stranger fell.

Sons of Cona! Fingal cried aloud, stop the hand of death.—Mighty was he that is now so low! and much is he mourned in Sora! The stranger will come towards his hall, and wonder why it is silent. The king is fallen, O stranger, and the joy of his house is ceased.——Listen to the sound of his woods: perhaps his ghost is[36] there; but he is far distant, on Morven, beneath the sword of a foreign foe.

Such were the words of Fingal, when the bard raised the song of peace; we stopped our uplifted swords, and spared the feeble foe. We laid Erragon in that tomb; and I raised the voice of grief: the clouds of night came rolling down, and the ghost of Erragon appeared to some.—His face was cloudy and dark; and an half-formed sigh is in his breast.——Blest be thy soul, O king of Sora! thine arm was terrible in war!

Lorma sat, in Aldo's hall, at the light of a flaming oak: the night came, but he did not return; and the soul of Lorma is sad.—What detains thee, hunter of Cona? for thou didst promise to return.——Has the deer been distant far; and do the dark winds sigh, round thee, on the heath? I am in the land of strangers, where is my friend, but Aldo? Come from thy echoing hills, O my best beloved!

Her eyes are turned toward the gate, and she listens to the rustling blast. She thinks it is Aldo's tread, and joy rises in her face:—but sorrow returns again, like a thin cloud on the moon.——And thou wilt not return, my love? Let me behold the face of the hill. The moon is in the east. Calm and bright is the breast of the lake! When shall I behold his dogs returning from the chace? When shall I hear his voice, loud and distant on the wind? Come from thy echoing hills, hunter of woody Cona!

His thin ghost appeared, on a rock, like the watry beam of the moon,[37] when it rushes from between two clouds, and the midnight shower is on the field.——She followed the empty form over the heath, for she knew that her hero fell.—I heard her approaching cries on the wind, like the mournful voice of the breeze, when it sighs on the grass of the cave.

She came, she found her hero: her voice was heard no more: silent she rolled her sad eyes; she was pale as a watry cloud, that rises from the lake, to the beam of the moon.[38]

Few were her days on Cona: she sunk into the tomb: Fingal commanded his bards; and they sung over the death of Lorma. The daughters[39] of Morven mourned her for one day in the year, when the dark winds of autumn returned.

Son of the distant land[40], thou dwellest in the field of fame: O let thy song rise, at times, in the praise of those that fell: that their thin ghosts may rejoice around thee; and the soul of Lorma come on a moon-beam[41], when thou liest down to rest, and the moon looks into thy cave. Then shalt thou see her lovely; but the tear is still on her cheek.

CONLATH and CUTHÓNA:

A POEM[1].

Did not Ossian hear a voice? or is it the sound of days that are no more? Often does the memory of former times come, like the evening sun, on my soul. The noise of the chace is renewed; and, in thought, I lift the spear. ——But Ossian did hear a voice: Who art thou, son of the night? The sons of little men[2] are asleep, and the midnight wind is in my hall. Perhaps it is the shield of Fingal that echoes to the blast, it hangs in Ossian's hall, and he feels it sometimes with his hands.——Yes!—I hear thee, my friend: long has thy voice been absent from mine ear! What brings thee, on thy cloud, to Ossian, son of the generous Morni? Are the friends of the aged near thee? Where is Oscar, son of fame?—He was often near thee, O Conlath, when the din of battle rose.

GHOST OF CONLATH.

Sleeps the sweet voice of Cona, in the midst of his rustling hall? Sleeps Ossian in his hall, and his friends without their fame? The sea rolls round the dark I-thona[3], and our tombs are not seen by the stranger.[4] How long shall our fame be unheard, son of the echoing Morven?[5]

OSSIAN.

O that mine eyes could behold thee, as thou sittest, dim, on thy cloud! Art thou like the mist of Lano; or an half-extinguished meteor?[6] Of what are the skirts of thy robe? Of what is thine airy bow?——But he is gone on his blast like the shadow of mist.[7]—Come from thy wall, my harp, and let me hear thy sound. Let the light of memory rise on I-thona; that I may behold my friends. And Ossian does behold his friends, on the dark-blue isle.—The cave of Thona appears, with its mossy rocks and bending trees. A stream roars at its mouth, and Toscar bends over its course. Fercuth is sad by his side: and the maid[8] of his love sits at a distance, and weeps. Does the wind of the waves deceive me? Or do I hear them speak?

TOSCAR.

The night was stormy. From their hills the groaning oaks came down. The sea darkly-tumbled beneath the blast, and the roaring waves were climbing against our rocks.—The lightning came often and shewed the blasted fern.—Fercuth! I saw the ghost of night[9]. Silent he stood, on that bank; his robe of mist flew on the wind.—I could behold his tears: an aged man he seemed, and full of thought.

FERCUTH.

It was thy father, O Toscar; and he foresees some death among his race. Such was his appearance on Cromla, before the great Ma-ronnan[10] fell.—— Ullin[11]! with thy hills of grass, how pleasant are thy vales! Silence is near thy blue streams, and the sun is on thy fields. Soft is the sound of the harp in Seláma[12], and pleasant[13] the cry of the hunter on Cromla. But we are in the dark I-thona, surrounded by the storm. The billows lift their white heads above our rocks: and we tremble amidst the night.

TOSCAR.

Whither is the soul of battle fled, Fercuth with the locks of age? I have seen thee undaunted in danger, and thine eyes burning with joy in the fight. Whither is the soul of battle fled? Our fathers never feared.—Go: view the settling sea: the stormy wind is laid. The billows still tremble[14] on the deep, and seem to fear the blast. But view the settling sea: morning is gray on our rocks. The sun will look soon from his east; in all his pride of light.

I lifted up my sails, with joy, before the halls of generous Conlath. My course was by the isle of waves,[15] where his love[16] pursued the deer. I saw her, like that beam of the sun that issues from the cloud. Her hair was on her heaving breast; she, bending forward, drew the bow: her white arm seemed, behind her, like the snow of Cromla:——Come to my soul, I said, thou huntress of the isle of waves![17] But she spends her time in tears, and thinks of the generous Conlath. Where can I find thy peace, Cuthona, lovely maid!

CU-THONA[18].

A distant steep bends over the sea, with aged trees and mossy rocks: the billows roll at its feet: on its side is the dwelling of roes. The people call it Ardven. There the towers of Mora rise.[19] There Conlath looks over the sea for his only love. The daughters of the chace returned, and he beheld their downcast eyes. Where is the daughter of Rumar? But they answered not.— My peace dwells on Ardven, son of the distant land!

TOSCAR.

And Cuthona shall return to her peace; to the halls[20] of generous Conlath. He is the friend of Toscar: I have feasted in his halls.—Rise, ye gentle breezes of Ullin,[21] and stretch my sails towards Ardven's shores. Cuthona shall rest on Ardven: but the days of Toscar will be sad.—I shall sit in my cave in the field of the sun. The blast will rustle in my trees, and I shall think it is Cuthona's voice. But she is distant far, in the halls of the mighty Conlath.

CUTHONA.

Oh![22] what cloud is that? It carries the ghosts of my fathers. I see the skirts of their robes, like gray and watry mist. When shall I fall, O Rumar?—Sad Cuthona sees[23] her death. Will not Conlath behold me, before I enter the narrow house?[24]

OSSIAN.

And he will behold thee, O maid: he comes along the rolling[25] sea. The death of Toscar is dark on his spear; and a wound is in his side. He is pale at the cave of Thona, and shews his ghastly wound[26]. Where art thou with thy tears, Cuthona? the chief of Mora dies.——The vision grows dim on my mind:—I behold the chiefs no more. But, O ye bards of future times, remember the fall of Conlath with tears: he fell before his day[27]; and sadness darkened in his hall. His mother looked to his shield on the wall, and it was bloody[28]. She knew that her hero died, and her sorrow was heard on Mora.

Art thou pale on thy rock, Cuthona, beside the fallen chiefs? The night comes, and the day returns, but none appears to raise their tomb. Thou frightnest the screaming fowls[29] away, and thy tears for ever flow. Thou art pale as a watry cloud, that rises from a lake.

The sons of the desart came, and they found her dead.[30] They raise a tomb over the heroes; and she rests at the side of Conlath.—Come not to my dreams, O Conlath; for thou hast received thy fame. Be thy voice far distant from my hall; that sleep may descend at night. O that I could forget my friends: till my footsteps cease to be seen! till I come among them with joy! and lay my aged limbs in the narrow house!

CARTHON[1]:
A POEM.

A tale of the times of old! The deeds of days of other years!—The murmur of thy streams, O Lora, brings back the memory of the past. The sound of thy woods, Garmallar, is lovely in mine ear. Dost thou not behold, Malvina, a rock with its head of heath? Three aged firs[2] bend from its face; green is the narrow plain at its feet; there the flower of the mountain grows, and shakes its white head in the breeze. The thistle is there alone, and sheds its aged beard. Two stones, half sunk in the ground, shew their heads of moss. The deer of the mountain avoids the place, for he beholds the gray ghost that guards it:[3] for the mighty lie, O Malvina, in the narrow plain of the rock. A tale of the times of old! the deeds of days of other years!

Who comes from the land of strangers, with his thousands around him? the sun-beam pours its bright stream before him; and his hair meets the wind of his hills. His face is settled from war. He is calm as the evening beam that looks, from the cloud of the west, on Cona's silent vale. Who is it but Comhal's son[4], the king of mighty deeds! He beholds his hills with joy, and bids a thousand voices rise.——Ye have fled over your fields, ye sons of the distant land! The king of the world sits in his hall, and hears of his people's flight. He lifts his red eye of pride, and takes his father's sword. Ye have fled over your fields, sons of the distant land!

Such were the words of the bards, when they came to Selma's halls.—A thousand lights[5] from the stranger's land rose, in the midst of the people. The feast is spread around; and the night passed away in joy.—Where is the noble Clessámmor[6], said the fair-haired Fingal? Where is the companion of my father, in the days[7] of my joy? Sullen and dark he passes his days in the vale of echoing Lora: but, behold, he comes from the hill, like a steed[8] in his strength, who finds his companions in the breeze; and tosses his bright mane in the wind.——Blest be the soul of Clessámmor, why so long from Selma?

Returns the chief, said Clessámmor, in the midst of his fame? Such was the renown of Comhal in the battles of his youth. Often did we pass over Carun to the land of the strangers: our swords returned, not unstained with blood: nor did the kings of the world rejoice.——Why do I remember the battles of my youth?[9] My hair is mixed with gray. My hand forgets to bend the bow: and I lift a lighter spear. O that my joy would return, as when I first beheld the maid; the white-bosomed daughter of strangers, Moina[10] with the dark-blue eyes!

Tell, said the mighty Fingal, the tale of thy youthful days. Sorrow, like a cloud on the sun, shades the soul of Clessámmor. Mournful are thy thoughts, alone, on the banks of the roaring Lora. Let us hear the sorrow of thy youth, and the darkness of thy days.

It was in the days of peace, replied the great Clessámmor, I came, in my bounding ship, to Balclutha's[11] walls of towers. The winds had roared behind my sails, and Clutha's[12] streams received my dark-bosomed vessel. Three days I remained in Reuthámir's halls, and saw that beam of light, his daughter. The joy of the shell went round, and the aged hero gave the fair. Her breasts were like foam on the wave, and her eyes like stars of light: her hair was dark as the raven's wing: her soul was generous and mild. My love for Moina was great: and my heart poured forth in joy.

The son of a stranger came; a chief who loved the white-bosomed Moina. His words were mighty in the hall, and he often half-unsheathed his sword.—Where, he said, is the mighty Comhal, the restless wanderer[13] of the heath? Comes he, with his host, to Balclutha, since Clessámmor is so bold?

My soul, I replied, O warrior! burns in a light of its own. I stand without fear in the midst of thousands, though the valiant are distant far.—Stranger! thy words are mighty, for Clessámmor is alone. But my sword trembles by my side, and longs to glitter in my hand.—Speak no more of Comhal, son of the winding Clutha!

The strength of his pride arose. We fought; he fell beneath my sword. The banks of Clutha heard his fall, and a thousand spears glittered around. I fought: the strangers prevailed: I plunged into the stream of Clutha. My white sails rose over the waves, and I bounded on the dark-blue sea.—Moina came to the shore, and rolled the red eye of her tears: her dark[14] hair flew on the wind; and I heard her cries.[15]—Often did I turn my ship! but the winds of the East prevailed. Nor Clutha ever since have I seen: nor Moina of the dark brown hair.—She fell in Balclutha: for I have seen her ghost. I knew her as she came through the dusky night, along the murmur of Lora: she was like the new moon[16] seen through the gathered mist: when the sky pours down its flaky snow, and the world is silent and dark.

Raise[17], ye bards, said the mighty Fingal, the praise of unhappy Moina. Call her ghost, with your songs, to our hills; that she may rest with the fair of Morven, the sun-beams of other days, and the delight of heroes of old.—I have seen the walls[18] of Balclutha, but they were desolate. The fire had resounded in the halls: and the voice of the people is heard no more. The stream of Clutha was removed from its place, by the fall of the walls.—The thistle shook, there, its lonely head: the moss whistled to the wind. The fox looked out, from the windows, the rank grass of the wall waved round his head.—Desolate is the dwelling of Moina, silence is in the house of her fathers.—Raise the song of mourning, O bards, over the land of strangers. They have but fallen before us: for, one day, we must fall.—Why dost thou build the hall, son of the winged days? Thou lookest from thy towers to-day; yet a few years, and the blast of the desert comes; it howls in thy empty court, and whistles round thy half-worn shield.—And let the blast of the desert come! we shall be renowned in our day. The mark of my arm shall be in the battle, and my name in the song of bards.—Raise the song; send round the shell: and let joy be heard in my hall.—When thou, sun of heaven, shalt fail! if thou shalt fail, thou mighty light! if thy brightness is for a season, like Fingal; our fame shall survive thy beams.

Such was the song of Fingal, in the day of his joy. His thousand bards leaned forward from their seats, to hear the voice of the king. It was like the music of the harp on the gale of the spring.—Lovely were thy thoughts, O Fingal! why had not Ossian the strength of thy soul?—But thou standest alone, my father; and who can equal the king of Morven?[19]

The night passed away in song, and morning returned in joy;—the mountains shewed their gray heads; and the blue face of ocean smiled.—The white wave is seen tumbling round the distant rock; the gray mist rises, slowly, from the lake. It came, in the figure of an aged man, along the silent plain. Its large limbs did not move in steps; for a ghost supported it in mid air. It came towards Selma's hall, and dissolved in a shower of blood.

The king alone beheld the terrible[20] sight, and he foresaw the death of the people. He came, in silence, to his hall; and took his father's spear.—The mail rattled on his breast. The heroes rose around. They looked, in silence, on each other, marking the eyes of Fingal.—They saw the battle in his face: the death of armies on his spear.—A thousand shields, at once, are placed on their arms; and they drew a thousand swords. The hall of Selma brightened around. The clang of arms ascends.—The gray dogs howl in their place. No word is among the mighty chiefs.—Each marked the eyes of the king; and half assumed his spear.

Sons of Morven, begun the king, this is no time to fill the shell. The battle darkens near us; and death hovers over the land. Some ghost, the friend of Fingal, has forewarned us of the foe.——The sons of the stranger come from the darkly-rolling sea. For, from the water, came the sign of Morven's gloomy danger.—Let each[21] assume his heavy spear, and gird on his father's sword.—Let the dark helmet rise on every head; and the mail pour its lightening from every side.—The battle gathers like a tempest, and soon shall ye hear the roar of death.

The hero moved on before his host, like a cloud before a ridge of heaven's[22] fire; when it pours on the sky of night, and mariners foresee a storm. On Cona's rising heath they stood: the white-bosomed maids beheld them above like a grove; they foresaw the death of their youths, and looked towards the sea with fear.—The white wave deceived them for distant sails, and the tear is on their cheek.

The sun rose on the sea, and we beheld a distant fleet.—Like the mist of ocean they came: and poured their youth upon the coast.—The chief was among them, like the stag in the midst of the herd.—His shield is studded with gold, and stately strode the king of spears.—He moved towards Selma; his thousands moved behind.

Go, with thy song of peace, said Fingal; go, Ullin, to the king of swords. Tell him that we are mighty in battle; and that the ghosts of our foes are many.—But renowned are they who have feasted in my halls! they shew the arms[23] of my fathers in a foreign land: the sons of the strangers wonder, and bless the friends of Morven's race; for our names have been heard afar; the kings of the world shook in the midst of their people.[24]

Ullin went with his song. Fingal rested on his spear: he saw the mighty foe in his armour: and he blest the stranger's son.

How stately art thou, son of the sea! said the king of woody Morven. Thy sword is a beam of might[25] by thy side: thy spear is a fir[26] that defies the storm. The varied face of the moon is not broader than thy shield.—Ruddy is thy face of youth! soft the ringlets of thy hair!—But this tree may fall; and his memory be forgot!—The daughter of the stranger will be sad, and look to the rolling sea:—the children will say, "We see a ship; perhaps it is the king of Balclutha." The tear starts from their mother's eye. Her thoughts are of him that sleeps in Morven.

Such were the words of the king, when Ullin came to the mighty Carthon: he threw down the spear before him; and raised the song of peace.

Come to the feast of Fingal, Carthon, from the rolling sea! partake the feast of the king, or lift the spear of war. The ghosts of our foes are many: but renowned are the friends of Morven!

Behold that field, O Carthon; many a green hill rises there, with mossy stones and rustling grass: these are the tombs of Fingal's foes, the sons of the rolling sea.

Dost thou speak to the feeble in arms, said Carthon, bard of the woody Morven? Is my face pale for fear, son of the peaceful song? Why, then, dost thou think to darken my soul with the tales of those who fell?—My arm has fought in the battle; my renown is known afar. Go to the feeble in arms, and bid them yield to Fingal.—Have not I seen the fallen Balclutha? And shall I feast with Comhal's son? Comhal! who threw his fire in the midst of my father's hall! I was young, and knew not the cause why the virgins wept. The columns of smoke pleased mine eye, when they rose above my walls; I often looked back, with gladness, when my friends fled along the hill.——But when the years of my youth came on, I beheld the moss of my fallen walls: my sigh arose with the morning, and my tears descended with night.—Shall I not fight, I said to my soul, against the children of my foes? And I will fight, O bard; I feel the strength of my soul.

His people gathered around the hero, and drew, at once, their shining swords. He stands, in the midst, like a pillar of fire; the tear half-starting from his eye; for he thought of the fallen Balclutha, and the crowded pride of his soul arose. Sidelong he looked up to the hill, where our heroes shone in arms; the spear trembled in his hand: and, bending forward, he seemed to threaten the king.

Shall I, said Fingal to his soul, meet, at once, the king?[27] Shall I stop him, in the midst of his course, before his fame shall arise? But the bard, here-after, may say, when he sees the tomb of Carthon; Fingal took his thou-sands, along with him, to battle, before the noble Carthon fell.——No:—bard of the times to come! thou shalt not lessen Fingal's fame. My heroes will fight the youth, and Fingal behold the battle. If he overcomes, I rush, in my strength, like the roaring stream of Cona.

Who, of my heroes,[28] will meet the son of the rolling sea? Many are his warriors on the coast; and strong is his ashen spear!

Cathul[29] rose, in his strength, the son of the mighty Lormar: three hundred youths attend the chief, the race[30] of his native streams. Feeble was his arm against Carthon, he fell; and his heroes fled.

Connal[31] resumed the battle, but he broke his heavy spear: he lay bound on the field: and Carthon pursued his people.

Clessámmor! said the king[32] of Morven, where is the spear of thy strength? Wilt thou behold Connal bound; thy friend, at the stream of Lora? Rise, in the light of thy steel, thou friend of Comhal.[33] Let the youth of Balclutha feel the strength of Morven's race.

He rose in the strength of his steel, shaking his grizly locks. He fitted the shield to his side; and rushed, in the pride of valour.

Carthon stood, on that heathy rock, and saw the heroes approach.[34] He loved the terrible joy of his face: and his strength, in the locks of age.——Shall I lift that spear, he said, that never strikes, but once, a foe? Or shall I, with the words of peace, preserve the warrior's life? Stately are his steps of age!—lovely the remnant of his years. Perhaps it is the love[35] of Moina; the father of car-borne Carthon. Often have I heard, that he dwelt at the echo-ing stream of Lora.

Such were his words, when Clessámmor came, and lifted high his spear. The youth received it on his shield, and spoke the words of peace.——Warrior of the aged locks! Is there no youth to lift the spear? Hast thou no son, to raise the shield before his father, and to meet the arm of youth? Is the spouse of thy love no more? or weeps she over the tombs of thy sons? Art thou of the kings of men? What will be the fame of my sword if thou shalt fall?

It will be great, thou son of pride! begun the tall Clessámmor, I have been renowned in battle; but I never told my name[36] to a foe. Yield to me, son of the wave, and then thou shalt know, that the mark of my sword is in many a field.

I never yielded, king of spears! replied the noble pride of Carthon: I have also fought in battles; and I behold my future fame. Despise me not, thou chief of men; my arm, my spear is strong. Retire among thy friends, and let young[37] heroes fight.

Why dost thou wound my soul, replied Clessámmor with a tear? Age does not tremble on my hand; I still can lift the sword. Shall I fly in Fingal's sight; in the sight of him I loved?[38] Son of the sea! I never fled: exalt thy pointed spear.

They fought, like two contending winds, that strive to roll the wave. Carthon bade his spear to err; for he still thought that the foe was the spouse of Moina.——He broke Clessámmor's beamy spear in twain: and seized his shining sword. But as Carthon was binding the chief; the chief drew the dagger of his fathers. He saw the foe's uncovered side; and opened, there, a wound.

Fingal saw Clessámmor low: he moved in the sound of his steel. The host stood silent, in his presence; they turned their eyes towards the hero.[39]——He came, like the sullen noise of a storm, before the winds arise: the hunter hears it in the vale, and retires to the cave of the rock.

Carthon stood in his place: the blood is rushing down his side: he saw the coming down of the king; and his hopes of fame arose[40]; but pale was his cheek: his hair flew loose, his helmet shook on high: the force of Carthon failed; but his soul was strong.

Fingal beheld the hero's blood; he stopt the uplifted spear. Yield, king of swords! said Comhal's son; I behold thy blood. Thou hast been mighty in battle; and thy fame shall never fade.

Art thou the king so far renowned, replied the car-borne Carthon? Art thou that light of death, that frightens the kings of the world?—But why should Carthon ask? for he is like the stream of his desart;[41] strong as a river, in his course: swift as the eagle of the sky.—O that I had fought with the king; that my fame might be great in the song! that the hunter, behold-ing my tomb, might say, he fought with the mighty Fingal. But Carthon dies unknown; he has poured out his force on the feeble.

But thou shalt not die unknown, replied the king of woody Morven: my bards are many, O Carthon, and their songs descend to future times. The children of the years to come shall hear the fame of Carthon; when they sit round the burning oak[42], and the night is spent in the songs of old. The hunter, sitting in the heath, shall hear the rustling blast; and, raising his eyes, behold the rock where Carthon fell. He shall turn to his son, and shew the place where the mighty fought; "There the king of Balclutha fought, like the strength of a thousand streams."

Joy rose in Carthon's face: he lifted his heavy eyes.——He gave his sword to Fingal, to lie within his hall, that the memory of Balclutha's king might remain on Morven.—The battle ceased along the field, for the bard had sung the song of peace. The chiefs gathered round the falling Carthon, and heard his words, with sighs. Silent they leaned on their spears, while Bal-clutha's hero spoke. His hair sighed in the wind, and his words were feeble.[43]

King of Morven, Carthon said, I fall in the midst of my course. A foreign tomb receives, in youth, the last of Reuthámir's race. Darkness dwells in Balclutha: and the shadows of grief in Crathmo.—But raise my remembrance on the banks of Lora: where my fathers dwelt. Perhaps the husband of Moina will mourn over his fallen Carthon.

His words reached the heart of Clessámmor: he fell, in silence, on his son. The host stood darkened around: no voice is on the plains of Lora.[44] Night came, and the moon, from the east, looked on the mournful field: but still they stood, like a silent grove that lifts its head on Gormal, when the loud winds are laid, and dark autumn is on the plain.

Three days they mourned over Carthon; on the fourth his father died. In the narrow plain of the rock they lie; and a dim ghost defends their tomb. There lovely Moina is often seen; when the sun-beam darts on the rock, and all around is dark. There she is seen, Malvina, but not like the daughters of the hill. Her robes are from the stranger's land; and she is still alone.

Fingal was sad for Carthon; he desired his bards to mark the day, when shadowy autumn returned. And often did they mark the day and sing the hero's praise. Who comes so dark from ocean's roar, like autumn's shadowy cloud? Death is trembling in his hand! his eyes are flames of fire!——Who roars along dark Lora's heath? Who but Carthon king of swords? The people fall! see! how he strides, like the sullen ghost of Morven!—But there he lies a goodly oak, which sudden blasts overturned! When shalt thou rise, Balclutha's joy! lovely car-borne Carthon?——Who comes so dark from ocean's roar, like autumn's shadowy cloud?

Such were the words of the bards, in the day of their mourning: I have accompanied[45] their voice; and added to their song. My soul has been mournful for Carthon; he fell in the days of his valour:[46] and thou, O Clessámmor! where is thy dwelling in the air?[47] —Has the youth forgot his wound? And flies he, on the clouds, with thee?——I feel the sun, O Malvina, leave me to my rest. Perhaps they may come to my dreams; I think I hear a feeble voice.—The beam of heaven delights to shine on the grave of Carthon: I feel it warm around.

O thou that rollest above[48], round as the shield of my fathers! Whence are thy beams, O sun! thy everlasting light? Thou comest forth, in thy awful beauty, and the stars hide themselves in the sky; the moon, cold and pale, sinks in the western wave. But thou thyself movest alone: who can be a companion of thy course! The oaks of the mountains fall: the mountains themselves decay with years; the ocean shrinks and grows again: the moon herself is lost in heaven; but thou art for ever the same; rejoicing in the brightness of thy course. When the world is dark with tempests; when thunder rolls, and lightning flies; thou lookest in thy beauty, from the clouds, and laughest at the storm. But to Ossian, thou lookest in vain; for he beholds thy beams no more; whether thy yellow hair flows on the eastern clouds, or thou tremblest at the gates of the west. But thou art perhaps, like me, for a season, and thy years will have an end. Thou shalt sleep in thy clouds, careless of the voice of the morning.——Exult then, O sun, in the strength of thy youth! Age is dark and unlovely; it is like the glimmering light of the moon[49], when it shines through broken clouds, and the mist is on the hills; the blast of the north is on the plain, the traveller shrinks in the midst of his journey.

THE

DEATH of CUCHULLIN:

A POEM[1].

Is the wind on Fingal's shield? Or is the voice of past times in my hall? Sing on, sweet voice, for thou art pleasant, and carriest away my night with joy. Sing on, O Bragéla, daughter of car-borne Sorglan!

It is the white wave of the rock, and not Cuchullin's sails. Often do the mists deceive me for the ship of my love! when they rise round some ghost, and spread their gray skirts on the wind. Why dost thou delay thy coming, son of the generous Semo?—Four times has autumn returned with its winds, and raised the seas of Togorma[2], since thou hast been in the roar of battles, and Bragéla distant far.—Hills of the isle of mist! when will ye answer to his hounds?——But ye are dark in your clouds, and sad Bragéla calls in vain. Night comes rolling down: the face of ocean fails. The heathcock's head is beneath his wing: the hind sleeps with the hart of the desert. They shall rise with the morning's light, and feed on the mossy stream. But my tears return with the sun, my sighs come on with the night. When wilt thou come in thine arms, O chief of mossy Tura?[3]

Pleasant is thy voice in Ossian's ear, daughter of car-borne Sorglan! But retire to the hall of shells; to the beam of the burning oak.——Attend to the murmur of the sea: it rolls at Dunscaich's[4] walls: let sleep descend on thy blue eyes, and the hero come to thy dreams.

Cuchullin sits at Lego's lake, at the dark rolling of waters. Night is around the hero; and his thousands spread on the heath: a hundred oaks burn in the midst, the feast of shells is smoking wide.—Carril strikes the harp, beneath a tree; his gray locks glitter in the beam; the rustling blast of night is near, and lifts his aged hair.—His song is of the blue Togorma, and of its chief, Cuchullin's friend.

Why art thou absent, Connal, in the day of the gloomy storm? The chiefs of the south have convened against the car-borne Cormac: the winds detain thy sails, and thy blue waters roll around thee. But Cormac is not alone: the son of Semo fights his battles. Semo's son his battles fights! the terror of the stranger! he that is like the vapour of death[5], slowly borne by sultry winds. The sun reddens in its presence, the people fall around.

Such was the song of Carril, when a son of the foe appeared; he threw down his pointless spear, and spoke the words of Torlath, Torlath the chief of heroes, from Lego's sable surge: he that led his thousands to battle, against car-borne Cormac, Cormac who was distant far, in Temora's[6] echoing halls: he learned to bend the bow of his fathers; and to lift the spear. Nor long didst thou lift the spear, mildly-shining beam of youth!

death stands dim behind thee, like the darkened half of the moon behind its growing light.

Cuchullin rose before the bard[7], that came from generous Torlath; he offered him the shell of joy, and honoured the son of songs. Sweet voice of Lego! he said, what are the words of Torlath? Comes he to our feast or battle, the car-borne son of Cantéla[8]?

He comes to thy battle, replied the bard, to the sounding strife of spears. ——When morning is gray on Lego, Torlath will fight on the plain: and wilt thou meet him, in thine arms, king of the isle of mist? Terrible is the spear of Torlath! it is a meteor of night. He lifts it, and the people fall: death sits in the lightning of his sword.

Do I fear, replied Cuchullin, the spear of car-borne Torlath? He is brave as a thousand heroes; but my soul delights in war. The sword rests not by the side of Cuchullin, bard of the times of old! Morning shall meet me on the plain, and gleam on the blue arms of Semo's son.—But sit thou, on the heath, O bard! and let us hear thy voice: partake of the joyful shell; and hear the songs of Temora.

This is no time, replied the bard, to hear the song of joy; when the mighty are to meet in battle like the strength of the waves of Lego. Why art thou so dark, Slimora[9]! with all thy silent woods? No green[10] star trembles on thy top; no moon-beam on thy side. But the meteors of death are there, and the gray watry forms of ghosts. Why art thou dark, Slimora! with thy silent woods?

He retired, in the sound of his song; Carril accompanied his voice. The music was like the memory of joys that are past, pleasant and mournful to the soul. The ghosts of departed bards heard it from Slimora's side. Soft sounds spread along the wood, and the silent valleys of night rejoice.—— So, when he sits in the silence of noon,[11] in the valley of his breeze, the humming of the mountain bee comes to Ossian's ear: the gale drowns it often in its course; but the pleasant sound returns again.[12]

Raise, said Cuchullin, to his hundred bards, the song of the noble Fingal: that song which he hears at night, when the dreams of his rest descend: when the bards strike the distant harp, and the faint light gleams on Selma's walls. Or let the grief of Lara rise, and the sighs of the mother of Calmar[13], when he was sought, in vain, on his hills; and she beheld his bow in the hall.——Carril, place the shield of Caithbat on that branch; and let the spear of Cuchullin be near; that the sound of my battle may rise with the gray beam of the east.

The hero leaned on his father's shield: the song of Lara rose. The hundred bards were distant far: Carril alone is near the chief. The words of the song were his; and the sound of his harp was mournful.

Alclétha[14] with the aged locks! mother of car-borne Calmar! why dost thou look towards the desert, to behold the return of thy son? These are not his heroes, dark on the heath: nor is that the voice of Calmar: it is but the distant grove, Alclétha! but the roar of the mountain wind!

Who[15] bounds over Lara's stream, sister of the noble Calmar? Does not Alclétha behold his spear? But her eyes are dim! Is it not the son of Matha, daughter of my love?

It is but an aged oak, Alclétha! replied the lovely weeping Alona[16]; it is but an oak, Alclétha, bent over Lara's stream. But who comes along the plain? sorrow is in his speed. He lifts high the spear of Calmar. Alclétha, it is covered with blood!

But it is covered with the blood of foes[17], sister of car-borne Calmar! his spear never returned unstained with blood[18], nor his bow from the strife of the mighty. The battle is consumed in his presence: he is a flame of death, Alona!——Youth[19] of the mournful speed! where is the son of Alclétha? Does he return with his fame? in the midst of his echoing shields?—— Thou art dark and silent!—Calmar is then no more. Tell me not, warrior, how he fell, for I cannot hear of his wound.——

Why dost thou look towards the desart, mother of car-borne[20] Calmar? ——

Such was the song of Carril, when Cuchullin lay on his shield: the bards rested on their harps, and sleep fell softly around.——The son of Semo was awake alone; his soul was fixed on the war.——The burning oaks began to decay; faint red light is spread around.—A feeble voice is heard: the ghost of Calmar came. He stalked[21] in the beam. Dark is the wound in his side. His hair is disordered and loose. Joy sits darkly[22] on his face: and he seems to invite Cuchullin to his cave.

Son of the cloudy night! said the rising chief of Erin; Why dost thou bend thy dark eyes on me, ghost of the car-borne[23] Calmar? Wouldest thou frighten me, O Matha's son! from the battles of Cormac? Thy hand was not feeble in war; neither was thy voice[24] for peace. How art thou changed, chief of Lara! if thou now dost advise to fly!——But, Calmar, I never fled. I never feared[25] the ghosts of the desart.[26] Small is their knowledge, and weak their hands; their dwelling is in the wind.——But my soul grows in danger, and rejoices in the noise of steel. Retire thou to thy cave; thou art not Calmar's ghost; he delighted in battle, and his arm was like the thunder of heaven.

He retired in his blast with joy, for he had heard the voice of his praise. The faint beam of the morning rose, and the sound of Caithbat's buckler spread. Green Ullin's[27] warriors convened, like the roar of many streams.— The horn of war is heard over Lego; the mighty Torlath came.

Why dost thou come with thy thousands, Cuchullin, said the chief of Lego. I know the strength of thy arm, and thy soul is an unextinguished fire.—Why fight we not on the plain, and let our hosts behold our deeds? Let them behold us like roaring waves, that tumble round a rock: the mariners hasten away, and look on their strife with fear.

Thou risest, like the sun, on my soul, replied the son of Semo. Thine arm is mighty, O Torlath! and worthy of my wrath. Retire, ye men of Ullin, to Slimora's shady side; behold the chief of Erin, in the day of his fame.——— Carril! tell to mighty Connal, if Cuchullin must fall, tell him I accused the winds which roar on Togorma's waves.—Never was he absent in battle, when the strife of my fame arose.—Let his[28] sword be before Cormac, like the beam of heaven: let his counsel sound in Temora in the day of danger.

He rushed, in the sound of his arms, like the terrible spirit of Loda[29], when he comes in the roar of a thousand storms, and scatters battles from his eyes.—He sits on a cloud over Lochlin's seas: his mighty hand is on his sword, and the winds lift his flaming locks.[30]—So terrible was Cuchullin in the day of his fame.—Torlath fell by his hand, and Lego's heroes mourned.—They gather around the chief like the clouds of the desart.—A thousand swords rose at once; a thousand arrows flew; but he stood like a rock in the midst of a roaring sea.———They fell around; he strode in blood: dark Slimora echoed wide.—The sons of Ullin came, and the battle spread over Lego.—The chief of Erin overcame; he returned over the field with his fame.———

But pale he returned! The joy of his face was dark. He rolled his eyes in silence.—The sword hung, unsheathed, in his hand, and his spear bent at every step.

Carril, said the king[31] in secret, the strength of Cuchullin fails. My days are with the years that are past: and no morning of mine shall arise.—They shall seek me at Temora, but I shall not be found. Cormac will weep in his hall, and say, "Where is Tura's[32] chief?"—But my name is renowned! my fame in the song of bards.———The youth will say in secret, O let me die as Cuchullin died; renown cloathed him like a robe; and the light of his fame is great. Draw the arrow from my side; and lay Cuchullin beneath that oak. Place the shield of Caithbat near, that they may behold me amidst the arms of my fathers.—

And is the son of Semo fallen[33], said Carril with a sigh?———Mournful are Tura's walls; and sorrow dwells at Dunscaich.—Thy spouse is left alone in her youth, the son[34] of thy love is alone.—He shall come to Bragéla, and ask her why she weeps.—He shall lift his eyes to the wall, and see his father's sword.—Whose sword is that? he will say: and the soul of his mother is sad. Who is that, like the hart of the desart, in the murmur of his course?—His eyes look wildly round in search of his friend.———Connal, son of Colgar, where hast thou been, when the mighty fell? Did the seas of Togorma[35] roll round thee? Was the wind of the south in thy sails? The mighty have fallen in battle, and thou wast not there.—Let none tell it in Selma, nor in Morven's woody land; Fingal will be sad, and the sons of the desart mourn.

By the dark rolling waves of Lego they raised the hero's tomb.——— Luäth[36], at a distance, lies, the companion of Cuchullin, at the chace.[37]———

Blest[38] be thy soul, son of Semo; thou wert mighty in battle.—Thy strength was like the strength of a stream: thy speed like the eagle's[39] wing.——Thy path in the battle was terrible: the steps of death were behind thy sword. ——Blest be thy soul, son of Semo; car-borne chief of Dunscaich!

Thou hast not fallen by the sword of the mighty, neither was thy blood on the spear of the valiant.—The arrow came, like the sting of death in a blast: nor did the feeble hand, which drew the bow, perceive it. Peace to thy soul, in thy cave, chief of the isle of Mist!

The mighty are dispersed at Temora: there is none in Cormac's hall. The king mourns in his youth, for he does not behold thy coming. The sound of thy shield is ceased: his foes are gathering round. Soft be thy rest in thy cave, chief of Erin's wars!

Bragéla will not hope thy return, or see thy sails in ocean's foam.——Her steps are not on the shore: nor her ear open to the voice of thy rowers.—She sits in the hall of shells, and sees the arms of him that is no more.—Thine eyes are full of tears, daughter of car-borne Sorglan!——Blest be thy soul in death, O chief of shady Cromla![40]

DAR-THULA:

A POEM[1].

Daughter of heaven[2], fair art thou! the silence of thy face is pleasant. Thou comest forth in loveliness: the stars attend thy blue steps[3] in the east. The clouds rejoice in thy presence, O moon, and brighten their dark-brown sides. Who is like thee in heaven, daughter of the night?[4] The stars are ashamed in thy presence, and turn aside their green,[5] sparkling eyes.—Whither dost thou retire from thy course, when the darkness[6] of thy countenance grows? Hast thou thy hall like Ossian? Dwellest thou in the shadow of grief? Have thy sisters fallen from heaven? Are they who rejoiced with thee, at night, no more?—Yes!—they have fallen, fair light! and thou dost often retire to mourn.——But thou thyself shalt fail, one night; and leave thy blue path in heaven. The stars will then lift their green[7] heads: they who were ashamed in thy presence, will rejoice.

Thou art now clothed with thy brightness: look from thy gates in the sky. Burst the cloud, O wind, that the daughter of night may look forth, that the shaggy mountains may brighten, and the ocean roll its blue[8] waves in light.

Nathos[9] is on the deep, and Althos that beam of youth, Ardan is near his brothers; they move in the gloom of their course. The sons of Usnoth move in darkness, from the wrath of car-borne Cairbar.[10]

Who is that dim, by their side? the night has covered her beauty. Her hair sighs on ocean's wind; her robe streams in dusky wreaths. She is like the fair spirit[11] of heaven, in the midst of his shadowy mist. Who is it but Dar-thula[12], the first of Erin's maids? She has fled from the love of Cairbar, with the car-borne[13] Nathos. But the winds deceive thee, O Dar-thula; and deny the woody Etha[14] to thy sails. These are not thy mountains, Nathos, nor is that the roar of thy climbing waves. The halls of Cairbar are near; and the towers of the foe lift their heads. Ullin[15] stretches its green head into the sea; and Tura's bay receives the ship. Where have ye been, ye southern winds! when the sons of my love were deceived? But ye have been sporting on plains, and pursuing the thistle's beard. O that ye had been rustling in the sails of Nathos, till the hills of Etha rose! till they rose in their clouds, and saw their coming chief! Long hast thou been absent, Nathos! and the day of thy return is past[16].

But the land of strangers saw thee, lovely: thou wast lovely in the eyes of Dar-thula. Thy face was like the light of the morning, thy hair like the raven's wing. Thy soul was generous and mild, like the hour of the setting sun. Thy words were the gale of the reeds, or the gliding stream of Lora.

But when the rage of battle rose, thou wast like[17] a sea in a storm; the clang of arms[18] was terrible: the host vanished at the sound of thy course.

——It was then Dar-thula beheld thee, from the top of her mossy tower: from the tower of Seláma[19], where her fathers dwelt.

Lovely art thou, O stranger! she said, for her trembling soul arose. Fair art thou in thy battles, friend of the fallen Cormac![20] Why dost thou rush on, in thy valour, youth of the ruddy look? Few are thy hands, in battle, against the car-borne[21] Cairbar!—O that I might be freed of his love![22] that I might rejoice in the presence of Nathos!——Blest are the rocks of Etha; they will behold his steps at the chace! they will see his white bosom, when the winds lift his raven[23] hair!

Such were thy words, Dar-thula, in Seláma's mossy towers. But, now, the night is round thee: and the winds have deceived thy sails. The winds have deceived thy sails, Dar-thula: their blustering sound is high. Cease a little while, O north wind, and let me hear the voice of the lovely. Thy voice is lovely, Dar-thula, between the rustling blasts.

Are these the rocks of Nathos, and the roar of his mountain-streams? Comes that beam of light from Usnoth's nightly hall? The mist rolls around, and the beam is feeble: but[24] the light of Dar-thula's soul is the car-borne chief[25] of Etha! Son of the generous Usnoth, why that broken sigh? Are we not[26] in the land of strangers, chief of echoing Etha?

These are not the rocks of Nathos, he replied, nor the roar of his streams. No light comes from Etha's halls, for they are distant far. We are in the land of strangers, in the land of car-borne[27] Cairbar. The winds have deceived us, Dar-thula. Ullin lifts here her green hills.[28]—Go towards the north, Althos; be thy steps, Ardan, along the coast; that the foe may not come in darkness, and our hopes of Etha fail.——

I will go towards that mossy tower, and see who dwells about the beam.—Rest, Dar-thula, on the shore! rest in peace, thou beam of light![29] the sword of Nathos is around thee, like the lightning of heaven.

He went. She sat alone, and heard the rolling of the wave. The big tear is in her eye; and she looks for the car-borne[30] Nathos.—Her soul trembles at the blast. And she turns her ear towards the tread of his feet.——The tread of his feet is not heard. Where art thou, son of my love! The roar of the blast is around me. Dark is the cloudy night.——But Nathos does not return. What detains thee, chief of Etha?—Have the foes met the hero in the strife of the night?—

He returned, but his face was dark: he had seen his departed friend.—It was the wall of Tura, and the ghost of Cuchullin stalked there. The sighing of his breast was frequent; and the decayed flame of his eyes terrible. His spear was a column of mist: the stars looked dim through his form. His voice was like hollow wind in a cave:[31] and he told the tale of grief. The soul of Nathos was sad, like the sun[32] in the day of mist, when his face is watry and dim.

Why art thou sad, O Nathos, said the lovely daughter of Colla? Thou art a pillar of light to Dar-thula: the joy of her eyes is in Etha's chief. Where is my friend[33], but Nathos? My father rests in the tomb.[34] Silence dwells on Seláma: sadness spreads on the blue streams of my land. My friends have fallen, with Cormac. The mighty were slain in the battle of Ullin.[35]

Evening darkened on the plain. The blue streams failed before mine eyes. The unfrequent blast came rustling in the tops of Seláma's groves. My seat was beneath a tree on the walls of my fathers. Truthil past before my soul; the brother of my love; he that was absent[36] in battle against the car-borne[37] Cairbar.

Bending on his spear, the gray-haired Colla came: his downcast face is dark, and sorrow dwells in his soul. His sword is on the side of the hero: the helmet of his fathers on his head.—The battle grows in his breast. He strives to hide the tear.

Dar-thula, he sighing said,[38] thou art the last of Colla's race. Truthil is fallen in battle. The king[39] of Seláma is no more.——Cairbar comes, with his thousands, towards Seláma's walls.—Colla will meet his pride, and revenge his son. But where shall I find thy safety, Dar-thula with the dark-brown hair! thou art lovely as the sun-beam of heaven, and thy friends are low!

And is the son of battle fallen? I said with a bursting sigh. Ceased the generous soul of Truthil to lighten through the field?—My safety, Colla, is in that bow; I have learned to pierce the deer. Is not Cairbar like the hart of the desart, father of fallen Truthil?

The face of age brightened with joy: and the crouded tears of his eyes poured down. The lips of Colla trembled. His gray beard whistled in the blast. Thou art the sister of Truthil, he said, and thou burnest in the fire of his soul. Take, Dar-thula, take that spear, that brazen shield, that burnished helmet: they are the spoils of a warrior: a son[40] of early youth.——When the light rises on Seláma, we go to meet the car-borne Cairbar.——But keep thou near the arm of Colla; beneath the shadow of my shield. Thy father, Dar-thula, could once defend thee; but age is trembling on his hand.——The strength of his arm has failed, and his soul is darkened with grief.

We passed the night in sorrow. The light of morning rose. I shone in the arms of battle. The gray-haired hero moved before. The sons of Seláma convened around the sounding shield of Colla. But few were they in the plain, and their locks were gray. The youths had fallen with Truthil, in the battle of car-borne Cormac.

Companions of my youth! said Colla, it was not thus you have seen me in arms. It was not thus I strode to battle, when the great Confadan fell. But ye are laden with grief. The darkness of age comes like the mist of the desart. My shield is worn with years; my sword is fixed[41] in its place. I said to my soul, thy evening shall be calm, and thy departure like a fading light. But the storm has returned; I bend like an aged oak. My boughs are fallen on Seláma, and I tremble in my place.——Where art thou, with thy fallen heroes, O my car-borne[42] Truthil! Thou answerest not from thy rushing blast; and the soul of thy father is sad. But I will be sad no more, Cairbar or Colla must fall. I feel the returning strength of my arm. My heart leaps at the sound of battle.

The hero drew his sword. The gleaming blades of his people rose. They moved along the plain. Their gray hair streamed in the wind.—Cairbar sat, at the feast, in the silent plain of Lona[43]. He saw the coming of the heroes, and he called his chiefs to battle.

Why[44] should I tell to Nathos, how the strife of battle grew! I have seen thee, in the midst of thousands, like the beam of heaven's fire; it is beautiful, but terrible; the people fall in its red[45] course.——The spear of Colla slew,[46] for he remembered the battles of his youth. An arrow came with its sound, and pierced the hero's side. He fell on his echoing shield. My soul started with fear; I stretched my buckler over him; but my heaving breast was seen. Cairbar came, with his spear, and he beheld Seláma's maid: joy rose on his dark-brown face; he stayed the lifted steel. He raised the tomb of Colla; and brought me weeping to Seláma. He spoke the words of love, but my soul was sad. I saw the shields of my fathers, and the sword of car-borne Truthil. I saw the arms of the dead, and the tear was on my cheek.

Then thou didst come, O Nathos: and gloomy Cairbar fled. He fled like the ghost of the desert before the morning's beam. His hosts were not near: and feeble was his arm against thy steel.

Why[47] art thou sad, O Nathos? said the lovely maid[48] of Colla.

I have met, replied the hero, the battle in my youth. My arm could not lift the spear, when first the danger rose; but my soul brightened before the war, as the green narrow vale, when the sun pours his streamy beams, before he hides his head in a storm.[49] My soul brightened in danger before I saw Seláma's fair; before I saw thee, like a star, that shines on the hill, at night; the cloud slowly comes,[50] and threatens the lovely light.

We are in the land of the foe, and the winds have deceived us, Dar-thula! the strength of our friends is not near, nor the mountains of Etha. Where shall I find thy peace, daughter of mighty Colla! The brothers of Nathos are brave: and his own sword has shone in war. But what are the sons of Usnoth to the host of car-borne[51] Cairbar! O that the winds had brought thy sails, Oscar[52] king of men! thou didst promise to come to the battles of fallen Cormac. Then would my hand be strong as the flaming arm of death. Cairbar would tremble in his halls, and peace dwell round the lovely Dar-thula. But why dost thou fall, my soul? The sons of Usnoth may prevail.

And they will prevail, O Nathos, said the rising soul of the maid: never shall Dar-thula behold the halls of gloomy Cairbar. Give me those arms of brass, that glitter to that passing meteor; I see them[53] in the dark-bosomed ship. Dar-thula will enter the battle of steel.—Ghost of the noble Colla! do I behold thee on that cloud? Who is that dim beside thee? It is the car-borne

Truthil. Shall I behold the halls of him that slew Seláma's chief! No: I will not behold them, spirits of my love!

Joy rose in the face of Nathos, when he heard the white-bosomed maid. Daughter of Seláma! thou shinest on my soul. Come, with thy thousands, Cairbar! the strength of Nathos is returned. And thou, O aged Usnoth, shalt not hear that thy son has fled. I remember thy words on Etha; when my sails begun to rise: when I spread them towards Ullin,[54] towards the mossy walls of Tura. Thou goest, he said, O Nathos, to the king of shields; to Cuchullin chief of men who never fled from danger. Let not thine arm be feeble: neither be thy thoughts of flight; lest the son of Semo say that Etha's race are weak. His words may come to Usnoth, and sadden his soul in the hall.——The tear was on his cheek.[55] He gave this shining sword.

I came to Tura's bay: but the halls of Tura were silent. I looked around, and there was none to tell of the chief of Dunscaich.[56] I went to the hall of his shells, where the arms of his fathers hung. But the arms were gone, and aged Lamhor[57] sat in tears.

Whence are the arms of steel, said the rising Lamhor? The light of the spear has long been absent from Tura's dusky walls.—Come ye from the rolling sea? Or from the mournful halls of Temora.[58]

We come from the sea, I said, from Usnoth's rising towers. We are the sons of Slis-sáma[59], the daughter of car-borne Semo. Where is Tura's chief, son of the silent hall? But why should Nathos ask? for I behold thy tears. How did the mighty fall, son of the lonely Tura?

He fell not, Lamhor replied, like the silent star of night, when it shoots[60] through darkness and is no more. But he was like a meteor that falls in[61] a distant land; death attends its red[62] course, and itself is the sign of wars. ——Mournful are the banks of Lego, and the roar of streamy Lara! There the hero fell, son of the noble Usnoth.

And the hero fell in the midst of slaughter, I said with a bursting sigh. His hand was strong in battle; and death was[63] behind his sword.—We came to Lego's mournful[64] banks. We found his rising tomb. His companions in battle are there; his bards of many songs. Three days we mourned over the hero: on the fourth, I struck the shield of Caithbat. The heroes gathered around with joy, and shook their beamy spears.

Corlath was near with his host, the friend of car-borne Cairbar. We came like a stream by night, and his heroes fell. When the people of the valley rose[65], they saw their blood with morning's light. But we rolled away, like wreaths of mist, to Cormac's echoing hall. Our swords rose to defend the king. But Temora's halls were empty. Cormac had fallen in his youth. The king of Erin was no more.

Sadness seized the sons of Ullin, they[66] slowly, gloomily retired: like clouds that, long having threatened rain, retire[67] behind the hills. The sons of Usnoth moved, in their grief, towards Tura's sounding bay. We passed by

Selama, and Cairbar retired like Lano's mist, when it is driven by the winds of the desart.[68]

It was then I beheld thee, O maid,[69] like the light of Etha's sun. Lovely is that beam, I said, and the crowded sigh of my bosom rose. Thou camest in thy beauty, Dar-thula, to Etha's mournful chief.——But the winds have deceived us, daughter of Colla, and the foe is near.

Yes!—the foe is near, said the rustling[70] strength of Althos[71]. I heard their clanging arms on the coast, and saw the dark wreaths of Erin's standard. Distinct is the voice of Cairbar[72], and loud as Cromla's falling stream. He had seen the dark ship on the sea, before the dusky night came down. His people watch on Lena's[73] plain, and lift ten thousand swords.

And let them lift ten thousand swords, said Nathos with a smile. The sons of car-borne Usnoth will never tremble in danger. Why dost thou roll with all thy foam, thou roaring sea of Ullin?[74] Why do ye rustle, on your dark wings, ye whistling tempests of the sky?—Do ye think, ye storms, that ye keep Nathos on the coast? No: his soul detains him, children of the night! ——Althos! bring my father's arms: thou seest them beaming to the stars. Bring the spear of Semo[75], it stands in the dark-bosomed ship.

He brought the arms. Nathos clothed his limbs in all their shining steel. The stride of the chief is lovely: the joy of his eyes terrible. He looks towards the coming of Cairbar. The wind is rustling in his hair. Dar-thula is silent at his side: her look is fixed on the chief. She strives to hide the rising sigh, and two tears swell in her eyes.[76]

Althos! said the chief of Etha, I see a cave in that rock. Place Dar-thula there: and let thy arm[77] be strong. Ardan! we meet the foe, and call to battle gloomy Cairbar. O that he came in his sounding steel, to meet the son of Usnoth!——Dar-thula! if thou shalt escape, look not on the falling Nathos. Lift thy sails, O Althos, towards the echoing groves of Etha.[78]

Tell to the chief[79], that his son fell with fame; that my sword did not shun the battle. Tell him I fell in the midst of thousands, and let the joy of his grief be great. Daughter of Colla! call the maids to Etha's echoing hall. Let their songs arise for Nathos, when shadowy autumn returns.—O that the voice of Cona[80] might be heard in my praise! then would my spirit rejoice in the midst of my mountain winds.[81]

And my voice shall praise thee, Nathos chief of the woody Etha! The voice of Ossian shall rise in thy praise, son of the generous Usnoth! Why was I not on Lena, when the battle rose? Then would the sword of Ossian have defended thee, or himself have fallen low.

We sat, that night, in Selma round the strength of the shell. The wind was abroad, in the oaks; the spirit of the mountain[82] shrieked.[83] The blast came rustling through the hall, and gently touched my harp. The sound was mournful and low, like the song of the tomb. Fingal heard it first, and the crowded sighs of his bosom rose.——Some of my heroes are low, said the gray-haired king of Morven. I hear the sound of death on the harp of my son.[84] Ossian, touch the sounding[85] string; bid the sorrow rise; that their spirits may fly with joy to Morven's woody hills.

I touched the harp before the king, the sound was mournful and low. Bend forward from your clouds, I said, ghosts of my fathers! bend; lay by the red terror of your course, and receive the falling chief; whether he comes from a distant land, or rises from the rolling sea. Let his robe of mist be near; his spear that is formed of a cloud. Place an half-extinguished meteor by his side, in the form of the hero's sword. And, oh! let his countenance be lovely, that his friends may delight in his presence. Bend from your clouds, I said, ghosts of my fathers! bend.

Such was my song, in Selma, to the lightly-trembling harp. But Nathos was on Ullin's[86] shore, surrounded by the night; he heard the voice of the foe amidst the roar of tumbling waves. Silent he heard their voice, and rested on his spear.

Morning rose, with its beams; the sons of Erin appear; like gray rocks, with all their trees, they spread along the coast. Cairbar stood, in the midst, and grimly smiled when he saw the foe.

Nathos rushed forward, in his strength; nor could Dar-thula stay behind. She came with the hero, lifting her shining spear. And who are these, in their armour, in the pride of youth? Who but the sons of Usnoth, Althos and dark-haired Ardan?

Come, said Nathos, come! chief of the high Temora! Let our battle be on the coast for the white-bosomed maid. His people are not with Nathos; they are behind that rolling sea. Why dost thou bring thy thousands against the chief of Etha? Thou didst fly[87] from him, in battle, when his friends were around him.[88]

Youth of the heart of pride, shall Erin's king fight with thee? Thy fathers were not among the renowned, nor of the kings of men. Are the arms of foes in their halls? Or the shields of other times? Cairbar is renowned in Temora, nor does he fight with little men.[89]

The tear starts from car-borne Nathos; he turned his eyes to his brothers. Their spears flew, at once, and three heroes lay on earth. Then the light of their swords gleamed on high; the ranks of Erin yield; as a ridge of dark clouds before a blast of wind.

Then Cairbar ordered his people, and they drew a thousand bows. A thousand arrows flew; the sons of Usnoth fell.[90] They fell like three young oaks which stood alone on the hill; the traveller saw the lovely trees, and wondered how they grew so lonely; the blast of the desert came, by night, and laid their green heads low; next day he returned, but they were withered, and the heath was bare.

Dar-thula stood in silent grief, and beheld their fall: no tear is in her eye: but her look is wildly sad. Pale was her cheek; her trembling lips broke short an half-formed word. Her dark hair flew on the wind.——But gloomy Cairbar came. Where is thy lover now? the car-borne chief of Etha? Hast thou beheld the halls of Usnoth? Or the dark-brown hills of Fingal? My battle had roared on Morven, did not the winds meet Dar-thula. Fingal himself would have been low, and sorrow dwelling in Selma.

Her shield fell from Dar-thula's arm, her breast of snow appeared. It appeared, but it was stained with blood for an arrow was fixed in her side. She fell on the fallen Nathos, like a wreath of snow. Her dark hair spreads on his face,[91] and their blood is mixing round.

Daughter of Colla! thou art low! said Cairbar's hundred bards; silence is at the blue streams of Seláma, for Truthil's[92] race have failed. When wilt thou rise in thy beauty, first of Erin's maids? Thy sleep is long in the tomb, and the morning distant far. The sun shall not come to thy bed, and say, Awake[93] Dar-thula! awake, thou first of women! the wind of spring is abroad. The flowers shake their heads on the green hills, the woods wave their growing leaves. Retire, O sun, the daughter of Colla is asleep. She will not come forth in her beauty: she will not move, in the steps of her loveliness.

Such was the song of the bards, when they raised the tomb. I sung, afterwards, over the grave, when the king of Morven came; when he came to green Ullin[94] to fight with car-borne Cairbar.

TEMORA:

AN

EPIC POEM[1].

The blue waves of Ullin roll in light. The green hills are covered with day. Trees shake their dusky heads in the breeze; and gray torrents pour their noisy streams.—Two green hills, with their aged oaks, surround a narrow plain. The blue course of the mountain-stream is there; Cairbar stands on its banks.——His spear supports the king: the red eyes of his fear are sad. Cormac rises in his soul, with all his ghastly wounds. The gray form of the youth appears in the midst of darkness, and the blood pours from his airy sides.—Cairbar thrice threw his spear on earth; and thrice he stroked his beard. His steps are short; he often stopt: and tossed his sinewy arms. He is like a cloud in the desert; that varies its form to every blast: the valleys are sad around, and fear, by turns, the shower.

The king, at length, resumed his soul, and took his pointed spear. He turned his eyes towards Lena[2]. The scouts of the ocean appeared. They appeared with steps of fear, and often looked behind. Cairbar knew that the mighty were near, and called his gloomy chiefs. The sounding steps of his heroes came. They drew, at once, their swords. There Morlath[3] stood with darkened face. Hidalla's bushy hair sighs in the wind. Red-haired Cormar bends on his spear, and rolls his side-long-looking eyes. Wild is the look of Malthos from beneath two shaggy brows.—Foldath stands like an oozy rock, that covers its dark sides with foam; his spear is like Slimora's fir, that meets the wind of heaven. His shield is marked with the strokes of battle; and his red eye despises danger. These and a thousand other chiefs surrounded car-borne Cairbar, when the scout of ocean came, Mor-annal[4], from streamy Lena.—His eyes hang forward from his face, his lips are trembling, pale.

Do the chiefs of Erin stand, he said, silent as the grove of evening? Stand they, like a silent wood, and Fingal on the coast? Fingal, who is terrible in battle, the king of streamy Morven.

And hast thou seen the warrior, said Cairbar with a sigh? Are his heroes many on the coast? Lifts he the spear of battle? Or comes the king in peace?

He comes not in peace, O Cairbar: for I have seen his forward spear[5]. It is a meteor of death: the blood of thousands is on its steel.——He came first to the shore, strong in the gray hair of age. Full rose his sinewy limbs, as he strode in his might. That sword is by his side which gives no second[6] wound. His shield is terrible, like the bloody moon, when it rises in a storm.——Then came Ossian king of songs; and Morni's son, the first of men. Connal leaps forward on his spear: Dermid spreads his dark-brown locks.—Fillan bends his bow: Fergus strides in the pride of youth. Who is that with aged locks? A dark shield is on his side. His spear trembles at every step; and age is on his limbs. He bends his dark face to the ground; the king of spears is sad!——It is Usnoth, O Cairbar, coming to revenge his sons. He sees green Ullin with tears, and he remembers the tombs of his children. But far before the rest, the son of Ossian comes, bright in the smiles of youth, fair as the first beams of the sun. His long hair falls on his back.—His dark brows are half hid beneath his helmet of steel. His sword hangs loose on the hero's side. His spear glitters as he moves. I fled from his terrible eyes, king of high Temora!

Then fly, thou feeble man, said the gloomy wrath of Foldath: fly to the grey streams of thy land, son of the little soul! Have not I seen that Oscar? I beheld the chief in battle. He is of the mighty in danger: but there are others who lift the spear.—Erin has many sons as brave: yes—more brave, O car-borne Cairbar!—Let Foldath meet him in the strength of his course, and stop this mighty stream.—My spear is covered with the blood of the valiant; my shield is like Tura's wall.

Shall Foldath alone meet the foe, replied the dark-browed Malthos? Are not they numerous on our coast, like the waters of a thousand streams? Are not these the chiefs who vanquished Swaran, when the sons of Erin fled? And shall Foldath meet their bravest hero? Foldath of the heart of pride! take the strength of the people by thy side; and let Malthos come. My sword is red with slaughter, but who has heard my words?[7]

Sons of green Erin, begun the mild Hidalla, let not Fingal hear your words: lest the foe rejoice, and his arm be strong in the land.—Ye are brave, O warriors, and like the tempests of the desart; they meet the rocks without fear, and overturn the woods in their course.—But let us move in our strength, and slow as a gathered cloud, when the winds drive it from behind.——Then shall the mighty tremble, and the spear drop from the hand of the valiant.—We see the cloud of death, they will say; and their faces will turn pale. Fingal will mourn in his age; and say that his fame is ceased.——Morven will behold his chiefs no more: the moss of years shall grow in Selma.

Cairbar heard their words, in silence, like the cloud of a shower: it stands dark on Cromla, till the lightning bursts its side; the valley gleams with red light; the spirits of the storm rejoice.——So stood the silent king of Temora; at length his words are heard.

Spread the feast on Lena: and let my hundred bards attend. And thou, red-hair'd Olla, take the harp of the king. Go to Oscar king of swords, and bid him to our feast. To-day we feast and hear the song; to-morrow break the spears. Tell him that I have raised the tomb of Cathol[8]; and that my bards have sung to his ghost.—Tell him that Cairbar has heard his fame at the stream of distant Carun[9].

Cathmor[10] is not here; the generous brother of Cairbar; he is not here with his thousands, and our arms are weak. Cathmor is a foe to strife at the feast: his soul is bright as the sun. But Cairbar shall fight with Oscar, chiefs of the high Temora! His words for Cathol were many; and the wrath of Cairbar burns. He shall fall on Lena: and my fame shall rise in blood.

The faces of the heroes brightened. They spread over Lena's heath. The feast of shells is prepared. The songs of the bards arose.

We heard[11] the voice of joy on the coast, and we thought that the mighty Cathmor came, Cathmor the friend of strangers! the brother of red-haired Cairbar. But their souls were not the same: for the light of heaven was in the bosom of Cathmor. His towers rose on the banks of Atha: seven paths led to his halls. Seven chiefs stood on those paths, and called the stranger to the feast! But Cathmor dwelt in the wood to avoid the voice of praise.

Olla came with his songs. Oscar went to Cairbar's feast. Three hundred heroes attended the chief, and the clang of their arms is terrible. The gray dogs bounded on the heath, and their howling is frequent. Fingal saw the departure of the hero: the soul of the king was sad. He dreads the gloomy Cairbar: but who of the race of Trenmor feared the foe?

My son lifted high the spear of Cormac: an hundred bards met him with songs. Cairbar concealed with smiles the death that was dark in his soul. The feast is spread, the shells resound; joy brightens the face of the host. But it was like the parting beam of the sun, when he is to hide his red head, in a storm.

Cairbar rose in his arms; darkness gathers on his brow. The hundred harps ceased at once. The clang[12] of shields is heard. Far distant on the heath Olla raised his song of woe. My son knew the sign of death; and rising seized his spear.

Oscar! said the dark-red Cairbar, I behold the spear[13] of Erin's kings. The spear of Temora[14] glitters in thy hand, son of the woody Morven! It was the pride of an hundred kings, the death of heroes of old. Yield it, son of Ossian, yield it to car-borne Cairbar.

Shall I yield, Oscar replied, the gift of Erin's injured king: the gift of fair-haired Cormac, when Oscar scattered his foes? I came to his halls of joy, when Swaran fled from Fingal. Gladness rose in the face of youth: he gave the spear of Temora. Nor did he give it to the feeble, O Cairbar, neither to the weak in soul. The darkness of thy face is not a storm to me; nor are thine eyes the flames of death. Do I fear thy clanging shield? Does my soul tremble at Olla's song? No: Cairbar, frighten thou the feeble; Oscar is like a rock.

And wilt thou not yield the spear, replied the rising pride of Cairbar? Are thy words mighty because Fingal is near, the gray-haired warrior of Morven? He has fought with little men. But he must vanish before Cairbar, like a thin pillar of mist before the winds of Atha[15].

Were he who fought with little men near the chief of Atha: Atha's chief would yield green Erin to avoid his rage. Speak not of the mighty, O Cairbar! but turn thy sword on me. Our strength is equal: but Fingal is renowned! the first of mortal men!

Their people saw the darkening chiefs. Their crowding steps are heard around. Their eyes roll in fire. A thousand swords are half unsheathed. Redhaired Olla raised the song of battle: the trembling joy of Oscar's soul arose: the wonted joy of his soul when Fingal's horn was heard.

Dark as the swelling wave of ocean before the rising winds, when it bends its head near the coast, came on the host of Cairbar.——Daughter of Toscar[16]! why that tear? He is not fallen yet. Many were the deaths of his arm before my hero fell!—Behold they fall before my son like the groves in the desart, when an angry ghost rushes through night, and takes their green heads in his hand! Morlath falls: Maronnan dies: Conachar trembles in his blood. Cairbar shrinks before Oscar's sword; and creeps in darkness behind his stone. He lifted the spear in secret, and pierced my Oscar's side. He falls forward on his shield: his knee sustains the chief: but his spear is in his hand. See gloomy Cairbar[17] falls. The steel pierced his forehead, and divided his red hair behind. He lay, like a shattered rock, which Cromla shakes from its side. But never more shall Oscar rise! he leans on his bossy shield. His spear is in his terrible hand: Erin's sons stood distant and dark. Their shouts arose, like the crowded noise of streams, and Lena echoed around.

Fingal heard the sound; and took his father's spear. His steps are before us on the heath. He spoke the words of woe. I hear the noise of battle: and Oscar is alone. Rise, ye sons of Morven, and join the hero's sword.

Ossian rushed along the heath. Fillan bounded over Lena. Fergus flew with feet of wind. Fingal strode in his strength, and the light of his shield is terrible. The sons of Erin saw it far distant; they trembled in their souls. They knew that the wrath of the king arose: and they foresaw their death. We first arrived; we fought; and Erin's chiefs withstood our rage. But when the king came, in the sound of his course, what heart of steel could stand! Erin fled over Lena. Death pursued their flight.

We saw Oscar leaning on his shield. We saw his blood around. Silence darkened on every hero's face. Each turned his back and wept. The king strove to hide his tears. His gray beard whistled in the wind. He bends his head over his son: and his words are mixed with sighs.

And art thou fallen, Oscar, in the midst of thy course? the heart of the aged beats over thee! He sees thy coming battles. He beholds the battles which ought to come, but they are cut off from thy fame. When shall joy dwell at Selma? When shall the song of grief cease on Morven? My sons fall by degrees: Fingal shall be the last of his race. The fame which I have received shall pass away: my age will be without friends. I shall sit like a grey cloud in my hall: nor shall I expect the return of a son, in the midst of his sounding arms. Weep, ye heroes of Morven! never more shall Oscar rise!

And they did weep, O Fingal; dear was the hero to their souls. He went out to battle, and the foes vanished; he returned, in peace, amidst their joy. No father mourned his son slain in youth; no brother his brother of love. They fell, without tears, for the chief of the people was low! Bran[18] is howling at his feet: gloomy Luäth is sad, for he had often led them to the chace; to the bounding roes of the desert.

When Oscar beheld his friends around, his white breast rose with a sigh.—The groans, he said, of my aged heroes, the howling of my dogs, the sudden bursts of the song of grief, have melted Oscar's soul. My soul, that never melted before; it was like the steel of my sword.—Ossian, carry me to my hills! Raise the stones of my fame. Place the horn of the deer, and my sword within my narrow dwelling.—The torrent hereafter may wash away[19] the earth of my tomb: the hunter may find the steel and say, "This has been Oscar's sword."

And fallest thou, son of my fame! And shall I never see thee, Oscar! When others hear of their sons, I shall not hear of thee. The moss is on the stones of his tomb, and the mournful wind is there. The battle shall be fought without him: he shall not pursue the dark-brown hinds. When the warrior returns from battles, and tells of other lands, he will say, I have seen a tomb, by the roaring stream, where a warrior darkly dwells: he was slain by car-borne Oscar, the first of mortal men.—I, perhaps, shall hear him, and a beam of joy will rise in my soul.

The night would have descended in sorrow, and morning returned in the shadow of grief: our chiefs would have stood like cold dropping rocks on Lena, and have forgot the war, had not the king dispersed his grief, and raised his mighty voice. The chiefs, as new-wakened from dreams, lift their heads around.

How long shall we weep on Lena; or pour our tears in Ullin? The mighty will not return. Oscar shall not rise in his strength. The valiant must fall one day, and be no more known on his hills.—Where are our fathers, O warriors! the chiefs of the times of old? They have set like stars that have shone, we only hear the sound of their praise. But they were renowned in their day, and the terror of other times. Thus shall we pass, O warriors, in the day of our fall. Then let us be renowned when we may; and leave our fame behind us, like the last beams of the sun, when he hides his red head in the west.

Ullin, my aged bard! take the ship of the king. Carry Oscar to Selma, and let the daughters of Morven weep. We shall fight in Erin for the race of fallen Cormac. The days of my years begin to fail: I feel the weakness of my arm. My fathers bend from their clouds, to receive their gray-haired son. But, Trenmor! before I go hence, one beam of my fame shall rise: so shall my days end, as my years begun, in fame: my life shall be one stream of light to other times.

Ullin rais'd his white sails: the wind of the south came forth. He bounded on the waves towards Selma's walls.—I remained in my grief, but my words were not heard.——The feast is spread on Lena: an hundred heroes reared the tomb of Cairbar: but no song is raised over the chief; for his soul had been dark and bloody. We remembered the fall of Cormac! and what could we say in Cairbar's praise?

The night came rolling down. The light of an hundred oaks arose. Fingal sat beneath a tree. The chief of Etha sat near the king, the gray-hair'd strength of Usnoth.

Old Althan[20] stood in the midst, and told the tale of fallen Cormac. Althan the son of Conachar, the friend of car-borne Cuchullin: he dwelt with Cormac in windy Temora, when Semo's son fought with generous Torlath.—The tale of Althan was mournful, and the tear was in his eye.

[21]The setting sun was yellow on Dora[22]. Gray evening began to descend. Temora's woods shook with the blast of the unconstant wind. A cloud, at length, gathered in the west, and a red star looked from behind its edge.—I stood in the wood alone, and saw a ghost on the darkening air. His stride extended from hill to hill: his shield was dim on his side. It was the son of Semo: I knew the sadness of his face. But he passed away in his blast; and all was dark around.——My soul was sad. I went to the hall of shells. A thousand lights arose: the hundred bards had strung the harp. Cormac stood in the midst, like the morning star[23], when it rejoices on the eastern hill, and its young beams are bathed in showers.—The sword of Artho[24] was in the hand of the king; and he looked with joy on its polished studs: thrice he attempted to draw it, and thrice he failed: his yellow locks are spread on his shoulders: his cheeks of youth are red.—I mourned over the beam of youth, for he was soon to set.

Althan! he said, with a smile, hast thou beheld my father? Heavy is the sword of the king, surely his arm was strong. O that I were like him in battle, when the rage of his wrath arose! then would I have met, like Cuchullin, the car-borne son of Cantéla! But years may come on, O Althan! and my arm be strong.—Hast thou heard of Semo's son, the chief of high Temora? He might have returned with his fame; for he promised to return to-night. My bards wait him with their songs, and my feast is spread.—

I heard the king in silence. My tears began to flow. I hid them with my gray locks; but he perceived my grief.

Son of Conachar! he said, is the king of Tura low? Why bursts thy sigh in secret? And why descends the tear?—Comes the car-borne Torlath? Or the sound of the red-haired Cairbar?——They come!—for I see thy grief; and Tura's king is low!—Shall I not rush to battle?—But I cannot lift the arms of my fathers!—O had mine arm the strength of Cuchullin, soon would

Cairbar fly; the fame of my fathers would be renewed; and the actions of other times!

He took his bow of yew. Tears flow from his sparkling eyes.—Grief saddens around: the bards bend forward from their harps. The blast touches their strings, and the sound of woe ascends.

A voice is heard at a distance, as of one in grief; it was Carril of other times, who came from the dark Slimora[25].—He told of the death of Cuchullin, and of his mighty deeds. The people were scattered around his tomb: their arms lay on the ground. They had forgot the battle, for the sound of his shield had ceased.

But who, said the soft-voiced Carril, come like the bounding roes? their stature is like the young trees of the plain, growing in a shower:—Soft and ruddy are their cheeks: but fearless souls look forth from their eyes!—— Who but the sons of Usnoth, the car-borne chiefs of Etha? The people rise on every side, like the strength of an half-extinguished fire, when the winds come suddenly from the desert, on their rustling wings.—The sound of Caithbat's shield was heard. The heroes saw Cuchullin[26], in the form of lovely Nathos. So rolled his sparkling eyes, and such were his steps on his heath.——Battles are fought at Lego: the sword of Nathos prevails. Soon shalt thou behold him in thy halls, king of woody Temora!——

And soon may I behold him, O Carril! replied the returning joy of Cormac. But my soul is sad for Cuchullin; his voice was pleasant in mine ear.——Often have we moved on Dora, at the chace of the dark-brown hinds: his bow was unerring on the mountains.—He spoke of mighty men. He told of the deeds of my fathers; and I felt the joy of my breast.——But sit thou, at the feast, O Carril; I have often heard thy voice. Sing in the praise of Cuchullin; and of that mighty stranger.

Day rose on Temora, with all the beams of the east. Trathin came to the hall, the son of old Gelláma[27].—I behold, he said, a dark cloud in the desert, king of Innis-fail! a cloud it seemed at first, but now a crowd of men. One strides before them in his strength; and his red hair flies in the wind. His shield glitters to the beam of the east. His spear is in his hand.

Call him to the feast of Temora, replied the king of Erin. My hall is the house of strangers, son of the generous Gelláma!—Perhaps it is the chief of Etha, coming in the sound of his renown.—Hail, mighty stranger, art thou of the friends of Cormac?—But Carril, he is dark, and unlovely; and he draws his sword. Is that the son of Usnoth, bard of the times of old?

It is not the son of Usnoth, said Carril, but the chief of Atha.——Why comest thou in thy arms to Temora, Cairbar of the gloomy brow? Let not thy sword rise against Cormac! Whither dost thou turn thy speed?

He passed on in his darkness, and seized the hand of the king. Cormac foresaw his death, and the rage of his eyes arose.—Retire, thou gloomy chief of Atha: Nathos comes with battle.——Thou art bold in Cormac's

hall, for his arm is weak.—The sword entered Cormac's side: he fell in the
halls of his fathers. His fair hair is in the dust. His blood is smoking round.

And art thou fallen in thy halls, I said[28], O son of noble Artho? The shield
of Cuchullin was not near. Nor the spear of thy father. Mournful are the
mountains of Erin, for the chief of the people is low!——Blest be thy soul,
O Cormac! thou art snatched from the midst of thy course.

My words came to the ears of Cairbar, and he closed us[29] in the midst of
darkness. He feared to stretch his sword to the bards[30]: though his soul was
dark. Three days we pined alone: on the fourth, the noble Cathmor came.—
He heard our voice from the cave; he turned the eye of his wrath on Cairbar.

Chief of Atha! he said, how long wilt thou pain my soul? Thy heart is like
the rock of the desart; and thy thoughts are dark.—But thou art the brother
of Cathmor, and he will fight thy battles.——But Cathmor's soul is not like
thine, thou feeble hand of war! The light of my bosom is stained with thy
deeds: the bards will not sing of my renown. They may say, "Cathmor was
brave, but he fought for gloomy Cairbar." They will pass over my tomb in
silence, and my fame shall not be heard.—Cairbar! loose the bards: they are
the sons of other times. Their voice shall be heard in other ages, when the
kings of Temora have failed.

We came forth at the words of the chief. We saw him in his strength. He
was like thy youth, O Fingal, when thou first didst lift the spear.—His face
was like the sunny field[31] when it is bright: no darkness moved[32] over his
brow. But he came with his thousands to Ullin; to aid the red-haired Cair-
bar: and now he comes to revenge his death, O king of woody Morven.——

And let him come, replied the king; I love a foe like Cathmor. His soul is
great: his arm is strong, and his battles are full of fame.——But the little
soul is like a vapour that hovers round the marshy lake: it never rises on the
green hill, lest the winds meet it there: its dwelling is in the cave, and it
sends forth the dart of death.

Usnoth! thou hast heard the fame of Etha's car-borne chiefs.—Our young
heroes, O warrior, are like the renown of our fathers.—They fight in youth,
and they fall: their names are in the song.—But we are old, O Usnoth, let us
not fall like aged oaks; which the blast overturns in secret. The hunter came
past, and saw them lying gray across a stream. How have these fallen, he
said, and whistling passed along.

Raise the song of joy, ye bards of Morven, that our souls may forget the
past.—The red stars look on us from the clouds, and silently descend. Soon
shall the gray beam of the morning rise, and shew us the foes of Cormac.
——Fillan! take the spear of the king; go to Mora's dark-brown side. Let
thine eyes travel over the heath, like flames of fire. Observe the foes of Fin-
gal, and the course of generous Cathmor. I hear a distant sound, like the
falling of rocks in the desart.——But strike thou thy shield, at times, that
they may not come through night, and the fame of Morven cease.—I begin
to be alone, my son, and I dread the fall of my renown.

The voice of the bards arose. The king leaned on the shield of Trenmor.—
Sleep descended on his eyes, and his future battles rose in his dreams. The
host are sleeping around. Dark-haired Fillan observed the foe. His steps are
on a distant hill: we hear, at times, his clanging shield.

One of the Fragments of Ancient Poetry lately published, gives a different account
of the death of Oscar, the son of Ossian. The translator, though he well knew the
more probable tradition concerning that hero, was unwilling to reject a poem,
which, if not really of Ossian's composition, has much of his manner, and concise
turn of expression. A more correct copy of that fragment, which has since come to
the translator's hands, has enabled him to correct the mistake, into which a similar-
ity of names had led those who handed down the poem by tradition.—The heroes of
the piece are Oscar the son of Caruth, and Dermid the son of Diaran. Ossian, or
perhaps his imitator, opens the poem with a lamentation for Oscar, and afterwards,
by an easy transition, relates the story of Oscar the son of Caruth, who seems to
have bore the same character, as well as name, with Oscar the son of Ossian.
Though the translator thinks he has good reason to reject the fragment as the com-
position of Ossian; yet as it is, after all, still somewhat doubtful whether it is or not,
he has here subjoined it. [M]

Why openest thou afresh the spring of my grief, O son of Alpin, inquiring how
Oscar[33] fell? My eyes are blind with tears; but memory beams on my heart. How can
I relate the mournful death of the head of the people! Chief[34] of the warriors, Oscar,
my son, shall I see thee no more!

He fell as the moon in a storm; as the sun from the midst of his course, when
clouds rise from the waste of the waves, when the blackness of the storm inwraps
the rocks of Ardannider. I, like an ancient oak on Morven, I moulder alone in my
place. The blast hath lopped my branches away; and I tremble at the wings of the
north. Chief[35] of the warriors, Oscar, my son! shall I see thee no more!

But, son of Alpin, the hero fell not harmless as the grass of the field; the blood of
the mighty was on his sword, and he travelled with death through the ranks of their
pride. But Oscar, thou son of Caruth, thou hast fallen low! No enemy fell by thy
hand. Thy spear was stained with the blood of thy friend.[36]

Dermid and Oscar were one: They reaped the battle together. Their friendship was
strong as their steel; and death walked between them to the field. They came on the
foe like two rocks falling from the brows of Ardven. Their swords were stained with
the blood of the valiant: warriors fainted at their names. Who was equal to[37] Oscar,
but Dermid? and who to Dermid, but Oscar?

They killed mighty Dargo in the field; Dargo who never fled in war.[38] His daugh-
ter was fair as the morn; mild as the beam of night. Her eyes, like two stars in a
shower: her breath, the gale of spring: her breasts, as the new-fallen snow floating
on the moving heath. The warriors saw her, and loved; their souls were fixed on the
maid. Each loved her as his fame; each must possess her or die. But her soul was
fixed on Oscar; the son of Caruth[39] was the youth of her love. She forgot the blood
of her father, and loved the hand that slew him.

Son of Caruth,[40] said Dermid, I love; O Oscar, I love this maid. But her soul cleaveth unto thee; and nothing can heal Dermid. Here, pierce this bosom, Oscar; relieve me, my friend, with thy sword.

My sword, son of Diaran,[41] shall never be stained with the blood of Dermid.

Who then is worthy to slay me, O Oscar son of Caruth? Let not my life pass away unknown. Let none but Oscar slay me. Send me with honour to the grave, and let my death be renowned.

Dermid, make use of thy sword; son of Diaran, wield thy steel. Would that I fell with thee! that my death came from the hand of Dermid!

They fought by the brook of the mountain, by the streams of Branno. Blood tinged the running water,[42] and curdled[43] round the mossy stones. The stately Dermid[44] fell; he fell, and smiled in death.

And fallest thou, son of Diaran, fallest thou by Oscar's hand! Dermid who never yielded[45] in war, thus do I see thee fall!——He went, and returned to the maid of his love; he returned,[46] but she perceived his grief.

Why that gloom, son of Caruth? what shades thy mighty soul?

Though once renowned for the bow, O maid, I have lost my fame. Fixed on a tree by the brook of the hill, is the shield of the valiant Gormur,[47] whom I slew in battle. I have wasted the day in vain, nor could my arrow pierce it.

Let me try, son of Caruth, the skill of Dargo's daughter. My hands were taught the bow: my father delighted in my skill.

She went. He stood behind the shield. Her arrow flew, and pierced his breast.[48]

Blessed be that hand of snow; and blessed that[49] bow of yew! Who[50] but the daughter of Dargo was worthy to slay the son of Caruth?[51] Lay me in the earth, my fair one; lay me by the side of Dermid.

Oscar! the maid replied,[52] I have the soul[53] of the mighty Dargo. Well pleased I can meet death. My sorrow I can end.[54]——She pierced her white bosom with the[55] steel. She fell; she trembled; and died.

By the brook of the hill their graves are laid; a birch's unequal shade covers their tomb. Often on their green earthen tombs the branchy sons of the mountain feed, when mid-day is all in flames, and silence over[56] all the hills.

CARRIC-THURA:

A POEM[1].

Hast[2] thou left thy blue course in heaven, golden-haired son[3] of the sky! The west has opened its gates; the bed of thy repose is there. The waves come to behold thy beauty: they lift their trembling heads: they see thee lovely in thy sleep; but they shrink away with fear. Rest, in thy shadowy cave, O sun! and let thy return be in joy.——But let a thousand lights arise to the sound of the harps of Selma: let the beam spread in the hall, the king of shells is returned! The strife of Crona[4] is past, like sounds that are no more: raise the song, O bards, the king is returned with his fame!

Such was the song of Ullin, when Fingal returned from battle: when he returned in the fair blushing of youth; with all his heavy locks. His blue arms were on the hero; like a gray[5] cloud on the sun, when he moves in his robes of mist, and shews but half his beams. His heroes follow the king: the feast of shells is spread. Fingal turns to his bards, and bids the song to rise.

Voices of echoing Cona! he said, O bards of other times! Ye, on whose souls the blue hosts of our fathers rise! strike the harp in my hall; and let Fingal hear the song. Pleasant is the joy of grief! it is like the shower of spring, when it softens the branch of the oak, and the young leaf lifts its green head. Sing on, O bards, to-morrow we lift the sail. My blue course is through the ocean, to Carric-thura's walls; the mossy walls of Sarno, where Comála dwelt. There the noble Cathulla spreads the feast of shells. The boars of his woods are many, and the sound of the chace shall arise.

Cronnan[6], son of song! said Ullin, Minona, graceful at the harp! raise the song of Shilric, to please the king of Morven. Let Vinvela come in her beauty, like the showery bow, when it shews its lovely head on the lake, and the setting sun is bright. And she comes, O Fingal! her voice is soft but sad.

VINVELA.

My love is a son of the hill. He pursues the flying deer. His gray dogs are panting around him; his bow-string sounds in the wind. Dost thou rest by the fount of the rock, or by the noise of the mountain-stream? the rushes are nodding with the wind, the mist is flying over the hill. I will approach my love unperceived, and see him from the rock. Lovely I saw thee first by the aged oak of Branno[7]; thou wert returning tall from the chace; the fairest among thy friends.

SHILRIC.

What voice is that I hear? that voice like the summer-wind.—I sit not by the nodding rushes; I hear not the fount of the rock. Afar, Vinvela[8], afar I go to the wars of Fingal. My dogs attend me no more. No more I tread the hill. No more from on high I see thee, fair-moving by the stream of the plain; bright as the bow of heaven; as the moon on the western wave.

VINVELA.

Then thou art gone, O Shilric! and I am alone on the hill. The deer are seen on the brow; void of fear they graze along. No more they dread the wind; no more the rustling tree. The hunter is far removed; he is in the field of graves. Strangers! sons of the waves! spare my lovely Shilric.

SHILRIC.

If fall I must in the field, raise high my grave, Vinvela. Gray stones and heaped-up earth, shall mark me to future times. When the hunter shall sit by the mound, and produce his food at noon, "Some warrior rests here," he will say; and my fame shall live in his praise. Remember me, Vinvela, when low on earth I lie!

VINVELA.

Yes!—I will remember thee—Indeed[9] my Shilric will fall. What shall I do, my love! when thou art gone for ever? Through these hills I will go at noon: I will go through the silent heath. There I will see the place of thy rest, returning from the chace. Indeed,[10] my Shilric will fall; but I will remember him.

And I remember the chief, said the king of woody Morven; he consumed the battle in his rage. But now my eyes behold him not. I met him, one day, on the hill; his cheek was pale; his brow was dark. The sigh was frequent in his breast: his steps were towards the desart. But now he is not in the crowd of my chiefs, when the sounds of my shields arise. Dwells he in the narrow house[11], the chief of high Carmora?[12]

Cronnan! said Ullin of other times, raise the song of Shilric; when he returned to his hills, and Vinvela was no more. He leaned on her gray mossy stone; he thought Vinvela lived. He saw her fair-moving[13] on the plain: but the bright form lasted not: the sun-beam fled from the field, and she was seen no more. Hear the song of Shilric, it is soft but sad.

I sit by the mossy fountain; on the top of the hill of winds. One tree is rustling above me. Dark waves roll over the heath. The lake is troubled below. The deer descend from the hill. No hunter at a distance is seen; no whistling cow-herd is nigh.[14] It is mid-day: but all is silent. Sad are my thoughts alone. Didst thou but appear, O my love, a wanderer on the heath! thy hair floating on the wind behind thee; thy bosom heaving on the sight; thine eyes full of tears for thy friends, whom the mist of the hill had concealed! Thee I would comfort, my love, and bring thee to thy father's house.

But is it she that there appears, like a beam of light on the heath? bright as the moon in autumn, as the sun in a summer-storm, comest thou, lovely[15] maid, over rocks, over mountains to me?——She speaks: but how weak her voice! like the breeze in the reeds of the pool.[16]

Returnest thou safe from the war? Where are thy friends, my love? I heard of thy death on the hill; I heard and mourned thee, Shilric!

Yes, my fair, I return; but I alone of my race. Thou shalt see them no more: their graves I raised on the plain. But why art thou on the desert hill? Why on the heath, alone?

Alone I am, O Shilric! alone in the winter-house. With grief for thee I expired.[17] Shilric, I am pale in the tomb.

She fleets, she sails away; as gray[18] mist before the wind!—and, wilt thou not stay, my love? Stay and behold my tears? fair thou appearest, Vinvela! fair thou wast, when alive!

By the mossy fountain I will sit; on the top of the hill of winds. When mid-day is silent around, converse, O my love, with me! come on the wings of the gale! on the blast of the mountain,[19] come! Let me hear thy voice, as thou passest, when mid-day is silent around.

Such was the song of Cronnan, on the night of Selma's joy. But morning rose in the east; the blue waters rolled in light. Fingal bade his sails to rise, and the winds come rustling from their hills. Inis-tore rose to sight, and Carric-thura's mossy towers. But the sign of distress was on their top: the green[20] flame edged with smoke. The king of Morven struck his breast: he assumed, at once, his spear. His darkened brow bends forward to the coast: he looks back to the lagging winds. His hair is disordered on his back. The silence of the king is terrible.

Night came down on the sea; Rotha's bay received the ship. A rock bends along the coast with all its echoing wood. On the top is the circle[21] of Loda, and the mossy stone of power. A narrow plain spreads beneath, covered with grass and aged trees, which the midnight winds, in their wrath, had torn from the shaggy rock. The blue course of a stream is there: and the lonely blast of ocean pursues the thistle's beard.

The flame of three oaks arose: the feast is spread around: but the soul of the king is sad, for Carric-thura's battling chief.[22] The wan, cold moon rose, in the east. Sleep descended on the youths: Their blue helmets glitter to the beam; the fading fire decays. But sleep did not rest on the king: he rose in the midst of his arms, and slowly ascended the hill to behold the flame of Sarno's tower.

The flame was dim and distant; the moon hid her red face in the east. A blast came from the mountain, and bore, on its wings, the spirit of Loda. He came to his place in his terrors[23], and he shook his dusky spear.—His eyes appear like flames in his dark face; and his voice is like distant thunder. Fingal advanced with the spear of his strength,[24] and raised his voice on high.

Son of night, retire: call thy winds and fly! Why dost thou come to my presence, with thy shadowy arms? Do I fear thy gloomy form, dismal spirit of Loda?[25] Weak is thy shield of clouds: feeble is that meteor, thy sword. The blast rolls them together; and thou thyself dost vanish. Fly from my presence son of night! call thy winds and fly!

Dost thou force me from my place, replied the hollow voice? The people bend before me. I turn the battle in the field of the valiant. I look on the nations and they vanish: my nostrils pour the blast of death. I come[26] abroad on the winds: the tempests are before my face. But my dwelling is calm, above the clouds, the fields of my rest are pleasant.

Dwell then in thy calm[27] field, said Fingal, and let Comhal's son be forgot. Do my steps ascend, from my hills, into thy peaceful plains? Do I meet thee, with a spear, on thy cloud, spirit of dismal Loda? Why then dost thou frown on Fingal? or shake thine airy spear? But thou frownest in vain: I never fled from mighty men. And shall the sons of the wind frighten the king of Morven? No: he knows the weakness of their arms.

Fly to thy land, replied the form: receive the wind and fly. The blasts are in the hollow of my hand: the course of the storm is mine. The king of Sora is my son, he bends at the stone of my power. His battle is around Carric-thura; and he will prevail. Fly to thy land, son of Comhal, or feel my flaming wrath.

He lifted high his shadowy spear; and bent forward his terrible height. But the king,[28] advancing, drew his sword; the blade of dark-brown Luno[29]. The gleaming path of the steel winds through the gloomy ghost. The form fell shapeless into air, like a column of smoke, which the staff of the boy disturbs, as it rises from the half-extinguished furnace.[30]

The spirit of Loda shrieked, as, rolled into himself, he rose on the wind. Inistore shook at the sound. The waves heard it on the deep: they stopped, in their course, with fear: the companions of Fingal started, at once; and took their heavy spears. They missed the king: they rose with rage; all their arms resound.

The moon came forth in the east. The king[31] returned in the gleam of his arms. The joy of his youths was great; their souls settled, as a sea from a storm. Ullin raised the song of gladness. The hills of Inistore rejoiced. The flame of the oak arose; and the tales of heroes are told.

But Frothal, Sora's battling[32] king, sits in sadness beneath a tree. The host spreads around Carric-thura. He looks towards the walls with rage. He longs for the blood of Cathulla, who, once, overcame the king[33] in war.——

When Annir reigned[34] in Sora, the father of car-borne[35] Frothal, a blast rose on the sea, and carried Frothal to Inistore. Three days he feasted in Sarno's halls, and saw the slow rolling eyes of Comála. He loved her, in the rage[36] of youth, and rushed to seize the white-armed maid. Cathulla met the chief. The gloomy battle rose, Frothal is bound in the hall: three days he pined alone. On the fourth, Sarno sent him to his ship, and he returned to his land. But wrath darkened in his soul against the noble Cathulla. When Annir's stone[37] of fame arose, Frothal came in his strength. The battle burned round Carric-thura, and Sarno's mossy walls.

Morning rose on Inistore. Frothal struck his dark-brown shield. His chiefs started at the sound; they stood, but their eyes were turned to the sea. They saw Fingal coming in his strength; and first the noble Thubar spoke.

Who comes like the stag of the mountain,[38] with all his herd behind him? Frothal, it is a foe; I see his forward spear. Perhaps it is the king of Morven, Fingal the first of men. His actions are well known on Gormal;[39] the blood of his foes is in Starno's halls. Shall I ask the peace[40] of kings? He is like the thunder[41] of heaven.

Son of the feeble hand, said Frothal, shall my days begin in darkness? Shall I yield before I have conquered in battle, chief of streamy Tora? The people would say in Sora, Frothal flew forth like a meteor; but the dark cloud met it, and it is no more. No: Thubar, I will never yield; my fame shall surround me like light. No: I will never yield, king[42] of streamy Tora.

He went forth with the stream of his people, but they met a rock: Fingal stood unmoved, broken they rolled back from his side. Nor did they roll in safety; the spear of the king pursued their flight. The field is covered with heroes. A rising hill preserved the flying host.[43]

Frothal saw their flight. The rage of his bosom rose. He bent his eyes to the ground, and called the noble Thubar.——Thubar! my people fled. My fame has ceased to rise. I will fight the king; I feel my burning soul.

Send a bard to demand the combat. Speak not against Frothal's words.—— But, Thubar! I love a maid; she dwells by Thano's stream, the white-bosomed daughter of Herman, Utha with the softly-rolling eyes. She feared the daughter of Inistore[44], and her soft sighs rose, at my departure.[45] Tell to Utha that I am low; but[46] that my soul delighted in her.

Such were his words, resolved to fight. But the soft sigh of Utha was near. She had followed her hero over the sea, in the armour of a man. She rolled her eye on the youth, in secret, from beneath a glittering helmet.[47] But now she saw the bard as he went, and the spear fell thrice from her hand. Her loose hair flew on the wind. Her white breast rose, with sighs. She lifted up her eyes to the king; she would speak, but thrice she failed.

Fingal heard the words of the bard; he came in the strength of steel. They mixed their deathful spears, and raised the gleam of their swords. But the steel of Fingal descended and cut Frothal's shield in twain. His fair side is exposed; half bent he foresees his death.

Darkness gathered on Utha's soul. The tear rolled down her cheek. She rushed to cover the chief with her shield; but a fallen oak met her steps. She fell on her arm of snow; her shield, her helmet flew wide. Her white bosom heaved to the sight; her dark-brown hair is spread on earth.

Fingal pitied the white-armed maid: he stayed the uplifted sword. The tear was in the eye of the king, as, bending forward, he spoke. King of streamy Sora! fear not the sword of Fingal. It was never stained with the blood of the vanquished; it never pierced a fallen foe. Let thy people rejoice along the blue waters of Tora:[48] let the maids of thy love be glad. Why shouldest thou fall in thy youth, king of streamy Sora?

Frothal heard the words of Fingal, and saw the rising maid: they[49] stood in silence, in their beauty: like two young trees of the plain, when the shower of spring is on their leaves, and the loud winds are laid.

Daughter of Herman, said Frothal, didst thou come from Tora's streams; didst thou come, in thy beauty, to behold thy warrior low? But he was low before the mighty, maid of the slow-rolling eye! The feeble did not overcome the son of car-borne Annir. Terrible art thou, O king of Morven! in battles of the spear. But, in peace, thou art like the sun, when he looks through a silent shower: the flowers lift their fair heads before him; and the gales shake their rustling wings. O that thou wert in Sora! that my feast were spread!—The future kings of Sora would see thy arms and rejoice. They would rejoice at the fame of their fathers, who beheld the mighty Fingal.

Son of Annir, replied the king, the fame of Sora's race shall be heard.—When chiefs are strong in battle, then does the song arise! But if their swords are stretched over the feeble: if the blood of the weak has stained their arms; the bard shall forget them in the song, and their tombs shall not be known. The stranger shall come and build there, and remove the heaped-up earth. An half-worn sword shall rise before him; and bending above it, he will say, "These are the arms of chiefs of old, but their names are not in song."——Come thou, O Frothal, to the feast of Inistore; let the maid of thy love be there; and our faces will brighten with joy.

Fingal took his spear, moving in the steps of his might. The gates of Carric-thura are opened.[50] The feast of shells is spread.——The voice of[51] music arose. Gladness brightened in the hall.——The voice of Ullin was heard; the harp of Selma was strung.—Utha rejoiced in his presence, and demanded the song of grief; the big tear hung in her eye, when the soft[52] Crimora spoke. Crimora the daughter of Rinval, who dwelt at Lotha's mighty stream.[53] The tale was long, but lovely; and pleased the blushing maid of Tora.[54]

CRIMORA[55].

Who cometh from the hill, like a cloud tinged with the beam of the west? Whose voice is that, loud as the wind, but pleasant as the harp of Carril?[56]

It is my love in the light of steel; but sad is his darkened brow. Live the mighty race of Fingal? or what disturbs my Connal?[57]

CONNAL.

They live. I saw them return from the chace, like a stream of light. The sun was on their shields. Like a ridge of fire they descended the hill. Loud is the voice of the youth; the war, my love, is near. To-morrow the terrible Dargo comes to try the force of our race. The race of Fingal he defies; the race of battle and wounds.

CRIMORA.

Connal, I saw his sails like gray mist on the sable[58] wave. They slowly came to land. Connal, many are the warriors of Dargo!

CONNAL.

Bring me thy father's shield; the bossy, iron shield of Rinval; that shield like the full moon when it moves[59] darkened through heaven.

CRIMORA.

That shield I bring, O Connal; but it did not defend my father. By the spear of Gormar he fell. Thou may'st fall, O Connal!

CONNAL.

Fall indeed I may: But raise my tomb, Crimora. Gray stones, a mound of earth, shall keep my memory.[60] Bend thy red eye over my tomb, and beat thy mournful heaving breast. Though fair thou art, my love, as the light; more pleasant than the gale of the hill; yet I will not stay. Raise my tomb, Crimora.

CRIMORA.

Then give me those arms of light;[61] that sword, and that spear of steel. I shall meet Dargo with thee, and aid my lovely Connal. Farewel, ye rocks of Ardven! ye deer! and ye streams of the hill!—We shall return no more. Our tombs are distant far.

And did they return no more? said Utha's bursting sigh. Fell the mighty in battle, and did Crimora live?—Her steps were lonely, and her soul was sad for Connal. Was he not young and lovely; like the beam of the setting sun? Ullin saw the virgin's tear, and took the softly-trembling harp: the song was lovely, but sad, and silence was in Carric-thura.

Autumn is dark on the mountains; gray mist rests on the hills. The whirlwind is heard on the heath. Dark rolls the river through the narrow plain. A tree stands alone on the hill, and marks the slumbering Connal. The leaves whirl round with the wind, and strew the grave of the dead. At times are seen here the ghosts of the deceased, when the musing hunter alone stalks slowly over the heath.

Who can reach the source of thy race, O Connal? and who recount thy fathers? Thy family grew like an oak on the mountain, which meeteth the wind with its lofty head. But now it is torn from the earth. Who shall supply the place of Connal?

Here was the din of arms; and here the groans of the dying. Bloody are the wars of Fingal! O Connal! it was here thou didst fall. Thine arm was like a storm; thy sword a beam of the sky; thy height, a rock on the plain; thine eyes, a furnace of fire. Louder than a storm was thy voice, in the battles of thy steel. Warriors fell by thy sword, as the thistle by the staff of a boy.

Dargo the mighty came on, like a cloud of thunder. His brows were contracted and dark.[62] His eyes like two caves in a rock. Bright rose their swords on each side; dire[63] was the clang of their steel.

The daughter of Rinval was near; Crimora bright in the armour of man; her yellow hair is loose behind, her bow is in her hand. She followed the youth to the war, Connal her much-beloved. She drew the string on Dargo; but erring pierced her Connal. He falls like an oak on the plain; like a rock from the shaggy hill. What shall she do, hapless maid!—He bleeds; her Connal dies. All the night long she cries, and all the day, O Connal, my love, and my friend! With grief the sad mourner dies.

Earth here incloses the loveliest pair on the hill. The grass grows between the stones of the tomb; I often sit in the mournful shade. The wind sighs through the grass; their memory rushes on my mind. Undisturbed you now sleep together; in the tomb of the mountain you rest alone.

And soft be your[64] rest, said Utha, children[65] of streamy Lotha. I will remember you with tears, and my secret song shall rise; when the wind is in the groves of Tora, and the stream is roaring near. Then shall ye come on my soul, with all your lovely grief.

Three days feasted the kings: on the fourth their white sails arose. The winds of the north carry the ship of Fingal[66] to Morven's woody land.——But the spirit of Loda sat, in his cloud, behind the ships of Frothal. He hung forward with all his blasts, and spread the white-bosomed sails.——The wounds of his form were not forgot; he still feared[67] the hand of the king.

THE
SONGS of SELMA[1].

Star of the descending[2] night! fair is thy light in the west! thou liftest thy unshorn head from thy cloud: thy steps are stately on thy hill. What dost thou behold in the plain? The stormy winds are laid. The murmur of the torrent comes from afar. Roaring waves climb the distant rock. The flies of evening are on their feeble wings, and the hum of their course is on the field. What dost thou behold, fair light? But thou dost smile and depart. The waves come with joy around thee, and bathe thy lovely hair. Farewel, thou silent beam!—Let the light of Ossian's soul arise.

And it does arise in its strength! I behold my departed friends. Their gathering is on Lora, as in the days that are past.[3]——Fingal comes like a watry column of mist; his heroes are around. And see the bards of the song, gray-haired Ullin; stately Ryno; Alpin[4], with the tuneful voice, and the soft complaint of Minona!——How are ye changed, my friends, since the days of Selma's feast! when we contended, like the gales of the spring, that, flying over the hill, by turns bend the feebly-whistling grass.

Minona then[5] came forth in her beauty; with down-cast look and tearful eye; her hair flew slowly on the blast that rushed unfrequent from the hill.——The souls of the heroes were sad when she raised the tuneful voice; for often had they seen the grave of Salgar[6], and the dark dwelling of white-bosomed Colma[7]. Colma left alone on the hill, with all her voice of music![8] Salgar promised to come: but the night descended round.—Hear the voice of Colma, when she sat alone on the hill!

COLMA.

It is night;—I am alone, forlorn on the hill of storms. The wind is heard in the mountain. The torrent shrieks[9] down the rock. No hut receives me from the rain; forlorn on the hill of winds.

Rise, moon! from behind thy clouds; stars of the night appear! Lead me, some light, to the place where my love rests from the toil of the chace! his bow near him, unstrung; his dogs panting around him. But here I must sit alone, by the rock of the mossy stream. The stream and the wind roar; nor can I hear the voice of my love.

Why delays my Salgar, why the son[10] of the hill, his promise? Here is the rock, and the tree; and here the roaring stream. Thou didst promise with night to be here. Ah! whither is my Salgar gone? With thee I would fly, my father; with thee, my brother[11] of pride. Our race have long been foes; but we are not foes, O Salgar!

Cease a little while, O wind! stream, be thou silent a while! let my voice be heard over the heath;[12] let my wanderer hear me. Salgar! it is I who call.[13] Here is the tree, and the rock. Salgar, my love! I am here. Why delayest thou thy coming?

Lo! the moon appeareth.[14] The flood is bright in the vale. The rocks are grey on the face of the hill.[15] But I see him not on the brow; his dogs before him tell not that he is coming.[16] Here I must sit alone.

But who are these that lie beyond me on the heath?[17] Are they my love and my brother?—Speak to me, O my friends! they answer not.[18] My soul is tormented with fears.——Ah! they are dead. Their swords are red from the fight. O my brother! my brother! why hast thou slain my Salgar? why, O Salgar! hast thou slain my brother? Dear were ye both to me! what shall I say in your praise? Thou wert fair on the hill among thousands; he was terrible in fight. Speak to me; hear my voice, sons of my love! But alas! they are silent; silent for ever! Cold[19] are their breasts of clay!

Oh! from the rock of the hill; from the top of the windy mountain,[20] speak ye ghosts of the dead! speak, I will not be afraid.—Whither are ye gone to rest? In what cave of the hill shall I find you?[21] No feeble voice is on the wind: no answer half-drowned in the storms of the hill.[22]

I sit in my grief. I wait for morning in my tears. Rear the tomb, ye friends of the dead; but close it not till Colma come. My life flies away like a dream: why should I stay behind? Here shall I rest with my friends, by the stream of the sounding rock. When night comes on the hill; when the wind is on the heath;[23] my ghost shall stand in the wind,[24] and mourn the death of my friends. The hunter shall hear from his booth. He shall fear but love my voice. For sweet shall my voice be for my friends; for pleasant were they both to me.[25]

Such was thy song, Minona softly-blushing maid[26] of Torman. Our tears descended for Colma, and our souls were sad.—Ullin came with the harp, and gave the song of Alpin.—The voice of Alpin was pleasant: the soul of Ryno was a beam of fire. But they had rested in the narrow house: and their voice was not heard in Selma.——Ullin had returned one day from the chace, before the heroes fell. He heard their strife on the hill; their song was soft but sad. They mourned the fall of Morar, first of mortal men. His soul was like the soul of Fingal; his sword like the sword of Oscar.—But he fell, and his father mourned: his sister's eyes were full of tears.——Minona's eyes were full of tears, the sister of car-borne Morar. She retired from the song of Ullin, like the moon in the west, when she foresees the shower, and hides her fair head in a cloud.—I touched the harp, with Ullin; the song of mourning rose.

RYNO.

The wind and the rain are over: calm is the noon of day. The clouds are divided in heaven. Over the green hills flies the inconstant sun. Red through the stony vale comes down the stream of the hill. Sweet are thy murmurs, O stream! but more sweet is the voice I hear. It is the voice of Alpin, the son of song, mourning for the dead. Bent is his head of age, and red his tearful eye. Alpin, thou son of song, why alone on the silent hill? why complainest thou, as a blast in the wood; as a wave on the lonely shore?

ALPIN.

My tears, O Ryno! are for the dead; my voice, for the inhabitants of the grave.[27] Tall thou art on the hill; fair among the sons of the plain.[28] But thou shalt fall like Morar[29]; and the mourner shall sit on thy tomb. The hills shall know thee no more; thy bow shall lie in the hall, unstrung.

Thou wert swift, O Morar! as a roe on the hill;[30] terrible as a meteor of fire. Thy wrath was as the storm. Thy sword in battle, as lightning in the field. Thy voice was like[31] a stream after rain; like thunder on distant hills. Many fell by thy arm; they were consumed in the flames of thy wrath.

But when thou didst return from war, how peaceful was thy brow! Thy face was like the sun after rain; like the moon in the silence of night; calm as the breast of the lake when the loud wind is laid.

Narrow is thy dwelling now; dark the place of thine abode. With three steps I compass thy grave, O thou who wast so great before! Four stones, with their heads of moss, are the only memorial of thee. A tree with scarce a leaf, long grass which whistles in the wind, mark to the hunter's eye the grave of the mighty Morar. Morar! thou art low indeed. Thou hast no mother to mourn thee; no maid with her tears of love. Dead is she that brought thee forth. Fallen is the daughter of Morglan.

Who on his staff is this? who is this, whose head is white with age, whose eyes are red with tears, who quakes at every step.—It is thy father[32], O Morar! the father of no son but thee. He heard of thy fame in battle; he heard of foes dispersed. He heard of Morar's fame; why did he not hear of his wound? Weep, thou father of Morar! weep; but thy son heareth thee not. Deep is the sleep of the dead; low their pillow of dust. No more shall he hear thy voice; no more shall he awake at thy call. When shall it be morn in the grave, to bid the slumberer awake?

Farewel, thou bravest of men! thou conqueror in the field! but the field shall see thee no more; nor the dark wood be lightened with the splendor of thy steel. Thou hast left no son. But the song shall preserve thy name. Future times shall hear of thee; they shall hear of the fallen Morar.

The grief of all arose, but most the bursting sigh of Armin[33]. He remembers the death of his son, who fell in the days of his youth. Carmor[34] was near the hero, the chief of the echoing Galmal. Why bursts the sigh of Armin, he said? Is there a cause to mourn? The song comes, with its music, to melt and please the soul. It is like soft mist, that, rising from a lake, pours on the silent vale; the green flowers are filled with dew, but the sun returns in his strength, and the mist is gone. Why art thou sad, O Armin, chief of sea-surrounded Gorma?

Sad! I am indeed: nor small my cause of woe!—Carmor, thou hast lost no son; thou hast lost no daughter of beauty. Colgar the valiant lives; and Annira fairest maid. The boughs of thy family flourish,[35] O Carmor! but Armin is the last of his race. Dark is thy bed, O Daura! and deep thy sleep in the tomb.—When shalt thou awake with thy songs? with all thy voice of music?

Rise, winds of autumn, rise; blow upon the dark heath![36] streams of the mountains, roar! howl, ye tempests, in the top of the oak![37] walk through broken clouds, O moon! show by intervals thy pale face! bring to my mind that sad night,[38] when all my children fell; when Arindal the mighty fell; when Daura the lovely failed.

Daura, my daughter! thou wert fair; fair as the moon on the hills of Fura;[39] white as the driven snow; sweet as the breathing gale. Arindal, thy bow was strong, thy spear was swift in the field: thy look was like mist on the wave; thy shield, a red cloud in a storm. Armar, renowned in war, came, and sought Daura's love; he was not long denied; fair was the hope of their friends.

Erath, son of Odgal, repined; for his brother was slain by Armar. He came disguised like a son of the sea: fair was his skiff on the wave; white his locks of age; calm his serious brow. Fairest of women, he said, lovely daughter of Armin! a rock not distant in the sea, bears a tree on its side; red shines the fruit afar. There Armar waits for Daura. I came to carry his love along the rolling sea.[40]

She went; and she called on Armar. Nought answered, but the son[41] of the rock. Armar, my love! my love! why tormentest thou me with fear? hear, son of Ardnart,[42] hear: it is Daura who calleth thee! Erath the traitor fled laughing to the land. She lifted up her voice, and cried for her brother and her father. Arindal! Armin! none to relieve your Daura.

Her voice came over the sea. Arindal my son descended from the hill; rough in the spoils of the chace. His arrows rattled by his side; his bow was in his hand: five dark gray dogs attended his steps. He saw fierce Erath on the shore: he seized and bound him to an oak. Thick bend[43] the thongs[44] of the hide around his limbs; he loads the wind with his groans.

Arindal ascends the wave[45] in his boat, to bring Daura to land. Armar came in his wrath, and let fly the gray-feathered shaft. It sung; it sunk in thy heart, O Arindal my son! for Erath the traitor thou diedst. The oar is stopped at once; he panted on the rock and expired. What is thy grief, O Daura, when round thy feet is poured thy brother's blood.

The boat is broken in twain by the waves.[46] Armar plunges into the sea, to rescue his Daura, or die. Sudden a blast from the hill comes over the waves. He sunk, and he rose no more.

Alone, on the sea-beat rock, my daughter was heard to complain. Frequent and loud were her cries; nor could her father relieve her.[47] All night I stood on the shore. I saw her by the faint beam of the moon. All night I heard her cries. Loud was the wind; and the rain beat hard on the side of the mountain.[48] Before morning appeared, her voice was weak. It died away, like the evening-breeze among the grass of the rocks. Spent with grief she expired. And left thee Armin alone: gone is my strength in the war, and fallen my pride among women.

When the storms of the mountain come;[49] when the north lifts the waves on high; I sit by the sounding shore, and look on the fatal rock. Often by the setting moon I see the ghosts of my children. Half-viewless, they walk in mournful conference together. Will none of you speak in pity? They do not regard their father. I am sad, O Carmor, nor small my cause of woe!

Such were the words of the bards in the days of song; when the king heard the music of harps, and the tales of other times. The chiefs gathered from all their hills, and heard the lovely sound. They praised the voice[50] of Cona! the first among a thousand bards. But age is now on my tongue; and my soul has failed. I hear, sometimes, the ghosts of bards, and learn their pleasant song. But memory fails in my mind; I hear the call of years. They say, as they pass along, why does Ossian sing? Soon shall he lie in the narrow house, and no bard shall raise his fame.

Roll on, ye dark-brown years, for ye bring no joy on your course. Let the tomb open to Ossian, for his strength has failed. The sons of song are gone to rest: my voice remains, like a blast, that roars, lonely, on a sea-surrounded rock, after the winds are laid. The dark moss whistles there, and the distant mariner sees the waving trees.

CALTHON and COLMAL:
A POEM[1].

Pleasant is the voice of thy song, thou lonely dweller of the rock. It comes on the sound of the stream, along the narrow vale. My soul awakes, O stranger! in the midst of my hall. I stretch my hand to the spear, as in the days of other years.—I stretch my hand, but it is feeble; and the sigh of my bosom grows.—Wilt thou not listen, son of the rock, to the song of Ossian? My soul is full of other times; the joy of my youth returns. Thus the sun[2] appears in the west, after the steps of his brightness have moved behind a storm; the green hills lift their dewy heads: the blue streams rejoice in the vale. The aged hero comes forth on his staff, and his grey hair glitters in the beam.

Dost thou not behold, son of the rock, a shield in Ossian's hall? It is marked with the strokes of battle; and the brightness of its bosses has failed. That shield the great Dunthalmo bore, the chief of streamy Teutha.—— Dunthalmo bore it in battle, before he fell by Ossian's spear. Listen, son of the rock, to the tale of other years.—

Rathmor was a chief of Clutha. The feeble dwelt in his hall. The gates of Rathmor were never closed; his feast was always spread. The sons of the stranger came, and blessed the generous chief of Clutha. Bards raised the song, and touched the harp: and joy brightened on the face of the mournful.—Dunthalmo came, in his pride, and rushed into the combat of Rathmor. The chief of Clutha overcame: the rage of Dunthalmo rose.—He came, by night, with his warriors; and the mighty Rathmor fell. He fell in his halls, where his feast was often spread for strangers.——

Colmar and Calthon were young, the sons of car-borne Rathmor. They came, in the joy of youth, into their father's hall. They behold him in his blood, and their bursting tears descend.—The soul of Dunthalmo melted, when he saw the children of youth; he brought them to Alteutha's[3] walls; they grew in the house of their foe.—They bent the bow in his presence; and came forth to his battles.

They saw the fallen walls of their fathers; they saw the green thorn in the hall. Their tears descended[4] in secret; and, at times, their faces were mournful. Dunthalmo beheld their grief: his darkening soul designed their death. He closed them in two caves, on the echoing banks of Teutha. The sun did not come there with his beams; nor the moon of heaven by night. The sons of Rathmor remained in darkness, and foresaw their death.

The daughter of Dunthalmo wept in silence, the fair-haired, blue-eyed Colmal[5]. Her eye had rolled in secret on Calthon; his loveliness swelled in her soul. She trembled for her warrior; but what could Colmal do? Her arm could not lift the spear; nor was the sword formed for her side. Her white breast never rose beneath a mail. Neither was her eye the terror of heroes. What canst thou do, O Colmal! for the falling chief?—Her steps are unequal; her hair is loose: her eye looks wildly through her tears.—She came, by night, to the hall[6]; and armed her lovely form in steel; the steel of a young warrior, who fell in the first of his battles.—She came to the cave of Calthon, and loosed the thong from his hands.

Arise, son of Rathmor, she said, arise, the night is dark. Let us fly to the king of Selma[7], chief of fallen Clutha! I am the son of Lamgal, who dwelt in thy father's hall. I heard of thy dark dwelling in the cave, and my soul arose. Arise, son of Rathmor, for the night is dark.——

Blest voice! replied the chief, comest thou from the darkly-rolling[8] clouds? for often the ghosts of his fathers descend to Calthon's dreams, since the sun has retired from his eyes, and darkness has dwelt around him. Or art thou the son of Lamgal, the chief I often saw in Clutha? But shall I fly to Fingal, and Colmar my brother low? Shall I fly to Morven, and the hero closed in night? No: give me that spear, son of Lamgal, Calthon will defend his brother.

A thousand warriors, replied the maid, stretch their spears round car-borne Colmar. What can Calthon do against a host so great? Let us fly to the king of Morven, he will come with battle. His arm is stretched forth to the unhappy; the lightning of his sword is round the weak.—Arise, thou son of Rathmor; the shades of night[9] will fly away. Dunthalmo will behold thy steps on the field,[10] and thou must fall in thy youth.

The sighing hero rose; his tears descend for car-borne Colmar. He came with the maid to Selma's hall; but he knew not that it was Colmal. The helmet cover'd her lovely face; and her breast[11] rose beneath the steel. Fingal returned from the chace, and found the lovely strangers. They were like two beams of light, in the midst of the hall.[12]

The king heard the tale of grief; and turned his eyes around. A thousand heroes half-rose before him; claiming the war of Teutha.—I came with my spear from the hill, and the joy of battle rose in my breast: for the king spoke to Ossian in the midst of the people.[13]

Son of my strength, he said,[14] take the spear of Fingal; go to Teutha's mighty[15] stream, and save the car-borne Colmar.—Let thy fame return before thee like a pleasant gale; that my soul may rejoice over my son, who renews the renown of our fathers.—Ossian! be thou a storm in battle; but mild when the foes are low!—It was thus my fame arose, O my son; and be thou like Selma's chief.—When the haughty come to my halls, my eyes behold them not. But my arm is stretched forth to the unhappy. My sword defends the weak.

I rejoiced in the words of the king: and took my rattling arms.—Diaran[16] rose at my side, and Dargo[17] king of spears.—Three hundred youths followed our steps: the lovely strangers were at my side. Dunthalmo heard the sound of our approach; he gathered the strength of Teutha.—He stood on a hill with his host; they were like rocks broken with thunder, when their bent trees are singed and bare, and the streams of their chinks have failed.

The stream of Teutha rolled, in its pride, before the gloomy foe. I sent a bard to Dunthalmo, to offer the combat on the plain; but he smiled in the darkness of his pride.—His unsettled host moved on the hill; like the mountain-cloud, when the blast has entered its womb, and scatters the curling gloom on every side.

They brought Colmar to Teutha's bank, bound with a thousand thongs. The chief is sad, but lovely,[18] and his eye is on his friends; for we stood, in our arms, on the opposite bank of Teutha.[19] Dunthalmo came with his spear, and pierced the hero's side: he rolled on the bank in his blood, and we heard his broken sighs.

Calthon rushed into the stream: I bounded forward on my spear. Teutha's race fell before us. Night came rolling down. Dunthalmo rested on a rock, amidst an aged wood. The rage of his bosom burned against the car-borne Calthon.—But Calthon stood in his grief; he mourned the fallen Colmar; Colmar slain in youth, before his fame arose.

I bade the song of woe to rise, to sooth the mournful chief; but he stood beneath a tree, and often threw his spear on earth.—The humid eye of Colmal rolled near in a secret tear: she foresaw the fall of Dunthalmo, or of Clutha's battling[20] chief.

Now half the night had passed away. Silence and darkness were on the field; sleep rested on the eyes of the heroes: Calthon's settling soul was still. His eyes were half-closed; but the murmur of Teutha had not yet failed in his ear.——Pale, and shewing his wounds, the ghost of Colmar came: he bended his head over the hero, and raised his feeble voice.

Sleeps the son of Rathmor in his might,[21] and his brother low? Did we not rise to the chace together, and pursue the dark-brown hinds? Colmar was not forgot till he fell; till death had blasted his youth. I lie pale beneath the rock of Lona. O let Calthon rise! the morning comes with its beams; and Dunthalmo will dishonour the fallen.

He passed away in his blast. The rising Calthon saw the steps of his departure.—He rushed in the sound of his steel; and unhappy Colmal rose. She followed her hero through night, and dragged her spear behind.—But when Calthon came to Lona's rock, he found his fallen brother—The rage of his bosom rose, and he rushed among the foe. The groans of death ascend. They close around the chief.—He is bound in the midst, and brought to gloomy Dunthalmo.—The shout of joy arose; and the hills of night replied.—

I started at the sound: and took my father's spear. Diaran rose at my side; and the youthful strength of Dargo. We missed the chief of Clutha, and our souls were sad.—I dreaded the departure of my fame; the pride of my valour rose.

Sons of Morven, I said, it is not thus our fathers fought. They rested not on the field of strangers, when the foe did not fall before them.——Their strength was like the eagles of heaven; their renown is in the song. But our people fall by degrees, and our fame begins to depart.——What shall the king of Morven say, if Ossian conquers not at Teutha? Rise in your steel, ye warriors, and follow the sound of Ossian's course. He will not return, but renowned, to the echoing walls of Selma.

Morning rose on the blue waters of Teutha; Colmal stood before me in tears. She told of the chief of Clutha: and thrice the spear fell from her hand. My wrath turned against the stranger; for my soul trembled for Calthon.

Son of the feeble hand, I said, do Teutha's warriors fight with tears? The battle is not won with grief; nor dwells the sigh in the soul of war.——Go to the deer of Carmun, or the lowing herds of Teutha.—But leave these arms, thou son of fear; a warrior may lift them in battle.——

I tore the mail from her shoulders. Her snowy breast appeared. She bent her red[22] face to the ground.—I looked in silence to the chiefs. The spear fell from my hand; and the sigh of my bosom rose.——But when I heard the name of the maid, my crowding tears descended.[23] I blessed the lovely beam of youth, and bade the battle move.

Why, son of the rock, should Ossian tell how Teutha's warriors died? They are now forgot in their land; and their tombs are not found on the heath.—Years came on with their tempests; and the green mounds mouldered away.—Scarce is the grave of Dunthalmo seen, or the place where he fell by the spear of Ossian.—Some gray warrior, half blind with age, sitting by night at the flaming oak of the hall, tells now my actions to his sons, and the fall of the dark Dunthalmo. The faces of youth bend sidelong towards his voice; surprize and joy burn in their eyes.—

I found the son of Rathmor[24] bound to an oak; my sword cut the thongs from his hands. And I gave him the white-bosomed Colmal.—They dwelt in the halls of Teutha; and Ossian returned to Selma.[25]

Note 17: Dargo, the son of Collath, is celebrated in other poems by Ossian. He is said to have been killed by a boar at a hunting party. The lamentation of his mistress, or wife, Mingala, over his body, is extant; but whether it is of Ossian's composition, I cannot determine. It is generally ascribed to him, and has much of his manner; but some traditions mention it as an imitation by some later bard.——As it has some poetical merit, I have subjoined it. [M]

The spouse of Dargo came in tears: for Dargo was no more! The heroes sigh over Lartho's chief: and what shall sad Mingala do? The dark soul vanished like morning mist, before the king of spears: but the generous glowed in his presence like the morning star.

Who was the fairest and most lovely? Who but Collath's stately son? Who sat in the midst of the wise, but Dargo of the mighty deeds?

Thy hand touched the trembling harp: Thy voice was soft as summer-winds.—Ah me! what shall the heroes say? for Dargo fell before a boar. Pale is the lovely cheek; the look of which was firm in danger!—Why hast thou failed on our hills, thou fairer than the beams of the sun?

The daughter of Adonfion was lovely in the eyes of the valiant; she was lovely in their eyes, but she chose to be the spouse of Dargo.

But thou art alone, Mingala! the night is coming with its clouds; where is the bed of thy repose? Where but in the tomb of Dargo?

Why dost thou lift the stone, O bard! why dost thou shut the narrow house? Mingala's eyes are heavy, bard! She must sleep with Dargo.

Last night I heard the song of joy in Lartho's lofty hall. But silence now dwells around my bed. Mingala rests with Dargo.[26]

LATHMON:

A POEM[1].

Selma, thy halls are silent. There is no sound in the woods of Morven. The wave tumbles alone on the coast. The silent beam of the sun is on the field. The daughters of Morven come forth, like the bow of the shower; they look towards green Ullin[2] for the white sails of the king. He had promised to return, but the winds of the north arose.

Who pours from the eastern hill, like a stream of darkness? It is the host of Lathmon. He was heard of the absence of Fingal. He trusts in the wind of the north. His soul brightens with joy. Why dost thou come, Lathmon? The mighty are not in Selma. Why comest thou with thy forward spear? Will the daughters of Morven fight? But stop, O mighty stream, in thy course! Does not Lathmon behold these sails? Why dost thou vanish, Lathmon, like the mist of the lake? But the squally storm is behind thee; Fingal pursues thy steps!

The king of Morven started from sleep, as we rolled on the dark-blue wave. He stretched his hand to his spear, and his heroes rose around. We knew that he had seen his fathers, for they often descended to his dreams, when the sword of the foe rose over the land; and the battle darkened before us.

Whither hast thou fled, O wind, said the king of Morven? Dost thou rustle in the chambers of the south, and pursue the shower in other lands? Why dost thou not come to my sails? to the blue face of my seas? The foe is in the land of Morven, and the king is absent. But let each bind on his mail, and each assume his shield. Stretch every spear over the wave; let every sword be unsheathed. Lathmon[3] is before us with his host: he that fled[4] from Fingal on the plains of Lona. But he returns, like a collected stream, and his roar is between our hills.

Such were the words of Fingal. We rushed into Carmona's bay. Ossian ascended the hill; and thrice struck his bossy shield. The rock of Morven replied; and the bounding roes came forth. The foes were troubled in my presence: and collected their darkened host; for I stood, like a cloud on the hill, rejoicing in the arms of my youth.

Morni[5] sat beneath a tree, at the roaring waters of Strumon[6]: his locks of age are gray: he leans forward on his staff; young Gaul is near the hero, hearing the battles of his youth.[7] Often did he rise, in the fire of his soul, at the mighty deeds of Morni.

The aged heard the sound of Ossian's shield: he knew the sign of battle. He started at once from his place. His gray hair parted on his back. He remembers the actions of other years. My son, he said to fair-haired Gaul, I hear the sound of battle. The king of Morven is returned, the sign of war is heard.[8] Go to the halls of Strumon, and bring his arms to Morni. Bring the arms which my father wore in his age,[9] for my arm begins to fail. Take thou thy armour, O Gaul; and rush to the first of thy battles. Let thine arm reach to the renown of thy fathers. Be thy course in the field, like the eagle's wing. Why shouldst thou fear death, my son! the valiant fall with fame; their shields turn the dark stream of danger away, and renown dwells on their gray[10] hairs. Dost thou not see, O Gaul, how the steps of my age are honoured? Morni moves forth, and the young meet him, with reverence, and turn their eyes, with silent joy, on his course. But I never fled from danger, my son! my sword lightened through the darkness of battle. The stranger melted before me; the mighty were blasted in my presence.

Gaul brought the arms to Morni: the aged warrior covered himself with steel. He took the spear in his hand, which was often[11] stained with the blood of the valiant. He came towards Fingal, his son attended his steps. The son of Comhal rejoiced over the warrior,[12] when he came in the locks of his age.

King of the[13] roaring Strumon! said the rising joy[14] of Fingal; do I behold thee in arms, after thy strength has failed? Often has Morni shone in battles, like the beam of the rising sun; when he disperses the storms of the hill, and brings peace to the glittering fields. But why didst thou not rest in thine age? Thy renown is in the song. The people behold thee, and bless the departure of mighty Morni. Why didst thou not rest in thine age? For the foe will vanish before Fingal.

Son of Comhal, replied the chief, the strength of Morni's arm has failed. I attempt to draw the sword of my youth, but it remains in its place. I throw the spear, but it falls short of the mark; and I feel the weight of my shield. We decay, like the grass of the mountain, and our strength returns no more. I have a son, O Fingal, his soul has delighted in the actions of Morni's youth; but his sword has not been lifted against the foe, neither has his fame begun. I come with him to battle; to direct his arm. His renown will be a sun[15] to my soul, in the dark hour of my departure. O that the name of Morni were forgot among the people! that the heroes would only say, "Behold the father of Gaul!"

King of Strumon, Fingal replied, Gaul shall lift the sword in battle. But he shall lift it before Fingal; my arm shall defend his youth. But rest thou in the halls of Selma; and hear of our renown. Bid the harp be strung; and the voice of the bard arise, that those who fall may rejoice in their fame; and the soul of Morni brighten with gladness.——Ossian! thou hast fought in battles: the blood of strangers is on thy spear: let thy course be with Gaul in the strife; but depart not from the side of Fingal; lest the foe find you alone; and your fame fail at once.[16]

I saw[17] Gaul in his arms, and my soul was mixed with his: for the fire of the battle was in his eyes! he looked to the foe with joy. We spoke the words of friendship in secret; and the lightning of our swords poured together; for we drew them behind the wood, and tried the strength of our arms on the empty air.

Night came down on Morven. Fingal sat at the beam of the oak. Morni sat by his side with all his gray waving locks. Their discourse is of other times, and the actions of their fathers. Three bards, at times, touched the harp; and Ullin was near with his song. He sung of the mighty Comhal; but darkness gathered[18] on Morni's brow. He rolled his red eye on Ullin; and the song of the bard ceased. Fingal observed the aged hero, and he mildly spoke.

Chief of Strumon, why that darkness? Let the days of other years be forgot. Our fathers contended in battle; but we meet together, at the feast. Our swords are turned on the foes, and they melt before us on the field. Let the days of our fathers be forgot, king[19] of mossy Strumon.

King of Morven, replied the chief, I remember thy father with joy. He was terrible in battle; the rage[20] of the chief was deadly. My eyes were full of tears, when the king of heroes fell. The valiant fall, O Fingal, and the feeble remain on the hills. How many heroes have passed away, in the days of Morni! And I did not shun the battle; neither did I fly from the strife of the valiant.

Now let the friends of Fingal rest; for the night is around; that they may rise, with strength, to battle against car-borne Lathmon. I hear the sound of his host, like thunder heard on a distant heath.[21] Ossian! and fair-haired Gaul! ye are swift[22] in the race. Observe the foes of Fingal from that woody hill. But approach them not, your fathers are not near to shield you. Let not your fame fall at once. The valour of youth may fail.

We heard the words of the chief with joy, and moved in the clang of our arms. Our steps are on the woody hill. Heaven burns with all its stars. The meteors of death fly over the field. The distant noise of the foe reached our ears. It was then Gaul spoke, in his valour; his hand half-unsheathed the sword.

Son of Fingal, he said, why burns the soul of Gaul? My heart beats high. My steps are disordered; and my hand trembles on my sword. When I look towards the foe, my soul lightens before me, and I see their sleeping host. Tremble thus the souls of the valiant in battles of the spear?——How would the soul of Morni rise if we should rush on the foe! Our renown would grow in the song; and our steps be stately in the eyes of the brave.

Son of Morni, I replied, my soul delights in battle. I delight to shine in battle alone, and to give my name to the bards. But what if the foe should prevail; shall I behold the eyes of the king? They are terrible in his displeasure, and like the flames of death.—But I will not behold them in his wrath. Ossian shall prevail or fall. But shall the fame of the vanquished rise?—They pass away like a shadow. But the fame of Ossian shall rise. His deeds shall be like his fathers. Let us rush in our arms; son of Morni, let us rush to battle. Gaul! if thou shalt return, go to Selma's lofty wall.[23] Tell to

Evirallin[24] that I fell with fame; carry this sword to Branno's daughter. Let her give it to Oscar, when the years of his youth shall arise.

Son of Fingal, Gaul replied with a sigh; shall I return after Ossian is low!—What would my father say, and Fingal king of men? The feeble would turn their eyes and say, "Behold the mighty[25] Gaul who left his friend in his blood!" Ye shall not behold me, ye feeble, but in the midst of my renown. Ossian! I have heard from my father the mighty deeds of heroes; their mighty deeds when alone; for the soul increases in danger.

Son of Morni, I replied and strode before him on the heath, our fathers shall praise our valour, when they mourn our fall. A beam of gladness shall rise on their souls, when their eyes are full of tears. They will say, "Our sons have not fallen like the grass of the field,[26] for they spread death around them."——But why should we think of the narrow house? The sword defends the valiant. But death pursues the flight of the feeble; and their renown is not heard.

We rushed forward through night; and came to the roar of a stream which bent its blue course round the foe, through trees that echoed to its noise, we came to the bank of the stream, and saw the sleeping host. Their fires were decayed on the plain; and the lonely steps of their scouts were distant far. I stretched my spear before me to support my steps over the stream. But Gaul took my hand, and spoke the words of the valiant.

Shall[27] the son of Fingal rush on a sleeping foe? Shall he come like a blast by night when it overturns the young trees in secret? Fingal did not thus receive his fame, nor dwells renown on the gray hairs of Morni, for actions like these. Strike, Ossian, strike the shield of battle, and let their thousands rise. Let them meet Gaul in his first battle, that he may try the strength of his arm.

My soul rejoiced over the warrior, and my bursting tears descended. And the foe shall meet Gaul, I said: the fame of Morni's son shall arise. But rush not too far, my hero: let the gleam of thy steel be near to Ossian. Let our hands join in slaughter.——Gaul! dost thou not behold that rock? Its gray side dimly gleams to the stars. If the foe shall prevail, let our back be towards the rock. Then shall they fear to approach our spears; for death is in our hands.

I struck thrice my echoing shield. The starting foe arose. We rushed on in the sound of our arms. Their crowded steps fly over the heath; for they thought that the mighty Fingal came; and the strength of their arms withered away. The sound of their flight was like that of flame, when it rushes through the blasted groves.

It was then the spear of Gaul flew in its strength: it was then his sword arose. Cremor fell; and mighty Leth. Dunthormo struggled in his blood. The steel rushed through Crotho's[28] side, as bent, he rose on his spear; the black stream poured from the wound, and hissed on the half-extinguished oak. Cathmin saw the steps of the hero behind him, and ascended a blasted tree; but the spear pierced him from behind. Shrieking, panting, he fell; moss and withered branches pursue his fall, and strew the blue arms of Gaul.

Such were thy deeds, son of Morni, in the first of thy battles. Nor slept the sword by thy side, thou last of Fingal's race! Ossian rushed forward in his strength, and the people fell before him; as the grass by the staff of the boy, when he whistles along the field, and the gray beard of the thistle falls. But careless the youth moves on; his steps are towards the desart.

Gray morning rose around us, the winding streams are bright along the heath. The foe gathered on a hill; and the rage of Lathmon rose. He bent the red eye of his wrath: he is silent in his rising grief. He often struck his bossy shield; and his steps are unequal on the heath. I saw the distant darkness of the hero, and I spoke to Morni's son.

Car-borne[29] chief of Strumon, dost thou behold the foe? They gather on the hill in their wrath. Let our steps be towards the king[30]. He shall rise in his strength, and the host of Lathmon vanish. Our fame is around us, warrior, the eyes of the aged[31] will rejoice. But let us fly, son of Morni, Lathmon descends the hill.

Then let our steps[32] be slow, replied the fair-haired Gaul; lest the foe say, with a smile, "Behold the warriors of night, they are, like ghosts, terrible in darkness, but they melt away before the beam of the east." Ossian, take the shield of Gormar who fell beneath thy spear, that the aged heroes may rejoice, when they shall behold the actions of their sons.

Such were our words on the plain, when Sulmath[33] came to car-borne Lathmon: Sulmath chief of Dutha at the dark-rolling stream of Duvranna[34]. Why dost thou not rush, son of Nuäth, with a thousand of thy heroes? Why dost thou not descend with thy host, before the warriors fly? Their blue arms are beaming to the rising light, and their steps are before us on the heath.

Son of the feeble hand, said Lathmon, shall my host descend! They[35] are but two, son of Dutha, and shall a thousand lift their steel! Nuäth would mourn, in his hall, for the departure of his fame. His eyes would turn from Lathmon, when the tread of his feet approached.——Go thou to the heroes, chief of Dutha, for I behold the stately steps of Ossian. His fame is worthy of my steel; let him fight with Lathmon.[36]

The noble Sulmath came. I rejoiced in the words of the king. I raised the shield on my arm; and Gaul placed in my hand the sword of Morni. We returned to the murmuring stream; Lathmon came in his strength. His dark host rolled, like the clouds, behind him: but the son of Nuäth was bright in his steel.

Son of Fingal, said the hero, thy fame has grown on our fall. How many lie there of my people by thy hand, thou king of men! Lift now thy spear against Lathmon; and lay the son of Nuäth low. Lay him low among his people,[37] or thou thyself must fall. It shall never be told in my halls that my warriors[38] fell in my presence; that they fell in the presence of Lathmon when his sword rested by his side: the blue eyes of Cutha[39] would roll in tears, and her steps be lonely in the vales of Dunlathmon.

Neither shall it be told, I replied, that the son of Fingal fled. Were his steps covered with darkness, yet would not Ossian fly; his soul would meet him and say, "Does the bard of Selma fear the foe?" No: he does not fear the foe. His joy is in the midst of battle.

Lathmon came on with his spear, and pierced the shield of Ossian. I felt the cold steel at my side; and drew the sword of Morni: I cut the spear in twain; the bright point fell glittering on the ground. The son of Nuäth burnt in his wrath, and lifted high his sounding shield. His dark eyes rolled above it, as bending forward, it shone like a gate of brass. But Ossian's spear pierced the brightness of its bosses, and sunk in a tree that rose behind. The shield hung on the quivering lance! but Lathmon still advanced. Gaul foresaw the fall of the chief, and stretched his buckler before my sword; when it descended, in a stream of light, over the king of Dunlathmon.

Lathmon beheld the son of Morni, and the tear started from his eye. He threw the sword of his fathers on the ground, and spoke the words of the valiant. Why should Lathmon fight against the first of mortal[40] men? Your souls are beams from heaven; your swords the flames of death. Who can equal the renown of the heroes, whose actions are so great in youth! O that ye were in the halls of Nuäth, in the green dwelling of Lathmon! then would my father say, that his son did not yield to the feeble.—But who comes, a mighty stream, along the echoing heath? the little hills are troubled before him, and a thousand spirits[41] are on the beams of his steel; the spirits[42] of those who are to fall by the arm of the king of resounding Morven.—Happy art thou, O Fingal, thy sons shall fight thy battles; they go forth before thee; and they return with the steps of renown.

Fingal came, in his mildness, rejoicing in secret over the actions of his son. Morni's face brightened with gladness, and his aged eyes looked faintly through the tears of joy. We came to the halls of Selma, and sat round the feast of shells. The maids of the song came into our presence, and the mildly blushing Evirallin. Her dark[43] hair spread on her neck of snow, her eye rolled in secret on Ossian; she touched the harp of music, and we blessed the daughter of Branno.

Fingal rose in his place, and spoke to Dunlathmon's battling king.[44] The sword of Trenmor trembled by his side, as he lifted up his mighty arm. Son of Nuäth, he said, why dost thou search for fame in Morven? We are not of the race of the feeble; nor do our swords gleam over the weak. When did we come to Dunlathmon,[45] with the sound of war? Fingal does not delight in battle, though his arm is strong. My renown grows on the fall of the haughty. The lightning[46] of my steel pours on the proud in arms. The battle comes; and the tombs of the valiant rise; the tombs of my people rise, O my fathers! and I at last must remain alone. But I will remain renowned, and the departure of my soul shall be one stream of light. Lathmon! retire to thy place. Turn thy battles to other lands. The race of Morven are renowned, and their foes are the sons of the unhappy.

OITHÓNA:

A POEM[1].

Darkness dwells around Dunlathmon, though the moon shews half her face on the hill. The daughter of night turns her eyes away; for she beholds the grief that is coming.—The son of Morni is on the plain; but there is no sound in the hall. No long-streaming[2] beam of light comes trembling through the gloom. The voice of Oithóna[3] is not heard amidst the noise of the streams of Duvranna.——

Whither art thou gone in thy beauty, dark-haired daughter of Nuäth? Lathmon is in the field of the valiant, but thou didst promise to remain in the hall; thou didst promise to remain in the hall till the son of Morni returned. Till he returned from Strumon, to the maid of his love. The tear was on thy cheek at his departure: the sigh rose in secret in thy breast. But thou dost not come to meet him, with songs, with the lightly-trembling sound of the harp.——

Such were the words of Gaul, when he came to Dunlathmon's towers. The gates were open and dark. The winds were blustering in the hall. The trees strowed the threshold with leaves; and the murmur of night was abroad.—Sad and silent, at a rock, the son of Morni sat: his soul trembled for the maid; but he knew not whither to turn his course. The son[4] of Leth stood at a distance, and heard the winds in his bushy hair. But he did not raise his voice, for he saw the sorrow of Gaul.

Sleep descended on the heroes.[5] The visions of night arose. Oithóna stood in a dream, before the eyes of Morni's son. Her dark[6] hair was loose and disordered: her lovely eye rolled[7] in tears. Blood stained her snowy arm. The robe half hid the wound of her breast. She stood over the chief, and her voice was heard.[8]

Sleeps the son of Morni, he that was lovely in the eyes of Oithóna? Sleeps Gaul at the distant rock, and the daughter of Nuäth low? The sea rolls round the dark isle of Tromáthon; I sit in my tears in the cave. Nor do I sit alone, O Gaul, the dark chief of Cuthal is there. He is there in the rage of his love.—And what can Oithóna do?

A rougher blast rushed through the oak. The dream of night departed. Gaul took his aspen spear; he stood in the rage of wrath.[9] Often did his eyes turn to the east, and accuse the lagging light.—At length the morning came forth. The hero lifted up the sail. The winds came rustling from the hill; and he bounded on the waves of the deep.—On the third day arose Tromathon[10], like a blue shield in the midst of the sea. The white wave roared against its rocks; sad Oithóna sat on the coast. She looked on the rolling waters, and her tears descend.——But when she saw Gaul in his arms, she started and turned her eyes away. Her lovely cheek is bent and red; her white arm trembles by her side.—Thrice she strove to fly from his presence; but her[11] steps failed her as she went.

Daughter of Nuäth, said the hero, why dost thou fly from Gaul? Do my eyes send forth the flame of death? Or darkens hatred in my soul? Thou art to me the beam of the east rising in a land unknown. But thou coverest thy face with sadness, daughter of high Dunlathmon![12] Is the foe of Oithóna near? My soul burns to meet him in battle. The sword trembles on the side of Gaul, and longs to glitter in his hand.——Speak, daughter of Nuäth, dost thou not behold my tears?

Car-borne[13] chief of Strumon, replied the sighing[14] maid, why comest thou over the dark-blue wave to Nuäth's mournful daughter? Why did I not pass away in secret, like the flower of the rock, that lifts its fair head unseen, and strows its withered leaves on the blast? Why didst thou come, O Gaul, to hear my departing sigh? I pass away in my youth; and my name shall not be heard. Or it will be heard with sorrow,[15] and the tears of Nuäth will fall. Thou wilt be sad, son of Morni, for the fallen[16] fame of Oithóna. But she shall sleep in the narrow tomb, far from the voice of the mourner. ——Why didst thou come, chief of Strumon, to the sea-beat rocks of Tromathon.

I came to meet thy foes, daughter of car-borne Nuäth! the death of Cuthal's chief darkens before me; or Morni's son shall fall.—Oithóna! when Gaul is low, raise my tomb on that oozy rock; and when the dark-bounding ship shall pass, call the sons of the sea; call them, and give this sword, that they may carry it to Morni's hall; that the grey-haired hero[17] may cease to look towards the desart for the return of his son.

And shall the daughter of Nuäth live, she replied with a bursting sigh? Shall I live in Tromáthon, and the son of Morni low? My heart is not of that rock; nor my soul careless as that sea, which lifts its blue waves to every wind, and rolls beneath the storm. The blast which shall lay thee low, shall spread the branches of Oithóna on earth. We shall wither together, son of car-borne Morni!——The narrow house is pleasant to me, and the gray stone of the dead: for never more will I leave thy rocks, sea-surrounded Tromáthon!—Night[18] came on with her clouds, after the departure of Lathmon, when he went to the wars of his fathers, to the moss-covered rock of Duthórmoth; night came on, and I sat in the hall, at the beam of the oak. The wind was abroad in the trees. I heard the sound of arms. Joy rose in my face; for I thought of thy return. It was the chief of Cuthal, the red-haired strength of Dunrommath. His eyes rolled in fire: the blood of my people was on his sword. They who defended Oithóna fell by the gloomy chief.—— What could I do? My arm was weak; it could not lift the spear. He took me in my grief, amidst my tears he raised the sail. He feared the returning strength of[19] Lathmon, the brother of unhappy Oithóna.——But behold, he comes with his people! the dark wave is divided before him!—Whither wilt thou turn thy steps, son of Morni? Many are the warriors of Dunrommath![20]

My steps never turned from battle, replied the hero, as he unsheathed his sword; and shall I begin to fear, Oithóna, when thy foes are near? Go to thy cave, daughter of Nuäth,[21] till our battle cease. Son of Leth, bring the bows of our fathers; and the sounding quiver of Morni. Let our three warriors bend the yew. Ourselves will lift the spear. They are an host on the rock; but our souls are strong.[22]

The daughter of Nuäth[23] went to the cave: a troubled joy rose on her mind, like the red path of the lightning on the stormy cloud.—Her soul was resolved, and the tear was dried from her wildly-looking eye.—Dunrommath slowly approached; for he saw the son of Morni. Contempt contracted his face, a smile is on his dark-brown cheek; his red eye rolled, half-conceal'd, beneath his shaggy brows.

Whence are the sons of the sea, begun the gloomy chief? Have the winds driven you to the rocks of Tromáthon? Or come you in search of the white-handed daughter of Nuäth?[24] The sons of the unhappy, ye feeble men, come to the hand of Dunrommath. His eye spares not the weak; and he delights in the blood of strangers. Oithóna is a beam of light, and the chief of Cuthal enjoys it in secret; wouldst thou come on its loveliness like a cloud, son of the feeble hand!—Thou mayst come, but shalt thou return to the halls of thy fathers?

Dost thou not know me, said Gaul, red-haired chief of Cuthal? Thy feet were swift on the heath, in the battle of car-borne Lathmon; when the sword of Morni's son pursued his host, in Morven's woody land. Dunrommath! thy words are mighty, for thy warriors gather behind thee. But do I fear them, son of pride? I am not of the race of the feeble.

Gaul advanced in his arms; Dunrommath shrunk behind his people. But the spear of Gaul pierced the gloomy chief, and his sword lopped off his head, as it bended in death.——The son of Morni shook it thrice by the lock; the warriors of Dunrommath fled. The arrows of Morven pursued them: ten fell on the mossy rocks. The rest lift the sounding sail, and bound on the echoing[25] deep.

Gaul advanced towards the cave of Oithóna. He beheld a youth leaning against a rock. An arrow had pierced his side; and his eye rolled faintly beneath his helmet.—The soul of Morni's son is sad, he came and spoke the words of peace.

Can the hand of Gaul heal thee, youth of the mournful brow? I have searched for the herbs of the mountains; I have gathered them on the secret banks of their streams. My hand has closed the wound of the valiant, and their eyes have blessed the son of Morni. Where dwelt thy fathers, warrior? Were they of the sons of the mighty? Sadness shall come, like night, on thy native streams; for thou art fallen in thy youth.——

My fathers, replied the stranger, were of the sons[26] of the mighty; but they shall not be sad; for my fame is departed like morning mist. High walls rise on the banks of Duvranna; and see their mossy towers in the stream; a rock ascends behind them with its bending firs.[27] Thou mayst behold it far distant. There my brother dwells. He is renowned in battle: give him this glittering helmet.

The helmet fell from the hand of Gaul; for it was the wounded Oithóna. She had armed herself in the cave, and came in search of death. Her heavy eyes are half closed; the blood pours from her side.[28]——

Son of Morni, she said, prepare the narrow tomb. Sleep comes, like a cloud,[29] on my soul. The eyes of Oithóna are dim. O had I dwelt at Duvranna, in the bright beam of my fame! then had my years come on with joy; and the virgins would bless my steps. But I fall in youth, son of Morni, and my father shall blush in his hall.——

She fell pale on the rock of Tromáthon. The mournful hero[30] raised her tomb.——He came to Morven; but we saw the darkness of his soul. Ossian took the harp in the praise of Oithóna. The brightness of the face of Gaul returned. But his sigh rose, at times, in the midst of his friends, like blasts that shake their unfrequent wings, after the stormy winds are laid.

CROMA:

A POEM[1].

It was the voice of my love! few are his visits to the dreams[2] of Malvina!
Open your airy halls, ye fathers of mighty Toscar.[3] Unfold the gates of your
clouds; the steps of Malvina's departure[4] are near. I have heard a voice in
my dream. I feel the fluttering of my soul. Why didst thou come, O blast,
from the dark-rolling[5] of the lake? Thy rustling wing was in the trees, the
dream of Malvina departed.[6] But she beheld her love, when his robe of mist
flew on the wind; the beam of the sun was on his skirts, they glittered like
the gold of the stranger. It was the voice of my love! few are his visits[7] to
my dreams!

But thou dwellest in the soul of Malvina, son of mighty Ossian. My sighs
arise with the beam of the east; my tears descend with the drops of night. I
was a lovely tree, in thy presence, Oscar, with all my branches round me;
but thy death came like a blast from the desert, and laid my green head low;
the spring returned with its showers, but no leaf of mine arose. The virgins
saw me silent in the hall, and they touched the harp of joy. The tear was on
the cheek of Malvina: the virgins beheld me in my grief. Why art thou sad,
they said; thou first of the maids of Lutha? Was he lovely as the beam of the
morning, and stately in thy sight?

Pleasant is thy song in Ossian's ear, daughter of streamy Lutha! Thou hast
heard the music of departed bards in the dream of thy rest, when sleep fell
on thine eyes, at the murmur of Moruth[8]. When thou didst return from the
chace, in the day of the sun, thou hast heard the music of the bards, and thy
song is lovely. It is lovely, O Malvina, but it melts the soul. There is a joy in
grief when peace dwells in the breast of the sad. But sorrow wastes the
mournful, O daughter of Toscar, and their days are few. They fall away, like
the flower on which the sun looks in his strength after the mildew has
passed over it, and its head is heavy with the drops of night. Attend to the
tale of Ossian, O maid; he remembers the days of his youth.

The king commanded; I raised my sails, and rushed into the bay of
Croma; into Croma's sounding bay in lovely Innis-fail[9]. High on the coast
arose the towers of Crothar king of spears; Crothar renowned in the battles
of his youth; but age dwelt then around the chief. Rothmar raised the sword
against the hero; and the wrath of Fingal burned. He sent Ossian to meet
Rothmar in battle, for the chief of Croma was the companion of his youth.

I sent the bard before me with songs; I came into the hall of Crothar.
There sat the hero[10] amidst the arms of his fathers, but his eyes had failed.
His gray locks waved around a staff, on which the warrior leaned. He

hummed the song of other times, when the sound of our arms reached his ears. Crothar rose, stretched his aged hand, and blessed the son of Fingal.

Ossian! said the hero, the strength of Crothar's arm has failed. O could I lift the sword, as on the day that Fingal fought at Strutha! He was the first of mortal[11] men; but Crothar had also his fame. The king of Morven praised me, and he placed on my arm the bossy shield of Calthar, whom the hero[12] had slain in war. Dost thou not behold it on the wall, for Crothar's eyes have failed? Is thy strength, like thy fathers, Ossian? let the aged feel thine arm.

I gave my arm to the king; he feels it with his aged hands. The sigh rose in his breast, and his tears descended. Thou art strong, my son, he said, but not like the king of Morven. But who is like that hero among the mighty in war! Let the feast of my halls[13] be spread; and let my bards raise the song. Great is he that is within my walls, sons of echoing Croma!

The feast is spread. The harp is heard; and joy is in the hall. But it was joy covering a sigh, that darkly dwelt in every breast. It was like the faint beam of the moon spread on a cloud in heaven. At length the music ceased, and the aged king of Croma spoke; he spoke without a tear, but the sigh[14] swelled in the midst of his voice.

Son of Fingal! dost thou not behold the darkness of Crothar's hall of shells?[15] My soul was not dark[16] at the feast, when my people lived.[17] I rejoiced in the presence of strangers, when my son shone in the hall. But, Ossian, he is a beam that is departed, and left no streak of light behind. He is fallen, son of Fingal, in the battles of his father.——Rothmar the chief of grassy Tromlo heard that my eyes had failed; he heard that my arms were fixed in the hall, and the pride of his soul arose. He came towards Croma; my people fell before him. I took my arms in the hall,[18] but what could sightless Crothar do? My steps were unequal; my grief was great. I wished for the days that were past. Days! wherein I fought; and conquered in the field of blood. My son returned from the chace; the fair-haired Fovar-gormo[19]. He had not lifted his sword in battle, for his arm was young. But the soul of the youth was great; the fire of valour burnt in his eyes. He saw the disordered steps of his father, and his sigh arose. King of Croma, he said, is it because thou hast no son; is it for the weakness of Fovar-gormo's arm that thy sighs arise? I begin, my father, to feel the strength of my arm; I have drawn the sword of my youth; and I have bent the bow. Let me meet this Rothmar, with the youths[20] of Croma: let me meet him, O my father; for I feel my burning soul.

And thou shalt meet him, I said, son of the sightless Crothar! But let others advance before thee, that I may hear the tread of thy feet at thy return; for my eyes behold thee not, fair-haired Fovar-gormo!——He went, he met the foe; he fell. The foe[21] advances towards Croma. He who slew my son is near, with all his pointed spears.

It is not time to fill the shell, I replied, and took my spear. My people saw the fire of my eyes, and they rose around. All night we strode along the heath. Gray morning rose in the east. A green narrow vale appeared before us; nor did it want its blue stream.[22] The dark host of Rothmar are on its banks, with all their glittering arms. We fought along the vale; they fled; Rothmar sunk beneath my sword. Day had not descended in the west when I brought his arms to Crothar. The aged hero felt them with his hands; and joy brightened in his soul.

The people gather to the hall; the sound of the shells is heard.[23] Ten harps are strung; five bards advance, and sing, by turns[24], the praise of Ossian; they poured forth their burning souls, and the harp[25] answered to their voice. The joy of Croma was great: for peace returned to the land. The night came on with silence, and the morning returned with joy. No foe came in darkness, with his glittering spear. The joy of Croma was great; for the gloomy Rothmar was fallen.

I raised my voice for Fovar-gormo, when they laid the chief in earth. The aged Crothar was there, but his sigh was not heard. He searched for the wound of his son, and found it in his breast. Joy rose in the face of the aged. He came and spoke to Ossian.

King of spears! he said, my son has not fallen without his fame. The young warrior did not fly; but met death, as he went forward in his strength. Happy are they who die in youth, when their renown is heard! The feeble will not behold them in the hall; or smile at their trembling hands. Their memory shall be honoured in the song; the young tear of the virgin falls. But the aged wither away, by degrees, and the fame of their youth begins to be forgot.[26] They fall in secret; the sigh of their son is not heard. Joy is around their tomb; and the stone of their fame is placed without a tear. Happy are they who die in youth, when their renown is around them!

Note 23: Those extempore compositions were in great repute among succeeding bards. The pieces extant of that kind shew more of the good ear, than of the poetical genius of their authors. The translator has only met with one poem of this sort, which he thinks worthy of being preserved. It is a thousand years later than Ossian, but the authors seem to have observed his manner, and adopted some of his expressions. The story of it is this. Five bards, passing the night in the house of a chief, who was a poet himself, went severally to make their observations on, and returned with an extempore description of, night. The night happened to be one in October, as appears from the poem; and in the north of Scotland, it has all that variety which the bards ascribe to it, in their descriptions. [M]

FIRST BARD.

Night is dull and dark. The clouds rest on the hills. No star with green trembling beam; no moon looks from the sky. I hear the blast in the wood; but I hear it distant far. The stream of the valley murmurs; but its murmur is sullen and sad. From the tree at the grave of the dead the long-howling owl is heard. I see a dim form on the plain!—It is a ghost!—it fades—it flies. Some funeral shall pass this way: the meteor marks the path.

The distant dog is howling from the hut of the hill. The stag lies on the mountain moss: the hind is at his side. She hears the wind in his branchy horns. She starts, but lies again.

The roe is in the cleft of the rock; the heath-cock's head is beneath his wing. No beast, no bird is abroad, but the owl and the howling fox. She on a leafless tree: he in a cloud on the hill.

Dark, panting, trembling, sad the traveller has lost his way. Through shrubs, through thorns, he goes, along the gurgling rill. He fears the rock and the fen. He fears the ghost of night. The old tree groans to the blast; the falling branch resounds. The wind drives the withered burs, clung together, along the grass. It is the light tread of a ghost!—He trembles amidst the night.

Dark, dusky, howling is night, cloudy, windy, and full of ghosts! The dead are abroad! my friends, receive me from the night.

SECOND BARD.

The wind is up. The shower descends. The spirit of the mountain shrieks. Woods fall from high. Windows flap. The growing river roars. The traveller attempts the ford. Hark that shriek! he dies:—The storm drives the horse from the hill, the goat, the lowing cow. They tremble as drives the shower, beside the mouldering bank.

The hunter starts from sleep, in his lonely hut; he wakes the fire decayed. His wet dogs smoke around him. He fills the chinks with heath. Loud roar two mountain streams which meet beside his booth.

Sad on the side of a hill the wandering shepherd sits. The tree resounds above him. The stream roars down the rock. He waits for the rising moon to guide him to his home.

Ghosts ride on the storm to-night. Sweet is their voice between the squalls of wind. Their songs are of other worlds.

The rain is past. The dry wind blows. Streams roar, and windows flap. Cold drops fall from the roof. I see the starry sky. But the shower gathers again. The west is gloomy and dark. Night is stormy and dismal; receive me, my friends, from night.

THIRD BARD.

The wind still sounds between the hills: and whistles through the grass of the rock. The firs fall from their place. The turfy hut is torn. The clouds, divided, fly over the sky, and shew the burning stars. The meteor, token of death! flies sparkling through the gloom. It rests on the hill. I see the withered fern, the dark-browed rock, the fallen oak. Who is that in his shrowd beneath the tree, by the stream?

The waves dark-tumble on the lake, and lash its rocky sides. The boat is brimful in the cove; the oars on the rocking tide. A maid sits sad beside the rock, and eyes the rolling stream. Her lover promised to come. She saw his boat, when yet it was light, on the lake. Is this his broken boat on the shore? Are these his groans on the wind?

Hark! the hail rattles around. The flaky snow descends. The tops of the hills are white. The stormy winds abate. Various is the night and cold; receive me, my friends, from night.

FOURTH BARD.

Night is calm and fair; blue, starry, settled is night. The winds, with the clouds, are gone. They sink behind the hill. The moon is up on the mountain. Trees glitter:[27] streams shine on the rock. Bright rolls the settled lake; bright the stream of the vale.

I see the trees overturned; the shocks of corn on the plain. The wakeful hind rebuilds the shocks, and whistles on the distant field.

Calm, settled, fair is night!—Who comes from the place of the dead? That form with the robe of snow; white arms and dark-brown hair! It is the daughter of the chief of the people; she that lately fell! Come, let us view thee, O maid! thou that hast been the delight of heroes! The blast drives the phantom away; white, without form, it ascends the hill.

The breezes drive the blue mist, slowly over the narrow vale. It rises on the hill, and joins its head to heaven.—Night is settled, calm, blue, starry, bright with the moon. Receive me not, my friends, for lovely is the night.

FIFTH BARD.

Night is calm, but dreary. The moon is in a cloud in the west. Slow moves that pale beam along the shaded hill. The distant wave is heard. The torrent murmurs on the rock. The cock is heard from the booth. More than half the night is past. The house-wife, groping in the gloom, rekindles the settled fire. The hunter thinks that day approaches, and calls his bounding dogs. He ascends the hill and whistles on his way. A blast removes the cloud. He sees the starry plough of the north. Much of the night is to pass. He nods by the mossy rock.

Hark! the whirlwind is in the wood! A low murmur in the vale! It is the mighty army of the dead returning from the air.

The moon rests behind the hill. The beam is still on that lofty rock. Long are the shadows of the trees. Now it is dark over all. Night is dreary, silent, and dark; receive me, my friends, from night.

THE CHIEF.

Let clouds rest on the hills: spirits fly and travellers fear. Let the winds of the woods arise, the sounding storms descend. Roar streams and windows flap, and green-winged meteors fly; rise the pale moon from behind her hills, or inclose her head in clouds; night is alike to me, blue, stormy, or gloomy the sky. Night flies before the beam, when it is poured on the hill. The young day returns from his clouds, but we return no more.

Where are our chiefs of old? Where our kings of mighty name? The fields of their battles are silent. Scarce their mossy tombs remain. We shall also be forgot. This lofty house shall fall. Our sons shall not behold the ruins in grass. They shall ask of the aged, "Where stood the walls of our fathers?"

Raise the song, and strike the harp; send round the shells of joy. Suspend a hundred tapers on high. Youths and maids begin the dance. Let some gray bard be near me to tell the deeds of other times; of kings renowned in our land, of chiefs we behold no more. Thus let the night pass until morning shall appear in our halls. Then let the bow be at hand, the dogs, the youths of the chace. We shall ascend the hill with day; and awake the deer.[28]

BERRATHON:

A POEM[1].

Bend thy blue course, O stream, round the narrow plain of Lutha[2]. Let the green woods hang over it from their mountains: and the sun look on it at noon. The thistle is there on its rock, and shakes its beard to the wind. The flower hangs its heavy head, waving, at times, to the gale. Why dost thou awake me, O gale, it seems to say, I am covered with the drops of heaven? The time of my fading is near, and the blast that shall scatter my leaves. To-morrow shall the traveller come, he that saw me in my beauty shall come; his eyes will search the field, but they will not find me?—So shall they search in vain, for the voice of Cona, after it has failed in the field. The hunter shall come forth in the morning, and the voice of my harp shall not be heard. "Where is the son of car-borne Fingal?" The tear will be on his cheek.

Then come thou, O Malvina[3], with all thy music, come; lay Ossian in the plain of Lutha: let his tomb rise in the lovely field.—Malvina! where art thou, with thy songs: with the soft sound of thy steps?—Son[4] of Alpin art thou near? where is the daughter of Toscar?

I passed, O son of Fingal, by Tar-lutha's[5] mossy walls. The smoke of the hall was ceased: silence was among the trees of the hill. The voice of the chace was over. I saw the daughters of the bow. I asked about Malvina, but they answered not. They turned their faces away: thin darkness covered their beauty. They were like stars, on a rainy hill, by night, each looking faintly through her mist.

Pleasant[6] be thy rest, O lovely beam! soon hast thou set on our hills! The steps of thy departure were stately, like the moon on the blue, trembling wave. But thou hast left us in darkness, first of the maids of Lutha! We sit, at the rock, and there is no voice; no light but the meteor of fire! Soon hast thou set, Malvina, daughter of generous Toscar!

But thou risest like the beam of the east, among the spirits of thy friends, where they sit in their stormy halls, the chambers of the thunder.——A cloud hovers over Cona: its blue curling sides are high. The winds are beneath it, with their wings; within it is the dwelling[7] of Fingal. There the hero sits in darkness; his airy spear is in his hand. His shield half covered with clouds, is like the darkened moon; when one half still remains in the wave, and the other looks sickly on the field.

His friends sit around the king, on mist; and hear the songs of Ullin: he strikes the half-viewless harp; and raises the feeble voice. The lesser heroes, with a thousand meteors, light the airy hall. Malvina rises, in the midst; a blush is on her cheek. She beholds the unknown faces of her fathers, and turns aside her humid eyes.

Art thou come so soon, said Fingal, daughter of generous Toscar? Sadness dwells in the halls of Lutha. My aged son[8] is sad. I hear the breeze of Cona, that was wont to lift thy heavy locks. It comes to the hall, but thou art not there; its voice is mournful among the arms of thy fathers. Go with thy rustling wing, O breeze! and sigh on Malvina's tomb. It rises yonder beneath the rock, at the blue stream of Lutha. The maids[9] are departed to their place; and thou alone, O breeze, mournest there.

But who comes from the dusky west, supported on a cloud? A smile is on his gray, watry face; his locks of mist fly on the wind: he bends forward on his airy spear: it is thy father, Malvina! Why shinest thou, so soon, on our clouds, he says, O lovely light of Lutha!—But thou wert sad, my daughter, for thy friends were passed away. The sons of little men[10] were in the hall; and none remained of the heroes, but Ossian king of spears.

And dost thou remember Ossian, car-borne Toscar[11] son of Conloch? The battles of our youth were many; our swords went together to the field. They saw us coming like two falling rocks; and the sons of the stranger fled. There come the warriors of Cona, they said; their steps are in the paths of the vanquished.[12]

Draw near, son of Alpin, to the song of the aged. The actions of other times are in my soul: my memory beams on the days that are past. On the days of the mighty Toscar, when our path was in the deep. Draw near, son of Alpin, to the last sound[13] of the voice of Cona.

The king of Morven commanded, and I raised my sails to the wind. Toscar chief of Lutha stood at my side, as I rose on the dark-blue wave. Our course was to sea-surrounded Berrathon[14], the isle of many storms. There dwelt, with his locks of age, the stately strength of Larthmor. Larthmor who spread the feast of shells to Comhal's mighty son,[15] when he went to Starno's halls, in the days of Agandecca. But when the chief was old, the pride of his son arose, the pride of fair-haired Uthal, the love of a thousand maids. He bound the aged Larthmor, and dwelt in his sounding halls.

Long pined the king in his cave, beside his rolling sea. Morning[16] did not come to his dwelling; nor the burning oak by night. But the wind of ocean was there, and the parting beam of the moon. The red star looked on the king, when it trembled on the western wave. Snitho came to Selma's hall: Snitho companion of Larthmor's youth. He told of the king of Berrathon: the wrath of Fingal rose. Thrice he assumed the spear, resolved to stretch his hand to Uthal. But the memory[17] of his actions rose before the king, and he sent his son and Toscar. Our joy was great on the rolling sea; and we often half-unsheathed our swords[18]. For never before had we fought alone, in the battles of the spear. Night came down on the ocean; the winds departed on their wings. Cold and pale is the moon. The red stars lift their heads.[19] Our course is slow along the coast of Berrathon; the white waves tumble on the rocks.

What voice is that, said Toscar, which comes between the sounds of the waves? It is soft but mournful, like the voice of departed bards. But I behold the maid[20], she sits on the rock alone. Her head bends on her arm of snow: her dark hair is in the wind. Hear, son of Fingal, her song, it is smooth as the gliding waters of Lavath.[21]—We came to the silent bay, and heard the maid of night.

How long will ye roll around me, blue-tumbling waters of ocean? My dwelling was not always in caves, nor beneath the whistling tree. The feast was spread in Torthóma's hall; my father delighted in my voice. The youths beheld me in the steps of my loveliness, and they blessed the dark-haired Nina-thoma. It was then thou didst come, O Uthal! like the sun of heaven. The souls of the virgins are thine, son of generous Larthmor! But why dost thou leave me alone in the midst of roaring waters. Was my soul dark with thy death? Did my white hand lift the sword? Why then hast thou left me alone, king of high Finthormo![22]

The tear started from my eye, when I heard the voice of the maid. I stood before her in my arms, and spoke the words of peace.——Lovely dweller of the cave, what sigh is in that breast? Shall Ossian lift his sword in thy presence, the destruction of thy foes?—Daughter of Torthóma, rise, I have heard the words of thy grief. The race of Morven are around thee, who never injured the weak. Come to our dark-bosomed ship, thou brighter than that setting moon. Our course is to the rocky Berrathon, to the echoing walls of Finthormo.——She came in her beauty, she came with all her lovely steps. Silent joy brightened in her face, as when the shadows fly from the field of spring; the blue-stream is rolling in brightness, and the green bush bends over its course.

The morning rose with its beams. We came to Rothma's bay. A boar rushed from the wood; my spear pierced his side.[23] I rejoiced over the blood[24], and foresaw my growing fame.——But now the sound of Uthal's train came from the high Finthormo; they spread over the heath to the chace of the boar. Himself comes slowly on, in the pride of his strength. He lifts two pointed spears. On his side is the hero's sword. Three youths carry his polished bows: the bounding of five dogs is before him. His warriors move on, at a distance, admiring the steps of the king. Stately was the son of Larthmor! but his soul was dark. Dark as the troubled face of the moon, when it foretels the storms.

We rose on the heath before the king; he stopt in the midst of his course. His warriors gathered around, and a gray-haired bard advanced. Whence are the sons of the strangers? begun the bard. The children of the unhappy come to Berrathon; to the sword of car-borne Uthal. He spreads no feast in his hall: the blood of strangers is on his streams. If from Selma's walls ye come, from the mossy walls of Fingal, chuse three youths to go to your king to tell of the fall of his people. Perhaps the hero may come and pour his blood on Uthal's sword; so shall the fame of Finthormo arise, like the growing tree of the vale.

Never will it rise, O bard, I said in the pride of my wrath. He would shrink in the presence of Fingal, whose eyes are the flames of death. The son of Comhal comes, and the kings vanish in his presence; they are rolled together, like mist, by the breath of his rage. Shall three tell to Fingal, that his people fell? Yes!—they may tell it, bard! but his people shall fall with fame.

I stood in the darkness of my strength; Toscar drew his sword at my side. The foe came on like a stream: the mingled sound of death arose. Man took man, shield met shield; steel mixed its beams with steel.—Darts hiss through air; spears ring on mails; and swords on broken bucklers bound. As the noise of an aged grove beneath the roaring wind, when a thousand ghosts break the trees by night, such was the din of arms.——But Uthal fell beneath my sword; and the sons of Berrathon fled.—It was then I saw him in his beauty, and the tear hung in my eye. Thou art fallen[25], young tree, I said, with all thy beauty round thee. Thou art fallen on thy plains, and the field is bare. The winds come from the desert, and there is no sound in thy leaves! Lovely art thou in death, son of car-borne Larthmor.

Nina-thoma sat on the shore, and heard the sound of battle. She turned her red eyes on Lethmal the gray-haired bard of Selma, for he had remained on the coast, with the daughter of Torthóma. Son of the times of old! she said, I hear the noise of death. Thy friends have met with Uthal and the chief is low! O that I had remained on the rock, inclosed with the tumbling waves! Then would my soul be sad, but his death would not reach my ear. Art thou fallen on thy heath, O son of high Finthormo! thou didst leave me on a rock, but my soul was full of thee. Son of high Finthormo! art thou fallen on thy heath?

She rose pale in her tears, and saw the bloody shield of Uthal; she saw it in Ossian's hand; her steps were distracted on the heath. She flew; she found him; she fell. Her soul came forth in a sigh. Her hair is spread on his face. My bursting tears descend. A tomb arose on the unhappy; and my song[26] was heard.

Rest, hapless children of youth! at the noise of that mossy stream. The virgins will see your tomb, at the chace, and turn away their weeping eyes. Your fame will be in the song; the voice of the harp will be heard in your praise. The daughters of Selma shall hear it; and your renown shall be in other lands.—Rest, children of youth, at the noise of the mossy stream.

Two days we remained on the coast. The heroes of Berrathon convened. We brought Larthmor to his halls; the feast of shells was spread.—The joy of the aged was great; he looked to the arms of his fathers; the arms which he left in his hall, when the pride of Uthal arose.——We were renowned before Larthmor, and he blessed the chiefs of Morven; but he knew not that his son was low, the stately strength of Uthal. They had told, that he had retired to the woods, with the tears of grief; they had told it, but he was silent in the tomb of Rothma's heath.

On the fourth day we raised our sails to the roar of the northern wind. Larthmor came to the coast, and his bards raised the song. The joy of the king was great, he looked to Rothma's gloomy heath; he saw the tomb of his son; and the memory of Uthal rose.——Who of my heroes, he said, lies there: he seems to have been of the kings of spears?[27] Was he renowned in my halls, before the pride of Uthal rose?

Ye are silent, ye sons of Berrathon, is the king of heroes low?—My heart melts for thee, O Uthal; though thy hand was against thy father.——O that I had remained in the cave! that my son had dwelt in Finthormo!——I might have heard the tread of his feet, when he went to the chace of the boar.—I might have heard his voice on the blast of my cave. Then would my soul be glad: but now darkness dwells in my halls.

Such were[28] my deeds, son of Alpin, when the arm of my youth was strong; such were the actions of Toscar, the car-borne son of Conloch. But Toscar is on his flying cloud; and I am alone at Lutha: my voice is like the last sound of the wind, when it forsakes the woods. But Ossian shall not be long alone, he sees the mist that shall receive his ghost. He beholds the mist that shall form his robe, when he appears on his hills. The sons of little[29] men shall behold me, and admire the stature of the chiefs of old. They shall creep to their caves, and look to the sky with fear; for my steps shall be in the clouds, and darkness shall roll on my side.

Lead, son of Alpin, lead the aged to his woods. The winds begin to rise. The dark wave of the lake resounds. Bends there not a tree from Mora with its branches bare? It bends, son of Alpin, in the rustling blast. My harp hangs on a blasted branch. The sound of its strings is mournful.——Does the wind touch thee, O harp, or is it some passing ghost!——It is the hand of Malvina! but bring me the harp, son of Alpin; another song shall rise. My soul shall depart in the sound; my fathers shall hear it in their airy hall.—Their dim faces shall hang, with joy, from their clouds; and their hands receive their son.

[30]The aged oak bends over the stream. It sighs with all its moss. The withered fern whistles near, and mixes, as it waves, with Ossian's hair.—— Strike the harp and raise the song: be near, with all your wings, ye winds. Bear the mournful sound away to Fingal's airy hall. Bear it to Fingal's hall, that he may hear the voice of his son; the voice of him that praised the mighty.—The blast of the north opens thy gates, O king, and I behold thee sitting on mist, dimly gleaming in all thine arms. Thy form now is not the terror of the valiant: but like a watery cloud; when we see the stars behind it with their weeping eyes. Thy shield is like the aged moon: thy sword a vapour half-kindled with fire. Dim and feeble is the chief, who travelled in brightness before.——

But thy steps[31] are on the winds of the desart, and the storms darken in thy hand. Thou takest the sun in thy wrath, and hidest him in thy clouds. The sons of little men are afraid; and a thousand showers descend.—

But when thou comest forth in thy mildness; the gale of the morning is near thy course. The sun laughs in his blue fields; and the gray stream winds in its valley.——The bushes shake their green heads in the wind. The roes bound towards the desart.

But there is a murmur in the heath! the stormy winds abate! I hear the voice of Fingal. Long has it been absent from mine ear!——Come, Ossian, come away, he says: Fingal has received his fame. We passed away, like flames that had shone for a season, our departure was in renown. Though the plains of our battles are dark and silent; our fame is in the four gray stones. The voice of Ossian has been heard; and the harp was strung in Selma.—Come Ossian, come away, he says, and fly with thy fathers on clouds.

And come I will,[32] thou king of men! the life of Ossian fails. I begin to vanish on Cona; and my steps are not seen in Selma. Beside the stone of Mora I shall fall asleep. The winds whistling in my grey hair shall not waken me.——Depart on thy wings, O wind: thou canst not disturb the rest of the bard. The night is long, but his eyes are heavy; depart, thou rustling blast.

But why art thou sad, son of Fingal? Why grows the cloud of thy soul? The chiefs of other times are departed; they have gone without their fame. The sons of future years shall pass away; and another race arise. The people are like the waves of ocean: like the leaves[33] of woody Morven, they pass away in the rustling blast, and other leaves lift their green heads.[34]—

Did thy beauty last, O Ryno[35]? Stood the strength of car-borne Oscar? Fingal himself passed away; and the halls of his fathers forgot his steps. ——And shalt thou remain, aged bard! when the mighty have failed?—— But my fame shall remain, and grow like the oak of Morven; which lifts its broad head to the storm, and rejoices in the course of the wind.

Note 35: Ryno, the son of Fingal, who was killed in Ireland, in the war against Swaran, [Fing. b. 5.] was remarkable for the beauty of his person, his swiftness and great exploits. Minvane[36], the daughter of Morni, and sister to Gaul so often mentioned in Ossian's compositions,[37] was in love with Ryno.—Her lamentation over her lover is[38] introduced as an episode in one of Ossian's great poems. The lamentation is the only part of the poem now extant, and as it has some poetical merit, I have subjoined it to this note. The poet represents Minvane as seeing, from one of the rocks of Morven, the fleet of Fingal returning from Ireland. [M]

She blushing sad, from Morven's rocks, bends over the darkly-rolling sea. She saw the youths in all their arms.—Where, Ryno, where art thou?

Our dark looks told that he was low!—That pale the hero flew on clouds! That in the grass of Morven's hills, his feeble voice was heard in wind!

And is the son of Fingal fallen, on Ullin's mossy plains? Strong was the arm that conquered him!—Ah me! I am alone.

Alone I will not be, ye winds! that lift my dark-brown hair. My sighs will not long mix with your stream; for I must sleep with Ryno.

I see thee not with beauty's steps returning from the chace.—The night is round Minvane's love; and silence dwells with Ryno.

Where are thy dogs, and where thy bow? Thy shield that was so strong? Thy sword like heaven's descending fire? The bloody spear of Ryno?

I see them mixed in thy ship;[39] I see them stained with blood.—No arms are in thy narrow hall, O darkly-dwelling Ryno!

When will the morning come, and say, arise, thou king of spears! arise, the hunters are abroad. The hinds are near thee, Ryno!

Away, thou fair-haired morning, away! the slumbering king hears thee not! The hinds bound over his narrow tomb; for death dwells round young Ryno.

But I will tread softly, my king! and steal to the bed of thy repose. Minvane will lie in silence, near her[40] slumbering Ryno.

The maids shall seek me; but they shall not find me: they shall follow my departure with songs. But I will not hear you, O maids: I sleep with fair-haired Ryno.

Advertisement.

Since the printing of the second Edition[1], Doctor Warner published a pamphlet, entitled, *Remarks on the History of Fingal and other Poems of Ossian.* The Doctor, it appears, is compiling a general history of Ireland, and is of opinion that Ossian, and the heroes he celebrates, were natives of that country. As he has advanced no argument to support so singular an opinion, I should have passed over his pamphlet in silence, had he not too precipitately accused me of a false quotation from O'Flaherty. I had said, in a note, on one of the lesser poems[2] of Ossian, that *Fingal is celebrated by the Irish historians, for his wisdom in making laws, his poetical genius, and his foreknowledge of events, and that O'Flaherty goes so far as to say, that Fingal's laws were extant, when he (O'Flaherty) wrote his Ogygia.* The Doctor denies that there is any such thing in O'Flaherty; and modestly quotes a passage from the same Author, which he supposes, I have misrepresented. I shall here give the whole paragraph, and the world will judge whether the Doctor has not been too hasty in his assertions. *Finnius ex Morniâ filia Thaddœi, filius Cuballi, jurisprudentia, super quâ scripta ejus hactenus extant, carminibus patriis, & ut quidam ferunt prophetiis celeberrimus, qui ob egregia sua, & militiæ suæ, facinora uberrimam vulgo, & poetis comminiscendi materiem relinquens, a nulla œtate reticebitur.* Ogyg. p. 338.

As the Doctor founds his claim of Ossian and his heroes, on the authority of some obscure passages in Keating and O'Flaherty, what he says on the subject stands self-confuted. These writers neither meet with, nor deserve credit. Credulous and partial, they have altogether disgraced the antiquities they meant to establish. Without producing records, or even following the ancient traditions of their country, they formed an ideal system of antiquity, from legends of modern invention. Sir James Ware, who was indefatigable in his researches, after the monuments of the Irish history, and had collected all the real, and pretendedly ancient manuscripts, concerning the antiquity of his nation, rejects as mere fiction and romance, all that is said concerning the times before Saint Patrick, and the reign of Leogaire, in the fifth century. I shall transcribe the passage, for the benefit of those who are compiling the history of Ireland from the *earliest ages,* and at the same time, caution them, not to look upon the antiquities of that country, through the false mediums of Keating and O'Flaherty: *Per exiguam superesse notitiam rerum in Hybernia gestarum ante exortam ibi evangelii auroram liquido constat. Neque me latet a viris nonnullis doctis plœraque quœ de antiquioribus illis temporibus ante S. Patricii in Hyberniam adventum traduntur, tanquam figmenta esse explosa. Notandum quidem descriptiones fere omnium quœ de illis temporibus (antiquioribus dico) extant, opera esse posteriorum seculorum.* Waræus de antiq. Præf. p. 1.

I must observe that the Doctor's claiming Ossian's poems (p. 8) *in forma pauperis*, not only invalidates his cause, but is also no very genteel compliment to the Irish nation. I am far from being of his opinion, that that nation can produce no monument of genius, but the works of Ossian, should these be tacitly ceded to them. On the contrary, I am convinced that Ireland has produced men of great and distinguished abilities, which, notwithstanding the Doctor's present opinion, I hope, will appear from his own history, even though he, confessedly, does not understand the language, or ancient records of that country.

THE

W O R K S

OF

O S S I A N,

THE

S O N of F I N G A L.

IN TWO VOLUMES.

Translated from the GALIC LANGUAGE

By JAMES MACPHERSON.

VOL. II. containing,

TEMORA, an Ancient EPIC POEM,

IN EIGHT BOOKS;

AND

SEVERAL OTHER POEMS.

THE THIRD EDITION.

To which is subjoined
A CRITICAL DISSERTATION on the
POEMS of OSSIAN. By HUGH BLAIR, D.D.

LONDON:

MDCCLXV.

A

D I S S E R T A T I O N.[1]

[2]The history of those nations which originally possessed the north of Europe, is little known.[3] Destitute of the use of letters, they themselves had not the means of transmitting their great actions to remote posterity. Foreign writers saw them only at a distance, and therefore their accounts are partial and undistinct.[4] The vanity of the Romans induced them to consider the nations beyond the pale of their empire as barbarians; and consequently their history unworthy of being investigated.[5] Some men, otherwise of great merit among ourselves, give into this confined opinion.[6] Having early imbibed their idea of exalted manners from the Greek and Roman writers, they scarcely ever afterwards have the fortitude to allow any dignity of character to any other ancient people.[7]

Without derogating from the fame of Greece and Rome, we may consider antiquity beyond the pale of their empire worthy of some attention. The nobler passions of the mind never shoot forth more free and unrestrained than in these times we call barbarous. That irregular manner of life, and those manly pursuits from which barbarity takes its name, are highly favorable to a strength of mind unknown in polished times. In advanced society the characters of men are more uniform and disguised. The human passions lie in some degree concealed behind forms, and artificial manners; and the powers of the soul, without an opportunity of exerting them, lose their vigor. The times of regular government, and polished manners, are therefore to be wished for by the feeble and weak in mind. An unsettled state, and those convulsions which attend it, is the proper field for an exalted character, and the exertion of great parts. Merit there rises always superior; no fortuitous event can raise the timid and mean into power. To those who look upon antiquity in this light, it is an agreeable prospect; and they alone can have real pleasure in tracing nations to their source.

The establishment of the Celtic states, in the north of Europe, is beyond the reach of their[8] written annals. The traditions and songs to which they trusted their history,[9] were lost, or altogether corrupted in their revolutions and migrations, which were so frequent and universal, that no kingdom in Europe is now possessed by its original inhabitants. Societies were formed, and kingdoms erected, from a mixture of nations, who, in process of time, lost all knowledge of their own origin.

If tradition could be depended upon, it is only among a people, from all time, free of intermixture with foreigners. We are to look for these among the mountains and inaccessible parts of a country: places, on account of their barrenness, uninviting to an enemy, or whose natural strength enabled the natives to repel invasions. Such are the inhabitants of the mountains of

Scotland. We, accordingly, find, that they differ materially from those who possess the low and more fertile part of the kingdom. Their language is pure and original, and their manners are those of an antient and unmixed race of men. Conscious of their own antiquity, they long despised others, as a new and mixed people. As they lived in a country only fit for pasture, they were free of that toil and business, which engross the attention of a commercial people. Their amusement consisted in hearing or repeating their songs and traditions, and these intirely turned on the antiquity of their nation, and the exploits of their forefathers. It is no wonder, therefore, that there are more remains of antiquity among them, than among any other people in Europe. Traditions, however, concerning remote periods, are only to be regarded, in so far as they co-incide with contemporary writers of undoubted credit and veracity.

No writers began their accounts from a more early period, than the historians of the Scots nation. Without records, or even tradition itself, they give a long list of antient kings, and a detail of their transactions, with a scrupulous exactness. One might naturally suppose, that, when they had no authentic annals, they should, at least, have recourse to the traditions of their country, and have reduced them into a regular system of history. Of both they seem to have been equally destitute. Born in the low country, and strangers to the ancient language of their nation, they contented themselves with copying from one another, and retailing the same fictions, in a new colour and dress.

John Fordun was the first who collected those fragments of the Scots history, which had escaped the brutal policy of Edward I. and reduced them into order. His accounts, in so far as they concerned recent transactions, deserved credit: beyond a certain period, they were fabulous and unsatisfactory. Some time before Fordun wrote, the king of England, in a letter to the pope, had run up the antiquity of his nation to a very remote æra. Fordun, possessed of all the national prejudice of the age, was unwilling that his country should yield, in point of antiquity, to a people, then its rivals and enemies. Destitute of annals in Scotland, he had recourse to Ireland, which, according to the vulgar errors of the times, was reckoned the first habitation of the Scots. He found, there, that the Irish bards had carried their pretensions to antiquity as high, if not beyond any nation in Europe. It was from them he took those improbable fictions, which form the first part of his history.

The writers that succeeded Fordun implicitly followed his system, though they sometimes varied from him in their relations of particular transactions, and the order of succession of their kings. As they had no new lights, and were, equally with him, unacquainted with the traditions of their country, their histories contain little information concerning the origin of the Scots. Even Buchanan himself, except the elegance and vigour of his stile, has very little to recommend him. Blinded with political prejudices, he seemed more anxious to turn the fictions of his predecessors to his own purposes, than to detect their misrepresentations, or investigate truth amidst the darkness which they had thrown round it. It therefore appears, that little can be collected from their own historians, concerning the first migration of the Scots into Britain.

That this island was peopled from Gaul admits of no doubt. Whether colonies came afterwards from the north of Europe is a matter of mere speculation. When South-Britain yielded to the power of the Romans, the unconquered nations to the north of the province were distinguished by the name of *Caledonians*. From their very name, it appears, that they were of those *Gauls*,[10] who possessed themselves originally of Britain. It is compounded of two *Celtic* words, *Caël* signifying *Celts*, or *Gauls*, and *Dun* or *Don, a hill*; so that *Caël-don*, or Caledonians, is as much as to say, the *Celts of the hill country*. The Highlanders, to this day, call themselves *Caël*, their language *Caëlic*, or *Galic*, and their country *Caëldoch*, which the Romans softened into *Caledonia*.[11] This, of itself, is sufficient to demonstrate, that they are the genuine descendents of the antient Caledonians, and not a pretended colony of *Scots*, who settled first in the north, in the third or fourth century.

From the double meaning of the word *Caël*, which signifies *strangers*, as well as *Gauls*, or *Celts*, some have imagined, that the ancestors of the Caledonians were of a different race from the rest of the Britons, and that they received their name upon that account. This opinion, say they, is supported by Tacitus, who, from several circumstances, concludes, that the Caledonians were of German extraction. A discussion of a point so intricate, at this distance of time, could neither be satisfactory nor important.

Towards the latter end of the third, and beginning of the fourth century, we meet with the *Scots* in the north. Porphyrius[12] makes the first mention of them about that time. As the *Scots* were not heard of before that period, most writers supposed them to have been a colony, newly come to Britain, and that the *Picts* were the only genuine descendents of the antient Caledonians. This mistake is easily removed. The Caledonians, in process of time, became naturally divided into two distinct nations, as possessing parts of the country intirely different in their nature and soil. The western coast of Scotland is hilly and barren; towards the east the country is plain, and fit for tillage. The inhabitants of the mountains, a roving and uncontrouled race of men, lived by feeding of cattle, and what they killed in hunting. Their employment did not fix them to one place. They removed from one heath to another, as suited best with their convenience or inclination. They were not, therefore, improperly called, by their neighbours, SCUITE, or *the wandering nation*; which is evidently the origin of the Roman name of *Scoti*.

On the other hand, the Caledonians, who possessed the east coast of Scotland, as the[13] division of the country was plain and fertile, applied themselves to agriculture, and raising of corn. It was from this, that the Galic name of the *Picts* proceeded; for they are called, in that language, *Cruithnich*, i.e. *the wheat or corn-eaters*. As the Picts lived in a country so different in its nature from that possessed by the Scots, so their national character suffered a material change. Unobstructed by mountains, or lakes, their communication with one another was free and frequent. Society, therefore, became sooner established among them, than among the Scots, and, consequently, they were much sooner governed by civil magistrates and laws. This, at last, produced so great a difference in the manners of the two nations, that they began to forget their common origin, and almost continual quarrels and animosities subsisted between them. These animosities, after some ages, ended in the subversion of the Pictish kingdom, but not in the total extirpation of the nation, according to most of the Scots writers, who seemed to think it more for the honour of their countrymen to annihilate, than reduce a rival people under their obedience. It is certain, however, that the very name of the Picts was lost, and those that remained were so compleatly incorporated with their conquerors, that they soon lost all memory of their own origin.—

The end of the Pictish government is placed so near that period, to which authentic annals reach, that it is matter of wonder, that we have no monuments of their language or history remaining. This favours the system I have laid down. Had they originally been of a different race from the Scots, their language of course would be different. The contrary is the case. The names of places in the Pictish dominions, and the very names of their kings, which are handed down to us, are of Galic original, which is a convincing proof, that the two nations were, of old, one and the same, and only divided into two governments, by the effect which their situation had upon the genius of the people.

The name of *Picts* was, perhaps,[14] given by the Romans to the Caledonians, who possessed the east coast of Scotland, from their painting their bodies.[15] This circumstance[16] made some imagine, that the Picts were of British extract, and a different race of men from the Scots. That more of the Britons, who fled northward from the tyranny of the Romans, settled in the low country of Scotland, than among the Scots of the mountains, may be easily imagined, from the very nature of the country. It was they who introduced painting among the Picts. From this circumstance proceeded the name of the latter, to distinguish them from the Scots, who never had that art among them, and from the Britons, who discontinued it after the Roman conquest.

The Caledonians, most certainly, acquired a considerable knowledge in navigation, by their living on a coast intersected with many arms of the sea, and, in islands, divided, one from another, by wide and dangerous firths. It . is, therefore, highly probable, that they, very early, found their way to the north of Ireland, which is within sight of their own country. That Ireland was first peopled from Britain is certain.[17] The vicinity of the two islands; the exact correspondence of the antient inhabitants of both, in point of manners and language, are sufficient proofs, even if we had not the testimony of[18] authors of undoubted veracity to confirm it. The abettors of the most romantic systems of Irish antiquities allow it; but they place the colony from Britain in an improbable and remote æra. I shall easily admit, that the colony of the *Firbolg*, confessedly the *Belgæ* of Britain, settled in the south of Ireland, before the *Caël*, or Caledonians, discovered the north: but it is not at all likely, that the migration of the Firbolg to Ireland happened many centuries before the Christian æra.[19]

Ossian, in the poem of Temora [Book II][20], throws considerable light on this subject. His accounts[21] agree so well with what the antients have delivered, concerning the first population and inhabitants of Ireland, that every unbiassed person will confess them more probable, than the legends handed down, by tradition, in that country. From him, it appears,[22] that, in the days of Trathal, grandfather to Fingal, Ireland was possessed by two nations; the *Firbolg* or *Belgæ* of Britain, who inhabited the south, and the *Caël*, who passed over from Caledonia and the Hebrides to Ulster. The two nations, as is usual among an unpolished and lately settled people, were divided into small dynasties, subject to petty kings, or chiefs, independent of one another. In this situation, it is probable, they continued long, without any material revolution in the state of the island, until Crothar, Lord of Atha, a country in Connaught, the most potent chief of the *Firbolg*, carried away Conlama, the daughter of Cathmin, a chief of the *Caël*, who possessed Ulster.

Conlama had been betrothed, some time before to Turloch, a chief of their own nation. Turloch resented the affront offered him by Crothar, made an irruption into Connaught, and killed Cormul, the brother of Crothar, who came to oppose his progress. Crothar himself then took arms, and either killed or expelled Turloch. The war, upon this, became general, between the two nations: and the Caël were reduced to the last extremity.—In this situation, they applied, for aid, to Trathal king of Morven, who sent his brother Conar, already famous for his great exploits, to their relief. Conar, upon his arrival in Ulster, was chosen king, by the unanimous consent of the Caledonian tribes, who possessed that country. The war was renewed with vigour and success; but the *Firbolg* appear to have been rather repelled than subdued. In succeeding reigns, we learn from episodes in the same poem, that the chiefs of Atha made several efforts to become monarchs of Ireland, and to expel the race of Conar.

To Conar succeeded his son Cormac [Book III], who appears to have reigned long. In his latter days he seems to have been driven to the last extremity, by an insurrection of the *Firbolg*, who supported the pretensions of the chiefs of Atha to the Irish throne. Fingal, who then was very young, came to the aid of Cormac, totally defeated Colc-ulla, chief of Atha, and re-established Cormac in the sole possession of all Ireland [Book IV]. It was then he fell in love with, and took to wife, Ros-crana, the daughter of Cormac, who was the mother of Ossian.

Cormac was succeeded in the Irish throne by his son, Cairbre; Cairbre by Artho, his son, who was the father of that Cormac, in whose minority the invasion of Swaran happened, which is the subject of the poem of *Fingal*. The family of Atha, who had not relinquished their pretensions to the Irish throne, rebelled in the minority of Cormac, defeated his adherents, and murdered him in the palace of Temora [Book I]. Cairbar, lord of Atha, upon this, mounted the throne. His usurpation soon ended with his life; for Fingal made an expedition into Ireland, and restored, after various vicissitudes of fortune, the family of Conar to the possession of the kingdom. This war is the subject of Temora; the events, though certainly heightened and embellished by poetry, seem, notwithstanding, to have their foundation in true history.

Ossian has not only preserved the history of the first migration of the Caledonians into Ireland, he has also delivered[23] some important facts, concerning the first settlement of the *Firbolg*, or *Belgæ of Britain*, in that kingdom, under their leader Larthon, who was ancestor to Cairbar and Cathmor, who successively mounted the Irish throne, after the death of Cormac, the son of Artho. I forbear to transcribe the passage, on account of its length. It is the song of Fonar, the bard; towards the latter end of the seventh book of Temora. As the generations from Larthon to Cathmor, to whom the episode is addressed, are not marked, as are those of the family of Conar, the first king of Ireland, we can form no judgment of the time of the settlement of the Firbolg. It is, however, probable, it was some time before the *Caël*, or Caledonians, settled in Ulster.—One important fact may be gathered from this history of Ossian,[24] that the Irish had no king before the latter end of the first century. Fingal lived, it is certain,[25] in the third century; so Conar, the first monarch of the Irish, who was his grand-uncle, cannot be placed farther back than the close of the first. The establishing of this fact, lays, at once, aside the pretended antiquities of the Scots and Irish, and cuts off[26] the long list of kings which the latter give us for a millennium before.

Of the affairs of Scotland, it is certain, nothing can be depended upon, prior to the reign of Fergus, the son of Erc, who lived in the fifth century. The true history of Ireland begins somewhat later than that period. Sir James Ware[27], who was indefatigable in his researches after the antiquities of his country, rejects, as mere fiction and idle romance, all that is related of the antient Irish, before the time of St. Patrick, and the reign of Leogaire. It is from this consideration, that he begins his history at the introduction of christianity, remarking, that all that is delivered down, concerning the times of paganism, were tales of late invention, strangely mixed with anachronisms and inconsistencies. Such being the opinion of Ware, who had collected with uncommon industry and zeal, all the real and pretendedly antient manuscripts, concerning the history of his country, we may, on his authority, reject the improbable and self-condemned tales of Keating and O'Flaherty. Credulous and puerile to the last degree, they have disgraced the antiquities they meant to establish. It is to be wished, that some able Irishman, who understands the language and records of his country, may redeem, ere it is too late, the genuine antiquities of Ireland, from the hands of these idle fabulists.

By comparing the history preserved by Ossian[28] with the legends of the Scots and Irish writers, and, by afterwards examining both by the test of the Roman authors, it is easy to discover which is the most probable. Probability is all that can be established on the authority of tradition, ever dubious and uncertain. But when it favours the hypothesis laid down by contemporary writers of undoubted veracity, and, as it were, finishes the figure of which they only drew the out-lines, it ought, in the judgment of sober reason, to be preferred to accounts framed in dark and distant periods, with little judgment, and upon no authority.

Concerning the period of more than a century, which intervenes between Fingal and the reign of Fergus, the son of Erc or Arcath, tradition is dark and contradictory. Some trace up the family of Fergus to a son of Fingal of that name, who makes a considerable figure in Ossian's poems. The three elder sons of Fingal, Ossian, Fillan, and Ryno, dying without issue, the succession, of course, devolved upon Fergus, the fourth son and his posterity. This Fergus, say some traditions, was the father of Congal, whose son was Arcath, the father of Fergus, properly called the first king of Scots, as it was in his time the *Caël*, who possessed the western coast of Scotland, began to be distinguished, by foreigners, by the name of *Scots*. From thence forward, the Scots and Picts, as distinct nations, became objects of attention to the historians of other countries. The internal state of the two Caledonian kingdoms has always continued, and ever must remain, in obscurity and fable.

It is in this epoch we must fix the beginning of the decay of that species of heroism, which subsisted in the days of Ossian.[29] There are three stages in human society. The first is the result of consanguinity, and the natural affection of the members of a family to one another. The second begins when property is established, and men enter into associations for mutual defence, against the invasions and injustice of neighbours. Mankind submit, in the third, to certain laws and subordinations of government, to which they trust the safety of their persons and property. As the first is formed on nature, so, of course, it is the most disinterested and noble. Men, in the last, have leisure to cultivate the mind, and to restore it, with reflection, to a primæval dignity of sentiment. The middle state is the region of compleat barbarism and ignorance. About the beginning of the fifth century, the Scots and Picts were advanced into the second stage, and, consequently, into those circumscribed sentiments, which always distinguish barbarity.—The events which soon after happened did not at all contribute to enlarge their ideas, or mend their national character.

About the year 426, the Romans, on account of domestic commotions, entirely forsook Britain, finding it impossible to defend so distant a frontier. The Picts and Scots, seizing this favourable opportunity, made incursions into the deserted province. The Britons, enervated by the slavery of several centuries, and those vices, which are inseparable from an advanced state of civility, were not able to withstand the impetuous, though irregular attacks of a barbarous enemy. In the utmost distress, they applied to their old masters, the Romans, and (after the unfortunate state of the Empire could not spare aid) to the Saxons, a nation equally barbarous and brave, with the enemies of whom they were so much afraid. Though the bravery of the Saxons repelled the Caledonian nations for a time, yet the latter found means to extend themselves, considerably, towards the South. It is, in this period, we must place the origin of the arts of civil life among the Scots. The seat of government was removed from the mountains to the plain and more fertile provinces of the South, to be near the common enemy, in case of sudden incursions. Instead of roving through unfrequented wilds, in search of subsistance, by means of hunting, men applied to agriculture, and raising of corn. This manner of life was the first means of changing the national character.—The next thing which contributed to it was their mixture with strangers.

In the countries which the Scots had conquered from the Britons, it is probable that most of the old inhabitants remained. These incorporating with the conquerors, taught them agriculture, and other arts, which they themselves had received from the Romans. The Scots, however, in number as well as power, being the most predominant, retained still their language, and as many of the customs of their ancestors, as suited with the nature of the country they possessed. Even the union of the two Caledonian kingdoms did not much affect the national character. Being originally descended from the same stock, the manners of the Picts and Scots were as similar as the different natures of the countries they possessed permitted.

What brought about a total change in the genius of the Scots nation, was their wars, and other transactions with the Saxons. Several counties in the south of Scotland were alternately possessed by the two nations. They were ceded, in the ninth age, to the Scots, and, it is probable, that most of the Saxon inhabitants remained in possession of their lands. During the several conquests and revolutions in England, many fled, for refuge, into Scotland, to avoid the oppression of foreigners, or the tyranny of domestic usurpers; in so much, that the Saxon race formed perhaps near one half of the Scottish kingdom. The Saxon manners and language daily gained ground, on the tongue and customs of the antient Caledonians, till, at last, the latter were entirely relegated to inhabitants of the mountains, who were still unmixed with strangers.

It was after the accession of territory which the Scots received, upon the retreat of the Romans from Britain, that the inhabitants of the Highlands were divided into clans. The king, when he kept his court in the mountains, was considered, by the whole nation, as the chief of their blood. Their small number, as well as the presence of their prince, prevented those divisions, which, afterwards, sprung forth into so many separate tribes. When the seat of government was removed to the south, those who remained in the Highlands were, of course, neglected. They naturally formed themselves into small societies, independent of one another. Each society had its own *regulus*, who either was, or in the succession of a few generations, was regarded as chief of their blood.—The nature of the country favoured an institution of this sort. A few valleys, divided from one another by extensive heaths and impassible mountains, form the face of the Highlands. In these valleys the chiefs fixed their residence. Round them, and almost within sight of their dwellings, were the habitations of their relations and dependents.

The seats of the Highland chiefs were neither disagreeable nor inconvenient. Surrounded with mountains and hanging woods, they were covered from the inclemency of the weather. Near them generally ran a pretty large river, which, discharging itself not far off, into an arm of the sea, or extensive lake, swarmed with variety of fish. The woods were stocked with wild-fowl; and the heaths and mountains behind them were the natural seat of the red deer and roe. If we make allowance for the backward state of agriculture, the valleys were not unfertile; affording, if not all the conveniences, at least the necessaries of life. Here the chief lived, the supreme judge and law-giver of his own people; but his sway was neither severe nor unjust. As the populace regarded him as the chief of their blood, so he, in return, considered them as members of his family. His commands therefore, though absolute and decisive, partook more of the authority of a father, than of the rigor of a judge.—Though the whole territory of the tribe was considered as the property of the chief, yet his vassals made him no other consideration for their lands than services, neither burdensome nor frequent. As he seldom went from home, he was at no expence. His table was supplied by his own herds, and what his numerous attendants killed in hunting.

In this rural kind of magnificence, the Highland chiefs lived, for many ages. At a distance from the seat of government, and secured, by the inaccessibleness of their country, they were free and independent. As they had little communication with strangers, the customs of their ancestors remained among them, and their language retained its original purity. Naturally fond of military fame, and remarkably attached to the memory of their ancestors, they delighted in traditions and songs, concerning the exploits of their nation, and especially of their own particular families. A succession of bards was retained in every clan, to hand down the memorable actions of their forefathers. As the æra of Fingal, on account of Ossian's poems, was the most remarkable, and his chiefs the most renowned names in tradition, the bards took care to place one of[30] them in the genealogy of every great family.—That part of the poems, which concerned the hero who was regarded as ancestor, was preserved, as an authentic record of the antiquity of the family, and was delivered down, from race to race, with wonderful exactness.[31]

The bards themselves, in the mean time, were not idle. They[32] erected their immediate patrons into heroes, and celebrated them in their songs. As the circle of their knowledge was narrow, their ideas were confined in proportion. A few happy expressions, and the manners they represent, may please those who understand the language; their obscurity and inaccuracy would disgust in a translation.—It was chiefly for this reason, that I kept wholly to the compositions of Ossian, in my former and present publication. As he acted in a more extensive sphere, his ideas are more noble and universal; neither has he so[33] many of those peculiarities, which are only understood in a certain period or country. The other bards have their beauties, but not in that species of composition in which Ossian excels.[34] Their rhimes, only calculated to kindle a martial spirit among the vulgar, afford very little pleasure to genuine taste. This observation only regards their poems of the heroic kind; in every other[35] species of poetry they are more successful. They express the tender melancholy of desponding love, with irresistible[36] simplicity and nature. So well adapted are the sounds of the words to the sentiments, that, even without any knowledge of the language, they pierce and dissolve the heart. Successful love is expressed with peculiar tenderness and elegance. In all their compositions, except the heroic, which was solely calculated to animate the vulgar, they give us the genuine language of the heart, without any of those affected ornaments of phraseology, which, though intended to beautify sentiments, divest them of their natural force. The ideas, it is confessed, are too local, to be admired, in another language; to those who are acquainted with the manners they represent, and the scenes they describe, they must afford the highest[37] pleasure and satisfaction.

It was the locality of his description and sentiment, that, probably, kept Ossian so long in the obscurity of an almost lost language. His ideas, though remarkably proper for the times in which he lived, are so contrary to the present advanced state of society, that more than a common mediocrity of taste is required, to relish his poems as they deserve.—Those who alone were capable to make a translation were, no doubt, conscious of this, and chose rather to admire their poet in secret, than see him received, with coldness, in an English dress.[38]

These were long my own sentiments, and accordingly, my first translations, from the Galic, were merely accidental. The publication, which soon after followed, was so well received, that I was obliged to promise to my friends a larger collection. In a journey through the Highlands and isles, and, by the assistance of correspondents, since I left that country, all the genuine remains of the works of Ossian have come to my hands. In the preceding volume compleat poems were only given. Unfinished and imperfect poems were purposely omitted; even some pieces were rejected, on account of their length, and others, that they might not break in upon that thread of connection, which subsists in the lesser compositions, subjoined to *Fingal*.—That the comparative merit of pieces was not regarded, in the selection, will readily appear to those who shall read, attentively, the present collection.—It is animated with the same spirit of poetry, and the same strength of sentiment is sustained throughout.

The opening of the poem of Temora made its appearance in the first collection of Ossian's works. The second book, and several other episodes, have only fallen into my hands lately. The story of the poem, with which I had been long acquainted, enabled me to reduce the broken members of the piece into the order in which they now appear. For the ease of the reader, I have divided it myself into books, as I had done before with the poem of *Fingal*. As to the merit of the poem I shall not anticipate the judgment of the public. My impartiality might be suspected, in my accounts of a work, which, in some measure, is become my own. If the poem of Fingal met with the applause of persons of genuine taste, I should also hope, that Temora will not displease them.

But what renders Temora infinitely more valuable than Fingal, is the light it throws on the history of the times.[39] The first population of Ireland, its first kings, and several circumstances, which regard its connection of old with the south and north of Britain, are presented to us, in several episodes. The subject and catastrophe of the poem are founded upon facts, which regarded the first peopling of that country, and the contests between the two British nations, which originally inhabited it.—In a preceding part of this dissertation, I have shewn how superior the probability of Ossian's traditions[40] is to the undigested fictions of the Irish bards, and the more recent and regular legends of both Irish and Scottish historians. I mean not to give offence to the abettors of the high antiquities of the two nations, though I have all along expressed my doubts, concerning the veracity and abilities of those who deliver down their antient history. For my own part, I prefer the national fame, arising from a few certain facts, to the legendary and uncertain annals of ages of remote and obscure antiquity. No kingdom now established in Europe, can pretend to equal antiquity with that of the Scots,[41] even according to my system, so that it is altogether needless to fix their[42] origin a fictitious millennium before.[43]

Since the publication of the poems contained in the first volume, many insinuations have been made, and doubts arisen, concerning their authenticity. I shall, probably, hear more of the same kind after the present poems shall make their appearance.[44] Whether these suspicions are suggested by prejudice, or are only the effects of ignorance of facts, I shall not pretend to determine.—To me they give no concern, as I have it always in my power to remove them. An incredulity of this kind is natural to persons, who confine all merit to their own age and country. These are generally the weakest, as well as the most ignorant, of the people. Indolently confined to a place, their ideas are narrow and circumscribed.—It is ridiculous enough to see such people as these are, branding their ancestors, with the despicable appellation of barbarians. Sober reason can easily discern, where the title ought to be fixed with more propriety.[45]

As prejudice is always the effect of ignorance, the knowing, the men of true taste, despise and dismiss it. If the poetry is good, and the characters natural and striking, to them it is a matter of indifference, whether the heroes were born in the little village of Angles in Juteland, or natives of the barren heaths of Caledonia. That honour which nations derive from ancestors, worthy, or renowned, is merely ideal. It may buoy up the minds of individuals, but it contributes very little to their importance in the eyes of others.—But of all those prejudices which are incident to narrow minds, that which measures the merit of performances by the vulgar opinion, concerning the country which produced them, is certainly the most ridiculous. Ridiculous, however, as it is, few have the courage to reject it; and, I am thoroughly convinced, that a few quaint lines of a Roman or Greek epigrammatist, if dug out of the ruins of Herculaneum, would meet with more cordial and universal applause, than all the most beautiful and natural rhapsodies of all the Celtic bards and Scandinavian Scalders that ever existed.[46]

While some doubt the authenticity of the compositions of Ossian, others strenuously endeavour to appropriate them to the Irish nation. Though the whole tenor of the poems sufficiently contradict so absurd an opinion, it may not be improper, for the satisfaction of some, to examine the narrow foundation, on which this extraordinary claim is built.[47]

Of all the nations descended from the antient *Celtæ*, the Scots and Irish are the most similar in language, customs, and manners. This argues a more intimate connection between them, than a remote descent from the great Celtic stock. It is evident, in short, that, at some one period or other, they formed one society, were subject to the same government, and were, in all respects, one and the same people. How they became divided, which the colony, or which the mother nation, does not fall now to be discussed.[48] The first circumstance that induced me to disregard the vulgarly-received opinion of the Hibernian extraction of the Scottish nation, was my observations on their antient language. That dialect of the Celtic tongue, spoken in the north of Scotland, is much more pure, more agreeable to its mother language, and more abounding with primitives, than that now spoken, or even that which has been writ for some centuries back, amongst the most unmixed part of the Irish nation. A Scotchman, tolerably conversant in his own language, understands an Irish composition, from that derivative analogy which it has to the *Galic* of North-Britain. An Irishman, on the other hand, without the aid of study, can never understand a composition in the *Galic* tongue.—This affords a proof, that the *Scotch Galic* is the most original, and, consequently, the language of a more antient and unmixed people. The Irish, however backward they may be to allow any thing to the prejudice of their antiquity, seem inadvertently to acknowledge it, by the very appellation they give to the dialect they speak.—They call their own language *Caëlic Eirinach*, i.e. *Caledonian Irish*, when, on the contrary, they call the dialect of North-Britain a *Chaëlic* or the *Caledonian tongue*, emphatically. A circumstance of this nature tends more to decide which is the most antient nation, than the united testimonies of a whole legion of ignorant bards and senachies, who, perhaps, never dreamed of bringing the Scots from Spain to Ireland, till some one of them, more learned than the rest, discovered, that the Romans called the first *Iberia*, and the latter *Hibernia*. On such a slight foundation were probably built those romantic fictions, concerning the Milesians of Ireland.

From internal proofs it sufficiently appears, that the poems published under the name of Ossian, are not of Irish composition. The favourite chimæra, that Ireland is the mother-country of the Scots, is totally subverted and ruined. The fictions concerning the antiquities of that country, which were forming for ages, and growing as they came down, on the hands of successive *senachies* and *fileas*, are found, at last, to be the spurious brood of modern and ignorant ages. To those who know how tenacious the Irish are, of their pretended *Iberian* descent, this alone is proof sufficient, that poems, so subversive of their system, could never be produced by an Hibernian bard.—But when we look to the language, it is so different from the Irish dialect, that it would be as ridiculous to think, that Milton's Paradise Lost could be wrote by a Scottish peasant, as to suppose, that the poems ascribed to Ossian were writ in Ireland.

The pretensions of Ireland to Ossian proceed from another quarter. There are handed down, in that country, traditional poems, concerning the *Fiona*, or the heroes of *Fion Mac Comnal*. This *Fion*, say the Irish annalists, was general of the militia of Ireland, in the reign of Cormac, in the third century. Where Keating and O'Flaherty learned, that Ireland had an *embodied* militia so early, is not easy for me to determine. Their information certainly did not come from the Irish poems, concerning *Fion*. I have just now, in my hands, all that remain, of those compositions; but, unluckily for the antiquities of Ireland, they appear to be the work of a very modern period. Every stanza, nay almost every line, affords striking proofs, that they cannot be three centuries old. Their allusions to the manners and customs of the fifteenth century, are so many, that it is matter of wonder to me, how any one could dream of their antiquity. They are entirely writ in that romantic taste, which prevailed two ages ago.—Giants, enchanted castles, dwarfs, palfreys, witches and magicians form the whole circle of the poet's invention. The celebrated *Fion* could scarcely move from one hillock to another, without encountering a giant, or being entangled in the circles of a magician. Witches, on broomsticks, were continually hovering round him, like crows; and he had freed enchanted virgins in every valley in Ireland. In short, *Fion*, great as he was, passed a disagreeable life.—Not only had he to engage all the mischiefs in his own country, foreign armies invaded him, assisted by magicians and witches, and headed by kings, as tall as the mainmast of a first rate.—It must be owned, however, that *Fion* was not inferior to them in height.

> A chos air *Cromleach*, druim-ard,
> Chos eile air Crom-meal dubh,
> Thoga *Fion* le lamh mhoir
> An d'uisge o *Lubhair* na sruth.[49]

> With one foot on *Cromleach* his brow,
> The other on *Crommal* the dark,
> *Fion* took up with his large hand
> The water from *Lubar* of the streams.

Cromleach and *Crommal* were two mountains in the neighbourhood of one another, in Ulster, and the river *Lubar* ran through the intermediate valley.[50] The property of such a monster as this *Fion*, I should never have disputed with any nation. But the bard himself, in the poem, from which the above quotation is taken, cedes him to Scotland.

> FION O ALBIN, siol nan laoich.
> FION *from* ALBION, *race of heroes*!

Were it allowable to contradict the authority of a bard, at this distance of time, I should have given as my opinion, that this enormous *Fion* was of the race of the Hibernian giants, of Ruanus, or some other celebrated name, rather than a native of Caledonia, whose inhabitants, now at least, are not remarkable for their stature.[51]

If *Fion* was so remarkable for his stature, his heroes had also other extraordinary properties. *In weight all the sons of strangers* yielded to the celebrated Ton-iosal; and for hardness of skull, and, perhaps, for thickness too, the valiant Oscar stood *unrivalled and alone*. Ossian himself had many singular and less delicate qualifications, than playing on the harp; and the brave Cuchullin[52] was of so diminutive a size, as to be taken for a child of two years of age, by the gigantic Swaran. To illustrate this subject, I shall here lay before the reader, the history of some of the Irish poems, concerning *Fion Mac Comnal*. A translation of these pieces, if well executed, might afford satisfaction[53] to the public. But this ought to be the work of a native of Ireland. To draw forth, from obscurity, the poems of my own country, has afforded ample employment to me;[54] besides, I am too diffident of my own abilities, to undertake such a work. A gentleman in Dublin accused me to the public, of committing blunders and absurdities, in translating the language of my own country, and that before any translation of mine appeared.[55] How the gentleman came to see my blunders before I committed them, is not easy to determine; if he did not conclude, that, as a Scotsman, and, of course descended of the Milesian race, I might have committed some of those oversights, which, perhaps very unjustly, are said to be peculiar to them.

From the whole tenor of the Irish poems, concerning the *Fiona*, it appears, that *Fion Mac Comnal* flourished in the reign of Cormac, which is placed, by the universal consent of the senachies, in the third century. They even fix the death of Fingal in the year 286, yet his son Ossian is made contemporary with St. Patrick, who preached the gospel in Ireland about the middle of the fifth age. Ossian, though, at that time, he must have been two hundred and fifty years of age, had a daughter young enough to become wife to the saint. On account of this family connection, *Patrick of the Psalms*, for so the apostle of Ireland is emphatically called in the poems, took great delight in the company of Ossian, and in hearing the great actions of his family. The saint sometimes threw off the austerity of his profession, drunk freely, and had his soul properly warmed with wine, in order to hear, with becoming enthusiasm, the poems of his father-in-law. One of the poems begins with this piece of useful information.

> Lo don rabh PADRIC na mhúr,
> Gun *Sailm* air uidh, ach a gól,
> Ghluais é thigh *Ossian* mhic *Fhion*,
> O san leis bu bhinn a ghloir.

The title of this poem is *Teantach mor na Fiona*. It appears to have been founded on the same story with the *battle of Lora*, one of the poems of the genuine Ossian.[56] The circumstances and catastrophe in both are much the same; but the *Irish Ossian* discovers the age in which he lived, by an unlucky anachronism. After describing the total route of Erragon, he very gravely concludes with this remarkable anecdote, that none of the foe escaped, but a few, who were allowed to go on a pilgrimage to the *Holy Land*. This circumstance fixes the date of the composition of the piece some centuries after the famous croisade; for, it is evident, that the poet thought the time of the croisade so antient, that he confounds it with the age of Fingal.—Erragon, in the course of this poem, is often called,

Riogh *Lochlin* an do shloigh,
King of Denmark of two nations,

which alludes to the union of the kingdoms of Norway and Denmark, a
circumstance which brings down the date of the piece to an æra, not far
remote.[57] Modern, however, as this pretended Ossian was, it is certain, he
lived before the Irish had dreamed of appropriating *Fion*, or *Fingal*, to
themselves. He concludes the poem, with this reflection:

Na fagha se comhthróm nan n'arm,
Erragon Mac Annir nan lánn glas
'San n'ALBIN ni n'abairtair Triath
Agus ghlaoite an n'*Fhiona* as.

"Had Erragon, son of Annir of gleaming swords, avoided the equal con-
test of arms, (single combat) no chief should have afterwards been num-
bered in ALBION, and the heroes of Fion should no more be named."

The next poem that falls under our observation is *Cath-cabhra*, or, *The
death of Oscar.* This piece is founded on the same story which we have in
the first book of Temora. So little thought the author of *Cath-cabhra* of
making Oscar his countryman, that, in the course of two hundred lines, of
which the poem consists, he puts the following expression thrice in the
mouth of the hero:

ALBIN an sa d'roina m'arach.——
ALBION *where I was born and bred.*

The poem contains almost all the incidents in the first book of Temora. In
one circumstance the bard differs materially from Ossian. Oscar, after he
was mortally wounded by Cairbar, was carried by his people to a neighbour-
ing hill, which commanded a prospect of the sea. A fleet appeared at a dis-
tance, and the hero exclaims with joy,

Loingeas mo shean-athair at'án
'S iad a tiáchd le cabhair chugain,
O ALBIN na n'ioma stuagh.

"It is the fleet of my grandfather, coming with aid to our field, from
ALBION of many waves!"——The testimony of this bard is sufficient to
confute the idle fictions of Keating and O'Flaherty; for, though he is far
from being antient, it is probable, he flourished a full century before these
historians.—He appears, however, to have been a much better christian than
chronologer; for *Fion*, though he is placed two centuries before St. Patrick,
very devoutly recommends the soul of his grandson to his Redeemer.

Duan a Gharibh Mac-Starn is another Irish poem in high repute. The grandeur of its images, and its propriety of sentiment, might have induced me to give a translation of it, had not I some expectations[58] of seeing it in the collection of the Irish Ossian's poems, promised more than a year since,[59] to the public. The author descends sometimes from the region of the sublime to low and indecent description; the last of which, the Irish translator, no doubt, will choose to leave in the obscurity of the original.—In this piece Cuchullin is used with very little ceremony, for he is oft called, the *dog of Tara*, in the county of Meath. This severe title of the *redoutable Cuchullin*, the most renowned of Irish champions, proceeded from the poet's ignorance of etymology. Cu, *voice*, or *commander*, signifies also a *dog*. The poet chose the last, as the most noble appellation for his hero.

The subject of the poem is the same with that of the epic poem of Fingal. *Garibh*[60] *Mac-Starn* is the same with Ossian's Swaran, the son of Starno.[61] His single combats with, and his victory over all the heroes of Ireland, excepting the *celebrated dog of Tara*, i.e. Cuchullin, afford matter for two hundred lines of tolerable poetry. *Garibh's*[62] progress in search of Cuchullin, and his intrigue with the gigantic Emir-bragal, that hero's wife, enables the poet to extend his piece to four hundred lines. This author, it is true, makes Cuchullin a native of Ireland; the gigantic Emir-bragal he calls *the guiding star of the women of Ireland*. The property of this enormous lady I shall not dispute with him, or any other. But, as he speaks with great tenderness of the *daughters of the convent*, and throws out some hints against the English nation, it is probable he lived in too modern a period to be intimately acquainted with the genealogy of Cuchullin.

Another Irish Ossian, for there were many, as appears from their difference in language and sentiment, speaks very dogmatically of *Fion Mac Comnal*, as an Irishman. Little can be said for the judgment of this poet, and less for his delicacy of sentiment. The history of one of his episodes may, at once, stand as a specimen of his want of both. Ireland, in the days of *Fion*, happened to be threatened with an invasion, by three great potentates, the kings of Lochlin, Sweden, and France. It is needless to insist upon the impropriety of a French invasion of Ireland; it is sufficient for me to be faithful to the language of my author. *Fion*, upon receiving intelligence of the intended invasion, sent Ca-olt, Ossian, and Oscar, to watch the bay, in which, it was apprehended, the enemy was to land. Oscar was the worst choice of a scout that could be made, for, brave as he was, he had the bad property of falling very often asleep on his post, nor was it possible to awake him, without cutting off one of his fingers, or dashing a large stone against his head. When the enemy appeared, Oscar, very unfortunately, was asleep. Ossian and Ca-olt consulted about the method of wakening him, and they, at last, fixed on the stone, as the less dangerous expedient.

Gun thog Caoilte a chlach, nach gán,
Agus a n'aighai' chiean gun bhuail;
Tri mil an tulloch gun chri',&c.

"Ca-olt took up a heavy stone, and struck it against the hero's head. The hill shook for three miles, as the stone rebounded and rolled away." Oscar rose in wrath, and his father gravely desired him to spend his rage on his enemies, which he did to so good purpose, that he singly routed a whole wing of their army. The confederate kings advanced, notwithstanding, till they came to a narrow pass, possessed by the celebrated Ton-iosal. This name is very significant of the singular property of the hero who bore it. Ton-iosal, though brave, was so heavy and unwieldy, that, when he sat down, it took the whole force of an hundred men to set him upright on his feet again. Luckily for the preservation of Ireland, the hero happened to be standing when the enemy appeared, and he gave so good an account of them, that *Fion*, upon his arrival, found little to do, but to divide the spoil among his soldiers.

All these extraordinary heroes, Fion, Ossian, Oscar and Ca-olt, says the poet, were

Siol ERIN na gorm lánn.
The sons of ERIN *of blue steel.*

Neither shall I much dispute the matter with him: He has my consent also to appropriate to Ireland the celebrated Ton-iosal. I shall only say, that they are different persons from those of the same name, in the Scotch poems; and that, though the stupenduous valour of the first is so remarkable, they have not been equally lucky with the latter, in their poet. It is somewhat extraordinary, that *Fion*, who lived some ages before St. Patrick, swears like a very good christian:

Air an Dia do chum gach *case.*
By God, who shaped every case.

It is worthy of being remarked, that, in the line quoted, Ossian, who lived in St. Patrick's days, seems to have understood something of the English, a language not then subsisting. A person, more sanguine for the honour of his country than I am, might argue, from this circumstance, that this pretendedly Irish Ossian was a native of Scotland; for my countrymen are universally allowed to have an exclusive right to the second-sight.

From the instances given, the reader may form a compleat idea of the Irish compositions concerning the *Fiona.* The greatest part of them make the heroes of *Fion,*

Siol ALBIN a n'nioma caoile.
The race of ALBION *of many firths.*

The rest make them natives of Ireland. But, the truth is, that their authority is of little consequence on either side. From the instances I have given, they appear to have been the work of a very modern period. The pious ejaculations they contain, their allusions to the manners of the times, fix them to the fifteenth century. Had even the authors of these pieces avoided all allusions to their own times, it is impossible that the poems could pass for ancient, in the eyes of any person tolerably conversant with the Irish tongue. The idiom is so corrupted and so many words borrowed from the English, that that language must have made considerable progress in Ireland before the poems were writ.

It remains now to shew, how the Irish bards begun to appropriate Ossian[63] and his heroes to their own country. After the English conquest, many of the natives of Ireland, averse to a foreign yoke, either actually were in a state of hostility with the conquerors, or at least, paid little regard to their government. The Scots, in those ages, were often in open war, and never in cordial friendship with the English. The similarity of manners and language, the traditions concerning their common origin, and above all, their having to do with the same enemy, created a free and friendly intercourse between the Scottish and Irish nations. As the custom of retaining bards and senachies was common to both; so each, no doubt, had formed a system of history, it matters not how much soever fabulous, concerning their respective origin. It was the natural policy of the times, to reconcile the traditions of both nations together, and, if possible, to deduce them from the same original stock.

The Saxon manners and language had, at that time, made great progress in the south of Scotland. The ancient language, and the traditional history of the nation, became confined entirely to the inhabitants of the Highlands, then fallen, from several concurring circumstances, into the last degree of ignorance and barbarism. The Irish, who, for some ages before the conquest, had possessed a competent share of that kind of learning, which then prevailed in Europe, found it no difficult matter to impose their own fictions on the ignorant Highland senachies. By flattering the vanity of the Highlanders, with their long list of Heremonian kings and heroes, they, without contradiction, assumed to themselves the character of being the mother-nation of the Scots of Britain. At this time, certainly, was established that Hibernian system of the original of the Scots, which afterwards, for want of any other, was universally received. The Scots of the low-country, who, by losing the language of their ancestors, lost, together with it, their national traditions, received, implicitly, the history of their country, from Irish refugees, or from Highland senachies, persuaded over into the Hibernian system.

These circumstances are far from being ideal. We have remaining many particular traditions, which bear testimony to a fact, of itself abundantly probable. What makes the matter incontestible is, that the antient traditional accounts of the genuine origin of the Scots, have been handed down without interruption. Though a few ignorant senachies might be persuaded out of their own opinion, by the smoothness of an Irish tale, it was impossible to eradicate, from among the bulk of the people, their own national traditions. These traditions afterwards so much prevailed, that the Highlanders continue totally unacquainted with the pretended Hibernian extract of the Scots nation. Ignorant chronicle writers, strangers to the antient language of their country, preserved only from falling to the ground, so improbable a story.

It was, during the period I have mentioned, that the Irish became acquainted with, and carried into their country, the compositions of Ossian. The scene of many of the pieces being in Ireland, suggested first to them a hint, of making both heroes and poet natives of that Island. In order to do this effectually, they found it necessary, to reject the genuine poems, as every line was pregnant with proofs of their Scottish original, and to dress up a fable, on the same subject, in their own language. So ill qualified, however, were their bards to effectuate this change, that amidst all their desires to make the *Fiona* Irishmen, they every now and then call them *Siol Albin*. It was, probably, after a succession of some generations, that the bards had effrontery enough to establish an Irish genealogy for *Fion*, and deduce him from the Milesian race of kings. In some of the oldest Irish poems, on the subject, the great-grand-father of *Fion* is made a Scandinavian; and his heroes are often called SIOL LOCHLIN NA BEUM; *i.e. the race of Lochlin of wounds*. The only poem that runs up the family of *Fion* to Nuades Niveus, king of Ireland, is evidently not above a hundred and fifty years old; for if I mistake not, it mentions the Earl of Tyrone, so famous in Elizabeth's time.[64]

This subject, perhaps, is pursued further than it deserves; but a discussion of the pretensions of Ireland to Ossian,[65] was become in some measure necessary. If the Irish poems, concerning the *Fiona*, should appear ridiculous, it is but justice to observe, that they are scarcely more so than the poems of other nations, at that period. On other subjects, the bards of Ireland have displayed a genius worthy of any age or nation.[66] It was, alone, in matters of antiquity, that they were monstrous in their fables. Their love-sonnets, and their elegies on the death of persons worthy or renowned, abound with such beautiful simplicity of sentiment, and wild harmony of numbers, that they[67] become more than an attonement for their errors, in every other species of poetry. But the beauty of these pieces, depends so much on a certain *curiosa felicitas* of expression in the original, that they must appear much to disadvantage in another language.

T E M O R A:

AN

EPIC POEM.

BOOK FIRST.

ARGUMENT to Book I.[1]

Cairbar, the son of Borbar-duthul, lord of Atha in Connaught, the most potent chief of the race of the Firbolg, having murdered, at Temora the royal palace, Cormac the son of Artho, the young king of Ireland, usurped the throne. Cormac was lineally descended from Conar the son of Trenmor, the great grandfather of Fingal, king of those Caledonians who inhabited the western coast of Scotland. Fingal resented the behaviour of Cairbar, and resolved to pass over into Ireland, with an army, to re-establish the royal family on the Irish throne. Early intelligence of his designs coming to Cairbar, he assembled some of his tribes in Ulster, and at the same time ordered his brother Cathmor to follow him speedily with an army, from Temora. Such was the situation of affairs when the Caledonian fleet appeared on the coast of Ulster.

The poem opens in the morning. Cairbar is represented as retired from the rest of the army, when one of his scouts brought him news of the landing of Fingal. He assembles a council of his chiefs. Foldath the chief of Moma haughtily despises the enemy; and is reprimanded warmly by Malthos. Cairbar, after hearing their debate, orders a feast to be prepared, to which, by his bard Olla, he invites Oscar the son of Ossian; resolving to pick a quarrel with that hero, and so have some pretext for killing him. Oscar came to the feast; the quarrel happened; the followers of both fought, and Cairbar and Oscar fell by mutual wounds. The noise of the battle reached Fingal's army. The king came on, to the relief of Oscar, and the Irish fell back to the army of Cathmor, who was advanced to the banks of the river Lubar, on the heath of Moilena. Fingal, after mourning over his grandson, ordered Ullin the chief of his bards to carry his body to Morven, to be there interred. Night coming on, Althan, the son of Conachar, relates to the king the particulars of the murder of Cormac. Fillan, the son of Fingal, is sent to observe the motions of Cathmor by night, which concludes the action of the first day. The scene of this book is a plain, near the hill of Mora, which rose on the borders of the heath of Moilena, in Ulster.

TEMORA: BOOK FIRST[2].

The blue waves of Ullin[3] roll in light. The green hills[4] are covered with day.
Trees shake their dusky heads in the breeze. Grey torrents pour their noisy
streams.—Two green hills, with aged oaks, surround a narrow plain. The
blue course of a stream is there; on its banks stood Cairbar[5] of Atha.——
His spear supports the king: the red eyes of his fear are sad. Cormac rises in
his soul, with all his ghastly wounds. The grey form of the youth appears in
darkness; blood pours from his airy sides.—Cairbar thrice threw his spear
on earth; and thrice he stroked his beard. His steps are short; he often stops:
and tosses his sinewy arms. He is like a cloud in the desert, that varies its
form to every blast: the valleys are sad around, and fear, by turns, the
shower.

The king, at length, resumed his soul, and took his pointed spear. He
turned his eyes to Moi-lena. The scouts of blue ocean came. They came with
steps of fear, and often looked behind. Cairbar knew that the mighty were
near, and called his gloomy chiefs.

The sounding steps of his warriors came. They drew, at once, their
swords. There Morlath[6] stood with darkened face. Hidalla's long hair sighs
in wind. Red-haired Cormar bends on his spear, and rolls his side-long-
looking eyes. Wild is the look of Malthos from beneath two shaggy
brows.—Foldath stands like an oozy rock, that covers its dark sides with
foam. His spear is like Slimora's fir, that meets the wind of heaven. His
shield is marked with the strokes of battle; and his red eye despises danger.
These and a thousand other chiefs surrounded car-borne Cairbar,[7] when the
scout of ocean came, Mor-annal[8], from streamy Moi-lena.—His eyes hang
forward from his face, his lips are trembling, pale.

Do the chiefs of Erin stand, he said, silent as the grove of evening? Stand
they, like a silent wood, and Fingal on the coast? Fingal, the terrible in
battle, the king of streamy Morven.—Hast thou seen the warrior? said Cair-
bar with a sigh. Are his heroes many of the coast? Lifts he the spear of
battle? Or comes the king in peace?

In peace he comes not, Cairbar.[9] I have seen his forward spear[10]. Is it a
meteor of death: the blood of thousands is on its steel.——He came first to
the shore, strong in the grey hair of age. Full rose his sinewy limbs, as he
strode in his might. That sword is by his side which gives no second[11]
wound. His shield is terrible, like the bloody moon ascending thro' a
storm.—Then came Ossian king of songs; and Morni's son, the first of
men. Connal leaps forward on his spear: Dermid spreads his dark-brown
locks.——Fillan bends his bow, the young hunter of streamy Moruth[12].—
But who is that before them, like the dreadful course of a stream! It is the
son of Ossian, bright between his locks. His long hair falls on his back.—
His dark brows are half-inclosed in steel. His sword hangs loose on his side.

His spear glitters as he moves. I fled from his terrible eyes, king of high Temora.

Then fly, thou feeble man, said Foldath in gloomy wrath: fly to the grey streams of thy land, son of the little soul! Have not I seen that Oscar? I beheld the chief in war. He is of the mighty in danger: but there are others who lift the spear.—Erin has many sons as brave, king of Temora of Groves! Let Foldath meet him in the strength of his course, and stop this mighty stream.—My spear is covered with the blood of the valiant; my shield is like the wall of Tura.

Shall Foldath[13] alone meet the foe? replied the dark-browed Malthos. Are they not numerous[14] on our coast, like the waters of many streams? Are not these the chiefs who vanquished Swaran, when the sons of Erin[15] fled? And shall Foldath meet their bravest heroes? Foldath of the heart of pride! take the strength of the people; and let Malthos come. My sword is red with slaughter, but who has heard my words[16]?

Sons of green Erin, said Hidalla[17], let not Fingal hear your words. The foe might rejoice, and his arm be strong in the land.—Ye are brave, O warriors, and like the storms of the desert;[18] they meet[19] the rocks without fear, and overturn the woods—But let us move in our strength, slow as a gathered cloud.——Then shall the mighty tremble; the spear shall fall from the hand of the valiant.—We see the cloud of death, they will say, while shadows fly over their face. Fingal will mourn in his age, and see his flying fame.—The steps of his chiefs will cease in Morven: the moss of years shall grow in Selma.

Cairbar heard their words, in silence, like the cloud of a shower: it stands dark on Cromla, till the lightning bursts its sides: the valley gleams with red light;[20] the spirits of the storm rejoice.——So stood the silent king of Temora; at length his words are heard.[21]

Spread the feast on Moi-lena: let my hundred bards attend. Thou, red-hair'd Olla, take the harp of the king. Go to Oscar chief of swords, and bid him to our feast.[22] To-day we feast and hear the song; to-morrow break the spears. Tell him that I have raised the tomb of Cathol[23]; that bards have sung to his ghost.[24]—Tell him that Cairbar has heard his fame at the stream of resounding Carun[25]. Cathmor[26] is not here, Borbar-duthul's generous race.[27] He is not here with his thousands, and our arms are weak. Cathmor is a foe to strife at the feast: his soul is bright as that sun. But Cairbar shall fight with Oscar, chiefs of the woody Temora! His words for Cathol were many; the wrath of Cairbar burns. He shall fall on Moi-lena: my fame shall rise in blood.

Their faces brightened round with joy. They spread over Moi-lena. The feast of shells is prepared. The songs of bards arise. We[28] heard[29] the voice of joy on the coast:[30] we thought that mighty Cathmor came. Cathmor the friend of strangers! the brother of red-haired Cairbar. Their souls were not the same. The light of heaven was in the bosom of Cathmor. His towers rose on the banks of Atha: seven paths led to his halls. Seven chiefs stood on the paths, and called the stranger to the feast! But Cathmor dwelt in the wood to avoid the voice of praise.

Olla came with his songs. Oscar went to Cairbar's feast. Three hundred warriors strode along Moi-lena of the streams. The grey dogs bounded on the heath, their howling reached afar. Fingal saw the departing hero: the soul of the king was sad. He dreaded Cairbar's gloomy thoughts, amidst the feast of shells.

My son raised high the spear of Cormac: an hundred bards met him with songs. Cairbar concealed with smiles the death that was dark in his soul. The feast is spread, the shells resound: joy brightens the face of the host. But it was like the parting beam of the sun, when he is to hide his red head in a storm.

Cairbar rose in his arms; darkness gathered on his brow. The hundred harps ceased at once. The clang[31] of shields was heard. Far distant on the heath Olla raised his song of woe. My son knew the sign of death; and rising seized his spear.

Oscar! said the dark-red Cairbar, I behold the spear[32] of Inisfail.[33] The spear of Temora[34] glitters in thy hand, son of woody Morven! It was the pride of an hundred[35] kings, the death of heroes of old. Yield it, son of Ossian, yield it to car-borne Cairbar.

Shall I yield, Oscar replied, the gift of Erin's injured king: the gift of fair-haired Cormac, when Oscar scattered his foes! I came to Cormac's halls of joy, when Swaran fled from Fingal. Gladness rose in the face of youth: he gave the spear of Temora. Nor did he give it to the feeble, O Cairbar, neither to the weak in soul. The darkness of thy face is no storm to me; nor are thine eyes the flames of death. Do I fear thy clanging shield? Tremble I at Olla's song? No: Cairbar, frighten the feeble; Oscar is a rock.

And wilt thou not yield the spear? replied the rising pride of Cairbar. Are thy words so mighty because Fingal is near? Fingal with aged locks from Morven's hundred groves! He has fought with little men. But he must vanish before Cairbar, like a thin pillar of mist before the winds of Atha[36].

Were he who fought with little men near Atha's darkening[37] chief: Atha's darkening chief[38] would yield green Erin his rage. Speak not of the mighty, O Cairbar! but turn thy sword on me. Our strength is equal: but Fingal is renowned! the first of mortal men!

Their people saw the darkening chiefs. Their crowding steps are heard around. Their eyes roll in fire. A thousand swords are half unsheathed. Red-haired Olla raised the song of battle: the trembling joy of Oscar's soul arose: the wonted joy of his soul when Fingal's horn was heard.

Dark as the swelling wave of ocean before the rising winds, when it bends its head near a coast, came on the host of Cairbar.——Daughter of Toscar[39]! why that tear? He is not fallen yet. Many were the deaths of his arm before my hero fell!—Behold they fall before my son like the groves in the desert, when an angry ghost rushes through night, and takes their green heads in his hand! Morlath falls: Maronnan dies: Conachar trembles in his blood. Cairbar shrinks before Oscar's sword; and creeps in darkness behind his stone. He lifted the spear in secret, and pierced my Oscar's side. He falls forward on his shield: his knee sustains the chief. But still his spear is in his hand.—See gloomy Cairbar[40] falls! The steel pierced his forehead, and divided his red hair behind. He lay, like a shattered rock, which Cromla shakes from its shaggy side.[41] But never more shall Oscar rise! he leans on his bossy shield. His spear is in his terrible hand: Erin's sons stood distant and dark. Their shouts arose, like crowded streams; Moi-lena echoed wide.

Fingal heard the sound; and took his father's spear.[42] His steps are before us on the heath. He spoke the words of woe. I hear the noise of war. Young Oscar is alone. Rise, sons of Morven; join the hero's sword.

Ossian rushed along the heath. Fillan bounded over Moi-lena. Fingal strode in his strength, and the light of his shield is terrible. The sons of Erin saw it far distant; they trembled in their souls. They knew that the wrath of the king arose: and they foresaw their death. We first arrived; we fought; and Erin's chiefs withstood our rage. But when the king came, in the sound of his course, what heart of steel could stand! Erin fled over Moi-lena. Death pursued their flight.

We saw Oscar on his shield. We saw his blood around. Silence darkened every face. Each turned his back and wept. The king strove to hide his tears. His grey beard whistled in the wind. He bent his head above his son.[43] His words were mixed with sighs.

And art thou fallen, Oscar, in the midst of thy course? the heart of the aged beats over thee! He sees thy coming wars. The wars which ought to come he sees, but they are cut off from thy fame. When shall joy dwell at Selma? When shall grief depart from Morven? My sons fall by degrees: Fingal shall be the last of his race. The fame which I have received shall[44] pass away: my age will be without friends. I shall sit a grey cloud in my hall: nor shall I hear the return of a son, in the midst of his sounding arms. Weep, ye heroes of Morven! never more shall Oscar rise!

And they did weep, O Fingal; dear was the hero to their souls. He went out to battle, and the foes vanished; he returned, in peace, amidst their joy. No father mourned his son slain in youth; no brother his brother of love. They fell, without tears, for the chief of the people was low! Bran[45] is howling at his feet: gloomy Luäth is sad, for he had often led them to the chace; to the bounding roe of the desert.

When Oscar saw his friends around, his breast[46] arose with sighs.[47]—The groans, he said, of aged chiefs; the howling of my dogs: the sudden bursts of songs of grief, have melted Oscar's soul. My soul, that never melted before; it was like the steel of my sword.—Ossian, carry me to my hills! Raise the stones of my renown. Place the horn of the deer, and my sword within my narrow dwelling.[48]—The torrent hereafter may raise the earth: the hunter may find the steel and say, "This has been Oscar's sword."[49]

And fallest thou, son of my fame! And shall I never see thee, Oscar! When others hear of their sons, I shall not hear of thee. The moss is on thy four grey stones; the mournful wind is there. The battle shall be fought without him: he shall[50] not pursue the dark-brown hinds. When the warrior returns from battles, and tells of other lands; I have seen a tomb, he will say, by the roaring stream, the dark dwelling of a chief. He fell by car-borne Oscar, the first of mortal men.—I, perhaps, shall hear his voice; and a beam of joy will rise in my soul.

The night would have descended in sorrow, and morning returned in the shadow of grief: our chiefs would have stood like cold dropping rocks on Moi-lena, and have forgot the war, did not the king disperse his grief, and raise his mighty voice. The chiefs, as new-wakened from dreams, lift up their heads around.

How long on Moi-lena shall we weep; or pour our tears in Ullin?[51] The mighty will not return. Oscar shall not rise in his strength. The valiant must fall one day, and be no more known on his hills.—Where are our fathers, O warriors! the chiefs of the times of old? They have set like stars that have shone, we only hear the sound of their praise. But they were renowned in their day,[52] the terror of other times. Thus shall we pass, O warriors, in the day of our fall. Then let us be renowned when we may; and leave our fame behind us, like the last beams of the sun, when he hides his red head in the west.[53]

Ullin, my aged bard! take the ship of the king. Carry Oscar to Selma of harps. Let the daughters of Morven weep. We shall fight in Erin for the race of fallen Cormac. The days of my years begin to fail: I feel the weakness of my arm. My fathers bend from their clouds, to receive their grey-hair'd son. But, before I go hence, one beam of fame shall rise: so shall my days end, as my years begun, in fame: my life shall be one stream of light to bards of other times.

Ullin rais'd his white sails: the wind of the south came forth. He bounded on the waves towards Selma.—[54] I remained in my grief, but my words were not heard.——The feast is spread on Moi-lena: an hundred heroes reared the tomb of Cairbar: but no song is raised over the chief: for his soul had been dark and bloody. The bards remembered the fall of Cormac! what could they say in Cairbar's praise?

The night came rolling down. The light of an hundred oaks arose. Fingal sat beneath a tree. Old Althan[55] stood in the midst. He told the tale of fallen Cormac. Althan the son of Conachar, the friend of car-borne Cuchullin: he dwelt with Cormac in windy Temora, when Semo's son fought with generous Torlath.[56]—The tale of Althan was mournful, and the tear was in his eye.[57]

[58]The setting sun was yellow on Dora[59]. Grey evening began to descend. Temora's woods shook with the blast of the unconstant wind. A cloud, at length, gathered in the west, and a red star looked from behind its edge.—I stood in the wood alone, and saw a ghost on the darkening air. His stride extended from hill to hill: his shield was dim on his side. It was the son of Semo: I knew the warrior's face. But he passed away in his blast; and all was dark around.—My soul was sad. I went to the hall of shells. A thousand lights arose: the hundred bards had strung the harp. Cormac stood in the midst, like the morning star, when it rejoices on the eastern hill, and its young beams are bathed in showers.[60]—The sword of Artho[61] was in the hand of the king; and he looked with joy on its polished studs: thrice he strove to draw it, and thrice he failed; his yellow locks are spread on his shoulders: his cheeks of youth are red.—I mourned over the beam of youth, for he was soon to set.

Althan! he said, with a smile, hast thou beheld my father? Heavy is the sword of the king, surely his arm was strong. O that I were like him in battle, when the rage of his wrath arose! then would I have met, like Cuchullin, the car-borne son of Cantéla! But years may come on, O Althan! and my arm be strong.—Hast thou heard of Semo's son, the chief[62] of high Temora? He might have returned with his fame; for he promised to return to-night. My bards wait him with songs; my feast is spread in Temora.[63]

I heard the king[64] in silence. My tears began to flow. I hid them with my aged locks; but he[65] perceived my grief.

Son of Conachar! he said, is the king of Tura[66] low? Why bursts thy sigh in secret? And why descends the tear?—Comes the car-borne Torlath? Or the sound of the red-haired Cairbar?——They come!—for I behold thy grief. Mossy Tura's king[67] is low!—Shall I not rush to battle?—But I cannot lift the spear!—O had mine arm the strength of Cuchullin, soon would Cairbar fly; the fame of my fathers would be renewed; and the deeds of other times!

He took his bow. The tears flow down, from both his sparkling eyes.—Grief saddens round: the bards bend forward, from their hundred harps. The lone blast touched their trembling strings. The sound[68] is sad and low.

A voice is heard at a distance, as of one in grief; it was Carril of other times, who came from dark Slimora[69].—He told of the death of Cuchullin, and of his mighty deeds. The people were scattered round his tomb: their arms lay on the ground. They had forgot the war, for he, their fire, was seen no more.

But who, said the soft-voiced Carril, come like the bounding roes? their stature is like the young trees of the plain,[70] growing in a shower:—Soft and ruddy are their cheeks; but fearless souls look forth from their eyes?—— Who but the sons of Usnoth[71], the car-borne chiefs of Etha?[72] The people rise on every side, like the strength of an half-extinguished fire, when the winds come, sudden, from the desert, on their rustling wings.[73]—The sound of Caithbat's[74] shield was heard. The heroes[75] saw Cuchullin[76] in Nathos. So rolled his sparkling eyes: his steps were such on heath.——Battles are fought at Lego: the sword of Nathos prevails. Soon shalt thou behold him in thy halls, king of Temora of Groves!

And soon may I behold the chief! replied the blue-eyed king. But my soul is sad for Cuchullin; his voice was pleasant in mine ear.—Often have we moved, on Dora, to the chace of the dark-brown hinds: his bow was unerring on the mountains.—He spoke of mighty men. He told of the deeds of my fathers; and I felt my joy.[77]—But sit thou at the feast, O bard,[78] I have often heard thy voice. Sing in the praise of Cuchullin; and of that mighty stranger[79].

Day rose on woody[80] Temora, with all the beams of the east. Trathin[81] came to the hall, the son of old Gelláma[82].—I behold, he said, a dark[83] cloud in the desert, king of Innisfail![84] a cloud it seemed at first, but now a croud of men. One strides before them in his strength; his red hair flies in wind. His shield glitters to the beam of the east. His spear is in his hand.

Call him to the feast of Temora, replied the king of Erin.[85] My hall is the house of strangers, son of the generous Gelláma!—Perhaps it is the chief of Etha, coming in the sound of his[86] renown.—Hail, mighty[87] stranger, art thou of the friends of Cormac?—But Carril, he is dark, and unlovely; and he draws his sword. Is that the son of Usnoth, bard of the times of old?

It is not the son of Usnoth, said Carril, but the chief of Atha.[88]——Why comest thou in thy arms to Temora, Cairbar[89] of the gloomy brow? Let not thy sword rise against Cormac! Whither dost thou turn thy speed?

He passed on in his darkness, and seized the hand of the king. Cormac foresaw his death, and the rage of his eyes arose.—Retire, thou gloomy[90] chief of Atha: Nathos comes with battle.—Thou art bold in Cormac's hall, for his arm is weak.—The sword entered the side of the king: he fell in the halls of his fathers. His fair hair is in the dust. His blood is smoking round.

And art thou fallen in thy halls,[91] O son of noble Artho? The shield of Cuchullin was not near. Nor the spear of thy father. Mournful are the mountains of Erin, for the chief of the people is low!——Blest be thy soul, O Cormac! thou art darkened in thy youth.

My[92] words came to the ears of Cairbar, and he closed us[93] in the midst of darkness. He feared to stretch his sword to the bards,[94] though his soul was dark. Long had[95] we pined alone: at length, the noble Cathmor[96] came.—He heard our voice from the cave; he turned the eye of his wrath on Cairbar.

Chief of Atha![97] he said, how long wilt thou pain my soul? Thy heart is like the rock of the desert;[98] and thy thoughts are dark.[99]—But thou art the brother of Cathmor, and he will fight thy battles.[100]——But Cathmor's[101] soul is not like thine, thou feeble hand of war! The light of my bosom is stained with thy deeds: the bards will not sing of my renown. They may say, "Cathmor was brave, but he fought for gloomy Cairbar." They will pass over my tomb in silence: my fame shall not be heard.—Cairbar! loose the bards: they are the sons of other[102] times. Their voice shall be heard in other years; after the kings of Temora have failed.——

We came forth at the words of the chief. We saw him in his strength. He was like thy youth, O Fingal, when thou first didst lift the spear.—His face was like the plain of the sun, when it is bright: no darkness travelled over his brow. But he came with his thousands to Ullin;[103] to aid the red-haired Cairbar: and now he comes to revenge his death, O king of woody Morven.——

And let him come, replied the king; I love a foe like Cathmor. His soul is great;[104] his arm is strong, his battles are full of fame.——But the little soul is a vapour that hovers round the marshy lake: it never rises on the green hill, lest the winds should meet it there: its dwelling is in the cave, it sends forth the dart of death.

Our young heroes, O warriors, are like the renown of our fathers.—They fight in youth; they fall: their names are in the song. Fingal is amidst his darkening years. He must not fall, as an aged oak, across a secret stream. Near it are the steps of the hunter, as it lies beneath the wind. "How has that tree fallen?" He, whistling, strides along.

Raise the song of joy, ye bards of Morven, that our souls may forget the past.—The red stars look on us from the clouds, and silently descend. Soon shall the grey beam of the morning rise, and shew us the foes of Cormac.——Fillan![105] take the spear of the king; go to Mora's dark-brown side. Let thine eyes travel over the heath, like flames of fire.[106] Observe the foes of Fingal, and the course of generous Cathmor. I hear a distant sound, like the falling of rocks in the desert.——But strike thou thy shield, at times, that they may not come through night, and the fame of Morven cease.—I begin to be alone, my son, and I dread the fall of my renown.

The voice of the bards arose. The king leaned on the shield of Trenmor.—Sleep descended on his eyes; his future battles rose in his dreams. The host are sleeping around. Dark-haired Fillan observed the foe. His steps are on a distant hill: we hear, at times, his clanging shield.

TEMORA:

AN

EPIC POEM.

BOOK SECOND.

ARGUMENT to Book II.

This book opens, we may suppose, about midnight, with a soliloquy of Ossian, who had retired, from the rest of the army, to mourn for his son Oscar. Upon hearing the noise of Cathmor's army approaching, he went to find out his brother Fillan, who kept the watch, on the hill of Mora, in the front of Fingal's army. In the conversation of the brothers, the episode of Conar, the son of Trenmor, who was the first king of Ireland, is introduced, which lays open the origin of the contests between the Caël and Firbolg, the two nations who first possessed themselves of that Island. Ossian kindles a fire on Mora; upon which Cathmor desisted from the design he had formed of surprising the army of the Caledonians. He calls a council of his chiefs; reprimands Foldath for advising a night-attack, as the Irish army were so much superior in number to the enemy. The bard Fonar introduces the story of Crothar, the ancestor of the king, which throws further light on the history of Ireland, and the original pretensions of the family of Atha, to the throne of that kingdom. The Irish chiefs lie down to rest, and Cathmor himself undertakes the watch. In his circuit, round the army, he is met by Ossian. The interview of the two heroes is described. Cathmor obtains a promise from Ossian, to order a funeral elegy to be sung over the grave of Cairbar; it being the opinion of the times, that the souls of the dead could not be happy, till their elegies were sung by a bard. Morning comes. Cathmor and Ossian part; and the latter, casually meeting with Carril the son of Kinfena, sends that bard, with a funeral song, to the tomb of Cairbar.

TEMORA: BOOK SECOND.

[1]Father of heroes, Trenmor! dweller[2] of eddying winds! where the dark-red course of[3] thunder marks the troubled clouds! Open thou thy stormy halls, and let the bards of old be near: let them draw near, with their songs and their half viewless harps. No dweller of misty valley comes; no hunter unknown at his streams; but the car-borne Oscar from the folds[4] of war. Sudden is thy change, my son, from what thou wert on dark Moi-lena! The blast folds thee in its skirt, and rustles along the sky.

Dost thou not behold thy father, at the stream of night? The chiefs of Morven sleep far-distant. They have lost no son. But ye have lost a hero, Chiefs of streamy[5] Morven! Who could equal his strength, when battle rolled against his side, like the darkness of crowded waters?——Why this cloud on Ossian's soul? It ought to burn in danger. Erin is near with her host. The king of Morven[6] is alone.—Alone thou shalt not be, my father, while I can lift the spear.

I rose, in my rattling arms.[7] I listened to the wind of night.[8] The shield of Fillan[9] is not heard. I shook for the son of Fingal. Why should the foe come, by night; and the dark-haired warrior fail?——Distant, sullen murmurs rise: like the noise of the lake of Lego, when its waters shrink, in the days of frost, and all its bursting ice resounds. The people of Lara look to heaven, and foresee the storm.—My steps are forward on the heath: the spear of Oscar in my hand. Red stars looked from high. I gleamed, along the night.—I saw Fillan silent before me, bending forward from Mora's rock. He heard the shout of the foe; the joy of his soul arose. He heard my sounding tread, and turned his lifted spear.

Comest thou, son of night, in peace? Or dost thou meet my wrath? The foes of Fingal are mine. Speak, or fear my steel.—I stand, not in vain,[10] the shield of Morven's race.

Never mayst thou stand in vain, son of blue-eyed Clatho. Fingal begins to be alone; darkness gathers on the last of his days. Yet he has two[11] sons who ought to shine in war. Who ought to be two beams of light, near the steps of his departure.

Son of Fingal, replied the youth, it is not long since I raised the spear. Few are the marks of my sword in battle, but my soul is fire. The chiefs of Bolga[12] crowd around the shield of generous Cathmor. Their gathering is on that heath. Shall my steps approach their host? I yielded to Oscar alone, in the strife of the race, on Cona.

Fillan, thou shalt not approach their host, nor fall before thy fame is known. My name is heard in song: when needful I advance.—From the skirts of night I shall view their gleaming tribes.—Why, Fillan, didst thou speak of Oscar, to call forth my sigh? I must forget[13] the warrior, till the storm is rolled away. Sadness ought not to dwell in danger, nor the tear in the eye of war. Our fathers forgot their fallen sons, till the noise of arms was past. Then sorrow returned to the tomb, and the song of bards arose.[14]

Conar[15] was the brother of Trathal, first of mortal men. His battles were on every coast. A thousand streams rolled down the blood of his foes. His fame filled green Erin, like a pleasant gale. The nations gathered in Ullin, and they blessed the king; the king of the race of their fathers, from the land of hinds.[16]

The chiefs[17] of the south were gathered, in the darkness of their pride. In the horrid cave of Moma[18], they mixed their secret words. Thither often, they said, the spirits of their fathers came; shewing their pale forms from the chinky rocks, and reminding them of the honor of Bolga.—Why should Conar reign, the son of streamy Morven?[19]

They came forth, like the streams of the desart, with the roar of their hundred tribes. Conar was a rock before them: broken they rolled on every side. But often they returned, and the sons of Ullin[20] fell. The king stood, among the tombs of his warriors, and darkly bent his mournful face. His soul was rolled into itself; he marked the place, where he was to fall; when Trathal came, in his strength, the chief of[21] cloudy Morven.—Nor did he come alone; Colgar[22] was at his side; Colgar the son of the king and of white-bosomed Solin-corma.

As Trenmor, cloathed with meteors, descends from the halls of thunder, pouring the dark storm before him over the troubled sea: so Colgar descended to battle, and wasted the echoing field. His father rejoiced over the hero: but an arrow came. His tomb was raised, without a tear. The king was to revenge his son.—He lightened forward in battle, till Bolga yielded at her streams.

When peace returned to the land, and his blue waves bore the king to Morven: then he remembered his son, and poured the silent tear. Thrice did the bards, at the cave of Furmóno, call the soul of Colgar. They called him to the hills of his land; he heard them in his mist. Trathal placed his sword in the cave, that the spirit of his son might rejoice.

[23]Colgar, son of Trathal, said Fillan, thou wert renowned in youth! But the king hath not marked my sword, bright-streaming on the field. I go forth with the crowd: I return, without my fame.——But the foe approaches, Ossian. I hear their murmur on the heath. The sound of their steps is like thunder, in the bosom of the ground, when the rocking hills shake their groves, and not a blast pours from the darkened sky.

Sudden I turned[24] on my spear, and raised the flame of an oak on high. I spread it large, on Mora's wind. Cathmor stopt in his course.—Gleaming he stood, like a rock, on whose sides are the wandering[25] of blasts; which seize its echoing streams and clothe them over with ice. So stood the friend[26] of strangers. The winds lift his heavy locks. Thou art the tallest of the race of Erin, king of streamy Atha!

First of bards, said Cathmor, Fonar[27], call the chiefs of Erin. Call red-hair'd Cormar, dark-browed Malthos, the side-long-looking gloom of Marónan. Let the pride of Foldath appear: the red-rolling eye of Turlótho. Nor let Hidalla be forgot; his voice, in danger, is like[28] the sound of a shower, when it falls in the blasted vale, near Atha's failing stream.[29]

They came, in their clanging arms. They bent forward to his voice, as if a spirit of their fathers spoke from a cloud of night.—Dreadful shone they to the light; like the fall of the stream of Brumo[30], when the meteor lights it, before the nightly stranger. Shuddering, he stops in his journey, and looks up for the beam of the morn.

[31]Why delights Foldath, said the king, to pour the blood of foes, by night? Fails his arm in battle, in the beams of day? Few are the foes before us, why should we clothe us in mist?[32] The valiant delight to shine, in the battles of their land.——

Thy counsel was in vain, chief of Moma; the eyes of Morven do not sleep. They are watchful, as eagles, on their mossy rocks.—Let each collect, beneath his cloud, the strength of his roaring tribe. To-morrow I move, in light, to meet the foes of Bolga!—Mighty[33] was he, that is low, the race of Borbar-Duthul!

Not unmarked, said Foldath, were my steps before thy race. In light, I met the foes of Cairbar; the warrior praised my deeds.—But his stone was raised without a tear? No bard sung[34] over Erin's king; and shall his foes rejoice along their mossy hills?—No: they must not rejoice: he was the friend of Foldath. Our words were mixed, in secret, in Moma's silent cave; whilst thou, a boy in the field, pursuedst the thistle's beard.—With Moma's sons I shall rush abroad, and find the foe, on his dusky hills. Fingal shall lie without his song, the grey-haired king of Selma.

Dost thou think, thou feeble man, replied the chief of Atha; dost[35] thou think that he[36] can fall, without his fame, in Erin? Could the bards be silent, at the tomb of the mighty Fingal?[37] The song would burst in secret; and the spirit of the king rejoice.—It is when thou shalt fall, that the bard shall forget the song. Thou art dark, chief of Moma, tho' thine arm is a tempest in war.—Do I forget the king of Erin, in his narrow house? My soul is not lost to Cairbar, the brother of my love. I marked the bright beams of joy, which travelled over his cloudy mind, when I returned, with fame, to Atha of the streams.

Tall they removed, beneath the words of the king; each to his own dark tribe; where, humming, they rolled on the heath, faint-glittering to the stars: like waves, in the rocky bay, before the nightly wind.——Beneath an oak, lay the chief of Atha: his shield, a dusky round, hung high. Near him, against a rock, leaned the stranger[38] of Inis-huna: that beam of light, with wandering locks, from Lumon of the roes.—At distance rose the voice of Fonar, with the deeds of the days of old. The song fails, at times, in Lubar's growing roar.

[39]Crothar, begun the bard, first dwelt at Atha's mossy stream. A thousand[40] oaks, from the mountains, formed his echoing hall. The gathering of the people was there, around the feast of the blue-eyed king.—But who, among his chiefs, was like the stately Crothar? Warriors kindled in his presence. The young sigh of the virgins rose. In Alnecma[41] was the warrior honoured; the first of the race of Bolga.

He pursued the chace in Ullin: on the moss-covered top of Drumárdo. From the wood looked the daughter of Cathmin, the blue-rolling eye of Con-láma. Her sigh rose in secret. She bent her head, midst her wandering locks. The moon looked in, at night, and saw the white-tossing of her arms; for she thought of the mighty Crothar, in the season of her dreams.

Three days feasted Crothar with Cathmin. On the fourth they awaked the hinds. Con-láma moved to the chace, with all her lovely steps. She met Crothar in the narrow path. The bow fell, at once, from her hand. She turned her face away, and half-hid it with her locks.——The love of Crothar rose. He brought the white-bosomed maid to Atha.——Bards raised the song in her presence; joy dwelt round the daughter of Ullin.[42]

The pride of Turloch rose, a youth who loved the white-handed Con-láma. He came, with battle, to Alnecma; to Atha of the roes. Cormul went forth to the strife, the brother of car-borne Crothar. He went forth, but he fell, and the sigh of his people rose.——Silent and tall, across the stream, came the darkening strength of Crothar: he rolled the foe from Alnecma, and returned, midst the joy of Con-láma.

Battle on battle comes. Blood is poured on blood. The tombs of the valiant rise. Erin's clouds are hung round with ghosts. The chiefs of the south gathered round the echoing shield of Crothar. He came, with death, to the paths of the foe. The virgins wept, by the streams of Ullin. They looked to the mist of the hill, no hunter descended from its folds. Silence darkened in the land: blasts sighed lonely on grassy tombs.

Descending like the eagle of heaven, with all his rustling wings, when he forsakes the blast with joy, the son of Trenmor came; Conar, arm of death, from Morven of the groves.—He poured his might along green Erin. Death dimly strode behind his sword. The sons of Bolga fled, from his course, as from a stream, that bursting from the stormy desart, rolls the fields together, with all their echoing woods.——Crothar[43] met him in battle: but Alnecma's warriors fled. The king of Atha slowly retired, in the grief of his soul. He, afterwards, shone in the south; but dim as the sun of Autumn; when he visits, in his robes of mist, Lara of dark streams. The withered grass is covered with dew: the field, tho' bright, is sad.

Why wakes the bard before me, said Cathmor, the memory of those who fled? Has some ghost, from his dusky cloud, bent forward to thine ear; to frighten Cathmor from the field with the tales of old? Dwellers of the folds[44] of night, your voice is but a blast to me; which takes the grey thistle's head, and strews its beard on streams. Within my bosom is a voice; others hear it not. His soul forbids the king of Erin to shrink back from war.

Abashed the bard sinks back in night: retired, he bends above a stream. His thoughts are on the days of Atha, when Cathmor heard his song with joy. His tears come rolling down: the winds are in his beard.

Erin sleeps around. No sleep comes down on Cathmor's eyes. Dark, in his soul, he saw the spirit of low-laid Cairbar. He saw him, without his song, rolled in a blast of night.——He rose. His steps were round the host. He struck, at times, his echoing shield. The sound reached Ossian's ear, on Mora of the hinds.[45]

Fillan, I said, the foes advance. I hear the shield of war. Stand thou in the narrow path. Ossian shall mark their course. If over my fall the host shall pour; then be thy buckler heard. Awake the king on his heath, lest his fame should cease.[46]

I strode, in all my rattling arms; wide-bounding over a stream that darkly-winded, in the field, before the king of Atha. Green Atha's king, with lifted spear, came forward on my course.—Now would we have mixed in horrid fray, like two contending ghosts, that bending forward, from two clouds, send forth the roaring winds; did not Ossian behold, on high, the helmet of Erin's kings. The eagle's wing spread above it, rustling in the breeze. A red star looked thro' the plumes. I stopt the lifted spear.

The helmet of kings is before me! Who art thou, son of night? Shall Ossian's spear be renowned, when thou art lowly-laid?——At once he dropt the gleaming lance. Growing before me seemed the form. He stretched his hand in night; and spoke the words of kings.

Friend of the spirit[47] of heroes, do I meet thee thus in shades? I have wished for thy stately steps in Atha, in the days of feasts.—Why should my spear now arise? The sun must behold us, Ossian; when we bend, gleaming, in the strife. Future warriors shall mark the place: and, shuddering, think of other years. They shall mark it, like the haunt of ghosts, pleasant and dreadful to the soul.

And shall it be forgot, I said, where we meet in peace? Is the remembrance of battles always pleasant to the soul? Do not we behold, with joy, the place where our fathers feasted? But our eyes are full of tears, on the field of their wars.—This stone shall rise, with all its moss, and speak to other years. "Here Cathmor and Ossian met! the warriors met in peace!"— When thou, O stone, shalt fail: and Lubar's stream roll quite away! then shall the traveller come, and bend here, perhaps, in rest. When the darkened moon is rolled over his head, our shadowy forms may come, and, mixing with his dreams, remind him of this place. But why turnest thou so dark away, son of Borbar-duthul[48]?

Not forgot, son of Fingal, shall we ascend these winds. Our deeds are streams of light, before the eyes of bards. But darkness is rolled on Atha: the king is low, without his song: still there was a beam towards Cathmor from his stormy soul; like the moon, in a cloud, amidst the dark-red course of thunder.

Son of Erin, I replied, my wrath dwells not, in his house[49]. My hatred flies, on eagle-wing from the foe that is low.—He shall hear the song of bards; Cairbar shall rejoice on his wind.

Cathmor's swelling soul arose: he took the dagger from his side; and placed it gleaming in my hand. He placed it, in my hand, with sighs, and, silent, strode away.——Mine eyes followed his departure. He dimly gleamed, like the form of a ghost, which meets a traveller, by night, on the dark-skirted heath. His words are dark like songs of old: with morning strides the unfinished shade away.

[50] Who comes from Lubar's vale? From the folds[51] of the morning mist? The drops of heaven are on his head. His steps are in the paths of the sad. It is Carril of other times. He comes from Tura's silent cave. I behold it dark in the rock, thro' the thin folds of mist. There, perhaps, Cuchullin sits, on the blast which bends its trees. Pleasant is the song of the morning from the bard of Erin!

The waves crowd away for fear: they hear the sound of thy coming forth, O sun!——Terrible is thy beauty, son of heaven, when death is folded in[52] thy locks; when thou rollest thy vapors before thee, over the blasted host. But pleasant is thy beam to the hunter, sitting by the rock in a storm, when thou lookest from thy[53] parted cloud, and brightenest his dewy locks; he looks down on the streamy vale, and beholds the descent of roes.——How long shalt thou rise on war, and roll, a bloody shield, thro' heaven? I see the deaths of heroes dark-wandering over thy face!——Why wander the words of Carril! does the son[54] of heaven mourn! he is unstained in his course, ever rejoicing in his fire.——Roll on, thou careless light; thou too, perhaps, must fall. Thy dun robe[55] may seize thee, struggling, in thy[56] sky.

Pleasant is the voice of the song,[57] O Carril, to Ossian's soul! It is like the shower of the morning, when it comes through the rustling vale, on which the sun looks thro' mist, just rising from his rocks.——But this is no time, O bard, to sit down, at the strife of song. Fingal is in arms on the vale. Thou seest the flaming shield of the king. His face darkens between his locks. He beholds the wide rolling of Erin.——

Does not Carril behold that tomb, beside the roaring stream? Three stones lift their grey heads, beneath a bending oak. A king is lowly laid: give thou his soul to the wind. He is the brother of Cathmor! open his airy hall.—Let thy song be a stream of joy to Cairbar's darkened ghost.

T E M O R A:

AN

EPIC POEM.

BOOK THIRD.

ARGUMENT to Book III.

Morning coming on, Fingal, after a speech to his people, devolves the command on Gaul, the son of Morni; it being the custom of the times, that the king should not engage, till the necessity of affairs required his superior valour and conduct.—The king and Ossian retire to the rock of Cormul, which overlooked the field of battle. The bards sing the war-song. The general conflict is described. Gaul, the son of Morni, distinguishes himself; kills Tur-lathon, chief of Moruth, and other chiefs of lesser name.—On the other hand, Foldath, who commanded the Irish army (for Cathmor, after the example of Fingal, kept himself for battle) fights gallantly; kills Connal, chief of Dun-lora, and advances to engage Gaul himself. Gaul, in the mean time, being wounded in the hand, by a random arrow, is covered by Fillan, the son of Fingal, who performs prodigies of valour. Night comes on. The horn of Fingal recalls his army. The bards meet them, with a congratulatory song, in which the praises of Gaul and Fillan are particularly celebrated. The chiefs sit down at a feast; Fingal misses Connal. The episode of Connal and Duth-caron is introduced; which throws further light on the ancient history of Ireland. Carril is dispatched to raise the tomb of Connal.—The action of this book takes up the second day, from the opening of the poem.

TEMORA: BOOK THIRD.

[1]Who is that, at blue-streaming Lubar; by the bending hill of the roes? Tall, he leans on an oak torn from high, by nightly winds.—Who but Comhal's son, brightening in the last of his fields? His grey hair is on the breeze: he half unsheaths the sword of Luno. His eyes are turned to Moi-lena, to the dark rolling[2] of foes.—Dost thou hear the voice of the king? It is like the bursting of a stream, in the desert, when it comes between its echoing rocks, to the blasted field of the sun.

Wide-skirted comes down the foe! Sons of woody Morven,[3] arise. Be ye like the rocks of my[4] land, on whose brown sides are the rolling of waters. A beam of joy comes on my soul; I see them mighty before me. It is when the foe is feeble, that the sighs of Fingal are heard; lest death should come, without renown, and darkness dwell on his tomb.—Who shall lead the war, against the host of Alnecma? It is, only when danger grows, that my sword shall shine.—Such was the custom, heretofore, of Trenmor the ruler of winds: and thus descended to battle the blue-shielded Trathal.

The chiefs bend towards the king: each darkly seems to claim the war. They tell, by halves, their mighty deeds: and turn their eyes on Erin. But far before the rest the son of Morni stood: silent he stood, for who had not heard of the battles of Gaul? They rose within his soul. His hand, in secret, seized the sword. The sword which he brought from Strumon, when the strength of Morni failed[5].

On his spear stood the son of Clatho[6] in the wandering of his locks. Thrice he raised his eyes to Fingal: his voice thrice failed him, as he spoke.—Fillan could not boast of battles; at once he strode away. Bent over a distant stream he stood: the tear hung in his eye. He struck, at times, the thistle's head, with his inverted spear.

Nor is he unseen of Fingal. Sidelong he beheld his son. He beheld him, with bursting joy; and turned, amidst his crowded soul. In silence turned the king towards Mora of woods. He hid the big tear with his locks.—At length his voice is heard.

[7]First of the sons of Morni; thou rock that defiest the storm! Lead thou my battle, for the race of low-laid Cormac. No boy's staff is thy spear: no harmless beam of light thy sword. Son of Morni of steeds, behold the foe; destroy.——Fillan, observe the chief: he is not calm in strife: nor burns he, heedless, in battle; my son, observe the king.[8] He is strong as Lubar's stream, but never foams and roars. High on cloudy Mora, Fingal shall behold the war. Stand, Ossian[9], near thy father, by the falling stream.— Raise the voice, O bards; Morven,[10] move beneath the sound. It is my latter field; clothe it over with light.

As the sudden rising of winds; or distant rolling of troubled seas, when some dark ghost, in wrath, heaves the billows over an isle, the seat of mist, on the deep, for many dark-brown years: so terrible is the sound of the host, wide-moving over the field. Gaul is tall before them: the streams glitter within his strides. The bards raised the song by his side; he struck his shield between. On the skirts of the blast, the tuneful voices rose.

On Crona, said the bards, there bursts a stream by night. It swells, in its own dark course, till morning's early beam. Then comes it white from the hill, with the rocks and their hundred groves. Far be my steps from Crona: Death is tumbling there. Be ye a stream from Mora, sons of cloudy Morven.

Who rises, from his car, on Clutha? The hills are troubled before the king! The dark woods echo round, and lighten at his steel. See him, amidst the foe, like Colgach's[11] sportful ghost; when he scatters the clouds, and rides the eddying winds! It is Morni[12] of the bounding steeds! Be like thy father, Gaul!

[13]Selma is opened wide. Bards take the trembling harps. Ten youths carry the oak of the feast. A distant sun-beam marks the hill. The dusky waves of the blast fly over the fields of grass.—Why art thou so silent, Morven?[14]— The king returns with all his fame. Did not the battle roar; yet peaceful is his brow? It roared, and Fingal overcame.—Be like thy father, Fillan.

They moved beneath the song.—High waved their arms, as rushy fields, beneath autumnal winds. On Mora stood the king in arms. Mist flies round his buckler broad; as, aloft, it hung on a bough, on Cormul's mossy rock.— In silence I stood by Fingal, and turned my eyes on Cromla's[15] wood: lest I should behold the host, and rush amidst my swelling soul. My foot is forward on the heath. I glittered, tall, in steel: like the falling stream of Tromo, which nightly winds bind over with ice.—The boy sees it, on high, gleaming to the early beam: towards it he turns his ear, and wonders why it is so silent.

Nor bent over a stream is Cathmor, like a youth in a peaceful field: wide he drew forward the war, a dark and troubled wave.—But when he beheld Fingal on Mora; his generous pride arose. "Shall the chief of Atha fight, and no king in the field? Foldath lead my people forth. Thou art a beam of fire."

Forth-issued the chief[16] of Moma, like a cloud, the robe of ghosts. He drew his sword, a flame, from his side; and bade the battle move.—The tribes, like ridgy waves, dark pour their strength around. Haughty is his stride before them: his red eye rolls in wrath.—He called the chief[17] of Dunratho[18]; and his words were heard.

Cormul, thou beholdest that path. It winds green behind the foe. Place thy people there; lest Morven[19] should escape from my sword.—Bards of green-valleyed Erin, let no voice of yours arise. The sons of Morven must fall without song. They are the foes of Cairbar. Hereafter shall the traveller meet their dark, thick mist on Lena, where it wanders, with their ghosts, beside the reedy lake. Never shall they rise, without song, to the dwelling of winds.

Cormul darkened, as he went: behind him rushed his tribe. They sunk beyond the rock: Gaul spoke to Fillan of Moruth;[20] as his eye pursued the course of the dark-eyed king[21] of Dunratho.

Thou beholdest the steps of Cormul; let thine arm be strong. When he is low, son of Fingal, remember Gaul in war. Here I fall forward into battle, amidst the ridge of shields.

The sign of death arose: the dreadful sound of Morni's shield. Gaul poured his voice between. Fingal rose, high on Mora. He saw them, from wing to wing, bending[22] in the strife. Gleaming, on his own dark hill, the strength[23] of Atha stood.—They[24] were like two spirits of heaven, standing each on his gloomy cloud; when they pour abroad the winds, and lift the roaring seas. The blue-tumbling of waves is before them, marked with the paths of whales. Themselves are calm and bright; and the gale lifts[25] their locks of mist.

What beam of light hangs high in air? It is Morni's dreadful sword.— Death is strewed on thy paths, O Gaul; thou foldest them together in thy rage.—Like a young oak falls Tur-lathon[26], with his branches round him. His high-bosomed spouse stretches her white arms, in dreams, to the return- ing king,[27] as she sleeps by gurgling Moruth, in her disordered locks. It is his ghost, Oichoma; the chief is lowly laid. Hearken not to the winds for Tur-lathon's echoing shield. It is pierced, by his streams, and its sound is past away.

Not peaceful is the hand of Foldath: he winds his course in blood. Connal met him in fight; they mixed their clanging steel.—Why should mine eyes behold them! Connal, thy locks are grey.—Thou wert the friend of strang- ers, at the moss-covered rock of Dunlora. When the skies were rolled together; then thy feast was spread. The stranger heard the winds without; and rejoiced at thy burning oak.—Why, son of Duth-caron, art thou laid in blood! The blasted tree bends above thee: thy shield lies broken near. Thy blood mixes with the stream; thou breaker of the shields!

[28]I took the spear, in my wrath; but Gaul rushed forward on the foe.[29] The feeble pass by his side; his rage is turned on Moma's chief. Now they had raised their deathful spears: unseen an arrow came. It pierced the hand of Gaul; his steel fell sounding to earth.——Young Fillan came[30], with Cormul's shield, and stretched it large before the king.[31] Foldath sent his shout abroad, and kindled all the field: as a blast that lifts the broad-winged flame, over Lumon's[32] echoing groves.

Son of blue-eyed Clatho, said Gaul, thou[33] art a beam from heaven; that coming on the troubled deep, binds up the tempest's wing.—Cormul is fallen before thee. Early art thou in the fame of thy fathers.—Rush not too far, my hero, I cannot lift the spear to aid. I stand harmless in battle: but my voice shall be poured abroad.—The sons of Morven[34] shall hear, and remember my former deeds.

His terrible voice rose on the wind, the host bend forward in the fight. Often had they heard him, at Strumon, when he called them to the chace of the hinds.——Himself stood tall, amidst the war, as an oak in the skirts of a storm, which now is clothed, on high, in mist: then shews its broad, waving head; the musing hunter lifts his eye from his own rushy field.

My soul pursues thee, O Fillan, thro' the path of thy fame. Thou rolledst the foe before thee.—Now Foldath, perhaps, would fly; but night came down with its clouds; and Cathmor's horn was heard.[35] The sons of Morven heard[36] the voice of Fingal, from Mora's gathered mist. The bards poured their song, like dew, on the returning war.

Who comes from Strumon, they said, amidst her wandering locks? She is mournful in her steps, and lifts her blue eyes towards Erin. Why art thou sad, Evir-choma[37]? Who is like thy chief in renown? He descended dreadful to battle; he returns, like a light from a cloud. He lifted the sword in wrath: they shrunk before blue-shielded Gaul!

Joy, like the rustling gale, comes on the soul of the king. He remembers the battles of old; the days, wherein his fathers fought. The days of old return on Fingal's mind, as he beholds the renown of his son. As the sun rejoices, from his cloud, over the tree his beams have raised, as it shakes its lonely head on the heath; so joyful is the king over Fillan.

As the rolling of thunder on hills, when Lara's fields are still and dark, such are the steps of Morven[38] pleasant and dreadful to the ear. They return with their sound, like eagles to their dark-browed rock, after the prey is torn on the field, the dun sons of the bounding hind. Your fathers rejoice from their clouds, sons of streamy Cona.[39]

Such was the nightly voice of bards, on Mora of the hinds. A flame rose, from an hundred oaks, which winds had torn from Cormul's steep. The feast is spread in the midst: around sat the gleaming chiefs. Fingal is there in his strength; the eagle-wing[40] of his helmet sounds: the rustling blasts of the west, unequal rushed thro' night. Long looked the king in silence round: at length, his words were heard.

My soul feels a want in our joy. I behold a breach among my friends.— The head of one tree is low: the squally wind pours in on Selma.—Where is the chief of Dun-lora? Ought he[41] to be forgot at the feast? When did he forget the stranger, in the midst of his echoing hall?—Ye are silent in my presence!—Connal is then no more.—Joy meet thee, O warrior, like a stream of light. Swift be thy course to thy fathers, in the folds of the mountain-winds.[42]—Ossian, thy soul is fire: kindle the memory of the king. Awake the battles of Connal, when first he shone in war. The locks of Connal were grey; his days of youth[43] were mixed with mine. In one day Duth-caron first strung our bows, against the roes of Dun-lora.

Many, I said, are our paths to battle, in green-hilled Inisfail.[44] Often did our sails arise, over the blue-tumbling waters;[45] when we came, in other days, to aid the race of Conar.

The strife roared once in Alnecma, at the foam-covered streams of Duth-úla[46]. With Cormac descended to battle Duth-caron from cloudy Morven.[47] Nor descended Duth-caron alone, his son was by his side, the long-haired youth of Connal, lifting the first of his spears. Thou didst command them, O Fingal, to aid the king of Erin.

Like the bursting strength of a stream,[48] the sons of Bolga rushed to war: Colc-ulla[49] was before them, the chief of blue-streaming Atha. The battle was mixed on the plain, like the meeting of two stormy seas.[50] Cormac[51] shone in his own strife, bright as the forms of his fathers. But, far before the rest, Duth-caron hewed down the foe. Nor slept the arm of Connal, by his father's side. Atha[52] prevailed on the plain: like scattered mist, fled the people of Ullin[53].

Then rose the sword of Duth-caron, and the steel of broad-shielded Connal. They shaded their flying friends, like two rocks with their heads of pine.—Night came down on Duth-ula: silent strode the chiefs over the field. A mountain-stream roared across the path, nor could Duth-caron bound over its course.—Why stands my father? said Connal.—I hear the rushing foe.

Fly, Connal, he said; thy father's strength begins to fail.—I come wounded from battle; here let me rest in night.—"But thou shalt not remain alone, said Connal's bursting sigh. My shield is an eagle's wing to cover the king of Dun-lora." He bends dark above the chief:[54] the mighty Duth-caron dies.

Day rose, and night returned. No lonely bard appeared, deep-musing on the heath: and could Connal leave the tomb of his father, till he should receive his fame?—He bent the bow against the roes[55] of Duth-ula; he spread the lonely feast.—Seven nights he laid his head on the tomb, and saw his father in his dreams. He saw him rolled dark, in a blast, like the vapor of reedy Lego.—At length the steps of Colgan[56] came, the bard of high Temora. Duth-caron received his fame, and brightened, as he rose on the wind.

Pleasant to the ear, said Fingal, is the praise of the kings of men; when their bows are strong in battle; when they soften at the sight of the sad.— Thus let my name be renowned, when bards shall lighten my rising soul. Carril, son of Kinfena; take the bards and raise a tomb. To night let Connal dwell, within his narrow house: let not the soul of the valiant wander on the winds.—Faint glimmers the moon on Moi-lena, thro' the broad-headed groves of the hill: raise stones, beneath its beams, to all the fallen in war.— Tho' no chiefs were they, yet their hands were strong in fight. They were my rock in danger: the mountain from which I spread my eagle-wings.— Thence am I renowned: Carril forget not the low.

Loud, at once, from the hundred bards, rose the song of the tomb. Carril strode before them, they are the murmur of streams behind him.[57] Silence dwells in the vales of Moi-lena, where each, with its own dark stream,[58] is winding between the hills. I heard the voice of the bards, lessening, as they moved along. I leaned forward from my shield; and felt the kindling of my soul. Half-formed the words of my song, burst forth upon the wind. So hears a tree, on the vale, the voice of spring around: it pours its green leaves to the sun, and shakes its lonely head. The hum of the mountain bee is near it; the hunter sees it, with joy, from the blasted heath.

Young Fillan, at a distance stood. His helmet lay glittering on the ground. His dark hair is loose to the blast: a beam of light is Clatho's son. He heard the words of the king, with joy; and leaned forward on his spear.

My son, said car-borne Fingal; I saw thy deeds, and my soul was glad. The fame of our fathers, I said, bursts from its gathered cloud.—Thou art brave, son of Clatho; but headlong in the strife. So did not Fingal advance, tho' he never feared a foe.—Let thy people be a ridge behind; they are thy strength in the field.—Then shalt thou be long renowned, and behold the tombs of thy fathers.[59] The memory of the past returns, my deeds in other years: when first I descended from ocean on the green-valleyed isle.—We bend towards the voice of the king. The moon looks abroad from her cloud. The grey-skirted mist is near, the dwelling of the ghosts.

Note 5: During Gaul's expedition to Tromathon, mentioned in the *poem of Oithona*, Morni his father died. Morni ordered the *sword of Strumon*, (which had been preserved, in the family, as a relique, from the days of Colgach, the most renowned of his ancestors) to be laid by his side, in the tomb: at the same time, leaving it in charge to his son, not to take it from thence, till he was reduced to the last extremity. Not long after, two of his brothers being slain, in battle, by Coldaronnan, chief of Clutha, Gaul went to his father's tomb to take the sword. His address to the spirit of the deceased hero, is the only part now remaining, of a poem of Ossian, on the subject. I shall here lay it before the reader.[60] [M]

GAUL.

"Breaker of echoing shields, whose head is deep in shades; hear me from the darkness of Clora, O son of Colgach, hear!

No rustling, like the eagle's wing, comes over the course of my streams. Deep-bosomed in the mist[61] of the desart, O king of Strumon, hear!

Dwellest thou in the shadowy breeze, that pours its dark wave over the grass? Cease to strew the beard of the thistle; O chief of Clora, hear!

Or ridest thou on a beam, amidst the dark trouble of clouds? Pourest thou the loud wind on seas, to roll their blue waves over isles? hear me, father of Gaul; amidst thy terrors, hear!

The rustling of eagles is heard, the murmuring oaks shake their heads on the hills: dreadful and pleasant is thy approach, friend of the dwelling of heroes.

MORNI.

Who awakes me, in the midst of my cloud, where my locks of mist spread on the winds? Mixed with the noise of streams, why rises the voice of Gaul?

GAUL.

My foes are around me, Morni: their dark ships descend from their waves. Give the sword of Strumon, that beam which thou hidest in thy night.

MORNI.

Take the sword of resounding Strumon; I look on thy war, my son; I look, a dim meteor, from my cloud: blue-shielded Gaul, destroy."

———————————

Note 56: Part of an old poem, on the loves of Fingal and Ros-crána, is still preserved, and goes under the name of this Colgan; but whether it is of his composition, or the production of a latter age, I shall not pretend to determine. Be that as it will, it appears, from the obsolete phrases which it contains, to be very ancient; and its poetical merit may perhaps excuse me, for laying a translation of it before the reader. What remains of the poem is a dialogue in a lyric measure, between Fingal and Ros-crána, the daughter of Cormac. She begins with a soliloquy, which is overheard by Fingal.[62] [M]

ROS-CRANA..

"By night, came a dream to Ros-crána! I feel my beating soul. No vision of the forms of the dead, came to the blue eyes of Erin. But, rising from the wave of the north, I beheld him bright in his locks. I beheld the son of the king. My beating soul is high. I laid my head down in night; again ascended the form. Why delayest thou thy coming, young rider of streamy[63] waves!

But, there, far-distant, he comes; where seas roll their green ridges in mist! Young dweller of my soul; why dost thou delay———

FINGAL.

It was the soft voice of Moi-lena! the pleasant breeze of the valley of roes! But why dost thou hide thee in shades? Young love of heroes rise.—Are not thy steps covered with light? In thy groves thou appearest,Ros-crána, like the sun in the gathering of clouds. Why dost thou hide thee in shades? Young love of heroes rise.

ROS-CRANA.

My fluttering soul is high!—Let me turn from the steps of the king. He has heard my secret voice, and shall my blue eyes roll, in his presence?—Roe of the hill of moss, toward thy dwelling I move. Meet me, ye breezes of Mora, as I move thro' the valley of winds.—But why should he ascend his ocean?—Son of heroes, my soul is thine!—My steps shall not move to the desart: the light of Ros-crána is here.

FINGAL.

It was the light tread of a ghost, the fair dweller of eddying winds. Why deceivest thou me, with thy voice? Here let me rest in shades.——Shouldst thou stretch thy white arm, from thy grove, thou sun-beam of Cormac of Erin!

ROS-CRANA.

He is gone! and my blue eyes are dim; faint-rolling, in all my tears. But, there, I behold him, alone; king of Morven,[64] my soul is thine. Ah me! what clanging of armour!—Colc-ulla of Atha is near!"—

Fingal, as we learn from the episode, with which the fourth book begins, under-took an expedition into Ireland, to aid Cormac Mac-conar against the insurrection of the Fir-bolg. It was then he saw, fell in love with, and married Ros-crána, the daughter of Cormac.——Some traditions give this poem to Ossian; but, from several circumstances, I conclude it to be an imitation, but a very happy one, of the manner of that poet.——The elegance of the sentiment, and beauty of the imagery, however, refer the composition of it to an æra of remote antiquity; for the nearer we approach to our own times, the less beautiful are the compositions of the bards.[65]
[M]

TEMORA:

AN

EPIC POEM.

BOOK FOURTH.

ARGUMENT to Book IV.

The second night continues. Fingal relates, at the feast, his own first ex-
pedition into Ireland, and his marriage with Ros-cránaa, the daughter of
Cormac, king of that island.——The Irish chiefs convene in the presence
of Cathmor. The situation of the king described. The story of Sul-malla,
the daughter of Conmor, king of Inis-huna, who, in the disguise of a
young warrior, had followed Cathmor to the war. The sullen behaviour of
Foldath, who had commanded in the battle of the preceding day, renews
the difference between him and Malthos; but Cathmor, interposing, ends
it. The chiefs feast, and hear the song of Fonar the bard. Cathmor returns
to rest, at a distance from the army. The ghost of his brother Cairbar
appears to him in a dream; and obscurely fortels the issue of the war.——
The soliloquy of the king. He discovers Sul-malla. Morning comes. Her
soliloquy closes the book.

TEMORA: BOOK FOURTH.

[1]Beneath an oak, said the king, I sat on Selma's streamy rock, when Connal rose, from the sea, with the broken spear of Duth-caron. Far-distant stood the youth, and turned away his eyes; for he remembered the steps of his father, on his own green hills. I darkened in my place: dusky thoughts rolled[2] over my soul. The kings of Erin rose before me. I half-unsheathed my sword.—Slowly approached the chiefs; they lifted up their silent eyes. Like a ridge of clouds, they wait for the bursting forth of my voice: it was to them, a wind from heaven to roll the mist away.

I bade my white sails to rise, before the roar of Cona's wind. Three hundred youths looked, from their waves, on Fingal's bossy shield. High on the mast it hung, and marked the dark-blue sea.—But when the night came down, I struck, at times, the warning boss: I struck, and looked on high, for fiery-haired Ul-erin[3].

Nor wanting[4] was the star of heaven: it travelled red between the clouds: I pursued the lovely beam, on the faint-gleaming deep.—With morning, Erin rose in mist. We came into the bay of Moi-lena, where its blue waters tumbled, in the bosom of echoing woods.—Here Cormac, in his secret hall, avoided the strength of Colc-ulla. Nor he alone avoids the foe: the blue eye of Ros-crana is there: Ros-crana[5], white-handed maid, the daughter of the king.

Grey, on his pointless spear, came forth the aged steps of Cormac. He smiled, from his waving locks, but grief was in his soul. He saw us few before him, and his sigh arose.—I see the arms of Trenmor, he said; and these are the steps of the king! Fingal! thou art a beam of light to Cormac's darkened soul.—Early is thy fame, my son: but strong are the foes of Erin. They are like the roar of streams in the land, son of car-borne Comhal.

Yet they may be rolled[6] away, I said in my rising soul. We are not of the race of the feeble, king of blue-shielded hosts. Why should fear come amongst us, like a ghost of night? The soul of the valiant grows, as foes increase in the field. Roll no darkness, king of Erin, of the young in war.

The bursting tears of the king came down. He seized my hand in silence.——"Race of the daring Trenmor,[7] I roll no cloud before thee. Thou burnest in the fire of thy fathers. I behold thy fame. It marks thy course in battles, like a stream of light.——But wait the coming of Cairbar[8]: my son must join thy sword. He calls the sons of Ullin,[9] from all their distant streams."

We came to the hall of the king, where it rose in the midst of rocks: rocks, on whose dark sides, were the marks of streams of old. Broad oaks bend around with their moss: the thick birch waves its green head.[10] Half-hid, in her shady grove, Ros-crana raised the song. Her white hands rose[11] on the harp. I beheld her blue-rolling eyes. She was like a spirit[12] of heaven half-folded in the skirt of a cloud.

Three days we feasted at Moi-lena: she rose bright amidst my troubled soul.—Cormac beheld me dark. He gave the white-bosomed maid.—She came with bending eye, amidst the wandering of her heavy locks.—She came.——Straight the battle roared.—Colc-ulla rushed;—I seized[13] my spear. My sword rose, with my people, against the ridgy foe. Alnecma fled. Colc-ulla fell. Fingal returned with fame.

He is renowned, O Fillan, who fights, in the strength of his people.[14] The bard pursues his steps, thro' the land of the foe.—But he who fights alone; few are his deeds to other times. He shines, to-day, a mighty light. To-morrow, he is low. One song contains his fame. His name is on one dark field. He is forgot, but where his tomb sends forth the tufts of grass.

Such were the words of Fingal, on Mora of the roes. Three bards, from the rock of Cormul, poured down the pleasant song. Sleep descended, in the sound, on the broad-skirted host. Carril returned, with the bards, from the tomb of Dun-lora's king.[15] The voice of morning shall not come, to the dusky bed of the hero.[16] No more shalt thou hear the tread of roes, around thy narrow house.

[17]As roll the troubled clouds, round a meteor of night, when they brighten their sides, with its light, along the heaving sea: so gathered Erin, around the gleaming form of Atha's king.[18] He, tall in the midst, careless lifts, at times, his spear: as swells or falls the sound of Fonar's distant harp.

[19]Near him leaned, against a rock, Sul-malla[20] of blue eyes, the white-bosomed daughter of Conmor king of Inis-huna. To his aid came blue-shielded Cathmor, and rolled his foes away. Sul-malla beheld him stately in the hall of feasts; nor careless rolled the eyes of Cathmor on the long-haired maid.

The third day arose, and Fithil[21] came from Erin of the streams. He told of the lifting up of the shield[22] on Morven,[23] and the danger of red-haired[24] Cairbar. Cathmor raised the sail at Cluba; but the winds were in other lands. Three days he remained on the coast, and turned his eyes on Conmor's halls.—He remembered the daughter of strangers, and his sigh arose.—Now when the winds awaked the wave: from the hill came a youth in arms; to lift the sword with Cathmor in his echoing field.——It was the white-armed Sul-malla: secret she dwelt beneath her helmet. Her steps were in the path of the king; on him her blue eyes rolled with joy, when he lay by his roaring streams.—But Cathmor thought, that, on Lumon, she still pursued the roes: or fair on a rock, stretched her white hand to the wind; to feel its course from Inis-fail,[25] the green dwelling of her love. He had promised to return, with his white-bosomed sails.——The maid is near thee, king of Atha,[26] leaning on her rock.

The tall forms of the chiefs stood around: all but dark-browed Foldath[27]. He stood beneath[28] a distant tree, rolled into his haughty soul. His bushy hair whistles in wind. At times, bursts the hum of a song.—He struck the tree, at length, in wrath; and rushed before the king.

Calm and stately, to the beam of the oak, arose the form of young Hidalla. His hair falls round his blushing cheek, in wreaths of waving light. Soft was his voice in Clon-ra[29], in the valley of his fathers; when[30] he touched the harp, in the hall, near his roaring streams.

King of Erin, said the youth,[31] now is the time of feasts. Bid the voice of bards arise, and roll the night away. The soul returns, from song, more terrible to war.—Darkness settles on Inis-fail:[32] from hill to hill bend the skirted clouds. Far and grey, on the heath, the dreadful strides of ghosts are seen: the ghosts of those who fell bend forward to their song.——Bid thou[33] the harps to rise, and brighten the dead, on their wandering blasts.

Be all the dead forgot, said Foldath's bursting wrath. Did not I fail in the field, and shall I hear the song? Yet was not my course harmless in battle: blood was a stream around my steps. But the feeble were behind me, and the foe has escaped my sword.—In Clon-ra's vale touch thou the harp; let Dura answer to thy voice;[34] while some maid looks, from the wood, on thy long, yellow locks.——Fly from Lubar's echoing plain: it is the field of heroes.

King of Temora[35], Malthos said, it is thine to lead in war. Thou art a fire to our eyes, on the dark-brown field. Like a blast thou hast past over hosts, and laid them low in blood; but who has heard thy words returning from the field?——The wrathful delight in death: their remembrance rests on the wounds of their spear. Strife is folded in their thoughts: their words are ever heard.——Thy course, chief of Moma, was like a troubled stream. The dead were rolled on thy path: but others also lift the spear. We were not feeble behind thee, but the foe was strong.

The king[36] beheld the rising rage, and bending forward of either chief: for half-unsheathed, they held their swords, and rolled their silent eyes.—Now would they have mixed in horrid fray, had not the wrath of Cathmor burned. He drew his sword: it gleamed thro' night, to the high-flaming oak.

Sons of pride, said the king, allay your swelling souls. Retire in night.— Why should my rage arise? Should I contend with both in arms?——It is no time for strife. Retire, ye clouds at my feast. Awake my soul no more.— They sunk from the king on either side; like[37] two columns of morning mist, when the sun rises, between them, on his glittering rocks. Dark is their rolling on either side; each towards its reedy pool.

Silent sat the chiefs at the feast. They looked, at times, on Atha's king, where he strode, on his rock, amidst his settling soul.—The host lay, at length, on the field: sleep descended on Moi-lena.—The voice of Fonar rose alone, beneath his distant tree. It rose in the praise of Cathmor son of Larthon[38] of Lumon. But Cathmor did not hear his praise. He lay at the roar of a stream. The rustling breeze of night flew over his whistling locks.

Cairbar[39] came to his dreams, half-seen from his low-hung cloud. Joy rose darkly in his face: he had heard the song of Carril[40].——A blast sustained his dark-skirted cloud; which he seized in the bosom of night, as he rose, with his fame, towards his airy hall. Half-mixed with the noise of the stream, he poured his feeble words.

Joy meet the soul of Cathmor: his voice was heard on Moi-lena. The bard gave his song to Cairbar: he travels on the wind. My form is in my father's hall, like the gliding of a terrible light, which winds thro'[41] the desert, in a stormy night.—No bard shall be wanting at thy tomb, when thou art lowly laid. The sons of song love the valiant.—Cathmor, thy name is a pleasant gale.—The mournful sounds arise! On Lubar's field there is a voice!— Louder still ye shadowy ghosts! the dead were full of fame.—Shrilly swells the feeble sound.—The rougher blast alone is heard!—Ah, soon is Cathmor low!

Rolled into himself he flew, wide on the bosom of his blast. The old oak felt his departure, and shook its whistling head. The king started[42] from rest, and took his deathful spear. He lifts his eyes around. He sees but dark-skirted night.

[43]It was the voice of the king; but now his form is gone. Unmarked is your path in the air, ye children of the night. Often, like a reflected beam, are ye seen in the desart wild; but ye retire in your blasts before our steps approach.—Go then, ye feeble race! knowledge with you there is none. Your joys are weak, and like the dreams of our rest, or the light-winged thought that flies across the soul.——Shall Cathmor soon be low? Darkly laid in his narrow house? where no morning comes with her half-opened eyes.—Away, thou shade! to fight is mine, all further thought away! I rush forth, on eagle wings, to seize my beam of fame.——In the lonely vale of streams, abides the little[44] soul.—Years roll on, seasons return, but he is still unknown.—In a blast comes cloudy death, and lays his grey head low. His ghost is rolled on[45] the vapour of the fenny field. Its course is never on hills, or mossy vales of wind.——So shall not Cathmor depart, no boy in the field was he, who only marks the bed of roes, upon the echoing hills. My issuing forth was with kings, and my joy in dreadful plains: where broken hosts are rolled away, like seas before the wind.

So spoke the king of Alnecma, brightening in his rising soul: valour, like a pleasant flame, is gleaming within his breast. Stately is his stride on the heath: the beam of east is poured around. He saw his grey host on the field, wide-spreading their ridges in light. He rejoiced, like a spirit of heaven, whose steps come forth on his seas, when he beholds them peaceful round, and all the winds are laid. But soon he awakes the waves, and rolls them large to some echoing coast.

On the rushy bank of a stream, slept the daughter of Inis-huna. The helmet[46] had fallen from her head. Her dreams were in the lands of her fathers. There morning was on the field: grey streams leapt down from the rocks; the breezes, in shadowy waves, fly o'er the rushy fields. There is the sound that prepares for the chace; and the moving of warriors from the hall.——But tall above the rest is the hero of streamy Atha: he bends his eye of love on Sul-malla, from his stately steps. She turns, with pride, her face away, and careless bends the bow.

Such were the dreams of the maid when Atha's warrior[47] came. He saw her fair face before him, in the midst of her wandering locks. He knew the maid of Lumon. What should Cathmor do?——His sigh arose: his tears came down. But straight he turned away.—This is no time, king of Atha, to wake thy secret soul. The battle is rolled before thee, like a troubled stream.

He struck that warning boss[48], wherein dwelt the voice of war. Erin rose around him like the sound of eagle-wings.—Sul-malla started from sleep, in her disordered locks. She seized the helmet from earth, and trembled in her place. Why should they know in Erin of the daughter of Inis-huna? for she remembered the race of kings, and the pride of her soul arose.

Her steps are behind a rock, by the blue-winding stream[49] of a vale: where dwelt the dark-brown hind ere yet the war arose. Thither came the voice of Cathmor, at times, to Sul-malla's ear. Her soul is darkly sad; she pours her words on wind.

[50]The dreams of Inis-huna departed: they are rolled away[51] from my soul. I hear not the chace in my land. I am concealed in the skirts of war. I look forth from my cloud, but no beam appears to light my path. I behold my warrior low; for the broad-shielded king is near; he that overcomes in danger; Fingal of the spears.[52]—Spirit of departed Conmor, are thy steps on the bosom of winds? Comest thou, at times, to other lands, father of sad Sul-malla? Thou dost come, for I have heard thy voice at night; while yet I rose on the wave to streamy Inis-fail.[53] The ghost of fathers, they say[54], can seize[55] the souls of their race, while they behold them lonely in the midst of woe. Call me, my father, when the king[56] is low on earth; for then I shall[57] be lonely in the midst of woe.

T E M O R A:

A N

E P I C   P O E M.

B O O K   F I F T H.

ARGUMENT to Book V.

Ossian,[1] after a short address to the harp of Cona, describes the arrangements of both armies on either side of the river Lubar. Fingal gives the command to Fillan: but, at the same time, orders Gaul, the son of Morni, who had been wounded in the hand in the preceding battle, to assist him with his counsel. The army of the Fir-bolg is commanded by Foldath. The general onset is described. The great actions of Fillan. He kills Rothmar and Culmin. But when Fillan conquers, in one wing, Foldath presses hard on the other. He wounds Dermid, the son of Duthno, and puts the whole wing to flight. Dermid deliberates with himself, and, at last, resolves to put a stop to the progress of Foldath, by engaging him in single combat.— When the two chiefs were approaching towards one another, Fillan came suddenly to the relief of Dermid; engaged Foldath, and killed him. The behaviour of Malthos towards the fallen Foldath. Fillan puts the whole army of the Fir-bolg to flight. The book closes with an address to Clatho, the mother of that hero.

TEMORA: BOOK FIFTH.

[2]Thou dweller between the shields that hang on high in Ossian's hall, descend from thy place, O harp, and let me hear thy voice.—Son of Alpin, strike the string; thou must awake the soul of the bard. The murmur of Lora's[3] stream has rolled the tale away.—I stand in the cloud of years: few are its openings towards the past, and when the vision comes it is but dim and dark.—I hear thee, harp of Cona;[4] my soul returns, like a breeze, which the sun brings back to the vale, where dwelt the lazy mist.

[5]Lubar is bright before me, in the windings of its vale. On either side, on their hills, rise the tall forms of the kings; their people are poured around them, bending forward to their words; as if their fathers spoke, descending from their winds.—But the kings were like two rocks in the midst, each with its dark head of pines, when they are seen in the desart, above low-sailing mist. High on their face are streams, which spread their foam on blasts.

Beneath the voice of Cathmor poured Erin, like the sound of flame. Wide they came down to Lubar; before them is the stride of Foldath. But Cathmor retired to his hill, beneath his bending oaks. The tumbling of a stream is near the king: he lifts, at times, his gleaming spear. It was a flame to his people, in the midst of war. Near him stood the daughter of Con-mor, leaning on her rock. She did not rejoice over the strife: her soul delighted not in blood. A valley[6] spreads green behind the hill, with its three blue streams. The sun is there in silence; and the dun mountain-roes come down. On these are turned the eyes of Inis-huna's white-bosomed maid.[7]

Fingal beheld,[8] on high, the son of Borbar-duthul: he saw the deep-rolling of Erin, on the darkened plain. He struck that warning boss, which bids the people obey; when he sends his chiefs before them, to the field of renown. Wide rose their spears to the sun; their echoing shields reply around.—Fear, like a vapor, did not wind among the host: for he, the king, war near, the strength of streamy Morven.[9]—Gladness brightened the hero, we heard his words of joy.

Like the coming forth of winds, is the sound of Morven's[10] sons! They are mountain waters, determined in their course. Hence is Fingal renowned, and his name in other lands. He was not a lonely beam in danger; for your steps were always near.—But never was I[11] a dreadful form, in your presence, darkened into wrath. My voice was no thunder to your ears: mine eyes sent forth no death.—When the haughty appeared, I beheld them not. They were forgot at my feasts: like mist they melted away.——A young beam is before you: few are his paths to war. They are few, but he is valiant: defend my dark-haired son. Bring him[12] back with joy: Hereafter he may stand alone. His form is like his fathers: his soul is a flame of their fire.——Son of car-borne Morni, move behind the son of Clatho:[13] let thy voice reach his ear, from the skirts of war. Not unobserved rolls battle, before thee, breaker of the shields.

The king strode, at once, away to Cormul's[14] lofty rock. As, slow, I lifted my steps behind; came[15] forward the strength of Gaul. His shield hung loose on its thong; he spoke, in haste, to Ossian.—Bind[16], son of Fingal, this shield, bind it high to the side of Gaul. The foe may behold it, and think I lift the spear. If I shall fall, let my tomb be hid in the field; for fall I must without my fame: mine arm cannot lift the steel. Let not Evir-choma hear it, to blush between her locks.——Fillan, the mighty behold us; let us not forget the strife. Why should they come, from their hills, to aid our flying field?

He strode onward, with the sound of his shield. My voice pursued him, as he went. Can the son of Morni fall without his fame in Erin? But the deeds of the mighty forsake their souls of fire. They rush careless over the fields of renown: their words are never heard.—I rejoiced over the steps of the chief: I strode to the rock of the king, where he sat in his wandering locks, amidst the mountain-wind.

In two dark ridges bend the hosts, towards each other, at Lubar. Here Foldath rose a pillar of darkness: there brightened the youth of Fillan. Each, with his spear in the stream, sent forth the voice of war.—Gaul struck the shield of Morven: at once they plunge in battle.—Steel poured its gleam on steel: like the fall of streams shone the field, when they mix their foam together, from two dark-browed rocks.—Behold he comes the son of fame: he lays the people low! Deaths sit on blasts around him!—Warriors strew thy paths, O Fillan!

[17]Rothmar, the shield of warriors, stood between two chinky rocks. Two oaks, which winds had bent from high, spread their branches on either side. He rolls his darkening eyes on Fillan, and silent, shades his friends. Fingal saw the approaching fight; and all his soul arose.—But as the stone of Loda[18] falls, shook, at once, from rocking Druman-ard, when spirits heave the earth in their wrath; so fell blue-shielded Rothmar.

Near are the steps of Culmin; the youth came, bursting into tears. Wrathful he cut the wind, ere yet he mixed his strokes with Fillan. He had first bent the bow with Rothmar, at the rock of his own blue streams. There they had marked the place of the roe, as the sun-beam flew over the fern.—Why, son of Cul-allin, dost thou rush on that beam[19] of light? it is a fire that consumes.—Youth of Strutha[20] retire. Your fathers were not equal, in the glittering strife of the field.

The mother of Culmin remains in the hall; she looks forth on blue-rolling Strutha. A whirlwind rises, on the stream, dark-eddying round the ghost of her son. His dogs[21] are howling in their place: his shield is bloody in the hall.—"Art thou fallen, my fair-haired son, in Erin's dismal war?"

As a roe, pierced in secret, lies panting, by her wonted streams, the hunter looks over her feet of wind, and remembers her stately bounding before: so lay the son of Cul-allin, beneath the eye of Fillan. His hair is rolled in a little stream: his blood wandered on his shield. Still his hand held the sword, that failed him in the day of his danger.[22]—"Thou art fallen, said Fillan, ere yet thy fame was heard.—Thy father sent thee to war: and he expects to hear thy deeds. He is grey, perhaps, at his streams, turning his dim eyes towards[23] Moi-lena. But thou shalt not return, with the spoil of the fallen foe."

Fillan poured the flight of Erin before him, over the echoing heath.—But, man on man, fell Morven before the dark-red rage of Foldath; for, far on the field, he poured the roar of half his tribes. Dermid[24] stood before him in wrath: the sons of Cona[25] gather round. But his shield is cleft by Foldath, and his people poured[26] over the heath.

Then said the foe, in his pride. They have fled, and my fame begins. Go, Malthos, and bid the king[27] to guard the dark-rolling of ocean; that Fingal may not escape from my sword. He must lie on earth. Beside some fen shall his tomb be seen. It shall rise without a song. His ghost shall hover in mist over the reedy pool.

Malthos heard, with darkening doubt; he rolled his silent eyes.—He knew the pride of Foldath, and looked up to the king on his hill; then, darkly turning, he[28] plunged his sword in war.

In Clono's[29] narrow vale, where[30] bent two trees above the streams,[31] dark in his grief stood Duthno's silent son. The blood poured from his thigh:[32] his shield lay broken near. His spear leaned against a stone; why, Dermid, why so sad?

I hear the roar of battle. My people are alone. My steps are slow on the heath; and no shield is mine.—Shall he then prevail?—It is then after Dermid is low![33] I will call thee forth, O Foldath, and meet thee yet in fight.

He took his spear, with dreadful joy. The son of Morni came.—"Stay, son of Duthno, stay thy speed; thy steps are marked with blood. No bossy shield is thine. Why shouldst thou fall unarmed?"—King of Strumon,[34] give thou thy shield. It has often rolled back the war. I shall stop the chief, in his course.—Son of Morni, dost thou behold that stone? It lifts its grey head thro' grass. There dwells a chief of the race of Dermid.—Place me there in night[35].

He slowly rose against the hill, and saw the troubled field. The gleaming ridges of the fight, disjoined and broken round.—As distant fires, on heath by night, now seem as lost in smoak, then rearing their red streams on the hill, as blow or cease the winds: so met the intermitting war the eye of broad-shielded Dermid.—Thro' the host are the strides of Foldath, like some dark ship on wintry waves, when it[36] issues from between two isles, to sport on echoing seas.[37]

Dermid, with rage, beheld his course. He strove to rush along. But he failed in the midst of his steps; and the big tear came down.—He sounded his father's horn; and thrice struck his bossy shield. He called thrice the name of Foldath, from his roaring tribes.—Foldath, with joy, beheld the chief: he lifted high his bloody spear.—As a rock is marked with streams, that fell troubled down its side in a storm; so, streaked with wandering blood, is the dark form[38] of Moma.

The host, on either side, withdrew from the contending of kings.—They raised, at once, their gleaming points.—Rushing came Fillan of Moruth.[39]Three paces back Foldath withdrew; dazzled with that beam of light, which came, as issuing from a cloud, to save the wounded hero.[40]— Growing in his pride he stood, and called forth all his steel.

As meet two broad-winged eagles, in their sounding strife, on the winds: so rushed the two chiefs, on Moi-lena, into gloomy fight.——By turns are the steps of the kings[41] forward on their rocks;[42] for now the dusky war seems to descend on their swords.—Cathmor feels the joy of warriors, on his mossy hill: their joy in secret when dangers rise equal to their souls. His eye is not turned on Lubar, but on Morven's[43] dreadful king; for he beheld him, on Mora, rising in his arms.

Foldath[44] fell on his shield; the spear of Fillan pierced the king. Nor looked the youth on the fallen, but onward rolled the war. The hundred voices of death arose.—"Stay, son of Fingal, stay thy speed. Beholdest thou not that gleaming form, a dreadful sign of death? Awaken not the king of Alnecma.[45] Return, son of blue-eyed Clatho."

Malthos[46] saw Foldath low. He darkly stood above the king.[47] Hatred was rolled from his soul. He seemed a rock in the desert, on whose dark side are the trickling of waters, when the slow-sailing mist has left it, and its trees are blasted with winds. He spoke to the dying hero, about the narrow house. Whether shall thy grey stone rise in Ullin? or in Moma's[48] woody land, where the sun looks, in secret, on the blue streams of Dalrutho[49]? There are the steps of thy daughter, blue-eyed Dardu-lena.

Rememberest thou her, said Foldath, because no son is mine; no youth to roll the battle before him, in revenge of me? Malthos, I am revenged. I was not peaceful in the field. Raise the tombs of those I have slain, around my narrow house. Often shall I forsake the blast, to rejoice above their graves; when I behold them spread around, with their long-whistling grass.

His soul rushed to the vales of Moma, and came to Dardu-lena's dreams, where she slept, by Dalrutho's stream, returning from the chace of the hinds. Her bow is near the maid, unstrung; the breezes fold her long hair on her breasts. Cloathed in the beauty of youth, the love of heroes lay. Dark-bending, from the skirts of the wood, her wounded father came.[50] He appeared, at times, then seemed as hid in mist.[51]—— Bursting into tears she rose: she knew that the chief was low. To her came a beam from his soul when folded in its storms. Thou wert the last of his race, blue-eyed Dardu-lena!

Wide-spreading over echoing Lubar, the flight of Bolga is rolled along. Fillan hung forward on their steps; and strewed, with dead, the heath.

Fingal rejoiced over his son.—Blue-shielded Cathmor rose.——[52] Son of Alpin, bring the harp: give Fillan's praise to the wind: raise high his praise, in my hall,[53] while yet he shines in war.

Leave, blue-eyed Clatho, leave thy hall. Behold that early beam of thine. The host is withered in its course. No further look—it is dark.——Light-trembling from the harp, strike, virgins, strike the sound.—No hunter he descends, from the dewy haunt of the bounding roe. He bends not his bow on the wind; or sends his grey arrow abroad.

Deep-folded in red war, the battle rolls against his side. Or, striding midst the ridgy strife, he pours the deaths of thousands forth. Fillan is like a spirit of heaven, that descends from the skirt of his blast. The troubled ocean feels his steps, as he strides from wave to wave. His path kindles behind him; islands shake their heads on the heaving seas.[54]

TEMORA:

AN

EPIC POEM.

BOOK SIXTH.

ARGUMENT to Book VI.

This book opens with a speech of Fingal, who sees Cathmor descending to the assistance of his flying army. The king dispatches Ossian to the relief of Fillan. He himself retires behind the rock of Cormul, to avoid the sight of the engagement between his son and Cathmor. Ossian advances. The descent of Cathmor described. He rallies the army, renews the battle, and, before Ossian could arrive, engages Fillan himself. Upon the approach of Ossian, the combat between the two heroes ceases. Ossian and Cathmor prepare to fight, but night coming on prevents them. Ossian returns to the place where Cathmor and Fillan fought. He finds Fillan mortally wounded, and leaning against a rock. Their discourse. Fillan dies: his body is laid, by Ossian, in a neighbouring cave.—The Caledonian army return to Fingal. He questions them about his son, and understanding that he was killed, retires, in silence, to the rock of Cormul.—Upon the retreat of the army of Fingal, the Fir-bolg advance. Cathmor finds Bran, one of the dogs of Fingal, lying on the shield of Fillan, before the entrance of the cave, where the body of that hero lay. His reflexions thereupon. He returns, in a melancholy mood, to his army. Malthos endeavours to comfort him, by the example of his father Borbar-duthul. Cathmor retires to rest. The song of Sul-malla concludes the book, which ends about the middle of the third night, from the opening of the poem.

TEMORA: BOOK SIXTH.

[1]Cathmor rises on his echoing[2] hill! Shall Fingal take the sword of Luno? But what should become of thy fame, son of white-bosomed Clatho? Turn not thine eyes from Fingal, daughter[3] of Inistore. I shall not quench thy early beam; it shines along my soul.—But rise, O wood-skirted Mora, rise, between the war and me! Why should Fingal behold the strife, lest his dark-haired warrior should fall!—Amidst the song, O Carril, pour the sound of the trembling harp: here are the voices of rocks, and bright tumbling of waters. Father of Oscar lift the spear; defend the young in arms. Conceal thy steps from Fillan's eyes.[4]—He must not know that I doubt his steel.—No cloud of mine shall rise, my son, upon thy soul of fire!

He sunk behind his rock, amidst the sound of Carril's song.—Brightening, in my growing soul, I took the spear of Temora[5]. I saw, along Moi-lena, the wild tumbling of battle, the strife of death, in gleaming rows, disjoined and broken round. Fillan is a beam of fire: from wing to wing is his wasteful course. The ridges of war melt before him. They are rolled, in smoak, from the fields.

[6]Now is the coming forth of Cathmor, in the armour of kings! Dark-rolled[7] the eagle's wing above his helmet of fire. Unconcerned are his steps, as if they were to the chace of Atha.[8] He raised, at times, his dreadful voice; Erin, abashed, gathered round.—Their souls returned back, like a stream: they wondered at the steps of their fear: for he rose, like the beam of the morning on a haunted heath: the traveller looks back, with bending eye, on the field of dreadful forms.

Sudden, from the rock of Moi-lena, are Sul-malla's trembling steps. An oak took the spear from her hand; half-bent she loosed the lance: but then are her eyes on the king, from amidst her wandering locks.—No friendly strife is before thee: no light contending of bows, as when the youth of Cluba[9] came forth beneath the eye of Conmor.

As the rock of Runo, which takes the passing clouds for its robe,[10] seems growing, in gathered darkness, over the streamy heath; so seemed the chief of Atha taller, as gathered his people round.—As different blasts fly over the sea, each behind its dark-blue wave, so Cathmor's words, on every side, poured his warriors forth.—Nor silent on his hill is Fillan; he mixed his words with his echoing shield. An eagle he seemed, with sounding wings, calling the wind to his rock, when he sees the coming forth of the roes, on Lutha's[11] rushy field.

Now they bent forward in battle: death's hundred voices rose; for the kings, on either side, were like fires on the souls of the people.—I[12]bounded along: high rocks and trees rushed tall between the war and me.—But I heard the noise of steel, between my clanging arms. Rising, gleaming, on the hill, I beheld the backward steps of hosts: their backward steps, on either side, and wildly-looking eyes. The chiefs were met in dreadful fight; the two blue-shielded kings. Tall and dark, thro' gleams of steel, are seen the striving heroes.—I rushed.—My fears for Fillan flew, burning across my soul.

I came; nor Cathmor fled; nor yet advanced: he sidelong stalked along. An icy rock, cold, tall he seemed. I called forth all my steel.—Silent awhile we strode, on either side of a rushing stream: then, sudden turning, all at once, we raised our pointed spears.—We raised our spears, but night came down. It is dark and silent around; but where the distant steps of hosts are sounding over the heath.

I came to the place where Fillan[13] fought. Nor voice, nor sound is there. A broken helmet lay on earth; a buckler cleft in twain. Where, Fillan, where art thou, young chief of echoing Morven? He heard me leaning against a rock, which bent its grey head over the stream. He heard; but sullen, dark he stood. At length I saw the chief.[14]

Why standest thou, robed in darkness, son of woody Selma? Bright is thy path, my brother, in this dark-brown field. Long has been thy strife in battle. Now the horn of Fingal is heard. Ascend to the cloud of thy father, to his hill of feasts. In the evening mist he sits, and hears the voice[15] of Carril's harp. Carry joy to the aged, young breaker of the shields.

Can the vanquished carry joy? Ossian, no shield is mine. It lies broken on the field. The eagle-wing of my helmet is torn. It is when foes fly before them that fathers delight in their sons. But their sighs burst forth, in secret, when their young warriors yield.—No: Fillan will not behold the king. Why should the hero mourn?

Son of blue-eyed Clatho,[16] why dost thou awake my soul? Wert thou not a burning fire before him; and shall he not rejoice?——Such fame belonged not to Ossian; yet was the king still a sun to me. He looked on my steps, with joy: shadows never rose on his face.—Ascend, O Fillan, to Mora: his feast is spread in the folds of mist.

Ossian, give me that broken shield: these feathers that are rolled in the wind. Place them near to Fillan, that less of his fame may fall. Ossian, I begin to fail.—Lay me in that hollow rock. Raise no stone above: lest one should ask about my fame. I am fallen in the first of my fields; fallen without renown. Let thy voice alone send joy to my flying soul. Why should the feeble[17] know where dwells the lost beam of Clatho?[18]

Is thy spirit on the eddying winds, blue-eyed king of shields?[19] Joy pursue my hero, thro' his folded clouds. The forms of thy fathers, O Fillan, bend to receive their son. I behold the spreading of their fire on Mora; the blue-rolling of their misty wreaths.—Joy meet thee my brother.——But we are dark and sad. I behold the foe round the aged, and the wasting away of his fame. Thou art left alone in the field, grey-haired king of Selma.

I laid him in the hollow rock, at the roar of the nightly stream. One red star looked in on the hero: winds lift, at times, his locks. I listened: no sound was heard: for the warrior slept.——As lightning on a cloud, a thought came rushing over my soul.—My eyes rolled in fire: my stride was in the clang of steel.

I will find thee, chief of Atha,[20] in the gathering of thy thousands. Why should that cloud escape, that quenched our early beam? Kindle your meteors,[21] my fathers, to light my daring steps. I will consume in wrath[22] ——Should I not return! the king is without a son, grey-haired amidst his foes. His arm is not as in the days of old: his fame grows dim in Erin. Let me not behold him from high,[23] laid low in his latter field.—But can I return to the king? Will he not ask about his son? "Thou oughtest to defend young Fillan."—I[24] will meet the foe.—Green Inisfail,[25] thy sounding tread is pleasant to my ear: I rush on thy ridgy host, to shun the eyes of Fingal. ——I hear the voice of the king, on Mora's misty top!—He calls his two sons; I come, my father, in my grief.—I come like an eagle, which the flame of night met in the desert, and spoiled of half his wings.

[26]Distant, round the king, on Mora, the broken ridges of Morven are rolled. They turned their eyes: each darkly bends, on his own ashen spear.—Silent stood the king in the midst. Thought on thought rolled over his soul. As waves on a secret mountain-lake, each with its back of foam.— He looked; no son appeared, with his long-beaming spear. The sighs rose, crowding, from his soul; but he concealed his grief.——At length I stood beneath an oak. No voice of mine was heard. What could I say to Fingal in his hour of woe?——His words rose, at length, in the midst: the people shrunk backward as he spoke[27].

Where is the son of Selma, he who led in war? I behold not his steps, among my people, returning from the field. Fell the young bounding roe, who was so stately on my hills?—He fell;—for ye are silent. The shield of war is broke.[28]——Let his armour be near to Fingal; and the sword of dark-brown Luno. I am waked on my hills: With morning I descend to war.

[29]High on Cormul's rock, an oak flamed to the wind. The grey skirts of mist are rolled around; thither strode the king in his wrath. Distant from the host he always lay, when battle burnt within his soul. On two spears hung his shield on high; the gleaming sign of death; that shield, which he was wont to strike, by night, before he rushed to war.—It was then his warriors knew, when the king was to lead in strife; for never was this buckler heard, till Fingal's wrath arose.—Unequal were his steps on high, as he shone in the beam of the oak; he was dreadful as the form of the spirit of night, when he cloaths, on hills, his wild gestures with mist, and, issuing forth, on the troubled ocean, mounts the car of winds.

Nor settled, from the storm, is Erin's sea of war; they glittered, beneath the moon, and, low-humming, still rolled on the field.—Alone are the steps of Cathmor, before them on the heath; he hung forward, with all his arms, on Morven's flying host. Now had he come to the mossy cave, where Fillan lay in night. One tree was bent above the stream, which glittered over the rock.——There shone to the moon the broken shield of Clatho's son; and near it, on grass, lay hairy-footed Bran[30]. He had missed the chief on Mora, and searched him along the wind. He thought that the blue-eyed hunter slept; he lay upon his shield. No blast came over the heath, unknown to bounding Bran.

Cathmor saw the white-breasted dog; he saw the broken shield. Darkness is blown back on his soul; he remembers the falling away of the people. They come, a stream; are rolled away; another race succeeds.—"But some mark the fields, as they pass, with their own mighty names. The heath, thro' dark-brown years, is theirs; some blue stream winds to their fame.— Of these be the chief of Atha, when he lays him down on earth. Often may the voice of future times meet Cathmor in the air: when he strides from wind to wind, or folds himself in the wing of a storm."

Green Erin gathered round the king, to hear the voice of his power. Their joyful faces bend, unequal, forward, in the light of the oak. They who were terrible were removed: Lubar[31] winds again in their host. Cathmor was that beam from heaven which shone when his people were dark. He was honoured in the midst. Their souls rose trembling[32] around. The king alone no gladness shewed; no stranger he to war!

Why is the king so sad, said Malthos eagle-eyed?—Remains there a foe at Lubar? Lives there among them, who can lift the spear? Not so peaceful was thy father, Borbar-dúthul[33], sovereign[34] of spears. His rage was a fire that always burned: his joy over fallen foes was great.—Three days feasted the grey-haired hero, when he heard that Calmar fell: Calmar, who aided the race of Ullin, from Lara of the streams.—Often did he feel, with his hands, the steel which, they said, had pierced his foe. He felt it with his hands, for Borbar-dúthul's eyes had failed.—Yet was the king a sun to his friends; a gale to lift their branches round. Joy was around him in his halls: he loved the sons of Bolga. His name remains in Atha, like the awful memory of ghosts, whose presence was terrible, but they blew the storm away.—Now let the voices[35] of Erin raise the soul of the king; he that shone when war was dark, and laid the mighty low.—Fonar, from that grey-browed rock, pour the tale of other times: pour it on wide-skirted Erin, as it settles round.

To me, said Cathmor, no song shall rise: nor Fonar sit on the rock of Lubar. The mighty there are laid low. Disturb not their rushing ghosts. Far, Malthos, far remove the sound of Erin's song. I rejoice not over the foe, when he ceases to lift the spear. With morning we pour our strength abroad. Fingal is wakened on his echoing hill.

Like waves, blown back by sudden winds, Erin retired, at the voice of the king. Deep-rolled into the field of night, they spread their humming tribes: Beneath his own tree, at intervals, each[36] bard sat down with his harp. They raised the song, and touched the string: each to the chief he loved.—Before a burning oak Sul-malla touched, at times, the harp. She touched the harp, and heard, between, the breezes in her hair.—In darkness near, lay the king of Atha, beneath an aged tree. The beam of the oak was turned from him; he saw the maid, but was not seen. His soul poured forth, in secret, when he beheld her tearful[37] eye.—But battle is before thee, son of Borbar-dúthul.

Amidst the harp, at intervals, she listened whether the warriors slept. Her soul was up; she longed, in secret, to pour her own sad song.—The field is silent. On their wings, the blasts of night retire. The bards had ceased; and meteors came, red-winding with their ghosts.—The sky grew dark: the forms of the dead were blended with the clouds. But heedless bends the daughter of Conmor, over the decaying flame. Thou wert alone in her soul, car-borne chief of Atha. She raised the voice of the song, and touched the harp between.

[38]Clun-galo came; she missed the maid.—Where art thou, beam of light? Hunters, from the mossy rock, saw you the blue-eyed fair?—Are her steps on grassy Lumon; near the bed of roes?—Ah me! I behold her bow in the hall. Where art thou, beam of light?

[39]Cease, love of Conmor, cease; I hear thee not on the ridgy heath. My eye is turned to the king, whose path is terrible in war. He for whom my soul is up, in the season of my rest.—Deep-bosomed in war he stands, he beholds me not from his cloud.—Why, sun of Sul-malla, dost thou not look forth?— I dwell in darkness here; wide over me flies the shadowy mist. Filled with dew are my locks: look thou from thy cloud, O sun of Sul-malla's soul.—

* * * * * * * * *

Note 18: In this, as well as the former publication, I have only admitted into the text compleat poems or independent episodes: the fragments which remain of the compositions of Ossian, I have chosen to throw, occasionally, into the notes. I shall here give a translation of a part of a poem concerning the death of Fillan. It is[40] a dialogue between Clatho the mother, and Bos-mina the sister, of that hero. [M]

CLATHO.

"Daughter of Fingal, arise: thou light between thy locks. Lift thy fair head from rest, soft-gliding sun-beam of Selma! I beheld thy arms, on thy breast, white-tossed amidst thy wandering locks: when the rustling breeze of the morning came from the desert of streams. Hast thou seen thy fathers, Bos-mina, descending in thy dreams? Arise, daughter of Clatho; dwells there aught of grief in thy soul?

BOS-MINA.

A thin form passed before me, fading as it flew: like the darkening wave of a breeze, along a field of grass. Descend, from thy wall, O harp, and call back the soul of Bos-mina, it has rolled away, like a stream. I hear thy pleasant sound.—I hear thee, O harp, and my voice shall rise.

How often shall ye rush to war, ye dwellers of my soul? Your paths are distant, kings of men, in Erin of blue streams. Lift thy wing, thou southern breeze, from Clono's darkening heath: spread the sails of Fingal towards the bays of his land.

But who is that, in his strength, darkening in the presence of war? His arm stretches to the foe, like the beam of the sickly sun; when his side is crusted with darkness; and he rolls his dismal course thro' the sky.—Who is it, but the father of Bos-mina? Shall he return till danger is past!

Fillan, thou art a beam by his side; beautiful, but terrible, is thy light. Thy sword is before thee, a blue fire of night. When shalt thou return to thy roes; to the streams of thy rushy fields? When shall I behold thee from Mora, while winds strew my long locks on moss![41]—But shall a young eagle return from the field where the heroes fall!

CLATHO.

Soft, as the song of Loda, is the voice of Selma's maid. Pleasant to the ear of Clatho is the name of the breaker of shields.—Behold, the king comes from ocean: the shield of Morven is borne by bards. The foe has fled before him, like the departure of mist.—I hear not the sounding wings of my eagle; the rushing forth of the son of Clatho.—Thou art dark, O Fingal; shall he not[47] return? *　*　*　*

T E M O R A:

AN

EPIC POEM.

BOOK SEVENTH.

ARGUMENT to Book VII.

This book begins, about the middle of the third night from the opening of the poem. The poet describes a kind of mist, which rose, by night, from the lake of Lego, and was the usual residence of the souls of the dead, during the interval between their decease and the funeral song. The appearance of the ghost of Fillan above the cave where his body lay. His voice comes to Fingal, on the rock of Cormul. The king strikes the shield of Trenmor, which was an infallible sign of his appearing in arms himself. The extraordinary effect of the sound of the shield. Sul-malla, starting from sleep, awakes Cathmor. Their affecting discourse. She insists with him, to sue for peace; he resolves to continue the war. He directs her to retire to the neighbouring valley of Lona, which was the residence of an old Druid, until the battle of the next day should be over. He awakes his army with the sound of his shield. The shield described. Fonar, the bard, at the desire of Cathmor, relates the first settlement of the Firbolg in Ireland, under their leader Larthon. Morning comes. Sul-malla retires to the valley of Lona. A Lyric song concludes the book.

TEMORA: BOOK SEVENTH.

[1]From the wood-skirted waters of Lego, ascend, at times, grey-bosomed mists, when the gates of the west are closed on the sun's eagle-eye. Wide, over Lara's stream, is poured the vapour dark and deep: the moon, like a dim shield, is swimming thro' its folds. With this, clothe the spirits of old their sudden gestures on the wind, when they stride, from blast to blast, along the dusky face of the night. Often, blended with the gale, to some warrior's grave, they roll the mist, a grey dwelling to his ghost, until the songs arise.

A sound came from the desert; the rushing course of Conar in winds.[2] He poured his deep mist on Fillan,[3] at blue-winding Lubar.—Dark and mournful sat the ghost, bending in[4] his grey ridge of smoak. The blast, at times, rolled him together: but the lovely form[5] returned again. It returned with slow-bending[6] eyes: and dark winding of locks of mist.

It is[7] dark. The sleeping host were still, in the skirts of night. The flame decayed, on the hill of Fingal; the king lay lonely on his shield. His eyes were half-closed in sleep; the voice of Fillan came. "Sleeps the husband of Clatho? Dwells the father of the fallen in rest? Am I forgot in the folds of darkness; lonely in the season of dreams?"[8]

Why art thou in the midst of my dreams, said Fingal, as, sudden, he rose?[9] Can I forget thee, my son, or thy path of fire in the field? Not such, on the soul of the king, come the deeds of the mighty in arms.[10] They are not there a beam of lightning, which is seen, and is then no more.—I remember thee, O Fillan, and my wrath begins to rise.

The king took his deathful spear, and struck the deeply-sounding shield: his shield[11] that hung high in night, the dismal sign of war!—Ghosts fled on every side, and rolled their gathered forms on the wind.—Thrice from the winding vale arose the voices of death.[12] The harps[13] of the bards, untouched, sound mournful over the hill.

He struck again the shield: battles rose in the dreams of his host.[14] The wide-tumbling strife is gleaming over their souls. Blue-shielded kings descend to war. Backward-looking armies fly; and mighty deeds are half-hid, in the bright gleams of steel.

But when the third sound arose; deer started from the clefts of their rocks. The screams of fowl are heard, in the desert, as each flew, frighted, on his blast.—The sons of Albion[15] half-rose, and half-assumed their spears.—But silence rolled back on the host: they knew the shield of the king. Sleep returned to their eyes: the field was dark and still.

[16]No sleep was thine in darkness, blue-eyed daughter of Conmor! Sulmalla heard the dreadful shield, and rose, amidst the night.—Her steps are towards the king of Atha.—Can danger shake his daring soul! In doubt, she stands, with bending eyes. Heaven burns with all its stars.

Again the shield resounds!—She rushed.—She stopt.—Her voice half-rose. It failed.—She saw him, amidst his arms, that gleamed to heaven's fire. She saw him dim in his locks, that rose to nightly wind.—Away, for fear, she turned her steps.——"Why should the king of Erin awake? Thou art not a dream to his rest, daughter of Inis-huna."

More dreadful rung the shield. Sul-malla starts. Her helmet falls. Loud-echoed Lubar's rock, as over it rolled the steel.—Bursting from the dreams of night, Cathmor half-rose, beneath his tree. He saw the form of the maid, above him, on the rock. A red star, with twinkling beam, looked down thro' her floating hair.

[17]Who comes thro' night to Cathmor, in the dark season[18] of his dreams? Bring'st thou ought of war? Who art thou, son of night?—Stand'st thou before me, a form of the times of old? A voice from the fold of a cloud, to warn me of Erin's danger?

Nor traveller of night[19] am I, nor voice from folded cloud: but[20] I warn thee of the danger of Erin. Dost thou hear that sound? It is not the feeble, king of Atha, that rolls his signs on night.

Let the warrior roll his signs;[21] to Cathmor they are the sound of harps. My joy is great, voice of night, and burns over all my thoughts. This is the music of kings, on lonely hills, by night; when they light their daring souls, the sons of mighty deeds! The feeble dwell alone, in the valley of the breeze; where mists lift their morning skirts, from the blue-winding streams.

Not feeble, thou leader of heroes,[22] were they, the fathers of my race. They dwelt in the darkness[23] of battle; in their distant lands. Yet delights not my soul, in the signs of death!—He[24], who never yields, comes forth: Awake[25] the bard of peace!

Like a rock with its trickling waters,[26] stood Cathmor in his tears. Her voice came, a breeze, on his soul, and waked the memory of her land; where she dwelt by her peaceful streams, before he came to the war of Conmor.

Daughter of strangers, he said; (she trembling turned away) long have I marked in her armour, the young[27] pine of Inis-huna.—But my soul, I said, is folded in a storm. Why should that beam arise, till my steps return in peace? Have I been pale in thy presence, when thou bidst me to fear the king?——The time of danger, O maid, is the season of my soul; for then it swells, a mighty stream, and rolls me on the foe.

Beneath the moss-covered rock of Lona, near his own winding[28] stream; grey in his locks of age, dwells Clonmal[29] king of harps. Above him is his echoing oak,[30] and the dun bounding of roes. The noise[31] of our strife reaches his ear, as he bends in the thoughts of years. There let thy rest be, Sul-malla, until our battle cease. Until I return, in my arms, from the skirts of the evening mist that rises, on Lona, round the dwelling of my love.

A light fell on the soul of the maid; it rose kindled before the king. She turned her face to Cathmor; her locks are struggling with winds.[32] Sooner[33] shall the eagle of heaven be torn, from the stream of his roaring wind, when he sees the dun prey, before him, the young sons of the bounding roe, than thou, O Cathmor, be turned from the strife of renown.——Soon may I see thee, warrior, from the skirts of the evening mist, when it is rolled around me, on Lona of the streams. While yet thou art distant far, strike, Cathmor, strike the shield, that joy may return to my darkened soul, as I lean on the mossy rock. But if thou shouldst fall——I am in the land of strangers;—O send thy voice, from thy cloud, to the maid of Inis-huna.

Young branch of green-headed Lumon, why dost thou shake in the storm? Often has Cathmor returned, from darkly-rolling wars. The darts of death are but hail to me; they have often bounded from[34] my shield. I have risen brightened from battle, like a meteor from a stormy cloud. Return not, fair beam, from thy vale, when the roar of battle grows. Then might the foe escape, as from my fathers of old.

They told to Son-mor[35], of Clunar[36], slain by Cormac the giver of shells.[37] Three days darkened Son-mor, over his brother's fall.—His spouse beheld the silent king, and foresaw his steps to war. She prepared the bow, in secret, to attend her blue-shielded hero. To her dwelt darkness, at Atha, when the warrior moved to his fields.[38]—From their hundred streams, by night, poured down the sons of Alnecma. They had heard the shield of the king, and their rage arose. In clanging arms, they moved along, towards Ullin the land of groves. Son-mor struck his shield, at times, the leader of the war.

Far behind followed Sul-allin[39], over the streamy hills. She was a light on the mountain, when they crossed the vale below. Her steps were stately on the vale, when they rose on the mossy hill.—She feared to approach the king, who left her in Atha of hinds.[40] But when the roar of battle rose; when host was rolled on host; when Son-mor burnt, like the fire of heaven in clouds, with her spreading hair came Sul-allin; for she trembled for her king.—He stopt the rushing strife to save the love of heroes.—The foe fled by night; Clunar slept without his blood; the blood which ought to be poured upon the warrior's tomb.

Nor rose the rage of Son-mor, but his days were dark and slow.[41] Sul-allin wandered, by her grey streams, with her tearful eyes. Often did she look, on the hero, when he was folded in his thoughts. But she shrunk from his eyes, and turned her lone steps away.—Battles rose, like a tempest, and drove the mist from his soul. He beheld, with joy, her steps in the hall, and the white rising of her hands on the harp.

[42]In his arms strode the chief of Atha, to where his shield hung, high, in night: high on a mossy bough, over Lubar's streamy roar. Seven bosses rose on the shield; the seven voices of the king, which his warriors received, from the wind, and marked over all their tribes.

On each boss is placed a star of night; Can-mathon with beams unshorn; Col-derna rising from a cloud: Uloicho robed in mist; and the soft beam of

Cathlin glittering on a rock. Fair-gleaming[43] on its own blue wave, Reldu-rath half-sinks its western light. The red eye of Berthin looks, through a grove, on the slow-moving hunter,[44] as he returns, through showery night,[45] with the spoils of the bounding roe.—Wide, in the midst, arose the cloud-less beams of Ton-théna; Ton-théna which[46] looked, by night, on the course of the sea-tossed Larthon: Larthon, the first of Bolga's race, who travelled on the winds[47].——White-bosomed spread the sails of the king, towards streamy Inisfail; dun night was rolled before him, with its skirts of mist. The winds were changeful in heaven,[48] and rolled him from wave to wave.—Then rose the fiery-haired Ton-théna, and laughed[49] from her parted cloud. Larthon[50] rejoiced at the guiding beam,[51] as it faint-gleamed on the tumbling waters.[52]

Beneath the spear of Cathmor, awaked[53] that voice which awakes the bards. They came, dark-winding, from every side; each, with the sound of his harp. Before them rejoiced the king, as the traveller, in the day of the sun; when he hears, far-rolling around, the murmur of mossy streams; streams that burst, in the desert, from the rock of roes.

Why, said Fonar, hear we the voice of the king, in the season of his rest? Were the dim forms of thy fathers bending in thy dreams? Perhaps they stand on that cloud, and wait for Fonar's song; often they come to the fields where their sons are to lift the spear.—Or shall our voice arise for him who lifts the spear no more; he that consumed the field, from Moma of the groves?

Not forgot is that cloud in war, bard of other times. High shall his tomb rise, on Moi-lena, the dwelling of renown. But, now, roll back my soul to the times of my fathers: to the years when first they rose, on Inis-huna's waves. Nor alone pleasant to Cathmor is the remembrance of wood-covered Lumon.—Lumon the land of streams,[54] the dwelling of white-bosomed maids.

[55]Lumon of foamy streams,[56] thou risest on Fonar's soul! Thy sun is on thy side, on the rocks of thy bending trees. The dun roe is seen from thy furze; the deer lifts his branchy head; for he sees, at times, the hound, on the half-covered heath. Slow, on the vale, are the steps of maids; the white-armed daughters of the bow: they lift their blue eyes to the hill, from amidst their wandering locks.—Not there is the stride of Larthon, chief of Inis-huna. He mounts the wave on his own dark oak, in Cluba's ridgy bay. That oak which he cut from Lumon, to bound along the sea. The maids turn their eyes away, lest the king should be lowly-laid; for never had they seen a ship, dark rider of the wave!

Now he dares to call the winds, and to mix with the mist of ocean. Blue Inis-fail rose, in smoak; but dark-skirted night came down. The sons of Bolga feared. The fiery haired Ton-théna rose. Culbin's bay received the ship, in the bosom of its echoing woods, There, issued a stream, from

Duthuma's horrid cave; where spirits gleamed, at times, with their half-finished forms.

Dreams descended on Larthon: he saw seven spirits of his fathers. He heard their half-formed words, and dimly beheld the times to come. He beheld the kings of Atha, the sons of future days. They led their hosts, along the field, like ridges of mist, which winds pour, in autumn, over Atha of the groves.

Larthon raised the hall of Samla[57], to the soft sound[58] of the harp. He went forth to the roes of Erin, to their wonted streams. Nor did he forget green-headed Lumon; he often bounded over his seas, to where white-handed Flathal[59] looked from the hill of roes. Lumon of the foamy streams, thou risest on Fonar's soul.

The beam awaked in the east.[60] The misty heads of the mountains rose. Valleys shew, on every side, the grey-winding of their streams. His host heard the shield of Cathmor: at once they rose around; like a crowded sea, when first it feels the wings of the wind. The waves know not whither to roll; they lift their troubled heads.

Sad and slow retired Sul-malla to Lona of the streams. She went—and often turned; her blue eyes rolled in tears. But when she came to the rock, that darkly covered Lona's vale: she looked, from her bursting soul, on the king; and sunk, at once, behind.

[61]Son of Alpin, strike the string. Is there ought of joy in the harp? Pour it then, on the soul of Ossian: it is folded in mist.—I hear thee, O bard, in my night. But cease the lightly-trembling sound. The joy of grief belongs to Ossian, amidst his dark-brown years.

Green thorn of the hill of ghosts, that shakest thy head to nightly winds! I hear no sound in thee; is there no spirit's windy skirt now rustling in thy leaves? Often are the steps of the dead, in the dark-eddying blasts; when the moon, a dun shield, from the east, is rolled along the sky.

Ullin, Carril and Ryno, voices of the days of old! Let me hear you, in the darkness of Selma, and awake the soul of songs.[62]——I hear you not, ye children of music,[63] in what hall of the clouds is your rest? Do you touch the shadowy harp, robed with morning mist, where the sun comes sounding forth[64] from his green-headed waves?

TEMORA:

AN

EPIC POEM.

BOOK EIGHTH.

ARGUMENT to Book VIII.

The fourth morning, from the opening of the poem, comes on. Fingal, still
continuing in the place, to which he had retired on the preceding night, is
seen, at intervals, thro' the mist, which covered the rock of Cormul. The
descent of the king is described. He orders Gaul, Dermid, and Carril the
bard, to go to the valley of Cluna, and conduct, from thence, to the Cale-
donian army, Ferad-artho, the son of Cairbre, the only person remaining
of the family of Conar, the first king of Ireland.—The king takes the
command of the army, and prepares for battle. Marching towards the
enemy, he comes to the cave of Lubar, where the body of Fillan lay. Upon
seeing his dog Bran, who lay at the entrance of the cave, his grief
returns.—Cathmor arranges the army of the Fir-bolg in order of battle.
The appearance of that hero. The general conflict is described. The
actions of Fingal and Cathmor. A storm. The total rout of the Fir-bolg.
The two kings engage, in a column of mist, on the banks of Lubar. Their
attitude and conference after the combat. The death of Cathmor.—Fingal
resigns the *spear of Trenmor* to Ossian. The ceremonies observed on that
occasion.——The spirit of Cathmor appears to Sul-malla, in the valley of
Lona. Her sorrow.—Evening comes on. A feast is prepared.—The coming
of Ferad-artho is announced by the songs of a hundred bards.—The poem
closes, with a speech of Fingal.

TEMORA: BOOK EIGHTH.

[1]As when the wintry winds have seized the waves of the mountain-lake, have seized them, in stormy night, and cloathed them over with ice; white, to the hunter's early eye, the billows still seem to roll. He turns his ear to the sound of each unequal ridge. But each is silent, gleaming, strewn with boughs and tufts of grass, which shake and whistle to the wind, over their grey seats of frost.—So silent shone to the morning the ridges of Morven's host, as each warrior looked up from his helmet towards the hill of the king; the cloud-covered hill of Fingal, where he strode, in the rolling[2] of mist. At times is the hero seen, greatly dim in all his arms. From thought to thought rolled the war, along his mighty soul.

Now is the coming forth of the king.—First appeared the sword of Luno; the spear half issuing from a cloud, the shield still dim in mist. But when the stride of the king came abroad, with all his grey, dewy locks in the wind; then rose the shouts of his host over every moving tribe. They gathered, gleaming, round, with all their echoing shields. So rise the green seas round a spirit, that comes down from the squally wind. The traveller hears the sound afar, and lifts his head over the rock. He looks on the troubled bay, and thinks he dimly sees the form. The waves sport, unwieldly,[3] round, with all their backs of foam.

Far-distant stood the son of Morni, Duthno's race, and Cona's bard. We stood far-distant; each beneath his tree. We shunned the eyes of the king; we had not conquered in the field.—A little stream rolled at my feet: I touched its light wave, with my spear. I touched it with my spear; nor there was the soul of Ossian. It darkly rose, from thought to thought, and sent abroad the sigh.

Son of Morni, said the king, Dermid, hunter of roes! why are ye dark, like two rocks, each with its trickling waters? No wrath gathers on the soul of Fingal, against the chiefs of men. Ye are my strength in battle; the kindling of my joy in peace. My early voice was a pleasant gale to your ears, when Fillan prepared the bow. The son of Fingal is not here, nor yet the chace of the bounding roes. But why should the breakers of shields stand, darkened, far away?

Tall they strode towards the king; they saw him turned to Mora's wind. His tears came down, for his blue-eyed son, who slept in the cave of streams. But he brightened before them, and spoke to the broad-shielded kings.

Crommal, with woody rocks, and misty top, the field of winds, pours forth, to the fight, blue Lubar's streamy roar. Behind it rolls clear-winding Lavath, in the still vale of deer. A cave is dark in a rock; above it strong-winged eagles dwell; broad-headed oaks, before it, sound in Cluna's wind. Within, in his locks of youth, is Ferad-artho[4], blue-eyed king, the son of broad-shielded Cairbar, from Ullin of the roes. He listens to the voice of Condan, as, grey, he bends in feeble light. He listens, for his foes dwell in the echoing halls of Temora. He comes, at times, abroad, in the skirts of mist, to pierce the bounding roes. When the sun looks on the field, nor by the rock, nor stream, is he! He shuns the race of Bolga, who dwell in his father's hall. Tell him, that Fingal lifts the spear, and that his foes, perhaps, may fail.

Lift up, O Gaul, the shield before him. Stretch, Dermid, Temora's spear. Be thy voice in his ear, O Carril, with the deeds of his fathers. Lead him to green Moilena, to the dusky field of ghosts; for there I fall forward, in battle, in the folds of war. Before dun night descends, come to high Dun-mora's top. Look, from the grey rolling of mist,[5] on Lena of the streams. If there my standard shall float on wind, over Lubar's gleaming course,[6] then has not Fingal failed in the last of his fields.

Such were his words: nor aught replied the silent, striding kings. They looked side-long, on Erin's host, and darkened, as they went.—Never before had they left the king, in the midst of the stormy field.—Behind them, touching at times his harp, the grey-haired Carril moved. He foresaw the fall of the people, and mournful was the sound!—It was like a breeze that comes, by fits, over Lego's reedy lake; when sleep half-descends on the hunter, within his mossy cave.

Why bends the bard of Cona, said Fingal, over his secret stream?—Is this a time for sorrow, father of low-laid Oscar? Be the warriors[7] remembered in peace; when echoing shields are heard no more. Bend, then, in grief, over the flood, where blows the mountain breeze. Let them pass on thy soul, the blue-eyed dwellers of Lena.[8]—But Erin rolls to war, wide-tumbling, rough, and dark. Lift, Ossian, lift the shield.—I am alone, my son!

As comes the sudden voice of winds to the becalmed ship of Inis-huna, and drives it large, along the deep, dark rider of the wave: so the voice of Fingal sent Ossian, tall, along the heath. He lifted high his shining shield, in the dusky wing of war: like the broad, blank moon, in the skirt of a cloud, before the storms arise.

Loud, from moss-covered Mora, poured down, at once, the broad-winged war. Fingal led his people forth; king of Morven of streams.—On high spreads the eagle's wing. His grey hair is poured on his shoulders broad. In thunder are his mighty strides. He often stood, and saw behind, the wide-gleaming rolling of armour.—A rock he seemed, grey over with ice, whose woods are high in wind. Bright streams leap from its head, and spread their foam on blasts.

Now he came to Lubar's cave, where Fillan darkly slept. Bran still lay on the broken shield: the eagle-wing is strewed on winds. Bright, from with-ered furze, looked forth the hero's spear.—Then grief stirred the soul of the king, like whirlwinds blackening on a lake. He turned his sudden step, and leaned on his bending spear.

White-breasted Bran came bounding with joy to the known path of Fingal. He came, and looked towards the cave, where the blue-eyed hunter lay, for he was wont to stride, with morning, to the dewy bed of the roe.—It was then the tears of the king came down, and all his soul was dark.—But as the rising wind rolls away the storm of rain, and leaves the white streams to the sun, and high hills with their heads of grass; so the returning war brightened the mind of Fingal. He bounded[9], on his spear, over Lubar, and struck his echoing shield. His ridgy host bend forward, at once, with all their pointed steel.

Nor Erin heard, with fear, the sound: wide they came rolling along. Dark Malthos, in the wing of war, looks forward from shaggy brows. Next rose that beam of light Hidalla; then the side-long-looking gloom of Maronnan. Blue-shielded Clonar lifts the spear; Cormar shakes his bushy locks on the wind.—Slowly, from behind a rock, rose the bright form of Atha. First appeared his two pointed spears, then the half of his burnished shield: like the rising of a nightly meteor, over the vale of ghosts. But when he shone all abroad: the hosts plunged, at once, into strife. The gleaming waves of steel are poured on either side.

As meet two troubled seas, with the rolling of all their waves, when they feel the wings of contending winds, in the rock-sided firth of Lumon; along the echoing hills is the dim course of ghosts: from the blast fall the torn groves on the deep, amidst the foamy path of whales.—So mixed the hosts!—Now Fingal; now Cathmor came abroad.—The dark tumbling of death is before them: the gleam of broken steel is rolled on their steps, as, loud, the high-bounding kings hewed down the ridge of shields.

Maronnan fell, by Fingal, laid large across a stream. The waters gathered by his side, and leapt grey over his bossy shield.—Clonar is pierced by Cathmor: nor yet lay the chief on earth. An oak seized his hair in his fall. His helmet rolled on the ground. By its thong, hung his broad shield; over it wandered his streaming blood. Tla-min[10] shall weep, in the hall, and strike her heaving breast.

Nor did Ossian forget the spear, in the wing of his war. He strewed the field with dead.—Young Hidalla came. Soft voice of streamy Clonra! Why dost thou lift the steel?—O that we met, in the strife of song, in thy own rushy vale!—Malthos beheld him low, and darkened as he rushed along. On either side of a stream, we bend in the echoing strife.—Heaven comes rolling down: around burst the voices of squally winds.—Hills are clothed, at times, in fire. Thunder rolls in wreaths of mist.—In darkness shrunk the foe: Morven's warriors stood aghast.—Still I bent over the stream, amidst my whistling locks.

Then rose the voice of Fingal, and the sound of the flying foe. I saw the king, at times, in lightning, darkly-striding in his might. I struck my echoing shield, and hung forward on the steps of Alnecma: the foe is rolled before me, like a wreath of smoak.

The sun looked forth from his cloud. The hundred streams of Moi-lena shone. Slow rose the blue columns of mist, against the glittering hill.—Where are the mighty kings?[11]—Nor by that stream, nor wood, are they!—I hear the clang of arms!—Their strife is in the bosom of mist.—Such is the contending of spirits in a nightly cloud, when they strive for the wintry wings of winds, and the rolling of the foam-covered waves.

I rushed along. The grey mist rose.—Tall, gleaming, they stood at Lubar.—Cathmor leaned against a rock. His half-fallen shield received the stream, that leapt from the moss above.—Towards him is the stride of Fingal; he saw the hero's blood. His sword fell slowly to his side.—He spoke, midst his darkening joy.

Yields the race of Borbar-duthul? Or still does he lift the spear? Not unheard is thy name, in Selma,[12] in the green dwelling of strangers. It has come, like the breeze of his desart, to the ear of Fingal.—Come to my hill of feasts: the mighty fail, at times. No fire am I to lowlaid foes: I rejoice not over the fall of the brave.—To close[13] the wound is mine: I have known the herbs of the hills. I seized their fair heads, on high, as they waved by their secret streams.—Thou art dark and silent, king of Atha of strangers.

By Atha of the streams,[14] he said, there rises a mossy rock. On its head is the wandering of boughs, within the course of winds. Dark, in its face, is a cave with its own loud rill.—There have I heard the tread of strangers[15], when they passed to my hall of shells. Joy rose, like a flame, on my soul: I blest the echoing rock. Here be my dwelling, in darkness, in my grassy vale. From this I shall mount the breeze, that pursues my thistle's beard; or look down, on blue-winding Atha, from its wandering mist.

Why speaks the king of the tomb?—Ossian! the warrior has failed!—Joy meet thy soul, like a stream, Cathmor, friend of strangers!—My son, I hear the call of years; they take my spear as they pass along. Why does not Fingal, they seem to say, rest within his hall? Dost thou always delight in blood? In the tears of the sad?—No: ye darkly-rolling years, Fingal delights not in blood. Tears are wintry streams that waste away my soul. But, when I lie down to rest, then comes the mighty voice of war. It awakes me, in my hall, and calls forth all my steel.—It shall call it forth no more; Ossian, take thou thy father's spear. Lift it, in battle, when the proud arise.

My fathers, Ossian, trace my steps; my deeds are pleasant to their eyes. Wherever I come forth to battle, on my field, are their columns of mist.—But mine arm rescued the feeble; the haughty found my rage was fire. Never over the fallen did mine eye rejoice. For this[16] my fathers shall meet me, at the gates of their airy halls, tall, with robes of light, with mildly-kindled eyes. But, to the proud in arms, they are darkened moons in heaven, which send the fire of night, red-wandering over their face.

Father of heroes, Trenmor, dweller of eddying winds! I give thy spear to Ossian, let thine eye rejoice. Thee have I seen, at times, bright from between thy clouds; so appear to my son, when he is to lift the spear: then shall he remember thy mighty deeds, though thou art now but a blast.

He gave the spear to my hand, and raised, at once, a stone on high, to speak to future times, with its grey head of moss. Beneath he placed a sword[17] in earth, and one bright boss from his shield. Dark in thought, a-while, he bends: his words, at length, came forth.

When thou, O stone, shalt moulder down, and lose thee, in the moss of years, then shall the traveller come, and whistling pass away.—Thou know'st not, feeble wanderer,[18] that fame once shone on Moi-lena. Here Fingal resigned his spear, after the last of his fields.—Pass away, thou empty shade; in thy voice there is no renown. Thou dwellest by some peaceful stream; yet a few years, and thou art gone. No one remembers thee, thou dweller of thick mist!—But Fingal shall be clothed with fame, a beam of light to other times; for he went forth, in echoing steel, to save the weak in arms.

Brightening in his fame, the king strode to Lubar's sounding oak, where it bent, from its rock, over the bright tumbling stream. Beneath it is a narrow plain, and the sound of the fount of the rock.—Here the standard[19] of Morven poured its wreaths on the wind, to mark the way of Ferad-artho, from his secret vale.——Bright, from his parted west, the sun of heaven looked abroad. The hero saw his people, and heard their shouts of joy. In broken ridges round, they glittered to the beam. The king rejoiced, as a hunter in his own green vale, when, after the storm is rolled away, he sees the gleaming sides of the rocks. The green thorn shakes its head in their face; from their top, look forward the roes.

[20]Grey, at his mossy cave, is bent the aged form of Clonmal. The eyes of the bard had failed. He leaned forward, on his staff. Bright in her locks, before him, Sul-malla listened to the tale; the tale of the kings of Atha, in the days of old. The noise of battle had ceased in his ear: he stopt, and raised the secret sigh. The spirits of the dead, they said, often lightened over his soul. He saw the king of Atha low, beneath his bending tree.

Why art thou dark, said the maid? The strife of arms is past. Soon[21] shall he come to thy cave, over thy winding streams. The sun looks from the rocks of the west. The mists of the lake arise. Grey, they spread on that hill, the rushy dwelling of roes. From the mist shall my king appear! Behold, he comes in his arms. Come to the cave of Clonmal, O my best beloved!

It was the spirit of Cathmor, stalking, large, a gleaming form. He sunk by the hollow stream, that roared between the hills.—"It was but the hunter, she said, who searches for the bed of the roe. His steps are not forth to war; his spouse expects him with night.—He shall, whistling, return, with the spoils of the dark-brown hinds."——Her eyes are turned to the hill; again the stately form came down. She rose, in the midst of joy. He retired in mist. Gradual vanish his limbs of smoak, and mix with the mountain-wind.—

Then she knew that he fell! "King of Erin art thou low!"—Let Ossian forget her grief; it wastes the soul of age[22].

Evening came down on Moi-lena. Grey rolled the streams of the land. Loud came forth the voice of Fingal: the beam of oaks arose. The people gathered round with gladness; with gladness blended with shades. They sidelong looked to the king, and beheld his unfinished joy.—Pleasant, from the way of the desert, the voice of music came. It seemed, at first, the noise of a stream, far-distant on its rocks. Slow it rolled along the hill like the ruffled wing of a breeze, when it takes the tufted beard of the rocks, in the still season of night.—It was the voice of Condan, mixed with Carril's trembling harp. They came with blue-eyed Ferad-artho, to Mora of the streams.

Sudden bursts the song from our bards, on Lena: the host struck their shields midst the sound. Gladness rose brightening on the king, like the beam of a cloudy day when it rises, on the green hill, before the roar of winds.—He struck the bossy shield of kings; at once they cease around. The people lean forward, from their spears, towards the voice of their land[23].

Sons of Morven, spread the feast; send the night away on song. Ye have shone around me, and the dark storm is past. My people are the windy rocks, from which I spread my eagle-wings, when I rush forth to renown, and seize it on its field.—Ossian, thou hast the spear of Fingal: it is not the staff of a boy with which he strews the thistle round, young wanderer of the field.—No: it is the lance of the mighty, with which they stretched forth their hands to death. Look to thy fathers, my son; they are awful beams.— With morning lead Ferad-artho forth to the echoing halls of Temora. Remind him of the kings of Erin; the stately forms of old.—Let not the fallen be forgot, they were mighty in the field. Let Carril pour his song, that the kings may rejoice in their mist.—To-morrow I spread my sails to Selma's shaded walls; where streamy Duthula winds through the seats of roes.—[24]

CATHLIN OF CLUTHA:

A

POEM.

ARGUMENT.

An address to Malvina, the daughter of Toscar.—The poet relates the arrival of Cathlin in Selma, to solicit aid against Duth-carmor of Cluba, who had killed Cathmol, for the sake of his daughter Lanul.—Fingal declining to make a choice among his heroes, who were all claiming the command of the expedition; they retired *each to his hill of ghosts*; to be determined by dreams. The spirit of Trenmor appears to Ossian and Oscar: they sail, from the bay of Carmona, and, on the fourth day, appear off the valley of Rath-col, in Inis-huna, where Duth-carmor had fixed his residence.——— Ossian dispatches a bard to Duth-carmor to demand battle.—Night comes on.—The distress of Cathlin of Clutha.—Ossian devolves the command on Oscar, who, according to the custom of the kings of Morven, before battle, retired to a neighbouring hill.—Upon the coming on of day, the battle joins.—Oscar and Duth-carmor meet. The latter falls.—Oscar carries the mail and helmet of Duth-carmor to Cathlin, who had retired from the field. Cathlin is discovered to be the daughter of Cathmol, in disguise, who had been carried off, by force, by, and had made her escape from, Duth-carmor.

CATHLIN OF CLUTHA: A POEM.

[1]Come, thou beam that art lonely, from watching in the night! The squally winds are around thee, from all their echoing hills. Red, over my hundred streams, are the light-covered paths of the dead. They rejoice, on the eddying winds, in the still season[2] of night.—Dwells there no joy in song, white hand of the harps of Lutha? Awake the voice of the string, and roll my soul to me. It is a stream that has failed.—Malvina pour the song.

I hear thee, from thy darkness, in Selma, thou that watchest, lonely, by night! Why didst thou with-hold the song, from Ossian's failing soul?—— As the falling brook to the ear of the hunter, descending from his storm-covered hill; in a sun-beam rolls the echoing stream; he hears, and shakes his dewy locks: such is the voice of Lutha, to the friend of the spirits of heroes.—My swelling bosom beats high. I look back on the days that are past.——Come, thou beam that art lonely, from the watching of night.

In the echoing bay of Carmona[3] we saw, one day, the bounding ship. On high, hung a broken shield; it was marked with wandering blood. Forward came a youth, in armour, and stretched his pointless spear. Long, over his tearful eyes, hung loose his disordered locks. Fingal gave the shell of kings. The words of the stranger arose.

In his hall lies Cathmol of Clutha, by the winding of his own dark streams. Duth-carmor saw white-bosomed Lánul[4], and pierced her father's side. In the rushy desert were my steps. He fled in the season of night. Give thine aid to Cathlin to revenge his father.——I sought thee not as a beam, in a land of clouds. Thou, like that sun, art known, king of echoing Selma.

Selma's king looked around. In his presence, we rose in arms. But who should lift the shield? for all had claimed the war. The night came down; we strode, in silence; each to his hill of ghosts: that spirits might descend, in our dreams, to mark us for the field.

We struck the shield of the dead, and raised the hum of songs. We thrice called the ghosts of our fathers. We laid us down in dreams.——Trenmor came, before mine eyes, the tall form of other years. His blue hosts were behind him in half-distinguished rows. Scarce seen in their strife in mist, or their stretching forward to deaths. I listened; but no sound was there. The forms were empty wind.

I started from the dream of ghosts. On a sudden blast flew my whistling hair. Low-sounding, in the oak, is the departure of the dead. I took my shield from its bough. Onward came the rattling of steel. It was Oscar[5] of Lego. He had seen his fathers.

As rushes forth the blast, on the bosom of whitening waves; so careless shall my course be, thro' ocean, to the dwelling of foes. I have seen the dead, my father. My beating soul is high. My fame is bright before me, like the streak of light on a cloud, when the broad sun comes forth, red traveller of the sky.

Grandson of Branno, I said; not Oscar alone shall meet the foe. I rush forward, thro' ocean, to the woody dwelling of heroes. Let us contend, my son, like eagles, from one rock; when they lift their broad wings, against the stream of winds.—We raised our sails in Carmona. From three ships, they marked my shield on the wave, as I looked on nightly Ton-thena[6], red wanderer[7] between the clouds.—Four days came the breeze abroad. Lumon came forward in mist. In winds were its hundred groves. Sun-beams marked, at times, its brown side. White, leapt the foamy streams from all its echoing rocks.

A green field, in the bosom of hills, winds silent with its own blue stream. Here, midst the waving of oaks, were the dwellings of kings of old. But silence, for many dark-brown years, had settled in grassy Rath-col[8], for the race of heroes had failed, along the pleasant vale.—Duth-carmor was here, with his people, dark rider of the wave. Ton-thena had hid her head in the sky. He bound his white-bosomed sails. His course is on the hills of Rath-col, to the seats of rocs.

We came. I sent the bard, with songs, to call the foe to fight. Duth-carmor heard him, with joy. The king's soul was[9] a beam of fire; a beam of fire, marked with smoak, rushing, varied, thro' the bosom of night. The deeds of Duth-carmor were dark, tho' his arm was strong.

Night came, with the gathering of clouds. By the beam of the oak we sat down. At a distance stood Cathlin of Clutha. I saw the changing[10] soul of the stranger. As shadows fly over the field of grass, so various is Cathlin's cheek. It was fair, within locks, that rose on Rath-col's wind. I did not rush, amidst his soul, with my words. I bade the song to rise.

Oscar of Lego, I said, be thine the secret hill[11], to night. Strike the shield, like Morven's kings. With day, thou shalt lead in war. From my rock, I shall see thee, Oscar, a dreadful form ascending in fight, like the appearance of ghosts, amidst the storms they raise.——Why should mine eyes return to the dim times of old, ere yet the song had bursted forth, like the sudden rising of winds?——But the years, that are past, are marked with mighty deeds. As the nightly rider of waves looks up to Ton-thena of beams: so let us turn our eyes to Trenmor, the father of kings.

Wide, in Caracha's echoing field, Carmal had poured his tribes. They were a dark ridge of waves; the grey-haired bards were like moving foam on their face. They kindled the strife around with their red-rolling eyes.—Nor alone were the dwellers of rocks; a son of Loda was there; a voice, in his own dark land, to call the ghosts from high.——On his hill, he had dwelt, in Lochlin, in the midst of a leafless grove. Five stones lifted, near, their heads. Loud-roared his rushing stream. He often raised his voice to winds, when meteors marked their nightly wings; when the dark-crusted[12] moon was rolled behind her hill. Nor unheard of ghosts was he!—They came with the sound of eagle-wings. They turned battle, in fields, before the kings of men.

But, Trenmor, they turned not from battle; he drew forward the troubled war; in its dark skirt was Trathal, like a rising light.—It was dark; and Loda's son poured forth his signs, on night.—The feeble were not before thee, son of other lands!

[13]Then rose the strife of kings, about the hill of night; but it was soft as two summer gales, shaking their light wings, on a lake.——Trenmor yielded to his son; for the fame of the king was heard.——Trathal came forth before his father, and the foes failed, in echoing Carácha. The years that are past, my son, are marked with mighty deeds[14].

* * * * * * * * * [15]

In clouds rose the eastern light. The foe came forth in arms. The strife is mixed at Rath-col, like the roar of streams. Behold the contending of kings! They meet beside the oak. In gleams of steel the dark forms are lost; such is the meeting of meteors, in a vale by night: red light is scattered round, and men foresee the storm.——Duth-carmor is low in blood. The son of Ossian overcame. Not harmless in battle was he, Malvina hand of harps!

Nor, in the field, are the steps of Cathlin. The stranger stood by a secret stream, where the foam of Rath-col skirted the mossy stones. Above, bends the branchy birch, and strews its leaves, on winds. The inverted spear of Cathlin touched, at times, the stream.——Oscar brought Duth-carmor's mail: his helmet with its eagle-wing. He placed them before the stranger, and his words were heard.——"The foes of thy father have failed. They are laid in the field of ghosts. Renown returns to Morven, like a rising wind. Why art thou dark, chief of Clutha? Is there cause for grief?"

Son of Ossian of harps, my soul is darkly sad. I behold the arms of Cathmol, which he raised in war. Take the mail[16] of Cathlin, place it high in Selma's hall; that thou mayst remember the hapless in thy distant land.

From white breasts descended the mail. It was the race of kings; the soft-handed daughter of Cathmol, at the streams of Clutha.—Duth-carmor saw her bright in the hall, he came, by night, to Clutha. Cathmol met him, in battle, but the warrior[17] fell. Three days dwelt the foe, with the maid. On the fourth she fled in arms. She remembered the race of kings, and felt her bursting soul.

Why, maid of Toscar of Lutha, should I tell how Cathlin failed? Her tomb is at rushy Lumon, in a distant land. Near it were the steps of Sul-malla, in the days of grief. She raised the song, for the daughter of strangers, and touched the mournful harp.

Come, from the watching of night, Malvina, lonely beam!

SUL-MALLA

OF

LUMON:

A

POEM.

ARGUMENT.

This poem, which, properly speaking, is a continuation of the last, opens with an address to Sul-malla, the daughter of the king of Inis-huna, whom Ossian met, at the chace, as he returned from the battle of Rath-col. Sul-malla invites Ossian and Oscar to a feast, at the residence of her father, who was then absent in the wars.——Upon hearing their name and family, she relates an expedition of Fingal into Inis-huna. She casually mentioning Cathmor, chief of Atha, (who then assisted her father against his enemies) Ossian introduces the episode of Culgorm and Surandronlo, two Scandinavian kings, in whose wars Ossian himself and Cathmor were engaged on opposite sides.——The story is imperfect, a part of the original being lost.—Ossian, warned, in a dream, by the ghost of Trenmor, sets sail from Inis-huna.

SUL-MALLA of LUMON: A POEM.

[1]Who moves so stately, on Lumon, at the roar of the foamy waters? Her hair falls upon her heaving breast. White is her arm behind, as slow she bends the bow. Why dost thou wander in desarts, like a light thro' a cloudy field? The young roes are panting, by their secret rocks.——Return, thou daughter of kings; the cloudy night is near.

It was the young branch of Lumon,[2] Sul-malla of blue eyes. She sent the bard from her rock, to bid us to her feast. Amidst the song we sat down, in Conmor's[3] echoing hall. White moved the hands of Sul-malla, on the trembling strings. Half-heard, amidst the sound, was the name of Atha's king: he that was absent in battle for her own green land.—Nor absent from her soul was he: he came midst her thoughts by night: Ton-thena looked in, from the sky, and saw her tossing arms.

The sound of the shells had ceased. Amidst long locks, Sul-malla rose. She spoke with bended eyes, and asked of our course thro' seas; "for of the kings of men are ye, tall riders of the wave[4]."——Not unknown, I said, at his streams is he, the father of our race. Fingal has been heard of at Cluba, blue-eyed daughter of kings.—Nor only, at Cona's stream, is Ossian and Oscar known. Foes trembled at our voice, and shrunk in other lands.

Not unmarked, said the maid, by Sul-malla, is the shield of Morven's king. It hangs high, in Conmor's[5] hall, in memory of the past; when Fingal came to Cluba, in the days of other years. Loud roared the boar of Culdarnu, in the midst of his rocks of woods. Inis-huna sent her youths, but they failed; and virgins wept over tombs.—Careless went the king[6] to Culdarnu. On his spear rolled the strength of the woods.—He was bright, they said, in his locks, the first of mortal men.—Nor at the feast were heard his words. His deeds passed from his soul of fire, like the rolling of vapours from the face of the wandering sun.—Not careless looked the blue eyes of Cluba on his stately steps. In white bosoms rose the king of Selma, in midst of their thoughts by night. But the winds bore the stranger to the echoing vales of his roes.——Nor lost to other lands was he, like a meteor that sinks in a cloud. He came forth, at times, in his brightness, to the distant dwelling of foes. His fame came, like the sound of winds, to Cluba's woody vale[7].

Darkness dwells in Cluba of harps: the race of kings is distant far; in battle is Conmor of spears;[8] and Lormar[9] king of streams. Nor darkening alone are they; a beam, from other lands, is nigh: the friend[10] of strangers in Atha, the troubler of the field. High, from their misty hills, look forth the blue eyes of Erin, for he is far away, young dweller of their souls.—Nor, harmless, white hands of Erin! is he[11] in the skirts of war; he rolls ten thousand before him, in his distant field.

Not unseen by Ossian, I said, rushed Cathmor from his streams, when he poured his strength on I-thorno[12], isle of many waves. In strife met two kings in I-thorno, Culgorm and Suran-drónlo: each from his echoing isle, stern hunters of the boar!

They met a boar, at a foamy stream: each pierced it with his steel. They strove for the fame of the deed: and gloomy battle rose. From isle to isle they sent a spear, broken and stained with blood, to call the friends of their fathers, in their sounding arms. Cathmor came, from Bolga,[13] to Culgorm, red-eyed king: I aided Suran-dronlo, in his land of boars.

We rushed on either side of a stream, which roared thro' a blasted heath. High broken rocks were round, with all their bending trees. Near are two circles of Loda, with the stone of power; where spirits descended, by night, in dark-red streams of fire.——There, mixed with the murmur of waters, rose the voice of aged men, they called the forms of night, to aid them in their war.

[14]Heedless I stood, with my people, where fell the foamy stream from rocks. The moon moved red from the mountain. My song, at times, arose. Dark on the other side, young Cathmor heard my voice; for he lay, beneath the oak, in all his gleaming arms.——Morning came; we rushed to fight: from wing to wing is the rolling of strife. They fell, like the thistle's head, beneath autumnal winds.

In armour came a stately form: I mixed my strokes with the king.[15] By turns our shields are pierced: loud rung our steely mails. His helmet fell to the ground. In brightness shone the foe. His eyes, two pleasant flames, rolled between his wandering locks.—I knew the king[16] of Atha, and threw my spear on earth.—Dark, we turned, and silent passed to mix with other foes.

Not so passed the striving kings[17]. They mixed in echoing fray; like the meeting of ghosts, in the dark wing of winds. Thro' either breast rushed the spears; nor yet lay the foes on earth. A rock received their fall; and half-reclined they lay in death. Each held the lock of his foe; and grimly seemed to roll his eyes. The stream of the rock leapt on their shields, and mixed below with blood.

The battle ceased in I-thorno. The strangers met in peace: Cathmor from Atha of streams, and Ossian, king of harps. We placed the dead in earth. Our steps were by Rúnar's bay. With the bounding boat, afar, advanced a ridgy wave. Dark was the rider of seas, but a beam of light was there, like the ray of the sun, in Stromlo's rolling smoak. It was the daughter[18] of Suran-dronlo, wild in brightened looks. Her eyes were wandering flames, amidst disordered locks. Forward is her white arm, with the spear; her high-heaving breast is seen, white as foamy waves that rise, by turns, amidst rocks. They are beautiful, but they are terrible, and mariners call the winds.

Come, ye dwellers of Loda! Carchar, pale in the midst of clouds! Sluthmor, that stridest in airy halls! Corchtur, terrible in winds! Receive, from his daughter's spear, the foes of Suran-dronlo.

No shadow, at his roaring streams; no mildly-looking form was he! When he took up his spear, the hawks shook their sounding wings: for blood was poured around the steps of dark-eyed Suran-dronlo.

He lighted me, no harmless beam, to glitter on his streams. Like meteors, I was bright, but I blasted the foes of Suran-dronlo.——

* * * * * * * * * * * * * *

Nor unconcerned heard Sul-malla, the praise of Cathmor of shields. He was within her soul, like a fire in secret heath, which awakes at the voice of the blast, and sends its beam abroad. Amidst the song removed the daughter of kings, like the soft sound[19] of a summer-breeze; when it lifts the heads of flowers, and curls the lakes and streams.[20]

By night came a dream to Ossian; without form stood the shadow of Trenmor. He seemed to strike the dim shield, on Selma's streamy rock. I rose, in my rattling steel; I knew that war was near. Before the winds our sails were spread; when Lumon shewed its streams to the morn.

Come from the watching of night, Malvina, lonely beam!

CATH-LODA:

A

POEM.

DUAN FIRST.

ARGUMENT.

Fingal, in one of his voyages to[1] the Orkney islands, was driven, by stress of weather, into a bay of Scandinavia, near the residence of Starno, king of Lochlin. Starno invites Fingal to a feast. Fingal, doubting the faith of the king, and mindful of his[2] former breach of hospitality, [Fingal, b.3.][3] refuses to go.——Starno gathers together his tribes: Fingal resolves to defend himself.——Night coming on, Duth-maruno proposes to Fingal, to observe the motions of the enemy.—The king himself undertakes the watch. Advancing towards the enemy, he, accidentally, comes to the cave of Turthor, where Starno had confined Conban-carglas, the captive daughter of a neighbouring chief.——Her story is imperfect, a part of the original being lost.—Fingal comes to a place of worship, where Starno and his son, Swaran, consulted the spirit of Loda, concerning the issue of the war.—The rencounter of Fingal and Swaran.—The *duan* concludes, with a description of the airy hall of Cruth-loda supposed to be the Odin of Scandinavia.

CATH-LODA: DUAN[4] FIRST.

A tale of the times of old!—Why, thou wanderer unseen, that bendest the thistle of Lora,—why, thou breeze of the valley, hast thou left mine ear? I hear no distant roar of streams, no sound of the harp, from the rocks! Come, thou huntress of Lutha, send back[5] his soul to the bard.

I look forward to Lochlin of lakes, to the dark, ridgy[6] bay of U-thórno, where Fingal descended from ocean, from the roar of winds. Few are the heroes of Morven, in a land unknown!—Starno sent a dweller of Loda, to bid Fingal to the feast; but the king remembered the past, and all his rage arose.

Nor Gormal's mossy towers, nor Starno shall Fingal behold. Deaths wander, like shadows, over his fiery soul. Do I forget that beam of light, the white-handed daughter[7] of kings? Go, son of Loda; his words are but blasts to Fingal: blasts, that, to and fro, roll the thistle, in autumnal vales.[8]

Duth-maruno[9], arm of death! Cromma-glas, of iron shields! Struthmor, dweller of battle's wing! Cormar, whose ships bound on seas, careless as the course of a meteor, on dark streaming[10] clouds! Arise, around me, children of heroes, in a land unknown. Let each look on his shield, like Trenmor, the ruler of battles. "Come down, said the king,[11] thou dweller between the harps. Thou shalt roll this stream away, or dwell[12] with me in earth."

Around him they rose in wrath.—No words came forth: they seized their spears. Each soul is rolled into itself.—At length the sudden clang is waked, on all their echoing shields.—Each took his hill, by night; at intervals, they darkly stood. Unequal bursts the hum of songs, between the roaring wind.—Broad over them rose the moon.—In his arms, came tall Duth-maruno; he from Croma-charn of rocks, stern hunter of the boar. In his dark boat he rose on waves, when Crumthormoth[13] awaked its woods. In the chace he shone, among his foes:—No fear was thine, Duth-maruno.

Son of Comhal, he said, my steps shall be forward thro' night.[14] From this shield I shall view them, over their gleaming tribes.[15] Starno, of lakes,[16] is before me, and Swaran, the foe of strangers. Their words are not in vain, by Loda's stone of power.—If Duth-maruno returns not, his spouse is lonely, at home, where meet two roaring streams, on Crathmo-craulo's plain. Around are hills, with their woods;[17] the ocean is rolling near. My son looks on screaming sea-fowl, young wanderer of the field. Give the head of a boar to Can-dona[18], tell him of his father's joy, when the bristly strength of I-thorno rolled on his lifted spear.[19]

Not forgetting my fathers, said Fingal, I have bounded over ridgy[20] seas: theirs were[21] the times of danger, in the days of old. Nor gathers[22] darkness on me, before foes, tho' I am young, in my locks.—Chief of Crathmo-craulo, the field of night is mine.

He[23] rushed, in all his arms, wide-bounding over Turthor's stream, that sent its sullen roar, by night, thro' Gormal's misty vale.—A moon-beam glittered on a rock; in the midst, stood a stately form; a form with floating locks, like Lochlin's white-bosomed maids.—Unequal are her steps, and short: she throws a broken song on wind. At times she tosses her white arms: for grief is[24] in her soul.

Torcul-torno[25], of aged locks![26] where now are thy steps, by Lulan? thou hast failed, at thine own dark streams, father of Conban-carglas![27] ——But I behold thee, chief of Lulan, sporting by Loda's hall, when the dark-skirted night is poured[28] along the sky.

Thou, sometimes, hidest the moon, with thy shield. I have seen her dim, in heaven. Thou kindlest thy hair into meteors, and sailest along the night.—Why am I forgot in my cave, king of shaggy boars? Look from the hall of Loda, on lonely Conban-carglas.[29]

"Who art thou, said Fingal, voice of night?"——She trembling, turned away. "Who art thou, in thy darkness?"——She shrunk into the cave.—— The king loosed the thong from her hands; he asked about her fathers.

Torcul-torno, she said, once dwelt at Lulan's foamy stream: he dwelt—— but, now, in Loda's hall, he shakes the sounding shell. He met Starno of Lochlin, in battle; long fought the dark-eyed kings. My father fell, at length,[30] blue-shielded Torcul-torno.

By a rock, at Lulan's stream, I had pierced the bounding roe. My white hand gathered my hair, from off the stream of winds.[31] I heard a noise. Mine eyes were up. My soft breast rose on high. My step was forward, at Lulan, to meet thee, Torcul-torno!

It was Starno, dreadful king!——His red eyes rolled on Conban-carglas.[32] Dark waved his shaggy brow, above his gathered smile. Where is my father, I said, he that was mighty in war? Thou are left alone among foes, daughter of Torcul-torno!

He took my hand. He raised the sail. In this cave he placed me dark. At times, he comes, a gathered mist. He lifts, before me, my father's shield. Often passes a beam[33] of youth, far-distant from my cave.[34] He dwells lonely in the soul of the daughter of Torcul-torno.[35]

Daughter[36] of Lúlan, said Fingal, white-handed Conban-carglas;[37] a cloud, marked with streaks of fire, is rolled along the[38] soul. Look not to that dark-robed moon; nor yet to those meteors of heaven; my gleaming steel is around thee, daughter of Torcul-torno.[39]

It is not the steel of the feeble, nor of the dark in soul. The maids are not shut in our[40] caves of streams; nor tossing their white arms alone. They bend, fair within their locks, above the harps of Selma. Their voice is not in the desart wild, young light of Torcul-torno.[41]

* * * * * * * * * * * * * * * * *
* * * * * * * * * * * * * * * *

Fingal, again, advanced his steps, wide thro' the bosom of night, to where the trees of Loda shook amidst squally winds. Three stones, with heads of moss, are there; a stream, with foaming course; and dreadful, rolled around them, is the dark-red cloud of Loda. From its top looked forward a ghost, half-formed of the shadowy smoak. He poured his voice, at times, amidst the roaring stream.—Near, bending beneath a blasted tree, two heroes received his words: Swaran of the lakes, and Starno foe of strangers.—On their dun shields, they darkly leaned: their spears are forward in night. Shrill sounds the blast of darkness, in Starno's floating beard.

They heard the tread of Fingal. The warriors rose in arms. "Swaran, lay that wanderer low, said Starno, in his pride. Take the shield of thy father; it is a rock in war."—Swaran threw his gleaming spear: it stood fixed in Loda's tree. Then came the foes forward, with swords. They mixed their rattling steel. Thro' the thongs of Swaran's shield rushed the blade[42] of Luno. The shield fell rolling on earth. Cleft the helmet[43] fell down. Fingal stopt the lifted steel. Wrathful stood Swaran, unarmed. He rolled his silent eyes, and threw his sword on earth. Then, slowly stalking over the stream, he whistled as he went.

Nor unseen of his father is Swaran. Starno turned away in wrath. His shaggy brows waved dark, above his gathered rage. He struck Loda's tree, with his spear; he raised the hum of songs.—They came to the host of Lochlin, each in his own dark path; like two foam-covered streams, from two rainy vales.

To Turthor's plain Fingal returned. Fair rose the beam of the east. It shone on the spoils of Lochlin in the hand of the king. From her cave came forth, in her beauty, the daughter of Torcul-torno. She gathered her hair from wind; and wildly raised her song. The song of Lulan of shells, where once her father dwelt.

She saw Starno's bloody shield. Gladness rose, a light, on her face. She saw the cleft helmet of Swaran[44]; she shrunk, darkened, from the king.[45] ——"Art thou fallen, by thy hundred streams, O love of Conban-carglas!"[46]——

* * * * * * * * * * * * * * * *
* * * * * * * * * * * * * * * *[47]

U-thorno, that risest in waters; on whose side are the meteors of night! I behold the dark moon descending behind thy echoing woods. On thy top dwells the misty Loda, the house of the spirits of men.—In the end of his cloudy hall bends forward Cruth-loda of swords. His form is dimly seen, amidst his wavy mist. His right-hand is on his shield: in his left is the half-viewless shell. The roof of his dreadful hall is marked with nightly fires.

The race of Cruth-loda advance, a ridge of formless shades. He reaches the sounding shell, to those who shone in war; but, between him and the feeble, his shield rises, a crust of darkness.[48] He is a setting meteor to the weak in arms.—Bright, as a rainbow on streams, came white-armed Conban-carglas.[49]——

* * * * * * * * * * * * * * * * *[50]

CATH-LODA:

A

POEM.

DUAN SECOND.

ARGUMENT.

Fingal returning, with day, devolves the command of the army on Duth-maruno, who engages the enemy, and drives them over the stream of Turthor. Fingal, after recalling his people, congratulates Duth-maruno on his success, but discovers, that that hero was mortally wounded in the engagement.—Duth-maruno dies. Ullin, the bard, in honour of the dead, introduces the episode of Colgorm and Strina-dona, with which the *duàn* concludes.

CATH-LODA: DUAN SECOND.

Where art thou, son of the king, said dark-haired Duth-maruno? Where hast thou failed, young beam of Selma?—He returns not from the bosom of night! Morning is spread on U-thorno: in his mist is the sun, on his hill.—Warriors, lift the shields, in my presence. He must not fall, like a fire from heaven, whose place is not marked on the ground.——He comes like an eagle, from the skirt of his squally wind! In his hand are the spoils of foes.—King of Selma, our souls were sad.

Near us are the foes, Duth-maruno. They come forward, like waves in mist, when their foamy tops are seen, at times, above the low-sailing vapour.—The traveller shrinks on his journey, and knows not whither to fly.—No trembling travellers are we!—Sons of heroes, call forth the steel.—Shall the sword of Fingal arise, or shall a warrior lead?

[1]The deeds of old, said Duth-maruno, are like paths to our eyes, O Fingal. Broad-shielded Trenmor is still seen, amidst his own dim years. Nor feeble was the soul of the king. There, no dark deed wandered in secret.——From their hundred streams came the tribes, to grassy Colglan-crona. Their chiefs were before them. Each strove to lead the war. Their swords were often half-unsheathed. Red rolled their eyes of rage. Separate they stood, and hummed their surly songs.——"Why should they yield to each other? their fathers were equal in war."

Trenmor was there, with his people, stately in youthful locks. He saw the advancing foe. The grief of his soul arose. He bade the chiefs to lead, by turns: they led, but they were rolled away.—From his own mossy hill, blue-shielded Trenmor came down. He led wide-skirted battle, and the strangers failed. Around him the dark-browed warriors came: they struck the shield of joy. Like a pleasant gale, the words of power rushed forth from Selma of kings. But the chiefs led, by turns, in war, till mighty danger rose: then was the hour of the king to conquer in the field.

"Not unknown, said Cromma-glas[2] of shields, are the deeds of our fathers.—But who shall now lead the war, before the race of kings? Mist settles on these four dark hills: within it let each warrior strike his shield. Spirits may descend in darkness, and mark us for the war."——They went, each to his hill of mist. Bards marked the sounds of the shields. Loudest rung thy boss, Duth-maruno. Thou must lead in war.

Like the murmur of waters, the race of U-thorno came down. Starno led the battle, and Swaran of stormy isles. They looked forward from iron shields, like Cruth-loda fiery-eyed, when he looks from behind the darkened moon, and strews his signs on night.

The foes met by Turthor's stream. They heaved like ridgy waves. Their echoing strokes are mixed. Shadowy death flies over the hosts. They were clouds of hail, with squally winds in their skirts. Their showers are roaring together. Below them swells the dark-rolling deep.

Strife of gloomy U-thorno, why should I mark thy wounds? Thou art with the years that are gone; thou fadest on my soul. Starno brought forward his skirt of war, and Swaran his own dark wing. Nor a harmless fire is Duth-maruno's sword.—Lochlin is rolled over her streams. The wrathful kings are folded in thoughts.[3] They roll their silent eyes, over the flight of their land.—The horn of Fingal was heard: the sons of woody Albion returned. But many lay, by Turthor's stream, silent in their blood.

Chief of Crom-charn,[4] said the king, Duth-maruno, hunter of boars! not harmless returns my eagle, from the field of foes. For this white-bosomed Lanul shall brighten, at her streams; Candona shall rejoice, at rocky Crathmo-craulo.[5]

Colgorm[6], replied the chief, was the first of my race in Albion; Colgorm, the rider of ocean, thro' its watry vales. He slew his brother in I-thorno[7]: he left the land of his fathers. He chose his place, in silence, by rocky Crathmo-craulo. His race came forth, in their years; they came forth to war, but they always fell. The wound of my fathers is mine, king of echoing isles!

He drew an arrow from his side. He fell pale, in a land unknown. His soul came forth to his fathers, to their stormy isle. There they pursued boars of mist, along the skirts of winds.——The chiefs stood silent around, as the stones of Loda, on their hill. The traveller sees them, thro' the twilight, from his lonely path. He thinks them the ghosts of the aged, forming future wars.

Night came down, on U-thorno. Still stood the chiefs in their grief. The blast hissed,[8] by turns, thro' every warrior's hair.—Fingal, at length, bursted[9] forth from the thoughts of his soul. He called Ullin of harps, and bade the song to rise.—No falling fire, that is only seen, and then retires in night; no departing meteor was Crathmo-craulo's chief.[10] He was like the strong-beaming sun, long rejoicing on his hill. Call the names of his fathers, from their dwellings old.

I-thorno[11], said the bard, that risest midst ridgy seas! Why is thy head so gloomy, in the ocean's mist? From thy vales came forth a race, fearless as thy strong-winged eagles; the race of Colgorm of iron shields, dwellers of Loda's hall.

In Tormoth's resounding isle, arose Lurthan, streamy hill. It bent its woody head above a silent vale. There, at foamy Cruruth's source, dwelt Rurmar, hunter of boars. His daughter was fair as a sun-beam, white-bosomed Strina-dona!

Many a king of heroes, and hero of iron shields; many a youth of heavy locks came to Rurmar's echoing hall. They came to woo the maid, the stately huntress of Tormoth wild.—But thou lookest careless from thy steps, high-bosomed Strina-dona!

If on the heath she moved, her breast was whiter than the down of Cana[12]; if on the sea-beat shore, than the foam of the rolling ocean. Her eyes were two stars of light; her face was heaven's bow in showers; her dark hair flowed round it, like the streaming clouds.—Thou wert the dweller of souls, white-handed Strina-dona!

Colgorm came, in his ship, and Corcul-Suran, king of shells. The brothers came, from I-thorno, to woo the sun-beam of Tormoth's isle.[13] She saw them in their echoing steel. Her soul was fixed on blue-eyed Colgorm.—Ul-lochlin's[14] nightly eye looked in, and saw the tossing arms of Strina-dona.

Wrathful the brothers frowned. Their flaming eyes, in silence, met. They turned away. They struck their shields. Their hands were trembling on their swords. They rushed into the strife of heroes, for long-haired Strina-dona.

Corcul-Suran fell in blood. On his isle, raged the strength of his father. He turned Colgorm, from I-thorno, to wander on all the winds.—In Crathmo-craulo's rocky field, he dwelt, by a foreign stream. Nor darkened the king alone, that beam of light was near, the daughter of echoing Tormoth, white-armed Strina-dona.[15]

CATH-LODA:

A

POEM.

DUAN THIRD.

ARGUMENT.

Ossian, after some general reflections, describes the situation of Fingal, and the position of the army of Lochlin.—The conversation of Starno and Swaran.—The episode of Corman-trunar and Foinar-bragal.—Starno, from his own example, recommends to Swaran, to surprize Fingal, who had retired alone to a neighbouring hill. Upon Swaran's refusal, Starno undertakes the enterprize himself, is overcome, and taken prisoner, by Fingal.—He is dismissed, after a severe reprimand for his cruelty.

CATH-LODA: DUAN THIRD.

Whence is the stream of years? Whither do they roll along? Where have they hid, in mist, their many-coloured sides? I look into the times of old, but they seem dim to Ossian's eyes, like reflected moon-beams, on a distant lake. Here rise the red beams of war!—There, silent, dwells a feeble race! They mark no years with their deeds, as slow they pass along.—Dweller between the shields; thou that awakest the failing soul, descend from thy wall, harp of Cona, with thy voices three! Come with that which kindles the past: rear the forms of old, on their own dark-brown years!

[1]U-thorno, hill of storms, I behold my race on thy side. Fingal is bending, in night, over Duth-maruno's tomb. Near him are the steps of his heroes, hunters of the boar.—By Turthor's stream the host of Lochlin is deep in shades. The wrathful kings stood on two hills; they looked forward from their bossy shields. They looked forward on the stars of night, red-wandering in the west. Cruth-loda bends from high, like a formless meteor in clouds. He sends abroad the winds, and marks them, with his signs. Starno foresaw, that Morven's king was never to yield in war.

He twice struck the tree in wrath. He rushed before his son. He hummed a surly song; and heard his hair in wind. Turned[2] from one another, they stood, like two oaks, which different winds had bent; each hangs over its own loud rill, and shakes its boughs in the course of blasts.

Annir, said Starno of lakes, was a fire that consumed of old. He poured death from his eyes, along the striving fields. His joy was in the fall of men. Blood, to him, was a summer stream, that brings joy to withered vales, from its own mossy rock.—He came forth to the lake Luth-cormo, to meet the tall Corman-trunar, he from Urlor of streams, dweller of battle's wing.

The chief of Urlor had come to Gormal, with his dark-bosomed ships; he saw the daughter of Annir, white-armed Foinar-bragal.[3] He saw her: nor careless rolled her eyes, on the rider of stormy waves. She fled to his ship in darkness, like a moon-beam thro' a nightly vale.—Annir pursued along the deep; he called the winds of heaven.—Nor alone was the king; Starno was by his side. Like U-thorno's young eagle, I turned my eyes on my father.

We came to[4] roaring Urlor. With his people came tall Corman-trunar. We fought; but the foe prevailed. In his wrath stood Annir of lakes.[5] He lopped the young trees, with his sword. His eyes rolled red in his rage. I marked the soul of the king, and I retired in night.—From the field I took a broken helmet: a shield that was pierced with steel: pointless was the spear in my hand. I went to find the foe.

On a rock sat tall Corman-trunar, beside his burning oak; and near him, beneath a tree, sat deep-bosomed Foinar-bragal. I threw my broken shield before her; and spoke the words of peace.—Beside his rolling sea, lies Annir of many lakes. The king was pierced in battle; and Starno is to raise his tomb. Me, a son of Loda, he sends to white-handed Foinar-bragal, to bid her send a lock from her hair, to rest with her father, in earth.—And thou king of roaring Urlor, let the battle cease, till Annir receive the shell, from fiery-eyed Cruth-loda.

[6]Bursting into tears, she rose, and tore a lock from her hair; a lock, which wandered, in the blast, along her heaving breast.—Corman-trunar gave the shell; and bade me to rejoice before him.—I rested in the shade of night; and hid my face in my helmet deep.—Sleep descended on the foe. I rose, like a stalking ghost. I pierced the side of Corman-trunar. Nor did Foinar-bragal escape. She rolled her white bosom in blood. Why then, daughter of heroes, didst thou wake my rage?—Morning rose. The foe were fled, like the departure of mist. Annir struck his bossy shield. He called his dark-haired son. I came, streaked with wandering blood: thrice rose the shout of the king, like the bursting forth of a squall of wind, from a cloud, by night.—We rejoiced, three days, above the dead, and called the hawks of heaven. They came, from all their winds, to feast on Annir's foes.—Swaran!—Fingal is alone[7], on his hill of night. Let thy spear pierce the king in secret; like Annir, my soul shall rejoice.

Son of Annir of Gormal, Swaran shall[8] not slay in shades. I move forth in light: the hawks rush from all their winds. They are wont to trace my course: it is not harmless thro' war.

Burning rose the rage of the king. He thrice raised his gleaming spear. But starting, he spared his son; and rushed into the night.—By Turthor's stream a cave is dark, the dwelling of Conban-carglas. There he laid the helmet of kings, and called the maid of Lulan, but she was distant far, in Loda's resounding hall.

Swelling in his rage, he strode, to where Fingal lay alone. The king was laid on his shield, on his own secret hill.—Stern hunter of shaggy boars, no feeble maid is laid before thee: no boy, on his ferny bed, by Turthor's murmuring stream. Here is spread the couch of the mighty, from which they rise to deeds of death. Hunter of shaggy boars awaken not the terrible.

Starno came murmuring on. Fingal arose in arms. "Who art thou, son of night?" Silent he threw the spear. They mixed their gloomy strife. The shield of Starno fell, cleft in twain. He is bound to an oak. The early beam arose.—Then Fingal beheld the king of Gormal.[9] He rolled a while his silent eyes. He thought of other days, when white-bosomed Agandecca moved like the music of songs.—He loosed the thong from his hands.—Son of Annir, he said, retire. Retire to Gormal of shells: a beam that was set returns. I remember thy white-bosomed daughter;——dreadful king away!——Go to thy troubled dwelling, cloudy foe of the lovely! Let the stranger shun thee, thou gloomy in the hall!

A tale of the times of old!

OINA-MORUL:

A

POEM.

ARGUMENT.

After an address to Malvina, the daughter of Toscar, Ossian proceeds to
relate his own expedition to Fuärfed, an island of Scandinavia.—Mal-
orchol, king of Fuärfed, being hard pressed in war, by Ton-thormod, chief
of Sar-dronlo, (who had demanded, in vain, the daughter of Mal-orchol in
marriage) Fingal sent Ossian to his aid.——Ossian, on the day after his
arrival, came to battle with Ton-thormod, and took him prisoner.—Mal-
orchol offers his daughter Oina-morul to Ossian; but he, discovering her
passion for Ton-thormod, generously surrenders her to her lover, and
brings about a reconciliation between the two kings.

OINA-MORUL: A POEM.

As flies the unconstant sun, over Larmon's grassy hill; so pass the tales of old, along my soul, by night. When bards are removed to their place; when harps are hung in Selma's hall; then comes a voice to Ossian, and awakes his soul. It is the voice of years that are gone: they roll before me, with all their deeds. I seize the tales, as they pass, and pour them forth in song. Nor a troubled stream is the song of the king, it is like the rising of music from Lutha of the strings.—Lutha of many strings, not silent are thy streamy rocks, when the white hands of Malvina move upon the harp.—Light of the shadowy thoughts, that fly across my soul, daughter of Toscar of helmets, wilt thou not hear the song! We call back, maid of Lutha, the years that have rolled away.

It was in the days of the king,[1] while yet my locks were young, that I marked Con-cathlin[2] , on high, from ocean's nightly wave. My course was towards the isle of Fuärfed, woody dweller of seas. Fingal had sent me to the aid of Mal-orchol, king of Fuärfed wild: for war was around him, and our fathers had met, at the feast.

In Col-coiled, I bound my sails, and sent my sword to Mal-orchol of shells. He knew the signal of Albion, and his joy arose. He came from his own high hall, and seized my hand in grief. "Why comes the race of heroes to a falling king? Ton-thormod of many spears is the chief of wavy Sardronlo. He saw and loved my daughter, white-bosomed Oina-mórul. He sought; I denied the maid; for our fathers had been foes.—He came, with battle, to Fuärfed. My people are rolled away.—Why comes the race of heroes to a falling king?"

I come not, I said, to look, like a boy, on the strife. Fingal remembers Mal-orchol, and his hall for strangers. From his waves, the warrior descended, on thy woody isle. Thou wert no cloud before him. Thy feast was spread with songs. For this my sword shall rise; and thy foes perhaps may fail.—Our friends are not forgot in their danger, tho' distant is our land.

Son[3] of the daring Trenmor, thy words are like the voice of Cruth-loda, when he speaks, from his parting cloud, strong dweller of the sky! Many have rejoiced at my feast; but they all have forgot Mal-orchol. I have looked towards all the winds, but no white sails were seen.—But steel[4] resounds in my hall; and not the joyful shells.—Come to my dwelling, race of heroes; dark-skirted night is near. Hear the voice of songs, from the maid of Fuärfed wild.

We went. On the harp arose the white hands of Oina-morul. She waked her own sad tale, from every trembling string. I stood in silence; for bright in her locks was the daughter of many isles. Her eyes were like[5] two stars, looking forward thro' a rushing shower. The mariner marks them on high, and blesses the lovely beams.—With morning we rushed to battle, to

Tormul's resounding stream: the foe moved to the sound of Ton-thormod's bossy shield. From wing to wing the strife was mixed. I met the chief of Sar-dronlo.[6] Wide flew his broken steel. I seized the king in fight.[7] I gave his hand, bound fast with thongs, to Mal-orchol, the giver of shells. Joy rose at the feast of Fuärfed,for the foe had failed.——Ton-thormod turned his face away, from Oina-morul of isles.

Son of Fingal, begun Mal-orchol, not forgot shalt thou pass from me. A light shall dwell in thy ship, Oina-morul of slow-rolling eyes. She shall kindle gladness, along thy mighty soul. Nor unheeded shall the maid move in Selma, thro' the dwelling of kings.

In the hall I lay in night. Mine eyes were half-closed in sleep. Soft music came to mine ear: it was like the rising breeze, that whirls, at first, the thistle's beard; then flies, dark-shadowy, over the grass. It was the maid of Fuärfed wild: she raised the nightly song; for she knew that my soul was a stream, that flowed at pleasant sounds.

Who looks, she said, from his rock, on ocean's closing mist? His long locks, like the raven's wing, are wandering on the blast. Stately are his steps in grief. The tears are in his eyes. His manly breast is heaving over his bursting soul.—Retire, I am distant far; a wanderer in lands unknown. Tho' the race of kings are around me, yet my soul is dark.—Why have our fathers been foes, Ton-thormod love of maids!

Soft voice of the streamy isle,[8] why dost thou mourn by night? The race of daring Trenmor are not the dark in soul. Thou shalt not wander, by streams unknown, blue-eyed Oina-morul.—Within this bosom is a voice; it comes not to other ears: it bids Ossian hear the hapless, in their hour of woe.—— Retire, soft singer by night; Ton-thormod shall not mourn on his rock.

With morning I loosed the king. I gave the long-haired maid. Mal-orchol heard my words, in the midst of his echoing halls.——"King of Fuärfed wild, why should Ton-thormod mourn? He is of the race of heroes, and a flame in war. Your fathers have been foes, but now their dim ghosts rejoice in death. They stretch their arms[9] of mist to the same shell in Loda. Forget their rage, ye warriors, it was the cloud of other years."——

Such were the deeds of Ossian, while yet his locks were young: tho' loveliness, with a robe of beams, clothed the daughter of many isles.—We call back, maid of Lutha, the years that have rolled away!

COLNA-DONA:

A

POEM.

ARGUMENT.

Fingal dispatches Ossian and Toscar[1] to raise a stone, on the banks of the stream of Crona, to perpetuate the memory of a victory, which he had obtained in that place. When they were employed in that work, Car-ul, a neighbouring chief, invited them to a feast.—They went: and Toscar fell desperately in love with Colna-dona, the daughter of Car-ul. Colna-dona became no less enamoured of Toscar. An incident, at a hunting-party, brings their loves to a happy issue.

COLNA-DONA: A POEM.

[2]Col-amon of troubled streams, dark wanderer of distant vales, I behold thy course, between trees, near Car-ul's echoing halls. There dwelt bright Colna-dona, the daughter of the king. Her eyes were rolling stars; her arms were white as the foam of streams. Her breast rose slowly to sight, like ocean's heaving wave. Her soul was a stream of light.— Who, among the maids, was like the love of heroes?

Beneath the voice of the king, we moved to Crona[3] of the streams, Toscar of grassy Lutha, and Ossian, young in fields. Three bards attended with songs. Three bossy shields were born before us: for we were to rear the stone, in memory of the past. By Crona's mossy course, Fingal had scattered his foes: he had rolled away the strangers, like a troubled sea. We came to the place of renown: from the mountains descended night. I tore an oak from its hill, and raised a flame on high. I bade my fathers to look down, from the clouds of their hall; for, at the fame of their race, they brighten in the wind.

I took a stone from the stream, amidst the song of bards. The blood of Fingal's foes hung curdled in its ooze. Beneath, I placed, at intervals, three bosses from the shields of foes, as rose or fell the sound of Ullin's nightly song. Toscar laid a dagger in earth, a mail of sounding steel. We raised the mould around the stone, and bade it speak to other years.

Oozy daughter of streams, that now art reared on high, speak to the feeble, O stone, after Selma's race have failed!— Prone, from the stormy night, the traveller shall lay him, by thy side: thy whistling moss shall sound in his dreams; the years that were past shall return.— Battles rise before him, blue-shielded kings descend to war: the darkened moon looks from heaven, on the troubled field.— He shall burst, with morning, from dreams, and see the tombs of warriors round. He shall ask about the stone, and the aged will reply, "This grey stone was raised by Ossian, a chief of other years!"

[4]From Col-amon came a bard, from Car-ul, the friend of strangers. He bade us to the feast of kings, to the dwelling of bright Colna-dona. We went to the hall of harps. There Car-ul brightened between his aged locks, when he beheld the sons of his friends, like two young trees with their leaves.[5]

Sons of the mighty, he said, ye bring back the days of old, when first I descended from waves, on Selma's streamy vale. I pursued Duth-mocarglos, dweller of ocean's wind. Our fathers had been foes, we met by Clutha's winding waters. He fled, along the sea, and my sails were spread behind him.— Night deceived me, on the deep. I came to the dwelling of kings, to Selma of high-bosomed maids.— Fingal came forth with his bards, and Conloch, arm of death. I feasted three days in the hall, and saw the blue-eyes of Erin, Ros-crana, daughter of heroes, light of Cormac's race.— Nor forgot did my steps depart: the kings gave their shields to Car-ul: they hang, on high, in Col-amon, in memory of the past.— Sons of the daring kings, ye bring back the days of old.

Car-ul placed[6] the oak of feasts. He took two bosses from our shields. He laid them in earth, beneath a stone, to speak to the hero's race. "When battle, said the king, shall roar, and our sons are to meet in wrath; my race shall look, perhaps, on this stone, when they prepare the spear.— Have not our fathers met in peace, they will say, and lay aside the shield?"

Night came down. In her long locks moved the daughter of Car-ul. Mixed with the harp arose the voice of white-armed Colna-dona.—Toscar darkened in his place, before the love of heroes. She came on his troubled soul, like a beam to the dark-heaving ocean: when it bursts from a cloud, and brightens the foamy side of a wave[7].

   *   *   *   *   *   *   *

   *   *   *   *   *   *   *

With morning we awaked the woods; and hung forward on the path of the roes. They fell by their wonted streams. We returned thro' Crona's vale. From the wood a youth came forward, with a shield and pointless spear. "Whence, said Toscar of Lutha, is the flying beam? Dwells there peace at Col-amon, round bright Colna-dona of harps?"

By Col-amon of streams, said the youth, bright Colna-dona dwelt. She dwelt; but her course is now in desarts, with the son of the king; he that seized[8] her soul as it wandered thro' the hall.

Stranger of tales, said Toscar, hast thou marked the warrior's course? He must fall,— give thou that bossy shield!— In wrath he took the shield. Fair behind it heaved[9] the breasts of a maid, white as the bosom of a swan, rising[10] on swift-rolling waves. It was Colna-dona of harps, the daughter of the king.— Her blue eyes had rolled on Toscar, and her love arose.

A

SPECIMEN

OF THE

ORIGINAL

OF

TEMORA.

BOOK SEVENTH.

A D V E R T I S E M E N T .

It is thought proper to give a specimen of the original Galic, for the satis-
faction of those who doubt the authenticity of Ossian's poems. The
seventh book of TEMORA is fixed on, for that purpose, not from any other
superior merit, than the variety of its versification. To print any part of the
former collection was unnecessary, as a copy of the originals lay, for many
months, in the bookseller's hands, for the inspection of the curious. Tho'
the erroneous orthography of the bards is departed from, in many
instances, in the following specimen, yet several quiescent consonants are
retained, to shew the derivation of the words. This circumstance may give
an uncouth appearance to the language, in the eyes of those who are
strangers to its harmony. They ought, however, to consider, that a lan-
guage is put to the severest test, when it is stripped of its own proper
characters; especially, when the power of *one* of them requires, some-
times, a combination of two or three Roman letters to express it.[1]

A SPECIMEN OF THE ORIGINAL OF TEMORA. BOOK SEVENTH.

O Linna doir-choille na *Leigo*,
Air uair, eri' ceo taobh-ghórm nan tón;
Nuair dhunas dorsa na h'oicha
Air iulluir-shuil greina nan speur.
Tomhail, mo *Lara* nan sruth,
Thaomas du'-nial, as doricha cruaim:
Mar ghlas-scia', roi taoma nan nial,
Snamh seachad, ta Gellach na h'oicha.
Le so edi' taisin o-shean
An dlu'-ghleus, a measc na gaoith,
'S iad leamnach, o osna gu osna,
Air du'-aghai' oicha nan sian.
An taobh oitaig, gu palin nan seoid,
Taomas iad ceäch nan speur,
Gorm-thalla do thannais nach béo,
Gu ám eri' fón marbh-rán nan teud.

Ta torman, a machair nan crán
Se *Conar* ri *Erin* at' án,
A taoma' ceo-tanais gu dlu'
Air *Faolan* aig *Lubhair* nan sru'
Muladach, suigha fo bhrón,
Dh'aom[2] an tais an ceach an loin.
Thaom osna, essin an fein,
Ach phil an cruth aluin, gu diän
Phíl é le chrom-shealla mál
Le cheo-leatain, mar shuibhal nan sian.
            'S doilleir so!
Ata na sloigh na nsuain, san ám,
An truscan cear na h'oicha:
Dh' ilsich teina an ri, gu ard,
Dh' aom é na aonar, air scia'.
Thuit codál, mo shuillin a ghaiscich,
Thanic guth *Fhaolan*, na chluais.

An codal so, don' fhear-phosda aig *Clatho*?
Am bail coni do m'athair, an suain?
Am bail cuina, 's mi 'ntruscan nan nial?
'S mi m' aonar an ám na h'oicha?

Cur son ta ú, a m' aslin fein?
Thubhart *Fion-ghael*, 's é'g eri grad.
An dith-chuin, d'omse, mo mhac,
Na shiubhal teina air Rethlan nan laoich?
Ni marsin, air anam an ri,
Thig gniomh seoid aluin na ncruai'-bheum.
Ni ndeallan iadse, a theichas an dubhra
Na h'oicha, 'snach fhág a lorg.
'S cuina liom *Faolan* na shuain:
'Ta m'anam aig eri' borb.

Ghluais an ri, le sleagh, gu grad,
Bhuail e nscia' as fuaimnach cop,
An scia' a dh' aom sa n'oicha ard,
Bal-mosgla' do cháth nan lót.
Air aomagh du' nan sliabh,
Air gaoith, theich treud nan tais:
O ghleanan cear nan ioma lúp,
'Mhosguil guth a bhais.

Bhuail é'n scia, an darra cuairt,
Ghluais coga, an aslin an t'shluaigh:
Bhith comh-sri nan lán glas—
A dealra'[3] air anam nan seoid,
Ciean-fheona a truita' gu cath,
Slua' a teicha,—gniomh bu chruai',
Leth-dhoilleir, an deallan na stalin.

Nuair dh' erich, an darra fuaim,[4]
Leum feigh, o chós nan cárn
Chluinte a screadan scé', sa n' fhasich——
Gach Ean, air osna fein.
Leth-erich siol *Albin* nam buaigh
Thog iad suas gach sleagh, bu ghlas:
Ach phíl sachir, air an t'shluaigh,[5]
Se bh' án scia' *Mhorbhein* na mfras.
Phíl codal, air suilin na mfear:
Bu dorcha, tróm a nglean.

Ni mo chodal, duitse é, sa nuair,
Nion shuil-ghórm *Chonmor* na mbuaigh,—
Chuala *Suil-mhalla* an fhuaim
Dh' erich i, sa n' oicha, le cruaim:
Ta ceum gu ri *Atha* na ncolg:

Ni mosguil cunart anam borb.
Tróm a shési,——a suilin sios.
Ta' nspeur an losga nan reul.

Chualas lé sciath na ncòp.
Ghluais;—ghrad shés an Oi:—
Dh' erich a gu'——ach dh' aom é sios.——
Chuinic ís é, na stalin chruai,
A dealra ri losga nan reul:
Chuinic is é, na leatan thróm.
Aig eri ri osna nan speur.
Thionta i ceamna, le fiamh,
Curson dhuisgimse Ri *Erin* na m *Bólg*,
Ni n' aslin do chodal u-fein,
A nion *Inis-uina* na ncólg.

Gu garg a mhosgul an torman;
On' oi thuit a cean-bhért sios:
Ta mforum, air carric nan sruth.
Plaosga, o aslin na h'oicha,
Ghluais *Cathmor* fa' chrán fein.
Chuinic é n' Oi bu tla,
Air carric *Lubhair* nan sliabh:
Dearg reul, a sealla sios,—
Measc siubhal a tróm chíabh.

Cia'ta roi Oicha gu *Cathmor*
An cear-amsair aslin fein?
Am bail fios duit, air sri na ncruai-bheum?
Cia ussa, mhic dubhra nan speur?
Na shés u, am fionas[6] an Ri,
Do chaol-thannais, on n' am o-shean;
Na nguth u, o neoil nam fras,
Le cunairt *Erin* na ncolg sean?

Ni mfear siubhail dubhra mi-fhein,
Ni nguth mi, o neol, na cruaim:
Ach ta m' fhocul, le cunairt na h'*Erin*.
An cualas duit coppan na fuaim?
Ni ntais é, Ri *Atha* nan sruth,
A thaomas an fhuaim air oicha.

Taomagh an seod a ghuth fein,
'S fon clarsich, do *Chathmor* an fhuaim,

Ta aitis, mhic dubhra nan speur,
Losga air m' anam, gun ghruaim.
Se ceoil chiean-fheona na ncruai-bheum,
A m' oicha, air asri nan siän,
Nuair lasas anam nan són;
A chlán an cruadal do miän.
Ta siol-meata a nconi, na mfiamh,
A ngleanan na n' osna tlá,
Far an aom ceo-maidin, ri sliabh,
O ghorm-shuibhal sruthan na mblár.

  Ni meata, chean-uia nan són,
An seans'ra', on thuit mi-fein,
Bu choni doigh dubhra nan tón,
An tir fhadda siol cholgach na mbeum.
Ach ni nsolas do m' anam tlá
Fuaim mhál a bhais on raoin,
Thig essin nach geil gu bráth;
Mosguil bard focuil a scaoin.—

  Mar charric, 's sruthan ri taobh,
'M fasich na mfaoin bhean,
Shes *Cathmor*, cean-feona nach maoin,—
An deoir——
Mar oitag, air anam le brón,
Thanic guth caoin na h'oi,
Mosgla cuina talamh nan bean
A caomh-choni aig sruthan na nglean;
Roi n' ám an d' thanic é gu borb
Gu cabhar *Chonmor* na ncolg fiar.

  A nion coigrich nan lán,
(Thionta i cean on d' shón)
'S fadda fa, m' shuil, an cruai,
Cran flathal *Inis-uina* nan tón.
Ta m' anam, do thubhairt mi-fein,
An truscan nan sian cear,
Car son a lassa an dealra so-fhein,
Gus am pil mi, an sí', on d' shliabh?

  Na ghlas m' aighai', na t' fhionas, a lamh-gheal,
'S tu togmhail do m' eagal an Ri?
'S ám[7] cunairt, annir nan tróm chiabh,
Am do m' anam, mór-thalla na sri!

Attas e, tomhail mar sruth,
A taomagh air *Cael* na ncruaí-bheum.

An taobh carric chosach, air *Lona*,
Mo chaochan, nan sruthan cróm,
Glas, a[8] nciabh na h' aose,
'Ta *Claon-mhal*, Ri clarsich nam fón.
O s' cion ta cran-darrach na mfuaim,
Agus siubhal nan rua-bhoc sliom,
'Ta forum na sri' na chluais
'S é'g aomagh à nsmuina nach tiom:
An sin bith do thalla, *Shul-mhalla*,
Gus an illsich[9] forum na mbeum:
Gus ám píl mi, an lassa na cruai',
O thruscan dubhra na bein:
On cheach do thrussas o *Lona*
Ma choni mo ruin fein.[10]

Thuit gath-soluis air anam na h'oi,
Las i suas, fa' choir an Ri:
Thionta i á h' aighai ri *Cathmor*,
A ciabh-bhóg ans' na h' osna á sri?

Reupar iulluir nan speür árd,
O mhór-srúth gaoith na nglean;
Nuair chi' é na ruai-bhuic, fa' choir,
Clán elid na mfaoin bhean,
Mu ntionta *Cathmor* na ncruai-bheum,
On d' srí mu n' erich dán.—
Faicimse u, ghasgaich na ngeur lán,
O thruscan an dubhra dú',
Nuair thogas ceo mu m' choni fein,
Air *Lona* na n' ioma srú'?
Nuair's fadda, o m' shuil, u sheoid!
Puail coppan na mfuaim árd.
Pillé solas, do m' anam,'s é nceö
'S mi aig aoma air carric liom fein.
Ach mo thuit u—mar ri coigrich ata mí!
Thigga' do ghuth o neoil,
Gu oi *Inis-uina*,'s i fán.

Og gheug *Lumoin* an fheur,
Com dh' aoma tu,'nstrachda nan sian?
'S tric thionta *Cathmor* ó nbhlár

Du'-thaomagh air aighai' nan sliabh.
Mar mhellain, do m' fein, ta sleagh nan lót,
'S iad prunagh air cós nan sciath;
Dh' erim, mo sholluis, on d' shrí;
Mar thein-oicha, o thaoma nan niäl
Na píl, a dheo-ghreina, on ghlean
Nuair dhluthichas forum na ncolg:
Eagal teachá do nabhad o m'lamh,
Mar theich iad, o shiean' sra' na m *Bólg*.

Chualas le *Sonmór* air *Cluanar*,
Thuit fa *Chormac* na ngeúr lán,
Tri lo dhorch an Ri,
Mu n' fhear, a gh' aom an sri na glean.
Chuinac min-bhean, an són á nceo.[11]
Phrosnich sud d' i siubhal gu sliabh,
Thog i bogha, fos n'iosal,
Gu dol marri laoch nan sciath.
Do n' ainir luigh dubhra air *Atha*,
Nuair shuilagh á ngaisgach gu gniomh.

O cheud sruthan aonach na h'oicha,
Thaom siol *Alnecma* sios.
Chualas scia' chasmachd an Ri,
Mhosguil a n' anam gu sri'
Bha' an siubhal, a mforum nan lán,
Gu *Ullin*, talamh na ncrán.
Bhuail *Sónmór*, air uari', an sciath
Cean-feona na mborb thriath.
Na ndeabh, lean *Sul-allin*
Air aoma na mfras,
Bu sholus ís, air aonach,
Nuair thaom iad air gleanta glas.
Ta ceamna flathail air lóm,
Nuair thog iad, ri aghai nan tóm.
B' eagal d' i sealla an Ri—
Dh' fhág i,'n *Atha* na mfri'.

Nuair dh' erich forum na mbeum,
Agus thaom iad, sa cheille, sa chath,
Loisg *Sonmor*, mar theina nan speur,
Thanic *Sul-aluin* na mflath.
A folt scaoilta, sa n' osna,
A h' anam aig osparn mon' Ri.

Dh' aom é an t' shri' mu rún nan laoich,
Theich nabhad fa' dhubhra nan speur
Luigh *Cluanar* gun fhuil,
Gun fhuil, air tigh caoil gun leus.——

Ni n' d' erich fearg *Shon-mhor* nan lán,
Bha' lo gu dorcha,'s gu mál:
Ghluais *Sul-allin* mu gorm-sru' fein,
A suil an reachda nan deuir.
Bu lionmhar a sealla, gu caoin
Air gaisgach sabhach nach faoin.
Ach thionta i a suillin tla,
O shealla, an laoch thuatal.
Mhosgul blair, mar fhorum nan nial,
Ghluais doran o anam mór,
Chunas a ceamna, le aitis,
'Sa lamh-gheal air clarsich na mfón.

Na chruai a ghluais an Ri, gun dail,
Bhuail é'n sciath chosach árd;
Gu árd, air darach nan sian,
Aig *Lubhair* na n'ioma sruth.
Seachd coppain a bh', air an scé,
Seachd focuil an Ri' do shluagh;
A thaomagh air osna nan speur,
Air finachá mór na m *Bólg.*

Air gach copan ta reül do n'oicha;
Cean-mathon nan ros gun scleo',
Caol-derna, o neoil aig eri',
Ul-oicho an truscan do cheö.
'Ta *Caon-cathlin,* air carric, a dealra
Reül-dura' ar gorm-thón on iar:
Leth-chellagh solus an uisce.
Ta *Ber-thein,* las-shuil nan sliabh,
Sealla sios, o choille sa n'aonach;
Air mál shiubhal, sélgair 's é triäl,
Roi ghleanan, an dubhra bhraonach,
Le faogh rua-bhuic nan leum árd.

Tomhail, a miän na scé,
'Ta lassa *Ton-theina,* gun neoil,
An rinnac a sheal, roi n'oicha,
Air *Lear-thon* a chuain mhoir;

Lear-thon, cean-feona na m *Bolg*
A nceud-fhear a shuibhail air gaoith.

Leathain scaoile seoil bhán an Ri.
Gu *Inis-fail* nan ioma sru?
Thaom oicha air aighai' a chuain,
Agus ceäch nan truscan du'.
Bha' gaoith a caochla dlu' sa nspeur.
Leum loingheas, o thòn gu tón;
Nuair dh' erich *Ton-theina* nan stuagh
Caon-shealla, o bhrista' nan nial,
B' aitis do *Learthon* tein-uil na mbuaigh,
A dealra air domhan nan sian.

Fa' sleagh *Chathmor* na ncolg sean
Dhuisge an guth, a dhuisga Baird.
Thaom iad du', o thaobh nan sliabh,
Le clarsich ghrin 's gach lamh.
Le aitis mór, shés rompa an Ri,
Mar fhear-siubhal, ri teas la'nglean.
Nuair chluinas é, fadda sa nréth,
Caoin thorman sruthan na mbean:
Sruthan a bhristas sa n' fhasich,
O charric thaobh-ghlas nan rua-bhoc.

Cur son chluinim guth ard an Ri—
N' ám codal, a n' oicha nan fras?
Am facas tanais nach beo,
Measc t'aslin aig aoma glas?
Air neoil am bail an aitach fuar,
Feaghai' fón *Fhonair* na mfleagh?
'S lionmhar an siubhal air réth,
Far an tog an siol an t'shleagh.
Na n' erich, ar cronan air thús,
Mu n' fhear, nach tog on t'shlea' gu brath;
Fear choscairt, air glean nan sloigh,
O *Mhoma* nan ioma bad?

Ni dith-chuin do m' dorcha na mblár
Chiean-fheona na mbard, o thús,
Togar cloch do aig *Lubhair* na ncárn,
Ait-coni dh' *Fholdath* 'sdo chliu.
Ach taom m'anam, air ám nan laoich,
Air na bliaghna', so n d' erich iad suas,

Air tón *Inis-uina* na ncolg.
Ni n' aitis, do *Chathmor* a bhain,
Cuina *Lumon* inis uina na nsloi?
Lumon talamh na nsruth,
Caon-choni na mbán-bhroilach Oi.

Lumon na sruth!
'Ta u dealra, air m' anam fein,
'Ta do ghrian, air do thaobh,
Air carric na ncrán bu tróm.

Tat' elid chear
Do dhearg bar-mhor, a measc na mbad
A faicin air sliabh.
An colg-chu, a siubhal grad.
Màl air an réth
Ta ceamna nan Oi:
Oi lamh-gheal nan teud
'S na bogha cróm, sa mhoi;
Togmhail an gorm-shuil tlá,
On leatain bhar-bhui, air sliabh na mflath.
Ni bail ceamna *Lear-thon* sa bhein,
Cean *Inis* na ngeug *uina*.

Ta ê togmhail du-dharach air tón,
A ncamis *Chluba*, nan ioma stua',
An du-dharach, bhuain é o *Lumon*,
Gu siubhal air aighai a chuain.
Thionta Oi an suillin tlá,
On Ri, mo ntuitagh é sios.
Ni mfacas leö riamh an long,
Cear mharcach a chuain mhoir.

Ghlaoi' anois, an Ri a ghaoith.
Measc ceó na marra glais.
Dh' erich *Inis-fail* gu gorm:
Thuit, gu dian, oicha na mfrais.
Bhuail eagal *Clan-Bholga* gu lua'
Ghlan neoil, o *Thon-theina* nan stua'
A ncamis *Chulbin* dh' atich an long
Far am fregra' coille do thón.
Bu chopach an sin an sru'
O charric *Duth-umha* na ncós,

'San dealra tannais nach beo
Le ncruith caochlach fein.

Thanic aslin gu *Lear-thon* nan long,
Seachd Samla do nlina nach beo,
Chualas a nguth brista, tróm:
Chunas an siol an ceö,
Chunas siol *Atha* na[12] ncolg—
'San clán ciean-uia' na m *Bolg*.
Thaom iad a mfeachda' fein,
Mar cheach a terna on bhein,
Nuair shiubhlas é glas, fa' osna,
Air *Atha* nan ioma dos.

Thog *Lear-thon* talla *Shamla*,
Ri caoin fhón clarsich nan teud.
Dh' aom eilid *Erin*, o cheamna
Aig aisra' glas nan sruth.
Nin dith-chuin do *Lumon* uina,
Na *Flathal*, gheal-lamhach na mbua'gh
'S í comhaid, air marcach nan tón
O Thulach nan eilid ruagh.

Lumon na sruth
Ta ú dealra' air m' anam fein!

Mhosguil gath soluis on ear,
Dh' erich árd-chiean cheäich na bein.
Chunas air cladach na ngleanan
A ncróm chaochan ghlas-sruthach fein.
Chualas sciath *Chathmor* na ncolg,
Mhosguil siol *Erin* na m *Bolg*.
Mar mhuir dhomhail, nuair ghluisas gu geur
Fuaim aitti, air aghai' nan speur:
Taoma tuin, o thaobh gu taobh,
Aig aomagh a nglas chiean bao;
Gun eolas, air siubhal a chuain.

Trom is mál, gu *Lon* na sruth
Ghluais *Suil-mhalla* nan rosc tlá;
Ghluais as thionta n' Oi le brón:
A gorm-shuil fa shilla blá.
Nuair thanic i gu carric chruai'
Du chromagh air gleanan an *Lón*

Sheal i, o bristagh a ceil,
Air Ri *Atha*——dh' aom i sios.

Puail teud, a mhic Alpain na mfón,
Ambail solas a nclarsich na nieöl?
Taom air *Ossian*, agus Ossun gu tróm,
Ta anam a snamh a nceö.

Chualas u, Bhaird, a m' oicha
Ach siubhla fón edrom uam fein!
'S aitis caoin thurra do dh' *Ossian*
A mbliaghna chear na h' aoise.[13]

Dhreun uaina thulloch nan tais
A thaomas do chean air gaoith oicha,
Ni bail t'fhorum na mchluais fein:
Na faital tannais, na d' gheug ghlais.
'S lionmhar ceamna na marbh bu treun
Air osna, dubh-aisra' na bein,
Nuair ghluisas a ghellach, an ear,
Mar ghlas-scia, du shiubhal nan speur.

Ullin, a Charril, a Raono
Guith amsair a dh' aom o-shean:
Cluinim siobh an dorchadas *Shelma*
Agus mosglibhse anam nan dán!

Ni ncluinim siobh shiol na mfón,
Cia an talla do neoil,'mbail ar suain
Na tribuail siobh, clarsach nach tróm,
An truscan ceo-madin 's cruaim.
Far an erich, gu fuaimar a ghrian
O stuaigh na ncean glas?

A CRITICAL

DISSERTATION

ON THE

POEMS OF OSSIAN,

THE

SON OF FINGAL.

BY

HUGH BLAIR D.D.

One of the Ministers of the High Church, and Professor of Rhetorick and
Belles-Lettres, in the University of Edinburgh.

A CRITICAL DISSERTATION ON THE POEMS OF OSSIAN.[1]

Among the monuments remaining of the ancient state of nations, few are more valuable than their poems or songs. History, when it treats of remote and dark ages, is seldom very instructive. The beginnings of society, in every country, are involved in fabulous confusion; and though they were not, they would furnish few events worth recording. But, in every period of society, human manners are a curious spectacle; and the most natural pictures of ancient manners are exhibited in the ancient poems of nations. These present to us, what is much more valuable than the history of such transactions as a rude age can afford, the history of human imagination and passion. They make us acquainted with the notions and feelings of our fellow-creatures in the most artless ages; discovering what objects they admired, and what pleasures they pursued, before those refinements of society had taken place, which enlarge indeed, and diversify the transactions, but disguise the manners of mankind.

Besides this merit, which ancient poems have with philosophical observers of human nature, they have another with persons of taste. They promise some of the highest beauties of poetical writing. Irregular and unpolished we may expect the productions of uncultivated ages to be; but abounding, at the same time, with that enthusiasm, that vehemence and fire, which are the soul of poetry. For many circumstances of those times which we call barbarous, are favourable to the poetical spirit. That state, in which human nature shoots wild and free, though unfit for other improvements, certainly encourages the high exertions of fancy and passion.

In the infancy of societies, men live scattered and dispersed, in the midst of solitary rural scenes, where the beauties of nature are their chief entertainment. They meet with many objects, to them new and strange; their wonder and surprize are frequently excited; and by the sudden changes of fortune occurring in their unsettled state of life, their passions are raised to the utmost. Their passions have nothing to restrain them: their imagination has nothing to check it. They display themselves to one another without disguise: and converse and act in the uncovered simplicity of nature. As their feelings are strong, so their language, of itself, assumes a poetical turn. Prone to exaggerate, they describe every thing in the strongest colours; which of course renders their speech picturesque and figurative. Figurative language owes its rise chiefly to two causes; to the want of proper names for objects, and to the influence of imagination and passion over the form of expression. Both these causes concur in the infancy of society. Figures are commonly considered as artificial modes of speech, devised by orators and poets, after the world had advanced to a refined state. The contrary of this is the truth. Men never have used so many figures of style, as in those rude ages, when, besides the power of a warm imagination to suggest lively images, the want of proper and precise terms for the ideas they would express, obliged them to have recourse to circumlocution, metaphor, comparison, and all those substituted forms of expression, which give a poetical air to language. An American chief, at this day, harangues at the head of his tribe, in a more bold metaphorical style, than a modern European would adventure to use in an Epic poem.

In the progress of society, the genius and manners of men undergo a change more favourable to accuracy than to sprightliness and sublimity. As the world advances, the understanding gains ground upon the imagination; the understanding is more exercised; the imagination, less. Fewer objects occur that are new or surprizing. Men apply themselves to trace the causes of things; they correct and refine one another; they subdue or disguise their passions; they form their exterior manners upon one uniform standard of politeness and civility. Human nature is pruned according to method and rule. Language advances from sterility to copiousness, and at the same time, from fervour and enthusiasm, to correctness and precision. Style becomes more chaste; but less animated. The progress of the world in this respect resembles the progress of age in man. The powers of imagination are most vigorous and predominant in youth; those of the understanding ripen more slowly, and often attain not their maturity, till the imagination begin to flag. Hence, poetry, which is the child of imagination, is frequently most glowing and animated in the first ages of society. As the ideas of our youth are remembered with a peculiar pleasure on account of their liveliness and vivacity; so the most ancient poems have often proved the greatest favourites of nations.

Poetry has been said to be more ancient than prose: and however paradoxical such an assertion may seem, yet, in a qualified sense, it is true. Men certainly never conversed with one another in regular numbers; but even their ordinary language would, in ancient times, for the reasons before assigned, approach to a poetical style; and the first compositions transmitted to posterity, beyond doubt, were, in a literal sense, poems; that is, compositions in which imagination had the chief hand, formed into some kind of numbers, and pronounced with a musical modulation or tone. Musick or song has been found coæval with society among the most barbarous nations. The only subjects which could prompt men, in their first rude state, to utter their thoughts in compositions of any length, were such as naturally assumed the tone of poetry; praises of their gods, or of their ancestors; commemorations of their own warlike exploits; or lamentations over their misfortunes. And before writing was invented, no other compositions, except songs or poems, could take such hold of the imagination and memory, as to be preserved by oral tradition, and handed down from one race to another.

Hence we may expect to find poems among the antiquities of all nations. It is probable too, that an extensive search would discover a certain degree of resemblance among all the most ancient poetical productions, from whatever country they have proceeded. In a similar state of manners, similar objects and passions operating upon the imaginations of men, will stamp their productions with the same general character. Some diversity will, no doubt, be occasioned by climate and genius. But mankind never bear such resembling features, as they do in the beginnings of society. Its subsequent revolutions give rise to the principal distinctions among nations; and divert, into channels widely separated, that current of human genius and manners, which descends originally from one spring. What we have been long accustomed to call the oriental vein of poetry, because some of the earliest poetical productions have come to us from the East, is probably no more oriental than occidental; it is characteristical of an age rather than a country; and belongs, in some measure, to all nations at a certain period. Of this the works of Ossian seem to furnish a remarkable proof.

Our present subject leads us to investigate the ancient poetical remains, not so much of the east, or of the Greeks and Romans, as of the northern nations; in order to discover whether the Gothic poetry has any resemblance to the Celtic or Galic, which we are about to consider. Though the Goths, under which name we usually comprehend all the Scandinavian tribes, were a people altogether fierce and martial, and noted, to a proverb, for their ignorance of the liberal arts, yet they too from the earliest times, had their poets and their songs. Their poets were distinguished by the title of *Scalders*, and their songs were termed *Vyses*.[2] Saxo Grammaticus, a Danish Historian of considerable note, who flourished in the thirteenth century, informs us that very many of these songs, containing the ancient traditionary stories of the country, were found engraven upon rocks in the old Runic character; several of which he has translated into Latin, and inserted into his History. But his versions are plainly so paraphrastical, and forced into such an imitation of the style and the measures of the Roman poets, that one can form no judgment from them of the native spirit of the original. A more curious monument of the true Gothic poetry is preserved by Olaus Wormius in his book de Literatura Runica. It is an Epicedium, or funeral song, composed by Regner Lodbrog; and translated by Olaus, word for word, from the original. This Lodbrog was a king of Denmark, who lived in the eighth century, famous for his wars and victories; and at the same time an eminent *Scalder* or poet. It was his misfortune to fall at last into the hands of one of his enemies, by whom he was thrown into prison, and condemned to be destroyed by serpents. In this situation he solaced himself with rehearsing all the exploits of his life. The poem is divided into twenty-nine stanzas, of ten lines each; and every stanza begins with these words, Pugnavimus Ensibus, We have fought with our swords. Olaus's version is in many places so obscure as to be hardly intelligible. I have subjoined the whole below, exactly as he has published it; and shall translate as much as may give the English reader an idea of the spirit and strain of this kind of poetry.[3]

"We have fought with our swords.—I was young, when, towards the east, in the bay of Oreon, we made torrents of blood flow, to gorge the ravenous beast of prey, and the yellow-footed bird. There resounded the hard steel upon the lofty helmets of men. The whole ocean was one wound. The crow waded in the blood of the slain. When we had numbered twenty years, we lifted our spears on high, and every where spread our renown. Eight barons we overcame in the east, before the port of Diminum; and plentifully we feasted the eagle in that slaughter. The warm stream of wounds ran into the ocean. The army fell before us. When we steered our ships into the mouth of the Vistula, we sent the Helsingians to the Hall of Odin. Then did the sword bite. The waters were all one wound. The earth was dyed red with the warm stream. The sword rung upon the coats of mail, and clove the bucklers in twain. None fled on that day, till among his ships Heraudus fell. Than him no braver baron cleaves the sea with ships; a chearful heart did he ever bring to the combat. Then the host threw away their shields, when the uplifted spear flew at the breasts of heroes. The sword bit the Scarfian rocks; bloody was the shield in battle, until Rafno the king was slain. From the heads of warriors the warm sweat streamed down their armour. The crows around the Indirian islands had an ample prey. It were difficult to single out one among so many deaths. At the rising of the sun I beheld the spears piercing the bodies of foes, and the bows throwing forth their steel-pointed arrows. Loud roared the swords in the plains of Lano.—The virgin long bewailed the slaughter of that morning."—In this strain the poet continues to describe several other military exploits. The images are not much varied; the noise of arms, the streaming of blood, and the feasting the birds of prey, often recurring. He mentions the death of two of his sons in battle; and the lamentation he describes as made for one of them is very singular. A Grecian or Roman poet would have introduced the virgins or nymphs of the wood, bewailing the untimely fall of a young hero. But, says our Gothic poet, "when Rogvaldus was slain, for him mourned all the hawks of heaven," as lamenting a benefactor who had so liberally supplied them with prey; "for boldly," as he adds, "in the strife of swords, did the breaker of helmets throw the spear of blood."

The poem concludes with sentiments of the highest bravery and contempt of death. "What is more certain to the brave man than death, though amidst the storm of swords, he stand always ready to oppose it? He only regrets this life who hath never known distress. The timorous man allures the devouring eagle to the field of battle. The coward, wherever he comes, is useless to himself. This I esteem honourable, that the youth should advance to the combat fairly matched one against another; nor man retreat from man. Long was this the warrior's highest glory. He who aspires to the love of virgins, ought always to be foremost in the roar of arms. It appears to me of truth, that we are led by the Fates. Seldom can any overcome the appointment of destiny. Little did I foresee that Ella[4] was to have my life in his hands, in that day when fainting I concealed my blood, and pushed forth my ships into the waves; after we had spread a repast for the beasts of prey throughout the Scottish bays. But this makes me always rejoice that in the halls of our father Balder [or Odin] I know there are seats prepared, where, in a short time, we shall be drinking ale out of the hollow skulls of our enemies. In the house of the mighty Odin, no brave man laments death. I come not with the voice of despair to Odin's hall. How eagerly would all the sons of Aslauga now rush to war, did they know the distress of their father, whom a multitude of venomous serpents tear! I have given to my children a mother who hath filled their hearts with valour. I am fast approaching to my end. A cruel death awaits me from the viper's bite. A snake dwells in the midst of my heart. I hope that the sword of some of my sons shall yet be stained with the blood of Ella. The valiant youths will wax red with anger, and will not sit in peace. Fifty and one times have I reared the standard in battle. In my youth I learned to dye the sword in blood: my hope was then, that no king among men would be more renowned than me. The goddesses of death will now soon call me; I must not mourn my death. Now I end my song. The goddesses invite me away; they whom Odin has sent to me from his hall. I will sit upon a lofty seat, and drink ale joyfully with the goddesses of death. The hours of my life are run out. I will smile when I die."

This is such poetry as we might expect from a barbarous nation. It breathes a most ferocious spirit. It is wild, harsh and irregular; but at the same time animated and strong; the style, in the original, full of inversions, and, as we learn from some of Olaus's notes, highly metaphorical and figured.

But when we open the works of Ossian, a very different scene presents itself. There we find the fire and the enthusiasm of the most early times, combined with an amazing degree of regularity and art. We find tenderness, and even delicacy of sentiment, greatly predominant over fierceness and barbarity. Our hearts are melted with the softest feelings, and at the same time elevated with the highest ideas of magnanimity, generosity, and true heroism. When we turn from the poetry of Lodbrog to that of Ossian, it is like passing from a savage desart, into a fertile and cultivated country. How is this to be accounted for? Or by what means to be reconciled with the remote antiquity attributed to these poems? This is a curious point; and requires to be illustrated.

That the ancient Scots were of Celtic original, is past all doubt. Their conformity with the Celtic nations in language, manners and religion, proves it to a full demonstration. The Celtæ, a great and mighty people, altogether distinct from the Goths and Teutones, once extended their dominion over all the west of Europe; but seem to have had their most full and compleat establishment in Gaul. Wherever the Celtæ or Gauls are mentioned by ancient writers, we seldom fail to hear of their Druids and their Bards; the institution of which two orders, was the capital distinction of their manners and policy. The Druids were their philosophers and priests; the Bards, their poets and recorders of heroic actions: And both these orders of men, seem to have subsisted among them, as chief members of the state, from time immemorial[5]. We must not therefore imagine the Celtæ to have been altogether a gross and rude nation. They possessed from very remote ages a formed system of discipline and manners, which appears to have had a deep and lasting influence. Ammianus Marcellinus gives them this express testimony, that there flourished among them the study of the most laudable arts; introduced by the Bards, whose office it was to sing in heroic verse, the gallant actions of illustrious men; and by the Druids, who lived together in colleges or societies, after the Pythagorean manner, and philosophizing upon the highest subjects, asserted the immortality of the human soul[6]. Though Julius Cæsar in his account of Gaul, does not expressly mention the Bards, yet it is plain that under the title of Druids, he comprehends that whole college or order; of which the Bards, who, it is probable, were the disciples of the Druids, undoubtedly made a part. It deserves remark, that according to his account, the Druidical institution first took rise in Britain, and passed from thence into Gaul; so that they who aspired to be thorough masters of that learning were wont to resort to Britain. He adds too, that such as were to be initiated among the Druids, were obliged to commit to their memory a great number of verses, insomuch that some employed twenty years in this course of education; and that they did not think it lawful to record these poems in writing, but sacredly handed them down by tradition from race to race[7].

So strong was the attachment of the Celtic nations to their poetry and their Bards, that amidst all the changes of their government and manners, even long after the order of the Druids was extinct, and the national religion altered, the Bards continued to flourish; not as a set of strolling songsters, like the Greek 'Αοιδοι or Rhapsodists, in Homer's time, but as an order of men highly respected in the state, and supported by a public establishment. We find them, according to the testimonies of Strabo and Diodorus, before the age of Augustus Cæsar; and we find them remaining under the same name, and exercising the same functions as of old, in Ireland, and in the north of Scotland, almost down to our own times. It is well known that in both these countries, every *Regulus* or chief had his own Bard, who was considered as an officer of rank in his court; and had lands assigned him, which descended to his family. Of the honour in which the Bards were held, many instances occur in Ossian's poems. On all important occasions, they were the ambassadors between contending chiefs; and their persons were held sacred. "Cairbar feared to stretch his sword to the bards, though his soul was dark ... Loose the bards, said his brother Cathmor, they are the sons of other times. Their voice shall be heard in other ages, when the kings of Temora have failed." (155)[8]

From all this, the Celtic tribes clearly appear to have been addicted in so high a degree to poetry, and to have made it so much their study from the earliest times, as may remove our wonder at meeting with a vein of higher poetical refinement among them, than was at first sight to have been expected among nations, whom we are accustomed to call barbarous. Barbarity, I must observe, is a very equivocal term; it admits of many different forms and degrees; and though, in all of them, it exclude polished manners, it is, however, not inconsistent with generous sentiments and tender affections[9]. What degrees of friendship, love and heroism, may possibly be found to prevail in a rude state of society, no one can say. Astonishing instances of them we know, from history, have sometimes appeared: and a few characters distinguished by those high qualities, might lay a foundation for a set of manners being introduced into the songs of the Bards, more refined, it is probable, and exalted, according to the usual poetical licence, than the real manners of the country. In particular, with respect to heroism; the great employment of the Celtic bards, was to delineate the characters, and sing the praises of heroes. So Lucan;

Vos quoque qui fortes animos, belloque peremptos,
Laudibus in longum vates diffunditis ævum
Plurima securi fudistis carmina Bardi.

Phars. 1.1. [447-9]

Now when we consider a college or order of men, who, cultivating poetry throughout a long series of ages, had their imaginations continually employed on the ideas of heroism; who had all the poems and panegyricks, which were composed by their predecessors, handed down to them with care; who rivalled and endeavoured to outstrip those who had gone before them, each in the celebration of his particular hero; is it not natural to think, that at length the character of a hero would appear in their songs with the highest lustre, and be adorned with qualities truly noble? Some of the qualities indeed which distinguish a Fingal, moderation, humanity, and clemency, would not probably be the first ideas of heroism occurring to a barbarous people: But no sooner had such ideas begun to dawn on the minds of poets, than, as the human mind easily opens to the native representations of human perfection, they would be seized and embraced; they would enter into their panegyricks; they would afford materials for succeeding bards to work upon, and improve; they would contribute not a little to exalt the publick manners. For such songs as these, familiar to the Celtic warriors from their childhood, and throughout their whole life, both in war and in peace, their principal entertainment, must have had a very considerable influence in propagating among them real manners nearly approaching to the poetical; and in forming even such a hero as Fingal. Especially when we consider that among their limited objects of ambition, among the few advantages which in a savage state, man could obtain over man, the chief was Fame, and that Immortality which they expected to receive from their virtues and exploits, in the songs of bards[10].

Having made these remarks on the Celtic poetry and Bards in general, I shall next consider the particular advantages which Ossian possessed. He appears clearly to have lived in a period which enjoyed all the benefit I just now mentioned of traditionary poetry. The exploits of Trathal, Trenmor, and the other ancestors of Fingal, are spoken of as familiarly known. Ancient bards are frequently alluded to. In one remarkable passage, Ossian describes himself as living in a sort of classical age, enlightened by the memorials of former times, which were conveyed in the songs of bards; and points at a period of darkness and ignorance which lay beyond the reach of tradition. "His words," says he, "came only by halves to our ears; they were dark as the tales of other times, before the light of the song arose." (113) Ossian, himself, appears to have been endowed by nature with an exquisite sensibility of heart; prone to that tender melancholy which is so often an attendant on great genius; and susceptible equally of strong and of soft emotions. He was not only a professed bard, educated with care, as we may easily believe, to all the poetical art then known, and connected, as he shews us himself, in intimate friendship with the other contemporary bards, but a warrior also; and the son of the most renowned hero and prince of his age. This formed a conjunction of circumstances, uncommonly favourable towards exalting the imagination of a poet. He relates expeditions in which he had been engaged; he sings of battles in which he had fought and overcome; he had beheld the most illustrious scenes which that age could exhibit, both of heroism in war, and magnificence in peace. For however rude the magnificence of those times may seem to us, we must remember that all ideas of magnificence are comparative; and that the age of Fingal was an æra of distinguished splendor in that part of the world. Fingal reigned over a considerable territory; he was enriched with the spoils of the Roman province; he was ennobled by his victories and great actions; and was in all respects a personage of much higher dignity than any of the chieftains, or heads of Clans, who lived in the same country, after a more extensive monarchy was established.

The manners of Ossian's age, so far as we can gather them from his writings, were abundantly favourable to a poetical genius. The two dispiriting vices, to which Longinus imputes the decline of poetry, covetousness and effeminacy, were as yet unknown. The cares of men were few. They lived a roving indolent life; hunting and war their principal employments; and their chief amusements, the musick of bards and "the feast of shells." The great object pursued by heroic spirits, was "to receive their fame," that is, to become worthy of being celebrated in the songs of bards; and "to have their name on the four grey stones." To die, unlamented by a bard, was deemed so great a misfortune, as even to disturb their ghosts in another state. "They wander in thick mists beside the reedy lake; but never shall they rise, without the song, to the dwelling of winds."[11] After death, they expected to follow employments of the same nature with those which had amused them on earth; to fly with their friends on clouds, to pursue airy deer, and to listen to their praise in the mouths of bards. In such times as these, in a country where poetry had been so long cultivated, and so highly honoured, is it any wonder that among the race and succession of bards, one Homer should arise; a man who, endowed with a natural happy genius, favoured by peculiar advantages of birth and condition, and meeting in the course of his life, with a variety of incidents proper to fire his imagination, and to touch his heart, should attain a degree of eminence in poetry, worthy to draw the admiration of more refined ages?

The compositions of Ossian are so strongly marked with characters of antiquity, that although there were no external proof to support that antiquity, hardly any reader of judgment and taste, could hesitate in referring them to a very remote æra. There are four great stages through which men successively pass in the progress of society. The first and earliest is the life of hunters; pasturage succeeds to this, as the ideas of property begin to take root; next agriculture; and lastly, commerce. Throughout Ossian's poems, we plainly find ourselves in the first of these periods of society; during which, hunting was the chief employment of men, and the principal method of their procuring subsistence. Pasturage was not indeed wholly unknown; for we hear of dividing the herd in the case of a divorce (69); but the allusions to herds and to cattle are not many; and of agriculture, we find no traces. No cities appear to have been built in the territories of Fingal. No arts are mentioned except that of navigation and of working in iron[12]. Every thing presents to us the most simple and unimproved manners. At their feasts, the heroes prepared their own repast; they sat round the light of the burning oak; the wind lifted their locks, and whistled through their open halls. Whatever was beyond the necessaries of life was known to them only as the spoil of the Roman province; "the gold of the stranger; the lights of the stranger; the steeds of the stranger, the children of the rein."

This representation of Ossian's times, must strike us the more, as genuine and authentick, when it is compared with a poem of later date, which Mr. Macpherson has preserved in one of his notes. It is that wherein five bards are represented as passing the evening in the house of a chief, and each of them separately giving his description of the night (189 ff.). The night scenery is beautiful; and the author has plainly imitated the style and manner of Ossian : But he has allowed some images to appear which betray a later period of society. For we meet with windows clapping, the herds of goats and cows seeking shelter, the shepherd wandering, corn on the plain, and the wakeful hind rebuilding the shocks of corn which had been overturned by the tempest. Whereas in Ossian's works, from beginning to end, all is consistent; no modern allusion drops from him; but every where, the same face of rude nature appears; a country wholly uncultivated, thinly inhabited, and recently peopled. The grass of the rock, the flower of the heath, the thistle with its beard, are the chief ornaments of his landscapes. "The desart," says Fingal, "is enough to me, with all its woods and deer." (101)[13]

The circle of ideas and transactions, is no wider than suits such an age: Nor any greater diversity introduced into characters, than the events of that period would naturally display. Valour and bodily strength are the admired qualities. Contentions arise, as is usual among savage nations, from the slightest causes. To be affronted at a tournament, or to be omitted in the invitation to a feast, kindles a war. Women are often carried away by force; and the whole tribe, as in the Homeric times, rise to avenge the wrong. The heroes show refinement of sentiment indeed on several occasions, but none of manners. They speak of their past actions with freedom, boast of their exploits, and sing their own praise. In their battles, it is evident that drums, trumpets, or bagpipes, were not known or used. They had no expedient for giving the military alarms but striking a shield, or raising a loud cry: And hence the loud and terrible voice of Fingal is often mentioned, as a necessary qualification of a great general; like the βοὴν ἀγαθὸς Μενέλαος of Homer. Of military discipline or skill, they appear to have been entirely destitute. Their armies seem not to have been numerous; their battles were disorderly; and terminated, for the most part, by a personal combat, or wrestling of the two chiefs; after which, "the bard sung the song of peace, and the battle ceased along the field." (132)[14]

The manner of composition bears all the marks of the greatest antiquity. No artful transitions; nor full and extended connection of parts; such as we find among the poets of later times, when order and regularity of composition were more studied and known; but a style always rapid and vehement; in narration concise even to abruptness, and leaving several circumstances to be supplied by the reader's imagination. The language has all that figurative cast, which, as I before shewed, partly a glowing and undisciplined imagination, partly the sterility of language and the want of proper terms, have always introduced into the early speech of nations; and in several respects, it carries a remarkable resemblance to the style of the Old Testament. It deserves particular notice, as one of the most genuine and decisive characters of antiquity, that very few general terms or abstract ideas, are to be met with in the whole collection of Ossian's works. The ideas of men, at first, were all particular. They had not words to express general conceptions. These were the consequence of more profound reflection, and longer acquaintance with the arts of thought and of speech. Ossian, accordingly, almost never expresses himself in the abstract. His ideas extended little farther than to the objects he saw around him. A public, a community, the universe, were conceptions beyond his sphere. Even a mountain, a sea, or a lake, which he has occasion to mention, though only in a simile, are for the most part particularized; it is the hill of Cromla, the storm of the sea of Malmor, or the reeds of the lake of Lego. A mode of expression, which whilst it is characteristical of ancient ages, is at the same time highly favourable to descriptive poetry. For the same reasons, personification is a poetical figure not very common with Ossian. Inanimate objects, such as winds, trees, flowers, he sometimes personifies with great beauty. But the personifications which are so familiar to later poets of Fame, Time, Terror, Virtue, and the rest of that class, were unknown to our Celtic bard. These were modes of conception too abstract for his age.

All these are marks so undoubted, and some of them too, so nice and deli-cate, of the most early times, as put the high antiquity of these poems out of question. Especially when we consider, that if there had been any imposture in this case, it must have been contrived and executed in the Highlands of Scotland, two or three centuries ago; as up to this period, both by manu-scripts, and by the testimony of a multitude of living witnesses, concerning the uncontrovertible tradition of these poems, they can clearly be traced. Now this is a period when that country enjoyed no advantages for a compo-sition of this kind, which it may not be supposed to have enjoyed in as great, if not in a greater degree, a thousand years before. To suppose that two or three hundred years ago, when we well know the Highlands to have been in a state of gross ignorance and barbarity, there should have arisen in that country a poet, of such exquisite genius, and of such deep knowledge of mankind, and of history, as to divest himself of the ideas and manners of his own age, and to give us a just and natural picture of a state of society ancienter by a thousand years; one who could support this counterfeited antiquity through such a large collection of poems, without the least incon-sistency; and who, possessed of all this genius and art, had at the same time the self-denial of concealing himself, and of ascribing his own works to an antiquated bard, without the imposture being detected; is a supposition that transcends all bounds of credibility.

There are, besides, two other circumstances to be attended to, still of greater weight, if possible, against this hypothesis. One is, the total absence of religious ideas from this work; for which the translator has, in his preface, given a very probable account, on the footing of its being the work of Ossian. The druidical superstition was, in the days of Ossian, on the point of its final extinction; and for particular reasons, odious to the family of Fingal; whilst the Christian faith was not yet established. But had it been the work of one, to whom the ideas of christianity were familiar from his infancy; and who had superadded to them also the bigotted superstition of a dark age and country; it is impossible but in some passage or other, the traces of them would have appeared. The other circumstance is, the entire silence which reigns with respect to all the great clans or families, which are now established in the Highlands. The origin of these several clans is known to be very ancient: And it is as well known, that there is no passion by which a native Highlander is more distinguished, than by attachment to his clan, and jealousy for its honour. That a Highland bard, in forging a work relating to the antiquities of his country, should have inserted no circumstance which pointed out the rise of his own clan, which ascertained its antiquity, or increased its glory, is of all suppositions that can be formed, the most improbable; and the silence on this head, amounts to a demonstration that the author lived before any of the present great clans were formed or known.

Assuming it then, as we well may, for certain, that the poems now under consideration, are genuine venerable monuments of very remote antiquity; I proceed to make some remarks upon their general spirit and strain. The two great characteristics of Ossian's poetry are, tenderness and sublimity. It breathes nothing of the gay and chearful kind; an air of solemnity and seriousness is diffused over the whole. Ossian is perhaps the only poet who never relaxes, or lets himself down into the light and amusing strain; which I readily admit to be no small disadvantage to him, with the bulk of readers. He moves perpetually in the high region of the grand and the pathetick. One key note is struck at the beginning, and supported to the end; nor is any ornament introduced, but what is perfectly concordant with the general tone or melody. The events recorded, are all serious and grave; the scenery throughout, wild and romantic. The extended heath by the sea shore; the mountain shaded with mist; the torrent rushing through a solitary valley; the scattered oaks, and the tombs of warriors overgrown with moss; all produce a solemn attention in the mind, and prepare it for great and extraordinary events. We find not in Ossian, an imagination that sports itself, and dresses out gay trifles to please the fancy. His poetry, more perhaps than that of any other writer, deserves to be stiled, *The Poetry of the Heart*. It is a heart penetrated with noble sentiments, and with sublime and tender passions; a heart that glows, and kindles the fancy; a heart that is full, and pours itself forth. Ossian did not write, like modern poets, to please readers and critics. He sung from the love of poetry and song. His delight was to think of the heroes among whom he had flourished; to recall the affecting incidents of his life; to dwell upon his past wars and loves and friendships; till, as he expresses it himself, "there comes a voice to Ossian and awakes his soul. It is the voice of years that are gone; they roll before me with all their deeds;"[15] and under this true poetic inspiration, giving vent to his genius, no wonder we should so often hear, and acknowledge in his strains, the powerful and ever-pleasing voice of nature.

———Arte, natura potentior omni.———
Est Deus in nobis, agitante calescimus illo. [Ovid, *Fasti*, 6.]

It is necessary here to observe, that the beauties of Ossian's writings cannot be felt by those who have given them only a single or hasty perusal. His manner is so different from that of the poets, to whom we are most accustomed; his style is so concise, and so much crowded with imagery; the mind is kept at such a stretch in accompanying the author; that an ordinary reader is at first apt to be dazzled and fatigued, rather than pleased. His poems require to be taken up at intervals, and to be frequently reviewed; and then it is impossible but his beauties must open to every reader who is capable of sensibility. Those who have the highest degree of it, will relish them the most.

As Homer is of all the great poets, the one whose manner, and whose times come the nearest to Ossian's, we are naturally led to run a parallel in some instances between the Greek and the Celtic bard. For though Homer lived more than a thousand years before Ossian, it is not from the age of the world, but from the state of society, that we are to judge of resembling times. The Greek has, in several points, a manifest superiority. He introduces a greater variety of incidents; he possesses a larger compass of ideas; has more diversity in his characters; and a much deeper knowledge of human nature. It was not to be expected, that in any of these particulars, Ossian could equal Homer. For Homer lived in a country where society was much farther advanced; he had beheld many more objects; cities built and flourishing; laws instituted; order, discipline, and arts begun. His field of observation was much larger and more splendid; his knowledge, of course, more extensive; his mind also, it shall be granted, more penetrating. But if Ossian's ideas and objects be less diversified than those of Homer, they are all, however, of the kind fittest for poetry: The bravery and generosity of heroes, the tenderness of lovers, the attachments of friends, parents, and children. In a rude age and country, though the events that happen be few, the undissipated mind broods over them more; they strike the imagination, and fire the passions in a higher degree; and of consequence become happier materials to a poetical genius, than the same events when scattered through the wide circle of more varied action, and cultivated life.

Homer is a more chearful and sprightly poet than Ossian. You discern in him all the Greek vivacity; whereas Ossian uniformly maintains the gravity and solemnity of a Celtic hero. This too is in a great measure to be accounted for from the different situations in which they lived, partly personal, and partly national. Ossian had survived all his friends, and was disposed to melancholy by the incidents of his life. But besides this, chearfulness is one of the many blessings which we owe to formed society. The solitary wild state is always a serious one. Bating the sudden and violent bursts of mirth, which sometimes break forth at their dances and feasts; the savage American tribes have been noted by all travellers for their gravity and taciturnity. Somewhat of this taciturnity may be also remarked in Ossian. On all occasions he is frugal of his words; and never gives you more of an image or a description, than is just sufficient to place it before you in one clear point of view. It is a blaze of lightning, which flashes and vanishes. Homer is more extended in his descriptions; and fills them up with a greater variety of circumstances. Both the poets are dramatick; that is, they introduce their personages frequently speaking before us. But Ossian is concise and rapid in his speeches, as he is in every other thing. Homer, with the Greek vivacity, had also some portion of the Greek loquacity. His speeches indeed are highly characteristical; and to them we are much indebted for that admirable display he has given of human nature. Yet if he be tedious any where, it is in these; some of them trifling; and some of them plainly unseasonable. Both poets are eminently sublime; but a difference may be remarked in the species of their sublimity. Homer's sublimity is accompanied with more impetuosity and fire; Ossian's with more of a solemn and awful grandeur. Homer hurries you along; Ossian elevates, and fixes you in astonishment. Homer is most sublime in actions and battles; Ossian, in description and sentiment. In the pathetick, Homer, when he chuses to exert it, has great power; but Ossian exerts that power much oftener, and has the character of tenderness far more deeply imprinted on his works. No poet knew better how to seize and melt the heart. With regard to dignity of sentiment, the pre-eminence must clearly be given to Ossian. This is indeed a surprising circumstance, that in point of humanity, magnanimity, virtuous feelings of every kind, our rude Celtic bard should be distinguished to such a degree, that not only the heroes of Homer, but even those of the polite and refined Virgil, are left far behind by those of Ossian.

After these general observations on the genius and spirit of our author, I now proceed to a nearer view, and more accurate examination of his works: and as Fingal is the first great poem in this collection, it is proper to begin with it. To refuse the title of an epic poem to Fingal, because it is not in every little particular, exactly conformable to the practice of Homer and Virgil, were the mere squeamishness and pedantry of criticism. Examined even according to Aristotle's rules, it will be found to have all the essential requisites of a true and regular epic; and to have several of them in so high a degree, as at first view to raise our astonishment on finding Ossian's composition so agreeable to rules of which he was entirely ignorant. But our astonishment will cease, when we consider from what source Aristotle drew those rules. Homer knew no more of the laws of criticism than Ossian. But guided by nature, he composed in verse a regular story, founded on heroic actions, which all posterity admired. Aristotle, with great sagacity and penetration, traced the causes of this general admiration. He observed what it was in Homer's composition, and in the conduct of his story, which gave it such power to please; from this observation he deduced the rules which poets ought to follow, who would write and please like Homer; and to a composition formed according to such rules, he gave the name of an epic poem. Hence his whole system arose. Aristotle studied nature in Homer. Homer and Ossian both wrote from nature. No wonder that among all the three, there should be such agreement and conformity.

The fundamental rules delivered by Aristotle concerning an epic poem, are these: That the action which is the ground work of the poem, should be one, compleat, and great; that it should be feigned, not merely historical; that it should be enlivened with characters and manners; and heightened by the marvellous.

But before entering on any of these, it may perhaps be asked, what is the moral of Fingal? For, according to M. Bossu, an epic poem is no other than an allegory contrived to illustrate some moral truth. The poet, says this critic, must begin with fixing on some maxim, or instruction, which he intends to inculcate on mankind. He next forms a fable, like one of Æsop's, wholly with a view to the moral; and having thus settled and arranged his plan, he then looks into traditionary history for names and incidents, to give his fable some air of probability. Never did a more frigid, pedantic notion, enter into the mind of a critic. We may safely pronounce, that he who should compose an epic poem after this manner, who should first lay down a moral and contrive a plan, before he had thought of his personages and actors, might deliver indeed very sound instruction, but would find few readers. There cannot be the least doubt that the first object which strikes an epic poet, which fires his genius, and gives him any idea of his work, is the action or subject he is to celebrate. Hardly is there any tale, any subject a poet can chuse for such a work, but will afford some general moral instruction. An epic poem is by its nature one of the most moral of all poetical compositions: But its moral tendency is by no means to be limited to some common-place maxim, which may be gathered from the story. It arises from the admiration of heroic actions, which such a composition is peculiarly calculated to produce; from the virtuous emotions which the characters and incidents raise, whilst we read it; from the happy impression which all the parts separately, as well as the whole taken together, leave upon the mind. However, if a general moral be still insisted on, Fingal obviously furnishes one, not inferior to that of any other Poet, viz. That Wisdom and Bravery always triumph over brutal force; or another nobler still; That the most compleat victory over an enemy is obtained by that moderation and generosity which convert him into a friend.

The unity of the Epic action, which, of all Aristotle's rules, is the chief and most material, is so strictly preserved in Fingal, that it must be perceived by every reader. It is a more compleat unity than what arises from relating the actions of one man, which the Greek critic justly censures as imperfect; it is the unity of one enterprise, the deliverance of Ireland from the invasion of Swaran: An enterprise, which has surely the full Heroic dignity. All the incidents recorded bear a constant reference to one end; no double plot is carried on; but the parts unite into a regular whole: And as the action is one and great, so it is an entire or compleat action. For we find, as the Critic farther requires, a beginning, a middle, and an end; a Nodus, or intrigue in the Poem; Difficulties occurring through Cuchullin's rashness and bad success; those difficulties gradually surmounted; and at last the work conducted to that happy conclusion which is held essential to

Epic Poetry. Unity is indeed observed with greater exactness in Fingal, than in almost any other Epic composition. For not only is unity of subject maintained, but that of time and place also. The Autumn is clearly pointed out as the season of the action; and from beginning to end the scene is never shifted from the heath of Lena, along the sea-shore. The duration of the action in Fingal, is much shorter than in the Iliad or Æneid. But sure, there may be shorter as well as longer Heroic Poems; and if the authority of Aristotle be also required for this, he says expressly that the Epic composition is indefinite as to the time of its duration. Accordingly the Action of the Iliad lasts only forty-seven days, whilst that of the Æneid is continued for more than a year.

Throughout the whole of Fingal, there reigns that grandeur of sentiment, style and imagery, which ought ever to distinguish this high species of poetry. The story is conducted with no small art. The Poet goes not back to a tedious recital of the beginning of the war with Swaran; but hastening to the main action, he falls in exactly, by a most happy coincidence of thought, with the rule of Horace.

> Semper ad eventum festinat, & in medias res,
> Non secus ac notas, auditorem rapit———
> Nec gemino bellum Trojanum orditur ab ovo.
>
> *De Arte Poet.*

He invokes no muse, for he acknowledged none; but his occasional addresses to Malvina, have a finer effect than the invocation of any muse. He sets out with no formal proposition of his subject; but the subject naturally and easily unfolds itself; the poem opening in an animated manner, with the situation of Cuchullin, and the arrival of a scout who informs him of Swaran's landing. Mention is presently made of Fingal, and of the expected assistance from the ships of the lonely isle, in order to give further light to the subject. For the poet often shows his address in gradually preparing us for the events he is to introduce; and in particular the preparation for the appearance of Fingal, the previous expectations that are raised, and the extreme magnificence fully answering these expectations, with which the hero is at length presented to us, are all worked up with such skillful conduct as would do honour to any poet of the most refined times. Homer's art in magnifying the character of Achilles has been universally admired. Ossian certainly shows no less art in aggrandizing Fingal. Nothing could be more happily imagined for this purpose than the whole management of the last battle, wherein Gaul the son of Morni, had besought Fingal to retire, and to leave to him and his other chiefs the honour of the day. The generosity of the King in agreeing to this proposal; the majesty with which he retreats to the hill, from whence he was to behold the engagement, attended by his Bards, and waving the lightning of his sword; his perceiving the chiefs overpowered by numbers, but from unwillingness to deprive them of the glory of victory by coming in person to their assistance, first sending

Ullin, the Bard, to animate their courage; and at last, when the danger becomes more pressing, his rising in his might, and interposing, like a divinity, to decide the doubtful fate of the day; are all circumstances contrived with so much art as plainly discover the Celtic Bards to have been not unpractised in Heroic poetry.

The story which is the foundation of the Iliad is in itself as simple as that of Fingal. A quarrel arises between Achilles and Agamemnon concerning a female slave; on which, Achilles, apprehending himself to be injured, withdraws his assistance from the rest of the Greeks. The Greeks fall into great distress, and beseech him to be reconciled to them. He refuses to fight for them in person, but sends his friend Patroclus; and upon his being slain, goes forth to revenge his death, and kills Hector. The subject of Fingal is this: Swaran comes to invade Ireland: Cuchullin, the guardian of the young King, had applied for assistance to Fingal, who reigned in the opposite coast of Scotland. But before Fingal's arrival, he is hurried by rash counsel to encounter Swaran. He is defeated; he retreats; and desponds. Fingal arrives in this conjuncture. The battle is for some time dubious; but in the end he conquers Swaran; and the remembrance of Swaran's being the brother of Agandecca, who had once saved his life, makes him dismiss him honourably. Homer it is true has filled up his story with a much greater variety of particulars than Ossian; and in this has shown a compass of invention superior to that of the other poet. But it must not be forgotten, that though Homer be more circumstantial, his incidents however are less diversified in kind than those of Ossian. War and bloodshed reign throughout the Iliad; and notwithstanding all the fertility of Homer's invention, there is so much uniformity in his subjects, that there are few readers, who before the close, are not tired of perpetual fighting. Whereas in Ossian, the mind is relieved by a more agreeable diversity. There is a finer mixture of war and heroism, with love and friendship, of martial, with tender scenes, than is to be met with, perhaps, in any other poet. The Episodes too, have great propriety; as natural, and proper to that age and country: consisting of the songs of Bards, which are known to have been the great entertainment of the Celtic heroes in war, as well as in peace. These songs are not introduced at random; if you except the Episode of Duchommar and Morna, in the first book, which though beautiful, is more unartful, than any of the rest; they have always some particular relation to the actor who is interested, or to the events which are going on; and, whilst they vary the scene, they preserve a sufficient connection with the main subject, by the fitness and propriety of their introduction.

As Fingal's love to Agandecca influences some circumstances of the Poem, particularly the honourable dismission of Swaran at the end; it was necessary that we should be let into this part of the hero's story. But as it lay without the compass of the present action, it could be regularly introduced no where, except in an Episode. Accordingly the poet, with as much propriety, as if Aristotle himself had directed the plan, has contrived an Episode for this purpose in the song of Carril, at the beginning of the third book.

The conclusion of the poem is strictly according to rule; and is every way noble and pleasing. The reconciliation of the contending heroes, the consolation of Cuchullin, and the general felicity that crowns the action, sooth the mind in a very agreeable manner, and form that passage from agitation and trouble, to perfect quiet and repose, which critics require as the proper termination of the Epic work. "Thus they passed the night in song, and brought back the morning with joy. Fingal arose on the heath; and shook his glittering spear in his hand. He moved first towards the plains of Lena; and we followed like a ridge of fire. Spread the sail, said the King of Morven, and catch the winds that pour from Lena.—We rose on the wave with songs; and rushed with joy through the foam of the ocean."—So much for the unity and general conduct of the Epic action in Fingal.

With regard to that property of the subject which Aristotle requires that it should be feigned not historical, he must not be understood so strictly, as if he meant to exclude all subjects which have any foundation in truth. For such exclusion would both be unreasonable in itself; and what is more, would be contrary to the practice of Homer, who is known to have founded his Iliad on historical facts concerning the war of Troy, which was famous throughout all Greece. Aristotle means no more than that it is the business of a poet not to be a mere annalist of Facts, but to embellish truth with beautiful, probable, and useful fictions; to copy nature, as he himself explains it, like painters, who preserve a likeness, but exhibit their objects more grand and beautiful than they are in reality. That Ossian has followed this course, and building upon true history, has sufficiently adorned it with poetical fiction for aggrandizing his characters and facts, will not, I believe, be questioned by most readers. At the same time, the foundation which those facts and characters had in truth, and the share which the poet himself had in the transactions which he records, must be considered as no small advantage to his work. For truth makes an impression on the mind far beyond any fiction; and no man, let his imagination be ever so strong, relates any events so feelingly as those in which he has been interested; paints any scene so naturally as one which he has seen; or draws any characters in such strong colours as those which he has personally known. It is considered as an advantage of the Epic subject to be taken from a period so distant, as by being involved in the darkness of tradition, may give licence to fable. Though Ossian's subject may at first view appear unfavourable in this respect, as being taken from his own times, yet when we reflect that he lived to an extreme old age; that he relates what had been transacted in another country, at the distance of many years, and after all that race of men who had been the actors were gone off the stage; we shall find the objection in a great measure obviated. In so rude an age, when no written records were known, when tradition was loose, and accuracy of any kind little attended to, what was great and heroic in one generation, easily ripened into the marvellous in the next.

The natural representation of human characters in an Epic Poem is highly essential to its merit: And in respect of this there can be no doubt of Homer's excelling all the heroic poets who have ever wrote. But though Ossian be much inferior to Homer in this article, he will be found to be equal at least, if not superior, to Virgil; and has indeed given all the display of human nature which the simple occurrences of his times could be expected to furnish. No dead uniformity of character prevails in Fingal; but on the contrary the principal characters are not only clearly distinguished, but sometimes artfully contrasted so as to illustrate each other. Ossian's heroes are, like Homer's, all brave; but their bravery, like those of Homer's too, is of different kinds. For instance; the prudent, the sedate, the modest and circumspect Connal, is finely opposed to the presumptuous, rash, over-bearing, but gallant and generous Calmar. Calmar hurries Cuchullin into action by his temerity; and when he sees the bad effect of his counsels, he will not survive the disgrace. Connal, like another Ulysses, attends Cuchullin to his retreat, counsels, and comforts him under his misfortune. The fierce, the proud, and high spirited Swaran is admirably contrasted with the calm, the moderate, and generous Fingal. The character of Oscar is a favourite one throughout the whole Poems. The amiable warmth of the young warrior; his eager impetuosity in the day of action; his passion for fame; his submission to his father; his tenderness for Malvina; are the strokes of a masterly pencil; the strokes are few; but it is the hand of nature, and attracts the heart. Ossian's own character, the old man, the hero, and the bard, all in one, presents to us through the whole work a most respect-able and venerable figure, which we always contemplate with pleasure. Cuchullin is a hero of the highest class; daring, magnanimous, and ex-quisitely sensible to honour. We become attached to his interest, and are deeply touched with his distress; and after the admiration raised for him in the first part of the Poem, it is a strong proof of Ossian's masterly genius that he durst adventure to produce to us another hero, compared with whom, even the great Cuchullin, should be only an inferior personage; and who should rise as far above him, as Cuchullin rises above the rest.

Here indeed, in the character and description of Fingal, Ossian triumphs almost unrivalled: For we may boldly defy all antiquity to shew us any hero equal to Fingal. Homer's Hector possesses several great and amiable quali-ties; but Hector is a secondary personage in the Iliad, not the hero of the work. We see him only occasionally; we know much less of him than we do of Fingal; who not only in this Epic Poem, but in Temora, and throughout the rest of Ossian's works, is presented in all that variety of lights, which give the full display of a character. And though Hector faithfully discharges his duty to his country, his friends, and his family, he is tinctured, however, with a degree of the same savage ferocity, which prevails among all the

Homeric heroes. For we find him insulting over the fallen Patroclus, with the most cruel taunts, and telling him when he lies in the agony of death, that Achilles cannot help him now; and that in a short time his body, stripped naked, and deprived of funeral honours, shall be devoured by the Vulturs[16]. Whereas in the character of Fingal, concur almost all the qualities that can ennoble human nature; that can either make us admire the hero, or love the man. He is not only unconquerable in war, but he makes his people happy by his wisdom in the days of peace (91). He is truly the father of his people. He is known by the epithet of "Fingal of the mildest look;" [87] and distinguished on every occasion, by humanity and generosity. He is merciful to his foes[17]; full of affection to his children; full of concern about his friends; and never mentions Agandecca, his first love, without the utmost tenderness. He is the universal protector of the distressed; "None ever went sad from Fingal." (99)——"O Oscar! bend the strong in arms; but spare the feeble hand. Be thou a stream of many tides against the foes of thy people; but like the gale that moves the grass, to those who ask thine aid. So Trenmor lived; such Trathal was; and such has Fingal been. My arm was the support of the injured; [and] the weak rested behind the lightning of my steel." (77)—These were the maxims of true heroism, to which he formed his grandson. His fame is represented as every where spread; the greatest heroes acknowledge his superiority; his enemies tremble at his name; and the highest encomium that can be bestowed on one whom the poet would most exalt, is to say, that his soul was like the soul of Fingal.

To do justice to the poet's merit, in supporting such a character as this, I must observe, what is not commonly attended to, that there is no part of poetical execution more difficult, than to draw a perfect character in such a manner, as to render it distinct and affecting to the mind. Some strokes of human imperfection and frailty, are what usually give us the most clear view, and the most sensible impression of a character; because they present to us a man, such as we have seen; they recall known features of human nature. When poets attempt to go beyond this range, and describe a faultless hero, they, for the most part, set before us, a sort of vague undistinguishable character, such as the imagination cannot lay hold of, or realize to itself, as the object of affection. We know how much Virgil has failed in this particular. His perfect hero, Æneas, is an unanimated, insipid personage, whom we may pretend to admire, but whom no one can heartily love. But what Virgil has failed in, Ossian, to our astonishment, has successfully executed. His Fingal, though exhibited without any of the common human failings, is nevertheless a real man; a character which touches and interests every reader. To this it has much contributed, that the poet has represented him as an old man; and by this has gained the advantage of throwing around him a great many circumstances, peculiar to that age, which paint him to the fancy in a more distinct light. He is surrounded with his family; he instructs his children in the principles of virtue; he is narrative of his past exploits; he is venerable with the grey locks of age; he is frequently disposed to moralize, like an old man, on human vanity and the prospect of death. There is more art, at least more felicity, in this, than may at first be imagined. For youth and old age, are the two states of human life, capable of being placed in the most picturesque lights. Middle age is more general and vague; and has fewer circumstances peculiar to the idea of it. And when any object is in a situation, that admits it to be rendered particular, and to be cloathed with a variety of circumstances, it always stands out more clear and full in poetical description.

Besides human personages, divine or supernatural agents are often introduced into epic poetry; forming what is called the machinery of it; which most critics hold to be an essential part. The marvellous, it must be admitted, has always a great charm for the bulk of readers. It gratifies the imagination, and affords room for striking and sublime description. No wonder therefore, that all poets should have a strong propensity towards it. But I must observe, that nothing is more difficult, than to adjust properly the marvellous with the probable. If a poet sacrifice probability, and fill his work with extravagant supernatural scenes, he spreads over it an appearance of romance and childish fiction; he transports his readers from this world, into a phantastick, visionary region; and loses that weight and dignity which should reign in epic poetry. No work, from which probability is altogether banished, can make a lasting or deep impression. Human actions and manners, are always the most interesting objects which can be presented to a human mind. All machinery, therefore, is faulty which withdraws these too much from view; or obscures them under a cloud of incredible fictions. Besides being temperately employed, machinery ought always to have some foundation in popular belief. A poet is by no means at liberty to invent what system of the marvellous he pleases: He must avail himself either of the religious faith, or the superstitious credulity of the country wherein he lives; so as to give an air of probability to events which are most contrary to the common course of nature.

In these respects, Ossian appears to me to have been remarkably happy. He has indeed followed the same course with Homer. For it is perfectly absurd to imagine, as some critics have done, that Homer's mythology was invented by him, in consequence of profound reflections on the benefit it would yield to poetry. Homer was no such refining genius. He found the traditionary stories on which he built his Iliad, mingled with popular legends, concerning the intervention of the gods; and he adopted these, because they amused the fancy. Ossian, in like manner, found the tales of his country full of ghosts and spirits: It is likely he believed them himself; and he introduced them, because they gave his poems that solemn and marvellous cast, which suited his genius. This was the only machinery he could employ with propriety; because it was the only intervention of supernatural beings, which agreed with the common belief of the country. It was happy; because it did not interfere in the least with the proper display of human characters and actions; because it had less of the incredible, than most other kinds of poetical machinery; and because it served to diversify the scene, and to heighten the subject by an awful grandeur, which is the great design of machinery.

As Ossian's mythology is peculiar to himself, and makes a considerable figure in his other poems, as well as in Fingal, it may be proper to make some observations on it, independent of its subserviency to epic composition. It turns for the most part on the appearances of departed spirits. These, consonantly to the notions of every rude age, are represented not as purely immaterial, but as thin airy forms, which can be visible or invisible at pleasure; their voice is feeble; their arm is weak; but they are endowed with knowledge more than human. In a separate state, they retain the same dispositions which animated them in this life. They ride on the wind; they bend their airy bows; and pursue deer formed of clouds. The ghosts of departed bards continue to sing. The ghosts of departed heroes frequent the fields of their former fame. "They rest together in their caves, and talk of mortal men. Their songs are of other worlds. They come sometimes to the ear of rest, and raise their feeble voice."[18] All this presents to us much the same set of ideas, concerning spirits, as we find in the eleventh book of the Odyssey, where Ulysses visits the regions of the dead: And in the twenty-third book of the Iliad, the ghost of Patroclus, after appearing to Achilles, vanishes precisely like one of Ossian's emitting a shrill, feeble cry, and melting away like smoke.

But though Homer's and Ossian's ideas concerning ghosts were of the same nature, we cannot but observe, that Ossian's ghosts are drawn with much stronger and livelier colours than those of Homer. Ossian describes ghosts with all the particularity of one who had seen and conversed with them, and whose imagination was full of the impression they had left upon it. He calls up those awful and tremendous ideas which the
——Simulacra modis pallentia miris, [Lucretius, 1. 123]
are fitted to raise in the human mind; and which, in Shakespear's style, "harrow up the soul." Crugal's ghost, in particular, in the beginning of the second book of Fingal, may vie with any appearance of this kind, described by any epic or tragic poet whatever. Most poets would have contented themselves with telling us, that he resembled, in every particular, the living Crugal; that his form and dress were the same, only his face more pale and sad; and that he bore the mark of the wound by which he fell. But Ossian sets before our eyes a spirit from the invisible world, distinguished by all those features, which a strong astonished imagination would give to a ghost. "A dark-red stream of fire comes down from the hill.[19] Crugal sat upon the beam; he that lately fell by the hand of Swaran,[20] striving in the battle of heroes. His face is like the beam of the setting moon. His robes are

of the clouds of the hill. His eyes are like two decaying flames. Dark is the wound of his breast ... The stars dim-twinkled through his form; and his voice was like the sound of a distant stream." The circumstance of the stars being beheld, "dim-twinkling through his form," is wonderfully pictur- esque; and conveys the most lively impression of his thin and shadowy substance. The attitude in which he is afterwards placed, and the speech put into his mouth, are full of that solemn and awful sublimity, which suits the subject. "Dim, and in tears, he stood and stretched his pale hand over the hero. Faintly he raised his feeble voice, like the gale of the reedy Lego.— My ghost, O Connal! is on my native hills; but my corse is on the sands of Ullin. Thou shalt never talk with Crugal, or find his lone steps in the heath. I am light as the blast of Cromla; and I move like the shadow of mist. Connal, son of Colgar! I see the dark cloud of death. It hovers over the plains of Lena. The sons of green Erin shall fall. Remove from the field of ghosts.—Like the darkened moon he retired in the midst of the whistling blast."

Several other appearances of spirits might be pointed out, as among the most sublime passages of Ossian's poetry. The circumstances of them are considerably diversified; and the scenery always suited to the occasion. "Oscar slowly ascends the hill. The meteors of night set on the heath before him. A distant torrent faintly roars. Unfrequent blasts rush through aged oaks. The half-enlightened moon sinks dim and red behind her hill. Feeble voices are heard on the heath. Oscar drew his sword."———Nothing can prepare the fancy more happily for the awful scene that is to follow. "Trenmor came from his hill, at the voice of his mighty son. A cloud, like the steed of the stranger, supported his airy limbs. His robe is of the mist of Lano, that brings death to the people. His sword is a green meteor, half- extinguished. His face is without form, and dark. He sighed thrice over the hero: And thrice, the winds of the night roared around. Many were his words to Oscar ... He slowly vanished, like a mist that melts on the sunny hill." (113) To appearances of this kind, we can find no parallel among the Greek or Roman poets. They bring to mind that noble description in the book of Job: "In thoughts from the visions of the night, when deep sleep falleth on men, fear came upon me, and trembling, which made all my bones to shake. Then a spirit passed before my face. The hair of my flesh stood up. It stood still; but I could not discern the form thereof. An image was before mine eyes. There was silence; and I heard a voice—Shall mortal man be more just than God[21]?"

As Ossian's supernatural beings are described with a surprising force of imagination, so they are introduced with propriety. We have only three ghosts in Fingal: That of Crugal, which comes to warn the host of impend- ing destruction, and to advise them to save themselves by retreat; that of Evirallin, the spouse of Ossian, which calls him to rise and rescue their son from danger; and that of Agandecca, which, just before the last engagement with Swaran, moves Fingal to pity, by mourning for the approaching destruction of her kinsmen and people. In the other poems, ghosts sometimes appear when invoked to foretell futurity; frequently, according to the notions of these times, they come as fore-runners of misfortune or death, to those whom they visit; sometimes they inform their friends at a distance, of their own death; and sometimes they are introduced to heighten the scenery on some great and solemn occasion. "A hundred oaks burn to the wind; and faint light gleams over the heath. The ghosts of Ardven pass through the beam; and shew their dim and distant forms. Comala is half-unseen on her meteor; and Hidallan is sullen and dim." (110)——"The awful faces of other times, looked from the clouds of Crona." (105)——"Fercuth! I saw the ghost of night. Silent he stood on that bank; his robe of mist flew on the wind. I could behold his tears. An aged man he seemed, and full of thought." (125)

The ghosts of strangers mingle not with those of the natives. "She is seen; but not like the daughters of the hill. Her robes are from the stranger's land; and she is still alone." (133) When the ghost of one whom we had formerly known is introduced, the propricty of the living character is still preserved. This is remarkable in the appearance of Calmar's ghost, in the poem entitled The Death of Cuchullin. He seems to forebode Cuchullin's death, and to beckon him to his cave. Cuchullin reproaches him for supposing that he could be intimidated by such prognostics. "Why dost thou bend thy dark eyes on me, ghost of the car-borne Calmar! Would'st thou frighten me, O Matha's son! from the battles of Cormac? Thy hand was not feeble in war; neither was thy voice for peace. How art thou changed, chief of Lara! if now thou dost advise to fly! ... Retire thou to thy cave: Thou art not Calmar's ghost: He delighted in battle; and his arm was like the thunder of heaven." Calmar makes no return to this seeming reproach: But, "He retired in his blast with joy; for he had heard the voice of his praise." (137) This is precisely the ghost of Achilles in Homer; who, notwithstanding all the dissatisfaction he expresses with his state in the region of the dead, as soon as he had heard his son Neoptolemus praised for his gallant behaviour, strode away with silent joy to rejoin the rest of the shades[22].

It is a great advantage of Ossian's mythology, that it is not local and temporary, like that of most other ancient poets; which of course is apt to seem ridiculous, after the superstitions have passed away on which it was founded. Ossian's mythology is, to speak so, the mythology of human nature; for it is founded on what has been the popular belief, in all ages and countries, and under all forms of religion, concerning the appearances of departed spirits. Homer's machinery is always lively and amusing; but far from being always supported with proper dignity. The indecent squabbles among his gods, surely do no honour to epic poetry. Whereas Ossian's machinery has dignity upon all occasions. It is indeed a dignity of the dark and awful kind; but this is proper; because coincident with the strain and spirit of the poetry. A light and gay mythology, like Homer's, would have been perfectly unsuitable to the subjects on which Ossian's genius was employed. But though his machinery be always solemn, it is not, however, always dreary or dismal; it is enlivened, as much as the subject would permit, by those pleasant and beautiful appearances, which he sometimes introduces, of the spirits of the hill. These are gentle spirits; descending on sun-beams; fair-moving on the plain; their forms white and bright; their voices sweet; and their visits to men propitious. The greatest praise that can be given, to the beauty of a living woman, is to say, "She is fair as the ghost of the hill[s]; when it moves in a sun-beam at noon, over the silence of Morven." (60)——"The hunter shall hear my voice from his booth. He shall fear, but love my voice. For sweet shall my voice be for my friends; for pleasant were they to me." (167)[23]

Besides ghosts, or the spirits of departed men, we find in Ossian some instances of other kinds of machinery. Spirits of a superior nature to ghosts are sometimes alluded to, which have power to embroil the deep; to call forth winds and storms, and pour them on the land of the stranger; to over-turn forests, and to send death among the people. (74, 120, 60, 113, 151) We have prodigies too; a shower of blood; and when some disaster is befall-ing at a distance, the sound of death heard on the strings of Ossian's harp (129, 145): all perfectly consonant, not only to the peculiar ideas of north-ern nations, but to the general current of a superstitious imagination in all countries. The description of Fingal's airy hall, in the poem called Berra-thon, and of the ascent of Malvina into it, deserves particular notice, as remarkably noble and magnificent. But above all, the engagement of Fingal with the spirit of Loda, in Carric-thura, cannot be mentioned without ad-miration. I forbear transcribing the passage, as it must have drawn the attention of every one who has read the works of Ossian. The undaunted courage of Fingal, opposed to all the terrors of the Scandinavian God; the appearance and the speech of that awful spirit; the wound which he receives, and the shriek which he sends forth, "as rolled into himself, he rose upon the wind;" are full of the most amazing and terrible majesty. [161] I know no passage more sublime in the writings of any uninspired author. The fiction is calculated to aggrandize the hero; which it does to a high degree; nor is it so unnatural or wild a fiction, as might at first be thought. According to the notions of those times, supernatural beings were material, and consequently, vulnerable. The spirit of Loda was not acknowl-edged as a deity by Fingal; he did not worship at the stone of his power; he plainly considered him as the God of his enemies only; as a local deity, whose dominion extended no farther than to the regions where he was worshiped; who had, therefore, no title to threaten him, and no claim to his submission. We know there are poetical precedents of great authority, for fictions fully as extravagant; and if Homer be forgiven for making Diomed attack and wound in battle, the gods whom that chief himself worshiped,

Ossian surely is pardonable for making his hero superior to the god of a foreign territory[24].

Notwithstanding the poetical advantages which I have ascribed to Ossian's machinery, I acknowledge it would have been much more beautiful and perfect, had the author discovered some knowledge of a supream Being. Although his silence on this head has been accounted for by the learned and ingenious translator in a very probable manner, yet still it must be held a considerable disadvantage to the poetry. For the most august and lofty ideas that can embellish poetry are derived from the belief of a divine admini-stration of the universe: And hence the invocation of a supream Being, or at least of some superior powers who are conceived as presiding over human affairs, the solemnities of religious worship, prayers preferred, and assis-tance implored on critical occasions, appear with great dignity in the works of almost all poets as chief ornaments of their compositions. The absence of all such religious ideas from Ossian's poetry, is a sensible blank in it, the more to be regretted, as we can easily imagine what an illustrious figure they would have made under the management of such a genius as his; and how finely they would have been adapted to many situations which occur in his works.

[25]After so particular an examination of Fingal, it were needless to enter into as full a discussion of the conduct of Temora, the other Epic Poem. Many of the same observations, especially with regard to the great charac-teristics of heroic poetry, apply to both. The high merit, however, of Temora, requires that we should not pass it by without some remarks.

The scene of Temora, as of Fingal, is laid in Ireland; and the action is of a posterior date. The subject is, an expedition of the hero, to dethrone and punish a bloody usurper, and to restore the possession of the kingdom to the posterity of the lawful prince; an undertaking worthy of the justice and heroism of the great Fingal. The action is one, and compleat. The poem opens with the descent of Fingal on the coast, and the consultation held among the chiefs of the enemy. The murder of the young prince Cormac, which was the cause of the war, being antecedent to the epic action, is introduced with great propriety as an episode in the first book. In the prog-ress of the poem, three battles are described, which rise in their importance above one another; the success is various, and the issue for some time doubtful; till at last, Fingal brought into distress, by the wound of his great general Gaul, and the death of his son Fillan, assumes the command him-self, and having slain the Irish king in single combat, restores the rightful heir to his throne.

Temora has perhaps less fire than the other epic poem; but in return it has more variety, more tenderness, and more magnificence. The reigning idea, so often presented to us of "Fingal in the last of his fields,"[26] is venerable and affecting; nor could any more noble conclusion be thought of, than the aged hero, after so many successful atchievements, taking his leave of battles, and with all the solemnities of those times resigning his spear to his son. The events are less crouded in Temora than in Fingal; actions and characters are more particularly displayed; we are let into the transactions of both hosts; and informed of the adventures of the night as well as of the day. The still pathetic, and the romantic scenery of several of the night adventures, so remarkably suited to Ossian's genius, occasion a fine diversity in the poem; and are happily contrasted with the military operations of the day.

In most of our author's poems, the horrors of war are softened by intermixed scenes of love and friendship. In Fingal, these are introduced as episodes; in Temora, we have an incident of this nature wrought into the body of the piece; in the adventure of Cathmor and Sulmalla. This forms one of the most conspicuous beauties of that poem. The distress of Sulmalla, disguised and unknown among strangers, her tender and anxious concern for the safety of Cathmor, her dream, and her melting remembrance of the land of her fathers; Cathmor's emotion when he first discovers her, his struggles to conceal and suppress his passion, lest it should unman him in the midst of war, though "his soul poured forth in secret, when he beheld her fearful eye;"[27] and the last interview between them, when overcome by her tenderness, he lets her know he had discovered her, and confesses his passion; are all wrought up with the most exquisite sensibility and delicacy.

Besides the characters which appeared in Fingal, several new ones are here introduced; and though, as they are all the characters of warriors, bravery is the predominant feature, they are nevertheless diversified in a sensible and striking manner. Foldath, for instance, the general of Cathmor, exhibits the perfect picture of a savage chieftain: Bold, and daring, but presumptuous, cruel, and overbearing. He is distinguished, on his first appearance, as the friend of the tyrant Cairbar; "His stride is haughty; his red eye rolls in wrath."[28] In his person and whole deportment, he is contrasted with the mild and wise Hidalla, another leader of the same army, on whose humanity and gentleness he looks with great contempt. He professedly delights in strife and blood. He insults over the fallen. He is imperious in his counsels, and factious when they are not followed. He is unrelenting in all his schemes of revenge, even to the length of denying the funeral song to the dead; which, from the injury thereby done to their ghosts, was in those days considered as the greatest barbarity. Fierce to the last, he comforts himself in his dying moments with thinking that his ghost shall often leave its blast to rejoice over the graves of those he had slain. Yet Ossian, ever prone to the pathetic, has contrived to throw into his account of the death, even of this man, some tender circumstances; by the moving description of his daughter Dardulena, the last of his race.

The character of Foldath tends much to exalt that of Cathmor, the chief commander, which is distinguished by the most humane virtues. He abhors all fraud and cruelty, is famous for his hospitality to strangers; open to every generous sentiment, and to every soft and compassionate feeling. He is so amiable as to divide the reader's attachment between him and the hero of the poem; though our author has artfully managed it so, as to make Cathmor himself indirectly acknowledge Fingal's superiority, and to appear somewhat apprehensive of the event, after the death of Fillan, which he knew would call forth Fingal in all his might. It is very remarkable, that although Ossian has introduced into his poems three compleat heroes, Cuchullin, Cathmor, and Fingal, he has, however, sensibly distinguished each of their characters. Cuchullin is particularly honourable; Cathmor particularly amiable; Fingal wise and great, retaining an ascendant peculiar to himself in whatever light he is viewed.

But the favourite figure in Temora, and the one most highly finished, is Fillan. His character is of that sort, for which Ossian shews a particular fondness; an eager, fervent young warrior, fired with all the impatient enthusiasm for military glory, peculiar to that time of life. He had sketched this in the description of his own son Oscar; but as he has extended it more fully in Fillan, and as the character is so consonant to the epic strain, though so far as I remember, not placed in such a conspicuous light by any other epic poet, it may be worth while to attend a little to Ossian's management of it in this instance.

Fillan was the youngest of all the sons of Fingal; younger, it is plain, than his nephew Oscar, by whose fame and great deeds in war, we may naturally suppose his ambition to have been highly stimulated. Withal, as he is younger, he is described as more rash and fiery. His first appearance is soon after Oscar's death, when he was employed to watch the motions of the foe by night. In a conversation with his brother Ossian, on that occasion, we learn that it was not long since he began to lift the spear. "Few are the marks of my sword in battle; by my soul is fire." (237) He is with some difficulty restrained by Ossian from going to attack the enemy; and complains to him, that his father had never allowed him any opportunity of signalizing his valour. "The king hath not remarked [marked] my sword; I go forth with the croud; I return without my fame." [228] Soon after, when Fingal according to custom was to appoint one of his chiefs to command the army, and each was standing forth, and putting in his claim to this honour, Fillan is presented in the following most picturesque and natural attitude. "On his spear stood the son of Clatho, in the wandering of his locks. Thrice he raised his eyes to Fingal: his voice thrice failed him as he spoke.—Fillan could not boast of battles—at once he strode away. Bent over a distant stream he stood; the tear hung in his eye. He struck, at times, the thistle's head, with his inverted spear." (245)[29] No less natural and beautiful is the description of Fingal's paternal emotion on this occasion. "Nor is he unseen of Fingal. Side-long he beheld his son. He beheld him with bursting joy. He hid the big tear with his locks, and turned amidst his crouded soul."[30] The command, for that day, being given to Gaul, Fillan rushes amidst the thickest of the foe, saves Gaul's life, who is wounded by a random arrow, and distinguishes himself so in battle, that "the days of old return on Fingal's mind, as he beholds the renown of his son. As the sun rejoices from the cloud, over the tree his beams have raised, whilst it shakes its lonely head on the heath, so joyful is the king over Fillan." (248) Sedate however and wise, he mixes the praise which he bestows on him with some reprehension of his rashness, "My son, I saw thy deeds, and my soul was glad. Thou art brave, son of Clatho, but headlong in the strife. So did not Fingal advance, though he never feared a foe. Let thy people be a ridge behind thee; they are thy strength in the field. Then shalt thou be long renowned, and behold the tombs of thy fathers." (250)

On the next day, the greatest and the last of Fillan's life, the charge is committed to him of leading on the host to battle. Fingal's speech to his troops on this occasion is full of noble sentiment; and where he recommends his son to their care, extremely touching. "A young beam is before you; few are his steps [paths] to war. They are few, but he is valiant; defend my dark-haired son. Bring him back with joy; hereafter he may stand alone. His form is like his fathers; his soul is a flame of their fire." (281) When the battle begins, the poet puts forth his strength to describe the exploits of the young hero; who, at last encountering and killing with his own hand Foldath the opposite general, attains the pinnacle of glory. In what follows, when the fate of Fillan is drawing near, Ossian, if any where, excels himself. Foldath being slain, and a general rout begun, there was no resource left to the enemy but in the great Cathmor himself, who in this extremity descends from the hill, where, according to the custom of those princes, he surveyed the battle. Observe how this critical event is wrought up by the poet. "Wide spreading over echoing Lubar, the flight of Bolga is rolled along. Fillan hung forward on their steps; and strewed the heath with dead.[31] Fingal rejoiced over his son.——Blue-shielded Cathmor rose.—Son of Alpin, bring the harp! Give Fillan's praise to the wind; raise high his praise in my hall, while yet he shines in war. Leave, blue-eyed Clatho! leave thy hall! behold that early beam of thine! The host is withered in its course. No farther look—it is dark—light trembling from the harp, strike, virgins! strike the sound." (267) The sudden interruption, and suspense of the narration on Cathmor's rising from his hill, the abrupt bursting into the praise of Fillan, and the passionate apostrophe to his mother Clatho, are admirable efforts of poetical art, in order to interest us in Fillan's danger; and the whole is heightened by the immediately following simile, one of the most magnificent and sublime that is to be met with in any poet, and which if it had been found in Homer, would have been the frequent subject of admiration to critics; "Fillan is like a spirit of heaven, that descends from the skirt of his blast. The troubled ocean feels his steps, as he strides from wave to wave. His path kindles behind him; islands shake their heads on the heaving seas."

But the poet's art is not yet exhausted. The fall of this noble young warrior, or in Ossian's stile, the extinction of this beam of heaven, could not be rendered too interesting and affecting. Our attention is naturally drawn towards Fingal. He beholds from his hill the rising of Cathmor, and the danger of his son But what shall he do? "Shall Fingal rise to his aid, and take the sword of Luno? What then should become of thy fame, son of white-bosomed Clatho?[32] Turn not thine eyes from Fingal, daughter of Inistore! I shall not quench thy early beam ... No cloud of mine shall rise, my son, upon thy soul of fire." (271) Struggling between concern for the fame, and fear for the safety of his son, he withdraws from the sight of the engagement; and dispatches Ossian in haste to the field, with this affectionate and delicate injunction. "Father of Oscar!" addressing him by a title which on this occasion has the highest propriety, "Father of Oscar! lift the spear; defend the young in arms. But conceal thy steps from Fillan's eyes: He must not know that I doubt his steel."——Ossian arrived too late.—But unwilling to describe Fillan vanquished, the poet suppresses all the circumstances of the combat with Cathmor; and only shews us the dying hero. We see him animated to the end with the same martial and ardent spirit; breathing his last in bitter regret for being so early cut off from the field of glory. "Ossian, lay me in that hollow rock. Raise no stone above me; least one should ask about my fame. I am fallen in the first of my fields; fallen without renown. Let thy voice alone, send joy to my flying soul. Why should the bard know where dwells the early-fallen Fillan?" (272)——He who after tracing the circumstances of this story, shall deny that our bard is possessed of high sentiment and high art, must be strangely prejudiced indeed. Let him read the story of Pallas in Virgil, which is of a similar kind; and after all the praise he may justly bestow on the elegant and finished description of that amiable author, let him say, which of the two poets unfold most of the human soul.——I wave insisting on any more of the particulars in Temora; as my aim is rather to lead the reader into the genius and spirit of Ossian's poetry, than to dwell on all his beauties.

The judgment and art discovered in conducting works of such length as Fingal and Temora, distinguish them from the other poems in this collection. The smaller pieces, however, contain particular beauties no less eminent. They are historical poems, generally of the elegiac kind; and plainly discover themselves to be the work of the same author. One consistent face of manners is every where presented to us; one spirit of poetry reigns; the masterly hand of Ossian appears throughout; the same rapid and animated style; the same strong colouring of imagination, and the same glowing sensibility of heart. Besides the unity which belongs to the compositions of one man, there is moreover a certain unity of subject which very happily connects all these poems. They form the poetical history of the age of Fingal. The same race of heroes whom we had met with in the greater poems, Cuchullin, Oscar, Connal and Gaul return again upon the stage; and Fingal himself is always the principal figure, presented on every occasion, with equal magnificence, nay rising upon us to the last. The circumstances of Ossian's old age and blindness, his surviving all his friends, and his relating their great exploits to Malvina, the spouse of mistress of his beloved son Oscar, furnish the finest poetical situations that fancy could devise for that tender pathetic which reigns in Ossian's poetry.

On each of these poems, there might be room for separate observations, with regard to the conduct and disposition of the incidents, as well as to the beauty of the descriptions and sentiments. Carthon is a regular and highly finished piece. The main story is very properly introduced by Clessammor's relation of the adventure of his youth; and this introduction is finely heightened by Fingal's song of mourning over Moina; in which Ossian, ever fond of doing honour to his father, has contrived to distinguish him, for being an eminent poet, as well as warrior. Fingal's song upon this occasion, when "his thousand Bards leaned forwards from their seats, to hear the voice of the King," [129] is inferior to no passage in the whole book; and with great judgment put in his mouth, as the seriousness, no less than the sublimity of the strain, is peculiarly suited to the Hero's character.[33] In Darthula, are assembled almost all the tender images that can touch the heart of man; Friendship, love, the affections of parents, sons, and brothers, the distress of the aged, and the unavailing bravery of the young. The beautiful address to the moon, with which the poem opens, and the transition from thence to the subject, most happily prepare the mind for that train of affecting events that is to follow. The story is regular, dramatic, interesting to the last. He who can read it without emotion may congratulate himself, if he pleases, upon being completely armed against sympathetic sorrow. As Fingal had no occasion of appearing in the action of this poem, Ossian makes a very artful transition from his narration, to what was passing in the halls of Selma. The sound heard there on the strings of his harp, the concern which Fingal shows on hearing it, and the invocation of the ghosts of their fathers, to receive the Heroes falling in a distant land, are introduced with great beauty of imagination to increase the solemnity, and to diversify the scenery of the poem.

Carric-thura is full of the most sublime dignity; and has this advantage of being more chearful in the subject, and more happy in the catastrophe than most of the other poems: Though tempered at the same time with episodes in that strain of tender melancholy, which seems to have been the great delight of Ossian and the Bards of his age. Lathmon is peculiarly distinguished, by high generosity of sentiment. This is carried so far, particularly in the refusal of Gaul, on one side, to take the advantage of a sleeping foe; and of Lathmon, on the other, to overpower by numbers the two young warriors, as to recall into one's mind the manners of Chivalry; some resemblance to which may perhaps be suggested by other incidents in this collection of Poems. Chivalry, however, took rise in an age and country too remote from those of Ossian to admit the suspicion that the one could have borrowed any thing from the other. So far as Chivalry had any real existence, the same military enthusiasm, which gave birth to it in the feudal times, might, in the days of Ossian, that is, in the infancy of a rising state, through the operation of the same cause, very naturally produce effects of the same kind on the minds and manners of men. So far as Chivalry was an ideal system existing only in romance, it will not be thought surprising, when we reflect on the account before given of the Celtic Bards, that this imaginary refinement of heroic manners should be found among them, as much, at least, as among the *Trobadores*, or strolling Provençal Bards, in the 10th or 11th century; whose songs, it is said, first gave rise to those romantic ideas of heroism, which for so long a time enchanted Europe[34]. Ossian's heroes have all the gallantry and generosity of those fabulous knights, without their extravagance; and his love scenes have native tenderness, without any mixture of those forced and unnatural conceits which abound in the old romances. The adventures related by our poet which resemble the most those of romance, concern women who follow their lovers to war disguised in the armour of men; and these are so managed as to produce, in the discovery, several of the most interesting situations; one beautiful instance of which may be seen in Carric-thura, and another in Calthon and Colmal.

Oithona presents a situation of a different nature. In the absence of her lover Gaul, she had been carried off and ravished by Dunrommath. Gaul discovers the place where she is kept concealed, and comes to revenge her. The meeting of the two lovers, the sentiments and the behaviour of Oithona on that occasion, are described with such tender and exquisite propriety, as does the greatest honour both to the art and to the delicacy of our author: and would have been admired in any poet of the most refined age. The conduct of Croma must strike every reader as remarkably judicious and beautiful. We are to be prepared for the death of Malvina, which is related in the succeeding Poem. She is therefore introduced in person; "she has heard a voice in a dream; she feels the fluttering of her soul;" and in a most moving lamentation addressed to her beloved Oscar, she sings her own Death Song. Nothing could be calculated with more art to sooth and comfort her, than the story which Ossian relates. In the young and brave Fovargormo, another Oscar is introduced; his praises are sung; and the happiness is set before her of those who die in their youth, "when their renown is around them; before the feeble behold them in the hall, and smile at their trembling hands."[35]

But no where does Ossian's genius appear to greater advantage, than in Berrathon, which is reckoned the conclusion of his songs, "The last sound of the Voice of Cona." [194]

> Qualis olor noto positurus littore vitam,
> Ingemit, et mæstis mulcens concentibus auras
> Præsago queritur venientia funera cantu.[36]

The whole train of ideas is admirably suited to the subject. Every thing is full of that invisible world, into which the aged Bard believes himself now ready to enter. The airy hall of Fingal presents itself to his view; "he sees the cloud [mist] that shall receive his ghost; he beholds the mist that shall form his robe when he appears on his hill;" and all the natural objects around him seem to carry the presages of death. "The thistle shakes its beard to the wind. The flower hangs its heavy head ... it seems to say, I am covered with the drops of heaven; the time of my departure is near, and the blast that shall scatter my leaves." [193] Malvina's death is hinted to him in the most delicate manner by the son of Alpin. His lamentation over her, her apotheosis, or ascent to the habitation of heroes, and the introduction to the story which follows from the mention which Ossian supposes the father of Malvina to make of him in the hall of Fingal, are all in the highest spirit of Poetry. "And dost thou remember Ossian, O Toscar son of Conloch?[37] The battles of our youth were many; our swords went together to the field."——— Nothing could be more proper than to end his songs with recording an exploit of the father of that Malvina, of whom his heart was now so full; and who, from first to last, had been such a favourite object throughout all his poems.

[38]The scene of most of Ossian's poems is laid in Scotland, or in the coast of Ireland opposite to the territories of Fingal. When the scene is in Ireland, we perceive no change of manners from those of Ossian's native country. For as Ireland was undoubtedly peopled with Celtic tribes, the language, customs, and religion of both nations were the same. They had been separated from one another by migration, only a few generations, as it should seem, before our poets age; and they still maintained a close and frequent intercourse. But when the poet relates the expeditions of any of his heroes to the Scandinavian coast, or to the islands of Orkney, which were then part of the Scandinavian territory, as he does in Carric-thura, Sulmalla of Lumon, and Cathloda, the case is quite altered. Those countries were inhabited by nations of the Teutonic descent, who in their manners and religious rites differed widely from the Celtæ; and it is curious and remarkable, to find this difference clearly pointed out in the poems of Ossian. His descriptions bear the native marks of one who was present in the expeditions which he relates, and who describes what he had seen with his own eyes. No sooner are we carried to Lochlin, or the islands of Inistore, than we perceive that we are in a foreign region. New objects begin to appear. We meet every where with the stones and circles of Loda, that is, Odin, the great Scandinavian deity.[39] We meet with the divinations and inchantments, for which it is well known those northern nations were early famous. "There, mixed with the murmur of waters, rose the voice of aged men, who called the forms of night to aid them in their war;" (302) whilst the Caledonian chiefs who assisted them, are described as standing at a distance, heedless of their rites. That ferocity of manners which distinguished those nations, also

becomes conspicuous. In the combats of their chiefs there is a peculiar savageness; even their women are bloody and fierce. (302 f.) The spirit, and the very ideas of Regner Lodbrog, that northern scalder whom I formerly quoted, occur to us again. "The hawks," Ossian makes one of the Scandinavian chiefs say, "rush from all their winds; they are wont to trace my course."—"We rejoiced three days above the dead, and called the hawks of heaven. They came from all their winds, to feast on the foes of Annir." (320)

Dismissing now the separate consideration of any of our author's works, I proceed to make some observations on his manner of writing, under the general heads of Description, Imagery, and Sentiment.

A poet of original genius is always distinguished by his talent for description[40]. A second rate writer discerns nothing new or peculiar in the object he means to describe. His conceptions of it are vague and loose; his expressions feeble; and of course the object is presented to us indistinctly and as through a cloud. But a true Poet makes us imagine that we see it before our eyes: he catches the distinguishing features; he gives it the colours of life and reality; he places it in such a light that a painter could copy after him. This happy talent is chiefly owing to a lively imagination, which first receives a strong impression of the object; and then, by a proper selection of capital picturesque circumstances employed in describing it, transmits that impression in its full force to the imaginations of others. That Ossian possesses this descriptive power in a high degree, we have a clear proof from the effect which his descriptions produce upon the imaginations of those who read him with any degree of attention and taste. Few poets are more interesting. We contract an intimate acquaintance with his principal heroes. The characters, the manners, the face of the country become familiar; we even think we could draw the figure of his ghosts: In a word, whilst reading him, we are transported as into a new region, and dwell among his objects as if they were all real.

It were easy to point out several instances of exquisite painting in the works of our author. Such, for instance, as the scenery with which Temora opens, and the attitude in which Cairbar is there presented to us (148); the description of the young prince Cormac, in the same book (153); and the ruins of Balclutha in Carthon (128). "I have seen the walls of Balclutha, but they were desolate. The fire had resounded in the halls; and the voice of the people is heard no more. The stream of Clutha was removed from its place by the fall of the walls. The thistle shook there its lonely head: The moss whistled to the wind. The fox looked out from the windows; the rank grass of the wall waved round his head. Desolate is the dwelling of Moina; silence is in the house of her fathers." Nothing also can be more natural and lively than the manner in which Carthon afterwards describes how the conflagration of his city affected him when a child: "Have I not seen the fallen Balclutha?[41] And shall I feast with Comhal's son? Comhal! who threw his fire in the midst of my father's hall! I was young, and knew not the cause why the virgins wept. The columns of smoke pleased mine eye, when they rose above my walls: I often looked back with gladness, when my friends fled along[42] the hill. But when the years of my youth came on, I beheld the moss of my fallen walls. My sigh arose with the morning; and my tears descended with night. Shall I not fight, I said to my soul, against the children of my foes? And I will fight, O Bard! I feel the strength of my soul." (130) In the same poem, the assembling of the chiefs round Fingal, who had been warned of some impending danger by the appearance of a prodigy, is described with so many picturesque circumstances, that one imagines himself present in the assembly. "The king alone beheld the terrible sight, and he foresaw the death of his [the] people. He came in silence to his hall, and took his father's spear; the mail rattled on his breast. The heroes rose around. They looked in silence on each other, marking the eyes of Fingal. They saw the battle in his face.——A thousand shields are placed at once on their arms; and they drew a thousand swords. The hall of Selma brightened around. The clang of arms ascends. The grey dogs howl in their place. No word is among the mighty chiefs. Each marked the eyes of the King; and half assumed his spear." (129)

It has been objected to Ossian, that his descriptions of military actions are imperfect, and much less diversified by circumstances than those of Homer. This is in some measure true. The amazing fertility of Homer's invention is no where so much displayed as in the incidents of his battles, and in the little history pieces he gives of the persons slain. Nor indeed, with regard to the talent of description, can too much be said in praise of Homer. Every thing is alive in his writings. The colours with which he paints are those of nature. But Ossian's genius was of a different kind from Homer's. It led him to hurry towards grand objects rather than to amuse himself with particulars of less importance. He could dwell on the death of a favorite hero: but that of a private man seldom stopped his rapid course. Homer's genius was more comprehensive than Ossian's. It included a wider circle of objects; and could work up any incident into description. Ossian's was more limited; but the region within which it chiefly exerted itself was the highest of all, the region of the pathetic and sublime.

We must not imagine, however, that Ossian's battles consist only of general indistinct description. Such beautiful incidents are sometimes introduced, and the circumstances of the persons slain so much diversified, as show that he could have embellished his military scenes with an abundant variety of particulars, if his genius had led him to dwell upon them. One man "is stretched[43] in the dust of his native land; he fell, where often he had spread the feast, and often raised the voice of the harp." (68) The maid of Inistore is introduced, in a moving apostrophe, as weeping for another (60); and a third, "as rolled in the dust he lifted his faint eyes to the king," is remembered and mourned by Fingal as the friend of Agandecca (87). The blood pouring from the wound of one who is slain by night, is heard "hissing on the half extinguished oak," which had been kindled for giving light: Another, climbing a tree to escape from his foe, is pierced by his spear from behind; "shrieking, panting he fell; whilst[44] moss and withered branches pursue his fall, and strew the blue arms of Gaul." (180) Never was a finer picture drawn of the ardour of two youthful warriors than the following: "I saw Gaul in his armour [arms], and my soul was mixed with his: For the fire of the battle was in his eyes; he looked to the foe with joy. We spoke the words of friendship in secret; and the lightening of our swords poured together. We drew them behind the wood, and tried the strength of our arms on the empty air." (178)

Ossian is always concise in his descriptions, which adds much to their beauty and force. For it is a great mistake to imagine, that a crowd of particulars, or a very full and extended style, is of advantage to description. On the contrary, such a diffuse manner for the most part weakens it. Any one redundant circumstance is a nuisance. It encumbers and loads the fancy, and renders the main image indistinct. "Obstat," as Quintilian says with regard to style, "quicquid non adjuvat." To be concise in description, is one thing; and to be general, is another. No description that rests in generals can possibly be good; it can convey no lively idea; for it is of particulars only that we have a distinct conception. But at the same time, no strong imagination dwells long upon any one particular; or heaps together a mass of trivial ones. By the happy choice of some one, or of a few that are the most striking, it presents the image more compleat, shows us more at one glance, than a feeble imagination is able to do, by turning its object round and round into a variety of lights. Tacitus is of all prose writers the most concise. He has even a degree of abruptness resembling our author: Yet no writer is more eminent for lively description. When Fingal, after having conquered the haughty Swaran, proposes to dismiss him with honour: "Raise to-morrow thy white sails to the wind, thou brother of Agandecca!" (101) he conveys, by thus addressing his enemy, a stronger impression of the emotions then passing within his mind, than if whole paragraphs had been spent in describing the conflict between resentment against Swaran and the tender remembrance of his ancient love. No amplification is needed to give us the most full idea of a hardy veteran, after the few following words: "His shield is marked with the strokes of battle; [and] his red eye despises danger." (148) When Oscar, left alone, was surrounded by foes, "he stood," it is said, "growing in his place, like the flood of the narrow vale;" (113) a happy representation of one, who, by daring intrepidity in the midst of danger, seems to increase in his appearance, and becomes more formidable every moment, like the sudden rising of the torrent hemmed in by the valley. And a whole crowd of ideas, concerning the circumstances of domestic sorrow occasioned by a young warrior's first going forth to battle, is poured upon the mind by these words; "Calmar leaned on his father's spear; that spear which he brought from Lara's hall, when the soul of his mother was sad." (75)

The conciseness of Ossian's descriptions is the more proper on account of his subjects. Descriptions of gay and smiling scenes may, without any disadvantage, be amplified and prolonged. Force is not the predominant quality expected in these. The description may be weakened by being diffuse, yet notwithstanding, may be beautiful still. Whereas, with respect to grand, solemn and pathetic subjects, which are Ossian's chief field, the case is very different. In these, energy is above all things required. The imagination must be seized at once, or not at all; and is far more deeply impressed by one strong and ardent image, than by the anxious minuteness of laboured illustration.

But Ossian's genius, though chiefly turned towards the sublime and pathetic, was not confined to it: In subjects also of grace and delicacy, he discovers the hand of a master. Take for an example the following elegant description of Agandecca, wherein the tenderness of Tibullus seems united with the majesty of Virgil. "The daughter of the snow overheard, and left the hall of her secret sigh. She came in all her beauty; like the moon from the cloud of the East. Loveliness was around her as light. Her steps were like the music of songs. She saw the youth and loved him. He was the stolen sigh of her soul. Her blue eyes rolled on him in secret: And she blest the chief of Morven." (73) Several other instances might be produced of the feelings of love and friendship painted by our author with a most natural and happy delicacy.

The simplicity of Ossian's manner adds great beauty to his descriptions, and indeed to his whole Poetry. We meet with no affected ornaments; no forced refinement; no marks either in style or thought of a studied endeavour to shine and sparkle. Ossian appears every where to be prompted by his feelings; and to speak from the abundance of his heart. I remember no more than one instance of what can be called quaint thought in this whole collection of his works. It is in the first book of Fingal, where from the tombs of two lovers two lonely yews are mentioned to have sprung, "whose branches wished to meet on high." (62) This sympathy of the trees with the lovers, may be reckoned to border on an Italian conceit; and it is somewhat curious to find this single instance of that sort of wit in our Celtic poetry.[45]

The "joy of grief," is one of Ossian's remarkable expressions, several times repeated. If any one shall think that it needs to be justified by a precedent, he may find it twice used by Homer; in the Iliad, when Achilles is visited by the ghost of Patroclus; and in the Odyssey, when Ulysses meets his mother in the shades. On both these occasions, the heroes, melted with tenderness, lament their not having it in their power to throw their arms round the ghost, "that we might," say they, "in a mutual embrace, enjoy the delight of grief."

——κρυεροῖο τεταρπώμεσθα γόοιο[46].

But in truth the expression stands in need of no defence from authority; for it is a natural and just expression; and conveys a clear idea of that gratification, which a virtuous heart often feels in the indulgence of a tender melancholy. Ossian makes a very proper distinction between this gratification, and the destructive effect of overpowering grief. "There is a joy in grief, when peace dwells in the breast[47] of the sad. But sorrow wastes the mournful, O daughter of Toscar, and their days are few." (187) To "give the joy of grief," generally signifies to raise the strain of soft and grave musick; and finely characterises the taste of Ossian's age and country. In those days, when the songs of bards were the great delight of heroes, the tragic muse was held in chief honour; gallant actions, and virtuous sufferings, were the chosen theme; preferably to that light and trifling strain of poetry and music, which promotes light and trifling manners, and serves to emasculate the mind. "Strike the harp in my hall," said the great Fingal, in the midst of youth and victory, "Strike the harp in my hall, and let Fingal hear the song. Pleasant is the joy of grief! It is like the shower of spring, when it softens the branch of the oak; and the young leaf lifts its green head. Sing on, O bards! To-morrow we lift the sail." (Carric-thura, 158)

Personal epithets have been much used by all the poets of the most ancient ages: and when well chosen, not general and unmeaning, they contribute not a little to render the style descriptive and animated. Besides epithets founded on bodily distinctions, akin to many of Homer's, we find in Ossian several which are remarkably beautiful and poetical. Such as, Oscar of the future fights [87], Fingal of the mildest look [87], Carril of other times [61], the mildly blushing Evirallin [181]; Bragela, the lonely sun-beam of Dunscaich [62]; a Culdee, the son of the secret cell [119].

But of all the ornaments employed in descriptive poetry, comparisons or similes are the most splendid. These chiefly form what is called the imagery of a poem: And as they abound so much in the works of Ossian, and are commonly among the favourite passages of all poets, it may be expected that I should be somewhat particular in my remarks upon them.

A poetical simile always supposes two objects brought together, between which there is some near relation or connection in the fancy. What that relation ought to be, cannot be precisely defined. For various, almost numberless, are the analogies formed among objects, by a sprightly imagination. The relation of actual similitude, or likeness of appearance, is far from being the only foundation of poetical comparison. Sometimes a resemblance in the effect produced by two objects, is made the connecting principle: Sometimes a resemblance in one distinguishing property or circumstance. Very often two objects are brought together in a simile, though they resemble one another, strictly speaking, in nothing, only because they raise in the mind a train of similar, and what may be called, concordant ideas; so that the remembrance of the one, when recalled, serves to quicken and heighten the impression made by the other. Thus, to give an instance from our poet, the pleasure with which an old man looks back on the exploits of his youth, has certainly no direct resemblance to the beauty of a fine evening; farther than that both agree in producing a certain calm, placid joy. Yet Ossian has founded upon this, one of the most beautiful comparisons that is to be met with in any poet. "Wilt thou not listen, son of the rock, to the song of Ossian? My soul is full of other times; the joy of my youth returns. Thus, the sun appears in the west, after the steps of his brightness have moved behind a storm. The green hills lift their dewy heads. The blue streams rejoice in the vale. The aged hero comes forth on his staff; and his grey hair glitters in the beam." (171) Never was there a finer group of objects. It raises a strong conception of the old man's joy and elation of heart, by displaying a scene, which produces in every spectator, a corresponding train of pleasing emotions; the declining sun looking forth in his brightness after a storm; the chearful face of all nature; and the still life finely animated by the circumstance of the aged hero, with his staff and his grey locks; a circumstance both extremely picturesque in itself, and pecu-liarly suited to the main object of the comparison. Such analogies and as-sociations of ideas as these, are highly pleasing to the fancy. They give opportunity for introducing many a fine poetical picture. They diversify the scene; they aggrandize the subject; they keep the imagination awake and sprightly. For as the judgment is principally exercised in distinguishing objects, and remarking the differences among those which seem like; so the highest amusement of the imagination is to trace likenesses and agreements among those which seem different.

The principal rules which respect poetical comparisons are, that they be introduced on proper occasions, when the mind is disposed to relish them; and not in the midst of some severe and agitating passion, which cannot admit this play of fancy; that they be founded on a resemblance neither too near and obvious, so as to give little amusement to the imagination in tracing it, nor too faint and remote, so as to be apprehended with difficulty; that they serve either to illustrate the principal object, and to render the conception of it, more clear and distinct; or at least, to heighten and embel-lish it, by a suitable association of images[48].

Every country has a scenery peculiar to itself; and the imagery of a good poet will exhibit it. For as he copies after nature, his allusions will of course be taken from those objects which he sees around him, and which have often struck his fancy. For this reason, in order to judge of the propriety of poetical imagery, we ought to be, in some measure, acquainted with the natural history of the country where the scene of the poem is laid. The introduction of foreign images betrays a poet, copying not from nature, but from other writers. Hence so many Lions, and Tygers, and Eagles and Serpents, which we meet with in the similes of modern poets; as if these animals had acquired some right to a place in poetical comparisons for ever, because employed by ancient authors. They employed them with propriety, as objects generally known in their country; but they are absurdly used for illustration by us, who know them only at second hand, or by description. To most readers of modern poetry, it were more to the purpose to describe Lions or Tygers by similes taken from men, than to compare men to Lions. Ossian is very correct in this particular. His imagery is, without exception, copied from that face of nature, which he saw before his eyes; and by consequence may be expected to be lively. We meet with no Grecian or Italian scenery; but with the mists, and clouds, and storms of a northern mountainous region.

No poet abounds more in similes than Ossian. There are in this collection as many, at least, as in the whole Iliad and Odyssey of Homer. I am indeed inclined to think, that the works of both poets are too much crowded with them. Similes are sparkling ornaments; and like all things that sparkle, are apt to dazzle and tire us by their lustre. But if Ossian's similes be too frequent, they have this advantage of being commonly shorter than Homer's; they interrupt his narration less; he just glances aside to some resembling object, and instantly returns to his former track. Homer's similes include a wider range of objects. But in return, Ossian's are, without exception, taken from objects of dignity, which cannot be said for all those which Homer employs. The Sun, the Moon, and the Stars, Clouds and Meteors, Lightning and Thunder, Seas and Whales, Rivers, Torrents, Winds, Ice, Rain, Snow, Dews, Mist, Fire and Smoke, Trees and Forests, Heath and Grass and Flowers, Rocks and Mountains, Music and Songs, Light and Darkness, Spirits and Ghosts; these form the circle, within which Ossian's comparisons generally run. Some, not many, are taken from Birds and Beasts; as Eagles, Sea Fowl, the Horse, the Deer, and the Mountain Bee; and a very few from such operations of art as were then known. Homer has diversified his imagery by many more allusions to the animal world; to Lions, Bulls, Goats, Herds of Cattle, Serpents, Insects; and to the various occupations of rural and pastoral life. Ossian's defect in this article, is plainly owing to the desert, uncultivated state of his country, which suggested to him few images beyond natural inanimate objects, in their rudest form. The birds and animals of the country were probably not numerous; and his acquaintance with them was slender, as they were little subjected to the uses of man.

The great objection made to Ossian's imagery, is its uniformity, and the too frequent repetition of the same comparisons. In a work so thick sown with similes, one could not but expect to find images of the same kind sometimes suggested to the poet by resembling objects; especially to a poet like Ossian, who wrote from the immediate impulse of poetical enthusiasm, and without much preparation of study or labour. Fertile as Homer's imagination is acknowledged to be, who does not know how often his Lions and Bulls and Flocks of Sheep, recur with little or no variation; nay, sometimes in the very same words? The objection made to Ossian is, however, founded, in a great measure, upon a mistake. It has been supposed by inattentive readers, that wherever the Moon, the Cloud, or the Thunder, returns in a simile, it is the same simile, and the same Moon, or Cloud, or Thunder, which they had met with a few pages before. Whereas very often the similes are widely different. The object, whence they are taken, is indeed in substance the same; but the image is new; for the appearance of the object is changed; it is presented to the fancy in another attitude; and cloathed with new circumstances, to make it suit the different illustration for which it is employed. In this, lies Ossian's great art; in so happily varying the form of the few natural appearances with which he was acquainted, as to make them correspond to a great many different objects.

Let us take for one instance the Moon, which is very frequently introduced into his comparisons; as in northern climates, where the nights are long, the Moon is a greater object of attention, than in the climate of Homer; and let us view how much our poet has diversified its appearance. The shield of a warrior is like "the darkened moon when it moves a dun circle through the heavens." (68)[49] The face of a ghost, wan and pale, is like "the beam of the setting moon." (65) And a different appearance of a ghost, thin and indistinct, is like "the new moon seen through the gathered mist, when the sky pours down its flaky snow, and the world is silent and dark;" (128) or in a different form still, it is like "the watry beam of the moon, when it rushes from between two clouds, and the midnight shower is on the field."(123) A very opposite use is made of the moon in the description of Agandecca: "She came in all her beauty, like the moon from the cloud of the East." (73) Hope, succeeded by disappointment, is "joy rising on her face, and sorrow returning again, like a thin cloud on the moon." (122) But when Swaran, after his defeat, is cheared by Fingal's generosity, "His face brightened like the full moon of heaven, when the clouds vanish away, and leave her calm and broad in the midst of the sky." (102) Vinvela is "bright as the moon when it trembles o'er the western wave;" (159)[50] but the soul of the guilty Uthal is "dark as the troubled face of the moon, when it foretels the storm[s]." (195) And by a very fanciful and uncommon allusion, it is said of Cormac, who was to die in his early years, "Nor long shalt [didst] thou lift the spear, mildly[-]shining beam of youth! Death stands dim behind thee, like the darkened half of the moon behind its growing light." (135 f.)

Another instance of the same nature may be taken from mist, which, as being a very familiar appearance in the country of Ossian, he applies to a variety of purposes, and pursues through a great many forms. Sometimes, which one would hardly expect, he employs it to heighten the appearance of a beautiful object. "The hair of Morna is like the mist of Cromla, when it curls on the rock, and shines to the beam of the west." (57)—"The song comes with its musick to melt and please the ear [soul]. It is like soft mist, that rising from a lake pours on the silent vale. The green flowers are filled with dew. The sun returns in its [his] strength, and the mist is gone[51]."

(169)—But, for the most part, mist is employed as a similitude of some disagreeable or terrible object. "The soul of Nathos was sad, like the sun in the day of mist, when his face is watery and dim." (141) "The darkness of old[52] age comes like the mist of the desert." (142) The face of a ghost is "pale as [like] the mist of Cromla." (84) "The gloom of battle is rolled along as mist that is poured on the valley, when storms invade the silent sun-shine of heaven." (67) Fame suddenly departing, is likened to "mist that flies away before the rustling wind of the vale." (102) A ghost, slowly vanishing, to "mist that melts by degrees[53] on the sunny hill." (113) Cairbar, after his treacherous assassination of Oscar, is compared to a pestilential fog. "I love a foe like Cathmor," says Fingal, "his soul is great; his arm is strong; his battles are full of fame. But the little soul is like a vapour that hovers round the marshy lake. It never rises on the green hill, lest the winds meet it there. Its dwelling is in the cave; and it sends forth the dart of death." (155)[54] This is a simile highly finished. But there is another which is still more striking, founded also on mist, in the 4th book of Temora. Two factious chiefs are contending; Cathmor the king interposes, rcbukes and silences them. The poet intends to give us the highest idea of Cathmor's superiority; and most effectually accomplishes his intention by the following happy image. "They sunk from the king on either side; like two columns of morning mist, when the sun rises between them, on his glittering rocks. Dark is their rolling on either side; each towards its reedy pool." [257] These instances may sufficiently shew with what richness of imagination Ossian's comparisons abound, and at the same time, with what propriety of judgment they are employed. If his field was narrow, it must be admitted to have been as well cultivated as its extent would allow.

As it is usual to judge of poets from a comparison of their similes more than of other passages, it will perhaps be agreeable to the reader, to see how Homer and Ossian have conducted some images of the same kind. This might be shewn in many instances. For as the great objects of nature are common to the poets of all nations, and make the general store-house of all imagery, the ground-work of their comparisons must of course be frequently the same. I shall select only a few of the most considerable from both poets. Mr. Pope's translation of Homer can be of no use to us here. The parallel is altogether unfair between prose, and the imposing harmony of flowing numbers. It is only by viewing Homer in the simplicity of a prose translation, that we can form any comparison between the two bards.

The shock of two encountering armies, the noise and the tumult of battle, afford one of the most grand and awful subjects of description; on which all epic poets have exerted their strength. Let us first hear Homer. The following description is a favourite one, for we find it twice repeated in the same words[55]. "When now the conflicting hosts joined in the field of battle, then were mutually opposed shields, and swords, and the strength of armed men. The bossy bucklers were dashed against each other. The universal tumult rose. There were mingled the triumphant shouts and the dying groans of the victors and the vanquished. The earth streamed with blood. As when winter torrents, rushing from the mountains, pour into a narrow valley, their violent waters. They issue from a thousand springs, and mix in the hollowed channel. The distant shepherd hears on the mountain, their roar from afar. Such was the terror and the shout of the engaging armies." In another passage, the poet, much in the manner of Ossian, heaps simile on simile, to express the vastness of the idea, with which his imagination seems to labour. "With a mighty shout the hosts engage. Not so loud roars the wave of ocean, when driven against the shore by the whole force of the boisterous north; not so loud in the woods of the mountain, the noise of the flame, when rising in its fury to consume the forest; not so loud the wind among the lofty oaks, when the wrath of the storm rages; as was the clamour of the Greeks and Trojans, when, roaring terrible, they rushed against each other[56]."

To these descriptions and similes, we may oppose the following from Ossian, and leave the reader to judge between them. He will find images of the same kind employed; commonly less extended; but thrown forth with a glowing rapidity which characterises our poet. "As autumn's dark storms pour from two echoing hills, towards each other, approached the heroes. As two dark streams from high rocks meet, and mix, and roar on the plain; loud, rough, and dark in battle, meet Lochlin and Inisfail. Chief mixed his strokes with chief, and man with man. Steel clanging, sounded on steel. Helmets are cleft on high; blood bursts and smoaks around ... As the troubled noise of the ocean, when roll the waves on high; as the last peal of the thunder of heaven, such is the noise of battle." (60)—"As roll a thousand waves to the rock, so Swaran's host came on; as meets a rock a thousand waves, so Inisfail met Swaran. Death raises all his voices around, and mixes with the sound of shields ... The field echoes from wing to wing, as a hundred hammers that rise by turns on the red son of the furnace." (60)——"As a hundred winds on Morven; as the streams of a hundred hills; as clouds fly successive over heaven; or as the dark ocean assaults the shore of the desart; so roaring, so vast, so terrible, the armies mixed on Lena's echoing heath." (77) In several of these images, there is a remarkable similarity to Homer's; but what follows is superior to any comparison that Homer uses on this subject. "The groan of the people spread over the hills; it was like the thunder of night, when the cloud bursts on Cona; and a thousand ghosts shriek at once on the hollow wind." (77) Never was an image of more awful sublimity employed to heighten the terror of battle.

Both poets compare the appearance of an army approaching, to the gathering of dark clouds. "As when a shepherd," says Homer, "beholds from the rock a cloud borne along the sea by the western wind; black as pitch it appears from afar, sailing over the ocean, and carrying the dreadful storm. He shrinks at the sight, and drives his flock into the cave: Such, under the Ajaces, moved on, the dark, the thickened phalanx to the war[57]."—"They came," says Ossian, "over the desert like stormy clouds, when the winds roll them over the heath; their edges are tinged with lightening; and the echoing groves foresee the storm." (117)[58] The edges of the cloud tinged with lightning, is a sublime idea; but the shepherd and his flock, render Homer's simile more picturesque. This is frequently the difference between the two poets. Ossian gives no more than the main image, strong and full. Homer adds circumstances and appendages, which amuse the fancy by enlivening the scenery.

Homer compares the regular appearance of an army, to "clouds that are settled on the mountain top, in the day of calmness, when the strength of the north wind sleeps[59]." Ossian, with full as much propriety, compares the appearance of a disordered army, to "the mountain[-]cloud, when the blast hath [has] entered its womb; and scatters the curling gloom on every side." (173) Ossian's clouds assume a great many forms; and, as we might expect from his climate, are a fertile source of imagery to him. "The warriors followed their chiefs, like the gathering of the rainy clouds, behind the red meteors of heaven." (56) An army retreating without coming to action, is likened to "clouds, that having long threatened rain, retire slowly behind the hills." (144)[60] The picture of Oithona, after she had determined to die, is lively and delicate. "Her soul was resolved, and the tear was dried from her wildly-looking eye. A troubled joy rose on her mind, like the red path of the lightning on a stormy cloud." (185)[61] The image also of the gloomy Cairbar, meditating, in silence, the assassination of Oscar, until the moment came when his designs were ripe for execution, is extremely noble, and complete in all its parts. "Cairbar heard their words in silence, like the cloud of a shower; it stands dark on Cromla, till the lightning bursts its side. The valley gleams with red light; the spirits of the storm rejoice. So stood the silent king of Temora; at length his words are heard." (149)

Homer's comparison of Achilles to the Dog-Star, is very sublime. "Priam beheld him rushing along the plain, shining in his armour, like the star of autumn; bright are its beams, distinguished amidst the multitude of stars in the dark hour of night. It rises in its splendor; but its splendor is fatal; betokening to miserable men, the destroying heat[62]." The first appearance of Fingal, is, in like manner, compared by Ossian, to a star or meteor. "Fingal, tall in his ship, stretched his bright lance before him. Terrible was the gleam of his [the] steel; it was like the green meteor of death, setting in the heath of Malmor, when the traveller is alone, and the broad moon is darkened in heaven." (76) The hero's appearance in Homer, is more magnificent; in Ossian, more terrible.

A tree cut down, or overthrown by a storm, is a similitude frequent among poets for describing the fall of a warrior in battle. Homer employs it often.

But the most beautiful, by far, of his comparisons, founded on this object, indeed one of the most beautiful in the whole Iliad, is that on the death of Euphorbus. "As the young and verdant olive, which a man hath reared with care in a lonely field, where the springs of water bubble around it; it is fair and flourishing; it is fanned by the breath of all the winds, and loaded with white blossoms; when the sudden blast of a whirlwind descending, roots it out from its bed, and stretches it on the dust[63]." To this, elegant as it is, we may oppose the following simile of Ossian's, relating to the death of the three sons of Usnoth. "They fell, like three young oaks which stood alone on the hill. The traveller saw the lovely trees, and wondered how they grew so lonely. The blast of the desert came by night, and laid their green heads low. Next day he returned; but they were withered, and the heath was bare." (146) Malvina's allusion to the same object, in her lamentation over Oscar, is so exquisitely tender, that I cannot forbear giving it a place also. "I was a lovely tree in thy presence, Oscar! with all my branches round me. But thy death came, like a blast from the desert, and laid my green head low. The spring returned with its showers; but no leaf of mine arose." (187) Several of Ossian's similes taken from trees, are remarkably beautiful, and diversified with well chosen circumstances; such as that upon the death of Ryno and Orla: "They have fallen like the oak of the desart; when it lies across a stream, and withers in the wind of the mountains [mountain]:" (95) Or that which Ossian applies to himself; "I, like an ancient oak in Morven, [I] moulder alone in my place; the blast hath lopped my branches away; and I tremble at the wings of the north." (156)

As Homer exalts his heroes by comparing them to gods, Ossian makes the same use of comparisons taken from spirits and ghosts. Swaran "roared in battle [in the midst of thousands], like the shrill spirit of a storm that sits dim on the clouds of Gormal, and enjoys the death of the mariner." (60) His people gathered around Erragon, "like [as] storms around the ghost of night, when he calls them from the top of Morven, and prepares to pour them on the land of the stranger." (120)——"They fell before my son, like [the] groves in the desert, when an angry ghost rushes through night, and takes their green heads in his hand." (151) In such images, Ossian appears in his strength; for very seldom have supernatural beings been painted with so much sublimity, and such force of imagination, as by this poet. Even Homer, great as he is, must yield to him in similes formed upon these. Take, for instance, the following, which is the most remarkable of this kind in the Iliad. "Meriones followed Idomeneus to battle, like Mars the destroyer of men, when he rushes to war. Terror, his beloved son, strong and fierce, attends him; who fills with dismay, the most valiant hero. They come from Thrace, armed against the Ephyrians and Phlegyans; nor do they regard the prayers of either; but dispose of success at their will[64]." The idea here, is undoubtedly noble: but observe what a figure Ossian sets before the astonished imagination, and with what sublimely terrible circumstances he has heightened it. "He rushed in the sound of his arms, like the dreadful spirit of Loda, when he comes in the roar of a thousand storms, and scatters battles from his eyes. He sits on a cloud over Lochlin's seas. His mighty hand is on his sword. [and] The winds lift his flaming locks. So terrible was Cuchullin in the day of his fame." (138)

Homer's comparisons relate chiefly to martial subjects, to the appearances and motions of armies, the engagement and death of heroes, and the various incidents of war. In Ossian, we find a greater variety of other subjects illustrated by similes; particularly, the songs of bards, the beauty of women, the different circumstances of old age, sorrow, and private distress; which give occasion to much beautiful imagery. What, for instance, can be more delicate and moving, than the following simile of Oithona's, in her lamentation over the dishonour she had suffered? "Chief of Strumon, replied the sighing maid, why didst thou come [why comest thou] over the dark blue wave to Nuath's mournful daughter? Why did not I pass away in secret, like the flower of the rock, that lifts its fair head unseen, and strews its withered leaves on the blast?" (184) The musick of bards, a favourite object with Ossian, is illustrated by a variety of the most beautiful appearances that are to be found in nature. It is compared to the calm shower of spring; to the dews of the morning on the hill of roes; to the face of the blue and still lake. (168 f., 62, 73, 158) Two similes on this subject, I shall quote, because they would do honour to any of the most celebrated classics. The one is; "Sit thou on the heath, O bard! and let us hear thy voice; it is pleasant as the gale of the spring [of spring] that sighs on the hunter's ear, when he wakens from dreams of joy, and has heard the music of the spirits of the hill." (96) The other contains a short, but exquisitely tender image, accompanied with the finest poetical painting. "The music of Carryl was like the memory of joys that are past, pleasant and mournful to the soul. The ghosts of departed bards heard it from Slimora's side. Soft sounds spread along the wood; and the silent valleys of night rejoice." (136) What a figure would such imagery and such scenery have made, had they been presented to us, adorned with the sweetness and harmony of the Virgilian numbers!

I have chosen all along to compare Ossian with Homer, rather than Virgil, for an obvious reason. There is a much nearer correspondence between the times and manners of the two former poets. Both wrote in an early period of society; both are originals; both are distinguished by simplicity, sublimity, and fire. The correct elegance of Virgil, his artful imitation of Homer, the Roman stateliness which he every where maintains, admit no parallel with the abrupt boldness, and enthusiastick warmth of the Celtic bard. In one article, indeed, there is a resemblance. Virgil is more tender than Homer; and thereby agrees more with Ossian; with this difference, that the feelings of the one are more gentle and polished, those of the other more strong; the tenderness of Virgil softens, that of Ossian dissolves and overcomes the heart.

A resemblance may be sometimes observed between Ossian's comparisons, and those employed by the sacred writers. They abound much in this figure, and they use it with the utmost propriety[65]. The imagery of Scripture exhibits a soil and climate altogether different from those of Ossian; a warmer country, a more smiling face of nature, the arts of agriculture and of rural life much farther advanced. The wine press, and the threshing floor, are often presented to us, the Cedar and the Palm-tree, the fragrance of perfumes, the voice of the Turtle, and the beds of Lillies. The similes are, like Ossian's, generally short, touching on one point of resemblance, rather than spread out into little episodes. In the following example may be perceived what inexpressible grandeur poetry receives from the intervention of the Deity. "The nations shall rush like the rushings of many waters; but God shall rebuke them, and they shall fly far off, and shall be chased as the chaff of the mountains before the wind, and like the down of the thistle before the whirlwind[66]."

Besides formal comparisons, the poetry of Ossian is embellished with many beautiful metaphors: Such as that remarkably fine one applied to Deugala; "She was covered with the light of beauty; but her heart was the house of pride." (69) This mode of expression, which suppresses the mark of comparison, and substitutes a figured description in room of the object described, is a great enlivener of style. It denotes that glow and rapidity of fancy, which without pausing to form a regular simile, paints the object at one stroke. "Thou art to me the beam of the east, rising in a land unknown." (184)—"In peace, thou art the gale of spring; in war, the mountain[-]storm." (101)——"Pleasant be thy rest, O lovely beam, soon hast thou set on our hills! The steps of thy departure were stately, like the moon on the blue trembling wave. But thou hast left us in darkness, first of the maids of Lutha! ... Soon hast thou set Malvina! [...] but thou risest, like the beam of the east, among the spirits of thy friends, where they sit in their stormy halls, the chambers of [the] thunder." (193) This is correct and finely supported. But in the following instance, the metaphor, though very beautiful at the beginning, becomes imperfect before it closes, by being improperly mixed with the literal sense. "Frothal[67] went forth with the stream of his people; but they met a rock; Fingal stood unmoved; broken they rolled back from his side. Nor did they roll in safety; the spear of the king pursued their flight." (162)

The hyperbole is a figure which we might expect to find often employed by Ossian; as the undisciplined imagination of early ages generally prompts exaggeration, and carries its objects to excess; whereas longer experience, and farther progress in the arts of life, chasten mens ideas and expressions. Yet Ossian's hyperboles appear not to me, either so frequent or so harsh as might at first have been looked for; an advantage owing no doubt to the more cultivated state, in which, as was before shewn, poetry subsisted among the ancient Celtæ, than among most other barbarous nations. One of the most exaggerated descriptions in the whole work, is what meets us at the beginning of Fingal, where the scout makes his report to Cuchullin of the landing of the foe. But this is so far from deserving censure that it merits praise, as being, on that occasion, natural and proper. The scout arrives, trembling and full of fears; and it is well known, that no passion disposes men to hyperbolize more than terror. It both annihilates themselves in their own apprehension, and magnifies every object which they view through the medium of a troubled imagination. Hence all those indistinct images of formidable greatness, the natural marks of a disturbed and con-fused mind, which occur in Moran's description of Swaran's appearance, and in his relation of the conference which they held together; not unlike the report, which the affrighted Jewish spies made to their leader of the land of Canaan. "The land through which we have gone to search it, is a land that eateth up the inhabitants thereof; and all the people that we saw in it, are men of a great stature: and there saw we giants, the sons of Anak, which come of the giants; and we were in our own sight as grasshoppers, and so were we in their sight."[68]

With regard to personifications, I formerly observed that Ossian was sparing, and I accounted for his being so. Allegorical personages he has none; and their absence is not to be regretted. For the intermixture of those shadowy Beings, which have not the support even of mythological or legen-dary belief, with human actors, seldom produces a good effect. The fiction becomes too visible and phantastick; and overthrows that impression of reality, which the probable recital of human actions is calculated to make upon the mind. In the serious and pathetick scenes of Ossian especially, allegorical characters would have been as much out of place, as in Tragedy; serving only unseasonably to amuse the fancy, whilst they stopped the current, and weakened the force of passion.

With apostrophes, or addresses to persons absent or dead, which have been, in all ages, the language of passion, our poet abounds; and they are among his highest beauties. Witness the apostrophe, in the first book of Fingal, to the maid of Inistore, whose lover had fallen in battle; and that inimitably fine one of Cuchullin to Bragela at the conclusion of the same book. He commands the harp to be struck in her praise; and the mention of Bragela's name, immediately suggesting to him a crowd of tender ideas; "Dost thou raise thy fair face from the rocks," he exclaims, "to find the sails of Cuchullin? The sea is rolling far distant, and its white foam shall deceive thee for my sails." And now his imagination being wrought up to conceive her as, at that moment, really in this situation, he becomes afraid of the harm she may receive from the inclemency of the night; and with an enthusiasm, happy and affecting, though beyond the cautious strain of modern poetry, "Retire," he proceeds, "retire, for it is night, my love, and the dark winds sigh in thy hair. Retire to the hall[s] of my feasts, and think of the times that are past; for I will not return till the storm of war has [is] ceased. O Connal, speak of wars and arms, and send her from my mind; for lovely with her raven[-]hair is the white-bosomed daughter of Sorglan." (62) This breathes all the native spirit of passion and tenderness.

The addresses to the sun (133), to the moon (140), and to the evening star (166), must draw the attention of every reader of taste, as among the most splendid ornaments of this collection. The beauties of each are too great, and too obvious to need any particular comment. In one passage only of the address to the moon, there appears some obscurity. "Whither dost thou retire from thy course, when the darkness of thy countenance grows? Hast thou thy hall like Ossian? Dwellest thou in the shadow of grief? Have thy sisters fallen from heaven? Are they who rejoiced with thee at night, no more? Yes, they have fallen, fair light! and thou dost often retire to mourn." We may be at a loss to comprehend, at first view, the ground of these speculations of Ossian, concerning the moon; but when all the circumstances are attended to, they will appear to flow naturally from the present situation of his mind. A mind under the dominion of any strong passion, tinctures with its own disposition, every object which it beholds. The old bard, with his heart bleeding for the loss of all his friends, is meditating on the different phases of the moon. Her waning and darkness, presents to his melancholy imagination, the image of sorrow; and presently the idea arises, and is indulged, that, like himself, she retires to mourn over the loss of other moons, or of stars, whom he calls her sisters, and fancies to have once rejoiced with her at night, now fallen from heaven. Darkness suggested the idea of mourning, and mourning suggested nothing so naturally to Ossian, as the death of beloved friends. An instance precisely similar of this influence of passion, may be seen in a passage which has always been admired of Shakespear's King Lear. The old man on the point of distraction, through the inhumanity of his daughters, sees Edgar appear disguised like a beggar and a madman.

> *Lear.* Didst thou give all to thy daughters? And art thou come to this? Couldest thou leave nothing? Didst thou give them all?
> *Kent.* He hath no daughters, Sir.
> *Lear.* Death, traitor! nothing could have subdued nature, To such a lowness, but his unkind daughters.
>
> *King Lear*, Act 3. Scene 5.

The apostrophe to the winds, in the opening of Darthula, is in the highest spirit of poetry. "But the winds deceive thee, O Darthula: and deny the woody Etha to thy sails. These are not thy mountains, Nathos, nor is that the roar of thy climbing waves. The halls of Cairbar are near, and the towers of the foe lift their head[s] ... Where have ye been, ye southern winds; when the sons of my love were deceived? But ye have been sporting on plains, and pursuing the thistle's beard. O that ye had been rustling in the sails of Nathos, till the hills of Etha rose! till they rose in their clouds, and saw their coming chief." (140) This passage is remarkable for the resemblance it bears to an expostulation with the wood nymphs, on their absence at a critical time; which, as a favourite poetical idea, Virgil has copied from Theocritus, and Milton has very happily imitated from both.

> Where were ye, nymphs! when the remorseless deep
> Clos'd o'er the head of your lov'd Lycidas?
> For neither were ye playing on the steep
> Where your old bards, the famous Druids, lie;
> Nor on the shaggy top of Mona, high,
> Nor yet where Deva spreads her wizard stream[69]

Having now treated fully of Ossian's talents, with respect to description and imagery, it only remains to make some observations on his sentiments. No sentiments can be beautiful without being proper; that is, suited to the character and situation of those who utter them. In this respect, Ossian is as correct as most writers. His characters, as above observed, are in general well supported; which could not have been the case, had the sentiments been unnatural or out of place. A variety of personages of different ages, sexes, and conditions, are introduced into his poems; and they speak and act with a propriety of sentiment and behaviour, which it is surprising to find in so rude an age. Let the poem of Darthula, throughout, be taken as an example.

But it is not enough that sentiments be natural and proper. In order to acquire any high degree of poetical merit, they must also be sublime and pathetick.

The sublime is not confined to sentiment alone. It belongs to description also; and whether in description or in sentiment, imports such ideas presented to the mind, as raise it to an uncommon degree of elevation, and fill it with admiration and astonishment. This is the highest effect either of eloquence or poetry: And to produce this effect, requires a genius glowing with the strongest and warmest conception of some object awful, great or magnificent. That this character of genius belongs to Ossian, may, I think, sufficiently appear from many of the passages I have already had occasion to quote. To produce more instances, were superfluous. If the engagement of Fingal with the spirit of Loda, in Carric-thura; if the encounters of the armies, in Fingal; if the address to the sun, in Carthon; if the similes founded upon ghosts and spirits of the night, all formerly mentioned, be not admitted as examples, and illustrious ones too, of the true poetical sublime, I confess myself entirely ignorant of this quality in writing.

All the circumstances, indeed, of Ossian's composition, are favourable to the sublime, more perhaps than to any other species of beauty. Accuracy and correctness; artfully connected narration; exact method and proportion of parts, we may look for in polished times. The gay and the beautiful, will appear to more advantage in the midst of smiling scenery and pleasurable themes. But amidst the rude scenes of nature, amidst rocks and torrents and whirlwinds and battles, dwells the sublime. It is the thunder and the light-

ning of genius. It is the offspring of nature, not of art. It is negligent of all
the lesser graces, and perfectly consistent with a certain noble disorder. It
associates naturally with that grave and solemn spirit, which distinguishes
our author. For the sublime, is an awful and serious emotion; and is height-
ened by all the images of Trouble, and Terror, and Darkness.

> Ipse pater, media nimborum in nocte, coruscâ
> Fulmina molitur dextrâ; quo maxima motu
> Terra tremit; fugere feræ; & mortalia corda
> Per gentes, humilis stravit pavor; ille, flagranti
> Aut Atho, aut Rhodopen, aut alta Ceraunia telo
> Dejicit.———

VIRG. Georg. I.

Simplicity and conciseness, are never-failing characteristics of the stile of
a sublime writer. He rests on the majesty of his sentiments, not on the pomp
of his expressions. The main secret of being sublime, is to say great things
in few, and in plain words: For every superfluous decoration degrades a
sublime idea. The mind rises and swells, when a lofty description or senti-
ment is presented to it, in its native form. But no sooner does the poet
attempt to spread out this sentiment or description, and to deck it round and
round with glittering ornaments, than the mind begins to fall from its high
elevation; the transport is over; the beautiful may remain, but the sublime is
gone. Hence the concise and simple style of Ossian, gives great advantage
to his sublime conceptions; and assists them in seizing the imagination with
full power.[70]

Sublimity as belonging to sentiment, coincides in a great measure with
magnanimity, heroism, and generosity of sentiment. Whatever discovers
human nature in its greatest elevation; whatever bespeaks a high effort of
soul; or shews a mind superior to pleasures, to dangers, and to death, forms
what may be called the moral or sentimental sublime. For this, Ossian is
eminently distinguished. No poet maintains a higher tone of virtuous and
noble sentiment, throughout all his works. Particularly in all the sentiments
of Fingal, there is a grandeur and loftiness proper to swell the mind with
the highest ideas of human perfection. Wherever he appears, we behold the
hero. The objects which he pursues, are always truly great; to bend the
proud; to protect the injured; to defend his friends; to overcome his enemies
by generosity more than by force. A portion of the same spirit actuates all
the other heroes. Valour reigns; but it is a generous valour, void of cruelty,
animated by honour, not by hatred. We behold no debasing passions among
Fingal's warriors; no spirit of avarice or of insult; but a perpetual contention
for fame; a desire of being distinguished an remembered for gallant actions;
a love of justice; and a zealous attachment to their friends and their country.
Such is the strain of sentiment in the works of Ossian.

But the sublimity of moral sentiments, if they wanted the softening of the
tender, would be in hazard of giving a hard and stiff air to poetry. It is not

enough to admire. Admiration is a cold feeling, in comparison of that deep interest, which the heart takes in tender and pathetick scenes; where, by a mysterious attachment to the objects of compassion, we are pleased and delighted, even whilst we mourn. With scenes of this kind, Ossian abounds; and his high merit in these, is incontestable. He may be blamed for drawing tears too often from our eyes; but that he has the power of commanding them, I believe no man, who has the least sensibility, will question. The general character of his poetry, is the heroic mixed with the elegiac strain; admiration tempered with pity. Ever fond of giving, as he expresses it, "the joy of grief," it is visible, that on all moving subjects, he delights to exert his genius; and accordingly, never were there finer pathetick situations, than what his works present. His great art in managing them lies in giving vent to the simple and natural emotions of the heart. We meet with no exaggerated declamation; no subtile refinements on sorrow; no substitution of description in place of passion. Ossian felt strongly himself; and the heart when uttering its native language never fails, by powerful sympathy, to affect the heart. A great variety of examples might be produced. We need only open the book to find them every where. What, for instance, can be more moving, than the lamentations of Oithona, after her misfortune? Gaul, the son of Morni, her lover, ignorant of what she had suffered, comes to her rescue. Their meeting is tender in the highest degree. He proposes to engage her foe, in single combat, and gives her in charge what she is to do, if he himself shall fall. "And shall the daughter of Nuäth live, she replied with a bursting sigh? Shall I live in Tromathon and the son of Morni low? My heart is not of that rock; nor my soul careless as that sea, which lifts its blue waves to every wind, and rolls beneath the storm. The blast, which shall lay thee low, shall spread the branches of Oithona on earth. We shall wither together, son of car-borne Morni! The narrow house is pleasant to me; and the grey stone of the dead; for never more will I leave thy rocks, sea-surrounded Tromathon! ... Chief of Strumon, why camest [comest] thou over the waves to Nuäth's mournful daughter? Why did not I pass away in secret, like the flower of the rock, that lifts its fair head unseen, and strews its withered leaves on the blast? Why didst thou come, O Gaul! to hear my departing sigh? ... O had I dwelt at Duvranna, in the bright beam[s] of my fame! Then had my years come on with joy; and the virgins would bless my steps. But I fall in youth, son of Morni, and my father shall blush in his hall." (184, 186))

Oithona mourns like a woman; in Cuchullin's expressions of grief after his defeat, we behold the sentiments of a hero, generous but desponding. The situation is remarkably fine. Cuchullin, rouzed from his cave, by the noise of battle, sees Fingal victorious in the field. He is described as kindling at the sight. "His hand is on the sword of his fathers; his red-rolling eyes on the foe. He thrice attempted to rush to battle; and thrice did Connal stop him;" suggesting, that Fingal was routing the foe; and that he ought not, by the show of superfluous aid, to deprive the king of any part of the honour of a victory, which was owing to him alone. Cuchullin yields to this generous sentiment; but we see it stinging him to the heart with the sense of his own disgrace. "Then, Carril, go, replied the chief, and greet the king of Morven. When Lochlin falls away like a stream after rain, and the noise of the battle is over, then be thy voice sweet in his ear, to praise the king of swords. Give him the sword of Caithbat; for Cuchullin is worthy no more to lift the arms of his fathers. But, O ye ghosts of the lonely Cromla! Ye souls of chiefs that are no more! Be ye the companions of Cuchullin, and talk to him in the cave of his sorrow. For never more shall I be renowned among the mighty in the land. I am like a beam that has shone: Like a mist that has fled away; when the blast of the morning came, and brightened the shaggy side of the hill. Connal! talk of arms no more: Departed is my fame. My sighs shall be on Cromla's wind; till my footsteps cease to be seen. And thou, white-bosomed Bragela! mourn over the fall of my fame; for vanquished, I will never return to thee, thou sun-beam of Dunscaich!" (88)

———————————————Æstuat Ingens

Uno in corde pudor, luctusque, & conscia virtus.[71]

Besides such extended pathetick scenes, Ossian frequently pierces the heart by a single unexpected stroke. When Oscar fell in battle, "No father mourned his son slain in youth; no brother, his brother of love; they fell without tears, for the chief of the people was low." (152) In the admirable interview of Hector with Andromache, in the sixth Iliad, the circumstance of the child in his nurse's arms, has often been remarked, as adding much to the tenderness of the scene. In the following passage relating to the death of Cuchullin, we find a circumstance that must strike the imagination with still greater force. "And is the son of Semo fallen? said Carril with a sigh. Mournful are Tura's walls, and sorrow dwells at Dunscaich. Thy spouse is left alone in her youth; the son of thy love is alone. He shall come to Bragela, and ask her why she weeps. He shall lift his eyes to the wall, and see his father's sword. Whose sword is that? he will say; and the soul of his mother is sad." (138) Soon after Fingal had shewn all the grief of a father's heart for Ryno, one of his sons, fallen in battle, he is calling, after his accustomed manner, his sons to the chase. "Call," says he, "Fillan and Ryno— But he is not here—My son rests on the bed of death." (103)—This unexpected start of anguish, is worthy of the highest tragic poet,

> If she come in, she'll sure speak to my wife—
> My wife!—my wife—What wife?—I have no wife—
> Oh insupportable! Oh heavy hour!
>
> *Othello*, Act 5. Scene 7.

The contrivance of the incident in both poets is similar; but the circumstances are varied with judgment. Othello dwells upon the name of wife, when it had fallen from him, with the confusion and horror of one tortured with guilt. Fingal, with the dignity of a hero, corrects himself, and suppresses his rising grief.

The contrast which Ossian frequently makes between his present and his former state, diffuses over his whole poetry, a solemn pathetick air, which cannot fail to make impression on every heart. The conclusion of the songs of Selma, is particularly calculated for this purpose. Nothing can be more poetical and tender, or can leave upon the mind, a stronger, and more affecting idea of the venerable aged bard. "Such were the words of the bards in the days of the song; when the king heard the music of harps, and the tales of other times. The chiefs gathered from all their hills, and heard the lovely sound. They praised the voice of Cona[72]; the first among a thousand bards. But age is now on my tongue, and my soul has failed. I hear, sometimes, the ghosts of bards, and learn their pleasant song. But memory fails on my mind; I hear the call of years. They say, as they pass along; Why does Ossian sing? Soon shall he lie in the narrow house, and no bard shall raise his fame. Roll on, ye dark-brown years! for ye bring no joy in your course. Let the tomb open to Ossian, for his strength has failed. The sons of the song are gone to rest. My voice remains, like a blast, that roars lonely on a sea-surrounded rock, after the winds are laid. The dark moss whistles there, and the distant mariner sees the waving trees." (170)

Upon the whole; if to feel strongly, and to describe naturally, be the two chief ingredients in poetical genius, Ossian must, after fair examination, be held to possess that genius in a high degree. The question is not, whether a few improprieties may be pointed out in his works; whether this, or that passage, might not have been worked up with more art and skill, by some writer of happier times? A thousand such cold and frivolous criticisms, are altogether indecisive as to his genuine merit. But, has he the spirit, the fire, the inspiration of a poet? Does he utter the voice of nature? Does he elevate by his sentiments? Does he interest by his descriptions? Does he paint to the heart as well as to the fancy? Does he make his readers glow, and tremble, and weep? These are the great characteristicks of true poetry. Where these are found, he must be a minute critic indeed, who can dwell upon slight defects. A few beauties of this high kind, transcend whole volumes of fault-less mediocrity. Uncouth and abrupt, Ossian may sometimes appear by reason of his conciseness. But he is sublime, he is pathetick, in an eminent degree. If he has not the extensive knowledge, the regular dignity of narra-tion, the fulness and accuracy of description, which we find in Homer and Virgil, yet in strength of imagination, in grandeur of sentiment, in native majesty of passion, he is fully their equal. If he flows not always like a clear stream, yet he breaks forth often like a torrent of fire. Of art too, he is far from being destitute; and his imagination is remarkable for delicacy as well as strength. Seldom or never is he either trifling or tedious; and if he be thought too melancholy, yet he is always moral. Though his merit were in other respects much less than it is, this alone ought to entitle him to high regard, that his writings are remarkably favourable to virtue. They awake the tenderest sympathies, and inspire the most generous emotions. No reader can rise from him, without being warmed with the sentiments of humanity, virtue and honour.

Though unacquainted with the original language, there is no one but must judge the translation to deserve the highest praise, on account of its beauty and elegance. Of its faithfulness and accuracy, I have been assured by persons skilled in the Galic tongue, who, from their youth, were acquainted with many of these poems of Ossian. To transfuse such spirited and fervid ideas from one language into another; to translate literally, and yet with such a glow of poetry; to keep alive so much passion, and support so much dignity throughout, is one of the most difficult works of genius, and proves the translator to have been animated with no small portion of Ossian's spirit.

The measured prose which he has employed, possesses considerable advantages above any sort of versification he could have chosen. Whilst it pleases and fills the ear with a variety of harmonious cadences, being, at the same time, freer from constraint in the choice and arrangement of words, it allows the spirit of the original to be exhibited with more justness, force, and simplicity. Elegant however, and masterly as Mr. Macpherson's translation is, we must never forget, whilst we read it, that we are putting the merit of the original to a severe test. For, we are examining a poet stripped of his native dress: divested of the harmony of his own numbers. We know how much grace and energy the works of the Greek and Latin poets receive from the charm of versification in their original languages. If then, destitute of this advantage, exhibited in a literal version, Ossian still has power to please as a poet; and not to please only, but often to command, to transport, to melt the heart; we may very safely infer, that his productions are the off-spring of true and uncommon genius; and we may boldly assign him a place among those, whose works are to last for ages.

A P P E N D I X.

The substance of the preceding Dissertation was originally delivered, soon after the first publication of Fingal, in the course of my lectures in the university of Edinburgh; and, at the desire of several of the hearers, was afterwards enlarged and given to the publick.

As the degree of antiquity belonging to the poems of Ossian, appeared to be a point which might bear dispute, I endeavoured, from internal evidence, to show that these poems must be referred to a very remote period; without pretending to ascertain precisely the date of their composition. I had not the least suspicion, when this Dissertation was first published, that there was any occasion for supporting their authenticity, as genuine productions of the Highlands of Scotland, as translations from the Galic language; nor forgeries of a supposed translator. In Scotland, their authenticity was never called in question. I myself had particular reasons to be fully satisfied concerning it. My knowledge of Mr. Macpherson's personal honour and integrity, gave me full assurance of his being incapable of putting such a gross imposition, first, upon his friends, and then upon the publick; and if this had not been sufficient, I knew, besides, that the manner in which these poems were brought to light, was entirely inconsistent with any fraud. An accidental conversation with a gentleman distinguished in the literary world[1], gave occasion to Mr. Macpherson's translating literally one or two small pieces of the old Galic poetry. These being shown to me and some others rendered us very desirous of becoming more acquainted with that poetry. Mr. Macpherson, afraid of not doing justice to compositions which he admired in the original, was very backward to undertake the task of translating; and the publication of *The fragments of ancient poems*, was with no small importunity extorted from him. The high reputation which these presently acquired, made it he thought unjust that the world should be deprived of the possession of more, if more of the same kind could be recovered: And Mr. Macpherson was warmly urged by several gentlemen of rank and taste, to disengage himself from other occupations, and to undertake a journey through the Highlands and Islands, on purpose to make a collection of those curious remains of ancient genius. He complied with their desire, and spent several months in visiting those remote parts of the country; during which time he corresponded frequently with his friends in Edinburgh, informed them of his progress, of the applications which he made in different quarters, and of the success which he met with; several letters of his, and of those who assisted him in making discoveries passed through my hands; his undertaking was the object of considerable attention; and returning at last, fraught with the poetical treasures of the north, he set himself to translate under the eye of some who were acquainted with the Galic language, and looked into his manuscripts; and by a large publication made an appeal to all the natives of the Highlands and Islands of Scotland, whether he had been faithful to his charge, and done justice to their well known and favourite poems.

Such a transaction certainly did not afford any favourable opportunity for carrying on an imposture. Yet in England, it seems, an opinion has prevailed with some, that an imposture has been carried on; that the poems which have been given to the world are not translations of the works of any old Galic Bard, but modern compositions, formed, as it is said, upon a higher plan of poetry and sentiment than could belong to an age and a country reputed barbarous: And I have been called upon and urged to produce some evidence for satisfying the world that they are not the compositions of Mr. Macpherson himself, under the borrowed name of Ossian.[2]

If the question had been concerning manuscripts brought from some distant or unknown region, with which we had no intercourse; or concerning translations from an Asiatic or American language which scarce any body understood, suspicions might naturally have arisen, and an author's assertions have been anxiously and scrupulously weighed. But in the case of a literal translation, professed to be given of old traditionary poems of our own country; of poems asserted to be known in the original to many thousand inhabitants of Great Britain, and illustrated too by many of their current tales and stories concerning them, such extreme scepticism is altogether out of place. For who would have been either so hardy or so stupid, as to attempt a forgery which could not have failed of being immediately detected? Either the author must have had the influence to engage, as confederates in the fraud, all the natives of the Highlands and Islands, dispersed as they are throughout every corner of the British dominions; or, we should, long ere this time, have heard their united voice exclaiming: "These are not our poems, nor what we were ever accustomed to hear from our bards or our fathers." Such remonstrances would, at least, have reached those who dwell in a part of the country which is adjacent to the Highlands; and must have come loud to the ears of such, especially, as were known to be the promoters of Mr. Macpherson's undertaking. The silence of a whole country in this case, and of a country, whose inhabitants are well known to be attached, in a remarkable degree, to all their own antiquities, is of as much weight as a thousand positive testimonies. And surely, no person of common understanding would have adventured, as Mr. Macpherson has done in his dissertation on Temora, to engage in a controversy with the whole Irish nation concerning these poems, and to insist upon the honour of them being due to Scotland, if they had been mere forgeries of his own; which the Scots, in place of supporting so ridiculous a claim, must have instantly rejected.

But as reasoning alone is apt not to make much impression, where suspicions have been entertained concerning a matter of fact, it was thought proper to have recourse to express testimonies. I have accordingly applied to several persons of credit and honour, both gentlemen of fortune, and clergymen of the established church, who are natives of the Highlands or Islands of Scotland, and well acquainted with the language of the country, desiring to know their real opinion of the translations published by Mr. Macpherson. Their original letters to me, in return, are in my possession. I shall give a fair and faithful account of the result of their testimony: And I have full authority to use the names of those gentlemen for what I now advance.

I must begin with affirming, that though among those with whom I have corresponded, some have had it in their power to be more particular and explicit in their testimony than others; there is not, however, one person, who insinuates the most remote suspicion that Mr. Macpherson has either forged, or adulterated any one of the Poems he has published. If they make any complaints of him, it is on account of his having omitted other poems which they think of equal merit with any which he has published. They all, without exception, concur in holding his translations to be genuine, and proceed upon their authenticity as a fact acknowledged throughout all those Northern Provinces; assuring me that any one would be exposed to ridicule among them, who should call it in question. I must observe, that I had no motive to direct my choice of the persons to whom I applied for information preferably to others, except their being pointed out to me, as the persons in their different counties who were most likely to give light on this head.

With regard to the manner in which the originals of these poems have been preserved and transmitted, which has been represented as so mysterious and inexplicable, I have received the following plain account: That until the present century, almost every great family in the Highlands had their own bard, to whose office it belonged to be master of all the poems and songs of the country; that among these poems the works of Ossian are easily distinguished from those of later bards by several peculiarities in his style and manner; that Ossian has been always reputed the Homer of the Highlands, and all his compositions held in singular esteem and veneration; that the whole country is full of traditionary stories derived from his poems, concerning Fingal and his race of heroes, of whom there is not a child but has heard, and not a district in which there are not places pointed out famous for being the scene of some of their feats of arms; that it was wont to be the great entertainment of the Highlanders, to pass the winter evenings in discoursing of the times of Fingal, and rehearsing these old poems, of which they have been all along enthusiastically fond; that when assembled at their festivals, or on any of their publick occasions, wagers were often laid who could repeat most of them, and to have store of them in their memories, was both an honourable and a profitable acquisition, as it procured them access into the families of their great men; that with regard to their antiquity, they are beyond all memory or tradition; insomuch that there is a word commonly used in the Highlands to this day, when they would express any thing which is of the most remote or unknown antiquity, importing, that it belongs to the age of Fingal.

I am farther informed, that after the use of letters was introduced into that part of the country, the bards and others began early to commit several of these poems to writing; that old manuscripts of them, many of which are now destroyed or lost, are known and attested to have been in the possession of some great families; that the most valuable of those which remained, were collected by Mr. Macpherson during his journey through that country; that though the poems of Ossian, so far as they were handed down by oral tradition, were no doubt liable to be interpolated, and to have their parts disjoined and put out of their natural order, yet by comparing together the different oral editions of them (if we may use that phrase) in different corners of the country, and by comparing these also with the manuscripts which he obtained, Mr. Macpherson had it in his power to ascertain, in a great measure, the genuine original, to restore the parts to their proper order, and to give the whole to the publick in that degree of correctness, in which it now appears.

I am also acquainted, that if enquiries had been made fifty or threescore years ago, many more particulars concerning these poems might have been learned, and many more living witnesses have been produced for attesting their authenticity; but that the manners of the inhabitants of the Highland counties have of late undergone a great change. Agriculture, trades, and manufactures, begin to take place of hunting, and the shepherd's life. The introduction of the busy and laborious arts has considerably abated that poetical enthusiasm which is better suited to a vacant and indolent state. The fondness of reciting their old poems decays; the custom of teaching them to their children is fallen into desuetude; and few are now to be found, except old men, who can rehearse from memory any considerable parts of them.

For these particulars, concerning the state of the Highlands and the transmission of Ossian's poems, I am indebted to the reverend and very learned and ingenious Mr. John Macpherson, minister of Slate in the Island of Sky, and to the reverend Mr. Donald Macqueen minister Kilmuir in Sky, Mr. Donald Macleod minister of Glenelg in Invernessshire, Mr. Lewis Grant minister of Duthel in Invernessshire, Mr. Angus Macneil minister of the Island of South Uist, Mr. Neil Macleod minister of Ross, in the Island of Mull, and Mr. Alexander Macaulay chaplain to the 88th Regiment.

The honourable colonel Hugh Mackay of Bighouse in the Shire of Sutherland, Donald Campbell of Airds in Argyleshire, Esq; Æneas Mackintosh of Mackintosh in Invernessshire, Esq; and Ronald Macdonell of Keappoch in Lochaber, Esq; captain in the 87th regiment commanded by colonel Fraser, all concur in testifying that Mr. Macpherson's collection consists of genuine Highland poems; known to them to be such, both from the general report of the country where they live, and from their own remembrance of the originals. Colonel Mackay asserts very positively, upon personal knowledge, that many of the poems published by Mr. Macpherson are true and faithful translations. Mr. Campbell declares that he has heard many of them, and captain Macdonell that he has heard parts of every one of them, recited in the original language.

James Grant of Rothiemurchus, Esq; and Alexander Grant, of Delrachny, Esq; both in the Shire of Inverness, desire to be named as vouchers for the poem of Fingal in particular. They remember to have heard it often in their younger days, and are positive that Mr. Macpherson has given a just translation of it.

Lauchlan Macpherson of Strathmashie in Invernessshire, Esq; gives a very full and explicit testimony, from particular knowledge, in the following words: That in the year 1760, he accompanied Mr. Macpherson during some part of his journey through the Highlands in search of the poems of Ossian; that he assisted him in collecting them; that he took down from oral tradition, and transcribed from old manuscripts by far the greatest part of those pieces Mr. Macpherson has published; that since the publication he has carefully compared the translation with the copies of the originals in his hands; and that he finds it amazingly literal, even to such a degree as often to preserve the cadence of the Galic versification. He affirms, that among the manuscripts which were at that time in Mr. Macpherson's possession, he saw one of as old a date as the year 1410.

Sir James Macdonald of Macdonald, in the Island of Sky, Baronet, assured me, that after having made, at my desire, all the enquiries he could in his part of the country, he entertained no doubt that Mr. Macpherson's collection consisted entirely of authentick Highland poems; that he had lately heard several parts of them repeated in the original, in the Island of Sky, with some variations from the printed translation, such as might naturally be expected from the circumstances of oral tradition; and some parts, in particular the episode of Fainasollis in the third book of Fingal, which agree literally with the translation; and added, that he had heard recitations of other poems not translated by Mr. Macpherson, but generally reputed to be of Ossian's composition, which were of the same spirit and strain with such as are translated, and which he esteemed not inferiour to any of them in sublimity of description, dignity of sentiment, or any other of the beauties of poetry. This last particular must have great weight; as it is well known how much the judgment of Sir James Macdonald deserves to be relied upon, in every thing that relates to literature and taste.[3]

The late reverend Mr. Alexander Macfarlane, minister of Arrachar in Dumbartonshire, who was remarkably eminent for his profound knowledge in Galic learning and antiquities, wrote to me soon after the publication of

Mr. Macpherson's work, terming it, a masterly translation; informing me that he had often heard several of these poems in the original, and remarked many passages so particularly striking beyond any thing he had ever read in any human composition, that he never expected to see a strength of genius able to do them thatjustice in a translation, which Mr. Macpherson has done.

Norman Macleod of Macleod, in the Island of Sky, Esq; Walter Macfarlane of Macfarlane in Dumbartonshire, Esq; Mr. Alexander Macmillan, deputy keeper of his Majesty's signet, Mr. Adam Fergusson, professor of moral philosophy in the University of Edinburgh, and many other gentlemen natives of the Highland counties, whom I had occasion to converse with upon this subject, declare, that though they cannot now repeat from memory any of these poems in the original, yet from what they have heard in their youth, and from the impression of the subject still remaining on their minds, they firmly believe those which Mr. Macpherson has published, to be the old poems of Ossian current in the country.

Desirous, however, to have this translation particularly compared with the oral editions of any who had parts of the original distinctly on their memory, I applied to several clergymen to make enquiry in their respective parishes concerning such persons; and to compare what they rehearsed with the printed version. Accordingly, from the reverend Mr. John Macpherson minister of Slate in Sky, Mr. Neil Macleod minister of Ross in Mull, Mr. Angus Macneil minister of South Uist, Mr. Donald Macqueen minister of Kilmuir in Sky, and Mr. Donald Macleod minister of Glenelg, I have had reports on this head, containing distinct and explicit testimonies to almost the whole epic poem of Fingal, from beginning to end, and to several also of the lesser poems, as rehearsed in the original, in their presence, by persons whose names and places of abode they mention, and compared by themselves with the printed translation. They affirm that in many places, what was rehearsed in their presence agreed literally and exactly with the translation. In some places they found variations from it, and variations even among different rehearsers of the same poem in the original; as words and stanzas omitted by some which others repeated, and the order and connection in some places changed. But they remark, that these variations are on the whole not very material; and that Mr. Macpherson seemed to them to follow the most just and authentic copy of the sense of his author. Some of these clergymen, particularly Mr. Neil Macleod, can themselves repeat from memory several passages of Fingal; the translation of which they assure me is exact. Mr. Donald Macleod acquaints me, that it was in his house Mr. Macpherson had the description of Cuchullin's horses and chariot, in the first book of Fingal, given him by Allan Macaskill schoolmaster. Mr Angus Macneil writes, that Mr. Macdonald, a parishioner of his, declares, that he has often seen and read a great part of an ancient manuscript, once in the possession of the family of Clanronald, and afterwards carried to Ireland, containing many of these poems; and that he rehearsed before him several passages out of Fingal, which agreed exactly with Mr. Macpherson's translation; that Neil Macmurrich, whose predecessors had for many generations been bards to the family of Clanronald, declared also in his presence, that he had often seen and read the same old manuscript; that he himself, gave to Mr. Macpherson a manuscript containing some of the poems which are now translated and published, and rehearsed before Mr. Macneil, in the original, the whole of the poem entitled Dar-thula, with very little variation from the printed translation. I have received the same testimony concerning this poem, Dar-thula, from Mr. Macpherson minister of Slate; and in a letter communicated to me from Lieutenant Duncan Macnicol, of the 88th regiment, informing me of its being recited in the original, in their presence, from beginning to end: On which I lay the more stress, as any person of taste who turns to that poem will see, that it is one of the most highly finished in the whole collection, and most distinguished for poetical and sentimental beauties: insomuch, that whatever genius could produce Dar-thula, must be judged fully equal to any performance contained in Mr. Macpherson's publication. I must add here, that though they who have compared the translation with what they have heard rehearsed in the original, bestow high praises both upon Mr. Macpherson's genius and his fidelity; yet I find it to be their general opinion, that in many places he has not been able to attain to the strength and sublimity of the original which he copied.

I have authority to say, in the name of Lieutenant Colonel Archibald Macnab of the 88th regiment, or regiment of Highland Voluntiers commanded by colonel Campbell, that he has undoubted evidence of Mr. Macpherson's collection being genuine, both from what he well remembers to have heard in his youth, and from his having heard very lately a considerable part of the poem of Temora rehearsed in the original, which agreed exactly with the printed version.

By the reverend Mr. Alexander Pope minister of Reay, in the shire of Caithness, I am informed, that twenty-four years ago, he had begun to make a collection of some of the old poems current in his part of the country; on comparing which, with Mr. Macpherson's work, he found in his collection the poem intitled, the battle of Lora, some parts of Lathmon, and the account of the death of Oscar. From the above mentioned Lieutenant Duncan Macnicol, testimonies have been also received to a great part of Fingal, to part of Temora, and Carric-thura, as well as to the whole of Dar-thula, as recited in his presence in the original, compared, and found to agree with the translation.

I myself read over the greatest part of the English version of the six books of Fingal, to Mr. Kenneth Macpherson of Stornoway in the Island of Lewis, merchant, in presence of the reverend Mr. Alexander Macaulay chaplain to the 88th regiment. In going along Mr. Macpherson vouched what was read

to be well known to him in the original, both the descriptions and the senti-
ments. In some places, though he remembered the story, he did not remem-
ber the words of the original; in other places, he remembered and repeated
the Galic lines themselves, which, being interpreted to me by Mr. Macaulay,
were found, upon comparison, to agree often literally with the printed ver-
sion, and sometimes with slight variations of a word or an epithet. This
testimony carried to me, and must have carried to any other who had been
present, the highest conviction; being precisely a testimony of that nature
which an Englishman well acquainted with Milton, or any favourite author,
would give to a foreigner, who shewed him a version of this author into his
own language, and wanted to be satisfied from what the Englishman could
recollect of the original, whether it was really a translation of Paradise Lost,
or a spurious work under that title which had been put into his hands.

The above-mentioned Mr. Alexander Macaulay, Mr. Adam Fergusson
professor of moral philosophy, and Mr. Alexander Fraser, governor to
Francis Stuart, Esq; inform me, that at several different times they were
with Mr. Macpherson, after he had returned from his journey through the
Highlands, and whilst he was employed in the work of translating; that they
looked into his manuscripts, several of which had the appearance of being
old; that they were fully satisfied of their being genuine Highland poems;
that they compared the translation in many places with the original; and
they attest it to be very just and faithful, and remarkably literal.

It has been thought worth while to bestow this attention on establishing
the authenticity of the works of Ossian, now in possession of the publick:
Because whatever rank they are allowed to hold as works of genius; what-
ever different opinions may be entertained concerning their poetical merit,
they are unquestionably valuable in another view; as monuments of the taste
and manners of an ancient age, as useful materials for enlarging our knowl-
edge of the human mind and character; and must, beyond all dispute, be
held as at least, one of the greatest curiosities, which have at any time
enriched the republick of letters. More testimonies to them might have been
produced by a more enlarged correspondence with the Highland counties:
But I apprehend, if any apology is necessary, it is for producing so many
names, in a question, where the consenting silence of a whole country, was
to every unprejudiced person, the strongest proof, that spurious composi-
tions, in the name of that country, had not been obtruded upon the world.

FINIS.

PREFACE to *The Poems of Ossian* (1773)

Without encreasing his genius, the Author may have improved his language, in the eleven years, that the following poems have been in the hands of the public. Errors in diction might have been committed at twenty-four, which the experience of a riper age may remove; and some exuberances in imagery may be restrained, with advantage, by a degree of judgment acquired in the progress of time. Impressed with this opinion, he ran over the whole with attention and accuracy; and, he hopes, he has brought the work to a state of correctness, which will preclude all future improvements.

The eagerness, with which these Poems have been received abroad, is a recompence for the coldness with which a few have affected to treat them at home. All the polite nations of Europe have transferred them into their respective languages; and they speak of him, who brought them to light, in terms that might flatter the vanity of one fond of fame. In a convenient indifference for a literary reputation, the Author hears praise without being elevated, and ribaldry, without being depressed. He has frequently seen the first bestowed too precipitately; and the latter is so faithless to its purpose, that it is often the only index to merit in the present age.

Though the taste, which defines genius, by the points of the compass, is a subject fit for mirth in itself, it is often a serious matter in the sale of a work. When rivers define the limits of abilities, as well the boundaries of countries, a Writer may measure his success, by the latitude under which he was born. It was to avoid a part of this inconvenience, that the Author is said, by some, who speak without any authority, to have ascribed his own productions to another name. If this was the case, he was but young in the art of deception. When he placed the poet in antiquity, the Translator should have been born on this side of the Tweed.

These observations regard only the frivolous in matters of literature; these, however, form a majority in every age and nation. In this country, men of genuine taste abound; but their still voice is drowned in the clamours of a multitude, who judge by fashion of poetry, as of dress. The truth is, to judge aright requires almost as much genius as to write well; and good critics are as rare as great poets. Though two hundred thousand Romans stood up, when Virgil came into the Theatre, Varius only could correct the Æneid. He that obtains fame must receive it through mere fashion; and gratify his vanity with the applause of men, of whose judgment he cannot approve.

The following Poems, it must be confessed, are more calculated to please persons of exquisite feelings of heart, than those who receive all their impressions by the ear. The novelty of cadence, in what is called a prose version, tho' not destitute of harmony, will not to common readers supply the absence of the frequent returns of rhime. This was the opinion of the Writer himself, tho' he yielded to the judgment of others, in a mode, which presented freedom and dignity of expression, instead of fetters, which cramp the thought, whilst the harmony of language is preserved. His intention was to publish in verse. The making of poetry, like any other handicraft, may be learned by industry; and he had served his apprenticeship, though in secret, to the muses.[1]

It is, however, doubtful, whether the harmony which these poems might derive from rhime, even in much better hands than those of the translator, could atone for the simplicity and energy, which they would lose. The determination of this point shall be left to the readers of this preface. The following is the beginning of a poem, translated from the Norse to the Gaëlic language; and, from the latter, transferred into English. The verse took little more time to the writer than the prose; and even he himself is doubtful (if he has succeeded in either) which of them is the most literal version.

FRAGMENT of a NORTHERN
TALE

Where Harold, with golden hair, spread o'er Lochlin[2] his high commands; where, with justice, he ruled the tribes, who sunk, subdued, beneath his sword; abrupt rises Gormal[3] in snow! The tempests roll dark on his sides, but calm, above, his vast forehead appears. White-issuing from the skirt of his storms, the troubled torrents pour down his sides. Joining, as they roar along, they bear the Torno, in foam, to the main.

Grey on the bank and far from men, half-covered by ancient pines, from the wind, a lonely pile exalts its head, long-shaken by the storms of the north. To this fled Sigurd, fierce in fight, from Harold the leader of armies, when fate had brightened his spear, with renown: When he conquered in that rude field, where Lulan's warriors fell in blood, or rose, in terror, on the waves of the main. Darkly sat the grey-haired chief; yet sorrow dwelt not in his soul. But when the warrior thought on the past, his proud heart heaved against his side: Forth-flew his sword from its place, he wounded Harold in all the winds.

One daughter, and only one, but bright in form and mild of soul, the last beam of the setting line, remained to Sigurd of all his race. His son, in Lulan's battle slain, beheld not his father's flight from his foes. Nor finished seemed the ancient line! The splendid beauty of bright-eyed Fithon, covered still the fallen king with renown. Her arm was white like Gormal's snow; her bosom whiter than the foam of the main, when roll the waves beneath the wrath of the winds. Like two stars were her radiant eyes, like two stars that rise on the deep, when dark tumult embroils the night. Pleasant are their beams aloft, as stately they ascend the skies.

Nor Odin forgot, in aught, the maid. Her form scarce equalled her lofty mind. Awe moved around her stately steps. Heroes loved - but shrunk away in their fears. Yet midst the pride of all her charms, her heart was soft, and her soul was kind. She saw the mournful with tearful eyes. Transient darkness arose in her breast. Her joy was in the chace. Each morning, when doubtful light wandered dimly on Lulan's waves, she rouzed the resounding woods, to Gormal's head of snow. Nor moved the maid alone, &c.

The same versified.

Where fair-haired Harold, o'er Scandinia reign'd
And held, with justice, what his valour gain'd,
Sevo, in snow, his rugged forehead rears
And, o'er the warfare of his storms, appears
Abrupt and vast.—White-wandering down his side
A thousand torrents, gleaming as they glide,
Unite below; and pouring through the plain
Hurry the troubled Torno to the main.
　　Grey, on the bank, remote from human kind,
By aged pines, half shelter'd from the wind,
A homely mansion rose, of antique form,
For ages batter'd by the polar storm.
To this fierce Sigurd fled, from Norway's lord,
When fortune settled, on the warrior's sword,
In that rude field, where Suecia's chiefs were slain,
Or forced to wander o'er the Bothnic main.
Dark was his life, yet undisturb'd with woes,
But when the memory of defeat arose,
His proud heart struck his side; he graspt the spear,
And wounded Harold in the vacant air.
　　One daughter only, but of form divine,
The last fair beam of the departing line,
Remain'd of Sigurd's race. His warlike son
Fell in the shock, which overturn'd the throne.
Nor desolate the house! Fionia's charms
Sustain'd the glory, which they lost in arms.
White was her arm, as Sevo's lofty snow,
Her bosom fairer, than the waves below,
When heaving to the winds. Her radiant eyes
Like two bright stars, exulting as they rise,
O'er the dark tumult of a stormy night
And gladd'ning heav'n, with their majestic light.
　　In nought is Odin to the maid unkind.
Her form scarce equals her exalted mind,
Awe leads her sacred steps where'er they move,
And mankind worship, where they dare not love.

But, mix'd with softness, was the virgin's pride,
Her heart had feelings, which her eyes deny'd.
Her bright tears started at another's woes,
While transient darkness on her soul arose.
    The chace she lov'd; when morn, with doubtful beam
Came dimly wandering o'er the Bothnic stream,
On Sevo's sounding sides, she bent the bow,
And rouz'd his forests to his head of snow.
Nor mov'd the maid alone; &c.

One of the chief improvements, on this edition, is the care taken, in arranging the poems in the order of time; so as to form a kind of regular history of the age to which they relate. The writer has now resigned them for ever to their fate. That they have been well received by the public, appears from an extensive sale; that they shall continue to be well received, he may venture to prophecy without the gift of that inspiration, to which poets lay claim. Through the medium of version upon version, they retain, in foreign languages, their native character of simplicity and energy. Genuine poetry, like gold, loses little, when properly transfused; but when a composition cannot bear the test of a literal version, it is a counterfeit which ought not to pass current. The operation must, however, be performed with skilful hands. A translator, who cannot equal his original, is incapable of expressing its beauties.

LONDON, Aug. 15, 1773.

REVISED ORDER IN EDITION OF 1773

Volume I

Preface

1)	Cath-loda [I-III]
2)	Comala
3)	Carric-thura
4)	Carthon
5)	Oina-morul
6)	Colna-dona
7)	Oithona
8)	Croma
9)	Calthon and Colmal
10)	The War of Caros
11)	Cathlin of Clutha
12)	Sul-malla of Lumon
13)	The War of Inis-thona
14)	The Songs of Selma
15)	Fingal [I-VI]
16)	Lathmon
17)	Dar-thula
18)	The Death of Cuthullin
19)	The Battle of Lora

Volume II

20) Temora [I-VIII]
21) Conlath and Cuthona
22) Berrathon
A Dissertation concerning the Æra of Ossian
A Dissertation concerning the Poems of Ossian
Critical Dissertation on the Poems of Ossian (Hugh Blair)

Secondary sources cited in editorial notes

GASKILL, Howard: 'What did James Macpherson really leave on display at his publisher's shop in 1762?', *Scottish Gaelic Studies*, 16 (1990), 67-89.

JIRICZEK, Otto L. (ed.): *James Macpherson's "Ossian". Faksimile-Neudruck der Erstausgabe von 1762/63 mit Begleitband: Die Varianten*, 3 vols (Heidelberg, 1940).
— 'Zur Bibliographie und Textgeschichte von Hugh Blairs Critical Dissertation on the Poems of Ossian', *Englische Studien*, 70 (1935), 181-89.

LAING, Malcolm (ed): *The Poems of Ossian, &c., containing the Poetical Works of James Macpherson, Esq., in Prose and Rhyme: with Notes and Illustrations*, 2 vols (Edinburgh, 1805; repr. 1971).

MEEK, Donald E.: 'The Gaelic Ballads of Scotland: Creativity and Adaptation', in *Ossian Revisited*, ed. H. Gaskill (Edinburgh, 1991), 19-48.

RAYNOR, David: 'Ossian and Hume', in *Ossian Revisited*, ed. H. Gaskill (Edinburgh, 1991), 147-63.

RIZZA, Steve: 'A Bulky and Foolish Treatise? Hugh Blair's "Critical Dissertation" Reconsidered', in *Ossian Revisited*, ed. H. Gaskill (Edinburgh, 1991), 129-46.

STAFFORD, Fiona: *The Sublime Savage: James Macpherson and the Poems of Ossian* (Edinburgh, 1988)

STERN, Ludwig Chr.: 'Die ossianischen Heldenlieder', *Zeitschrift für vergleichende Litteraturgeschichte*, 8 (1895), 50-86, 143-74.

THOMSON, Derick S.: *The Gaelic Sources of Macpherson's "Ossian"* (Edinburgh, 1952)

NOTES

Fragments of Ancient Poetry

1.   *The reference is to* Pharsalia, *1. 447 ff. Cf. Blair,* Dissertation, *p. 351. For the significance of the Latin tag, see Fiona Stafford,* Sublime Savage, *pp. 100 ff.*

2.   *According to his letter to Henry Mackenzie of 1797, Hugh Blair* "wrote the Preface ... in consequence of the conversations I had held with Mr Macpherson".

3.   *The translator had indeed seen such a poem, for instance in the important early 16th-century collection, the* Book of the Dean of Lismore, *whose preservation we owe to Macpherson.*

4.   *Echoed by Macpherson in both his* Dissertations - *see pp. 52, 215.*

5.   *Cf.* 'Carric-thura', *pp. 158 f.*

6.   oak of Branno;] oak; 1st ed.

7.   the place of thy rest,] where often thou sattest 1st ed.

8.   *Cf.* 'Carric-thura', *pp. 159 f.*

9.   alone.] as I sit alone. 1st ed.

10.   summer-storm,] summer-storm? 1st ed.

11.   comest thou ... to me?] *added* 2nd ed.

12.   thin-wavering] trembling 1st ed.

13.   no voice but] no voice is heard except 1st ed.

14.   voice] voice! 1st ed.

15.   *Cf.* 'Carric-thura', *pp. 163 f.*

16.   Like ... the hill.] In a line they descended the hill. 1st ed.

17.   They slowly came to land.] They came to land. 1st ed.

18.   Bend thy ... sighs.] *added* 2nd ed.

19.   *Cf.* 'Carric-thura', *p. 165.*

20.   thro'] through 1st ed.

21.   Appear ... from a cloud.] *added* 2nd ed.

22.   *The plot of this* Fragment, *itself based on an authentic ballad, is loosely adapted in the third Book of* 'Fingal' - *see pp. 77 f.*

23.   sons of the hill/sons of the mountain = *deer*

24.   oak] roe 1st ed.

25.   *Later inserted, with some emendation, as a footnote in the fragment of* 'Temora' *published in the* Fingal *volume in 1762 (here pp. 156 f.), but omitted from the completed epic in 1763. This* Fragment *was the first specimen of Celtic poetry produced by Macpherson for John Home in Moffat in 1759.*

26.   *In 1762 a new paragraph is inserted here - see p. 156.*

27.   crudled] curdled 1762

28.   Nothing was held by the ancient Highlanders more essential to their glory, than to die by the hand of some person worthy or renowned. This was the occasion of Oscur's contriving to be slain by his mistress, now that he was weary of life. In those early times, suicide was utterly unknown among that people, and no traces of it are found in the old poetry. Whence the translator suspects the account that follows of the daughter of Dargo killing herself, to be the interpolation of some later Bard. [M]
Note deleted 1762

29.   He came ... in his arms.] *added* 2nd ed.

30. *In a note to Book II of* 'Fingal', *Macpherson refers to this* Fragment *as* not the work of Ossian, though it is writ in his manner - *see p. 70, note 62.*

31. Supposed to be Fergus II. This fragment is reckoned not altogether so ancient as most of the rest. [M]

32. *Cf.* 'Songs of Selma', *p. 166.*

33. what shall ... in fight.] *added* 2nd ed.

34. No feeble ... the hill.] *added* 2nd ed.

35. *Cf.* 'Songs of Selma', *pp. 169 f.*

36. Dark is ... voice of music?] *added* 2nd ed.

37. top of the oak!] trees! 1st ed.

38. when Daura ... children died.] when Daura the lovely died. 1st ed.

39. Arindel, thy ... in a storm.] *added* 2nd ed.

40. hear, ... hear:] come, ... come; 1st ed.

41. dark] *added* **2nd ed.**

42. The oar ... expired.] *added* 2nd ed.

43. I saw ... moon.] *added* 2nd ed.

44. And left ... among women.] O lay me soon by her side. 1st ed.

45. Half-viewless,] Indistinct, 1st ed.

46. speak ... They] speak to me?—But they 1st ed.

47. *Cf.* 'Songs of Selma', *pp. 167 f.*

48. shall] shalt 1st ed. 2nd ed. (*corrected in* 'Songs of Selma', 1762)

49. *Added* 2nd ed.

50. This is the opening of the epic poem mentioned in the preface. The two following fragments are parts of some episodes of the same work. [M]
Cf. 'Fingal' I, *p. 50.*

51. The aspen or poplar tree. [M]

52. Garve signifies a man of great size. [M]
In the epic of 'Fingal', *Garve is rechristened* Swaran. *Curiously enough, this change is anticipated by Blair in his* Preface *to the* Fragments (Swarthan).

53. *Cf.* 'Fingal' I, *pp. 57 f.*

54. The signification of the names in this fragment are. Dubhchomar, a black, well shaped man; Muirne or Morna, a woman beloved by all. Cormac-cairbre, an un-equalled and rough warrior. Cromleach, a crooked hill. Mugruch, a surly gloomy man. Tarman, thunder. Moinie, soft in temper and person. [M]

55. *Cf.* 'Fingal' V, *p. 94.*

56. The signification of the names in this fragment are; Gealchossack, white-legged. Tuathal-Teachtmhar, the surly, but fortunate man. Lambhdearg, bloody-hand. Ulfadha, long-beard. Firchios, the conqueror of men. [M]

57. Allad is plainly a Druid consulted on this occasion. [M]

Advertisement to first edition of *Fingal*

1. *Macpherson's reticence is abandoned in 1763 with the appearance of* Temora: "The following poems are inscribed to the Earl of Bute, in obedience to whose commands, they were translated from the original Galic of Ossian, the son of Fingal, by his Lordship's most obedient, and most obliged, humble servant, James Macpherson." *Cf. also the more elaborate dedication in the 1765 edition, p. 41.*

Preface to first edition of *Fingal*

1.	*At this point Macpherson inserts a detailed plot-summary of* 'Fingal', *such as is found in the* Argument *preceding each individual* Book *in the 1765 edition. It has therefore been omitted here.*

2.	*The reference is to John Macpherson's* Critical Dissertations on the Origin ... of the Ancient Caledonians *which appeared posthumously in 1768. Cf. the* Dissertation *preceding* Temora, *p. 215, note 43.*

A Dissertation concerning the Antiquity, &c. of the Poems of Ossian

1.	*In the extensively revised edition of 1773 this is renamed:* 'A Dissertation concerning the Æra of Ossian'. *It should be noted that Macpherson's later revisions of both his* Dissertations *are based on this, the 1765 version. This is in contrast to the actual poems where he generally uses the originals of 1762 and 1763 as his point of departure.*

2.	Plin.1. 6. [M]

3.	Cæs. 1. 5. Tac. Agric. 1. 1.c.2. [M]

4.	Cæsar. Pomp. Mel. Tacitus. [M]

5.	Diod. Sic.1. 5. [M]

6.	extract.] extract; but even the ancient Germans themselves were Gauls. 1773

7.	By ... writer.] *deleted* 1773

8.	The Germans,] The present Germans, 1773

9.	Strabo, 1. 7. [M]

10.	ancient Daæ, ... Germany.] ancient Scandinavians, who crossed, in an early period, the Baltic. 1773

11.	Cæs. 1. 6. Liv. 1. 5. Tac. de mor. Germ. [M]

12.	it is certain,] anciently, 1773

13.	customs;] customs, till they were dissipated, in the Roman empire; 1773

14.	a cunning ... tribe of men] these priests 1773

15.	Cæs. 1. 6. [M]

16.	Fer-gubreth, *the man to judge.* [M]

17.	The poems that celebrate .. public.] The traditions concerning Trathal and Cormac, ancestors to Fingal, are full of the particulars of the fall of the Druids: a singular fate, it must be owned, of priests, who had once established their superstition! 1773

18.	the nobility] the better sort 1773

19.	as the poems ... call] as tradition ... calls 1773

20.	make ... Druids,] disliked the Druids, 1773

21.	mythology.] mythology. But gods are not necessary, when the poet has genius. [It is hard ...] 1773

22.	Had Ossian ... beings.] Had the poet brought down gods, as often as Homer hath done, to assist his heroes, his work had not consisted of eulogiums on men, but of hymns to superior beings. 1773

23.	To .... that write] Those who write 1773

24.	account for Ossian's ... own times.] excuse the author's silence concerning the religion of ancient times. 1773

25.	is the same ... endued with reason.] would betray ignorance of the history of mankind. 1773

26.   divinity.] divinity. The Indians, who worship no God, believe that he exists. [It would be ...] 1773

27.   to Ossian ... narrow mind,] to the author of these poems, 1773

28.   Ossian's] his 1773

29.   he had no knowledge ... religion.] he has not alluded to Christianity or any of its rites, in his poems; which ought to fix his opinions, at least, to an æra prior to that religion. Conjectures, on this subject, must supply the place of proof. 1773

30.   who were the more ready ... before.] who were ready to hearken to their doctrines, if the religion of the Druids was exploded long before. 1773

31.   Culdich. [M]

32.   This dispute is still extant,] This dispute, they say, is extant, 1773

33.   What ... times.] Tradition here steps in with a kind of proof. 1773

34.   Carac'huil, *terrible eye.* Carac-'healla, *terrible look.* Carac-challamh, *a sort of upper garment.* [M]

35.   in the poems of Ossian,] *deleted* 1773

36.   Car-avon, *Winding river.* [M]

37.   Ossian, ... Carun.] In one of the many lamentations of the death of Oscar, a battle which he fought against Caros, king of ships, on the banks of the winding Carun, is mentioned amongst his great actions. 1773

38.   in Ossian's poems,] *deleted* 1773

39.   in the poems] in traditions 1773

40.   Some people ... those times.] Some people may imagine, that the allusions to the Roman history might have been derived, by tradition, from learned men, more than from ancient poems. This must then have happened at least three hundred years ago, as these allusions are mentioned often in the compositions of those times. 1773

41.   to give ... remote.] to allude to the Roman times. 1773

42.   that he has advanced,] *deleted* 1773

43.   But should we ... ancestors.] *deleted* 1773

44.   authenticity] antiquity 1773

45.   the works of Ossian.] the more ancient poems. 1773

46.   His ... his] Their ... their 1773

47.   Tacitus de mor. Germ. [M]

48.   Abbé de la Blet[t]erie *Remarques sur la Germanie.* [M]

49.   *In 1773 the rest of the* 'Dissertation' *is omitted and replaced by the following concluding paragraph:* What is advanced, in this short Dissertation, it must be confessed, is mere conjecture. Beyond the reach of records, is settled a gloom, which no ingenuity can penetrate. The manners described, in these poems, suit the ancient Celtic times, and no other period, that is known in history. We must, therefore, place the heroes far back in antiquity; and it matters little, who were their cotemporaries in other parts of the world. If we have placed Fingal in his proper period, we do honour to the manners of barbarous times. He exercised every manly virtue in Caledonia, while Heliogabalus disgraced human nature at Rome.

50.   *The following two paragraphs - It is therefore ... ravages of time. - are found only in the 1765 edition. The 1762 original continues at this point:* It was a gentleman, who has himself made a figure in the poetical world, that gave him the first hint concerning a literal prose translation. He tried it at his desire, and the specimen was approved. Other gentlemen were earnest in exhorting him to bring more to the

light, and it is to their uncommon zeal that the world owes the Galic poems, if they have any merit.// It was at first intended to make a general collection of all the ancient pieces of genius to be found in the Galic language; but the translator had his reasons for confining himself to the remains of the works of Ossian. [The action of the poem ...]

51.   in a great measure] irrecoverably 1762
52.   of them] *added* 1765
53.   To speak of ... And all] To say anything concerning the poetical merit of the poems, would be an anticipation of the judgment of the public. The poem which stands first in the collection is truly epic. The characters are strongly marked, and the sentiments breathe heroism. The subject of it is an invasion of Ireland by Swaran king of Lochlin, which is the name of Scandinavia in the Galic language. Cuchullin, general of the Irish tribes in the minority of Cormac king of Ireland, upon intelligence of the invasion, assembled his forces near Tura, a castle on the coast of Ulster. The poem opens with the landing of Swaran, councils are held, battles fought, and Cuchullin is, at last, totally defeated. In the mean time, Fingal, king of Scotland, whose aid was sollicited before the enemy landed, arrived and expelled them from the country. This war, which continued but six days and as many nights, is, including the episodes, the whole story of the poem. The scene is the heath of Lena near a mountain called Cromleach in Ulster.// All [that can be said ...] 1762

Fingal Book I.

1.   *The more or less authentic* Cuchullin *(Cù Chulainn) is in the 1773 edition replaced throughout by* Cuthullin, *a change anticipated in Macpherson's first note to the 1765 edition (here note 3) on the basis of a fanciful etymology - cf. the fun poked at the Irish dog (= Gaelic* cù*) in the* Dissertation *preceding* Temora, *p. 221. In* 'Fragment' XIV, *on which the opening five paragraphs of* 'Fingal' *are based,* Cuchullin *is called* Cuchulaid.
2.   *The summarizing* Arguments *are an innovation introduced in* Temora (1763). *Those for* Fingal *in 1765 are taken more or less verbatim from the* Preface *to the first edition.*
3.   Cuchullin, or rather Cuth-Ullin, *the voice of Ullin,* a poetical name given the son of Semo by the bards, from his commanding the forces of the Province of Ulster against the Ferbolg or Belgæ, who were in possession of Connaught. Cuchullin when very young married Bragela the daughter of Sorglan, and passing over into Ireland, lived for some time with Connal, grandson by a daughter to Congal the petty king of Ulster. His wisdom and valour in a short time gained him such reputation, that in the minority of Cormac the supreme king of Ireland, he was chosen guardian to the young king, and sole manager of the war against Swaran king of Lochlin. After a series of great actions he was killed in battle somewhere in Connaught, in the twenty-seventh year of his age. He was so remarkable for his strength, that to describe a strong man it has passed into a proverb, "He has the strength of Cuchullin." They shew the remains of his palace at Dunscaich in the Isle of Skye; and a stone to which he bound his dog Luath, goes still by his name. [M] Cuchullin, or ... possession of Connaught.] Cuchullin the son of Semo and grandson to Caithbat a druid celebrated in tradition for his wisdom and valour. [Cuchullin when very young ...] 1762 1773
4.   leaf.] sound. 1773

5.   Cairbar or Cairbre signifies a strong man. [M]

6.   We may conclude from Cuchullin's applying so early for foreign aid, that the Irish were not then so numerous as they have since been; which is a great presumption against the high antiquities of that people. We have the testimony of Tacitus that one legion only was thought sufficient, in the time of Agricola, to reduce the whole island under the Roman yoke; which would not probably have been the case had the island been inhabited for any number of centuries before. [M]

Cuchullin having previous intelligence of the invasion intended by Swaran, sent scouts all over the coast of Ullin or Ulster, to give early notice of the first appearance of the enemy, at the same time that he sent Munan the son of Stirmal to implore the assistance of Fingal. He himself collected the flower of the Irish youth to Tura, a castle on the coast, to stop the progress of the enemy till Fingal should arrive from Scotland. [We may conclude ...] 1762

7.   Moran signifies many; and Fithil, or rather Fili, *an inferior bard.* [M]

8.   Fingal the son of Comhal, and Morna the daughter of Thaddu. His grandfather was Trathal, and great grandfather Trenmor, both of whom are often mentioned in the poem.—Trenmor, according to tradition, had two sons; Trathal, who succeeded him in the Kingdom of Morven, and Conar, called by the bards *Conar the great*, who was elected king of all Ireland, and was the ancestor of that Cormac who sat on the Irish throne when the invasion of Swaran happened. It may not be improper here to observe, that the accent ought always to be placed on the last syllable of Fingal. [M]

—Trenmor, according ... syllable of Fingal.] *(only)* 1765

9.   the king ... hills] Fingal, king of desarts, 1773

10.   on green Ullin's plains.] to green Erin of streams. 1773

11.   rock of ice.] glittering rock. 1773

12.   *In the 1762 edition (and only there) Macpherson draws attention to the parallel with Milton*: ——His ponderous shield/ Behind him cast; the broad circumference/ Hung on his shoulders like the Moon. [*Paradise Lost*, 1.284 ff.].

13.   his dark host ... around him.] like a cloud of mist on the silent hill. 1762 1773

14.   *This makes more sense in 'Fragment' XIV where* Swaran *is still called* Garve *(Gaelic garbh = rough, thick, brawny - cf. above, p. 28, note 52).*

15.   windy walls.] walls of wind. 1762

16.   of stormy hills.] of Selma of storms? 1773

17.   Meal-mór—*a great hill.* [M]

18.   strife.] side. 1773

19.   Malmor.] his land! 1773

20.   Cabait, or rather Cathbait, grandfather to the hero, was so remarkable for his valour, that his shield was made use of to alarm his posterity to the battles of the family. We find Fingal making the same use of his own shield in the 4th book.—— A horn was the most common instrument to call the army together before the invention of bagpipes. [M]

In the text of 1773 Cabait *becomes* Semo, *without this change being reflected in the note, which remains the same, apart from the omission of* before the invention of bagpipes. *For a similar inconsistency, cf. below, note 28.*

21.   Cu-raoch signifies *the madness of battle.* [M]

22.   Cruth-geal——*fair-complexioned.* [M]

23.   Cu-thón—*the mournful sound of waves.* [M]

24. like] *deleted* 1773
25. Crom-leach signified a place of worship among the Druids. It is here the proper name of a hill on the coast of Ullin or Ulster. [M]
26. [*gr.q.*] Homer, Il. 5. v. 522. So when th' embattled clouds in dark array,/ Along the skies their gloomy lines display;/ The low-hung vapours motionless and still/ Rest on the summits of the shaded hill. POPE. [M]
Note deleted 1773
27. Shall] Or shall 1762 1773
28. Ireland so called from a colony that settled there called Falans.—Innis-fail, *i.e.* the island of the Fa-il or Falans. [M]
In the text of 1773 Inis-fail *is changed here (and throughout) to* Erin, *though the note - absurdly - remains the same. Cf. above, note 20.*
29. Connal, the friend of Cuchullin, was the son of Cathbait prince of Tongorma or the *island of the blue waves*, probably one of the Hebrides. His mother was Fioncoma the daughter of Congal. He had a son by Foba of Conachar-nessar, who was afterwards king of Ulster. For his services in the war against Swaran he had lands conferred on him, which, from his name, were called Tir-chonnuil or Tir-connel, *i.e.* the land of Connal. [M]
Cathbait] Caithbait 1773
king of Ulster.] petty king of Ulster. 1773
Cf. 'Death of Cuchullin', *p. 135, note 2.*
30. wilt thou lift] shalt thou lift up 1762
31. Erin, a name of Ireland; from *ear* or *iar* West, and *in* an island. This name was not always confined to Ireland, for there is the highest probability that the *Ierne* of the ancients was Britain to the North of the Forth.—For Ierne is said to be to the North of Britain, which could not be meant of Ireland. STRABO, l. 2. & 4. CASAUB. l. 1. [M]
32. like] *deleted* 1773
33. Cálm-er, *a strong man*. [M]
34. The Galic name of Scandinavia in general; in a more confined sense that of the peninsula of Jutland. [M]
general; ... Jutland.] general. 1773
35. Innis-tore, *the island of whales*, the ancient name of the Orkney islands. [M]
36. of the heath!] of Lara of hinds! 1773
37. the oaks ... shore.] and Morven ecchoes over all her oaks! 1773
38. Cathbat] Câthba 1773
39. Dubhchomar, *a black well-shaped man*. [M]
Duchomar] Duchômar 1773
40. Fear-guth,—*the man of the word*, or a commander of an army. [M]
41. Be thou like a roe or young hart on the mountains of Bether. SOLOMON's Song. [ii.17] [M]
Note deleted 1773
42. This passage alludes to the manner of burial among the ancient Scots. They opened a grave six or eight feet deep: the bottom was lined with fine clay; and on this they laid the body of the deceased, and, if a warrior, his sword, and the heads of twelve arrows by his side. Above they laid another stratum of clay, in which they placed the horn of a deer, the symbol of hunting. The whole was covered with a fine

mold, and four stones placed on end to mark the extent of the grave. These are the four stones alluded to here. [M]

43.   on the hill.] in Erin. 1773

44.   like] *deleted* 1773

45.   death to the people.] the death of thousands along. 1773

46.   the chiefs of Cromla] the strong in arms 1773

47.   The grave.——The house appointed for all living. JOB. [xxx.23]. [M]
Note deleted 1773

48.   Muirne or Morna, *a woman beloved by all*. [M]
The affecting episode of Morna *is the subject of* 'Fragment' XV.

49.   Cormac-cairbar.] strong-armed Cormac! 1773

50.   But ... Cromla.] But thou art snow on the heath; thy hair is the mist of Cromla. 1773

51.   like] *deleted* 1773

52.   white-armed] fair-haired 1773

53.   Torman, *Thunder*. This is the true origin of the Jupiter Taramis of the ancients. [M]

54.   said, his ... sword.] said, long shall Morna wait for Câthba! Behold this sword unsheathed! Here wanders the blood of Câthba. [Long ...] 1773

55.   said the maid ... eye.] said the wildly bursting voice of the maid. 1773

56.   heath;] hill; 1762 hills, 1773

57.   She alludes to his name——*the dark man*. [M]

58.   blood] wandering blood 1773

59.   Duchomar.] me in youth! 1773

60.   Moina, *soft in temper and person*. [M]

61.   groans.] sighs. 1762 1773

62.   It was the opinion then, as indeed it is to this day, of some of the highlanders, that the souls of the deceased hovered round their living friends; and sometimes appeared to them when they were about to enter on any great undertaking. [M]

63.   HOM. [*gr.q.*]. As torrents roll encreas'd by numerous rills/ With rage impetuous down the ecchoing hills;/ Rush to the vales, and pour'd along the plain,/ Roar thro' a thousand channels to the main. POPE. *Aut ubi decursu rapido de montibus altis,/ Dant sonitum spumosi amnes, & in æquora currunt,/ Quisque suum populatus iter.* VIRG. [M]
No references are given. They appear to be to Iliad, *4.452 ff. (cf.11.492 ff.);* Æneid, *12.523 ff.; cf. also below, note 77.*
Note deleted 1773

64.   steep] deep 1773 (*error repeated in subsequent editions*)

65.   rolling above, ... hill.] travelling above, and dark-brown night sits on half the hill. Through the breaches of the tempest look forth the dim faces of ghosts. [So fierce ...] 1773

66.   winter-stream.] winter-storm 1773

67.   As when the hollow rocks retain/ The sound of blustering wind. MILTON [M]
(only) 1762

68.   *For the authentic sources and the resonance of the following passage amongst contemporaries, see Thomson, pp. 19 f.*

69.   golden] sun-streaked 1773

70.   high-leaping] wide-leaping 1773

71. on the heath.] on a ridge of rocks. 1773
72. dark-maned,] thin-maned 1762 1773
73. A hill of Lochlin. [M] *(only)* 1765
74. strong stormy son] strong-armed son 1773
75. son of Arno,] *deleted* 1773
76. woods] pines 1773
77. The reader may compare this passage with a similar one in Homer, *Iliad.* 4, v. 446. Now shield with shield, with helmet helmet clos'd,/ To armour armour, lance to lance oppos'd,/ Host against host, with shadowy squadrons drew,/ The sounding darts in iron tempests flew,/ With streaming blood the slipp'ry fields are dy'd,/ And slaughter'd heroes swell the dreadful tide. POPE. Statius has very happily imitated Homer. *Jam clypeus clypeis, umbone repellitur umbo,/ Ense minax ensis, pede pes, & cuspide cuspis, &c.* Arms on armour crashing, bray'd/ Horrible discord, and the madding wheels/ Of brazen chariots rag'd, &c. MILTON. [M]
Note deleted 1773
78. As two dark] Like two deep 1773
79. twang] murmur 1762 1773
80. Sithallin signifies *a handsome man*;—Fiòna, *a fair maid*;—and Ardan, *pride.* [M]
Sithallin] Sithâllin 1773
81. The Isle of Sky; not improperly called the *isle of mist*, as its high hills, which catch the clouds from the western ocean, occasion almost continual rains. [M]
82. One of Cuchullin's horses. Dubhstron-gheal. [M]
83. Sith-fadda, *i.e. a long stride.* [M]
84. *The maid of Inistore* was the daughter of Gorlo king of Inistore or Orkney islands. Trenar was brother to the king of Iniscon, supposed to be one of the islands of Shetland. The Orkneys and Shetland were at that time subject to the king of Lochlin. We find that the dogs of Trenar are sensible at home of the death of their master, the very instant he is killed.——It was the opinion of the times, that the souls of heroes went immediately after death to the hills of their country, and the scenes they frequented the most happy time of their life. It was thought too that dogs and horses saw the ghosts of the deceased. [M]
85. spirit] ghost 1762 1773
86. the youth] thy love 1773
87. heath] hill 1773
88. so Innis-fail met Swaran.] so Erin met Swaran of spears. 1773
89. As when two black clouds/ With heaven's artillery fraught, come rattling on/ Over the Caspian. MILTON [*Paradise Lost*, 2.714 ff.] [M]
Note deleted 1773
90. The ancient manner of preparing feasts after hunting, is handed down by tradition.——A pit lined with smooth stones was made; and near it stood a heap of smooth flat stones of the flint kind. The stones as well as the pit were properly heated with heath. Then they laid some venison in the bottom, and a stratum of the stones above it; and thus they did alternately till the pit was full. The whole was covered over with heath to confine the steam. Whether this is probable I cannot say; but some pits are shewn, which the vulgar say, were used in that manner. [M]
91. Cean-feana, *i.e. the head of the people.* [M]
92. Ullin's] Erin's 1773

93. him that came from] him from 1762 1773

94. Ossian the son of Fingal and author of the poem. One cannot but admire the address of the poet in putting his own praise so naturally into the mouth of Cuchullin. The Cona here mentioned is perhaps that small river that runs through Glenco in Argyleshire. One of the hills which environ that romantic valley is still called Scornafena, or the hill of Fingal's people. [M]
Ossian ... mouth of Cuchullin.] *deleted* 1773

95. This episode is introduced with propriety. Calmar and Connal, two of the Irish heroes, had disputed warmly before the battle about engaging the enemy. Carril endeavours to reconcile them with the story of Cairbar and Grudar; who, tho' enemies before, fought *side by side* in the war. The poet obtained his aim, for we find Calmar and Connal perfectly reconciled in the third book. [M]

96. Golb-bhean, as well as Cromleach, signifies *a crooked hill*. It is here the name of a mountain in the county of Sligo. [M]
It is ... Sligo.] *(only)* 1765

97. Lubar—a river in Ulster. *Labhar*, loud, noisy. [M]

98. like a sun-beam,] *deleted* 1773

99. Brassolis signifies *a woman with a white breast*. [M]

100. night.] night, when its edge heaves white on the view, from the darkness, which covers its orb. [Her voice ...] 1773

101. these two lonely yews, ... high.] these two lonely yews sprung from their tombs, and wish to meet on high. 1762 these lonely yews sprung from their tombs, and shade them from the storm. 1773
In 1762 and 1773 sprung *is preterite, in 1765 presumably past participle. Laing (1:48, n. 74) suspects the radical alteration of the second clause in 1773 to have been provoked by Blair's criticism that the* "sympathy of the trees with the lovers, might be reckoned to border on an Italian conceit; and it is somewhat curious to find this single instance of that sort of wit in our Celtic poetry." *- see above,, p. 381.*

102. Homer compares soft piercing words to the fall of snow. [*gr.q.*] [*Iliad* 3.222 f.] But when he speaks, what elocution flows!/ Like the soft fleeces of descending snows. POPE. [M]
Note deleted 1773

103. Dunscaich.] Dunscaith 1773

104. Bragéla was the daughter of Sorglan, and the wife of Cuchullin.—Cuchullin, upon the death of Artho, supreme king of Ireland, passed over into Ireland, probably by Fingal's order, to take upon him the administration of affairs in that kingdom during the minority of Cormac the son of Artho. He left his wife Bragéla in Dunscaich, the seat of the family, in the isle of Sky, where the remains of his palace is still shewn; and a stone, to which he bound his dog Luath, goes still by his name. [M] *(only)* 1765
He left ... by his name.] *cf. above, note 3.*

105. sigh] sing 1784-85 *(and subsequent editions)*
A miscorrection of sign *(owing to a defective* h *in the edition of 1773 - see Jiriczek, 3:60)*

106. raven-hair] flowing hair 1773

107. of the desart] of Selma 1773

108. It was long the opinion of the ancient Scots, that a ghost was heard shrieking near the place where a death was to happen soon after. The accounts given, to this

day, among the vulgar, of this extraordinary matter, are very poetical. The ghost comes mounted on a meteor, and surrounds twice or thrice the place destined for the person to die; and then goes along the road through which the funeral is to pass, shrieking at intervals; at last, the meteor and ghost disappear above the burial place. [M]

The 1773 edition, here as often elsewhere, turns the similes into metaphors: His spear is a blasted pine. His shield the rising moon.

Fingal Book II.

1.　The scene of Connal's repose is familiar to those who have been in the Highlands of Scotland. The poet removes him to a distance from the army, to add more horror to the description of Crugal's ghost by the loneliness of the place. It perhaps will not be disagreeable to the reader, to see how two other ancient poets handled a similar subject. [*gr.q.*] HOM. Il. 23. When lo! the shade, before his closing eyes,/ Of sad Patroclus rose or seem'd to rise,/ In the same robe he living wore, he came/ In stature, voice, and pleasing look the same./ The form familiar hover'd o'er his head,/ And sleeps Achilles thus? the phantom said. POPE. [*l.q.*] Æn. lib. 2. When Hector's ghost before my sight appears:/ A bloody shroud he seem'd, and bath'd in tears./ Such as he was, when, by Pelides slain,/ Thessalian coursers drag'd him o'er the plain./ Swoln were his feet, as when the thongs were thrust/ Through the bor'd holes, his body black with dust./ Unlike that Hector, who return'd from toils/ Of war triumphant, in Æacian spoils:/ Or him, who made the fainting Greeks retire,/ And launch'd against their navy Phrygian fire./ His hair and beard stood stiffen'd with his gore;/ And all the wounds he for his country bore. DRYDEN. [M]

The scene ... familiar] The scene here described will appear natural 1773

As Laing points out (1:57, n.1) the original use of is familiar *might suggest Macpherson's having forgotten that he has set the scene in Ireland. As usual the 1773 edition omits the references to Homer and Virgil.*

2.　coming] rushing 1773

3.　like] *deleted* 1773

4.　son of the hill?] the departed Crugal? 1773

5.　ghost,] spirit 1773

6.　Ullin.] Erin 1773

7.　Connal the son of Caithbat, the friend of Cuchullin, is sometimes, as here, called the son of Colgar; from one of that name who was the founder of his family. [M] (*only*) 1765

Cf. 'Death of Cuchullin', *p. 138.*

8.　[*gr.q.*] HOM. Il. 23. v. 100. Like a thin smoke he sees the spirit fly,/ And hears a feeble, lamentable cry. POPE. [M]

Note deleted 1773

9.　and ride ... desart.] and scarcely seen, pass over the desert? 1773

10.　like the son of heaven.] like the sun of heaven. 1762 the sun of heaven! 1773

That the aberrant son *of 1765 might be a misprint - cf.* 'Fingal' IV, *p. 84 - is suggested by the obviously correct* sun of heaven *in* 'Carthon'; *not to mention the obviously incorrect* son-beam *initially perpetrated on p. 69 (note 58). On the other hand, at the beginning of* 'Carthon', *the sun is addressed as* son of the sky, *and* son of heaven *may be found in all three editions in the second book of* 'Temora' - *see p. 242.*

11. Dunscaich;] Erin! 1773
12. in the caves of Lena.] across thy ear. 1773
13. The poet teaches us the opinions that prevailed in his time concerning the state of separate souls. From Connal's expression, "That the stars dim-twinkled through the form of Crugal," and Cuchullin's reply, we may gather that they both thought the soul was material; something like the εἴδωλον of the ancient Greeks. [M]
14. hand; yet will I not] hand, yet I will not 1762 hand! yet I will not 1773
15. shield of Caithbat, it] shield. It 1773
16. of the stormy hills;] of his stormy isles; 1773
17. ——As when heaven's fire/ Hath scath'd the forest oaks, or mountain pines/ With singed tops, their stately growth tho' bare/ Stand on the blasted heath. MILTON. [*Paradise Lost*, 1.612 ff.] [M]
Note deleted 1773
18. blue, gray mist] blue mist 1773
19. and ... silent.] and silence spread over his isle. 1773
20. rose] rose rustling 1773
21. moved ... groves.] moved stately before them the king. 1773
22. beam.] beam! Dimly gleam the hills around, and shew indistinctly their oaks! 1773
23. Innis-fail] Erin 1773
This change is frequent, but not consistent. In the first edition the spelling is usually Inisfail, *in 1773* Inis-fail.
24. shore.] coast; when mariners, on shores unknown, are trembling at veering winds! 1773
25. Swart,] Swarth, 1773
26. the king of shields,] the youth along! 1773
27. son,] chief 1773
28. Ullin's lovely] Erin's streamy 1773
29. of Dunscaich;] of my love. 1773
30. Ullin] Erin 1773
31. Innis-fail,] Erin 1773
32. ——As evening mist/ Ris'n from a river o'er the marish glides/ And gathers ground fast at the lab'rer's heel/ Homeward returning MILTON [*Paradise Lost*, 12.629 ff.] [M]
Note deleted 1773
33. rolled along ... valley,] poured along, as mist that is rolled on a valley, 1773
34. The chief] Cuthullin 1773
35. The ancient Scots, as well as the present highlanders, drunk in shells; hence it is that we so often meet, in the old poetry, with the *chief of shells*, and *the halls of shells*. [M]
36. Crugal had married Degrena but a little time before the battle, consequently she may with propriety be called a stranger in the hall of her sorrow. [M]
37. Deo-ghréna signifies a *sun-beam*. [M]
38. Green,] Pale, 1773
39. *Mediisque in millibus ardet.* VIRG. [*Æneid*, 1.491] [M]
Note deleted 1773
40. firs] pines 1773

41.   Virgil and Milton have made use of a comparison similar to this; I shall lay both before the reader, and let him judge for himself which of these two great poets have best succeeded. [*l.q.*] [*Æneid*,12.701 ff.] Like Eryx or like Athos great he shews/ Or father Appenine when white with snows;/His head divine obscure in clouds he hides,/ And shakes the sounding forest on his sides. DRYDEN. On th' other side Satan alarm'd,/ Collecting all his might, dilated stood/ Like Teneriff or Atlas unremov'd;/ His stature reach'd the sky. MILTON. [*Paradise Lost*, 4.985 ff.] [M]
Note deleted 1773

42.   Innis-fail,] Erin 1773

43.   of light.] of gems. 1773

44.   heaven.] heaven; and dreadful change is expected by men. 1773

45.   Dusronnal] Stronnal 1762 Sronnal 1773

46.   night.] night; distant, withered, dark they stand, with not a leaf to shake in the gale. 1773

47.   lovely] *deleted* 1773

48.   chief ... hinds.] king of resounding Selma! 1773

49.   like] *deleted* 1773

50.   pleasant] pleasing, in grief, 1773

51.   the noble son of Damman.] the son of the noble Damman. 1773

52.   of the hill.] of heaven. 1773

53.   Muri, say the Irish bards, was an academy in Ulster for teaching the use of arms. The signification of the word is a *cluster of people*; which renders the opinion probable. Cuchullin is said to have been the first who introduced into Ireland complete armour of steel. He is famous, among the Senachies, for teaching horsemanship to the Irish, and for being the first who used a chariot in that kingdom; which last circumstance was the occasion of Ossian's being so circumstantial in his description of Cuchullin's car, in the first book. [M]
Muri, ... in the first book.] An academy in Ulster for teaching the use of arms. 1762 A place in Ulster. 1773

54.   the noble son of Damman.] the son of noble Damman. 1773

55.   snow-white bull] bull of snow 1762

56.   him,] the chief, 1773

57.   hills] plain 1773

58.   sun-beam] son-beam 1765

59.   He ... Malmor.] He is a rock on Malmor. 1773

60.   like] *deleted* 1773

61.   Grumal] Gormal 1762 1765 (*misprint*)

62.   The unfortunate death of this Ronan is the subject of the ninth fragment of ancient poetry published last year [*1760*]; it is not the work of Ossian, though it is writ in his manner, and bears the genuine marks of antiquity.—The concise expressions of Ossian are imitated, but the thoughts are too jejune and confined to be the production of that poet.—Many poems go under his name that have been evidently composed since his time; they are very numerous in Ireland, and some have come to the translator's hands. They are trivial and dull to the last degree; swelling into ridiculous bombast, or sinking into the lowest kind of prosaic style. [M]
Note deleted 1773

63.   Galvina] Galbina 1773 (*in text, but not in the* Argument)

64.   white] fair 1773
65.   the feathered dart.] the arrow he threw. 1762 1773

Fingal Book III.

1.   The second night, since the opening of the poem, continues; and Cuchullin, Connal, and Carril still sit in the place described in the preceding book. The story of Agandecca is introduced here with propriety, as great use is made of it in the course of the poem, and as it, in some measure, brings about the catastrophe. [M]
2.   Tura:] Selma: 1773
3.   man] dweller 1773
4.   like] *deleted* 1773
5.   Starno was the father of Swaran as well as Agandecca.——His fierce and cruel character is well marked in other poems concerning the times. [M]
6.   hall] halls 1765
7.   This passage most certainly alludes to the religion of Lochlin, and *the stone of power* here mentioned is the image of one of the deities of Scandanavia. [M]
8.   Fingal king of the desart;] the king of Selma; 1773
9.   to Albion's windy hills:] to Selma's hall: 1773
10.   went.] attended his steps. 1773
11.   before him] to the maid, 1773
12.   lonely] distant 1773
13.   The king of snow] Starno 1773
Starno is here poetically called the king of snow, from the great quantities of snow that fall in his dominions. [M]
Note deleted 1773
14.   hero.] king. 1773
15.   the hill of Cona.] resounding Cona. 1773
16.   of snow;] of the snow; 1762 of Lochlin; 1773
17.   All the North-west coast of Scotland probably went of old under the name of Morven, which signifies a ridge of very high hills. [M]
18.   like] *deleted* 1773
19.   Morven.] resounding Morven. 1773
20.   spear of Fingal ... Gormal.] spear of Selma was red in blood. 1773
Gormal is the name of a hill in Lochlin, in the neighbourhood of Starno's palace. [M] (*only*) 1765
21.   with her loose raven locks.] with loosely flowing locks. 1773
22.   sighs,] broken sighs, 1773
23.   raven hair.] softest soul. 1773
24.   round ... Agandecca.] round her narrow dwelling. 1773
25.   This is the only passage in the poem that has the appearance of religion.——But Cuchullin's apostrophe to this spirit is accompanied with a doubt; so that it is not easy to determine whether the hero meant a superior being, or the ghosts of deceased warriors, who were supposed in those times to rule the storms, and to transport themselves in a gust of wind from one country to another. [M]
26.   Alclétha, her lamentation over her son is introduced in the poem concerning the death of Cuchullin, printed in this collection. [M] (*only*) 1765
27.   when ... grass.] to lighten, to restore the isle! 1773
28.   warrior; he] chief. He 1773

29.   Lara's hall,] Lara, 1773
30.   sad.] sad; the soul of the lonely Alcletha, waining [*sic*] in the sorrow of years.
[But slowly ...] 1773
31.   the plains of Cona.] the plain. 1773
32.   [*gr.q.*] HOM. Il. 15. [610 ff.] So some tall rock o'erhangs the hoary main,/ By
winds assail'd, by billows beat in vain,/ Unmov'd it hears, above, the tempests
blow,/ And sees the watry mountains break below. POPE. [M]
Note deleted 1773
33.   king of ... hill.] king. 1773
34.   of Innis-fail!] of Erin's race! 1773
35.   the dark mighty man;] the mighty stranger. 1773
36.   flew like lightning;] as lightning gleamed along: 1773
37.   him.] him. Dimly seen, as lightens the night, he strides largely from hill to
hill. [Bloody was ...] 1773
38.   Myself,] Ossian, 1773
Here the poet celebrates his own actions, but he does it in such a manner that we
are not displeased. The mention of the great actions of his youth immediately
suggests to him the helpless situation of his age. We do not despise him for selfish
praise, but feel his misfortunes. [M]
Note deleted 1773
39.   his aged locks, and his] his locks; his 1773
40.   lovely] valiant 1773
41.   arms:] arm: 1762 1773
42.   What the Craca here mentioned was, is not, at this distance of time, easy to
determine. The most probable opinion is, that it was one of the Shetland isles.—
There is a story concerning a daughter of the king of Craca in the sixth book. [M]
Cf. p. 102. The episode of Fainasóllis *is an adaptation of the subject of* 'Fragment'
VI, *itself based on authentic sources (and closer to them) - see Thomson, pp. 29 ff.*
43.   O chief] O prince 1762 1773
44.   chief of shells,] chief of the generous shells 1762 1773
45.   like] *deleted* 1773
46.   rolling] roaring 1773
47.   the unhappy children] the hapless lovers 1762 1773
48.   ye children of the race;] ye, that are swift in the race! 1773
49.   of roaring winds;] in my presence 1773
50.   like ... Cona.] like distant sounds in woods. 1773
51.   of the storm] of war 1773
52.   Gaul, the son of Morni, was chief of a tribe that disputed long, the pre-
eminence, with Fingal himself. They were reduced at last to obedience, and Gaul,
from an enemy, turned Fingal's best friend and greatest hero. His character is some-
thing like that of Ajax in the Iliad; a hero of more strength than conduct in battle.
He was very fond of military fame, and here he demands the next battle to him-
self.—The poet, by an artifice, removes Fingal, that his return may be the more
magnificent. [M]
53.   The poet prepares us for the dream of Fingal in the next book. [M]
54.   the now mournful] *deleted* 1773

Fingal Book IV.

1.   Fingal being asleep, and the action suspended by night, the poet introduces the story of his courtship of Evirallin the daughter of Branno. The episode is necessary to clear up several passages that follow in the poem; at the same time that it naturally brings on the action of the book, which may be supposed to begin about the middle of the third night from the opening of the poem.——This book, as many of Ossian's other compositions, is addressed to the beautiful Malvina the daughter of Toscar. She appears to have been in love with Oscar, and to have affected the company of the father after the death of the son. [M]

For the authentic Gaelic sources of Ossian's courtship of Evirallin, see Thomson, pp. 31 ff.

2.   sorrow.] grief! 1773

3.   love of Cormac.] daughter of Branno! 1773

4.   Duma-riccan's] Dumariccan's 1762 1773

5.   pierced] broke on 1762 1773

6.   The poet addresses himself to Malvina the daughter of Toscar. [M] *(only)* 1765

7.   The poet returns to his subject. If one could fix the time of the year in which the action of the poem happened, from the scene described here, I should be tempted to place it in autumn.—The trees shed their leaves, and the winds are variable, both which circumstances agree with that season of the year. [M]

8.   chief] prince 1762 1773

9.   Ossian gives the reader a high idea of himself. His very song frightens the enemy. This passage resembles one in the eighteenth Iliad, where the voice of Achilles frightens the Trojans from the body of Patroclus.—Forth march'd the chief, and distant from the crowd/ High on the rampart rais'd his voice aloud./ So high his brazen voice the hero rear'd,/ Hosts drop their arms and trembled as they fear'd. POPE. [M]

Note deleted 1773

10.   lovely in] pleasant to 1773

11.   son] sun 1762 1773

Cf. above, p. 65, note 10.

12.   thou daughter] fair wanderer 1773

13.   of the storm.] of ecchoing Selma! 1773

14.   cloud, ... Cona.] cloud on Cona's eddying winds. 1773

15.   king of hills] king of Selma 1773

16.   graceful] *deleted* 1773

17.   son] red son 1773

18.   Ossian never fails to give a fine character of his beloved son. His speech to his father is that of a hero; it contains the submission due to a parent, and the warmth that becomes a young warrior. There is a propriety in dwelling here on the actions of Oscar, as the beautiful Malvina, to whom the book is addressed, was in love with that hero. [M]

Note deleted 1773

19.   The war-song of Ullin varies from the rest of the poem in the versification. It runs down like a torrent; and consists almost intirely of epithets. The custom of encouraging men in battle with extempore rhymes, has been carried down almost to our own times. Several of these war-songs are extant, but the most of them are only

a group of epithets, without beauty or harmony, utterly destitute of poetical merit. [M]

The war-song ... epithets.] *deleted* 1773

20.   of the desart] of Selma 1773

21.   shower.] shower. Silence attends its slow progress aloft; but the tempest is soon to arise. [Swaran beheld ...] 1773

22.   Th' imperial ensign, which full high advanc'd,/ Shone like a meteor streaming to the wind. MILTON. [*Paradise Lost*, 1.534 f.] [M]

Note deleted 1773

23.   steel] blades 1762 shields 1773

24.   Fingal's standard was distinguished by the name of *sun-beam*; probably on account of its bright colour, and its being studded with gold. To begin a battle is expressed, in old composition, by *lifting of the sun-beam*. [M]

For the authentic background, see Meek, p. 43.

25.   of the hill] of Selma 1773

26.   are blowing.] blow on her ruffled wing. 1773

27.   [*l.q*] VIRG. [*Georg.* 1.440 ff.] Above the rest the sun, who never lies,/ Foretels the change of weather in the skies./ For if he rise, unwilling to his race,/ Clouds on his brow and spots upon his face;/ Or if thro' mists he shoots his sullen beams,/ Frugal of light, in loose and straggling streams,/ Suspect a drisling day. DRYDEN. [M]

Note deleted 1773

28.   [*l.q*.] VIRG. [*Georg.* 1.356 ff.] For ere the rising winds begin to roar,/ The working seas advance to wash the shore;/ Soft whispers run along the leafy wood,/ And mountains whistle to the murm'ring flood. DRYDEN. [M]

Note deleted 1773

29.   [*l.q*.] VIRG. [*Æneid*, 4.165] The rapid rains, descending from the hills,/ To rolling torrents swell the creeping rills. DRYDEN. [M]

Note deleted 1773

30.   daughter of the hill,] daughter of Toscar, 1773

31.   for bloody was the blue steel] for bloody were the blue blades 1762 Bloody were the blue swords 1773

32.   grave of the son of Mathon;] grave of Mathon; 1773

33.   aspen] pointed 1773

34.   king of swords.] king of Selma! 1773

35.   sorrow.] grief. 1773

36.   like a beam ... like a mist] a beam ... a mist 1773

37.   of Dunscaich.] of my soul! 1773

Fingal Book V.

1.   Lamderg] Lamdarg 1762 1765 1773

In the body of the poem he is called Lamderg, as indeed he is in 'Fragment' XVI. But see 'Fingal' III, above, p. 76.

2.   The fourth day still continues. The poet by putting the narration in the mouth of Connal, who still remained with Cuchullin on the side of Cromla, gives propriety to the praises of Fingal. The beginning of this book, in the original, is one of the most beautiful parts of the poem. The versification is regular and full, and agrees very well with the sedate character of Connal.——No poet has adapted the cadence

of his verse more to the temper of the speaker, than Ossian has done. It is more than probable that the whole poem was originally designed to be sung to the harp, as the versification is so various, and so much suited to the different passions of the human mind. [M]

Note deleted 1773

3.   Now .... spoke] On Cromla's resounding side, Connal spoke 1773
4.   overturned.] torn from all their rocks! 1773
5.   chief of the lonely hills.] king of resounding Selma! 1773
6.   like] *deleted* 1773
7.   met in ... people.] met, in fight. 1773
8.   This passage resembles one in the twenty-third Iliad. - Close lock'd above their heads and arms are mixt;/ Below their planted feet at distance fixt;/ Now to the grasp each manly body bends;/ The humid sweat from ev'ry pore descends;/ Their bones resound with blows: sides, shoulders, thighs,/ Swell to each gripe, and bloody tumours rise. POPE. [M]

Note deleted 1773

Macpherson makes use of standard Gaelic ballad imagery for such contests - cf. also the wrestling match between Fingal and Gaul in 'Fragment' VIII.

9.   to the grasp of his foe.] to his hero's grasp. 1762 1773
10.   Sons of ... Fingal,] Sons of distant Morven, said Fingal, 1773
11.   pursue ... Lena;] pursue Lochlin over Lena, 1773
12.   flew ... over] flew sudden across 1773
13.   like a cloud] so dark and sad, 1773
14.   dark-brown] dark-red 1773
15.   The story of Orla is so beautiful and affecting in the original, that many are in possession of it in the north of Scotland, who never heard a syllable more of the poem. It varies the action, and awakes the attention of the reader when he expected nothing but languor in the conduct of the poem, as the great action was over in the conquest of Swaran. [M]

Note deleted 1773

16.   desart.] desart: be thou the friend of Fingal. 1773
17.   hair?] shield? 1773
18.   stream of night.] ruffled stream.
19.   Loda] Lota 1773 (*throughout this episode*)
20.   voice ... hall.] voice, and brighten within his hall. 1773
21.   heroes.] chiefs. 1773
22.   The sons of the feeble] The feeble 1773
23.   sound.] sound! But the winds drive it beyond the steep. It sinks from sight, and darkness prevails. 1773
24.   rest, and be ... valiant.] rest. A neighbour to the brave let him lie. 1773
25.   Perhaps some] Some 1773
26.   on the heath of Lena.] on Lena's resounding plains! 1773
27.   mouth of the song,] bard of song, 1773
28.   Lamh-dhearg signifies *bloody hand*. Gelchossa, *white-legged*. Tuathal, *surly*. Ulfadda, *long-beard*. Ferchios, *the conqueror of men*. [M]

For the following episode, cf. 'Fragment' XVI (with its cliff-hanging end).

29.   tomb, and Ullin] place: dumb is Ullin, 1773
30.   Gelchossa,] *deleted* 1773

31. Selma's] Tura's 1773
32. Selma,] Tura, 1773
33. with the gloomy Ulfadda.] with great Ulfada. 1773
In 'Fragment' XVI *he had been (suitably)* hairy.
34. I am ... sorrow.] I sit in grief. 1773
35. Bran is a common name of gray-hounds to this day. It is a custom in the north of Scotland, to give the names of the heroes mentioned in this poem, to their dogs; a proof that they are familiar to the ear, and their fame generally known. [M]
36. may be] moves stately 1773
37. Allad is plainly a druid: he is called the son of the rock, from his dwelling in a cave; and the circle of stones here mentioned is the pale of the druidical temple. He is here consulted as one who had a supernatural knowledge of things; from the druids, no doubt, came the ridiculous notion of the second sight, which prevailed in the highlands and isles. [M]
38. of Gelchossa.] of the bright Gelchossa! 1773
39. came like a cloud] came, in darkness, 1773
40. Selma.] Tura. 1773
41. on Cromla.] in his halls. 1773
42. The reader will find this passage altered from what it was in the fragments of ancient poetry.——It is delivered down very differently by tradition, and the translator has chosen that reading which favours least of bombast. [M]
Note deleted 1773
43. Selma.] Tura. 1773
44. tell the king of Morven] tell to Selma's king, 1773
45. love, the ... woman said,] love, she trembling said? 1773
46. the snow of Cromla!] the snow! 1773
47. Cromla?] Tura? 1773
48. dead.] cold. 1773
49. Loda.] Lota! 1773
50. Loda.] Lota weep! 1773
51. [*gr.q.*] HOM.. Il. 16. [483 ff.] ——as the mountain oak/ Nods to the ax, till with a groaning sound/ It sinks, and spreads its honours on the ground. POPE. [M]
Note deleted 1773
52. ——a bow/ Conspicuous with three lifted colours gay./ ——What mean those colour'd streaks in heav'n./ Distended as the brow of God appeas'd,/ Or serve they as a flow'ry verge to bind/ The fluid skirts of that same watry cloud? MILTON. [M] (*only*) 1762
53. hills,] swords, 1773
54. the blast of the desart.] the passing blast. 1773
55. Dunscaich,] Erin, 1773
56. battle] battles 1762 1773
57. soul;] mind: 1773
58. of Dunscaich.] of his love! 1773
59. ——Others more mild/ Retreated in a silent valley, sing/ With notes angelical.——/ ——The harmony,/ What could it less when spirits immortal sing?/ Suspended hell, and took with ravishment/ The thronging audience. MILTON. [M] (*only*) 1762

Fingal Book VI.

1.   This book opens with the fourth night, and ends on the morning of the sixth day. The time of five days, five nights, and a part of the sixth day is taken up in the poem. The scene lies in the heath of Lena, and the mountain Cromla on the coast of Ulster. [M]

Note deleted 1773

2.   come] came 1762

3.   down ... steep.] down. Darkness rests on the steeps of Cromla. 1773

4.   of the ... Ullin;] of Erin's waves: 1773

5.   tuneful] *deleted* 1773

6.   Cromla, with ... steeps,] Cromla, 1773

7.   blasts.] winds. 1773

8.   By the strength of the shell is meant the liquor the heroes drunk: of what kind it was, cannot be ascertained at this distance of time. The translator has met with several ancient poems that mention wax-lights and wine as common in the halls of Fingal. The names of both are borrowed from the Latin, which plainly shews that our ancestors had them from the Romans, if they had them at all. The Caledonians in their frequent incursions to the province, might become acquainted with those conveniencies of life, and introduce them into their own country, among the booty which they carried from South Britain. [M]

By the strength .... several ancient poems that] The ancient Celtæ brewed beer, and they were no strangers to mead. Several poems [mention ...] 1773

The names ... at all.] *deleted* 1773

9.   noise] dismal noise 1773

10.   Trenmor was great grandfather to Fingal. The story is introduced to facilitate the dismission of Swaran. [M]

11.   but ... slew it.] but it rolled in death on the spear of Trenmor. 1773

12.   in the grove.] behind the groves. 1773

13.   beauty.] youth. 1773

14.   Trenmor.] mighty Trenmor. 1773

15.   shore of ... Gormal;] shore; 1773

16.   all over.] from death. 1773

17.   in the halls of Gormal;] in the hall; 1773

18.   ground, for he ... like a beam] ground. She was to him a beam 1773

19.   families] fathers 1773

20.   of the waves of Lochlin;] of resounding Lochlin! 1773

21.   heathy] *deleted* 1773

22.   the mossy towers of] *deleted* 1773

23.   thou noble king of Morven.] king of ecchoing Selma! 1773

24.   but ... cease.] What avails it, when our strength hath ceased? 1773

25.   It was ... times.] "Where, Carril," said the great Fingal, "Carril of other times! [Where is ...] 1773

26.   battle] battles 1762 1773

Since we have had evidence of only one lost battle, the singular of 1765 provides the best reading - cf. Book V, p. 95, note 56; Book VI, p. 104 (always victorious in the battles of other spears!); also below, note 27.

27.   for ... victorious.] till now unconquered in war. 1773

Cf. above, note 26.

28. wind of the vale.] wind, along the brightening vale. 1773
29. ; and tell him ... sun of heaven.] : his fame shall never fail. Many have been overcome in battle; whose renown arose from their fall. 1773
30. the sounding] *deleted* 1773
31. This passage alludes to the religion of the king of Craca. See a note on a similar subject in the third book. [M]
See ... book.] *deleted* 1773
Cf. p.77, note 42; also 'Temora' II, *p. 239, note 30.*
32. times,] times, continued the great Fingal, 1773
33. heroes.] chiefs. 1773
34. on gray-headed Cromla.] on Cromla's side. 1773
35. Ullin] Erin 1773
36. the heath.] the divided heath. 1762
37. Gaul king] Gaul, chief 1773
38. swords] blades 1762 steel 1773
39. king] chief 1773
40. desolate.] silent and lonely. 1773
41. like] *deleted* 1773
42. of the desart;] of thy land: 1773
43. This is the only passage in the poem, wherein the wars of Fingal against the Romans are alluded to:——The Roman emperor is distinguished in old compositions by the title of *king of the world.* [M]
44. Connan was of the family of Morni. He is mentioned in several other poems, and always appears with the same character. The poet passed him over in silence till now, and his behaviour here deserves no better usage. [M]
45. sorrow,] grief, 1773
46. son of Erin.] chief of Erin! 1773
47. sorrow, ... lived.] grief, till Erin failed at her streams. 1773
48. desart.] world. 1773
49. winds of night] breeze of night, 1773
50. The practice of singing when they row is universal among the inhabitants of the north-west coast of Scotland and the isles. It deceives time, and inspirits the rowers. [M]
51. Fingal king of shells.] Fingal of generous shells. 1773
52. like a ridge of fire.] in all our arms. 1773
53. king of Morven,] king, 1773
54. ocean.] deep. 1773
It is allowed by the best critics that an epic poem ought to end happily. This rule, in its most material circumstances, is observed by the three most deservedly celebrated poets, Homer, Virgil, and Milton; yet, I know not how it happens, the conclusions of their poems throw a melancholy damp on the mind. One leaves his reader at a funeral; another at the untimely death of a hero; and the third in the solitary scenes of an unpeopled world. [*gr.q.*] HOMER. Such honours Ilion to her hero paid,/ And peaceful slept the mighty Hector's shade. POPE. [*l.q.*]. VIRGIL. He rais'd his arm aloft; and at the word/ Deep in his bosom drove the shining sword./ The streaming blood distain'd his arms around,/ And the disdainful soul came rushing thro' the wound. DRYDEN. They, hand in hand, with wand'ring steps and slow,/ Through Eden took their solitary way. MILTON. [M]

Note deleted 1773

Comala

1.   This poem is valuable on account of the light it throws on the antiquity of Ossian's compositions. The Caracul mentioned here is the same with Caracalla the son of Severus, who in the year 211 commanded an expedition against the Caledonians.—The variety of the measure shews that the poem was originally set to music, and perhaps presented before the chiefs upon solemn occasions.——Tradition has handed down the story more complete than it is in the poem.—"Comala, the daughter of Sarno king of Inistore or Orkney islands, fell in love with Fingal the son of Comhal at a feast, to which her father had invited him, [Fingal, B. III.] upon his return from Lochlin, after the death of Agandecca. Her passion was so violent, that she followed him, disguised like a youth, who wanted to be employed in his wars. She was soon discovered by Hidallan the son of Lamor, one of Fingal's heroes, whose love she had slighted some time before—Her romantic passion and beauty recommended her so much to the king, that he had resolved to make her his wife; when news was brought him of Caracul's expedition. He marched to stop the progress of the enemy, and Comala attended him.——He left her on a hill, within sight of Caracul's army, when he himself went to battle, having previously promised, if he survived, to return that night." The sequel of the story may be gathered from the poem itself. [M]

Though the 1765 edition does not use preceding Arguments *for the shorter poems, the first note clearly functions as such in each case, and these notes are in fact adopted (or at least adapted) as* Arguments *in the edition of 1773.*

2.   Melilcoma,—*soft-rolling eye.* [M]
3.   And night comes on,] Night comes apace, 1773
4.   [*l.q.*] VIRG. [*Æneid, 2.522 f.*] ————dreadful sounds I hear,/ And the dire forms of hostile gods appear. DRYDEN. [M]
5.   Dersagrena, *the brightness of a sun-beam.* [M]
6.   Comala, *the maid of the pleasant brow.* [M]
7.   blue-rolling] blue 1773
8.   Carun or Cara'on, *a winding river.*—This river retains still the name of Carron, and falls into the Forth some miles to the North of Falkirk. ——*Gentesque alias cum pelleret armis/ Sedibus, aut victas vilem servaret in usum/ Servitii, hic contenta suos defendere fines/ Roma securigeris prætendit mænia Scotis:/ Hic spe progressus posita, Caronis ad undam/ Terminus Ausonii signat divortia regni.* BUCHANAN. [M]

Mentioned also in the Dissertation *preceding* 'Fingal' - *see p. 47, and Macpherson's note where the anglicised spelling is given as* Car-avon.

9.   heard on thy banks;] heard; 1773
10.   light] gleam 1773
11.   departed] *deleted* 1773
12.   light,] beam, 1773
13.   the beam] the coming forth 1773
14.   Hidallan was sent by Fingal to give notice to Comala of his return; he, to revenge himself on her for slighting his love some time before, told her that the king was killed in battle. He even pretended that he carried his body from the field to be

buried in her presence; and this circumstance makes it probable that the poem was presented of old. [M]

Perhaps Malcolm Laing (1:219, n. 7) is worth quoting here: "The poem itself is an ambitious imitation of the Song of Solomon, with a regular chorus of bards from [*Mason's*] Caractacus. But when we contemplate such outrageous fictions, as a dramatic poem upon the subject of Caracalla's expedition against the Caledonians, a Celtic drama, performed of old (in the third century) in the Highlands of Scotland, with a Greek chorus as revived by Mason, we are at a loss whether to admire the effrontery of the translator, or the credulous simplicity of the public."

15.   Roll ... roll] Dwell ... dwell 1773
16.   hunter.] king. 1773
17.   grassy] sounding 1773
18.   of her sorrow!] in her grief. 1773
19.   lightening] lightning 1773
20.   chief] king 1773
21.   By *the son of the rock* she means a druid. It is probable that some of the order of the druids remained as late as the beginning of the reign of Fingal; and that Comala had consulted one of them concerning the event of the war with Caracul. [M]

son] dweller 1773 (*both text and note*)

22.   voice like ... my hills.] voice, or was it the breeze of my hills? 1773
23.   Galmal,] Ardven, 1773
24.   O my dove *that art* in the clefts of the rock, in the secret *places* of the stairs, let me see thy countenance, let me hear thy voice. SOLOMON's Song. [ii.14] [M]
Note deleted 1773
25.   over,] past, 1773

The winter is past, the rain is over and gone. SOLOMON's Song. [ii.13] [M]
Note deleted 1773

26.   Cona.] Ardven! 1773
27.   Perhaps the poet alludes to the Roman eagle. [M]
28.   Galmal?] Ardven? 1773
29.   The sequel of the story of Hidallan is introduced, as an episode, in the poem which immediately follows in this collection. [M]

introduced,] introduced in another poem. 1773 (*rest of note deleted*)

30.   wind of the hills.] winds of heaven! 1773
31.   roll] gleam 1773
32.   Sarno the father of Comala died soon after the flight of his daughter.——Fidallan was the first king that reigned in Inistore. [M]
33.   The angel ended, and in Adam's ear/ So charming left his voice, that he a while/ Thought him still speaking, still stood fix'd to hear. MILTON. [*Paradise Lost*, 8.1 ff.] [M]
Note deleted 1773
34.   roll] gleam 1773

The War of Caros

1.   Caros is probably the noted usurper Carausius, by birth a Menapian, who assumed the purple in the year 284; and, seizing on Britain, defeated the emperor Maximian Herculius in several naval engagements, which gives propriety to his

being called in this poem *the king of ships.*——He repaired Agricola's wall, in order to obstruct the incursions of the Caledonians; and when he was employed in that work, it appears he was attacked by a party under the command of Oscar the son of Ossian. This battle is the foundation of the present poem, which is addressed to Malvina the daughter of Toscar. [M]

2.   Crona is the name of a small stream which runs into the Carron. On its banks is the scene of the preceding dramatic poem. [M]

On ... preceding poem.] *deleted* 1773

3.   Who *is* this that cometh out of the wilderness like pillars of smoke. SOLO-MON's Song. [iv.9] [M]

Note deleted 1773

4.   Ryno is often mentioned in the ancient poetry.——He seems to have been a bard, of the first rank, in the days of Fingal. [M]

5.   The Roman eagle. [M]

6.   Agricola's wall which Carausius repaired. [M]

7.   sound of his song.] murmur of his song. 1762 murmur of songs. 1773

8.   ——As when the hollow rocks retain/ The sound of blustering winds.—— MILTON. [*Paradise Lost*, 2.285 f.] [M]

Note deleted 1773

9.   waters.] waves. 1773

10.   The river Carron. [M]

11.   This is the scene of Comala's death, which is the subject of the dramatic poem.——The poet mentions her in this place, in order to introduce the sequel of Hidallan's story, who, on account of her death, had been expelled from the wars of Fingal. [M]

12.   hero,] chief, 1773

13.   the chief] Hidallan, 1773

14.   Hidallan.] the chief. 1773

15.   helmet.] brow. 1773

16.   This is perhaps that small stream, still retaining the name of Balva, which runs through the romantic valley of Glentivar in Stirlingshire. Balva signifies *a silent stream*; and Glentivar, *the sequestered vale.* [M]

17.   feared.] fled. 1773

18.   moulder ... banks.] moulder away. 1773

19.   roaring] winding 1773

20.   discourse] converse 1762 1773

21.   meteor] green meteor 1762 1773

22.   ——*caput obscura nitidum ferrugine texit.* VIRG. [M]

Note deleted 1773

Laing (1:245, n.19) - who is not as conscientious as he might be in attributing his detections to Macpherson himself - here quotes Dryden's translation of Georgica 1: "Clouds on his brow, and spots upon his face."

23.   but ... Cona.] but again he looks forth from his darkness on the green hills of Cona. 1773

24.   like] *deleted* 1773

25.   This passage is very like the soliloquy of Ulysses upon a similar occasion. [*gr.q.*] HOM. Il. 11. What farther subterfuge, what hopes remain?/ What shame, inglorious if I quit the plain?/ What danger, singly if I stand the ground,/ My friends

all scatter'd, all the foes around?/ Yet wherefore doubtful? let this truth suffice;/ The brave meets danger, and the coward flies:/ To die or conquer proves a hero's heart,/ And knowing this, I know a soldier's part. POPE. [M]
Note deleted 1773
26.   stood dilated] stood, growing 1762 1773
27.   like a flood swelling in a narrow vale.] like the flood of the narrow vale. 1762 like a flood in a vale. 1773
28.   sorrow,] grief; 1773
29.   friends:] friend: 1762 1773
30.   of Ossian.] of me! 1773
31.   winds] breeze 1773

The War of Inis-thona

1.   Inis-thona, *i.e. the island of waves*, was a country of Scandinavia subject to its own king, but depending upon the kingdom of Lochlin.—This poem is an episode introduced in a great work composed by Ossian, in which the actions of his friends, and his beloved son Oscar, were interwoven.——The work itself is lost, but some episodes, and the story of the poem, are handed down by tradition. There are some now living, who, in their youth, have heard the whole repeated. [M]
The cynical might agree with Laing here (1:255, n.1): "it appears that the translator had provided for the discovery of future epic poems in the Highlands."
In 1773 the note is deleted and the poem preceded by the following Argument: Reflections on the poet's youth. An apostrophe to Selma. Oscar obtains leave to go to Inis-thona, an island of Scandinavia. The mournful story of Argon and Ruro, the two sons of the king of Inis-thona. Oscar revenges their death, and returns in triumph to Selma. A soliloquy by the poet himself.
2.   Travelling in the greatness of his strength. ISAIAH. lxiii.1. [M]
Note deleted 1773
3.   my heart feels] I feel 1773
4.   This is Branno, the father of Everallin, and grandfather to Oscar; he was of Irish extraction and lord of the country round the lake of Lego.—His great actions are handed down by tradition, and his hospitality has passed into a proverb. [M]
5.   like the] a 1773
6.   Leather thongs were used in Ossian's time, instead of ropes. [M]
in Ossian's time,] among the Celtic nations, 1773
7.   king] *deleted* 1773
8.   ghosts contended.] spirits were striving in winds. 1773
9.   Cormalo had resolved on a war against his father-in-law Annir king of Inis-thona, in order to deprive him of his kingdom: the injustice of his designs was so much resented by Fingal, that he sent his grandson, Oscar, to the assistance of Annir. Both armies came soon to a battle, in which the conduct and valour of Oscar obtained a complete victory. An end was put to the war by the death of Cormalo, who fell in a single combat, by Oscar's hand.—Thus is the story delivered down by tradition; though the poet, to raise the character of his son, makes Oscar himself propose the expedition. [M]
10.   comes like a cloud] comes like cloud 1762 comes a cloud 1773
11.   It was thought, in those days of heroism, an infringement upon the laws of hospitality, to ask the name of a stranger, before he had feasted three days in the

great hall of the family. *He that asks the name of the stranger*, is, to this day, an opprobrious term applied, in the north, to the inhospitable. [M] (*only*) 1765

12.   *To rejoice in the shell* is a phrase for feasting sumptuously and drinking freely. I have observed in a preceding note, that the ancient Scots drunk in shells.

I have ... shells.] *deleted* 1773

Cf. 'Fingal' II, *p. 67, note. 35.*

13.   the hunters.] their repose. 1773

14.   The notion of Ossian concerning the state of the deceased, was the same with that of the ancient Greeks and Romans. They imagined that the souls pursued, in their separate state, the employments and pleasures of their former life. [*l.q.*] Virg. *Æneid* 6.651 ff.] The chief beheld their chariots from afar;/ Their shining arms and coursers train'd to war:/ Their lances fix'd in earth, their steeds around,/ Free from the harness, graze the flow'ry ground./ The love of horses which they had, alive,/ And care of chariots, after death survive. Dryden. [*gr.q.*] Hom. Odyss. 11. Now I the strength of Hercules behold,/ A tow'ring spectre of gigantic mold;/ Gloomy as night he stands in act to throw/ Th' aerial arrow from the twanging bow./ Around his breast a wond'rous zone is roll'd/ Where woodland monsters grin in fretted gold,/ There sullen lions sternly seem to roar,/ The bear to growl, to foam the tusky boar,/ There war and havock and destruction stood,/ And vengeful murder red with human blood. Pope. [M]

All quotations deleted 1773

15.   dark-rolling] *deleted* 1773

16.   Lano was a lake of Scandinavia, remarkable, in the days of Ossian, for emitting a pestilential vapour in autumn. *And thou, O valiant Duchomar, like the mist of marshy Lano; when it sails over the plains of autumn, and brings death to the people.* Fingal, B. I. [M]

people.] host. 1773 (*though this does not correspond to the text*)

See above, p. 57; cf. also 'War of Caros', *p. 112.*

17.   By *the honour of the spear* is meant a kind of tournament practised among the ancient northern nations. [M]

18.   loved ... Lano.] was seized in his love. 1773

19.   Lano's chief] Cormalo 1773

20.   fell.] fell in blood. 1773

21.   dark-haired] long-haired 1773

22.   him.] in shades! 1773

23.   I charge you, O ye daughters of Jerusalem, by the foes, and by the hinds of the field, that ye stir not up, nor awake my love, till he please. Solomon's Song. [viii.4] [M] (*only*) 1762

The Battle of Lora

1.   This poem is compleat; nor does it appear from tradition, that it was introduced, as an episode, into any of Ossian's great works.—It is called, in the original, *Duan a Chuldich*, or the *Culdee's poem*, because it was addressed to one of the first Christian missionaries, who were called, from their retired life, Culdees, or *sequestered persons.*—The story bears a near resemblance to that which was the foundation of the Iliad. Fingal, on his return from Ireland, after he had expelled Swaran from that kingdom, made a feast to all his heroes: he forgot to invite Maronnan and Aldo, two chiefs, who had not been along with him on his expedition.

They resented his neglect; and went over to Erragon king of Sora, a country of Scandinavia, the declared enemy of Fingal. The valour of Aldo soon gained him a great reputation in Sora: and Lorma the beautiful wife of Erragon fell in love with him.—He found means to escape with her, and to come to Fingal, who resided then in Selma on the western coast.—Erragon invaded Scotland, and was slain in battle by Gaul the son of Morni, after he had rejected terms of peace offered him by Fingal.—In this war Aldo fell, in a single combat, by the hands of his rival Erragon; and the unfortunate Lorma afterwards died of grief. [M]

This poem ... foundation of the Iliad.] *deleted* 1773

The poem is normally called, in the original, 'Teanntachd mhór na Féinne', as Macpherson well knew (see the 'Dissertation' preceding Temora, p. 219). For his use of the genuine sources here, see Thomson, pp.42 ff. Cf. also below, note 32.

2.   the voice of thy songs?] thy voice of songs? 1762 1773

3.   The poet alludes to the religious hymns of the Culdees. [M]

4.   Erragon, or Ferg-thonn, signifies *the rage of the waves*; probably a poetical name given him by Ossian himself; for he goes by the name of Annir in tradition. [M]

5.   has] have 1762 1773

6.   The beauty of Israel is slain on thy high places: how are the mighty fallen! 2 SAM. ii.19. How are the mighty fallen in the midst of the battle! O Jonathan, thou wast slain in thine high places. 2 SAM. ii.25. [M]

Note deleted 1773

7.   This was at Fingal's return from his war against Swaran. [M]

8.   Ullin's] Erin's 1773

9.   of echoing Sora.] of other lands! 1773

10.   dark-brown] yellow 1773

11.   rolling] troubled 1773

12.   said ... Morven,] said Fingal rising in wrath: 1773

13.   wrath] rage 1773

14.   has ... Sora?] has dishonoured my name in Sora? 1773

15.   Comhal the Father of Fingal was slain in battle, against the tribe of Morni, the very day that Fingal was born; so that he may, with propriety, be said to have been *born in the midst of battles.* [M]

16.   is in the song:] is only in song. 1773

17.   Neart-mór, *great strength.* Lora, *noisy.* [M]

In the text of 1773 the name is given as Nartmor.

18.   king] chief 1773

19.   begun the chief,] said Nartmor, 1773

20.   night.] night; when they sail along her skirts, and give the light that has failed o'er her orb. 1773

21.   Bos-mhina, *soft and tender hand.* She was the youngest of Fingal's children. [M]

22.   These were probably horses taken in the incursions of the Caledonians into the Roman province, which seems to be intimated in the phrase of the *steeds of strangers.* [M]

Note deleted 1773

23. In her right ... peace.] In her right hand was seen a sparkling shell. In her left an arrow of gold. The first, the joyful mark of peace! The latter, the sign of war. 1773

24. Sanctified girdles, till very lately, were kept in many families in the north of Scotland; they were bound about women in labour, and were supposed to alleviate their pains, and to accelerate the birth. They were impressed with several mystical figures, and the ceremony of binding them about the woman's waist, was accompanied with words and gestures which shewed the custom to have come originally from the druids. [M]

25. women; the] maids. The 1773

26. blue] bright 1773

27. The Roman emperors. These shells were some of the spoils of the province. [M]
These ... province.] *deleted* 1773

28. mighty] *deleted* 1773

29. actions] deeds 1773 *(frequent change)*

30. of the tomb.] that rises from death! 1773

31. Fear-cuth, the same with Fergus, *the man of the word*, or a commander of an army. [M]

32. The poet addresses himself to the Culdee. [M]
Note (together with the address in the text: O son of the rock,*) deleted* 1773
In authentic tradition this particular sequestered person *is usually St. Patrick with whom Ossian engages in debate and who prods him into communicating his reminiscences (cf* Dissertation *preceding* Temora, *p. 219). Elsewhere Macpherson (authentically but disingenuously) disguises Patrick as the* son of Alpin *(son of Calpurnius* = Mac Calpuirn = Mac [C]Alpin).

33. He spake; and to confirm his words out-flew/ Millions of flaming swords, drawn from the thighs/ Of mighty Cherubim; the sudden blaze/ Far round illumin'd hell. MILTON. [*Paradise Lost*, 1.663 ff.] [M]
Note deleted 1773

34. I have observed in a former note, that the standard of Fingal was called the sun-beam from its being studded with stones and gold. [M]
See above, 'Fingal' IV, p. 87, note 24.
Note deleted 1773

35. the battle ... side.] the battle falls around his steps: death dimly stalks along by his side! 1773

36. ghost is] ghost is murmuring 1773

37. like the watry beam of the moon,] like a watry beam of feeble light: 1773

38. silent ... moon.] Silent she rolled her eyes. She was pale and wildly sad! 1773

39. The daughters of Israel went yearly to lament the daughter of Jephthah the Gileadite four days in a year. JUDGES xi. 40. [M]
Note deleted 1773

40. The poet addresses himself to the Culdee. [M]

41. moon-beam] feeble beam 1773
Be thou on a moon-beam, O Morna, near the window of my rest; when my thoughts are of peace; and the din of arms is over. FINGAL, B.1. [M]
See above, p. 58.

Conlath and Cuthóna

1.   Conlath was the youngest of Morni's sons, and brother to the celebrated Gaul, who is so often mentioned in Ossian's poems. He was in love with Cuthóna the daughter of Rumar, when Toscar the son of Kinfena, accompanied by Fercuth his friend, arrived, from Ireland, at Mora where Conlath dwelt. He was hospitably received, and according to the custom of the times, feasted, three days, with Conlath. On the fourth he set sail, and coasting the *island of waves*, probably, one of the Hebrides, he saw Cuthóna hunting, fell in love with her, and carried her away, by force, in his ship. He was forced, by stress of weather, into I-thona a desart isle. In the mean time Conlath, hearing of the rape, sailed after him, and found him on the point of sailing for the coast of Ireland. They fought; and they, and their followers fell by mutual wounds. Cuthóna did not long survive: for she died of grief the third day after. Fingal, hearing of their unfortunate death, sent Stormal the son of Moran to bury them, but forgot to send a bard to sing the funeral song over their tombs. The ghost of Conlath came, long after, to Ossian, to intreat him to transmit, to posterity, his and Cuthóna's fame. For it was the opinion of the times, that the souls of the deceased were not happy, till their elegies were composed by a bard.——— Thus is the story of the poem handed down by tradition. [M]
Gaul, who ... poems.] Gaul. 1773
Thus ... tradition.] *deleted* 1773
2.   The sons of little men] The children of the feeble 1773
3.   I-thonn, *island of waves*, one of the uninhabited western isles. [M]
4.   by the stranger.] in our isle. 1773
5.   of the echoing Morven?] of resounding Selma? 1773
6.   meteor?] meteor of fire? 1773
7.   shadow of mist.] shade of a wandering cloud. 1773
8.   Cuthóna the daughter of Rumar, whom Toscar had carried away by force. [M]
9.   It was long thought, in the north of Scotland, that storms were raised by the ghosts of the deceased. This notion is still entertained by the vulgar; for they think that whirlwinds, and sudden squalls of wind are occasioned by spirits, who transport themselves, in that manner, from one place to another. [M]
10.   Ma-ronnan was the brother of Toscar: the translator has a poem in his possession concerning the extraordinary death of that hero. [M]
11.   Ullin] Erin 1773
Ulster in Ireland. [M]
Note deleted 1773
12.   Selámath - *beautiful to behold*, the name of Toscar's palace, on the coast of Ulster, near the mountain Cromla the scene of the epic poem. [M]
Like Selma, *formed from Gaelic* seall *(= look) and* math *(= good). Cf. 'Darthula', p. 141, note 19. Macpherson later had his own Speyside Belvedere designed for himself by Adam, and christened it* Belleville.
13.   pleasant] lovely 1762 1773
14.   ———the face of ocean sleeps,/ And a still horror saddens all the deeps. POPE's Homer. [*Iliad*, 7.73 *f.*] [M]
Note deleted 1773
15.   isle of waves,] a desart isle, 1773
16.   his love] Cuthona 1773
17.   isle of waves!] desart isle! 1773

18. Cu-thona, *the mournful sound of the waves*; a poetical name given her by Ossian, on account of her mourning to the sound of the waves; her name in tradition is Gorm-huil, *the blue-eyed maid*. [M]
by Ossian,] *deleted* 1773

19. The people call it Ardven. There the towers of Mora rise.] The people call it Mora. There the towers of my love arise. 1773
Here and below, Ardven *becomes* Mora *in 1773*.

20. halls] towers 1773

21. Ullin,] Erin. 1773

22. Oh!] Ha! 1773

23. sees] foresees 1773

24. The grave. [M]

25. rolling] heaving 1773

26. [*l.q.*] VIRG. [*Æneid,* 1.357 ff.] ——the ghost appears/ Of her unhappy Lord: the spectre stares,/ And with erected eyes his bloody bosom bares. DRYDEN. [M]
Note deleted 1773

27. *Nam quia nec fato, merita nec morte peribat,/ Sed misera ante diem, &.c.* VIRG. [*Æneid,* 4.620 f.] [M]
Note deleted 1773

28. It was the opinion of the times, that the arms left by the heroes at home, became bloody the very instant their owners were killed, though at ever so great a distance. [M]

29. The situation of Cuthona is like that of Rizpah, Saul's mistress, who sat by her sons after they had been hanged by the Gibeonites.—And Rizpah, the daughter of Aiah, took sackcloth, and spread it for her upon the rock, from the beginning of the harvest until water dropped on them out of heaven, and suffered neither the birds of the air to rest on them by day, nor the beasts of prey by night. 2 SAM. xxi.10. [M]
Note deleted 1773

30. The sons of the desart ... dead.] The sons of green Selma came. They found Cuthona cold. 1773

Carthon

1. This poem is compleat, and the subject of it, as of most of Ossian's compositions, tragical. In the time of Comhal the son of Trathal, and father of the celebrated Fingal, Clessámmor the son of Thaddu and brother of Morna, Fingal's mother, was driven by a storm into the river Clyde, on the banks of which stood Balclutha, a town belonging to the Britons between the walls. He was hospitably received by Reuthámir, the principal man in the place, who gave him Moina his only daughter in marriage. Reuda, the son of Cormo, a Briton who was in love with Moina, came to Reuthámir's house, and behaved haughtily towards Clessámmor. A quarrel insued, in which Reuda was killed; the Britons, who attended him pressed so hard on Clessámmor, that he was obliged to throw himself into the Clyde, and swim to his ship. He hoisted sail, and the wind being favourable, bore him out to sea. He often endeavoured to return, and carry off his beloved Moina by night; but the wind continuing contrary, he was forced to desist.

Moina, who had been left with child by her husband, brought forth a son, and died soon after.——Reuthámir named the child Carthon, *i.e. the murmur of waves*, from the storm which carried off Clessámmor his father, who was supposed to have been cast away. When Carthon was three years old, Comhal the father of Fingal, in one of his expeditions against the Britons, took and burnt Balclutha. Reuthámir was killed in the attack: and Carthon was carried safe away by his nurse, who fled farther into the country of the Britons. Carthon, coming to man's estate was resolved to revenge the fall of Balclutha on Comhal's posterity. He set sail, from the Clyde, and, falling on the coast of Morven, defeated two of Fingal's heroes, who came to oppose his progress. He was, at last, unwittingly killed by his father Clessámmor, in a single combat. This story is the foundation of the present poem, which opens on the night preceding the death of Carthon, so that what passed before is introduced by way of episode. The poem is addressed to Malvina the daughter of Toscar. [M]

For the authentic sources, which of course offer a variation on a common theme in early literature (cf. the German Hildebrandslied*), see Thomson, pp. 48 ff.; also Meek, p. 34, who points out that Macpherson's main source-poem, 'Bás Chonlaoich', originated in Scotland.*

2.   firs] pines 1773
3.   the gray ghost that guards it:] a dim ghost standing there. 1773
It was the opinion of the times, that deer saw the ghosts of the dead. To this day, when beasts suddenly start without any apparent cause, the vulgar think that they see the spirits of the deceased. [M]
4.   Fingal returns here, from an expedition against the Romans, which was celebrated by Ossian in a particular poem which is in the translator's possession. [M]
a particular ... possession.] a poem called *the strife of Crona*. 1762 1773
Cf. 'Carric-thura', *p. 158, note 4.*
5.   Probably wax-lights; which are often mentioned as carried, among other booty, from the Roman province. [M]
Cf. 'Fingal' VI, *p. 99, note 8.*
6.   Clessamh-mór, *mighty deeds.* [M]
7.   the companion of my father, in the days] the brother of Morna, in the hour 1773
8.   Hast thou given the horse strength? Hast thou clothed his neck with thunder? He paweth in the valley, and rejoiceth in his strength. JOB. [xxxi.19]. [*gr.q.*] HOM. Il. 6. The wanton courser thus with reins unbound,/ Breaks from his stall, and beats the trembling ground;/ His head, now freed, he tosses to the skies;/ His mane dishevel'd o'er his shoulders flies;/ He snuffs the females in the distant plain,/ And springs, exulting. POPE. [*l.q.*] VIRG. Freed from his keepers, thus with broken reins,/ The wanton courser prances o'er the plains:/ Or in the pride of youth o'erleaps the mounds,/ And snuffs the females in forbidden grounds./ ——O'er his shoulders flows his waving mane:/ He neighs, he snorts, he bears his head on high. DRYDEN. [M]
Note deleted 1773
9.   the battles of my youth?] the times of our war? 1773
10.   Moina, *soft in temper and person.* We find the British names in this poem derived from the Galic, which is a proof that the ancient language of the whole island was one and the same. [M]
11.   Balclutha, *i.e. the town of Clyde,* probably the *Alcluth* of Bede. [M]
Presumably Dumbarton.

12.   Clutha, or Cluäth, the Galic name of the river Clyde, the signification of the word is *bending*, in allusion to the winding course of that river. From Clutha is derived its Latin name, Glotta. [M]

13.   The word in the original here rendered by *restless wanderer*, is *Scuta*, which is the true origin of the *Scoti* of the Romans; an opprobrious name imposed by the Britons, on the Caledonians, on account of the continual incursions into their country. [M]

14.   dark] loose 1773

15.   her cries.] her mournful, distant cries. 1773

16.   [*l.q.*] VIRG. [*Æneid*, 6.450 ff.] Not far from these Phoenician Dido stood,/ Fresh from her wound, her bosom bath'd in blood./ Whom when the Trojan hero hardly knew/ Obscure in shades, and with a doubtful view,/ Doubtful as he who runs thro' dusky night,/ Or thinks he sees the moon's uncertain light, &c. DRYDEN. [M]

Note deleted 1773

17.   The title of this poem, in the original, is *Duan na nlaoi, i.e. The Poem of the Hymns:* probably on account of its many digressions from the subject, all which are in a lyric measure, as this song of Fingal. Fingal is celebrated by the Irish historians for his wisdom in making laws, his poetical genius, and his foreknowledge of events.—O'Flaherty goes so far as to say, that Fingal's laws were extant in his own time. [M]

18.   The reader may compare this passage with the three last verses of the 13th chapter of Isaiah, where the prophet fortels the destruction of Babylon. [M]

Note deleted 1773

19.   Morven?] Selma? 1773

20.   terrible] *deleted* 1773

21.   [*gr.q.*] HOM. ii. 382. His sharpen'd spear let every Grecian wield,/ And every Grecian fix his brazen shield, &c. POPE. Let each/ His adamantine coat gird well, and each/ Fit well his helm, gripe fast his orbed shield,/ Borne ev'n or high; for this day will pour down,/ If I conjecture right, no drizling shower,/ But rattling storm of arrows barb'd with fire. MILTON. [*Paradise Lost*, 6.541 ff.] [M]

Note deleted 1773

22.   heaven's] green 1762 1773

23.   It was a custom among the ancient Scots, to exchange arms with their guests, and those arms were preserved long in the different families, as monuments of the friendship which subsisted between their ancestors. [M]

24.   people.] host. 1773

25.   might] fire 1773

26.   fir] pine 1773

27.   the king?] the youth? 1773

28.   heroes,] chiefs, 1773

29.   Cath-'huil, *the eye of battle*. [M]

30.   It appears, from this passage, that clanship was established, in the days of Fingal, though not on the same footing with the present tribes in the north of Scotland. [M]

Contrast with this Blair's information in the Preface to the Fragments, *above, p. 5.*

31.   This Connal is very much celebrated, in ancient poetry, for his wisdom and valour: there is a small tribe still subsisting, in the North, who pretend they are descended from him. [M]

32.   Fingal did not then know that Carthon was the son of Clessámmor. [M]

33.   Comhal.] valiant Comhal. 1773

34.   on that heathy rock, ... approach.] on a rock; he saw the hero rushing on. 1773

35.   love] husband 1773

36.   To tell one's name to an enemy was reckoned, in those days of heroism, a manifest evasion of fighting him; for, if it was once known, that friendship subsisted, of old, between the ancestors of the combatants, the battle immediately ceased; and the ancient amity of their forefathers was renewed. *A man who tells his name to his enemy,* was of old an ignominious term for a coward. [M]

37.   young] younger 1773

38.   loved?] love? 1773

39.   towards the hero.] to the king. 1773

40.   This expression admits of a double meaning, either that Carthon hoped to acquire glory by killing Fingal; or to be rendered famous by falling by his hand. The last is the most probable, as Carthon is already wounded. [M]

41.   desart;] hills; 1773

42.   In the north of Scotland, till very lately, they burnt a large trunk of an oak at their festivals; it was called *the trunk of the feast.* Time had so much consecrated the custom, that the vulgar thought it a kind of sacrilege to disuse it. [M]

43.   words were feeble.] voice was sad and low. 1773

44.   plains of Lora.] plain. 1773

45.   I have accompanied] Ossian often joined 1773

46.   valour] youth 1773

47.   air?] wind? 1773

48.   This passage is something similar to Satan's address to the Sun, in the fourth book of Paradise Lost.—O thou that with surpassing glory crown'd,/ Looks from thy sole dominion like the god/ Of this new world; at whose sight all the stars/ Hide their diminish'd heads; to thee I call,/ But with no friendly voice, and add thy name/ O Sun! [4.32 ff.] [M]
Note deleted 1773

49.   [*l.q.*] VIRG. [*Æneid,* 6.270 ff.] Thus wander travellers in woods by night,/ By the moon's doubtful, and malignant light:/ When Jove in dusky clouds involves the skies,/ And the faint crescent shoots by fits before their eyes. DRYDEN. [M] (*only*) 1762

The Death of Cuchullin

1.   Tradition throws considerable light on the history of Ireland, during the long reign of Fingal, the son of Comhal, in Morven.—Arth, the son of Cairbre, supreme king of Ireland, dying, was succeeded by his son Cormac, a minor.——The petty kings and chiefs of the tribes met at Temora, the royal palace, in order to chuse, out of their own number, a guardian to the young king. Disputes, concerning the choice of a proper person, run high, and it was resolved to end all differences by giving the tuition of the young king to Cuchullin, the son of Semo, who had rendered himself famous by his great actions, and who resided, at the time, with Connal, the son of Caithbat, in Ulster.

Cuchullin was but three and twenty years old, when he assumed the management of affairs in Ireland: and the invasion of Swaran happened two years after. In the twenty-seventh year of Cuchullin's age, and the third of his administration, Torlath, the son of Cantéla, one of the chiefs of that colony of Belgæ, who were in possession of the south of Ireland, set up for himself in Connaught, and advanced towards Temora, in order to dethrone Cormac, who, excepting Feradath, afterwards king of Ireland, was the only one of the Scotch race of kings existing in that country. Cuchullin marched against him, came up with him at the lake of Lego, and totally defeated his forces. Torlath fell in the battle by Cuchullin's hand; but as he himself pressed too eagerly on the flying enemy, he was mortally wounded by an arrow, and died the second day after.

The good fortune of Cormac fell with Cuchullin: many set up for themselves, and anarchy and confusion reigned. At last Cormac was taken off; and Cairbar, lord of Atha, one of the competitors for the throne, having defeated all his rivals, became sole monarch of Ireland.——The family of Fingal, who were in the interest of Cormac's family, were resolved to deprive Cairbar of the throne he had usurped; in particular, Oscar the son of Ossian had determined the revenge the death of Cathol, his friend, who had been assassinated by Cairbar.—The threats of Oscar reached Cairbar's ears: he invited him in a friendly manner to a feast which he had prepared at the royal palace of Temora, resolving to pick a quarrel, and have some pretext for killing him.

The quarrel happened; the followers of both fought, and Cairbar and Oscar fell by mutual wounds: in the mean time Fingal arrived from Scotland with an army, defeated the friends of Cairbar, and re-established the family of Cormac in the possession of the kingdom.——The present poem concerns the death of Cuchullin. It is, in the original, called *Duan loch Leigo*, i.e. *The Poem of Lego's Lake*, and is an episode introduced in a great poem, which celebrated the last expedition of Fingal into Ireland. The greatest part of the poem is lost, and nothing remains but some episodes, which a few old people in the north of Scotland retain on memory.—— Cuchullin is the most famous champion in the Irish traditions and poems; in them he is always called the *redoubtable Cuchullin*; and the fables concerning his strength and valour are innumerable. Ossian thought his expedition against the Fir-bolg, or Belgæ of Britain, a subject fit for an epic poem; which was extant till of late, and was called *Tora-na-tana*, or a *Dispute about Possessions*, as the war which was the foundation of it, was commenced by the British Belgæ, who inhabited Ireland, in order to extend their territories.—The fragments that remain of this poem are animated with the genuine spirit of Ossian; so that there can be no doubt that it was of his composition. [M]

[§ 2] one of the chiefs ... south of Ireland,] *(only) 1765*
who, excepting Feradath ... existing in that country.] *(only)* 1765
[§ 3] At last Cormac was taken off; and Cairbar, lord of Atha,] At last Cormac was taken off, nobody knew how; Cairbar, [one of the ...] 1762
In 1773 the note as Argument *is amended and reduced to:*
Cuthullin, after the arms of Fingal had expelled Swaran from Ireland, continued to manage the affairs of that kingdom as the guardian of Cormac the young king. In the third year of Cuthullin's administration, Torlath, the son of Cantéla, rebelled in Connaught; and advanced to Temora to dethrone Cormac. Cuthullin marched against him, came up with him at the lake of Lego, and totally defeated his forces. Torlath

fell in battle by Cuthullin's hand; but as he too eagerly pressed on the enemy, he was mortally wounded. The affairs of Cormac, though for some time supported by Nathos, as mentioned in the preceding poem ['Dar-thula'], fell into confusion at the death of Cuthullin. Cormac himself was slain by the rebel Cairbar; and the re-establishment of the royal family of Ireland, by Fingal, furnishes the subject of the epic poem of Temora.

Given the changes, it is difficult to argue here with Laing's conclusion (1:352) that the 'Death of Cuchullin' *was originally intended as an episode in* 'Temora', *which celebrates Fingal's last expedition into Ireland, and of which only the first book had been composed when the* Fingal *volume appeared.* "But the translator, who had already prepared us, in Inisthona, for an additional epic poem on the exploits of his beloved Oscar and his friends, has here [*in the note to the first editions*] provided for the subsequent appearance, not only of the Temora, but of a fourth epic poem ... which remains to be discovered, in due time, in the Highlands of Scotland."

2.	Togorma, *i.e. The island of blue waves*, one of the Hebrides, was subject to Connal, the son of Caithbat, Cuchullin's friend.—He is sometimes called the son of Colgar, from one of that name who was the founder of the family.——Connal, a few days before the news of Torlath's revolt came to Temora, had sailed to Togorma, his native isle; where he was detained by contrary winds during the war in which Cuchullin was killed. [M]

Cf. 'Fingal' I, *p. 56, note 29.*

3.	of mossy Tura?] of Erin's wars? 1773

4.	Dunscaich's] Dunscai's 1773

The 1773 edition opts here and below either for Dunscai *or* Dunscäi.

5.	[*gr.q.*] Hom. Il. 5. As vapours blown by Auster's sultry breath,/ Pregnant with plagues, and shedding seeds of death,/ Beneath the rage of burning Sirius rise,/ Choke the parch'd earth, and blacken all the skies. Pope. [M]

Note deleted 1773

6.	The royal palace of the Irish kings; Teamhrath according to some of the bards. [M]

7.	The bards were the heralds of ancient times; and their persons were sacred on account of their office. In later times they abused that privilege; and as their persons were inviolable, they satyrised and lampooned so freely those who were not liked by their patrons, that they became a public nuisance. Screened under the character of heralds, they grosly abused the enemy when he would not accept the terms they offered. [M]

8.	Cean-teola', *head of a family.* [M]

9.	Slia'-mór, *great hill.* [M]

10.	green] *deleted* 1773

11.	of noon,] of the day, 1773

12.	again.] again! Slant looks the sun on the field; gradual grows the shade of the hill! 1773

13.	Calmar the son of Matha. His death is related at large, in the third book of Fingal. He was the only son of Matha; and the family was extinct in him.—The seat of the family was on the banks of the river Lara, in the neighbourhood of Lego, and probably near the place where Cuchullin lay; which circumstance suggested to him, the lamentation of Alclétha over her son. [M]

14.   Ald-cla'tha, *decaying beauty:* probably a poetical name given the mother of Calmar, by the bard himself. [M]

15.   Alcletha speaks. Calmar had promised to return, by a certain day, and his mother and his sister Alona are represented by the bard as looking, with impatience, towards that quarter where they expected Calmar would make his first appearance. [M]

16.   Alúine, *exquisitely beautiful.* [M]

17.   Alclétha speaks. [M]

18.   From the blood of the slain, from the fat of the mighty, the bow of Jonathan returned not back, and the sword of Saul returned not empty. 2 Sam. i. 22. [M]
Note deleted 1773

19.   She addresses herself to Larnir, Calmar's friend, who had returned with the news of his death. [M]

20.   car-borne] low-laid 1773

21.   stalked] stalked dimly 1773

22.   darkly] pale 1773

23.   car-borne] noble 1773

24.   See Calmar's speech, in the first book of Fingal. [M]
Note deleted 1773
See p. 56.

25.   See Cuchullin's reply to Connal, concerning Crugal's ghost. Fing. b. 2. [M]
Note deleted 1773
See pp. 65 f.

26.   of the desart.] of night. 1773

27.   Ullin's] Erin's 1773

28.   his] this 1762 1765

29.   Loda, in the third book of Fingal, is mentioned as a place of worship in Scandinavia: by the *spirit of Loda*, the poet probably means Odin, the great deity of the northern nations. He is described here with all his terrors about him, not unlike Mars, as he is introduced in a simile, in the seventh Iliad [207 ff.]. [*gr.q.*] So stalks in arms the grisly god of Thrace,/ When Jove to punish faithless men prepares,/ And gives whole nations to the waste of wars. POPE. [M]
terrors about him,] terrors. 1773 (*rest of note deleted*)

30.   locks.] locks! The waning moon half-lights his dreadful face. His features blended in darkness arise to view. [So terrible ...] 1773

31.   king] chief 1773

32.   Tura's] Erin's 1773

33.   The Irish historians have placed Cuchullin in the first century.—The translator has given his reasons for fixing him in the third, in the dissertation which is prefixed to this collection. In other particulars the accounts of Keating and O'Flaherty coincide pretty nearly with Ossian's poems, and the traditions of the Highlands and Isles. They say that he was killed in the twenty-seventh year of his age, and they give him a great character for his wisdom and valour. [M]
Note deleted 1773
The Irish historians are of course right, certainly as far as the dominant tradition is concerned where the Ulster and Fingalian cycles are never mixed. For evidence that this could and did in fact happen in Gaelic Scotland, see Stern, pp. 80 ff., 151.

34. Conloch, who was afterwards very famous for his great exploits in Ireland. He was so remarkable for his dexterity in handling the javelin, that when a good marksman is described, it has passed into a proverb, in the north of Scotland, *He is unerring as the arm of Conloch.* [M]

35. Togorma] Cogorma 1773

36. Luäth] Luath 1762 1773

It was of old, the custom to bury the favourite dog near the master. This was not peculiar to the ancient Scots, for we find it practised by many other nations in their ages of heroism.——There is a stone shewn still at Dunscaich in the isle of Sky, to which Cuchullin commonly bound his dog Luäth.—The stone goes by his name to this day. [M]

37. lies ... chace.] lies. The song of bards rose over the dead. 1773

38. This is the song of the bards over Cuchullin's tomb. Every stanza closes with some remarkable title of the hero, which was always the custom in funeral elegies.—The verse of the song is a lyric measure, and it was of old sung to the harp. [M]

The verse ... harp.] *deleted* 1773

39. They were swifter than eagles, they were stronger than lions. 2 Sam. i. 23. [M]

Note deleted 1773

40. Cromla!] Tura! 1773

Dar-thula

1. It may not be improper here, to give the story which is the foundation of this poem, as it is handed down by tradition.—Usnoth, lord of Etha, which is probably that part of Argyleshire which is near Loch Eta, an arm of the sea in Lorn, had three sons, Nathos, Althos, and Ardan by Slis-sáma, the daughter of Semo and sister to the celebrated Cuchullin. The three brothers, when very young, were sent over to Ireland, by their father, to learn the use of arms, under their uncle Cuchullin, who made a great figure in that kingdom. They were just landed in Ulster when the news of Cuchullin's death arrived. Nathos, though very young, took the command of Cuchullin's army, made head against Cairbar the usurper, and defeated him in several battles. Cairbar at last having found means to murder Cormac the lawful king, the army of Nathos shifted sides, and he himself was obliged to return into Ulster, in order to pass over into Scotland.

Dar-thula, the daughter of Colla, with whom Cairbar was in love, resided, at that time, in Seláma a castle in Ulster: she saw, fell in love, and fled with Nathos; but a storm rising at sea, they were unfortunately driven back on that part of the coast of Ulster, where Cairbar was encamped with his army, waiting for Fingal, who meditated an expedition into Ireland, to re-establish the Scotch race of kings on the throne of that kingdom. The three brothers, after having defended themselves, for some time, with great bravery, were overpowered and slain, and the unfortunate Dar-thula killed herself upon the body of her beloved Nathos.

Ossian opens the poem, on the night preceding the death of the sons of Usnoth, and brings in, by way of episode, what passed before. He relates the death of Dar-thula differently from the common tradition; his account is the most probable, as suicide seems to have been unknown in those early times: for no traces of it are found in the old poetry. [M]

[§ 2] army, waiting for Fingal ... kingdom.] army. 1762 1773
[§ 3] Ossian opens the poem,] The poem opens, 1773
He relates] It relates 1773
his account] this account 1773

The last three changes are consistent with a general tendency in the revised edition, particularly evident in the Dissertations, *to downplay the significance of Ossian himself. Macpherson was perhaps motivated by professional jealousy. Both believers and detractors found indications in the 1773 edition of his asserting his own claim to the primary authorship of the poems.*

For Macpherson's adaptation of the Story of Deirdre, "one of the oldest in Scottish, as distinct from Irish, tradition", *see Thomson, pp. 53 ff.*

2. The address to the moon is very beautiful in the original. It is in a lyric measure, and appears to have been sung to the harp. [M]
Note deleted 1773
3. steps] course 1773
4. daughter of the night?] light of the silent night? 1773
5. green,] *deleted* 1773
6. The poet means the moon in her wane. [M]
Note deleted 1773
7. grccn] *deleted* 1773
8. blue] white 1773
9. Nathos signifies *youthful*, Ailthos, *exquisite beauty*, Ardan, *pride.* [M]
10. car-borne Cairbar.] Cairbar of Erin. 1773
Cairbar, who murdered Cormac king of Ireland, and usurped the throne. He was afterwards killed by Oscar the son of Ossian in a single combat. The poet, upon other occasions, gives him the epithet of red-haired. [M]
11. spirit] ghost 1762
12. Dar-thúla, or Dart-'huile, *a woman with fine eyes.* She was the most famous beauty of antiquity. To this day, when a woman is praised for her beauty, the common phrase is, that *she is as lovely as Dar-thula.* [M]
13. with the car-borne] with blue-shielded 1773
14. Etha] Etha, 1762 1773
15. Ullin] Erin 1773
16. That is, the day appointed by destiny. We find no deity in Ossian's poetry, if fate is not one; of that he is very full in some of his poems in the translator's hands. [M]
Note deleted 1773
17. like] *deleted* 1773
18. of arms] of thy arms 1762 1773
19. The poet does not mean that Seláma which is mentioned as the seat of Toscar in Ulster, in the poem of Conlath and Cuthona. The word in the original signifies either *beautiful to behold*, or a place *with a pleasant or wide prospect.* In those times, they built their houses upon eminences, to command a view of the country, and to prevent their being surprized: many of them, on that account, were called Seláma. The famous Selma of Fingal is derived from the same root. [M]
The poet ... Cuthona.] *deleted* 1773
in the original] *deleted* 1773
Cf. above, 'Conlath and Cuthona', p. 125, note 12.

20. Cormac the young king of Ireland, who was murdered by Cairbar. [M]
was murdered] was privately murdered 1762 1773
21. car-borne] dark-browed 1773 (*from 1796 - Laing excepted* - dark-brown)
22. That is, of the love of Cairbar. [M]
23. raven] flowing 1773
24. feeble: but] feeble and distant far. But 1773
25. is the car-borne chief] dwells in the chief 1773
26. Are we not] Are we 1773
See *Jiriczek, 3:104. The omission of not is probably a mistake. The* land of strangers
means Morven for Dar-thula, for Nathos Ireland. That is, for Dar-thula it betokens
successful escape, for Nathos doom.
27. car-borne] cruel 1773
28. Ullin lifts here her green hills.] Erin lifts here her hills. 1773
29. thou beam of light!] thou lovely light! 1773
30. for the car-borne] for returning 1773
31. cave:] cave: his eye a light seen afar. 1773
32. [*l.q.*] VIRG. [*Georgica*, 1.444 f.] —Thro' mists he shoots his sullen beams,/
Frugal of light, in loose and straggling streams. DRYDEN. [M]
Quoted at greater length in 'Fingal' IV, *above p. 87, note 27.*
Note deleted 1773
33. [*gr.q.*] HOM. vi. 411. [M]
Note deleted 1773
From Andromache's speech to Hector: No parent now remains my grief to share,/
No father's aid, no mother's tender care. POPE. (*Laing, 1:388*)
34. My father rests in the tomb.] My father, my brother is fallen! 1773
35. battle of Ullin.] battles of Erin. Hear, son of Usnoth! hear, O Nathos, my tale
of grief. 1773
36. The family of Colla preserved their loyalty to Cormac long after the death of
Cuchullin. [M]
Note deleted 1773
37. car-borne] haughty 1773
38. Dar-thula, he sighing said,] "Dar-thula, my daughter," he said, 1773
39. king] chief 1773
It is very common, in Ossian's poetry, to give the title of King to every chief that
was remarkable for his valour. [M]
Note deleted 1773
40. The poet, to make the story of Dar-thula's arming herself for battle, more
probable, makes her armour to be that of a very young man, otherwise it would
shock all belief, that she, who was very young, should be able to carry it. [M]
Note deleted 1773
41. It was the custom of those times, that every warrior at a certain age, or when
he became unfit for the field, fixed his arms, in the great hall, where the tribe
feasted, upon joyful occasions. He was afterwards never to appear in battle; and this
stage of life was called the *time of fixing of the arms.* [M]
those times,] ancient times 1773
42. car-borne] beloved 1773
43. Lona, *a marshy plain.* It was the custom, in the days of Ossian, to feast after a
victory. Cairbar had just provided an entertainment for his army, upon the defeat of

Truthil the son of Colla, and the rest of the party of Cormac, when Colla and his aged warriors arrived to give him battle. [M]

It was ... victory.] *deleted* 1773

44.   The poet avoids the description of the battle of Lona, as it would be improper in the mouth of a woman, and could have nothing new, after the numerous descriptions, of that kind, in his other poems. He, at the same time, gives an opportunity to Dar-thula to pass a fine compliment on her lover. [M]

The poet avoids] The poet, by an artifice, avoids 1762 1773

his other poems.] the rest of the poems. 1773

45.   red] dreadful 1773

46.   slew,] flew, (*later editions, including Laing - not registered by Jiriczek*)

47.   It is usual with Ossian, to repeat, at the end of the episodes, the sentence which introduced them. It brings back the mind of the reader to the main story of the poem. [M]

Note deleted 1773

The dùnadh, whereby the opening words or syllables of a poem are repeated at the end, is a formal closing device which Macpherson would have observed in his genuine sources. The 'Lay of Fraoch', the first Gaelic ballad translated into English (by Jerome Stone, 1756 in the Scots *Magazine), begins and ends with a sigh.*

48.   maid] daughter 1773

49.   storm.] storm. The lonely traveller feels a mournful joy. He sees the darkness, that slowly comes. [My soul ...] 1773

50.   slowly comes,] advances, 1773

51.   car-borne] dark-browed 1773

Cf. above, note 21.

52.   Oscar, the son of Ossian, had long resolved on the expedition, into Ireland, against Cairbar, who had assassinated his friend Cathol, the son of Moran, an Irishman of noble extraction, and in the interest of the family of Cormac. [M]

53.   them] them dimly 1773

54.   Ullin,] Erin, 1773

55.   on his cheek.] on my father's cheek. 1773

56.   chief of Dunscaich.] son of generous Semo. 1773

57.   Lamh-mhor, *mighty-hand.* [M]

58.   the mournful halls of Temora.] Temora's mournful halls? 1762 1773

Temora was the royal palace of the supreme kings of Ireland. It is here called mournful, on account of the death of Cormac, who was murdered there by Cairbar who usurped his throne. [M]

59.   Slis-seamha, *soft bosom.* She was the wife of Usnoth and daughter of Semo the chief of the *isle of mist.* [M]

60.   shoots] flies 1773

61.   falls in] shoots into 1773

62.   red] green 1762 dreary 1773

63.   and death was] Death dimly sat 1773

64.   mournful] sounding 1773

65.   And it came to pass that night, that the angel of the Lord went out, and smote in the camp of the Assyrians, an hundred fourscore and five thousand: and when they rose early in the morning, behold, they were all dead men. 2 KINGS xix. 35. [M] (*only*) 1762

66. Ullin, they] Erin. They 1773
67. retire] vanish 1773
68. when ... desart.] when driven before the winds. 1773
69. O maid,] O Dar-thula, 1773
70. rustling] rushing 1773
71. Althos had just returned from viewing the coast of Lena, whither he had been sent by Nathos, the beginning of the night. [M]
72. Cairbar had gathered an army, to the coast of Ulster, in order to oppose Fingal, who prepared for an expedition into Ireland to re-establish the house of Cormac on the throne, which Cairbar had usurped. Between the wings of Cairbar's army was the bay of Tura, into which the ship of the sons of Usnoth was driven: so that there was no possibility of their escaping. [M]
73. The scene of the present poem is nearly the same with that of the epic poem in this collection. The heath of Lena and Tura are often mentioned. [M]
Note deleted 1773
The epic poem is 'Fingal'.
74. Ullin?] Erin? 1773
75. Semo was grandfather to Nathos by the mother's side. The spear mentioned here was given to Usnoth on his marriage, it being the custom then for the father of the lady to give his arms to his son-in-law. The ceremony used upon these occasions is mentioned in other poems. [M]
76. eyes.] radiant eyes! 1773
77. arm] arm, my brother, 1773
78. of Etha.] of my land. 1773
79. Usnoth. [M]
80. of Cona] of Cona, that Ossian 1773
Ossian, the son of Fingal, is, often, poetically called the voice of Cona. [M]
Note deleted 1773
81. my mountain winds.] the rushing winds.
82. By the spirit of the mountain is meant that deep and melancholy sound which precedes a storm; well known to those who live in a high country. [M]
83. shrieked.] roared. 1773
84. harp of my son.] harp. 1773
85. sounding] trembling 1773
86. Ullin's] Erin's 1773
87. He alludes to the flight of Cairbar from Seláma. [M]
88. around him.] around his spear. 1773
89. little men.] feeble men! 1773
90. fell.] fell in blood. 1773
91. Her dark hair spreads on his face,] Her hair spreads wide on his face. 1773
92. Truthil was the founder of Dar-thula's family. [M]
93. Rise up, my love, my fair one, and come away. For lo, the winter is past, the rain is over, and gone. The flowers appear on the earth; the time of singing is come, and the voice of the turtle is heard in our land. The fig-tree putteth forth her green figs, and the vines, *with* the tender grape, give a *good* smell. Arise, my love, my fair one, and come away. SOLOMON's Song. [ii.10] [M]
Note deleted 1773
94. Ullin] Erin

Temora [1761/62]

1.   Though the history which is the foundation of the present poem, was given in the notes on the two pieces preceding, it may not be here improper to recapitulate some part of what has been said.—Immediately after the death of Cuchullin, Cairbar, lord of Atha, openly set up for himself in Connaught, and having privately murdered young king Cormac, became, without opposition, sole monarch of Ireland. The murder of Cormac was so much resented by Fingal, that he resolved on an expedition into Ireland against Cairbar. Early intelligence of his designs came to Cairbar, and he had gathered the tribes together into Ulster, to oppose Fingal's landing; at the same time his brother Cathmor kept himself with an army near Temora.—This Cathmor is one of the finest characters in the old poetry. His humanity, generosity, and hospitality, were unparalleled: in short, he had no fault, but too much attachment to so bad a brother as Cairbar.—The present poem has its name from Temora, the royal palace of the Irish kings, near which the last and decisive battle was fought between Fingal and Cathmor. What has come to the translator's hands, in a regular connection, is little more than the opening of the poem.—This work appears, from the story of it, which is still preserv'd, to have been one of the greatest of Ossian's compositions. The variety of the characters makes it interesting; and the war, as it is carried on by Fingal and Cathmor, affords instances of the greatest bravery, mixed with incomparably generous actions and sentiments. One is at a loss for which side to declare himself: and often wishes, when both commanders march to battle, that both may return victorious. At length the good fortune of Fingal preponderates, and the family of Cormac are re-established on the Irish throne.

The Irish traditions relate the affair in another light, and exclaim against Fingal for appointing thirty judges, or rather tyrants, at Temora, for regulating the affairs of Ireland. They pretend to enumerate many acts of oppression committed by those judges; and affirm, that both they and a part of Fingal's army, which was left in Ireland to enforce their laws, were at last expelled the kingdom.—Thus the Irish traditions, say the historians of that nation. It is said, however, that those gentlemen sometimes create facts, in order afterwards to make remarks upon them; at least, that they adopt for real facts, the traditions of their bards, when they throw lustre on the ancient state of their country.

The present poem opens in the morning. Cairbar is represented as retired from the rest of the Irish chiefs, and tormented with remorse for the murder of Cormac, when news was brought him of Fingal's landing. What passed, preceding that day, and is necessary to be known for carrying on the poem, is afterwards introduced by way of episode. [M]

This poem is substantially, though by no means wholly, identical with the first book of the completed epic 'Temora', published in 1763 after the translator's hands had been fortunate enough to lay hold of the missing materials. It is clear from the note that the expansion was projected at an early stage, since the story is already outlined here, the elaboration presumably being made dependent on the financial success of Fingal. The first book of 'Temora' appears to be the only part grounded in authentic sources, for which see Thomson, pp. 59 ff. It should be noted that, despite the publication of the whole work in 1763, the text of the initial version is still included in the first volume of the collected Works of 1765 (though not the Poems of 1773) which is why it is reproduced here. Since the reader has the opportunity of comparing it for himself with the later reworking, the notes will generally be confined to significant variants within the same version. The only difference of any consequence in the actual plot is the removal of Fergus and Usnoth from the completed epic. Admirers of Cesarotti, whose fine Ossianic translations are a milestone in Italian literature, might be relieved to learn that his apparent aberrations in the translation of 'Temora' are to be explained by his continuing to use this, the first version, for his rendering of the first book of the completed epic.

2.   The scene described here is nearly that of the epic poem, Fingal. In this neighbourhood also the sons of Usnoth were killed. [M]

3.   Mór-lath, *great in the day of battle.* Hidalla', *wildly looking hero.* Cor-mar, *expert at sea.* Málth-os, *slow to speak.* Foldath, *generous.* [M]
wildly looking] mildly looking (*completed epic: all editions*)
The later reading is included here, since Hidalla's character makes it likely that wildly is a misprint. The name itself furnishes one of Macpherson's more impenetrable etymologies (though allaidh - *pronounced* alli - *does mean "wild", "fierce"). Cf. Jiriczek, 3:226.*

4.   Mór-annail, *strong breath*; a very proper name for a scout. [M]

5.   Mor-annal here alludes to the particular appearance of Fingal's spear.——If a man, upon his first landing in a strange country, kept the point of his spear forward, it denoted in those days that he came in a hostile manner, and accordingly he was treated as an enemy; if he kept the point behind him, it was a token of friendship, and he was immediately invited to the feast according to the hospitality of the times. [M]

6.   This was the famous sword of Fingal, made by Luno, a smith of Lochlin, and after him poetically called the *son of Luno:* it is said of this sword, that it killed a man at every stroke; and that Fingal never used it, but in times of the greatest danger. [M]

7.   That is, who has heard my vaunting? He intended the expression as a rebuke to the self-praise of Foldath. [M]

8.   Cathol the son of Maronnan, or Moran, was murdered by Cairbar, for his attachment to the family of Cormac. He had attended Oscar to the *war of Inis-thona*, where they contracted a great friendship for one another. Oscar, immediately after the death of Cathol, had sent a formal challenge to Cairbar, which he prudently declined, but conceived a secret hatred against Oscar, and had beforehand contrived to kill him at the feast, to which he here invites him. [M]

9.   He alludes to the battle of Oscar against Caros, *king of ships*; who is supposed to be the same with Carausius the usurper. [M]

10.   Cath-mór, *great in battle.* Cairbar takes advantage of his brother's absence, to perpetrate his ungenerous designs against Oscar; for the noble spirit of Cathmor, had he been present, would not have permitted the laws of that hospitality, for which he was so renowned himself, to be violated. The brothers form a contrast; we do not detest the mean soul of Cairbar more, than we admire the disinterested and generous mind of Cathmor. [M]

11.   Fingal's army heard the joy that was in Cairbar's camp. The character given of Cathmor is agreeable to the times. Some, through ostentation, were hospitable; and others fell naturally into a custom handed down from their ancestors. But what marks strongly the character of Cathmor, is his aversion to praise; for he is

represented to dwell in a wood to avoid the thanks of his guests; which is still a higher degree of generosity than that of Axylus in Homer: for the poet does not say, but the good man might, at the head of his own table, have heard with pleasure the praise bestowed on him by the people he entertained. [*gr.q.*] HOM. [*Iliad*] 6.12. Next Teuthras' son distain'd the sands with blood,/ Axylus, hospitable, rich and good:/ In fair Arisbe's walls, his native place,/ He held his seat; a friend to human race./ Fast by the road, his ever open door/ Oblig'd the wealthy, and reliev'd the poor. POPE. [M]

In the Temora *volume the translator will dispense altogether with such references and parallel passages.*

The build-up of Cathmor anticipates the major role Macpherson already envisages for him in the completed epic.

12.   When a chief was determined to kill a man that was in his power already, it was usual to signify, that his death was intended, by the sound of a shield struck with the blunt end of a spear; at the same time that a bard at a distance raised the *death-song*. A ceremony of another kind was long used in Scotland upon such occasions. Every body has heard that a bull's head was served up to Lord Douglas in the castle of Edinburgh, as a certain signal of his approaching death. [M]

13.   Cormac, the son of Arth, had given the spear, which is here the foundation of the quarrel, to Oscar when he came to congratulate him, upon Swaran's being expelled from Ireland. [M]

14.   Ti'-mór-ri', *the house of the great king*, the name of the royal palace of the supreme kings of Ireland. [M]

The ancient seat of the Irish kings, Temair *or* Teamhair *(= "wall"), in Meath, called* Temoria *by O'Flaherty. Although Macpherson seems to have been unaware of this,* Temora, Tura *and* Tara *are all forms of the same word - see Stern, p. 67.*

15.   Atha, *shallow river*: the name of Cairbar's seat in Connaught. [M]

16.   The poet means Malvina, the daughter of Toscar, to whom he addressed that part of the poem, which related to the death of Oscar her lover. [M]

17.   The Irish historians place the death of Cairbar, in the latter end of the third century: they say, he was killed in battle against Oscar the son of Ossian, but deny that he fell by his hand. As they have nothing to go upon but the traditions of their bards, the translator thinks that the account of Ossian is as probable: at the worst, it is but opposing one tradition to another. [M]

18.   Bran was one of Fingal's dogs.—He was so remarkable for his fleetness, that the poet, in a piece which is not just now in the translator's hands, has given him the same properties with Virgil's Camilla. [M]

For Bran *as a dog's name, cf.* 'Fingal' V, *p. 94, note 35 ; Fingal's* Bran *is introduced in the very next book, above, p. 103. In authentic tradition he is indeed Fionn's hound, endowed with semi-human properties.*

19.   wash away] raise 1762

20.   Althan, the son of Conachar, was the chief bard of Arth king of Ireland. After the death of Arth, Althan attended his son Cormac, and was present at his death.— He had made his escape from Cairbar, by the means of Cathmor, and coming to Fingal, related, as here, the death of his master Cormac. [M]

21.   Althan speaks. [M]

22.   Doira, *the woody side of a mountain*; it is here a hill in the neighbourhood of Temora. [M]

23. [*l.q.*] VIRG. [*Æneid*, 8.588 ff.] So from the seas exerts his radiant head,/ The star, by whom the lights of heav'n are led:/ Shakes from his rosy locks the pearly dews;/ Dispels the darkness, and the day renews. DRYDEN. [M]
24. Arth, or Artho, the father of Cormac king of Ireland. [M]
25. Slimora, a hill in Connaught, near which Cuchullin was killed. [M]
26. That is, they saw a manifest likeness between the person of Nathos and Cuchullin. [M]
27. Geal-lamha, *white-handed*. [M]
28. Althan speaks. [M]
29. That is, himself and Carril, as it afterwards appears. [M]
30. The persons of the bards were so sacred, that even he, who had just murdered his sovereign, feared to kill them. [M]
31. like the sunny field] like the plain of the sun 1762
32. moved] travelled 1762
33. Oscar] Oscur 'Fragment' VII.
This and other name changes are effected throughout, and will be indicated only once.
34. Chief] Prince 'Fragment' VII.
35. Chief] Prince 'Fragment' VII.
36. But, son of Alpin ... blood of thy friend.] *added* 1762
It is as difficult to forgive this easy "transition", whereby the original Fragment *is appropriated to another* Oscar, *the son of* Caruth - *and which for Laing (2:393) amounts to an avowal of the whole imposture - as it is to understand how Macpherson, who had already been collecting for some years, should still have been ignorant of the authentic traditions about the death of Oscur when he presented the poem to John Home in the autumn of 1759.*
37. equal to] a match for 'Fragment' VII.
38. who never fled in war.] before invincible. 'Fragment' VII.
39. the son of Caruth] my son 'Fragment' VII.
40. Caruth,] Oscian, 'Fragment' VII.
41. Diaran,] Morny 'Fragment' VII.
42. the running water,] the silvery stream, 'Fragment' VII.
43. curdled] crudled 'Fragment' VII.
44. The stately Dermid] Dermid the graceful 'Fragment' VII.
45. who never yielded] invincible 'Fragment' VII.
46. of his love; he returned,] whom he loved; returned, 'Fragment' VII.
47. the valiant Gormur, whom I slew in battle.] Gormur the brave, whom in battle I slew. 'Fragment' VII.
48. *The original* Fragment *contains a note about suicide which is omitted here.*
49. that] thy 'Fragment' VII.
50. Who] I fall resolved on death: and who 'Fragment' VII.
51. the son of Caruth?] me? 'Fragment' VII.
52. the maid replied,] *added* 1762
53. the soul] the blood, the soul 'Fragment' VII.
54. end.] end thus. 'Fragment' VII.
55. with the] with 'Fragment' VII.
56. over] is over 'Fragment' VII.

Carric-thura

1.   Fingal, returning from an expedition which he had made into the Roman province, resolved to visit Cathulla king of Inis-tore, and brother to Comála, whose story is related, at large, in the dramatic poem, published in this collection. Upon his coming in sight of Carric-thura, the palace of Cathulla, he observed a flame on its top, which, in those days, was a signal of distress. The wind drove him into a bay, at some distance from Carric-thura, and he was obliged to pass the night on the shore. Next day he attacked the army of Frothal king of Sora who had besieged Cathulla in his palace of Carric-thura, and took Frothal himself prisoner, after he had engaged him in a single combat. The deliverance of Carric-thura is the subject of the poem, but several other episodes are interwoven with it. It appears from tradition, that this poem was addressed to a Culdee, or one of the first Christian missionaries, and that the story of the *Spirit of Loda*, supposed to be the ancient Odin of Scandinavia, was introduced by Ossian in opposition to the Culdee's doctrine. Be this as it will, it lets us into Ossian's notions of a superior being; and shews that he was not addicted to the superstition which prevailed all the world over, before the introduction of Christianity. [M]

'Carric-thura', *together with* 'Carthon', 'Dar-thula' *and the* 'Songs of Selma', *perhaps the most popular and influential of all of the Ossianic poems, incorporates* 'Fragments' I, II, IV *and* V.

2.   The song of Ullin, with which the poem opens, is in a lyric measure. It was usual with Fingal, when he returned from his expeditions, to send his bards singing before him. This species of triumph is called, by Ossian, the *song of victory*. [M]

3.   *It should perhaps be noted that the Gaelic words for sun and moon* (grian *and* gealach) *are both in fact feminine.*

4.   strife of Crona] strife of Carun 1773

Ossian has celebrated the *strife of Crona*, in a particular poem. This poem is connected with it, but it was impossible for the translator to procure that part which relates to Crona, with any degree of purity. [M]

Cf. above 'Carthon', *p. 127, note 4. Laing comments (1:415):* "as Fingal had also returned in Carthon from the strife of Crona, the text was altered in the improved editions, without a correspondent alteration in the notes."

5.   gray] light 1773

6.   One should think that the parts of Shilric and Vinvela were represented by Cronnan and Minona, whose very names denote that they were singers, who performed in public. Cronnan signifies *a mournful sound*; Minona, or Mín-'ónn, *soft air*. All the dramatic poems of Ossian appear to have been presented before Fingal, upon solemn occasions. [M]

Laing comments (1:417, n. 10): "This, and the next episode, are the two first Fragments, inserted in Carric-thura as a dramatic interlude, performed in the Highlands before Fingal. An heroic poem, with short dramas by way of episodes, is a species of composition unknown to Aristotle, and we may conceive the improvement of which the Aeneid would have been susceptible, if Virgil had introduced his pastorals as dramatic poems, exhibited before Aeneas at the courts of Dido, Acestes, or Evander ..." *To some extent Laing's irony misfires here, for not only does Macpherson's mixing of the genres represent an important proto-romantic feature of his work, but it is also - quite remarkably - anticipated in his authentic sources (see Meek, p. 22; also p. 25 , for the bringing together of poetry and prose).*

7. Bran, or Branno, signifies *a mountain-stream:* it is here some river known by that name, in the days of Ossian. There are several small rivers in the north of Scotland still retaining the name of Bran; in particular one which falls into the Tay at Dunkeld. [M]

8. Bhín-bheul, *a woman with a melodious voice.* Bh in the Galic Language has the same sound with the *v* in English. [M]

9. —Indeed] ; alas! 1773

10. Indeed,] Alas! 1773

11. The grave. [M]

12. Carn-mór, *high rocky hill.* [M]

13. The distinction, which the ancient Scots made between good and bad spirits, was, that the former appeared sometimes in the day-time in lonely unfrequented places, but the latter seldom but by night, and always in a dismal gloomy scene. [M]
seldom] never 1762 1773
always] *(only) 1765*

14. no ... nigh.] *deleted* 1773

15. lovely] O 1773

16. pool.] lake 1773

17. expired.] fell. 1773

18. gray] *deleted* 1773

19. on the wings of the gale! on the blast of the mountain,] on the light-winged gale! on the breeze of the desart, 1773

20. green] warning 1773

21. *The circle of Loda* is supposed to be a place of worship among the Scandinavians, as the spirit of Loda is thought to be the same with their god Odin. [M]

22. battling chief.] chief distrest. 1773

23. He is described, in a simile, in the poem concerning the death of Cuchullin. [M]
See above, p. 138.

24. of his strength,] in night, 1773

25. dismal spirit of Loda?] spirit of dismal Loda? 1773

26. There is a great resemblance between the terrors of this mock divinity, and those of the true God, as they are described in the 18th Psalm. [M]
Note deleted 1773

27. calm] pleasant 1773

28. But the king,] Fingal, 1773

29. The famous sword of Fingal, made by Lun, or Luno, a smith of Lochlin. [M]
Cf. above, 'Temora', p. 148, note 6.

30. *Fingal's encounter with the Spirit of Loda seems to have been inspired by a ballad on Fionn's combat with the Muilgheartach, a one-eyed monster from Lochlin, through whom blades pass like knives through a flame - see Thomson, pp. 51 ff.*

31. The king] Fingal 1773

32. battling] wrathful 1773

33. the king] him 1773

34. Annir was also the father of Erragon, who was king after the death of his brother Frothal. The death of Erragon is the subject of *the battle of Lora*, a poem in this collection. [M]
king] killed 1765 *(misprint?)*

35. car-borne] sea-borne 1773
36. rage] flame 1773
37. That is, after the death of Annir. To erect the stone of one's fame, was, in other words, to say that the person was dead. [M]
38. mountain,] desart, 1773
39. on Gormal;] in Lochlin; 1773
40. Honourable terms of peace. [M]
41. He is like the thunder] His sword is the bolt 1773
42. king] chief 1773
43. flying host.] foe. 1773
44. daughter of Inistore] the low-laid Comála 1773
By the daughter of Inistore, Frothal means Comála, of whose death Utha probably had not heard; consequently she feared that the former passion of Frothal for Comála might return. [M]
Note deleted 1773
45. her soft sighs rose, at my departure.] her secret sighs rose, when I spread the sail. 1773
46. Utha ... but] Utha of harps, [that my soul ...] 1773
47. a glittering helmet.] her steel. 1773
48. along the blue waters of Tora:] by thy native streams. 1773
49. Frothal and Utha. [M]
50. opened.] opened wide.
51. The voice of] The soft sound of 1773
52. There is a propriety in introducing this episode, as the situations of Crimora and Utha were so similar. [M]
53. Lotha's mighty stream.] Lotha's roaring stream! 1773
Lotha was the ancient name of one of the great rivers in the north of Scotland. The only one of them that still retains a name of a like sound is Lochy, in Invernessshire; but whether it is the river mentioned here, the translator will not pretend to say. [M]
54. maid of Tora.] Utha. 1773
55. Cri-móra, *a woman of a great soul.* [M]
56. Perhaps the Carril mentioned here is the same with Carril the son of Kinfena, Cuchullin's bard. The name itself is proper to any bard, as it signifies *a sprightly and harmonious sound.* [M]
Here, as in note 23 above, the original spelling of Cuchullin *is preserved in the edition of 1773.*
57. disturbs my Connal?] darkens in Connal's soul? 1773
Connal, the son of Diaran, was one of the most famous heroes of Fingal; he was slain in a battle against Dargo a Briton; but whether by the hand of the enemy, or that of his mistress, tradition does not determine. [M]
58. sable] dark-brown 1773
59. full moon when it moves] full-orbed moon when she moves 1773
60. keep my memory.] send my name to other times. 1773
61. of light;] that gleam; 1773
62. like a cloud ... contracted and dark.] darkening in his rage. His brows were gathered into wrath. 1773
63. dire] loud 1773
64. your] their 1773 (*address transferred to third person throughout paragraph*)

65. children] hapless children 1773
66. carry the ship of Fingal] drove Fingal 1773
67. The story of Fingal and the spirit of Loda, supposed to be the famous Odin, is the most extravagant fiction in all Ossian's poems. It is not, however, without precedents in the best poets; and it must be said for Ossian, that he says nothing but what perfectly agreed with the notions of the times, concerning ghosts. They thought the souls of the dead were material, and consequently susceptible of pain. Whether a proof could be drawn from this passage, that Ossian had no notion of a divinity, I shall leave to others to determine: it appears, however, that he was of opinion, that superior beings ought to take no notice of what passed among men. [M]

The Songs of Selma
1.   This poem fixes the antiquity of a custom, which is well known to have prevailed afterwards, in the north of Scotland, and in Ireland. The bards, at an annual feast, provided by the king or chief, repeated their poems, and such of them as were thought, by him, worthy of being preserved, were carefully taught to their children, in order to have them transmitted to posterity.——It was one of those occasions that afforded the subject of the present poem to Ossian.—It is called in the original, The Songs of Selma, which title it was thought proper to adopt in the translation.
     The poem is entirely lyric, and has a great variety of versification. The address to the evening star, with which it opens, has, in the original, all the harmony that numbers could give it; flowing down with all that tranquillity and softness, which the scene described naturally inspires.—Three of the songs which are introduced in this piece, were published among the fragments of ancient poetry, printed last year. [M]
The 'Fragments' in question are X, XII *and* XI.
In 1773 the note is replaced by the following Argument:
Address to the evening star. An apostrophe to Fingal and his times. Minona sings before the king the song of the unfortunate Colma; and the bards exhibit other specimens of their talents; according to an annual custom established by the monarchs of the ancient Caledonians.
2.   of the descending] of the falling 1762 of descending 1773
3.   that are past.] of other years. 1773
4.   Alpin is from the same root with Albion, or rather Albin, the ancient name of Britain; Alp *high*, in *land*, or *country*. The present name of our island has its origin in the Celtic tongue; so that those who derived it from any other, betrayed their ignorance of the ancient language of our country.——*Britain* comes from *Breac't in, variegated island*, so called from the face of the country, from the natives painting themselves, or from their party-coloured cloaths. [M]
Britain comes from] (*only*) 1765
Breac't ... cloaths.] Brait or Braid, extensive; and *in*, land. 1773
5.   Minona then] Minona 1762 1773
Ossian introduces Minona, not in the ideal scene in his own mind, which he had described; but at the annual feast of Selma, where the bards repeated their works before Fingal. [M] (*only*) 1762 1773
6.   Sealg-'er, *a hunter.* [M]
The original spelling in 'Fragment' X - Shalgar - corresponds to Gaelic pronunciation.

7.   Cul-math, *a woman with fine hair*. [M]

8.   music!] song! 1773

9.   shrieks] pours 1773

10. the son] the chief 1773

11. my father ... my brother] from my father ... from my brother 1773

A considerable improvement - the punctuation in 'Fragment' X is unfortunately departed from in 1762 and 1765, so that the meaning is not immediately apparent (and translators such as Goethe should be congratulated for divining it).

12. over the heath;] around. 1773

13. I who call.] Colma who calls. 1773

14. the moon appeareth.] the calm moon comes forth. 1773

15. face of the hill.] steep. 1773

16. his dogs ... coming.] His dogs come not before him, with tidings of his near approach. 1773

17. But ... heath?] Who lie on the heath beside me? 1773

18. they answer not.] To Colma they give no reply. Speak to me: I am alone! [My soul ...] 1773

19. Cold] Cold, cold 1773

20. mountain,] steep, 1773

21. you?] the departed? 1773

22. storms of the hill.] storm! 1773

23. when ... heath;] when the loud winds arise; 1773

24. wind,] blast, 1773

25. they both to me.] her friends to Colma! 1773

26. maid] daughter 1773

27. voice ... grave.] voice for those that have passed away. 1773

28. plain.] vale. 1773

29. Mór-ér, *great man*. [M]

30. hill;] desart; 1773

31. like] *deleted* 1773

32. Torman, the son of Carthul, lord of I-mora, one of the western isles. [M]

33. Armin, *a hero*. He was chief or petty king of Gorma, i.e. *the blue island*, supposed to be one of the Hebrides. [M]

34. Cear-mór, *a tall dark-complexioned man*. [M]

35. family flourish,] house ascend, 1773

36. blow upon the dark heath!] blow along the heath! 1773

37. howl, ye tempests, in the top of the oak!] roar, tempests, in the groves of my oaks! 1773

38. that sad night,] the night, 1773

39. on the hills of Fura;] on Fura; 1773

Fuar-a, *cold island*. [M]

40. along the rolling sea.] *deleted* 1773

41. By *the son of the rock* the poet means the echoing back of the human voice from a rock. The vulgar were of opinion, that this repetition of sound was made by a spirit within the rock; and they, on that account, called it *mac-talla*; *the son who dwells in the rock*. [M]

Elsewhere, however, by son of the rock the poet seems to mean some kind of hermit: Allad, the Druid, in 'Fingal' V (p. 94, note 37); another Druid in 'Comála' (p. 107, note 21); or his famous Culdee, as in 'The Battle of Lora' *(beginning, and p. 121, note 32), and* 'Calthon and Colmal', *p. 171.*

42. Ardnart,] Arnart 1773
43. bend] fly 1762 wind 1773
44. The poet here only means that Erath was bound with leathern thongs. [M]
45. wave] deep 1762 1773
46. by the waves.] *deleted* 1773
47. cries; nor ... relieve her.] cries. What could her father do? 1773
48. on the side of the mountain.] on the hill. 1773
49. of the mountain come;] aloft arise: 1773
50. Ossian is sometimes poetically called *the voice of Cona*. [M]

Calthon and Colmal

1. This piece, as many more of Ossian's compositions, is addressed to one of the first Christian missionaries.—The story of the poem is handed down, by tradition, thus—In the country of the Britons between the walls, two chiefs lived in the days of Fingal, Dunthalmo, lord of Teutha, supposed to be the Tweed; and Rathmor, who dwelt at Clutha, well known to be the river Clyde.——Rathmor was not more renowned for his generosity and hospitality, than Dunthalmo was infamous for his cruelty and ambition.—Dunthalmo, through envy, or on account of some private feuds, which subsisted between the families, murdered Rathmor at a feast; but being afterwards touched with remorse, he educated the two sons of Rathmor, Calthon and Colmar, in his own house.—They growing up to man's estate, dropped some hints that they intended to revenge the death of their father, upon which Dunthalmo shut them up in two caves on the banks of Teutha, intending to take them off privately.—Colmal, the daughter of Dunthalmo, who was secretly in love with Calthon, helped him to make his escape from prison, and fled with him to Fingal, disguised in the habit of a young warrior, and implored his aid against Dunthalmo.——Fingal sent Ossian with three hundred men, to Colmar's relief.—Dunthalmo having previously murdered Colmar, came to a battle with Ossian; but he was killed by that hero, and his army totally defeated.

   Calthon married Colmal, his deliverer; and Ossian returned to Morven. [M]

2. If chance the radiant sun with farewel sweet/ Extend his evening beam, the fields revive,/ The birds their notes renew, and bleating herds/ Attest their joy, that hill and valley rings. MILTON. [*Paradise Lost*, 2.492 ff.] —The fair sun-shine in summer's day;/ —When a dreadful storm away is flit/ Through the broad world doth spread his goodly ray;/ At sight whereof each bird that sits on spray,/ And every beast that to his den was fled,/ Come forth afresh out of their late dismay,/ And to the light lift up their drooping head. SPENCER. [M]

Note deleted 1773

That Macpherson quotes the latter sonnet is regarded by Laing (1:474, n. 1) as proof that he consulted Newton's edition of Milton for parallel passages (the Spenser is also quoted by Newton).

3. Al-teutha, or rather Balteutha, *the town of Tweed*, the name of Dunthalmo's seat. It is observable that all the names in this poem, are derived from the Galic language; which, as I have remarked in a preceding note, is a proof that it was once the universal language of the whole island. [M]

as I ... note,] *deleted* 1773

"Clutha and Teutha are the Clyde and the Tweed; and as Balclutha was Dumbarton, or the town of Clyde, Balteutha must have been Berwick upon Tweed." (*Laing, 1:476*)

Cf. above, 'Carthon', *p. 128, note 11*.

4.   descended] rushed forth 1773

5.   Caol-mhal, *a woman with small eye-brows*; small eye-brows were a distinguishing part of beauty in Ossian's time: and he seldom fails to give them to the fine women of his poems. [M]

6.   That is, the hall where the arms taken from enemies were hung up as trophies. Ossian is very careful to make his stories probable; for he makes Colmal put on the arms of a youth killed in his first battle, as more proper for a young woman, who cannot be supposed strong enough to carry the armour of a full-grown warrior. [M] *Cf.* 'Dar-thula', *p. 142, note 40*.

7.   Fingal. [M]

8.   darkly-rolling] *deleted* 1773

9.   shades of night] shadows 1762 1773

10.   Dunthalmo ... field,] Arise, or thy steps may be seen, 1773

11.   face; and her breast rose] face. Her bosom heaved 1773

12.   hall.] hall of shells. 1773

13.   the people.] a thousand chiefs. 1773

14.   he said,] began the king,

15.   mighty] rushing 1773

16.   Diaran, father of that Connal who was unfortunately killed by Crimora, his mistress. [M]

17.   *Macpherson's note and the lamentation of the widow of Dargo may be found appended to the text of* 'Calthon and Colmal', *pp. 174 f.*

18.   lovely,] stately. 1773

19.   on ... Teutha.] whilst Teutha's waters rolled between. 1773

20.   battling] warlike

21.   might,] night, 1762 1773

22.   red] blushing 1773

23.   descended.] rushed down. 1773

24.   son of Rathmor] Calthon 1773 (= *note* 1762 1765)

25.   Teutha; and Ossian returned to Selma.] Teutha. 1773

26.   *This touching lament does indeed have some* poetical merit. *In Macpherson's time it was still sung by thousands in the Highlands and Islands, and this rendering is probably as close as he ever gets to faithful translation. For the original, see Thomson, p. 55 ff.*

Lathmon

1.   Lathmon a British prince, taking advantage of Fingal's absence in Ireland, made a descent on Morven, and advanced within sight of Selma the royal palace. Fingal arrived in the mean time, and Lathmon retreated to a hill, where his army was surprised by night, and himself taken prisoner by Ossian and Gaul the son of Morni. This exploit of Gaul and Ossian bears a near resemblance to the beautiful episode of Nisus and Euryalus in Virgil's ninth Æneid. The poem opens, with the first appearance of Fingal on the coast of Morven, and ends, it may be supposed, about noon the next day. The first paragraph is in a lyric measure, and appears to

have been sung, of old, to the harp, as a prelude to the narrative part of the poem, which is in heroic verse. [M]

absence in Ireland,] absence on an expedition in Ireland, 1773

royal palace.] royal residence. 1773

This exploit of Gaul and Ossian ... Æneid.] *deleted* 1773

The first paragraph ... heroic verse.] *deleted* 1773

2.   Ullin] Erin 1773

3.   It is said, by tradition, that it was the intelligence of Lathmon's invasion, that occasioned Fingal's return from Ireland; though Ossian, more poetically, ascribes the cause of Fingal's knowledge to his dream. [M]

4.   He alludes to a battle wherein Fingal had defeated Lathmon. The occasion of this first war, between those heroes, is told by Ossian in another poem, which the translator has seen. [M]

The occasion ... has seen.] *deleted* 1773

5.   Morni was chief of a numerous tribe, in the days of Fingal and his father Comhal. The last mentioned hero was killed in battle against Morni's tribe; but the valour and conduct of Fingal reduced them, at last, to obedience. We find the two heroes perfectly reconciled in this poem. [M]

6.   Stru'-moné, *stream of the hill*. Here the proper name of a rivulet in the neighbourhood of Selma. [M]

7.   youth.] father. 1773

8.   the sign of war is heard.] his signals are spread on the wind. 1773

9.   arms ... age,] shield of my father's latter years. 1773

10. gray] aged 1773

11. often] *deleted* 1773

12. rejoiced over the warrior,] arose before him with joy 1773

13. King of the] Chief of 1773

14. joy] soul 1773

15. sun] light 1773

16. at once.] in my presence. 1773

17. Ossian speaks. The contrast between the old and young heroes is strongly marked. The circumstance of the latter's drawing their swords is well imagined, and agrees with the impatience of young soldiers, just entered upon action. [M]

18. Ullin had chosen ill the subject of his song. The *darkness which gathered on Morni's brow*, did not proceed from any dislike he had to Comhal's name, though they were foes, but from his fear that the song would awaken Fingal to remembrance of the feuds which had subsisted of old between the families. Fingal's speech on this occasion abounds with generosity and good sense. [M]

19. king] hero 1773

20. This expression is ambiguous in the original. It either signifies that Comhal killed many in battle, or that he was implacable in his resentment. The translator has endeavoured to preserve the same ambiguity in the version; as it was probably designed by the poet. [M]

Note deleted 1773

21. heard on a distant heath.] moving on the hills. 1773

22. swift] young and swift 1773

23. wall.] hall. 1773

24.   Ossian had married her a little time before. The story of his courtship of this lady is introduced, as an episode, in the fourth book of Fingal. [M]
Note deleted 1773

25.   the mighty] *deleted* 1773

26.   like the grass of the field,] unknown: 1773

27.   This proposal of Gaul is much more noble, and more agreeable to true heroism, than the behaviour of Ulysses and Diomed in the Iliad, or that of Nisus and Euryalus in the Æneid. What his valour and generosity suggested became the foundation of his success. For the enemy being dismayed with the sound of Ossian's shield, which was the common signal of battle, thought that Fingal's whole army came to attack them; so that they fly in reality from an army, not from two heroes; which reconciles the story to probability. [M]
Note deleted 1773

28.   Crotho's] Crotha's 1765

29.   Car-borne is a title of honour bestowed, by Ossian, indiscriminately on every hero; as every chief, in his time, kept a chariot or litter by way of state. [M]
Note deleted 1773

For which the evident reason is that between 1765 and 1773 Ossian had become significantly more discriminating - witness the multifarious substitutions for car-borne in the revised edition.

30.   Fingal. [M]

31.   Fingal and Morni. [M]

32.   The behaviour of Gaul, throughout this poem, is that of a hero in the most exalted sense. The modesty of Ossian, concerning his own actions, is not less remarkable than his impartiality with regard to Gaul, for it is well known that Gaul afterwards rebelled against Fingal, which might be supposed to have bred prejudices against him in the breast of Ossian. But as Gaul, from an enemy, became Fingal's firmest friend and greatest hero, the poet passes over one slip in his conduct, on account of his many virtues. [M]
Note deleted 1773

33.   Suil-mhath, *a man of good eye-sight.* [M]

34.   Dubh-bhranna, *dark mountain-stream.* What river went by this name, in the days of Ossian, is not easily ascertained, at this distance of time. A river in Scotland, which falls into the sea at Banff, still retains the name of Duvran. If that is meant, by Ossian, in this passage, Lathmon must have been a prince of the Pictish nation, or those Caledonians who inhabited of old the eastern coast of Scotland. [M]
meant, by Ossian, in] meant in 1773

35.   Ossian seldom fails to give his heroes, though enemies, that generosity of temper which, it appears from his poems, was a conspicuous part of his own character. Those who too much despise their enemies do not reflect, that the more they take from the valour of their foes, the less merit they have themselves in conquering them. The custom of depreciating enemies is not altogether one of the refinements of modern heroism. This railing disposition is one of the capital faults in Homer's characters, which, by the bye, cannot be imputed to the poet, who kept to the manners of the times in which he wrote. Milton has followed Homer in this respect; but railing is less shocking in infernal spirits, who are the objects of horror, than in heroes, who are set up as patterns of imitation. [M]
Note deleted 1773

36. let ... Lathmon.] let us contend in fight. 1773
37. people,] warriors, 1773
38. warriors] people 1773
39. Cutha appears to have been Lathmon's wife or mistress. [M]
Note deleted 1773
40. mortal] *deleted* 1773
41. spirits] ghosts 1762 1773
42. spirits] ghosts 1762 1773
It was thought, in Ossian's time, that each person had his attending spirit. The traditions concerning this opinion are dark and unsatisfactory. [M]
43. dark] *deleted* 1773
44. Dunlathmon's battling king.] Lathmon king of spears. 1773
45. come to Dunlathmon,] rouse thee, O Lathmon, 1773
46. lightning] light 1773

Oithóna

1.   Gaul, the son of Morni, attended Lathmon into his own country, after his being defeated in Morven, as related in the preceding poem. He was kindly entertained by Nuäth, the father of Lathmon, and fell in love with his daughter Oithóna.——The lady was no less enamoured of Gaul, and a day was fixed for their marriage. In the mean time Fingal, preparing for an expedition into the country of the Britons, sent for Gaul. He obeyed, and went; but not without promising to Oithóna to return, if he survived the war, by a certain day.—Lathmon too was obliged to attend his father Nuäth in his wars, and Oithóna was left alone at Dunlathmon, the seat of the family.—Dunrommath, lord of Cuthal, supposed to be one of the Orkneys, taking advantage of the absence of her friends, came and carried off, by force, Oithóna, who had formerly rejected his love, into Tromáthon, a desert island, where he concealed her in a cave.

Gaul returned on the day appointed; heard of the rape, and sailed to Tromáthon, to revenge himself on Dunrommath. When he landed, he found Oithóna disconsolate, and resolved not to survive the loss of her honour.—She told him the story of her misfortunes, and she scarce ended, when Dunrommath, with his followers, appeared at the further end of the island. Gaul prepared to attack him, recommending to Oithóna to retire, till the battle was over.—She seemingly obeyed; but she secretly armed herself, rushed into the thickest of the battle, and was mortally wounded.— Gaul pursuing the flying enemy, found her just expiring on the field: he mourned over her, raised her tomb, and returned to Morven.——Thus is the story handed down by tradition; nor is it given with any material difference in the poem, which opens with Gaul's return to Dunlathmon, after the rape of Oithóna. [M]
[§ 1] Dunrommath, lord of Cuthal] D..., lord of Uthal *(all editions - misprint)*
This note is taken over unaltered as the Argument *in 1773, despite the fact that there the* preceding poem *is not* 'Lathmon' *but* 'Colna-dona'.
2.   Some gentle taper/ ——visit us/ With thy long levelled rule of streaming light. MILTON. [*Comus*, 337 ff.] [M]
Note deleted 1773
3.   Oi-thóna, *the virgin of the wave.* [M]
4.   Morlo, the son of Leth, is one of Fingal's most famous heroes. He and three other men attended Gaul on his expedition to Tromáthon. [M]

5.   heroes.] chiefs. 1773
6.   dark] *deleted* 1773
7.   rolled] rolled deep 1773
8.   heard.] feebly heard. 1773
9.   of wrath.] of his soul. 1773
10.   [*gr.q.*] Hom. Od. v. 280. Then swell'd to sight Phæacia's dusky coast,/ And woody mountains half in vapours lost;/ That lay before him indistinct and vast,/ Like a broad shield amid the watry waste. [Pope.] Tróm-thón, *heavy or deep-sounding wave.* [*M*]
Reference to Homer deleted 1773
11.   but her] thrice her 1773
12.   high Dunlathmon!] car-borne Nuäth! 1773
13.   Car-borne] Young 1773
14.   sighing] *deleted* 1773
15.   sorrow,] grief; 1773
16.   fallen] departed 1773
17.   hero] chief 1773
18.   Oithóna relates how she was carried away by Dunrommath. [M]
19.   strength of] *deleted* 1773
20.   of Dunrommath!] of thy foe! 1773
21.   daughter of Nuäth,] my love, 1773
22.   strong.] strong in war! 1773
23.   The daughter of Nuäth] Oithóna 1773
24.   daughter of Nuäth?] maid? 1773
25.   echoing] troubled 1773
26.   sons] race 1773
27.   firs.] pines. 1773
28.   side.] heaving side. 1773
29.   Sleep comes, like a cloud,] Sleep grows, like darkness, 1773
30.   hero] warrior 1773

Croma

1.   Malvina the daughter of Toscar is overheard by Ossian lamenting the death of Oscar her lover. Ossian, to divert her grief, relates his own actions in an expedition which he undertook, at Fingal's command, to aid Crothar the petty king of Croma, a country in Ireland, against Rothmar who invaded his dominions. The story is delivered down thus, in tradition. Crothar king of Croma being blind with age, and his son too young for the field, Rothmar the chief of Tromlo resolved to avail himself of the opportunity offered of annexing the dominions of Crothar to his own. He accordingly marched into the country subject to Crothar, but which he held of Arth or Artho, who was, at the time, supreme king of Ireland.

Crothar being, on account of his age and blindness, unfit for action, sent for aid to Fingal king of Scotland; who ordered his son Ossian to the relief of Crothar. But before his arrival Fovar-gormo, the son of Crothar, attacking Rothmar, was slain himself, and his forces totally defeated. Ossian renewed the war; came to battle, killed Rothmar, and routed his army. Croma being thus delivered of its enemies, Ossian returned to Scotland. [M]

2.   few are his visits to the dreams] seldom art thou in the dreams 1773

3.   ye fathers of mighty Toscar.] O father of Toscar of shields! 1773
4.   of Malvina's departure] of Malvina 1773
5.   dark-rolling] dark-rolling face 1773

As Jiriczek points out (3:131), the initial reading of dark-rolling *as a verbal noun can be supported by reference to* 'Temora' V: I behold ... the blue-rolling of their misty wreaths (*see p. 272*).

6.   departed.] fled. 1773
7.   few are his visits] seldom comes he 1773

Laing (1:537 f., n. 2) suspects that the avoidance of visit *in the opening paragraph in the later edition - apart from being designed to conceal a debt to James Thomson - might have been occasioned by Macpherson's having difficulty finding a Gaelic equivalent (he had in the meantime caused an "original" version of* 'Malvina's Dream' *to be put into circulation). If so, it would not be the only instance of Macpherson's demonstrably adjusting his English to accord with a Gaelic text designed to prove the authenticity of Ossian. Temora, as first published in 1763, concludes with* A Specimen of the Original *of the seventh book of the epic. When the* Works *appear in 1765, the Gaelic remains the same, but the English has undergone certain transformations which bring it into a much closer relationship to its putative original. Cf. p. 279, note 10.*

8.   Mor'-ruth, *great stream.* [M]
9.   *Innis-fail,* one of the ancient names of Ireland. [M]
10.   hero] chief 1773
11.   mortal] *deleted* 1773
12.   hero] king 1773
13.   halls] hall 1773
14.   but the sigh] but sorrow 1773
15.   hall of shells?] joy? 1773
16.   dark] sad 1773
17.   lived.] lived before me. 1773
18.   in the hall,] in my wrath, 1773
19.   Faobhar-gorm, *the blue point of steel.* [M]
20.   youths] sons 1773
21.   The foe] Rothmar 1773
22.   nor did it want its blue stream.] nor wanting was its winding stream. 1773
23.   the sound of the shells is heard.] the shells of the feast are heard. 1762 1773
24.   *Macpherson's note and the accompanying poem have been inserted at the end of the text of* 'Croma', *pp. 189 ff..*
25.   harp] string 1773
26.   youth begins to be forgot.] youth, while yet they live, is all forgot. 1773
27.   glitter:] glister: 1762 1773
28.   *This poem, which has come to be known as* 'The Six Bards', *is one of the pieces transmitted by Blair to Gray and Shenstone, prior to the publication of the* Fragments. *The (English) verse original, together with the printed prose version, may be found in Laing, 2:414 ff. Gray considered it as inferior in kind to the other* Fragments, *since it was merely descriptive. For Laing* "it is far superior, as it is purely descriptive, (in which Macpherson certainly excelled) without any insipid fable, and with less of that false pathos and affected sublimity which render Ossian

such strange bombast." *Whatever, it is certainly the work of a poet and deserves to be better known (19th century editions of Ossian usually omit it).*

Berrathon

1.   This poem is reputed to have been composed by Ossian, a little time before his death; and consequently it is known in tradition by no other name than *Ossian's last hymn.* The translator has taken the liberty to call it *Berrathon,* from the episode concerning the re-establishment of Larthmor king of that island, after he had been dethroned by his own son Uthal. Fingal in his voyage to Lochlin [Fing. B. III.] whither he had been invited by Starno the father of Agandecca, so often mentioned in Ossian's poems, touched at Berrathon, an island of Scandinavia, where he was kindly entertained by Larthmor the petty king of the place, who was a vassal of the supreme kings of Lochlin. The hospitality of Larthmor gained him Fingal's friendship, which that hero manifested, after the imprisonment of Larthmor by his own son, by sending Ossian and Toscar, the father of Malvina so often mentioned, to rescue Larthmor, and to punish the unnatural behaviour of Uthal. Uthal was handsome to a proverb, and consequently much admired by the ladies. Nina-thoma the beautiful daughter of Torthóma, a neighbouring prince, fell in love and fled with him. He proved unconstant; for another lady, whose name is not mentioned, gaining his affections, he confined Nina-thoma to a desert island near the coast of Berrathon. She was relieved by Ossian, who, in company with Toscar, landing on Berrathon, defeated the forces of Uthal, and killed him in a single combat. Nina-thoma, whose love not all the bad behaviour of Uthal could erase, hearing of his death, died of grief. In the mean time Larthmor is restored, and Ossian and Toscar returned in triumph to Fingal.

The present poem opens with an elegy on the death of Malvina the daughter of Toscar, and closes with presages of the poet's death. It is almost altogether in a lyric measure, and has that melancholy air which distinguishes the remains of the works of Ossian. If ever he composed any thing of a merry turn it is long since lost. The serious and melancholy make the most lasting impressions on the human mind, and bid fairest for being transmitted from generation to generation by tradition. Nor is it probable that Ossian dealt much in chearful composition. Melancholy is so much the companion of a great genius, that it is difficult to separate the idea of levity from chearfulness, which is sometimes the mark of an amiable disposition, but never the characteristic of elevated parts. [M]

[§ 1]This poem ... his own son Uthal.] *deleted* 1773

so often mentioned in Ossian's poems,] *deleted* 1773

[§ 2] presages of the poet's death.] presages of Ossian's death. 1773 (*rest of note deleted*)

2.   Lutha, *swift stream.* It is impossible, at this distance of time, to ascertain where the scene here described lies. Tradition is silent on that head, and there is nothing in the poem from which a conjecture can be drawn. [M]

It is impossible ... drawn.] *deleted* 1773

3.   Mal-mhina, *soft or lovely brow. Mh* in the Galic language has the same sound with *v* in English. [M]

Note deleted 1773

4.   Tradition has not handed down the name of this son of Alpin. His father was one of Fingal's principal bards, and he appears himself to have had a poetical genius. [M]
Tradition ... Alpin.] *deleted* 1773
appears himself to have] *deleted* 1773
5.   Tar-lutha's] Tor-lutha's 1773
6.   Ossian speaks. He calls Malvina a beam of light, and continues the metaphor throughout the paragraph. [M]
7.   The description of this ideal palace of Fingal is very poetical, and agreeable to the notions of those times, concerning the state of the deceased, who were supposed to pursue, after death, the pleasures and employments of their former life. The situation of Ossian's heroes, in their separate state, if not entirely happy, is more agreeable, than the notions of the ancient Greeks concerning their departed heroes. See Hom. Odyss. l. II. [M]
very poetical, and] *deleted* 1773
The situation of Ossian's heroes,] The situation of the Celtic, 1773
Reference to Homer deleted 1773
8.   Ossian; who had a great friendship for Malvina, both on account of her love for his son Oscar, and her attention to his own poems. [M]
to his own poems.] to himself. 1773
9.   That is, the young virgins who sung the funeral elegy over her tomb. [M]
10.   Ossian, by way of disrespect, calls those, who succeeded the heroes whose actions he celebrates, *the sons of little men*. Tradition is entirely silent concerning what passed in the north, immediately after the death of Fingal and all his heroes; but it appears from that term of ignominy just mentioned, that the actions of their successors were not to be compared to those of the renowned Fingalians. [M]
Ossian ... *little men.*] *deleted* 1773
but it appears ... , that the actions] by which it would seem that the actions 1773
11.   Toscar was the son of that Conloch, who was also father to the lady, whose unfortunate death is related in the last episode of the second book of Fingal. [M]
The reference is to Galvina - *see above, p. 70.*
12.   vanquished.] flying! 1773
13.   Ossian seems to intimate by this expression, that this poem was the last of his composition; so that there is some foundation for the traditional title of *the last hymn of Ossian.* [M]
Note deleted 1773
14.   Barrathón, *a promontory in the midst of waves.* The poet gives it the epithet of sea-surrounded, to prevent its being taken for a peninsula in the literal sense. [M]
The poet ... literal sense.] *deleted* 1773
15.   Comhal's mighty son,] Fingal 1773
16.   Morning] Day 1762 1773
17.   The meaning of the poet is, that Fingal remembered his own great actions, and consequently would not sully them by engaging in a petty war against Uthal, who was so far his inferior in valour and power. [M]
18.   The impatience of young warriors, going on their first expedition, is well marked by their half-drawing their swords. The modesty of Ossian, in his narration of a story which does him so much honour, is remarkable; and his humanity to Nina-thoma would grace a hero of our own polished age. Though Ossian passes over his

own actions in silence, or slightly mentions them; tradition has done ample justice to his martial fame, and perhaps has exaggerated the actions of the poet beyond the bounds of credibility. [M]
Note deleted 1773
19.	heads.] heads on high. 1773
20.	Nina-thoma the daughter of Torthóma, who had been confined to a desart island by her lover Uthal. [M]
21.	waters of Lavath.] stream. 1773
22.	Finthormo, the palace of Uthal. The names in this episode are not of a Celtic original; which makes it probable that Ossian founds his poem on a true story. [M]
original; ... true story.] original. 1773
23.	his side.] his side, and he fell. 1773
24.	Ossian thought that his killing the boar, on his first landing in Berrathon, was a good omen of his future success in that island. The present highlanders look, with a degree of superstition, upon the success of their first action, after they have engaged in any desperate undertaking. [M]
Ossian thought] Ossian might have thought 1773
25.	To mourn over the fall of their enemies was a practice universal among Ossian's heroes. This is more agreeable to humanity, than the shameful insulting of the dead, so common in Homer, and after him, servilely copied by all his imitators, the humane Virgil not excepted, who have been more successful in borrowing the imperfections of that great poet, than in their imitations of his beauties. Homer, it is probable, gave the manners of the times in which he wrote, not his own sentiments: Ossian also seems to keep to the sentiments of his heroes. The reverence, which the most barbarous highlanders have still for the remains of the deceased, seems to have descended to them from their most remote ancestors. [M]
Ossian's heroes.] the Celtic heroes. 1773
Homer, it is probable ... their most remote ancestors.] *deleted* 1773
26.	my song] my song of woe 1773
27.	of spears?] of men. 1773
28.	Ossian speaks. [M]
29.	little] feeble 1773
30.	Here begins the lyric piece, with which, tradition says, Ossian concluded his poems.—It is set to music, and still sung in the north, with a great deal of wild simplicity, but little variety of sound. [M]
Note deleted 1773
31.	This magnificent description of the power of Fingal over the winds and storms, and the image of his taking the sun, and hiding him in the clouds, do not correspond with the preceding paragraph, where he is represented as a feeble ghost, and no more the TERROR OF THE VALIANT; but it agrees with the notion of the times concerning the souls of the deceased, who, it was supposed, had the command of the winds and storms, but in combat were not a match for valiant men.
	It was the immoderate praise bestowed by the poets on their departed friends, that gave the first hint to superstition to deify the deceased heroes; and those new divinities owed all their attributes to the fancy of the bard who sung their elegies.
	We do not find, that the praises of Fingal had this effect upon his countrymen; but that is to be imputed to the idea they had of power, which they always connected with bodily strength and personal valour, both which were dissolved by death. [M]

[§ 1] This magnificent description] This description 1773
but in combat ... valiant men.] but took no concern in the affairs of men. 1762 1773
[§ 2-3] *deleted* 1773
32.   And come I will,] I come, I come, 1773
Cf. Goethe's 'Ganymed': "Ich komme, ich komme!"
33.   The same thought may be found almost in the same words, in Homer, [*Iliad*]
vi. 46. [*gr.q.*] Mr. Pope falls short of his original; in particular he has omitted
altogether the beautiful image of the wind strewing the withered leaves on the
ground. - Like leaves on trees the race of men are found,/ Now green in youth, now
with'ring on the ground;/ Another race the following spring supplies;/ They fall
successive, and successive rise. POPE. [M]
Note deleted 1773
Laing's comment on this (1:576 f., n. 23) issues in the unmasking of the author of
Ecclesiasticus *as a plagiarist:* "it is evident, that the son of Sirach, like the father of
Ossian, enriched a pretended translation from the Hebrew, with the choicest
passages of the Greek poets. But the generations of men compared, with Horace, to
the waves of ocean, and, with Homer, to the annual succession of leaves,
demonstrates only the want of original genius in us moderns, who can conceive
nothing similar, or superior, to the classics, without imitation."
34.   heads.] heads on high. 1773
35.   *Macpherson's note, together with Minvane's lament, is appended to the text*
of 'Berrathon', *pp. 198 f..*
36.   Minvane] Minvâne 1773 (*throughout*)
37.   so often mentioned in Ossian's compositions,] *deleted* 1773
38.   is] follows. 1773 (*rest of note deleted*)
39.   ship;] deep ship; 1773
40.   near her] nor disturb the 1773

Advertisement (appended to *Fingal*)
1.   *By this is meant the second edition of* Fingal *which appeared in January*
1762, almost immediately after the first.
2.   *See* 'Carthon', *p. 128, n. 17.*

A Dissertation (preceding *Temora*)
1.   A Dissertation] A Dissertation concerning the Poems of Ossian 1773
2.   *The first two paragraphs are new and replace the opening paragraph of the*
1763 original edition which reads: Nations, small in their beginnings and slow in
their progress to maturity, cannot, with any degree of certainty, be traced to their
source. The first historians, in every country, are, therefore, obscure and unsatis-
factory. Swayed by a national partiality, natural to mankind, they adopted uncertain
legends and ill-fancied fictions, when they served to strengthen a favourite system,
or to throw lustre on the antient state of their country. Without judgment or
discernment to separate the probable and more antient traditions, from ill-digested
tales of late invention, they jumbled the whole together, in one mass of anachro-
nisms and inconsistencies. Their accounts, however, though deduced from æras too
remote to be known, were received with that partial credulity which always dis-
tinguishes an unpolished age. Mankind had neither abilities nor inclination to
dispute the truth of relations, which, by throwing lustre on their ancestors, flattered

their own vanity. - Such were the historians of Europe, during the dark ages, which succeeded the subversion of the Roman empire. When learning began to revive, men looked into antiquity with less prejudiced eyes. They chose rather to trust their national fame to late and well-attested transactions, than draw it from ages, dark and involved in fable.

3. is little known.] is less known than their manners. 1773
4. and therefore ... undistinct.] and described them as they found them. 1773
5. investigated.] investigated. Their manners and singular character were matters of curiosity, as they committed them to record. [Some men ...] 1773
6. this confined opinion.] confined ideas on this subject. 1773
7. any other ancient people] any nation destitute of the use of letters. 1773
8. their] *deleted* 1773
9. The establishment ... trusted their history,] The Romans give the first and, indeed, the only authentic accounts of the northern nations. Destitute of the use of letters, they themselves had no means of transmitting their history to posterity. Their traditions and songs [were lost ...] 1763
10. of those *Gauls*,] of those *Celts*, or *Gauls*, 1763
11. and their ... *Caledonia.*] *added* 1765
12. St. Hierom. ad Ctesiphon. [M]
13. the] their 1763
14. was, perhaps,] is said to have been 1773
15. bodies.] bodies. The story is silly and the argument is absurd. But let us revere antiquity in her very follies. [This circumstance ...] 1773
16. circumstance] circumstance, affirm some antiquaries, 1773
17. is certain.] is, at length, a matter that admits of no doubt. 1773
18. Dio. Sic. l.5. [M]
19. Christian æra] incarnation 1763
20. *Unlike the* Dissertation *preceding* Fingal, *this one preserves from the first edition the practice of placing the notes in the margin, rather than the foot of the page. Where appropriate they are here inserted in square brackets in the text. The references to the Books of* 'Temora' *are deleted in 1773.*
21. Ossian ... His accounts] The poem of Temora throws considerable light on this subject. The accounts given in it [agree ...] 1773
Cf. similar changes below, and in the Dissertation *preceding* Fingal, *all of which might seem designed to downplay the significance of Ossian himself.*
22. From him, it appears] It appears, 1773
23. Ossian ... delivered] Temora contains not only the history of the first migration of the Caledonians into Ireland; it also preserves [some ...] 1773
24. history of Ossian,] history, 1773
25. it is certain,] it is supposed, 1773
26. The establishing ... cuts off] To establish this fact, is to lay, at once, aside the pretended antiquities of the Scots and Irish, and to get quit of [the long list ...] 1773
27. War. de antiq. Hybern. præ. p.1. [M]
28. preserved by Ossian] in these poems 1773
29. Ossian.] Fingal. 1773
30. As the æra ... one of] As Fingal and his chiefs were the most renowned names in tradition, the bards took care to place [them ...] 1773

31.   That part ... exactness.] They became famous among the people, and an object of fiction and poetry to the bards. 1773

32.   themselves ... They] *deleted* 1773

33.   that I kept ... neither has he so] that I have rejected wholly the works of the bards in my publication. Ossian acted in a more extensive sphere, and his ideas ought to be more noble and universal; neither gives he, I presume, so [many ...] 1773

34.   but ... excels.] but not in this species of composition. 1773

35.   other] inferior 1773

36.   irresistible] *deleted* 1773

37.   the highest] *deleted* 1773

38.   It was the locality ... English dress.] It was the locality of their description and sentiment, that, probably, has kept them in the obscurity of an almost lost language. The ideas of an unpolished period are so contrary to the present advanced state of society, that more than a common mediocrity of taste is required to relish them as they deserve. Those who alone are capable of transferring ancient poetry into a modern language, might be better employed in giving originals of their own, were it not for that wretched envy and meanness which affects to despise contemporary genius. My first publication was merely accidental. Had I then met with less approbation, my after pursuits would have been more profitable; at least I might have continued to be stupid, without being branded with dulness. 1773

In 1773 the following two paragraphs - These were ... displeases them. - *are deleted. Continues:* These poems ... - *see below, note 39*

39.   But ... times.] These poems may furnish light to antiquaries, as well as some pleasure to the lovers of poetry. [The first ...] 1773

Follows: branded with dulness. - *see above, note 38*

40.   Ossian's traditions] this system 1773

41.   that of the Scots,] those of Ireland and Scotland, 1763 that of the Scots, inconsiderable as it may appear in other respects, [even ...] 1773

42.   their] its 1773

43.   before.] before. This subject I have only lightly touched upon, as it is to be discussed, with more perspicuity, and at much greater length, by a gentleman, who has thoroughly examined the antiquities of Britain and Ireland. 1763

The reference is to John Macpherson - cf. the final paragraph of the Preface *to the first edition of* Fingal, *above, p. 38.*

44.   I shall ... appearance.] *deleted* 1773

45.   ignorance of facts, ... fixed with more propriety.] malice, I neither know nor care. Those who have doubted my veracity have paid a compliment to my genius; and were even the allegation true, my self-denial might have atoned for my fault. Without vanity I say it, I think I could write tolerable poetry; and I assure my antagonists, that I should not translate what I could not imitate. 1773

46.   As prejudice is always the effect of ignorance... Scalders that ever existed.] As prejudice is the effect of ignorance, I am not surprized at its being general. An age that produces few marks of genius ought to be sparing of admiration. The truth is, the bulk of mankind have ever been led, by reputation more than taste, in articles of literature. If all the Romans, who admired Virgil, understood his beauties, he would have scarce deserved to have come down to us, through so many centuries. Unless genius were in fashion, Homer himself might have written in vain. He that wishes

to come with weight, on the superficial, must skim the surface, in their own shallow way. Were my aim to gain the many, I would write a madrigal sooner than an heroic poem. Laberius himself would be always sure of more followers than Sophocles. 1773

47.   While some doubt ... claim is built.] Some who doubt the authenticity of this work, with peculiar acuteness appropriate them *[sic]* to the Irish nation. Tho' it is not easy to conceive how these poems can belong to Ireland and to me, at once, I shall examine the subject, without further animadversion on the blunder. 1773

48.   does not ... discussed.] I have in another work amply discussed. 1773
A reference to Macpherson's own Introduction to the History of Great Britain and Ireland *(1771).*

49.   sruth.] fruth. 1765 1773
The correct form of the 1763 original has been restored here.

50.   *Fion* took up with his large hand ... the intermediate valley.] *Fion*, says the Irish bard, sometimes placed one foot on the mountain *Cromleach*, his other foot on the hill of *Crommal*, and, in that position, washed his hands, in the river *Lubar*, which ran thro' the intermediate valley. [The property ...] 1763

51.   stature.] stature. As for the poetry, I leave it to the reader. 1773

52.   Cuchullin] Cuthullin 1773

53.   satisfaction] satisfaction, in an uncommon way, 1773

54.   afforded ... to me;] wasted all the time I had allotted for the muses; 1773

55.   In Faulkner's Dublin Journal, of the 1st December, 1761, appeared the following Advertisement: "Speedily will be published, by a gentleman of this kingdom, who hath been, for some time past, employed in translating and writing Historical Notes to

F I N G A L ,   A   P o e m ,

Originally wrote in the Irish or Erse language. In the preface to which, the translator, who is a perfect master of the Irish tongue, will give an account of the manners and customs of the antient Irish or Scotch; and, therefore, most humbly intreats the public, to wait for his edition, which will appear in a short time, as he will set forth all the blunders and absurdities in the edition now printing in London, and shew the ignorance of the English translator, in his knowledge of Irish grammar, not understanding any part of that accidence." [M]

Advertisement:] Advertisement: two weeks before my first publication appeared in London. 1773
The promise of the Advertisement *- presumably only intended as a spoiler - was not to be fulfilled.*

56.   *Lora,* ... Ossian.] *Lora.* 1773

57.   which brings ... remote] which happened under Margaret de Waldemar, in the close of the fourteenth age. 1773

58.   expectations] expectations, which are now over, 1773

59.   promised more than a year since] promised twelve years since, 1773

60.   *Garibh*] *Caribh* 1773

61.   *In the* Fragments *(though not in Blair's* Preface*) he is still called* Garve, *as indeed he should have remained, were authentic tradition to have been respected.*

62.   *Garibh's*] *Caribh's* 1773

63.   Ossian] the Scottish Ossian 1773

64.   It was, during ... Elizabeth's time.] *paragraph deleted* 1773

65. Ireland to Ossian,] Ireland, 1773
66. genius ... nation.] genius for poetry. 1773
67. abound ... that they] abound with simplicity and a wild harmony of numbers. They 1773

Temora Book I.

1. *Original in antiqua, unlike the* Arguments *to* 'Fingal'. *In 1763 the title page of the epic poem itself is preceded by an* Advertisement: The poem that stands first in this collection had its name from TEMORA, the royal palace of the first Irish kings of the Caledonian race, in the province of Ulster.

2. The first book of Temora made its appearance in the collection of lesser pieces, which were subjoined to the epic poem of Fingal. When that collection was printed, little more than the opening of the present poem came, in a regular connection, to my hands. The second book, in particular, was very imperfect and confused. By means of my friends, I collected since all the broken fragments of Temora, that I formerly wanted; and the story of the poem, which was accurately preserved by many, enabled me to reduce it into that order in which it now appears. The title of Epic was imposed on the poem by myself. The technical terms of criticism were totally unknown to Ossian. Born in a distant age, and in a country remote from the seats of learning, his knowledge did not extend to Greek and Roman literature. If therefore, in the form of his poems, and in several passages of his diction, he resembles Homer, the similarity must proceed from nature, the original from which both drew their ideas. It is from this consideration that I have avoided, in this volume, to give parallel passages from other authors, as I had done, in some of my notes, on the former collection of Ossian's poems. It was far from my intention to raise my author into a competition with the celebrated names of antiquity. The extensive field of renown affords ample room to all the poetical merit which has yet appeared in the world, without overturning the character of one poet, to raise that of another on its ruins. Had Ossian even superior merit to Homer and Virgil, a certain partiality, arising from the fame deservedly bestowed upon them by the sanction of so many ages, would make us overlook it, and give them the preference. Tho' their high merit does not stand in need of adventitious aid, yet it must be acknowledged, that it is an advantage to their fame, that the posterity of the Greeks and Romans, either do not at all exist, or are not now objects of contempt or envy to the present age.

Tho' this poem of Ossian has not perhaps all the *minutiæ*, which Aristotle, from Homer, lays down as necessary to the conduct of an epic poem, yet, it is presumed, it has all the grand essentials of the epopoea. Unity of time, place, and action is preserved throughout. The poem opens in the midst of things; what is necessary of preceding transactions to be known, is introduced by episodes afterwards; not formally brought in, but seemingly rising immediately from the situation of affairs. The circumstances are grand, and the diction animated; neither descending into a cold meanness, nor swelling into ridiculous bombast.

The reader will find some alterations in the diction of this book. These are drawn from more correct copies of the original which came to my hands, since the former publication. As the most part of the poem is delivered down by tradition, the text is sometimes various and interpolated. After comparing the different readings, I always made choice of that which agreed best with the spirit of the context. [M]

New (i.e. not in version first published in Fingal *in 1761/62)*
Note deleted 1773
3.   Ullin] Erin 1773
4.   The green hills] The mountains 1773
5.   Cairbar, the son of Borbar-duthul, was descended lineally from Larthon the chief of the Firbolg, the first colony who settled in the south of Ireland. The Caël were in possession of the northern coast of that kingdom, and the first monarchs of Ireland were of their race. Hence arose those differences between the two nations, which terminated, at last, in the murder of Cormac, and the usurpation of Cairbar, lord of Atha, who is mentioned in this place. [M]
6.   Mór-lath, *great in the day of battle.* Hidalla', *mildly looking hero.* Cor-mar, *expert at sea.* Málth-os, *slow to speak.* Foldath, *generous.*

Foldath, who is here strongly marked, makes a great figure in the sequel of the poem. His fierce, uncomplying character is sustained throughout. He seems, from a passage in the second book, to have been Cairbar's greatest confidant, and to have had a principal hand in the conspiracy against Cormac king of Ireland. His tribe was one of the most considerable of the race of the Fir-bolg. [M]
Second paragraph new
7.   car-borne Cairbar,] the king of Erin, 1773
8.   Mór-annal, *strong-breath*; a very proper name for a scout. 1763 1773 (*also first version* 1765 - *see above, p. 148, note 4*)
9.   Cairbar.] king of Erin.
10.   Mor-annal here alludes to the particular appearance of Fingal's spear.——If a man, upon his first landing in a strange country, kept the point of his spear forward, it denoted in those days that he came in a hostile manner, and accordingly he was treated as an enemy; if he kept the point behind him, it was a token of friendship, and he was immediately invited to the feast, according to the hospitality of the times. [M]
11.   This was the famous sword of Fingal, made by Luno, a smith of Lochlin, and after him poetically called the *son of Luno:* it is said of this sword, that it killed a man at every stroke; and that Fingal never used it but in times of the greatest danger. [M]
12.   In some traditions Fergus the son of Fingal, and Usnoth chief of Etha, immediately follow Fillan in the list of the chiefs of Morven; but as they are not afterwards mentioned at all in the poem, I look upon the whole sentence to be an interpolation, and have therefore rejected it. [M]
New
Note deleted 1773
Laing (2:15 f., n. 7) is perhaps worth quoting here: "In the first book of Temora annexed to Fingal, in 1762, the passage partly *rejected* as an *interpolation,* stood originally thus: 'Fillan bends his bow: Fergus strides in the pride of youth. Who is that with aged locks? A dark shield is on his side. His spear trembles at every step; and age is on his limbs. He bends his dark face to the ground; the king of spears is sad!——It is Usnoth, O Cairbar, coming to revenge his sons. He sees green Ullin with tears, and he remembers the tombs of his children. But far before the rest, the son of Ossian comes, bright in the smiles of youth, fair as the first beams of the sun. His long hair falls on his back.——His dark brows are half hid beneath his helmet of steel,' &c. ... In this description of the Celtic Apollo, the first design was to connect

the poem with Dar-thula and the Children of Usnoth, which immediately preceded this book in the collection of the lesser poems annexed to Fingal. When the Temora, however, was published entire, the first part of the passage was expunged, and the later altered; as the translator, in the course of composition, had either forgotten old Usnoth, or had found no opportunity to introduce him and Fergus again into the poem."

The apparent reinstatement of Fergus *and* Usnoth *into the poem by Cesarotti has given the odd critic an opportunity to expatiate on bold interpolations and the daring liberties taken with the "original" - cf. above, p. 148, note 1.*

13.   The opposite characters of Foldath and Malthos are strongly marked in sub-sequent parts of the poem. They appear always in opposition. The feuds between their families, which were the source of their hatred to one another, are mentioned in other poems. [M]

New

14.   numerous] *deleted* 1773
15.   Erin] green Erin 1773
16.   That is, who has heard my vaunting? He intended the expression as a rebuke to the self-praise of Foldath. [M]
17.   Hidalla was the chief of Clonra, a small district on the banks of the lake of Lego. The beauty of his person, his eloquence and genius for poetry are afterwards mentioned. [M]

New

18.   of the desert;] in war. 1773
19.   they meet] Ye are like storms which meet 1773
20.   red light;] heaven's flame; 1773
21.   are heard.] broke forth. 1773
22.   feast.] joy. 1773
23.   Cathol the son of Maronnan, or Moran, was murdered by Cairbar, for his attachment to the family of Cormac. He had attended Oscar to the *war of Inis-thona*, where they contracted a great friendship for one another. Oscar, immediately after the death of Cathol, had sent a formal challenge to Cairbar, which he prudently declined, but conceived a secret hatred against Oscar, and had beforehand contrived to kill him at the feast, to which he here invites him. [M]
24.   have sung to his ghost.] gave his friend to the winds. 1773
25.   He alludes to the battle of Oscar against Caros, *king of ships*; who is supposed to be the same with Carausius the usurper. [M]
26.   Cathmor] Cathmor my brother 1773

Cathmor, *great in battle*, the son of Borbar-duthul, and brother of Cairbar king of Ireland, had, before the insurrection of the Firbolg, passed over into Inis-huna, supposed to be a part of South-Britain, to assist Conmor king of that place against his enemies. Cathmor was successful in the war, but, in the course of it, Conmor was either killed, or died a natural death. Cairbar, upon intelligence of the designs of Fingal to dethrone him, had dispatched a messenger for Cathmor, who returned into Ireland a few days before the opening of the poem.

Cairbar here takes advantage of his brother's absence, to perpetrate his ungenerous designs against Oscar; for the noble spirit of Cathmor, had he been present, would not have permitted the laws of that hospitality, for which he was so renowned himself, to be violated. The brothers form a contrast: we do not detest the mean soul

of Cairbar more, than we admire the disinterested and generous mind of Cathmor.
[M]
[§ 1] the son of Borbar-duthul ... opening of the poem.] *new*
27.   here, ... race.] here. 1773
28.   We] The chiefs of Selma 1773
29.   Fingal's army heard the joy that was in Cairbar's camp. The character given of
Cathmor is agreeable to the times. Some, through ostentation, were hospitable; and
others fell naturally into a custom handed down from their ancestors. But what
marks strongly the character of Cathmor, is his aversion to praise; for he is repre-
sented to dwell in a wood to avoid the thanks of his guests; which is still a higher
degree of generosity than that of Axylus in Homer: for the poet does not say, but the
good man might, at the head of his own table, have heard with pleasure the praise
bestowed on him by the people he entertained.

No nation in the world carried hospitality to a greater length than the antient
Scots. It was even infamous, for many ages, in a man of condition, to have the door
of his house shut at all, LEST, as the bards express it, THE STRANGER SHOULD COME
AND BEHOLD HIS CONTRACTED SOUL. Some of the chiefs were possessed of this hospi-
table disposition to an extravagant degree; and the bards, perhaps upon a selfish
account, never failed to recommend it, in their eulogiums. *Cean-uia' na dai'*, or *the
point to which all the roads of the strangers lead*, was an invariable epithet given
by them to the chiefs; on the contrary, they distinguished the inhospitable by the
title of *the cloud which the strangers shun*. This last however was so uncommon,
that in all the old poems I have ever met with, I found but one man branded with
this ignominious appellation; and that, perhaps, only founded upon a private
quarrel, which subsisted between him and the patron of the bard, who wrote the
poem.

We have a story of this hospitable nature, handed down by tradition, concerning
one of the first Earls of Argyle. This nobleman, hearing that an Irishman, of great
quality, intended to make him a visit, with a very numerous retinue of his friends
and dependants, burnt the castle of Dunora, the seat of his family, lest it should be
too small to entertain his guests, and received the Irish in tents on the shore.
Extravagant as this behaviour might seem in our days, it was admired and
applauded in those times of hospitality, and the Earl acquired considerable fame by
it, in the songs of the bards.

The open communication with one another, which was the consequence of their
hospitality, did not a little tend to improve the understanding and enlarge the ideas
of the ancient Scots. It is to this cause, we must attribute that sagacity and sense,
which the common people, in the highlands, possess, still, in a degree superior even
to the vulgar of more polished countries. When men are crowded together in great
cities they see indeed many people, but are acquainted with few. They naturally
form themselves into small societies, and their knowledge scarce extends beyond
the alley or street they live in: add to this that the very employment of a mechanic
tends to contract the mind. The ideas of a peasant are still more confined. His
knowledge is circumscribed within the compass of a few acres; or, at most, extends
no further than the nearest market town. The manner of life among the inhabitants
of the highlands is very different from these. As their fields are barren, they have
scarce any domestic employment. Their time is spent therefore in an extensive
wilderness, where they feed their cattle, and these, by straying far and wide, carry

their keepers after them, at times, to all the different settlements of the clans. There they are received with hospitality and good cheer, which, as they tend to display the minds of the hosts, afford an opportunity to the guests to make their observations on the different characters of men; which is the true source of knowledge and acquired sense. Hence it is that a common highlander is acquainted with a greater number of characters, than any of his own rank living in the most populous cities. [M]

New after first paragraph (from which quoted Homer/Pope is here omitted - cf. above, p. 150. note 1.)

All but first two paragraphs deleted 1773

30.   heard ... coast:] heard their joy. 1773

31.   When a chief was determined to kill a person already in his power, it was usual to signify that his death was intended, by the sound of a shield struck with the blunt end of a spear; at the same time that a bard at a distance raised the *death-song*. A ceremony of another kind was long used in Scotland upon such occasions. Every body has heard that a bull's head was served up to Lord Douglas in the castle of Edinburgh, as a certain signal of his approaching death. [M]

A ceremony ... approaching death.] *deleted* 1773

32.   Cormac, the son of Arth, had given the spear, which is here the foundation of the quarrel, to Oscar when he came to congratulate him, upon Swaran's being expelled from Ireland. [M]

33.   Inisfail.] Erin. 1773

34.   Ti-mor-rath, *the house of good fortune*, the name of the royal palace of the supreme kings of Ireland. [M]

Ti-mor-rath ... *fortune*,] Ti'-mór-ri', *the house of the great king*, 1762 1763 1773 (*also first version* 1765)

Cf. above, p. 150, note 14.

35.   *Hundred* here is an indefinite number, and is only intended to express a great many. It was probably the hyperbolical phrases of bards, that gave the first hint to the Irish Senachies to place the origin of their monarchy in so remote a period, as they have done. [M]

New

36.   Atha, *shallow river:* the name of Cairbar's seat in Connaught. [M]

37.   darkening] haughty 1773

38.   Atha's darkening chief] Atha's chief 1763 1773

39.   The poet means Malvina, the daughter of Toscar, to whom he addresses that part of the poem, which relates to the death of Oscar her lover. [M]

The poet means] *deleted* 1773

he addresses] is addressed 1773

40.   The Irish historians place the death of Cairbar, in the latter end of the third century: they say, he was killed in battle against Oscar the son of Ossian, but deny that he fell by his hand. As they have nothing to go upon but the traditions of their bards, the translator thinks that the account of Ossian is as probable: at the worst, it is but opposing one tradition to another.

It is, however, certain that the Irish historians disguise, in some measure, this part of their history. An Irish poem on this subject, which, undoubtedly, was the source of their information, concerning the battle of Gabhra, where Cairbar fell, is just now in my hands. The circumstances are less to the disadvantage of the character of Cairbar, than those related by Ossian. As a translation of the poem (which, tho' evidently no very ancient composition, does not want poetical merit) would extend this note to too great a length, I shall only give the story of it, in brief, with some extracts from the original Irish.

Oscar, says the Irish bard, was invited to a feast, at Temora, by Cairbar king of Ireland. A dispute arose between the two heroes, concerning the exchange of spears, which was usually made, between the guests and their host, upon such occasions. In the course of their altercation, Cairbar said, in a boastful manner, that he would hunt on the hills of Albion, and carry the spoils of it into Ireland, in spite of all the efforts of its inhabitants. The original words are; *Briathar buan sin; Briathar buan/ A bheireadh an Cairbre rua',/ Gu tuga' se sealg, agus creach/ A h'ALBIN an la'r na mhaireach.* Oscar replied, that, the next day, he himself would carry into Albion the spoils of the five provinces of Ireland; in spite of the opposition of Cairbar. *Briathar eile an aghai' sin/ A bheirea' an t'Oscar, og, calma/ Gu'n tugadh se sealg agus creach/ Do dh'ALBIN an la'r na mhaireach, &c.* Oscar, in consequence of his threats, begun to lay waste Ireland; but as he returned with the spoil into Ulster, through the narrow pass of Gabhra (*Caoil-ghlen-Ghabhra*) he was met, by Cairbar, and a battle ensued, in which both the heroes fell by mutual wounds. The bard gives a very curious list of the followers of Oscar, as they marched to battle. They appear to have been five hundred in number, commanded, as the poet expresses it, by *five heroes of the blood of kings.* This poem mentions Fingal, as arriving from Scotland, before Oscar died of his wounds. [M]

New apart from first paragraph

As they have ... one tradition to another.] *deleted* 1773

the Irish historians] the Irish bards 1773

The circumstances ... related by Ossian.] *deleted* 1773

41.   side.] side; when the green-vallied Erin shakes its mountains, from sea to sea! 1773

42.   his father's spear.] the spear of Selma. 1773

43.   his son.] the chief. 1773

44.   The fame ... shall] My fame begins to 1773

45.   Bran was one of Fingal's dogs.—He was so remarkable for his fleetness, that the poet, in a piece which is not just now in the translator's hands, has given him the same properties with Virgil's Camilla. Bran signifies *a mountain-stream.* [M]

The etymological explanation is new.

He was... Virgil's Camilla.] *deleted* 1773

For Bran *cf. first version, above, p. 152, note 18.*

46.   his breast] his white breast 1763 (*also first version* 1765) his heaving breast 1773

47.   with sighs.] *deleted* 1773

48.   within my narrow dwelling.] by my side. 1773

49.   sword."] sword, the pride of other years!" 1773

50.   him: he shall] thee. Thou shalt 1773

51.   or pour our tears in Ullin?] How long pour in Erin our tears? 1773

52.   day,] years: 1773

53.   west.] west. The traveller mourns his absence, thinking of the flame of his beams. 1773

54.   The poet speaks in his own person. [M]

New

Note deleted 1773

55.   Althan, the son of Conachar, was the chief bard of Arth king of Ireland. After the death of Arth, Althan attended his son Cormac, and was present at his death.— He had made his escape from Cairbar, by the means of Cathmor, and coming to Fingal, related, as here, the death of his master Cormac. [M]

56.   fought with generous Torlath.] fell at Lego's stream. 1773

57.   eye.] eye, when he spoke. 1773

58.   Althan speaks. [M]

59.   Doira, *the woody side of a mountain*; it is here a hill in the neighbourhood of Temora. [M]

60.   showers.] showers. Bright and silent is its progress aloft, but the cloud, that shall hide it, is near! [The sword of Artho ...] 1773

61.   Arth or Artho, the father of Cormac king of Ireland. [M]

62.   chief] ruler 1773

63.   in Temora.] in the hall of kings. 1773

64.   the king] Cormac 1773

65.   he] the king 1773

66.   the king of Tura] the son of Semo

Cuchullin is called the king of Tura from a castle of that name on the coast of Ulster, where he dwelt, before he undertook the management of the affairs of Ireland, in the minority of Cormac. [M]

New and preserved in 1773, despite Cuthullin's now being called the son of Semo. *As Laing observes (2:38, n. 31):* "the alteration of phraseology, in the improved edition, has introduced perpetual contradiction between the text and the notes."

67.   king] chief 1773

68.   The prophetic sound, mentioned in other poems, which the harps of the bards emitted before the death of a person worthy and renowned. It is here an omen of the death of Cormac, which, soon after, followed. [M]

New

69.   Slimora, a hill in Connaught, near which Cuchullin was killed. [M]

70.   of the plain,] in the valley, 1773

71.   Usnoth chief of Etha, a district on the western coast of Scotland, had three sons, Nathos, Althos and Ardan, by Slis-sáma the sister of Cuchullin. The three brothers, when very young, were sent over to Ireland by their father, to learn the use of arms under their uncle, whose military fame was very great in that kingdom. They had just arrived in Ulster when the news of Cuchullin's death arrived. Nathos, the eldest of the three brothers, took the command of Cuchullin's army, and made head against Cairbar the chief of Atha. Cairbar having, at last, murdered young king Cormac, at Temora, the army of Nathos shifted sides, and the brothers were obliged to return into Ulster, in order to pass over into Scotland. The sequel of their mournful story is related, at large, in the poem of Dar-thula. [M]

New

In part verbatim quotation of introductory note to 'Dar-thula' *(see above, p. 140, note 1). According to Laing (2:39):* "The introduction of the sons of Usnoth into the episode, was a branch of the original plan, of representing old Usnoth as an actor in the poem, listening to the episode, and ready to revenge the death of his son."

72.   the car-borne chiefs of Etha?] chief of streamy Etha? 1773

73.   wings.] wings. Sudden glows the dark brow of the hill; the passing mariner lags, on his winds. [The sound ...] 1773

74.   Caithbait was grandfather to Cuchullin; and his shield was made use of to alarm his posterity to the battles of the family. [M]

New

75.   heroes] warriors 1773

76.   That is, they saw a manifest likeness between the person of Nathos and Cuchullin. [M]

77.   my joy.] my rising joy. 1773

78.   O bard,] O Carril, 1773 (*also first version*)

79.   Cuchullin; and of that mighty stranger.] Cuthullin. Sing of Nathos of Etha! 1773

Nathos the son of Usnoth. [M]

New

80.   woody] *deleted* 1773 (*= original version*)

81.   Trathin] Crathin 1773

82.   Geal-lamha, *white-handed*. [M]

83.   dark] *deleted* 1773

84.   Innisfail!] Erin! 1773

85.   king of Erin.] the brightening king. 1773

86.   in the sound of his] in all his 1773

87.   From this expression, we understand, that Cairbar had entered the palace of Temora, in the midst of Cormac's speech. [M]

New

88.   but the chief of Atha.] It is Cairbar thy foe. 1773

89.   Cairbar] chief 1773

90.   gloomy] *deleted* 1773

91.   halls,] halls? said Carril. 1773

Althan speaks. [M]

92.   My] His 1773

93.   That is, himself and Carril, as it afterwards appears. [M]

94.   The persons of the bards were so sacred, that even he, who had just murdered his sovereign, feared to kill them. [M]

95.   had] *deleted* 1773 (*= original version*)

96.   Cathmor appears the same disinterested hero upon every occasion. His humanity and generosity were unparalleled: in short, he had no fault, but too much attachment to so bad a brother as Cairbar. His family connection with Cairbar prevails, as he expresses it, over every other consideration, and makes him engage in a war, of which he did not approve. [M]

New

97.   Chief of Atha!] Brother of Cathmor, 1773

98.   like the rock of the desart;] is a rock. 1773

99.   dark.] dark and bloody! 1773

100. and he will fight thy battles.] and Cathmor shall shine in thy war. 1773

101. Cathmor's] My 1773

102. other] future 1773

103. to Ullin;] *deleted* 1773

104. And let him come, replied the king; I love a foe like Cathmor. His soul is great;] Let Cathmor come, replied the king, I love a foe so great. His soul is bright. 1773

105. Fillan! take] Fillan! my son, take thou 1773

106. heath, ... fire.] heath. 1773

Temora Book II.

1.   Addresses to the spirits of deceased warriors are common, in the compositions of Ossian. He, however, expresses them in such language as prevents all suspicion of his paying divine honours to the dead, as was usual among other nations.—From the sequel of this apostrophe, it appears, that Ossian had retired from the rest of the army to mourn, in secret, over the death of his son Oscar. This indirect method of narration has much of the nature of the Drama, and is more forcible than a regular historical chain of circumstances. The abrupt manner of Ossian may often render him obscure to inattentive readers. Those who retain his poems, on memory, seem to be sensible of this; and usually give the history of the pieces minutely before they begin to repeat the poetry.

Tho' this book has little action, it is not the least important part of Temora. The poet, in several episodes, runs up the cause of the war to the very source. The first population of Ireland, the wars between the two nations who originally possessed that island, its first race of kings, and the revolutions of its government, are important facts, and are delivered by the poet, with so little mixture of the fabulous, that one cannot help preferring his accounts to the improbable fictions of the Scotch and Irish historians. The Milesian fables of those gentlemen bear about them the marks of a late invention. To trace their legends to their source would be no difficult task; but a disquisition of this sort would extend this note too far. [M]

[§ 1] as was usual among other nations.] as was usual among other unenlightened nations. 1763

First paragraph deleted 1773

[§ 2] The Milesian fables of those gentlemen] The Milesian fables 1773

2.   dweller] High dweller 1773

3.   course of] *deleted* 1773

4.   folds] fields 1773

5.   streamy] resounding 1773

6.   Morven] Selma 1773

7.   in my rattling arms.] in all my arms. 1773

8.   wind of night.] wind. 1773

9.   We understand, from the preceding book, that Cathmor was near with an army. When Cairbar was killed, the tribes who attended him fell back to Cathmor; who, as it afterwards appears, had taken a resolution to surprize Fingal by night. Fillan was dispatched to the hill of Mora, which was in the front of the Caledonians, to observe the motions of Cathmor. In this situation were affairs when Ossian, upon hearing the noise of the approaching enemy, went to find out his brother. Their conversation naturally introduces the episode, concerning Conar the son of Trenmor the first Irish monarch, which is so necessary to the understanding the foundation of the rebellion and usurpation of Cairbar and Cathmor.—Fillan was the youngest of the sons of Fingal, then living. He and Bosmina, mentioned in the *battle of Lora*, were the only children of the king, by Clatho the daughter of Cathulla king of Inis-tore,

whom he had taken to wife, after the death of Ros-crana, the daughter of Cormac Mac-Conar king of Ireland. [M]

10.   stand, not in vain,] stand not, in vain, 1763 1773

11.   That is, two sons in Ireland. Fergus, the second son of Fingal, was, at that time, on an expedition, which is mentioned in one of the lesser poems of Ossian. He according to some traditions, was the ancestor of Fergus, the son of Erc or Arcath, commonly called *Fergus the second* in the Scotch histories. The beginning of the reign of Fergus, over the Scots, is placed, by the most approved annals of Scotland, in the fourth year of the fifth age: a full century after the death of Ossian. The genealogy of his family is recorded thus by the highland Senachies; *Fergus Mac-Arcath Mac-Chongael, Mac-Fergus, Mac Fion-gäel na buai': i.e.* Fergus the son of Arcath, the son of Congal, the son of Fergus, the son of Fingal *the victorious*. This subject is treated more at large, in the dissertation prefixed to the poem. [M]

12.   The southern parts of Ireland went, for some time, under the name of Bolga, from the Fir-bolg or Belgæ of Britain, who settled a colony there. *Bolg* signifies *a quiver*, from which proceeds *Fir-bolg*, i.e. *bow-men*; so called from their using bows, more than any of the neighbouring nations. [M]

13.   It is remarkable, that, after this passage, Oscar is not mentioned in all Temora. The situations of the characters who act in the poem are so interesting, that others, foreign to the subject, could not be introduced with any lustre. Tho' the episode, which follows, may seem to flow naturally enough from the conversation of the brothers, yet I have shewn, in a preceding note, and, more at large, in the dissertation prefixed to this collection, that the poet had a farther design in view. It is highly probable, tho' the Irish annalists do not agree with Ossian in other particulars, that the Conar here mentioned is the same with their *Conar-mór*, i.e. *Conar the great*, whom they place in the first century. [M]

It is remarkable, that, after] After 1773

It is highly probable ... first century.] *deleted* 1773

14.   arose.] arose. The memory of those, who fell, quickly followed the departure of war: When the tumult of battle is past, the soul, in silence, melts away, for the dead. 1773

15.   Conar, the first king of Ireland, was the son of Trenmor, the great-grand-father of Fingal. It was on account of this family-connection, that Fingal was engaged in so many wars in the cause of the race of Conar. Tho' few of the actions of Trenmor are mentioned in Ossian's poems, yet, from the honourable appellations bestowed on him, we may conclude that he was, in the days of the poet, the most renowned name of antiquity. The most probable opinion concerning him is, that he was the first, who united the tribes of the Caledonians, and commanded them, in chief, against the incursions of the Romans. The genealogists of the North have traced his family far back, and given a list of his ancestors to *Cuanmór nan lan*, or Conmor of the swords, who according to them, was the first who crossed the *great sea*, to Caledonia, from which circumstance his name proceeded, which signifies *Great ocean*. Genealogies of so ancient a date, however, are little to be depended upon. [M]

mentioned in Ossian's poems ... the most] mentioned, he was the most 1773

16.   of hinds.] of Selma. 1773

17.   The chiefs of the Fir-bolg who possessed themselves of the south of Ireland, prior, perhaps, to the settlement of the *Caël* of Caledonia, and the Hebrides, in Ulster. From the sequel, it appears that the Fir-bolg were, by much, the most power-

ful nation; and it is probable that the Caël must have submitted to them, had they not received succours from their mother-country, under the command of Conar. [M]

18.   Moma] Muma 1763 1773 (*but only here - cf.* 'Temora' V, *p. 266, note 48*)

As Jiriczek points out (3:152), Mumu is the ancient name of Munster.

19.   reign, ... streamy Morven?] reign, they said, the son of resounding Morven? 1773

20.   Ullin] Selma 1773

21.   the chief of] the brother from 1773

22.   Colg-er, *fiercely-looking warrior.* Sulin-corma, *blue eyes.* Colgar was the eldest of the sons of Trathal: Comhal, who was the father of Fingal, was very young when the present expedition to Ireland happened. It is remarkable, that, of all his ancestors, the poet makes the least mention of Comhal; which, probably, proceeded from the unfortunate life and untimely death of that hero. From some passages, concerning him, we learn, indeed, that he was brave, but he wanted conduct, and, as Ossian expresses it, *his soul was dark.* This impartiality, with respect to a character so near him, reflects honour on the poet. [M]

of all his ancestors, the poet] of all the ancestors of Fingal, tradition 1773

he wanted conduct, ... honour on the poet.] he wanted conduct. 1773

As is evident from such changes, the Macpherson of 1773 clearly feels that rather more than his fair share of honour has been reflected on Ossian.

23.   The poet begins here to mark strongly the character of Fillan, who is to make so great a figure in the sequel of the poem. He has the impatience, the ambition and fire which are peculiar to a young hero. Kindled with the fame of Colgar, he forgets his untimely fall.—From Fillan's expressions in this passage, it would seem, that he was neglected by Fingal, on account of his youth. [M]

The poet] The poem 1773

sequel of the poem.] sequel. 1773

24.   Sudden I turned on my spear,] Ossian turned sudden on his spear. 1773

25.   *As Jiriczek notes (3:153), such combinations of singular participial noun with plural verb may be found elsewhere in Ossian - e.g.* are the rolling of waters, are the trickling of waters *(pp. 245, 266)*

26.   Cathmor is distinguished, by this honourable title, on account of his generosity to strangers, which was so great as to be remarkable even in those days of hospitality. [M]

27.   *Fónar, the man of song.* Before the introduction of Christianity a name was not imposed upon any person, till he had distinguished himself by some remarkable action, from which his name should be derived. Hence it is that the names in the poems of Ossian, suit so well with the characters of the persons who bear them. [M]

Hence ... bear them.] *deleted* 1773

"At that rate," *writes Laing (2:64),* "Fonar must have gone without a name till he became a bard; and the greater part of the Celtic heroes, unless distinguished by some remarkable exploit, must have been nameless till their death. Characteristical names, like those of modern comedies, are a sufficient proof that such fictitious personages ... are all the produce of the author's invention. Ossian, Oscar, Cairbar, Fingal, and the few historical names introduced into the poems, are not susceptible of such characteristical etymologies; and Homer, whose personages are all real, might have taught his Highland competitor, that even before the introduction of Christianity, no man, whether distinguished or not by some remarkable action, could remain without a name from his birth." *It is just as well there is no* Dances with Wolves *in Ossian - but then there are no wolves either, and that too was held against Macpherson.*

28.   like] *deleted* 1773

29.   failing stream.] falling stream. Pleasant is its sound, on the plain, whilst broken thunder travels over the sky! 1773

falling (*all later editions, including Laing) is likely to be a misprint, since we know from* 'Temora' I, *note 36, that* Atha *means* shallow river *and we are told here that the vale has been* blasted. *It is the shower, not the stream, which* falls.

30.   Brumo was a place of worship (Fing. b. 6.) in Craca, which is supposed to be one of the isles of Shetland. It was thought, that the spirits of the deceased haunted it, by night, which adds more terror to the description introduced here. *The horrid circle of Brumo, where often, they said, the ghosts of the dead howled round the stone of fear.* Fing. [M]

See above, p. 102, note 31.

31.   From this passage, it appears, that it was Foldath who had advised the night-attack. The gloomy character of Foldath is properly contrasted to the generous, the open Cathmor. Ossian is peculiarly happy in opposing different characters, and, by that means, in heightening the features of both. Foldath appears to have been the favourite of Cairbar, and it cannot be denied but he was a proper enough minister to such a prince. He was cruel and impetuous, but seems to have had great martial merit. [M]

Ossian is peculiarly happy ... martial merit.] *deleted* 1773

32.   mist?] shades? 1773

33.   By this exclamation Cathmor intimates that he intends to revenge the death of his brother Cairbar. [M]

34.   To have no funeral elegy sung over his tomb, was, in those days, reckoned the greatest misfortune that could befal a man; as his soul could not otherwise be admitted to the *airy hall of his fathers.* [M]

in those days,] among the Celtæ 1773

35.   the chief of Atha; dost] Cathmor, half-enraged; Dost ... 1773

36.   that he] Fingal 1773

37.   of the mighty Fingal?] of Selma's king? 1773

38.   the stranger] the fair stranger 1773

By *the stranger of Inis-huna,* is meant Sulmalla, the daughter of Conmor king of Inis-huna, the ancient name of that part of South-Britain, which is next to the Irish coast.—She had followed Cathmor in disguise. Her story is related at large in the fourth book. [M]

39.   Crothar was the ancestor of Cathmor, and the first of his family, who had settled in Atha. It was in his time, that the first wars were kindled between the Fir-bolg and Caël. The propriety of the episode is evident; as the contest which originally rose between Crothar and Conar, subsisted afterwards between their posterity, and was the foundation of the story of the poem. [M]

40.   From this circumstance we may learn that the art of building with stone was not known in Ireland so early as the days of Crothar. When the colony were long settled in the country, the arts of civil life began to increase among them, for we find mention made of the *towers of Atha* in the time of Cathmor, which could not well be applied to wooden buildings. In Caledonia they begun very early to build

with stone. None of the houses of Fingal, excepting Ti-foirmal, were of wood. Ti-foirmal was the great hall where the bards met to repeat their compositions annually, before they submitted them to the judgment of the king in Selma. By some accident or other, this wooden house happened to be burnt, and an ancient bard, in the character of Ossian, has left us a curious catalogue of the furniture which it contained. The poem is not just now in my hands, otherwise I would lay here a translation of it before the reader. It has little poetical merit, and evidently bears the marks of a period much later than that wherein Fingal lived. [M]

period ... Fingal lived.] later period. 1773

41.   Alnecma, or Alnecmacht, was the ancient name of Connaught. Ullin is still the Irish name of the province of Ulster. To avoid the multiplying of notes, I shall here give the signification of the names in this episode. Drumárdo, *high-ridge.* Cathmin, *calm in battle.* Con-lámha [*corrected from* Cón-lamha], *soft hand.* Turloch, *man of the quiver.* Cor-mul, *blue eye.* [M]

42.   Ullin.] Cathmin. 1773

43.   The delicacy of the bard, with regard to Crothar, is remarkable. As he was the ancestor of Cathmor, to whom the episode is addressed, the bard softens his defeat, by only mentioning that his *people fled.*—Cathmor took the song of Fonar in an unfavourable light. The bards, being of the order of the Druids, who pretended to a foreknowledge of events, were supposed to have some supernatural prescience of futurity. The king thought, that the choice of Fonar's song proceeded, from his foreseeing the unfortunate issue of the war; and that his own fate was shadowed out, in that of his ancestor Crothar. The attitude of the bard, after the reprimand of his patron, is picturesque and affecting. We admire the speech of Cathmor, but lament the effect it has on the feeling soul of the good old poet. [M]

The delicacy of the bard ... is remarkable.] The delicacy here ... is proper. 1773

44.   folds] skirts 1773

45.   Mora of the hinds.] Mora's mossy brow. 1773

46.   cease.] fly away. 1773

47.   spirit] spirits 1763 1773

48.   Borbar-duthul, *the surly warrior of the dark-brown eyes.* That his name suited well with his character, we may easily conceive, from the story delivered concerning him, by Malthos, toward the end of the sixth book. He was the brother of that Colculla, who is mentioned in the episode which begins the fourth book. [M]

49.   house] earth 1773

The grave, often poetically called a house. This reply of Ossian abounds with the most exalted sentiments of a noble mind. Tho', of all men living, he was the most injured by Cairbar, yet he lays aside his rage as the *foe was low.* How different is this from the behaviour of the heroes of other ancient poems!—*Cynthius aurem vellit.* [M]

The grave ... house.] *deleted* 1773

This reply of Ossian abounds with the most exalted sentiments] This reply abounds with the sentiments 1773

"Touched the ear of the translator himself." (*Laing, 2:76*)

50.   The morning of the second day, from the opening of the poem, comes on.— After the death of Cuchullin, Carril, the son of Kinfena, his bard, retired to the cave of Tura, which was in the neighbourhood of Moi-lena, the scene of the poem of Temora. His casual appearance here enables Ossian to fulfil immediately the

promise he had made to Cathmor, of causing the *funeral song* to be pronounced over the tomb of Cairbar.—The whole of this passage, together with the address of Carril to the sun, is a lyric measure, and was, undoubtedly, intended as a relief to the mind, after the long narrative which preceded it. Tho' the lyric pieces, scattered through the poems of Ossian, are certainly very beautiful in the original, yet they must appear much to disadvantage, stripped of numbers, and the harmony of rhime. In the recitative or narrative part of the poem, the original is rather a measured sort of prose, than any regular versification; but it has all that variety of cadences, which suit the different ideas, and passions of the speakers.——This book takes up only the space of a few hours. [M]

—The whole of this passage ... speakers.——] *deleted* 1773

51. folds] skirts 1773

52. folded in] descending on 1773

53. lookest from thy] shewest thyself from the 1773

54. son] sun 1763

Cf. above, 'Fingal' II, *p. 65, note 10.*

55. dun robe] darkening hour 1773

By the *dun robe* of the sun, is probably meant an eclipse. [M]

Note deleted 1773

56. in thy] as thou rollest through thy 1773

57. song,] bard: 1773

Temora Book III.

1. This sudden apostrophe, concerning Fingal, the attitude of the king, and the scenery in which he is placed, tend to elevate the mind to a just conception of the succeeding battle. The speech of Fingal is full of that magnanimous generosity which distinguishes his character throughout. The groupe of figures, which the poet places around his father, are picturesque, and described with great propriety. The silence of Gaul, the behaviour of Fillan, and the effect which both have on the mind of Fingal, are well imagined.—His speech upon the occasion is very beautiful in the original. Broken and unequal, the numbers represent the agitation of his mind, divided between the admiration excited by the silence of Gaul, (when others boasted of their own actions) and his natural affection for Fillan, which the behaviour of that valiant youth had raised to the highest pitch. [M]

Note deleted 1773

2. rolling] moving 1773

3. Morven,] Selma 1773

4. my] our 1773

5. Strumon, *stream of the hill*, the name of the seat of the family of Gaul, in the neighbourhood of Selma. [M]

The rest of the note, together with the accompanying poem, may be found immediately following the end of 'Temora' III, *pp. 250 f..*

6. stood the son of Clatho,] leans Fillan of Selma, 1773

Clatho was the daughter of Cathulla, king of Inistore. Fingal, in one of his expeditions to that island, fell in love with Clatho, and took her to wife, after the death of Ros-cràna, the daughter of Cormac, king of Ireland.

Clatho was the mother of Ryno, Fillan, and Bosmina, mentioned in the *battle of Lora*, one of the lesser poems printed in Vol. I. Fillan is often called the son of Clatho, to distinguish him from those sons which Fingal had by Ros-cránа. [M]

[§ 2] *Lora*, ... Vol. I.] *Lora.* 1773

The note has been adjusted to take account of the new ordering of the poems, but, curiously, not of the change in the text.

7. Gaul, the son of Morni, next to Fingal, is the most renowned character introduced by Ossian in his poems. He is, like Ajax in the Iliad, distinguished by his manly taciturnity. The honourable epithets bestowed on him here, by Fingal, are amazingly expressive in the original. There is not a passage in all Temora, which loses so much in the translation as this. The first part of the speech is rapid and irregular, and is peculiarly calculated to animate the soul to war.—Where the king addresses Fillan, the versification changes to a regular and smooth measure. The first is like torrents rushing over broken rocks; the second like the course of a full-flowing river, calm but majestic. This instance serves to shew, how much it assists a poet to alter the measure, according to the particular passion, that he intends to excite in his reader. [M]

Note deleted 1773

8. king.] chief! 1773

9. Ullin being sent to Morven with the body of Oscar, Ossian attends his father, in quality of chief bard. [M]

10. Morven,] Selma 1773

11. There are some traditions, but, I believe, of late invention, that this Colgach was the same with the Galgacus of Tacitus. He was the ancestor of Gaul, the son of Morni, and appears, from some, really ancient, traditions, to have been king, or Vergobret, of the Caledonians; and hence proceeded the pretensions of the family of Morni to the throne, which created a good deal of disturbance, both to Comhal and his son Fingal. The first was killed in battle by that tribe; and it was after Fingal was grown up, that they were reduced to obedience. Colgach signifies *fiercely-looking*; which is a very proper name for a warrior, and is probably the origin of Galgacus; tho' I believe it a matter of mere conjecture, that the Colgach here mentioned was the same with that hero.—I cannot help observing, with how much propriety the song of the bards is conducted. Gaul, whose experience might have rendered his conduct cautious in war, has the example of his father, just rushing to battle, set before his eyes. Fillan, on the other hand, whose youth might make him impetuous and unguarded in action, is put in mind of the sedate and serene behaviour of Fingal upon like occasions. [M]

with how much propriety the song of the bards is conducted.] that the song of the bards is conducted with propriety. 1773

12. The expedition of Morni to Clutha, alluded to here, is handed down in tradition. The poem, on which the tradition was founded, is now lost. [M]

The poem, ... is now lost.] *deleted* 1773

13. Ossian is peculiarly happy, in his descriptions of still life; and these acquire double force, by his placing them near busy and tumultuous scenes. This antithesis serves to animate and heighten the features of poetry. [M]

Note deleted 1773

14. Morven?] O Selma! 1773

15. The mountain Cromla was in the neighbourhood of the scene of this poem; which was nearly the same with that of Fingal. [M]

16. the chief] Foldath 1773

17. called the chief] calls Cormul chief 1773

18. Dun-ratho, *a hill, with a plain on its top.* Corm-uil, *blue eye.* Foldath dispatches, here, Cormul to lie in ambush behind the army of the Caledonians. This speech suits well with the character of Foldath, which is, throughout, haughty and presumptuous. Towards the latter end of this speech, we find the opinion of the times, concerning the unhappiness of the souls of those who were buried without the funeral song. This doctrine, no doubt, was inculcated by the bards, to make their order respectable and necessary. [M]

This speech suits well] This speech suits 1773

This doctrine, no doubt, was] This doctrine was 1773

19. Morven] Selma 1773

20. Moruth;] Selma; 1773

21. king] chief 1773

22. bending] bending at once 1773

23. By the *strength of Atha,* is meant Cathmor. The expression is common in Homer, and other ancient poets. [M]

Note deleted 1773

24. The two kings. [M]

Note deleted 1773

25. lifts] lifts slowly 1773

26. Tur-lathon, *broad trunk of a tree.* Móruth, *great stream.* Oichaoma, *mild maid.* Dun-lora, *the hill of the noisy stream.* Duth-caron, *dark-brown man.* [M]

27. king,] chief, 1773

28. The poet speaks in his own person. [M]

Note deleted 1773 (*paragraph begins:* Ossian took the spear, in his wrath;)

29. on the foe.] on Foldath. 1773

30. Fillan had been dispatched by Gaul to oppose Cormul, who had been sent by Foldath to lie in ambush behind the Caledonian army. It appears that Fillan had killed Cormul, otherwise he could not be supposed to have possessed himself of the shield of that chief. The poet being intent upon the main action, passes over slightly this feat of Fillan. [M]

The poet ... of Fillan.] *deleted* 1773

31. king.] chief. 1773

32. Lumon, *bending hill;* a mountain in Inis-huna, or that part of South-Britain which is over-against the Irish coast. [M]

33. thou] O Fillan, thou 1773

34. Morven] Selma 1773

35. was heard.] was heard from high 1763 is heard on high 1773

36. Morven heard] Selma hear 1773

37. Evir-choama, *mild and stately maid,* the wife of Gaul. She was the daughter of Casdu-conglas, chief of I-dronlo, one of the Hebrides. [M]

Evir-choama *(all editions) appears to be a misprint for* Evir-chaoma - *cf. above, note 26:* Oichaoma, *mild maid.* See Jiriczek, 3:157.

38. Morven] Selma 1773

39. Cona.] Selma! 1773

40.   From this, and several other passages, in this poem, it appears, that the kings of Morven and Ireland had a plume of eagle's feathers, by way of ornament, in their helmets. It was from this distinguished mark that Ossian knew Cathmor, in the second book; which custom, probably, he had borrowed, from the former monarchs of Ireland, of the race of the Caël or Caledonians. [M]
From this, ... the kings of Morven] The kings of Caledonia 1773
which custom, ... or Caledonians.] *deleted* 1773
41.   he] Connal 1773
42.   in the folds of the mountain-winds.] along the roaring winds. 1773
43.   After the death of Comhal, and during the usurpation of the tribe of Morni, Fingal was educated in private by Duth-caron. It was then he contracted that inti-macy, with Connal the son of Duth-caron, which occasions his regretting so much his fall. When Fingal was grown up, he soon reduced the tribe of Morni; and, as it appears from the subsequent episode, sent Duth-caron and his son Connal to the aid of Cormac, the son of Conar, king of Ireland, who was driven to the last extremity, by the insurrections of the Firbolg. This episode throws farther light on the contests between the Caël and Firbolg; and is the more valuable upon that account. [M]
and is ... account.] *deleted* 1773
44.   green-hilled Inisfail.] green-vallied Erin. 1773
45.   waters;] waves; 1763 1773
46.   Duth-úla, a river in Connaught; it signifies, *dark-rushing water*. [M]
47.   Morven.] Selma. 1773
48.   of a stream,] of ocean, 1773
49.   Colc-ulla, *firm look in readiness*; he was the brother of Borbar-duthul, the father of Cairbar and Cathmor, who after the death of Cormac, the son of Artho, successively mounted the Irish throne. [M]
50.   plain, like ... seas.] plain. 1773
51.   Cormac, the son of Conar, the second king of Ireland, of the race of the Cale-donians. This insurrection of the Firbolg happened towards the latter end of the long reign of Cormac. From several episodes and poems, it appears, that he never possessed the Irish throne peaceably.—The party of the family of Atha had made several attempts to overturn the succession in the race of Conar, before they effected it, in the minority of Cormac, the son of Artho.—Ireland, from the most ancient accounts concerning it, seems to have been always so disturbed by domestic commotions, that it is difficult to say, whether it ever was, for any length of time, subject to one monarch. It is certain, that every province, if not every small district, had its own king. One of these petty princes assumed, at times, the title of king of Ireland, and, on account of his superior force, or in cases of publick danger, was acknowledged by the rest as such; but the succession, from father to son, does not appear to have been established.—It was the divisions amongst themselves, arising from the bad constitution of their government, that, at last, subjected the Irish to a foreign yoke. [M]
From several episodes ... he] He 1773
52.   Atha] Colc-ulla 1773
53.   Ullin.] Cormac. 1773
The inhabitants of Ullin or Ulster, who were of the race of the Caledonians, seem, alone, to have been the firm friends to the succession in the family of Conar. The

Firbolg were only subject to them by constraint, and embraced every opportunity to throw off their yoke. [M]

Note unaltered 1773

54.   the chief:] his father. 1773

55.   roes] rose 1773 (*presumably misprint - all later editions, including Laing*)

56.   Colgan, the son of Cathmul, was the principal bard of Cormac Mac-Conar, king of Ireland. [M]

For the rest of Macpherson's note and Colgan's poem on the love of Fingal and Ros-cräna, see above, pp. 256 f. (following the dialogue of Morni and Gaul).

57.   him.] his steps. 1773

58.   stream,] rill 1773

59.   of thy fathers.] of the old. 1773

60.   is the only part ... before the reader.] is the subject of the following short poem. 1773

Laing (2:88, n. 2) thinks the sword of Strumon *to be a product of Macpherson's reading of the* sword of Angantyr *in one of Percy's* Five pieces of Runic poetry ('The Incantation of Hervor') *which appeared in 1763 when* Temora *was already at press. Hence it was too late to integrate the poem, other than in the form of a note.*

61.   mist] midst 1773

62.   Part of an old poem, ... overheard by Fingal.] The following dialogue, on the loves of Fingal and Ros-crana, may be ascribed to him. [*i.e.* Colgan] 1773

63.   streamy] stormy 1773

64.   Morven,] Selma, 1773

65.   Fingal, as we learn ... compositions of the bards.] *deleted* 1773

Temora Book IV.

1.   This episode has an immediate connection with the story of Connal and Duth-caron, in the latter end of the third book. Fingal, sitting beneath an oak, near the palace of Selma, discovers Connal just landing from Ireland. The danger which threatened Cormac king of Ireland induces him to sail immediately to that island.— The story is introduced, by the king, as a pattern for the future behaviour of Fillan, whose rashness in the preceding battle is reprimanded. [M]

2.   rolled] flew 1773

3.   Ul-erin, *the guide to Ireland,* a star known by that name in the days of Fingal, and very useful to those who sailed, by night, from the Hebrides, or Caledonia, to the coast of Ulster. We find, from this passage, that navigation was considerably advanced, at this time, among the Caledonians. [M]

We find ... Caledonians.] *deleted* 1773

4.   wanting] absent 1773

5.   Ros-cräna, *the beam of the rising sun;* she was the mother of Ossian. The Irish bards relate strange fictions concerning this princess. The character given of her here, and in other poems of Ossian, does not tally with their accounts. Their stories, however, concerning Fingal, if they mean him by *Fion Mac-Comnal,* are so inconsistent and notoriously fabulous, that they do not deserve to be mentioned; for they evidently bear, along with them, the marks of late invention. [M]

The character ... their accounts.] *deleted* 1773

6. Cormac had said that his foes were *like the roar of streams*, and Fingal continues the metaphor. The speech of the young hero is spirited, and consistent with that sedate intrepidity, which eminently distinguishes his character throughout. [M]

7. ——"Race of the daring Trenmor,] "Race of the daring Trenmor!" at length he said, 1773

It should be noted that the variable-length dashes, which are such a distinctive feature of the earlier editions and which presumably indicate pauses for the reader (aloud) of the text, are dispensed with in that of 1773.

8. Cairbar, the son of Cormac, was afterwards king of Ireland. His reign was short. He was succeeded by his son Artho, the father of that Cormac who was murdered by Cairbar the son of Borbar-duthul.—Cairbar, the son of Cormac, long after his son Artho was grown to man's estate, had, by his wife Beltanno, another son, whose name was Ferad-artho.—He was the only one remaining of the race of Conar the first king of Ireland, when Fingal's expedition against Cairbar the son of Borbar-duthul happened. See more of Ferad-artho in the eighth book. [M]

9. Ullin,] Erin, 1773

10. waves its green head.] is waving near. 1773

11. rose] move 1773

12. The attitude of Ros-crana is aptly illustrated by this simile; for the ideas of those times, concerning the spirits of the deceased, were not so gloomy and disagreeable, as those of succeeding ages. The spirits of women, it was supposed, retained that beauty, which they possessed while living, and transported themselves, from place to place, with that gliding motion, which Homer ascribes to the gods. The descriptions which poets, less antient than Ossian, have left us of those beautiful figures, that appeared sometimes on the hills, are elegant and picturesque. They compare them to the *rain-bow on streams:* or, *the gliding of sun-beams on the hills.* I shall here translate a passage of an old song, where both these beautiful images are mentioned together.

A chief who lived three centuries ago, returning from the war, understood that his wife or mistress was dead. The bard introduces him speaking the following soliloquy, when he came, within sight of the place, where he had left her, at his departure.

"My soul darkens in sorrow. I behold not the smoak of my hall. No grey dog bounds at my streams. Silence dwells in the valley of trees.

Is that a rain-bow on Crunath? It flies:—and the sky is dark. Again, thou movest, bright, on the heath, thou sun-beam cloathed in a shower!—Hah! it is she, my love: her gliding course on the bosom of winds!"

In succeeding times the beauty of Ros-crana passed into a proverb; and the highest compliment, that could be paid to a woman, was to compare her person with *the daughter of Cormac.* "'S tu fein an Ros-crána,/ Siol Chormaec na n'ioma lán." [M]

[§ 1] The attitude of Ros-crana is aptly] The attitude of Ros-crana is 1773

I shall here translate ... mentioned together.] *deleted* 1773

13. rushed;—I seized] came: I took 1763 appeared: I took 1773

14. people.] host. 1773

15. king.] chief. 1773

16. of the hero.] of Duth-caron. 1773

17. The poet changes the scene to the Irish camp. The images introduced here are magnificent, and have that sort of *terrible beauty*, if I may use the expression, which

occurs so frequently in the compositions of Ossian. The troubled motion of the army, and the sedate and careless attitude of Cathmor, form a contrast, which, as I have before remarked, heightens the features of description, and is calculated to enliven poetry. [M]

Note deleted 1773

18.   Atha's king.] Cathmor. 1773

19.   In order to illustrate this passage, I shall give, here, the history on which it is founded, as I have gathered it from other poems. The nation of the Firbolg who inhabited the south of Ireland, being originally descended from the Belgæ, who possessed the south and south-west coast of Britain, kept up, for many ages, an amicable correspondence with their mother-country; and sent aid to the British Belgæ, when they were pressed by the Romans or other new-comers from the continent. Con-mor, king of Inis-huna, (that part of South-Britain which is over-against the Irish coast) being attacked, by what enemy is not mentioned, sent for aid to Cairbar, lord of Atha, the most potent chief of the Firbolg. Cairbar dispatched his brother Cathmor to the assistance of Conmor. Cathmor, after various vicissitudes of fortune, put an end to the war, by the total defeat of the enemies of Inis-huna, and returned in triumph to the residence of Con-mor. There, at a feast, Sul-malla, the daughter of Con-mor, fell desperately in love with Cathmor, who, before her passion was disclosed, was recalled to Ireland by his brother Cairbar, upon the news of the intended expedition of Fingal, to re-establish the family of Conar on the Irish throne.—The wind being contrary, Cathmor remained, for three days, in a neighbouring bay, during which time Sul-malla disguised herself, in the habit of a young warrior, and came to offer him her service, in the war. Cathmor accepted of the proposal, sailed for Ireland, and arrived in Ulster a few days before the death of Cairbar. [M]

as I have gathered it from other poems.] as I have gathered it from tradition. 1773

20.   Sul-malla, *slowly rolling eyes.* Caon-mór, *mild and tall.* Inis-huna, *green island.* [M]

21.   Fithil, *an inferior bard.* It may either be taken here for the proper name of a man, or in the literal sense, as the bards were the heralds and messengers of those times. Cathmor, it is probable, was absent, when the rebellion of his brother Cairbar, and the assassination of Cormac, king of Ireland, happened. The traditions, which are handed down with the poem, say that Cathmor and his followers had only arrived, from Inis-huna, three days before the death of Cairbar, which sufficiently clears his character from any imputation of being concerned in the conspiracy, with his brother. [M]

The traditions ... say that Cathmor and his followers] Cathmor and his followers 1773

22.   The ceremony which was used by Fingal, when he prepared for an expedition, is related, by Ossian, in one of his lesser poems. A bard, at midnight, went to the hall, where the tribes feasted upon solemn occasions, raised the *war-song,* and thrice called the Spirits of their deceased ancestors to come, *on their clouds,* to behold the actions of their children. He then fixed the *shield of Trenmor,* on a tree on the rock of Selma, striking it, at times, with the blunt end of a spear, and singing the war-song between. Thus he did, for three successive nights, and in the mean time, messengers were dispatched to convene the tribes; or, as Ossian expresses it, *to call them from all their streams.* This phrase alludes to the situation of the residences of the clans, which were generally fixed in valleys, where the torrents of the

neighbouring mountains were collected into one body, and became *large streams* or rivers.—*The lifting up of the shield*, was the phrase for beginning a war. [M] is related, by Ossian, in one of his lesser poems.] is related thus in tradition. 1773 or, as Ossian expresses it,] or, to use an ancient expression, 1773

Laing, (2:123, n. 8):"This tradition, I believe, is transcribed from some account of the mode of declaring war among the American tribes."

23.   on Morven,] in Selma: 1773
24.   red-haired] *deleted* 1773
25.   Inis-fail,] Erin, 1773
26.   king of Atha,] O Cathmor! 1773
27.   The surly attitude of Foldath, is a proper preamble to his after behaviour. Chaffed with the disappointment of the victory which he promised himself, he becomes passionate and over-bearing. The quarrel which succeeds between him and Malthos was, no doubt, introduced by the poet, to raise the character of Cathmor, whose superior worth shines forth, in his manly manner of ending the difference between the chiefs. [M]

was ... introduced by the poet, to] is introduced, to 1773
28.   stood beneath] leaned against 1773
29.   Claon-rath, *winding field*. The *th* are seldom pronounced audibly in the Galic language. [M]
30.   fathers; when] fathers. Soft was his voice when 1773

Such repetition of clauses (Soft was his voice) *is a distinctive feature of the 1773 edition, only occasional instances of which are signalled here.*

31.   the youth,] Hidalla, 1773
32.   Inis-fail:] Erin. 1773
33.   Bid thou] Bid, O Cathmor, 1773
34.   thy voice;] the voice of Hidalla. 1773
35.   Temora,] Erin, 1773

This speech of Malthos is, throughout, a severe reprimand to the blustering behaviour of Foldath. It abounds with that laconic eloquence, and indirect manner of address, which is so justly admired in the short speech of Ajax, in the ninth book of the Iliad. [M]

It abounds ... Iliad.] *deleted* 1773
36.   The king] Cathmor 1773
37.   The poet could scarcely find, in all nature, a comparison so favourable as this to the superiority of Cathmor over his two chiefs. I shall illustrate this passage with another from a fragment of an ancient poem, just now in my hands.—"As the sun is above the vapours, which his beams have raised; so is the soul of the king above the sons of fear. They roll dark below him; he rejoices in the robe of his beams. But when feeble deeds wander on the soul of the king, he is a darkened sun rolled along the sky: the valley is sad below: flowers wither beneath the drops of the night." [M] The poet could ... so favourable as this, to] This comparison is favourable to 1773
38.   Lear-thon, *sea-wave*, the name of the chief of that colony of the Fir-bolg, which first migrated into Ireland. Larthon's first settlement in that country is related in the seventh book. He was the ancestor of Cathmor; and is here called *Larthon of Lumon*, from a high hill of that name in Inis-huna, the ancient seat of the Fir-bolg.——The poet preserves the character of Cathmor throughout. He had mentioned, in the first book, the aversion of that chief to praise, and we find him here

lying at the side of a stream, that the noise of it might drown the voice of Fonar, who, according to the custom of the times, sung his eulogium in his *evening song*. Tho' other chiefs, as well as Cathmor, might be averse to hear their own praise, we find it the universal policy of the times, to allow the bards to be as extravagant as they pleased in their encomiums on the leaders of armies, in the presence of their people. The vulgar, who had no great ability to judge for themselves, received the characters of their princes, entirely upon the faith of the bards. The good effects which an high opinion of its ruler has upon a community, are too obvious to require explanation; on the other hand, distrust of the abilities of leaders produce the worst consequences. [M]

——The poet preserves ... throughout.] The character of Cathmor is preserved. 1773 (*but the following* He *is allowed to stand*)

The good effects ... worst consequences.] *deleted* 1773

39.   Cairbar] His brother 1773

40.   Carril, the son of Kinfena, by the orders of Ossian, sung the funeral elegy at the tomb of Cairbar. See the second book, towards the end. In all the poems of Ossian, the visits of ghosts, to their living friends, are short, and their language obscure, both which circumstances tend to throw a solemn gloom on these super-natural scenes. Towards the latter end of the speech of the ghost of Cairbar, he fortels the death of Cathmor, by enumerating those signals which, according to the opinion of the times, preceded the death of a person renowned. It was thought that the ghosts of deceased bards sung, for three nights preceding the death (near the place where his tomb was to be raised) round an unsubstantial figure which represented the body of the person who was to die. [M]

In all the poems of Ossian,] In all these poems 1773

41.   winds thro'] darts across 1773

42.   The king started] Cathmor starts 1773

43.   The soliloquy of Cathmor abounds with that magnanimity and love of fame which constitute the hero. Tho' staggered at first with the prediction of Cairbar's ghost, he soon comforts himself with the agreeable prospect of his future renown; and like Achilles, prefers a short and glorious life, to an obscure length of years in retirement and ease. [M]

The soliloquy of Cathmor abounds ... the hero.] The soliloquy of Cathmor suits the magnanimity of his character. 1773

44.   little] narrow 1773

From this passage we learn in what extreme contempt an indolent and unwarlike life was held in those days of heroism. Whatever a philosopher may say, in praise of quiet and retirement, I am far from thinking, but they weaken and debase the human mind. When the faculties of the soul are not exerted, they lose their vigour, and low and circumscribed notions take the place of noble and enlarged ideas. Action, on the contrary, and the vicissitudes of fortune which attend it, call forth, by turns, all the powers of the mind, and, by exercising, strengthen them. Hence it is, that in great and opulent states, when property and indolence are secured to individuals, we seldom meet with that strength of mind, which is so common in a nation, not far advanced in civilization. It is a curious, but just observation; that great kingdoms seldom produce great characters, which must be altogether attributed to that indo-lence and dissipation, which are the inseparable companions of too much property and security. Rome, it is certain, had more real great men within it, when its power was confined within the narrow bounds of Latium, than when its dominion extended over all the known world; and one petty state of the Saxon heptarchy had, perhaps, as much genuine spirit in it, as the two British kingdoms united. As a state, we are much more powerful than our ancestors, but we would lose by comparing individuals with them. [M]

From this passage ... heroism.] An indolent and unwarlike life was held in extreme contempt. 1773

An illuminating expansion of the ideas contained in the second paragraph of the 'Dissertation' preceding Temora - this note is omitted by Laing and most later editions.

45.   rolled on] folded in 1773

46.   The discovery which succeeds this circumstance is well imagined, and naturally conducted. The silence of Cathmor upon this occasion is more expressive of the emotions of his soul, than any speech which the poet could put into his mouth. [M]

Note deleted 1773

47.   Atha's warrior] Cathmor of Atha 1773

48.   In order to understand this passage, it is necessary to look to the description of Cathmor's shield, which the poet has given us in the seventh book. This shield had seven principal bosses, the sound of each of which, when struck with a spear, conveyed a particular order from the king to his tribes. The sound of one of them, as here, was the signal for the army to assemble. [M]

shield, which the poet has given us in] shield in 1773

49.   This was not the valley of Lona to which Sul-malla afterwards retired. [M]

See 'Temora' V, p. 263, note 6.

50.   Of all passages in the works of Ossian these lyric pieces lose most, by a literal prose translation, as the beauty of them does not so much depend, on the strength of thought, as on the elegance of expression and harmony of numbers. It has been observed, that an author is put to the severest test, when he is stript of the ornaments of versification, and delivered down in another language in prose. Those, therefore, who have seen how awkward a figure even Homer and Virgil make, in a version of this sort, will think the better of the compositions of Ossian. [M]

Note deleted 1773

51.   rolled away] dispersed 1773

52.   of the spears.] from Selma of spears! 1773

53.   streamy Inis-fail.] Erin of the streams. 1773

54.   Con-mor, the father of Sul-malla, was killed in that war, from which Cathmor delivered Inis-huna. Lormar his son succeeded Conmor. It was the opinion of the times, when a person was reduced to a pitch of misery, which could admit of no alleviation, that the ghosts of his ancestors *called his soul away*. This supernatural kind of death was called *the voice of the dead*; and is believed by the superstitious vulgar to this day.

There is no people in the world, perhaps, who gave more universal credit to apparitions, and the visits of the ghosts of the deceased to their friends, than the common highlanders. This is to be attributed as much, at least, to the situation of the country they possess, as to that credulous disposition which distinguishes an unenlightened people. As their business was feeding of cattle, in dark and extensive desarts, so their journeys lay over wide and unfrequented heaths, where, often, they were obliged to sleep in the open air, amidst the whistling of winds, and roar of waterfalls. The gloominess of the scenes around them was apt to beget that melancholy disposition of mind, which most readily receives impressions of the extraordinary and supernatural kind. Falling asleep in this gloomy mood, and their dreams being disturbed by the noise of the elements around, it is no matter of wonder, that they thought they heard the *voice of the dead*. This *voice of the dead*, however, was, perhaps, no more than a shriller whistle of the winds in an old tree, or in the chinks of a neighbouring rock. It is to this cause I ascribe those many and improbable tales of ghosts, which we meet with in the highlands: for, in other respects, we do not find that the highlanders are more credulous than their neighbours. [M]

[§ 2] There is no people ... than the common highlanders.] There is no people ... than the ancient Scots. 1773

that the highlanders are more credulous] that the inhabitants are more credulous 1773

55.   can seize] call away 1773
56.   when the king] When Cathmor 1773
57.   I shall] shall Sul-malla 1773

Temora Book V.
1.   Ossian,] The poet, 1773
2.   These abrupt addresses give great life to the poetry of Ossian. They are all in a lyric measure. The old men, who retain, on memory, the compositions of Ossian, shew much satisfaction when they come to those parts of them, which are in rhime, and take great pains to explain their beauties, and inculcate the meaning of their obsolete phrases, on the minds of their hearers. This attachment does not proceed from the superior beauty of these lyric pieces, but rather from a taste for rhime which the modern bards have established among the highlanders. Having no genius themselves for the sublime and pathetic, they placed the whole beauty of poetry in the returning harmony of similar sounds. The seducing charms of rhime soon weaned their countrymen from that attachment they long had to the recitative of Ossian: and, tho' they still admired his compositions, their admiration was founded more on his antiquity, and the detail of facts which he gave, than on his poetical excellence. Rhiming, in process of time, became so much reduced into a system, and was so universally understood, that every cow-herd composed tolerable verses. These poems, it is true, were a description of nature; but of nature in its rudest form; a group of uninteresting ideas dressed out in the flowing harmony of mono-tonous verses. Void of merit as those vulgar compositions were, they fell little short of the productions of the regular bards; for when all poetical excellence is confined to sounds alone, it is within the power of every one possessed of a good ear. [M] *Note deleted* 1773

3.   Lora is often mentioned; it was a small and rapid stream in the neighbourhood of Selma. There is no vestige of this name now remaining; tho' it appears from a very old song, which the translator has seen, that one of the small rivers on the north-west coast was called Lora some centuries ago. [M]

4.   Cona;] Selma! 1773
5.   From several passages in the poem we may form a distinct idea of the scene of the action of Temora. At a small distance from one another rose the hills of Mora

and Lona: the first possessed by Fingal, the second by the army of Cathmor. Through the intermediate plain ran the small river Lubar, on the banks of which all the battles were fought, excepting that between Cairbar and Oscar, related in the first book. This last mentioned engagement happened, to the north of the hill of Mora, of which Fingal took possession, after the army of Cairbar fell back to that of Cathmor. At some distance, but within sight of Mora, towards the west, Lubar issued from the mountain of Crommal, and after a short course thro' the plain of Moi-lena, discharged itself into the sea near the field of battle. Behind the mountain of Crommal ran the small stream of Lavath, on the banks of which Ferad-artho, the son of Cairbre, the only person remaining of the race of Conar, lived concealed in a cave, during the usurpation of Cairbar, the son of Borbar-duthul. [M]
Lona:] Lora 1773 (*misprint - note omitted by Laing*)
6.   It was to this valley Sul-malla retired, during the last and decisive battle between Fingal and Cathmor. It is described in the seventh book, where it is called the vale of Lona, and the residence of a Druid. [M]
7.   Inis-huna's white-bosomed maid.] Sul-malla in her thoughtful mood. 1773
8.   beheld,] beholds Cathmor, 1773
9.   Morven.] Selma. 1773
10.   Morven's] Selma's 1773
11.   I] Fingal 1773
12.   him] Fillan 1773
13.   son of Clatho:] the youth.
14.   The rock of Cormul rose on the hill of Mora, and commanded a prospect of the field of battle. The speech of Fingal, which immediately precedes this passage, is worthy of being remarked, as the language, not only, of a warlike but a good king. The confidence which his people reposed in him, was as much the result of his clemency and military merit, as the consequence of that affection which men, un-corrupted with the vices of advanced society, naturally have for the chief of their blood and hereditary prince. [M]
The confidence which his people reposed in him ... hereditary prince.] The mutual confidence which subsisted between him and his people, the result of his clemency and their dutiful behaviour towards him, is worthy of being imitated in a more polished age than that in which he lived. 1763
Note deleted 1773
15.   As, slow ... came] Intermitting darts the light, from his shield, as, slow the king of heroes moves. Sidelong rolls his eye o'er the heath, as forming advance the lines. Graceful, fly his half-grey locks, round his kingly features, now lightened with dreadful joy. Wholly mighty is the chief! Behind him dark and slow I moved. Straight came [forward the strength of Gaul.] 1773
16.   It is necessary to remember, that Gaul was wounded; which occasions his requiring here the assistance of Ossian to bind his shield on his side. [M]
17.   Roth-mar, *the sound of the sea before a storm*. Druman-ard, *high ridge*. Culmin, *soft-haired*. Cull-allin, *beautiful locks*. Strutha, *streamy river*. [M]
18.   By the stone of Loda, as I have remarked in my notes on some other poems of Ossian, is meant a place of worship among the Scandinavians. Ossian, in his many expeditions to Orkney and Scandinavia, became acquainted with some of the rites of the religion which prevailed in those countries, and frequently alludes to them in his poems. There are some ruins, and circular pales of stone, remaining still in Orkney,

and the islands of Shetland, which retain, to this day, the name of *Loda* or *Loden*. They seem to have differed materially, in their construction, from those Druidical monuments which remain in Britain, and the western isles. The places of worship among the Scandinavians were originally rude and unadorned. In after ages, when they opened a communication with other nations, they adopted their manners, and built temples. That at Upsal, in Sweden, was amazingly rich and magnificent. Haquin, of Norway, built one, near Drontheim, little inferior to the former; and it went always under the name of Loden. *Mallet, introduction a l'histoire de Danne-marc.* [M]

Loda, as I have remarked ... , is] Loda is 1773

Ossian, in his many expeditions] The Caledonians in their many expeditions 1773

and frequently alludes to them in his poems.] and the ancient poetry frequently alludes to them. 1773

Cf. Blair, p. 370, note 24: "In confirmation of Ossian's topography, it is proper to acquaint the reader that in these islands, as I have been well informed, there are many pillars, and circles of stones, still remaining, known by the name of the stones and circles of Loda, or Loden; to which some degree of superstitious regard is annexed to this day."

Also Laing, 2:152, n. 11: "I know not whether Blair's information was derived from Macpherson, or Macpherson's from Blair; but the name of *Loda* or *Loden* was never heard in these islands, nor ever applied to the circle of stones: and the passage from Mallet is an absolute misquotation. Mallet's words, from Olaus Wormius, are precisely these, 'that Haco, early of Norway, (anno 979) had built a temple at *Laden*, near Drontheim, nothing inferior to that at Upsal.' Laden, the name of the district where the temple stood, has been evidently converted into Loden and Loda, from its supposed affinity to the name of Odin."

The Copenhagen-based Paul Henri Mallet's Introduction á l'histoire de Dannemarc *(1755), and his* Monumens de la mythologie et de la poésie des Celtes, et particu-lièrement des anciens Scandinaves *(1756) provided extremely important documents for 18th century primitivist thought, and especially for Northern Europeans suffer-ing from a sense of cultural deficit. It should be noted that Ossianism and Scandi-navianism tend to go together, at least until after 1800, with Mallet and Macpher-son mutually reinforcing one another. For what Laing does not mention is that, when he reissues his works in 1787 and 1790, Mallet welcomes Ossian, observes the identity between Odin and the Spirit of Loda, generally approves of Macpherson's revelations and finds in the Ossianic poetry an interesting confirmation of Scandi-navian mythology.*

19. The poet, metaphorically, calls Fillan a beam of light. Culmin, mentioned here, was the son of Clonmar, chief of Strutha, by the beautiful Cul-allin. She was so remarkable for the beauty of her person, that she is introduced, frequently, in the similies and allusions of antient poetry. *Mar Chul-aluin Strutha nan sian;* is a line of Ossian in another poem; i.e. *Lovely as Cul-allin of Strutha of the storms.* [M]

is a line of Ossian in another poem; i.e.] *deleted* 1773

20. Youth of Strutha] Son of Cul-allin 1773

21. Dogs were thought to be sensible of the death of their master, let it happen at ever so great a distance. It was also the opinion of the times, that the arms which warriors left at home became bloody, when they themselves fell in battle. It was from those signs that Cul-allin is supposed to understand that her son is killed; in

which she is confirmed by the appearance of his ghost.—Her sudden and short exclamation, on the occasion, is more affecting than if she had extended her complaints to a greater length. The attitude of the fallen youth, and Fillan's reflexions over him, are natural and judicious, and come forcibly back on the mind, when we consider, that the supposed situation of the father of Culmin, was so similar to that of Fingal, after the death of Fillan himself. [M]

exclamation, on the occasion, is more affecting] exclamation is more judicious in the poet, 1773

are natural and judicious, and] *deleted* 1773

22.   day of his] midst of 1763 1773

23.   turning his dim eyes towards] and his eyes are towards 1763 His eyes are toward 1773

24.   This Dermid is, probably, the same with *Dermid O duine*, who makes so great a figure in the fictions of the Irish bards. [M]

Note deleted 1773

25.   Cona] Selma 1773

26.   poured] fly 1773

27.   the king] Cathmor 1773

Cathmor. [M]

Note deleted 1773

28.   to the king on his hill; then, darkly turning, he] to Fingal on his hills: then, darkly turning, in doubtful mood, he 1773

hills *presumably misprint, but taken over by later editions, including Laing.*

29.   This valley had its name from Clono, son of Lethmal of Lora, one of the ancestors of Dermid, the son of Duthno. His history is thus related in an old poem. In the days of Conar, the son of Trenmor, the first king of Ireland, Clono passed over into that kingdom, from Caledonia, to aid Conar against the Fir-bolg. Being remarkable for the beauty of his person, he soon drew the attention of Sulmin, the young wife of an Irish chief. She disclosed her passion, which was not properly returned by the Caledonian. The lady sickened, thro' disappointment, and her love for Clono came to the ears of her husband. Fired with jealousy, he vowed revenge. Clono, to avoid his rage, departed from Temora, in order to pass over into Scotland; and being benighted in the valley mentioned here, he laid him down to sleep. *There*, (to use the words of the poet) *Lethmal descended in the dreams of Clono; and told him that danger was near.* For the reader's amusement I shall translate the vision, which does not want poetical merit. [M]

(to use the words of the poet)] *deleted* 1773

For the reader's amusement ... poetical merit.] *deleted* 1773

Ghost of LETHMAL.

"Arise from thy bed of moss; son of low-laid Lethmal, arise. The sound of the coming of foes, descends along the wind.

CLONO.

Whose voice is that, like many streams, in the season of my rest?

Ghost of LETHMAL.

Arise, thou dweller of the souls of the lovely; son of Lethmal, arise.

CLONO.

How dreary is the night! The moon is darkened in the sky; red are the paths of ghosts, along its sullen face! Green-skirted meteors set around. Dull is the roaring of streams, from the valley of dim forms. I hear thee, spirit of my father, on the eddying course of the wind. I hear thee, but thou bendest not, forward, thy tall form, from the skirts of night."

As Clono prepared to depart, the husband of Sulmin came up, with his numerous attendants. Clono defended himself, but, after a gallant resistance, he was over-powered and slain. He was buried in the place where he was killed, and the valley was called after his name. Dermid, in his request to Gaul the son of Morni, which immediately follows this paragraph, alludes to the tomb of Clono, and his own connection with that unfortunate chief. [M]

30. where] were 1765

31. streams,] stream 1763 1773

32. from his thigh:] from the side of Dermid. 1773

33. low!] slow! 1773 (*misprint - corrected in Laing, and other 19th century editions*)

34. King of Strumon,] Son of Morni! 1773

35. The brevity of the speech of Gaul, and the laconic reply of Dermid, are judi-cious and well suited to the hurry of the occasion. The incidents which Ossian has chosen to diversify his battles, are interesting, and never fail to awaken our atten-tion. I know that want of particularity in the wounds, and diversity in the fall of those that are slain, have been among the objections, started, to the poetical merit of Ossian's poems. The criticism, without partiality I may say it, is unjust, for our poet has introduced as great a variety of this sort, as he, with propriety, could within the compass of so short poems. It is confessed, that Homer has a greater variety of deaths than any other poet that ever appeared. His great knowledge in anatomy can never be disputed; but, I am far from thinking, that his battles, even with all their novelty of wounds, are the most beautiful parts of his poems. The human mind dwells with disgust upon a protracted scene of carnage; and, tho' the introduction of the terrible is necessary to the grandeur of heroic poetry, yet I am convinced, that a medium ought to be observed. [M]

Note deleted 1773

36. it] she 1773

37. echoing seas.] resounding ocean! 1773

38. form] chief 1773

39. Moruth.] Selma. 1773

The rapidity of this verse, which indeed is but faintly imitated in the translation, is amazingly expressive in the original. One hears the very rattling of the armour of Fillan. The intervention of Fillan is necessary here; for as Dermid was wounded before, it is not to be supposed, he could be a match for Foldath. Fillan is often, poetically called the *son of Moruth*, from a stream of that name in Morven, near which he was born. [M]

Note deleted 1773

40. hero.] chief. 1773

41. Fingal and Cathmor. [M]

42. rocks;] rocks above; 1773

43. Morven's] Selma's 1773

44.   The fall of Foldath, if we may believe tradition, was predicted to him, before he had left his own country to join Cairbar, in his designs on the Irish throne. He went to the cave of Moma, to enquire of the spirits of his fathers, concerning the success of the enterprise of Cairbar. The responses of oracles are always attended with obscurity, and liable to a double meaning: Foldath, therefore, put a favourable interpretation on the prediction, and pursued his adopted plan of aggrandizing himself with the family of Atha. I shall, here, translate the answer of *the ghosts of his ancestors*, as it was handed down by tradition. Whether the legend is really ancient, or the invention of a late age, I shall not pretend to determine, tho', from the phraseology, I should suspect the last.

FOLDATH, *addressing the spirits of his fathers.*

"Dark, I stand in your presence; fathers of Foldath, hear. Shall my steps pass over Atha, to Ullin of the roes?

The Answer.

Thy steps shall pass over Atha, to the green dwelling of kings. There shall thy stature arise, over the fallen, like a pillar of thunder-clouds. There, terrible in darkness, shalt thou stand, till the *reflected beam*, or *Clon-cath* of Moruth, come; Moruth of many streams, that roars in distant lands."

Cloncath, or *reflected beam*, say my traditional authors, was the name of the sword of Fillan; so that it was, in the latent signification of the word *Clon-cath*, that the deception lay. My principal reason for introducing this note, is, that if this tradition is equally ancient with the poem, which, by the bye, is doubtful, it serves to shew, that the religion of the Fir-bolg differed from that of the Caledonians, as we never find the latter enquiring of the spirits of their deceased ancestors. [M]

[§ 1] I shall, here, translate ... suspect the last. *deleted* 1773

[§ 4] that if this tradition is ... it serves] that this tradition serves 1773

45.   Alnecma.] Erin. 1773

46.   The characters of Foldath and Malthos are well sustained. They were both dark and surly, but each in a different way. Foldath was impetuous and cruel. Malthos stubborn and incredulous. Their attachment to the family of Atha was equal; their bravery in battle the same. Foldath was vain and ostentatious: Malthos unindulgent but generous. His behaviour here, towards his enemy Foldath, shews, that a good heart often lies concealed under a gloomy and sullen character. [M]

are well sustained.] are sustained. 1773

47.   king.] chief. 1773

48.   Moma was the name of a country in the south of Connaught, once famous for being the residence of an Arch-druid. The cave of Moma was thought to be inhabited by the spirits of the chiefs of the Fir-bolg, and their posterity sent to enquire there, as to an oracle, concerning the issue of their wars. [M]

Cf. 'Temora' II, *p. 238, note 18.*

49.   Dal-ruäth, *parched or sandy field.* The etymology of Dardu-lena is uncertain. The daughter of Foldath was, probably, so called, from a place in Ulster, where her father had defeated part of the adherents of Artho, king of Ireland. Dor-du-lena; *the dark wood of Moi-lena.* As Foldath was proud and ostentatious, it would appear, that he transferred the name of a place, where he himself had been victorious, to his daughter. [M]

50.   came.] seemed to come. 1773

51.   seemed as hid] hid himself 1773

52.   These sudden transitions from the subject are not uncommon in the composi-
tions of Ossian. That in this place has a peculiar beauty and propriety. The
suspence, in which the mind of the reader is left, conveys the idea of Fillan's danger
more forcibly home, than any description the poet could introduce. There is a sort of
eloquence, in silence with propriety. A minute detail of the circumstances of an
important scene is generally cold and insipid. The human mind, free and fond of
thinking for itself, is disgusted to find every thing done by the poet. It is, therefore,
his business only to mark the most striking out-lines, and to allow the imaginations
of his readers to finish the figure for themselves.

   The address to Clatho, the mother of Fillan, which concludes this book, if we
regard the versification of the original, is one of the most beautiful passages in the
poem. The wild simplicity and harmony of its cadences are inimitably beautiful. It is
sung still by many in the north, and is distinguished by the name of *Laoi chaon
Chlatho:* i.e. *The harmonious hymn of Clatho.* The book ends in the afternoon of
the third day, from the opening of the poem. [M]
[§ 1] These sudden transitions ... beauty and propriety.] *deleted* 1773
any description the poet could introduce.] any description that could be introduced.
1773
[§ 2] The address to Clatho ... *The harmonious hymn of Clatho.*] *deleted* 1773
Laing (2:164) observes: "The poet's address to Clatho in person, to leave her hall in
Selma, in order to behold her son Fillan in Ireland, as if she were alive and present
both at the song and at the battle, is one of those extravagant efforts of affected
inspiration, in which all distinctions of time and place are confounded." *The
comment perhaps reveals more about Laing's limitations than the inadequacies of
Ossian. The first part of Macpherson's note, which Laing ignores (and which
Macpherson himself later truncates), draws attention to one of those features of
Ossian which, for contemporaries, distinguished the poetry as genuinely "popular"
and/or archaic and appealed most to the aesthetic sensibilities of the coming
literary avant-garde. As Blair observes (and Macpherson here echoes?), we find in
Ossian:* "No artful transitions; nor full and extended connexion of parts; such as we
find among the poets of later times when order and regularity of composition were
more studied and known; but a style always rapid and vehement; in narration
concise even to abruptness, and leaving several circumstances to be supplied by the
reader's imagination." *(see, p. 354; cf. also his comments on this passage itself, p.
373). From here it is not very far to Herder and the* "Sprünge und kühne Würfe"
*which he finds in folk-song (and Ossian), and which left a deep impact on Goethe's
early lyric (and his* Faust*). But then it is also not very far from what Jerome Stone
found in the (authentic)* 'Lay of Fraoch', *an example of a composition* "in which
energy is more sought after than neatness, and the strictness of connexion less
adverted to than the design of moving the passions and affecting the heart." *(cf.*
'Dar-thula', *p. 143, note 47).*
53.   in my hall,] in mine ear, 1773
54.   seas.] seas! Leave, blue-eyed Clatho, leave thy hall! 1773

Temora Book VI.
1.   I have, in a preceding note, observed that the abrupt manner of Ossian
partakes much of the nature of the Drama. The opening of this book is a confirma-
tion of the justness of this observation. Instead of a long detail of circumstances

delivered by the poet himself, about the descent of Cathmor from the hill, whereon he sat to behold the battle, he puts the narration in the mouth of Fingal. The relation acquires importance from the character of the speaker. The concern which Fingal shews, when he beholds the *rising of Cathmor*, raises our ideas of the valour of that hero to the highest pitch. The apostrophes which are crowded on one another, are expressive of the perturbation of Fingal's soul, and of his fear for his son, who was not a match for the king of Ireland. The conduct of the poet in removing Fingal from the sight of the engagement, is very judicious; for the king might be induced, from seeing the inequality of the combat between Fillan and Cathmor, to come to battle himself, and so bring about the catastrophe of the poem prematurely. The removal of Fingal affords room to the poet for introducing those affecting scenes which immediately succeed, and are among the chief beauties of the poem.—They who can deny art to Ossian, in conducting the catastrophe of Temora, are certainly more prejudiced against the age he lived in, than is consistent with good sense. I cannot finish this note, without observing the delicacy and propriety of Fingal's address to Ossian. By the appellation of the *father of Oscar*, he raises at once, in the mind of the hero, all that tenderness for the safety of Fillan, which a situation so similar to that of his own son, when he fell, was capable to suggest. [M]

Note replaced by Fingal speaks. 1773

*For Macpherson's observations on Ossian's abrupt manner and its affinity to drama, see above, '*Temora' II, *note 1. In the light of the (later deleted) praise of Ossian's judicious handling of the subject here and also the stress laid in the '*Dissertation' *on the value of '*Temora' *as a historical document, it does not perhaps require the acumen of a Laing (2:172, n. 1) to wonder* "whether the death of Fillan, in consequence of the removal of Fingal from the sight of the engagement, was an historical fact recorded by Ossian, or a mere epic artifice, employed to retard the catastrophe of the poem." *It cannot very well have been both.*

2.   echoing] *deleted* 1773
3.   daughter] fair daughter 1773
4.   Fillan's eyes.] Fillan. 1773
5.   The *spear of Temora* was that which Oscar had received, in a present, from Cormac, the son of Artho, king of Ireland. It was of it that Cairbar made the pretext for quarrelling with Oscar, at the feast, in the first book. After the death of Oscar we find it always in the hands of Ossian. It is said, in another poem, that it was preserved, as a relique, at Temora, from the days of Conar, the son of Trenmor, the first king of Ireland. [M]

After the death of Oscar ... king of Ireland.] *deleted* 1773

6.   The appearance of Cathmor is magnificent: his unconcerned gait, and the effect which his very voice has upon his flying army, are circumstances calculated to raise our ideas of his superior merit and valour. Ossian is very impartial with regard to his enemies: this, however, cannot be said of other poets of great eminence and unquestioned merit. Milton, of the first class of poets, is undoubtedly the most irreprehensible in this respect; for we always pity or admire his Devil, but seldom detest him, even tho' he is the arch enemy of our species. Mankind generally takes sides with the unfortunate and daring. It is from this disposition that many readers, tho' otherwise good christians, have almost wished success to Satan, in his desperate and daring voyage from hell, through the regions of chaos and night. [M]

Note deleted 1773

7.   Dark-rolled] Dark-waves 1773

In both cases the apparently idiosyncratic hyphen alters the stress and has the effect of making dark *part of the verb which therefore opens the sentence. Such constructions seem to be modelled on the natural inversions of Gaelic which is a verb-subject-object language. Instances of this and other estranging devices, designed to suggest translation, are presumably what Percy had in mind when he criticized Macpherson's* "studied affectation of Erse idiom".

8.   Atha.] Erin. 1773

9.   Cluba] Inis-huna 1773

Clu-ba, *winding bay*, an arm of the sea in Inis-huna, or the western coast of South-Britain. It was in this bay that Cathmor was wind-bound when Sul-malla came, in the disguise of a young warrior, to accompany him in his voyage to Ireland. Conmor, the father of Sul-malla, as we learn from her soliloquy, at the close of the fourth book, was dead before the departure of his daughter. [M]

Again, despite the change in the text, the note remains unaltered in 1773.

10.   for its robe,] as they fly, 1773

11.   Lutha was the name of a valley in Morven, in the days of Ossian. There dwelt Toscar the son of Conloch, the father of Malvina, who, upon that account, is often called *the maid of Lutha*. Lutha signifies *swift stream*. [M]

Morven, in the days of Ossian.] Morven. 1773

12.   people.—I] hosts. Ossian 1773

13.   The scenery of the place where Fillan fought, and the situation of that hero, are picturesque and affecting. The distress, which succeeds, is heightened by Ossian's being ignorant, for some time, that his brother was wounded. This kind of suspence is frequent in Ossian's poems. The more unexpected a thing is, the greater impression it makes on the mind when it comes. [M]

Note deleted 1773

14.   chief.] hero 1763 1773

15.   voice] sound 1773

16.   Clatho,] Clatho! O Fillan, 1773

17.   the feeble] the bard 1763 1773

18.   the lost beam of Clatho?] the early-fallen Fillan? 1763

The fragment of a poem on the death of Fillan, *quoted here by Macpherson, has been inserted at the end of* 'Temora' VI - *see above, pp. 275 f.*

19.   blue-eyed king of shields?] O Fillan, young breaker of shields! 1773

20.   chief of Atha,] king of Erin! 1773

21.   meteors,] meteors on your hills, 1763 1773

22.   wrath—] wrath. 1773

Here the sentence is designedly left unfinished by the poet. The sense is, that he was resolved, like a destroying fire, to consume Cathmor, who had killed his brother. In the midst of this resolution, the situation of Fingal suggests itself to him, in a very strong light. He resolves to return to assist the king in prosecuting the war.——But then his shame for not defending his brother, recurs to him.—He is determined again to go and find out Cathmor.—We may consider him, as in the act of advancing towards the enemy, when the horn of Fingal sounded on Mora, and called back his people to his presence.—This soliloquy is natural: the resolutions which so suddenly follow one another, are expressive of a mind extremely agitated with sorrow and conscious shame; yet the behaviour of Ossian, in his execution of the commands of Fingal, is so irreprehensible, that it is not easy to determine where he failed in his duty. The truth is, that when men fail in designs which they ardently wish to accomplish, they naturally blame themselves, as the chief cause of their disappointment. The comparison, with which the poet concludes his soliloquy, is very fanciful; and well adapted to the ideas of those, who live in a country, where lightning is extremely common. [M]

unfinished by the poet.] unfinished. 1773

The comparison ... extremely common.] *deleted* 1773

Given that the sentence is designedly left unfinished (though in 1773 apparently no longer by Ossian), it seems somewhat strange that the revised edition has it end with a full-stop.

23.   him from high,] him, 1773

24.   I] Ossian 1773

25.   Inisfail,] Erin, 1773

26.   This scene is solemn. The poet always places his chief character amidst objects which favour the sublime. The face of the country, the night, the broken remains of a defeated army, and, above all, the attitude and silence of Fingal himself, are circumstances calculated to impress an awful idea on the mind. Ossian is most successful in his night-descriptions. Dark images suited the melancholy temper of his mind. His poems were all composed after the active part of his life was over, when he was blind, and had survived all the companions of his youth: we therefore find a veil of melancholy thrown over the whole. [M]

This scene is] "This scene, says an ingenious writer, and a good judge, is 1773 *(entire note within quotation marks)*

Who the ingenious writer *and* good judge *is, I am not sure. Blair, who surely influenced Macpherson here, has much to say both about Ossian's solemnity and his sublimity, though he does not mention this particular scene. Perhaps Kames (Henry Home) is meant. Unfortunately, this, together with Macpherson's next note, in which the same writer is quoted, is omitted by Laing.*

27.   The abashed behaviour of the army of Fingal proceeds rather from shame than fear. The king was not of a tyrannical disposition: *He*, as he professes himself in the fifth book, *never was a dreadful form, in their presence, darkened into wrath. His voice was no thunder to their ears: his eye sent forth no death.*—The first ages of society are not the times of arbitrary power. As the wants of mankind are few, they retain their independence. It is an advanced state of civilization that moulds the mind to that submission to government, of which ambitious magistrates take advantage, and raise themselves into absolute power.

It is a vulgar error, that the common Highlanders lived, in abject slavery, under their chiefs. Their high ideas of, and attachment to, the heads of their families, probably, led the unintelligent into this mistake.—When the honour of the tribe was concerned, the commands of the chief were obeyed, without restriction: but, if individuals were oppressed, they threw themselves into the arms of a neighbouring clan, assumed a new name, and were encouraged and protected. The fear of this desertion, no doubt, made the chiefs cautious in their government. As their consequence, in the eyes of others, was in proportion to the number of their people, they took care to avoid every thing that tended to diminish it.

It was but very lately that the authority of the laws extended to the Highlands. Before that time the clans were governed, in civil affairs, not by the verbal

commands of the chief, but by what they called *Clechda*, or the traditional pre-
cedents of their ancestors. When differences happened between individuals, some of
the oldest men in the tribe were chosen umpires between the parties, to decide
according to the *Clechda*. The chief interposed his authority, and, invariably,
enforced the decision.—In their wars, which were frequent, on account of family-
feuds, the chief was less reserved in the execution of his authority; and even then he
seldom extended it to the taking the life of any of his tribe.—No crime was capital,
except murder; and that was very unfrequent in the highlands. No corporal punish-
ment, of any kind, was inflicted. The memory of an affront of this sort would
remain, for ages in a family, and they would seize every opportunity to be revenged,
unless it came immediately from the hands of the chief himself; in that case it was
taken, rather as a fatherly correction, than a legal punishment for offences. [M]
New opening paragraph 1773: I owe the first paragraph of the following note to the
same pen. *(see above, note 26)*
The abashed behaviour ... absolute power.] "The abashed behaviour ... absolute
power." 1784-85, 1790, 1796
28.   broke.] cleft in twain. 1773
29.   This rock of Cormul is often mentioned in the preceding part of the poem. It
was on it Fingal and Ossian stood to view the battle. The custom of retiring from
the army, on the night prior to their engaging in battle, was universal among the
kings of the Caledonians.—Trenmor, the most renowned of the ancestors of Fingal,
is mentioned as the first who instituted this custom. Succeeding bards attributed it
to a hero of a latter period.——In an old poem, which begins with *Mac-Arcath nan
ceud sról*, this custom of retiring from the army, before an engagement, is
numbered, among the wise institutions of Fergus, the son of Arc or Arcath, the first
king of Scots. I shall here translate the passage; in some other note I may, probably,
give all that remains of the poem. *Fergus of the hundred streams, son of Arcath who
fought of old: thou didst first retire at night: when the foe rolled before thee, in
echoing fields. Nor bending in rest is the king: he gathers battles in his soul. Fly,
son of the stranger; with morn he shall rush abroad.* When, or by whom, this poem
was writ, is uncertain. It has much of the spirit of the ancient composition of the
Scottish bards; and seems to be a close imitation of the manner of Ossian. [M]
Mac-Arcath nan ceud sról,] *Mac-Arcath na ceud sról,* 1763 1773
It has much of the spirit ... the manner of Ossian.] *deleted 1773*
The promise of a full translation was apparently never to be fulfilled.
30.   This circumstance, concerning Bran, the favourite dog of Fingal, is perhaps,
one of the most affecting passages in the poem. I remember to have met with an old
poem, composed long after the time of Ossian, wherein a story of this sort is very
happily introduced. In one of the invasions of the Danes, Ullin-clundu, a consider-
able chief, on the western coast of Scotland, was killed in a rencounter with a flying
party of the enemy, who had landed, at no great distance, from the place of his resi-
dence. The few followers who attended him were also slain.—The young wife of
Ullin-clundu, who had not heard of his fall, fearing the worst, on account of his long
delay, alarmed the rest of his tribe, who went in search of him along the shore. They
did not find him; and the beautiful widow became disconsolate. At length he was
discovered, by means of his dog, who sat on a rock beside the body, for some
days.—The poem is not just now in my hands; otherwise its poetical merit might

induce me to present the reader with a translation of it. The stanza concerning the dog, whose name was Du-chos, or *Blackfoot*, is very descriptive.

"Dark-sided Du-chos! feet of wind! cold is thy seat on rocks. He (the dog) sees the roe; his ears are high; and half he bounds away. He looks around; but Ullin sleeps; he droops again his head. The winds come past; dark Du-chos thinks, that Ullin's voice is there. But still he beholds him silent, laid amidst the waving heath. Dark-sided Du-chos, his voice no more shall send thee over the heath!" [M]

[§ 1] This circumstance ... in the poem.] *deleted* 1773
an old poem, composed long after the time of Ossian,] an old poem, 1773
The poem is not just now ... translation of it.] *deleted* 1773
is very descriptive.] is descriptive. 1773

31.   In order to illustrate this passage, it is proper to lay before the reader the scene of the two preceding battles. Between the hills of Mora and Lona lay the plain of Moi-lena, thro' which ran the river Lubar. The first battle, wherein Gaul, the son of Morni, commanded on the Caledonian side, was fought on the banks of Lubar. As there was little advantage obtained, on either side, the armies, after the battle, retained their former positions.

In the second battle, wherein Fillan commanded, the Irish, after the fall of Foldath, were driven up the hill of Lona; but, upon the coming of Cathmor to their aid, they regained their former situation, and drove back the Caledonians, in their turn: so that *Lubar winded again in their host.* [M]

32.   trembling] with ardour 1773

33.   Borbar-duthul, the father of Cathmor, was the brother of that Colc-ulla, who is said, in the beginning of the fourth book, to have rebelled against Cormac king of Ireland. Borbar-duthul seems to have retained all the prejudice of his family against the succession of the posterity of Conar, on the Irish throne. From this short episode we learn some facts which tend to throw light on the history of the times. It appears, that, when Swaran invaded Ireland, he was only opposed by the Caël, who possessed Ulster, and the north of that island. Calmar, the son of Matha, whose gallant behaviour and death are related in the third book of Fingal, was the only chief of the race of the Fir-bolg, that joined the Caël, or Irish Caledonians, during the invasion of Swaran. The indecent joy, which Borbar-duthul expressed, upon the death of Calmar, is well suited with that spirit of revenge, which subsisted, universally, in every country where the feudal system was established.—It would appear that some person had carried to Borbar-duthul that weapon, with which, it was pretended, Calmar had been killed. [M]

This note, with its interesting comment on the feudal system, is one of increasingly many arbitrarily omitted by Laing.

34.   sovereign] king 1763 1773

35.   *The voices of Erin,* a poetical expression for the bards of Ireland. [M]

36.   Not only the kings, but every petty chief, had their bards attending them, in the field, in the days of Ossian; and these bards, in proportion to the power of the chiefs, who retained them, had a number of inferior bards in their train. Upon solemn occasions, all the bards, in the army, would join in one chorus; either when they celebrated their victories, or lamented the death of a person, worthy and renowned, slain in the war. The words were of the composition of the arch-bard, retained by the king himself, who generally attained to that high office on account of his superior genius for poetry. As the persons of the bards were sacred, and the

emoluments of their office considerable, the order, in succeeding times, became very numerous and insolent. It would appear, that, after the introduction of Christianity, some served in the double capacity of bards and clergymen. It was, from this circumstance, that they had the name of *Chlére*, which is, probably, derived from the latin Clericus. The *Chlére*, be their name derived from what it will, became, at last, a public nuisance; for, taking advantage of their sacred character, they went about, in great bodies, and lived, at discretion, in the houses of the chiefs; till another party, of the same order, drove them away by mere dint of satire. Some of the indelicate disputes of these worthy poetical combatants are handed down, by tradition, and shew how much the bards, at last, abused the privileges, which the admiration of their countrymen had conferred on the order.—It was this insolent behaviour that induced the chiefs to retrench their number, and to take away those privileges which they were no longer worthy to enjoy. Their indolence, and disposition to lampoon, extinguished all the poetical fervour, which distinguished their predecessors, and makes us the less regret the extinction of the order. [M]
, in the days of Ossian;] *deleted* 1773
37.   tearful] fearful 1763 1773
38.   Clun-galo, *white knee*, the wife of Conmor, king of Inis-huna, and the mother of Sul-malla. She is here represented, as missing her daughter, after she had fled with Cathmor. This song is very beautiful in the original. The expressive cadences of the measure are inimitably suited to the situation of the mind of Sul-malla. [M]
white knee,] *deleted* 1773
This song ... the mind of Sul-malla.] *deleted* 1773
39.   Sul-malla replies to the supposed questions of her mother. Towards the middle of this paragraph she calls Cathmor *the sun of her soul*, and continues the metaphor throughout. Those, who deliver this song down by tradition, say that there is a part of the original lost.—This book ends, we may suppose, about the middle of the third night, from the opening of the poem. [M]
Those, who deliver ... original lost.] *deleted* 1773
40.   In this, as well ... the death of Fillan. It is] *deleted* 1773
41.   on moss!] on their blasts! 1773
42.   he not] the warrior never 1773

Temora Book VII.
1.   No poet departs less from his subject than Ossian. No far-fetched ornaments are introduced; the episodes rise from, and are indeed essential to, the story of the poem. Even his lyric songs, where he most indulges the extravagance of fancy, naturally spring from his subject. Their propriety and connection with the rest of the poem, shew that the Celtic bard was guided by judgment, amidst the wildest flights of imagination. It is a common supposition among mankind, that a genius for poetry and sound sense seldom center in the same person. The observation is far from being just; for true genius and judgment must be inseparable. The wild flights of fancy, without the guidance of judgment, are, as Horace observes, like the dreams of a sick man, irksome and confused. Fools can never write good poems. A warm imagination, it is true, domineers over a common portion of sense; and hence it is that so few have succeeded in the poetical way. But when an uncommon strength of judgment, and a glowing fancy, are properly tempered together, they, and they only, produce genuine poetry.

The present book is not the least interesting part of Temora. The awful images, with which it opens, are calculated to prepare the mind for the solemn scenes which are to follow. Ossian, always, throws an air of consequence on every circumstance which relates to Fingal. The very sound of his shield produces extraordinary effects; and these are heightened, one above another, in a beautiful climax. The distress of Sul-malla, and her conference with Cathmor, are very affecting. The description of his shield is a curious piece of antiquity; and is a proof of the early knowledge of navigation among the inhabitants of Britain and Ireland. Ossian, in short, throughout this book, is often sublime; and always pathetic.

Lego, so often mentioned by Ossian, was a lake, in Connaught, in which the river Lara emptied itself. On the banks of this lake dwelt Branno, the father-in-law of Ossian, whom the poet often visited before and after the death of Evir-allin. This circumstance, perhaps, occasioned the partiality, with which he always mentions Lego and Lara; and accounts for his drawing so many of his images from them. The signification of Leigo, is, *the lake of disease*, probably so called, on account of the morasses which surrounded it.

As the mist, which rose from the lake of Lego, occasioned diseases and death, the bards feigned, as here, that it was the residence of the ghosts of the deceased, during the interval between their death and the pronouncing of the funeral elegy over their tombs; for it was not allowable, without that ceremony was performed, for the spirits of the dead to mix with their ancestors, *in their airy halls*. It was the business of the spirit of the nearest relation to the deceased, to take the mist of Lego, and pour it over the grave. We find here Conar, the son of Trenmor, the first king of Ireland, according to Ossian, performing this office for Fillan, as it was in the cause of the family of Conar, that that hero was killed. The description of the appearance of the ghost is picturesque and solemn, imposing a still attention to the speech that follows it, which, with great propriety, is short and awful. [M]

[§ 4] the first king of Ireland, according to Ossian,] the first king of Ireland, 1773
Between the second and third paragraphs the original 1763 edition inserts, as a specimen of the harmony of Galic versification without rhime, *the first twelve lines in Gaelic, identical with those reproduced in the* Specimen, *p. 329.*
In 1773 the note is transferred to some warrior's grave *near the end of the first paragraph of the text, and reduced to* As the mist ... that that hero was killed. *(= final paragraph of note, minus last sentence - and preceding reference to Ossian)*
2.   the rushing course of Conar in winds.] it was Conar, king of Inis-fail. 1763 1773
Exceptionally, the reason for the 1765 deviation is not that advanced in notes 10, 19 and 28 below.
3.   He poured his deep mist on Fillan,] He poured his mist on the grave of Fillan, 1763 1773
4.   bending in] in 1763 1773
5.   the lovely form] the form 1763 1773
6.   slow-bending] bending 1763 1773
7.   It has been observed, that Ossian takes great delight in describing night-scenes. This, in some measure, is to be attributed to his melancholy disposition, which delighted to dwell upon solemn objects. Even other poets, of a less serious turn than Ossian, have best succeeded in descriptions of this sort. Solemn scenes make the most lasting impressions on the imagination; gay and light objects only

touch the surface of the soul, and vanish. The human mind is naturally serious: levity and chearfulness may be amiable, but they are too often the characteristics of weakness of judgment, and a deplorable shallowness of soul.—The night-descriptions of Ossian were in high repute among succeeding bards. One of them delivered a sentiment, in a distich, more favourable to his taste for poetry, than to his gallantry towards the ladies. I shall here give a translation of it.

"More pleasant to me is the night of Cona, dark-streaming from Ossian's harp; more pleasant it is to me, than a white-bosomed dweller between my arms; than a fair-handed daughter of heroes, in the hour of rest."

Tho' tradition is not very satisfactory concerning the history of this poet, it has taken care to inform us, that he was *very old* when he wrote the distich. He lived (in what age is uncertain) in one of the western isles, and his name was Turloch Ciabhglas, or *Turloch of the grey locks.* [M]

[§ 1] It has been observed that Ossian ... I shall give here a translation of it.] The following is the singular sentiment of a frigid bard. 1773

[§ 3] wrote the distich.] wrote the distich, a circumstance, which we might have supposed, without the aid of tradition. 1773

He lived ... *grey locks.] deleted* 1773

The observer of Ossian's delight in night-scenes is presumably Blair.

8.   dreams?"] night?" 1763 1773

9.   Why art thou ... rose?] Why dost thou mix, said the king, with the dreams of thy father? 1763 1773

10.   Not such ... mighty in arms.] Not such come the deeds of the valiant on the soul of Fingal. 1763 1773

The deviations of the text of 1765 from that (those) of 1763 and 1773, minor as they may seem, are particularly frequent and marked in the seventh Book of 'Temora'. The reason for this appears to be an attempt to bring the English more closely into line with the Gaelic Specimen at the end of the volume - and it is, as an examination of this particular paragraph proves. By 1773 Macpherson has, perhaps, ceased to care and largely reverts to the original English text (the Gaelic Specimen is in any case omitted).

11.   Succeeding bards have recorded many fables, concerning this wonderful shield. They say, that Fingal, in one of his expeditions into Scandinavia, met, in one of the islands of Juteland, with Luno, a celebrated magician. This Luno was the Vulcan of the north, and had made compleat suits of armour for many of the heroes of Scandinavia. One disagreeable circumstance was, that every person who wanted to employ Luno to make armour for him, was obliged to overcome him, at his own magic art.—Fingal, unskilled in spells or enchantments, effected with dint of prowess, what others failed in, with all their supernatural art. When Luno demanded a trial of skill from Fingal, the king drew his sword, cut off the skirts of the magician's robe, and obliged him, bare as he was, to fly before him. Fingal pursued, but Luno, coming to the sea, by his magic art, walked upon the waves. Fingal pursued him in his ship, and, after a chace of ten days, came up with him, in the isle of Sky, and obliged him to erect a furnace, and make him this shield, and his famous sword, poetically called, *the son of Luno.*—Such are the strange fictions which the modern Scotch and Irish bards have formed on the original of Ossian. [M]

Note deleted 1773

Laing (2:201, n. 6) has great fun with this: "Fingal's wonderful shield, of which the very sound produced a climax of such extraordinary effects, is struck to no purpose, neither to awaken the host, nor to alarm the scouts. And Fingal is introduced as sounding his shield, with much the same propriety as if, in Addison's Campaign, Marlborough had been employed in tuning his kettle-drums on the night preceding the battle of Blenheim."

12.   voices of death.] voice of deaths 1763 1773

13.   It was the opinion of the times, that, on the night preceding the death of a person worthy and renowned, the harps of those bards, who were retained by his family, emitted melancholy sounds. This was attributed, to use Ossian's expression, to *the light touch of ghosts;* who were supposed to have a fore-knowledge of events. The same opinion prevailed long in the north, and the particular sound was called, *the warning voice of the dead. The voice of deaths,* mentioned in the preceding sentence, was of a different kind. Each person was supposed to have an attendant spirit, who assumed his form and voice, on the night preceding his death, and appeared, to some, in the attitude, in which the person was to die. The VOICES OF DEATH were the foreboding shrieks of those spirits. [M]
the opinion of the times,] the opinion of ancient times, 1773

14.   host.] people. 1763

15.   Albion] Morven 1763 Selma 1773

16.   A bard, several ages more modern than Ossian, was so sensible of the beauty of this passage, as to give a close imitation of it, in a poem, concerning the great actions of Keneth Mac-Alpin, king of Scotland, against the Picts. As the poem is long, I shall only give here the story of it, with a translation of that paragraph, which bears the nearest resemblance to the passage of Temora just now before me. When Keneth was making preparations for that war, which terminated in the subversion of the Pictish kingdom, Flathal, his sister, had demanded permission from him, of attending him in the expedition; in order to have a share in revenging the death of her father Alpin, who had been barbarously murdered by the Picts. The king, tho' he, perhaps, approved of the gallant disposition of his sister, refused, on account of her sex, to grant her request. The heroine, however, dressed herself in the habit of a young warrior; and, in that disguise, attended the army, and performed many gallant exploits. On the night preceding the final overthrow of the Picts, Keneth, as was the custom among the kings of Scots, retired to a hill, without the verge of the camp, to meditate on the dispositions he was to make in the approaching battle. Flathal, who was anxious about the safety of her brother, went, privately, to the top of an adjoining rock, and kept watch there to prevent his being surprized by the enemy.——Keneth fell asleep, in his arms; and Flathal observed a body of the Picts surrounding the hill, whereon the king lay.—The sequel of the story may be gathered from the words of the bard.

"Her eyes, like stars, roll over the plain. She trembled for Alpin's race. She saw the gleaming foe. Her steps arose: she stopt.—'Why should he know of Flathal? he the king of men!—But hark! the sound is high.—It is but the wind of night, lone-whistling in my locks.—I hear the echoing shields!'—Her spear fell from her hand. The lofty rock resounds.—He rose, a gathered cloud.

'Who wakes Conad of Albion, in the midst of his secret hill? I heard the soft voice of Flathal. Why, maid, dost thou shine in war? The daughters roll their blue eyes, by the streams. No field of blood is theirs.'

'Alpin of Albion was mine, the father of Flathal of harps. He is low, mighty Conad, and my soul is fire. Could Flathal, by the secret stream, behold the blood of her foes? I am a young eagle, on Dura, king of Drum-albin of winds.'"—

In the sequel of the piece, the bard does not imitate Ossian, and his poem is so much the worse for it.—Keneth, with his sister's assistance, forced his way thro' the advanced parties of the enemy, and rejoined his own army. The bard has given a catalogue of the Scotch tribes, as they marched to battle; but, as he did not live near the time of Keneth, his accounts are to be little depended on. [M]

Note deleted 1773

17.   The rapid manner of Ossian does not often allow him to mark the speeches with the names of the persons who speak them. To prevent the obscurity, which this might occasion, I have, sometimes, used the freedom to do it in the translation. In the present dialogue between Cathmor and Sul-malla, the speeches are so much marked with the characters of the speakers, that no interpolation is necessary to distinguish them from one another. [M]

Note deleted 1773

For which the evident reason is that Macpherson has meanwhile decided that his text would indeed be clearer if he inserted the odd she said *or* he replied. *Occasionally such additions have been noted here.*

18.   dark season] season 1763 1773

19.   traveller of night] lonely scout 1763 1773

Again the English of 1765 is closer to the Gaelic of the Specimen. *Unless otherwise noted, it may be assumed that this is always the case when the 1765 text of* 'Temora' VII *deviates markedly from that of the other two editions.*

20.   cloud: but] cloud, she said; but 1773

21.   signs;] signs, he replied; 1773

22.   thou leader of heroes,] king of men, 1763 1773

23.   darkness] folds 1763 1773

24.   Fingal is said to have never been overcome in battle. From this proceeded that title of honour which is always bestowed on him in tradition. *Fiön-ghal na buai'*, FINGAL OF VICTORIES. In a poem, just now in my hands, which celebrates some of the great actions of Arthur the famous British hero, that appellation is often bestowed on him.—The poem, from the phraseology, appears to be ancient; and is, perhaps, tho' that is not mentioned, a translation from the Welsh language. [M]

25.   Awake] O send 1763 1773

26.   Like a rock with its trickling waters,] Like a dropping rock, in the desart, 1763 1773

It is the dropping rock *which has been preserved for posterity.* Presumably, dropping *means shedding drops, i.e. dripping (cf* 'Temora' I, *p. 231:* like cold dropping rocks on Moi-lena). *Be that as it may, here as elsewhere in this Book of the epic - and whatever the provenance of the Gaelic -, the 1765 text might be considered by some to be the more pleasing.*

27.   marked in her armour, the young] thee in thy steel, young 1763 1773

28.   winding] blue 1763 loud 1773

The Gaelic of the Specimen *has* cróm (crom = "bend"; "bent"; *cognate with Old Celtic and German "krumm").* Whatever metrical constraints Macpherson - or whoever composed the Specimen - might have subjected himself to, whatever rules of assonance and rhyme he was observing, one finds it difficult to imagine that it

would have defeated his ingenuity to make the stream blue. Perhaps he simply felt a
winding one yielded better poetry. Assuming that the Gaelic was modelled on the
English of 1763 (and not the other way round, which is a possibility, though not
very likely), it does not seem bound by strict fidelity to its source. Hence the
attempt, in the English of 1765, to iron out the discrepancies.

29.   Claon-mal, *crooked eye-brow.* From the retired life of this person, it appears,
that he was of the order of the Druids; which supposition is not, at all, invalidated
by the appellation of *king of harps,* here bestowed on him; for all agree that the
bards were of the number of the Druids originally. [M]

it appears, that] is insinuated, that 1773

30.   oak,] tree, 1763 1773

31.   By this circumstance, the poet insinuates, that the valley of Lona was very
near the field of battle. In this indirect manner of narration, consists the great differ-
ence between poetical and historical narration. [M]

narration.] stile. 1763

Note deleted 1773

32.   her locks are struggling with winds.] from amidst her waving locks. 1763
1773

33.   In after ages, the allusions of the bards, to particular passages of the works of
Ossian, were very numerous. I have met with a poem, which was writ three centu-
ries ago, in which the bard recommends, to a lady of his own times, the behaviour of
Sul-malla, in this place. The poem has little to recommend it, excepting the
passage, of which I am to give a translation here. The bards, when they alluded to
the works of Ossian, seem to have caught some portion of his fire: upon other occa-
sions, their compositions are little more than a group of epithets reduced into meas-
ure. Only their poems, upon martial subjects, fall under this censure. Their love
sonnets, and pastoral verses, are far from wanting their beauties; but a great deal of
these depend upon a certain *curiosa felicitas* of expression in the original; so that
they would appear greatly to their disadvantage in another language. What the
modern bards are most insupportable in, are their nauseous panegyrics upon their
patrons. We see, in them, a petty tyrant, whose name was never heard, beyond the
contracted limits of his own valley, stalking forth in all the trappings of a finished
hero. From their frequent allusions, however, to the entertainments which he gave,
and the *strength of his cups,* we may easily guess from whence proceeded the praise
of an indolent and effeminate race of men: for the bards, from the great court paid,
originally, to their order, became, at last, the most flagitious and dispirited of all
mortals. Their compositions, therefore, on this side of a certain period, are dull and
trivial to the highest degree. By lavishing their praises upon unworthy objects, their
panegyricks became common and little regarded; they were thrust out of the houses
of the chiefs, and wandered about, from tribe to tribe, in the double capacity of poet
and harper. Galled with this usage, they betook themselves to satire and lampoon,
so that the compositions of the bards, for more than a century back, are almost alto-
gether of the sarcastical kind. In this they succeeded well; for as there is no
language more copious than the Galic, so there is scarcely any equally adapted to
those quaint turns of expression which belong to satire.—Tho' the chiefs dis-
regarded the lampoons of the bards, the vulgar, out of mere fear, received them into
their habitations, entertained them, as well as their circumstances would allow, and

kept existing, for some years, an order, which, by their own mismanagement, had deservedly fallen into contempt.

To return to an old poem, which gave occasion to this note. It is an address to the wife of a chief, upon the departure of her husband to war. The passage, which alludes to Sul-malla, is this:

"Why art thou mournful on rocks; or lifting thine eyes on waves? His ship has bounded towards battle. His joy is in the murmur of fields. Look to the beams of old, to the virgins of Ossian of harps. Sul-malla keeps not her eagle, from the field of blood. She would not tear her eagle, from the sounding course of renown." [M]

[§ 3] She would not tear her eagle,] She would not tear thee, O Cathmor, 1763
Note deleted 1773

34.   bounded from] rattled along 1773

35.   Són-mor, *tall handsome man.* He was the father of Borbar-duthul, chief of Atha, and grandfather to Cathmor himself. The propriety of this episode is evident. But, tho' it appears here to be only introduced as an example to Sul-malla; the poet probably had another design in view, which was further to illustrate the antiquity of the quarrel between the Firbolg and Caël. [M]
The propriety of this episode ... Firbolg and Caël.] *deleted* 1773

36.   Cluan-er, *man of the field.* This chief was killed in battle by Cormac Mac-Conar, king of Ireland, the father of Roscrana, the first wife of Fingal. The story is alluded to in other poems. [M]
in other poems.] in some ancient poems. 1773

37.   slain by Cormac the giver of shells.] who was slain by Cormac in fight. 1763 1773

38.   when the warrior moved to his fields.] when he was not there. 1763 1773

39.   Suil-alluin, *beautiful eye*, the wife of Son-mor. [M]

40.   Atha of hinds.] echoing Atha. 1763 1773

41.   dark and slow.] silent and dark. 1763 1773

42.   The poet returns to his subject. The description of the shield of Cathmor is valuable, on account of the light it throws on the progress of arts in those early times. Those who draw their ideas of remote antiquity from their observations on the manners of modern savage nations, will have no high opinion of the workmanship of Cathmor's shield. To remove some part of their prejudice, I shall only observe, that the Belgæ of Britain, who were the ancestors of the Firbolg, were a commercial people; and commerce, we might prove, from many shining examples of our own times, is the proper inlet of arts and sciences, and all that exalts the human mind. To avoid multiplying notes, I shall give here the signification of the names of the stars, engraved on the shield. Cean-mathon, *head of the bear.* Col-derna, *slant and sharp beam.* Ul-oicho, *ruler of night.* Cathlin, *beam of the wave.* Reul-durath, *star of the twilight.* Berthin, *fire of the hill.* Tonthéna, *meteor of the waves.* These etymologies, excepting that of Cean-mathon, are pretty exact. Of it I am not so certain; for it is not very probable, that the Firbolg had distinguished a constellation, so very early as the days of Larthon, by the name of the bear. [M]
The poet returns to his subject ... all that exalts the human mind.] *deleted* 1773
For Laing (2:212, n. 23) the shield is a "plain imitation of the shield of Achilles, of which the boss or centre was occupied by the sun, moon, and earth, the Pleiades, Hyades, Orion, and the Bear".

43.   Fair-gleaming] Laughing, 1763 Smiling 1773

44. on the slow-moving hunter,] on the hunter, 1763 1773
45. through showery night,] by night, 1763 1773
46. Ton-théna; Ton-théna which] Ton-thena, that star which 1763 1773
47. *To travel on the winds*, a poetical expression for sailing. [M]
48. The winds were changeful in heaven,] Unconstant blew the winds, 1763 1773
49. laughed] smiled 1773
50. Larthon is compounded of *Lear*, sea, and *thon*, wave. This name was given to the chief of the first colony of the Firbolg, who settled in Ireland, on account of his knowledge of navigation. A part of an old poem is still extant, concerning this hero. The author of it, probably, took the hint from the episode in this book, relating to the first discovery of Ireland by Larthon. It abounds with those romantic fables of giants and magicians, which distinguish the compositions of the less ancient bards. The descriptions, contained in it, are ingenious and proportionable to the magnitude of the persons introduced; but, being unnatural, they are insipid and tedious. Had the bard kept within the bounds of probability, his genius was far from being contemptible. The exordium of his poem is not destitute of merit; but it is the only part of it, that I think worthy of being presented to the reader.

"Who first sent the black ship, thro' ocean, like a whale thro' the bursting of foam?—Look, from thy darkness, on Cronath, Ossian of the harps of old!—Send thy light on the blue-rolling waters, that I may behold the king.——I see him dark in his own shell of oak! sea-tossed Larthon, thy soul is fire.—It is careless as the wind of thy sails; as the wave that rolls by thy side. But the silent green isle is before thee, with its sons, who are tall as woody Lumon; Lumon which sends, from its top, a thousand streams, white-wandering down its sides."—

It may, perhaps, be for the credit of this bard, to translate no more of this poem, for the continuation of his description of the Irish giants betrays his want of judgment. [M]

[§ 1] The author of it, probably ... discovery of Ireland by Larthon.] *deleted* 1773
[§ 2] thy soul is fire.] thy soul is strong.] 1763 1773
51. rejoiced at the guiding beam,] blessed the well-known beam, 1763 1773
52. the tumbling waters.] the deep. 1763 1773
53. awaked] rose 1763 1773
54. the land of streams,] of the streams 1763 1773
55. Lumon, as I have remarked in a preceding note, was a hill, in Inis-huna, near the residence of Sul-malla. This episode has an immediate connection with what is said of Larthon, in the description of Cathmor's shield. We have there hinted to us only Larthon's first voyage to Ireland; here his story is related, at large, and a curious description of his invention of ship-building. This concise, but expressive, episode has been much admired in the original. Its brevity is remarkably suited to the hurry of the occasion. [M]

Lumon, as I ... note, was] Lumon was 1773
We have there hinted ... the hurry of the occasion.] *deleted* 1773
See. 'Temora' III, *p. 247, note 32.*
56. of foamy streams,] of the streams, 1763 1773
57. Samla, *apparitions*, so called from the vision of Larthon, concerning his posterity. [M]
58. soft sound] music 1763 1773
59. Flathal, *heavenly, exquisitely beautiful*. She was the wife of Larthon. [M]

60.   The beam awaked in the east.] Morning pours from the east. 1763 1773

61.   The original of this lyric ode is one of the most beautiful passages of the poem. The harmony and variety of its versification prove, that the knowledge of music was considerably advanced in the days of Ossian. See the specimen of the original. [M]

The last sentence is added in 1765. In 1763 eight lines of the Specimen *are actually quoted at this point:* Puail teud, [a] mhic Alpain nam són ... *etc. - see p. 341.*
Note deleted 1773

62.   in the darkness of Selma, and awake the soul of songs.] while yet it is dark, to please and awake my soul. 1763 1773

63.   ye children of music,] ye sons of song; 1763 1773

64.   the sun comes sounding forth] the rustling sun comes forth 1763 1773

Temora Book VIII.

1.   In the course of my notes, I have made it more my business to explain, than to examine, critically, the works of Ossian. The first is my province, as the person best acquainted with them, the second falls to the share of others. I shall, however, observe, that all the precepts, which Aristotle drew from Homer, ought not to be applied to the composition of a Celtic bard; nor ought the title of the latter to the *epopœa* to be disputed, even if he should differ in some circumstances, from a Greek poet.—Some allowance should be made for the different manners of nations. The genius of the Greeks and Celtæ was extremely dissimilar. The first were lively and loquacious; a manly conciseness of expression distinguished the latter. We find, accordingly, that the compositions of Homer and Ossian are marked with the general and opposite characters of their respective nations, and, consequently, it is improper to compare the *minutiæ* of their poems together. There are, however, general rules, in the conduct of an epic poem, which, as they are natural, are likewise, universal. In these the two poets exactly correspond. This similarity, which could not possibly proceed from imitation, is more decisive, with respect to the grand essentials of the *epopœa*, than all the precepts of Aristotle.

Ossian is now approaching to the grand catastrophe. The preparations he has made, in the preceding book, properly introduce the magnificence of description, with which the present book opens, and tend to shew that the Celtic bard had more art, in working up his fable, than some of those, who closely imitated the perfect model of Homer. The transition from the pathetic to the sublime is easy and natural. Till the mind is opened, by the first, it scarcely can have an adequate comprehension of the second. The soft and affecting scenes of the seventh book form a sort of contrast to, and consequently heighten, the features of the more grand and terrible images of the eighth.

The simile, with which the book opens, is, perhaps, the longest, and the most minutely descriptive, of any in the works of Ossian. The images of it are only familiar to those who live in a cold and mountainous country. They have often seen a lake suddenly frozen over, and strewed with withered grass, and boughs torn, by winds, from the mountains, which form its banks; but, I believe, few of them would be of the mind of the ancient bard, who preferred these winter scenes to the irriguous vales of May.—*To me,* says he, *bring back my woods, which strew their leaves on blasts: spread the lake below, with all its frozen waves. Pleasant is the breeze on the bearded ice; when the moon is broad in heaven, and the spirit of the mountain roars. Roll away the green vales of May; they are thoughts of maids,* &c. Such are the words of this winter poet, but what he afterwards adds, gives us to understand, that those frigid scenes were not his sole delight: for he speaks, with great tenderness, of the *oak-lighted hall of the chief;* and the *strength of the shells, at night, when the course of winds is abroad.*

If the simile of a frozen lake aptly illustrates the stillness and silent expectation of an army, lying under arms, waiting for the coming of their king, so the comparison of the sudden rising of waves, around a spirit, is also very expressive of the tumultuous joy of Fingal's army, upon the appearance of that hero.——An ancient bard, sensible of the beauty of this passage, has happily imitated it, in a poem, concerning Kenneth Mac Alpin, king of Scotland.—I had occasion to quote this piece, in a note [*16*] in the preceding book. Kenneth had retired privately, by night, to a hill, in the neighbourhood of his army, and, upon his return, next morning, the bard says, *that he was like the form of a spirit, returning to his secret bay. In the skirt of a blast he stands. The waves lift their roaring heads. Their green backs are quivering round. Rocks eccho back their joy.*[M]
Note deleted 1773

The simile with which the book opens may well be Ossian's longest, and most minutely descriptive. But as Laing comments (2:231, n. 2): "The waves of a mountain lake suddenly frozen into the form of ridges, are undoubtedly picturesque; and the only objection to an image, 'familiar,' as it seems, 'to those only who reside in a cold and mountainous country,' is, that it never yet was realized, as every lake must acquire a plain superficies when frozen."

2.   rolling] folds 1763 1773
3.   unwieldly,] unwieldy, 1763 1773
Presumably 1765 intends the adverb.
4.   Ferad-artho was the son of Cairbar Mac-Cormac king of Ireland. He was the only one remaining of the race of Conar, the son of Trenmor, the first Irish monarch, according to Ossian. In order to make this passage thoroughly understood, it may not be improper to recapitulate some part of what has been said in preceding notes.—Upon the death of Conar the son of Trenmor, his son Cormac succeeded on the Irish throne. Cormac reigned long. His children were, Cairbar, who succeeded him, and Ros-crana, the first wife of Fingal. Cairbar, long before the death of his father Cormac, had taken to wife Bos-gala, the daughter of Colgar, one of the most powerful chiefs in Connaught, and had, by her, Artho, afterwards king of Ireland. Soon after Artho arrived at man's estate, his mother Bos-gala died, and Cairbar took to wife Beltanno, the daughter of Conachar of Ullin, who brought him a son, whom he called Ferad-artho, i.e. *a man in the place of Artho.* The occasion of the name was this. Artho, when his brother was born, was absent, on an expedition to the south of Ireland. A false report was brought to his father that he was killed.—*Cairbar,* to use the words of the poem on the subject, *darkened for his fair-haired son. He turned to the young beam of light, the son of Beltanno of Conachar. Thou shalt be Ferad-artho, he said, a fire before thy race.* Cairbar, soon after, died, nor did Artho long survive him. Artho was succeeded, in the Irish throne, by his son Cormac, who in his minority, was murdered by Cairbar, the son of Borbar-duthul.— Ferad-artho, says tradition, was very young, when the expedition of Fingal, to settle him on the throne of Ireland, happened. During the short reign of young Cormac, Ferad-artho lived at the royal palace of Temora. Upon the murder of the king,

Condan, the bard, conveyed Ferad-artho, privately, to the cave of Cluna, behind the mountain Crommal, in Ulster, where they both lived concealed, during the usurpation of the family of Atha. All these particulars, concerning Ferad-artho, may be gathered from the compositions of Ossian: A bard, less ancient, has delivered the whole history, in a poem just now in my possession. It has little merit, if we except the scene between Ferad-artho, and the messengers of Fingal, upon their arrival, in the valley of Cluna. After hearing of the great actions of Fingal, the young prince proposes the following questions concerning him, to Gaul and Dermid.—"Is the king tall as the rock of my cave? Is his spear a fir of Cluna? Is he a rough-winged blast, on the mountain, which takes the green oak by the head, and tears it from its hill?—Glitters Lubar within his strides, when he sends his stately steps along?—— Nor is he tall, said Gaul, as that rock: nor glitter streams within his strides, but his soul is a mighty flood, like the strength of Ullin's seas." [M]

royal palace of Temora.] royal residence of Temora. 1773

All these particulars ... compositions of Ossian.] *deleted* 1773

A bard, less ancient,] A late bard 1773

5.   rolling of mist,] folds of mist, 1763 skirts of mist, 1773

6.   course,] stream, 1763 1773

7.   Oscar and Fillan are here, emphatically called *the warriors*. Ossian was not forgetful of them, *when*, to use his own expression, *peace returned to the land*. His plaintive poems, concerning the death of these young heroes, were very numerous. I had occasion, in a preceding note, to give a translation of one of them, (a dialogue between Clatho and Bos-mina). In this I shall lay before the reader a fragment of another. The greatest, and, perhaps, the most interesting part of the poem, is lost. What remains, is a soliloquy of Malvina, the daughter of Toscar, so often mentioned in Ossian's compositions. She sitting alone, in the vale of Moi-lutha, is represented as descrying, at a distance, the ship which carried the body of Oscar to Morven.

"Malvina is like the bow of the shower, in the secret valley of streams; it is bright, but the drops of heaven roll on its blended light. They say, that I am fair within my locks, but, on my brightness, is the wandering of tears. Darkness flies over my soul, as the dusky wave of the breeze, along the grass of Lutha.—Yet have not the roes failed me, when I moved between the hills. Pleasant, beneath my white hand, arose the sound of harps. What then, daughter of Lutha, travels over thy soul, like the dreary path of a ghost, along the nightly beam?—Should the young warrior fall, in the roar of his troubled fields!—Young virgins of Lutha arise, call back the wandering thoughts of Malvina. Awake the voice of the harp, along my echoing vale. Then shall my soul come forth, like a light from the gates of the morn, when clouds are rolled around them, with their broken sides.

Dweller of my thoughts, by night, whose form ascends in troubled fields, why dost thou stir up my soul, thou far-distant son of the king?—Is that the ship of my love, its dark course thro' the ridges of ocean? How art thou so sudden, Oscar, from the heath of shields?"——

The rest of this poem, it is said, consisted of a dialogue between Ullin and Malvina, wherein the distress of the latter is carried to the highest pitch. [M]

[§ 1] Oscar and Fillan are here ... body of Oscar to Morven.] Malvina is supposed to speak the following soliloquy. 1773

[§ 4] The rest of this poem, it is said, consisted] The rest of this poem consisted 1773

Since in 1773 the first paragraph has been replaced by a single terse introductory sentence which makes no mention of warriors, *one wonders about the point of the note. But the revised edition is full of such inconsistencies.*

8.   Lena.] the tomb. 1763 1773

9.   The poetical hyperboles of Ossian were, afterwards, taken in the literal sense, by the ignorant vulgar; and they firmly believed, that Fingal, and his heroes, were of a gigantic stature. There are many extravagant fictions founded upon the circumstance of Fingal leaping at once over the river Lubar. Many of them are handed down in tradition. The Irish compositions concerning Fingal invariably speak of him as a giant. Of these Hibernian poems there are now many in my hands. From the language, and allusions to the times in which they were writ, I should fix the date of their composition in the fifteenth and sixteenth centuries. In some passages, the poetry is far from wanting merit, but the fable is unnatural, and the whole conduct of the pieces injudicious. I shall give one instance of the extravagant fictions of the Irish bards, in a poem which they, most unjustly, ascribe to Ossian. The story of it is this.—Ireland being threatened with an invasion from some part of Scandinavia, Fingal sent Ossian, Oscar and Ca-olt, to watch the bay, in which, it was expected, the enemy was to land. Oscar, unluckily, fell asleep, before the Scandinavians appeared; and, great as he was, says the Irish bard, he had one bad property, that no less could waken him, before his time, than cutting off one of his fingers, or throwing a great stone against his head; and it was dangerous to come near him on those occasions, till he had recovered himself, and was fully awake. Ca-olt, who was employed by Ossian to waken his son, made choice of throwing the stone against his head, as the least dangerous expedient. The stone, rebounding from the hero's head, shook, as it rolled along, the hill for three miles round. Oscar rose in rage, fought bravely, and, singly, vanquished a wing of the enemy's army.—Thus the bard goes on, till Fingal put an end to the war, by the total rout of the Scandinavians. Puerile, and even despicable, as these fictions are, yet Keating and O'Flaherty have no better authority than the poems which contain them, for all that they write concerning Fion Mac-comnal, and the pretended militia of Ireland. [M]

The poetical hyperboles of Ossian ... handed down in tradition.] *deleted* 1773

10.   Tla-min, *mildly-soft.* The loves of Clonar and Tlamin were rendered famous in the north, by a fragment of a Lyric poem, still preserved, which is ascribed to Ossian. Be it the composition of whom it will, its poetical merit may, perhaps, excuse me, for inserting it here. It is a dialogue between Clonar and Tla-min. She begins with a soliloquy, which he overhears.

"Clonar, son of Conglas of I-mor, young hunter of dun-sided roes! where art thou laid, amidst rushes, beneath the passing wing of the breeze?—I behold thee, my love, in the plain of thy own dark streams! The clung thorn is rolled by the wind, and rustles along his shield. Bright in his locks he lies: the thoughts of his dreams fly, darkening, over his face. Thou thinkest of the battles of Ossian, young son of the echoing isle!

Half-hid, in the grove, I sit down. Fly back, ye mists of the hill. Why should ye hide her love from the blue eyes of Tla-min of harps?

CLONAR.

As the spirit, seen in a dream, flies off from our opening eyes, we think, we behold his bright path between the closing hills; so fled the daughter of Clun-gal, from the sight of Clonar of shields. Arise, from the gathering of trees; blue-eyed Tlamin arise.

TLAMIN.

I turn me away from his steps. Why should he know of my love! My white breast is heaving over sighs, as foam on the dark course of streams.—But he passes away, in his arms!—Son of Conglas, my soul is sad.

CLONAR.

It was the shield of Fingal! the voice of kings from Selma of harps!—My path is towards green Erin. Arise, fair light, from thy shades. Come to the field of my soul, there is the spreading of hosts. Arise, on Clonar's troubled soul, young daughter of blue-shielded Clungal."——

Clungal was the chief of I-mor, one of the Hebrides. [M]

[§ 1] a fragment of a Lyric poem, still preserved, which is ascribed to Ossian ... It is a dialogue] a fragment of a lyric poem. It is a dialogue 1773

11.   Fingal and Cathmor. The conduct of the poet, in this passage, is remarkable. His numerous descriptions of single combats had already exhausted the subject. Nothing new, nor adequate to our high idea of the kings, could be said. Ossian, therefore, throws a *column of mist* over the whole, and leaves the combat to the imagination of the reader.—Poets have almost universally failed in their descriptions of this sort. Not all the strength of Homer could sustain, with dignity, the *minutiæ* of a single combat. The throwing of a spear, and the braying of a shield, as some of our own poets most elegantly express it, convey no grand ideas. Our imagination stretches beyond, and, consequently, despises, the description. It were, therefore, well, for some poets, in my opinion, (tho' it is, perhaps, somewhat singular) to have, sometimes, like Ossian, thrown *mist* over their single combats. [M]

The conduct of the poet ... remarkable. His] The conduct here is perhaps proper. The 1773

Ossian, therefore, throws ... and leaves the combat] A *column of mist* is thrown over the whole, and the combat is left 1773

convey no grand ideas.] convey no magnificent, tho' they are striking ideas.

, like Ossian, thrown *mist*] thrown mist 1773

12.   in Selma,] at Atha, 1763 1773

13.   Fingal is very much celebrated, in tradition, for his knowledge of the virtues of herbs. The Irish poems, concerning him, often represent him, curing the wounds which his chiefs received in battle. They fable concerning him, that he was in possession of a cup, containing the essence of herbs, which instantaneously healed wounds. The knowledge of curing the wounded, was, till of late, universal among the Highlanders. We hear of no other disorder, which required the skill of physic. The wholesomeness of the climate, and an active life, spent in hunting, excluded diseases. [M]

14.   streams,] stream, 1763 1773

15.   The hospitable disposition of Cathmor was unparalleled. He reflects, with pleasure, even in his last moments, on the relief he had afforded to strangers. The very tread of their feet was pleasant in his ear.—His hospitality was not passed unnoticed by succeeding bards; for, with them, it became a proverb, when they described the hospitable disposition of a hero, *that he was like Cathmor of Atha, the friend of strangers*. It will seem strange, that, in all the Irish traditions, there is no mention made of Cathmor. This must be attributed to the revolutions and domestic

confusions which happened in that island, and utterly cut off all the real traditions concerning so ancient a period. All that we have related of the state of Ireland before the fifth century is of late invention, and the work of ill informed senachies and injudicious bards. [M]

The hospitable disposition ... unparalleled. He reflects] Cathmor reflects 1773

passed unnoticed by succeeding bards;] passed unnoticed by the bards; 1773

Irish traditions,] Irish poems, 1773

Laing comments (2:251, n. 23): "This note is an answer to one of Warner's Remarks on Ossian, 'That Cormac was not murdered in his youth by Cairbar, nor indeed murdered at all; that Cairbar was not his enemy who openly set up for himself, but his son whom he loved and resigned his crown to; and he had no such brother as Cathmor, a man in the moon; or at least no where else, as brother of Cairbar, but in the poet's fancy.' [Ferdinando] WARNER's *Remarks on Ossian,* 1763, p. 26."

16. We see, from this passage, that, even in the times of Ossian, and, consequently, before the introduction of christianity, they had some idea of rewards and punishments after death.—Those who behaved, in life, with bravery and virtue, were received, with joy, to the airy halls of their fathers: but *the dark in soul,* to use the expression of the poet, were spurned away *from the habitation of heroes, to wander on all the winds.* Another opinion, which prevailed in those times, tended not a little to make individuals emulous to excel one another in martial atchievements. It was thought, that, in the *hall of clouds,* every one had a seat, raised above others, in proportion as he excelled them, in valour, when he lived.—The simile in this paragraph is new, and, if I may use the expression of a bard, who alludes to it, *beautifully terrible.*

Mar dhubh-reûl, an croma nan speur,/ A thaomas teina na h'oicha,/ Deargsruthach, air h'aighai' fein. [M]

We see, from this passage, ... rewards and punishments] The Celtic nations had some idea of rewards, and perhaps of punishments 1773

The simile in this paragraph ... air h'aighai' fein.] *deleted* 1773

By omitting any reference to the passage *and its* simile *in the later edition, Macpherson successfully orphans the note. As to the content, Laing (2:253, n. 24) suspects the influence of* 'Regner Lodbrog's Death Song' *which Macpherson would have known from Blair's* 'Dissertation'.

17. There are some stones still to be seen in the north, which were erected, as memorials of some remarkable transactions between the ancient chiefs. There are generally found, beneath them, some piece of arms, and a bit of half-burnt wood. The cause of placing the last there is not mentioned in tradition. [M]

18. wanderer,] man, 1763 1773

19. The erecting of his standard on the bank of Lubar, was the signal, which Fingal, in the beginning of the book, promised to give to the chiefs, who went to conduct Ferad-artho to the army, should he himself prevail in battle. This standard here (and in every other part of Ossian's poems, where it is mentioned) is called, the *sun-beam.* The reason of this appellation, I gave, more than once, in my notes in the preceding volume. [M]

(and in every other part of Ossian's poems, where it is mentioned)] *deleted* 1773

I gave ... preceding volume.] I gave in my notes on the poem intitled Fingal. 1773

Cf. 'Fingal' IV, *above, p. 87, note 24.*

20.   The poet changes the scene to the valley of Lona, whither Sul-malla had been sent, by Cathmor, before the battle. Clonmal, an aged bard, or rather druid, as he seems here to be endued with a prescience of events, had long dwelt there, in a cave. This scene is awful and solemn, and calculated to throw a melancholy gloom over the mind. [M]

The poet changes the scene] The scene is changed to 1773

This scene is awful and solemn, and] This scene is 1773

21.   Cathmor had promised, in the seventh book, to come to the cave of Clonmal, after the battle was over. [M]

22.   The abrupt manner, in which Ossian quits the story of Sul-malla, is judicious. His subject led him immediately to relate the restoration of the family of Conar to the Irish throne; which we may consider effectually done, by the defeat and death of Cathmor, and the arrival of Ferad-artho in the Caledonian army. To pursue, here, the story of the *maid of Inis-huna*, which was foreign to the subject, would be altogether inconsistent with the rapid manner of Ossian, and a breach on unity of time and action, one of the fundamental essentials of the *epopœa*, the rules of which our Celtic bard gathered from nature, not from the precepts of critics.—Neither did the poet totally desert the beautiful Sul-malla, deprived of her lover, and a stranger, as she was, in a foreign land. Tradition relates, that Ossian, the next day after the decisive battle between Fingal and Cathmor, went to find out Sul-malla, in the valley of Lona. His address to her, which is still preserved, I here lay before the reader.

"Awake, thou daughter of Conmor, from the fern-skirted cavern of Lona. Awake, thou sun-beam in desarts; warriors one day must fail. They move forth, like terrible lights; but, often, their cloud is near.—Go to the valley of streams, to the wandering of herds, on Lumon; there dwells, in his lazy mist, the man of many days. But he is unknown, Sul-malla, like the thistle of the rocks of roes; it shakes its grey beard, in the wind, and falls, unseen of our eyes.—Not such are the kings of men, their departure is a meteor of fire, which pours its red course, from the desart, over the bosom of night.

He is mixed with the warriors of old, those fires that have hid their heads. At times shall they come forth in song. Not forgot has the warrior failed.—He has not seen, Sul-malla, the fall of a beam of his own: no fair-haired son, in his blood, young troubler of the field.—I am lonely, young branch of Lumon, I may hear the voice of the feeble, when my strength shall have failed in years, for young Oscar has ceased, on his field."—* * *

The rest of the poem is lost; from the story of it, which is still preserved, we understand, that Sul-malla returned to her own country. Sul-malla makes a considerable figure in the poem which immediately follows in this volume; her behaviour in that piece accounts for that partial regard with which the poet speaks of her throughout Temora. [M]

[§ 1] The abrupt manner ... in a foreign land.] *deleted* 1773

His address to her ... reader.] His address to her follows. 1773

[§ 4] The rest of the poem ... that Sul-malla returned] Sul-malla returned 1773

Sul-malla makes] She makes 1773

the poem which ... in this volume;] in another poem of Ossian; 1763 in another poem 1773

the poet speaks of her] the poet ought to speak of her 1773

23. Before I finish my notes, it may not be altogether improper to obviate an objection, which may be made to the credibility of the story of Temora, as related by Ossian. It may be asked, whether it is probable, that Fingal could perform such actions as are ascribed to him in this book, at an age when his grandson, Oscar, had acquired so much reputation in arms. To this it may be answered, that Fingal was but very young [book 4th] when he took to wife Ros-crana, who soon after became the mother of Ossian. Ossian was also extremely young when he married Ever-allin, the mother of Oscar. Tradition relates, that Fingal was but eighteen years old at the birth of his son Ossian; and that Ossian was much about the same age, when Oscar, his son, was born. Oscar, perhaps, might be about twenty, when he was killed, in the battle of Gabhra, [book 1st] so the age of Fingal, when the decisive battle was fought between him and Cathmor, was just fifty-six years. In those times of activity and health, the natural strength and vigour of a man was little abated, at such an age; so that there is nothing improbable in the actions of Fingal, as related in this book. [M]

the story of Temora, as related by Ossian.] the story of Temora. 1773

Laing comments (2:261, n. 34): "In this *traditionary* attempt to reconcile contradictions, the translator forgets, that in the former collection of Gaelic poems, Fingal opposed Caracalla in 208, and Oscar encountered Carausius in 286; an interval of almost eighty years, which renders the grandfather's age upwards of a hundred at the date of his last exploits in Temora ..."

24. *The concluding comment shall be Laing's (2:264):* "With a genius for poetry far superior to either [Wilkie or Glover], or perhaps to any contemporary poet, Gray excepted, Macpherson was released even from the rules of versification; and if we may judge from the subjects which he had provided, the pretended translator might have produced, each year, an epic poem like an annual novel, had the Temora been equally successful with Fingal."

Cathlin of Clutha

1. The traditions, which accompany this poem, inform us, that both it, and the succeeding piece, went, of old, under the name of *Laoi-Oi-lutha*; i.e. the *hymns of the maid of Lutha.* They pretend also to fix the time of its composition to the third year after the death of Fingal; that is, during the expedition of Fergus the son of Fingal, to the banks of *Uisca duthon.* In support of this opinion, the Highland senachies have prefixed to this poem, an address of Ossian, to Congal the young son of Fergus, which I have rejected, as having no manner of connection with the rest of the piece.——It has poetical merit; and, probably, it was the opening of one of Ossian's other poems, tho' the bards injudiciously transferred it to the piece now before us.

"Congal son of Fergus of Durath, thou light between thy locks, ascend to the rock of Selma, to the oak of the breaker of shields. Look over the bosom of night, it is streaked with the red paths of the dead: look on the night of ghosts, and kindle, O Congal, thy soul. Be not, like the moon on a stream, lonely in the midst of clouds: darkness closes around it; and the beam departs.—Depart not, son of Fergus, ere thou markest the field with thy sword. Ascend to the rock of Selma; to the oak of the breaker of shields." [M]

[§ 1] that both it, and the succeeding piece, went,] that it went, 1773
the *hymns*] the *hymn* 1773

2.   still season] season 1763 1773

3.   Car-mona, *bay of the dark brown hills,* an arm of the sea, in the neighbour-hood of Selma.—In this paragraph are mentioned the signals presented to Fingal, by those who came to demand his aid. The suppliants held, in one hand, a shield covered with blood, and, in the other, a broken spear; the first a symbol of the death of their friends, the last an emblem of their own helpless situation. If the king chose to grant succours, which generally was the case, he reached to them *the shell of feasts,* as a token of his hospitality and friendly intentions towards them.

It may not be disagreeable to the reader to lay here before him the ceremony of the Cran-tara, which was of a similar nature, and, till very lately, used in the High-lands.—When the news of an enemy came to the residence of the chief, he immedi-ately killed a goat with his own sword, dipped the end of an half-burnt piece of wood in the blood, and gave it to one of his servants, to be carried to the next hamlet. From hamlet to hamlet this *tessera* was carried with the utmost expedition, and, in the space of a few hours, the whole clan were in arms, and convened in an appointed place; the name of which was the only word that accompanied the deliv-ery of the *Cran-tara.* This symbol was the manifesto of the chief, by which he threatened fire and sword to those of his clan, that did not immediately appear at his standard. [M]

Laing (2:270, n. 3): "Unfortunately, in all the applications to Fingal for aid, no allusion to these symbols has occurred till now, towards the conclusion of the poems."

4.   Lánul, *full-eyed,* a surname which, according to tradition, was bestowed on the daughter of Cathmol, on account of her beauty; this tradition, however, may have been founded on that partiality, which the bards have shewn to *Cathlin of Clutha;* for according to them, no *falshood could dwell in the soul of the lovely.* [M]

5.   Oscar is here called *Oscar of Lego,* from his mother being the daughter of Branno, a powerful chief, on the banks of that lake. It is remarkable that Ossian addresses no poem to Malvina, in which her lover Oscar was not one of the princi-pal actors. His attention to her, after the death of his son, shews that delicacy of sentiment is not confined, as some fondly imagine, to our own polished times. [M]

6.   Ton-thena, *fire of the wave,* was that remarkable star, which, as has been mentioned in the seventh book of Temora, directed the course of Larthon to Ireland. It seems to have been well known to those, who sailed on that sea, which divides Ireland from South-Britain. As the course of Ossian was along the coast of Inis-huna, he mentions with propriety, that star which directed the voyage of the colony from that country to Ireland. [M]

7.   wanderer] traveller 1763 1773

8.   Rath-col, *woody field,* does not appear to have been the residence of Duth-carmor: he seems rather to have been forced thither by a storm; at least I should think that to be the meaning of the poet, from his expression, that *Ton-thena had hid her head,* and that *he bound his white-bosomed sails;* which is as much as to say, that the weather was stormy, and that Duth-carmor put in to the bay of Rathcol for shelter. [M]

9.   was] was like 1763 1773

10.   changing] changeful 1773

From this circumstance, succeeding bards feigned that Cathlin, who is here in the disguise of a young warrior, had fallen in love with Duth-carmor at a feast, to which he had been invited by her father. Her love was converted into detestation for him, after he had murdered her father. But *as those rain-bows of heaven are changeful*, say my authors, speaking of women, she felt the return of her former passion, upon the approach of Duth-carmor's danger.—I myself, who think more favourably of the sex, must attribute the agitation of Cathlin's mind to her extream sensibility to the injuries done her by Duth-carmor: and this opinion is favoured by the sequel of the story. [M]

11.   This passage alludes to the well known custom among the ancient kings of Scotland, to retire from their army on the night preceding a battle.——The story which Ossian introduces in the next paragraph, concerns the fall of the Druids, of which I gave some account in the dissertation prefixed to the preceding volume. It is said in many old poems, that the Druids, in the extremity of their affairs, had solic- ited and obtained aid from Scandinavia. Among the auxiliaries there came many pretended magicians, which circumstance Ossian alludes to, in his description of the *son of Loda.*—Magic and incantation could not, however, prevail: for Trenmor, assisted by the valour of his son Trathal, entirely broke the power of the Druids. [M] the fall of the Druids, of which ... volume.] fall of the Druids. 1773

For the well known custom, *cf. above, 'Temora' VI, p. 273, note 29, where we are tantalized with the prospect of a poem on the subject.*

12.   dark-crusted] dark-robed 1773
13.   Trenmor and Trathal. Ossian introduced this episode, as an example to his son, from ancient times. [M]
14.   Those who deliver down this poem in tradition, lament that there is a great part of it lost. In particular they regret the loss of an episode, which was here intro- duced, with the sequel of the story of Carmal and his Druids. Their attachment to it was founded on the descriptions of magical inchantments which it contained. [M]
15.   *asterisks deleted* 1773
16.   mail] male 1765
17.   warrior] hero 1763 1773

Sul-malla of Lumon

1.   The expedition of Ossian to Inis-huna happened a short time before Fingal passed over into Ireland, to dethrone Cairbar the son of Borbar-duthul. Cathmor, the brother of Cairbar, was aiding Conmor, king of Inis-huna, in his wars, at the time that Ossian defeated Duth-carmor, in the valley of Rath-col. The poem is more interesting, that it contains so many particulars concerning those personages, who make so great a figure in Temora.

The exact correspondence in the manners and customs of Inis-huna, as here described, to those of Caledonia, leaves no room to doubt, that the inhabitants of both were originally the same people. Some may alledge, that Ossian might transfer, in his poetical descriptions, the manners of his own nation to foreigners. The objec- tion is easily answered: for had Ossian used that freedom in this passage, there is no reason why he should paint the manners of the Scandinavians so different from those of the Caledonians. We find however, the former very different in their customs and superstitions from the nations of Britain and Ireland. The Scandinavian manners are remarkably barbarous and fierce, and seem to mark out a nation much less advanced in civil society, than the inhabitants of Britain were in the times of Ossian. [M]

[§ 2] for had Ossian used ... We find however, the former] Why has he not done this
with regard to the inhabitants of Scandinavia?—We find the latter 1763 1773
in civil society,] in a state of civilization, 1763 1773
Had Laing chosen to include this note, he might have detected the influence of Blair
- cf. p. 349.
2.   of Lumon,] of green Inis-huna, 1773
3.   Conmor's] Cluba's 1773
4.   Sul-malla here discovers the quality of Ossian and Oscar, from their stature
and stately gait. Among nations, not far advanced in civilization, a superior beauty
and stateliness of person were inseparable from nobility of blood. It was from these
qualities, that those of family were known by strangers, not from tawdry trappings
of state injudiciously thrown round them. The cause of this distinguishing property,
must, in some measure, be ascribed to their unmixed blood. They had no induce-
ment to intermarry with the vulgar: and no low notions of interest made them devi-
ate from their choice, in their own sphere. In states, where luxury has been long
established, I am told, that beauty of person is, by no means, the characteristic of
antiquity of family. This must be attributed to those enervating vices, which are
inseparable from luxury and wealth. A great family, (to alter a little the words of the
historian) it is true, like a river, becomes considerable from the length of its course,
but, as it rolls on, hereditary distempers, as well as property, flow successively into
it. [M]
I am told, that] *deleted* 1773
Again, Laing does not consider this note - or indeed any other in the poem - worthy
of inclusion.
5.   Conmor's] my father's 1773
6.   the king] Fingal 1773
7.   Too partial to our own times, we are ready to mark out remote antiquity, as the
region of ignorance and barbarism. This, perhaps, is extending our prejudices too
far. It has been long remarked, that knowledge, in a great measure, is founded on a
free intercourse between mankind; and that the mind is enlarged in proportion to the
observations it has made upon the manners of different men and nations.—If we
look, with attention, into the history of Fingal, as delivered by Ossian, we shall find
that he was not altogether a poor ignorant hunter, confined to the narrow corner of
an island. His expeditions to all parts of Scandinavia, to the north of Germany, and
the different states of Great Britain and Ireland, were very numerous, and performed
under such a character, and at such times, as gave him an opportunity to mark the
undisguised manners of mankind.—War and an active life, as they call forth, by
turns, all the powers of the soul, present to us the different characters of men: in
times of peace and quiet, for want of objects to exert them, the powers of the mind
lie concealed, in a great measure, and we see only artificial passions and
manners.—It is from this consideration I conclude, that a traveller of penetration
could gather more genuine knowledge from a tour of ancient Gaul, than from the
minutest observation of all the artificial manners, and elegant refinements of
modern France. [M]
8.   Conmor of spears;] my father Conmor: 1773
9.   Lormar] Lormar my brother, 1773
Lormar was the son of Conmor, and the brother of Sul-malla. After the death of
Conmor, Lormar succeeded him in the throne. [M]

10. Cathmor, the son of Borbar-duthul. It would appear, from the partiality with which Sul-malla speaks of that hero, that she had seen him, previous to his joining her father's army; tho' tradition positively asserts, that it was, after his return, that she fell in love with him. [M]

11. he] Cathmor 1773

12. I-thorno, says tradition, was an island of Scandinavia. In it, at a hunting party, met Culgorm and Suran-dronlo, the kings of two neighbouring isles. They differed about the honour of killing a boar; and a war was kindled between them.—From this episode we may learn, that the manners of the Scandinavians were much more savage and cruel, than those of Britain.——It is remarkable, that the names, introduced in this story, are not of Galic original, which circumstance affords room to suppose, that it had its foundation in true history. [M]

13. Bolga,] Erin, 1773

14. From the circumstance of Ossian not being present at the rites, described in the preceding paragraph, we may suppose that he held them in contempt. This difference of sentiment, with regard to religion, is a sort of argument, that the Caledonians were not originally a colony of Scandinavians, as some have imagined. Concerning so remote a period, mere conjecture must supply the place of argument and positive proofs. [M]

15. king.] chief. 1773

16. the king] Cathmor 1773

17. Culgorm and Suran-dronlo. The combat of the kings and their attitude in death are highly picturesque, and expressive of that ferocity of manners, which distinguished the northern nations.—The wild melody of the versification of the original, is inimitably beautiful, and very different from the rest of the works of Ossian. [M]
The wild melody ... works of Ossian.] *deleted* 1773

18. Tradition has handed down the name of this princess. The bards call her Runo-forlo, which has no other sort of title for being genuine, but its not being of Galic original; a distinction, which the bards had not the art to preserve, when they feigned names for foreigners. The highland senachies, who very often endeavoured to supply the deficiency, they thought they found in the tales of Ossian, have given us the continuation of the story of the daughter of Suran-dronlo. The catastrophe is so unnatural, and the circumstances of it so ridiculously pompous, that for the sake of the inventors, I shall conceal them.

The wildly beautiful appearance of Runo-forlo, made a deep impression on a chief, some ages ago, who was himself no contemptible poet. The story is romantic, but not incredible, if we make allowances for the lively imagination of a man of genius. Our chief sailing, in a storm, along one of the islands of Orkney, saw a woman, in a boat, near the shore, whom he thought, as he expresses it himself, *as beautiful as a sudden ray of the sun, on the dark-heaving deep*. The verses of Ossian, on the attitude of Runo-forlo, which was so similar to that of the woman in the boat, wrought so much on his fancy, that he fell desperately in love.—The winds, however, drove him from the coast, and, after a few days, he arrived at his residence in Scotland.—There his passion increased to such a degree, that two of his friends, fearing the consequence, sailed to the Orkneys, to carry to him the object of his desire.—Upon enquiry they soon found the nymph, and carried her to the enamoured chief; but mark his surprize, when, instead *of a ray of the sun*, he saw a skinny fisher-woman, more than middle-aged, appearing before him.—Tradi tion here ends the story: but it may be easily supposed that the passion of the chief soon subsided. [M]

19.   the soft sound] the voice 1773

20.   streams.] streams. The rustling sound gently spreads o'er the vale, softly-pleasing as it saddens the soul. 1773

Cath-loda: Duan First

1.   in one of his voyages to] when very young, making a voyage to 1773

2.   his] a 1773

3.   [Fingal, b.3.]] *deleted* 1773

4.   The bards distinguished those compositions, in which the narration is often interrupted, by episodes and apostrophes, by the name of *Duän*. Since the extinction of the order of the bards, it has been a general name for all ancient compositions in verse.—The abrupt manner in which the story of this poem begins, may render it obscure to some readers; it may not therefore be improper, to give here the traditional preface, which is generally prefixed to it. Two years after he took to wife Ros-crana, the daughter of Cormac, king of Ireland, Fingal undertook an expedition into Orkney, to visit his friend Cathulla, king of Inistore. After staying a few days at Carric-thura, the residence of Cathulla, the king set sail, to return to Scotland; but a violent storm arising, his ships were driven into a bay of Scandinavia, near Gormal, the seat of Starno, king of Lochlin, his avowed enemy. Starno, upon the appearance of strangers on his coast, summoned together the neighbouring tribes, and advanced, in a hostile manner, towards the bay of U-thorno, where Fingal had taken shelter. Upon discovering who the strangers were, and fearing the valour of Fingal, which he had, more than once, experienced before, he resolved to accomplish by treachery, what he was afraid he should fail in by open force. He invited, therefore, Fingal to a feast, at which he intended to assassinate him. The king prudently declined to go, and Starno betook himself to arms.——The sequel to the story may be learned from the poem itself. [M]

Byron was grateful to Macpherson's duan for providing him with a rhyme for Don Juan.

5.   send back] roll back 1763 Malvina, call back 1773

6.   ridgy] billowy 1773

7.   Agandecca, the daughter of Starno, whom her father killed, on account of her discovering to Fingal, a plot laid against his life. Her story is related at large, in the third book of Fingal. [M]

8.   are but blasts ... autumnal vales.] are wind to Fingal: wind, that, to and fro, drives the thistle in autumns dusky vale. 1773

9.   Duth-maruno is a name very famous in tradition. Many of his great actions are handed down, but the poems, which contained the detail of them, are long since lost. He lived, it is supposed, in that part of the north of Scotland, which is over against Orkney. Duth-maruno, Cromma-glas, Struthmor, and Cormar, are mentioned, as attending Comhal, in his last battle against the tribe of Morni, in a poem, which is still preserved. It is not the work of Ossian; the phraseology betrays it to be a modern composition. It is something like those trivial compositions, which the Irish bards forged, under the name of Ossian, in the fifteenth and sixteenth centuries.—Duth-maruno signifies, *black and steady*; Cromma-glas, *bending and swarthy*; Struthmor, *roaring stream*; Cormar, *expert at sea*. [M]

10.   dark streaming] dark-rolling 1763 1773
11.   said the king,] thus Trenmor said, 1773
12.   dwell] waste 1773
13.   Crumthormoth, one of the Orkney or Shetland islands. The name is not of Galic original. It was subject to its own petty king, who is mentioned in one of Ossian's poems. [M]
14.   Son of Comhal, ... night.] Son of daring Comhal, shall my steps be forward thro' night? 1773
15.   I shall ... tribes.] shall I ... tribes? 1773
16.   Starno, of lakes,] Starno king of lakes, 1773
17.   with their woods;] with echoing woods, 1773
18.   Cean-daona, *head of the people,* the son of Duth-maruno. He became after-wards famous, in the expeditions of Ossian, after the death of Fingal. The tradi-tional tales concerning him are very numerous, and, from the epithet, in them, bestowed on him *(Candona of boars)* it would appear, that he applied himself to that kind of hunting, which his father, in this paragraph, is so anxious to recommend to him. As I have mentioned the traditional tales of the Highlands, it may not be improper here, to give some account of them. After the expulsion of the bards, from the houses of the chiefs, they, being an indolent race of men, owed all their subsis-tence to the generosity of the vulgar, whom they diverted with repeating the compo-sitions of their predecessors, and running up the genealogies of their entertainers to the family of their chiefs. As this subject was, however, soon exhausted, they were obliged to have recourse to invention, and form stories having no foundation in fact which were swallowed, with great credulity, by an ignorant multitude. By frequent repeating, the fable grew upon their hands, and, as each threw in whatever circum-stance he thought conducive to raise the admiration of his hearers, the story became, at last, so devoid of all probability, that even the vulgar themselves did not believe it. They, however, liked the tales so well, that the bards found their advantage in turning professed tale-makers. They then launched out into the wildest regions of fiction and romance. I firmly believe, there are more stories of giants, enchanted castles, dwarfs, and palfreys, in the Highlands, than in any country in Europe. These tales, it is certain, like other romantic compositions, have many things in them unnatural, and, consequently, disgustful to true taste, but, I know not how it happens, they command attention more than any other fictions I ever met with.— The extream length of these pieces is very surprising, some of them requiring many days to repeat them, but such hold they take of the memory, that few circumstances are ever omitted by those who have received them only from oral tradition: What is more amazing, the very language of the bards is still preserved. It is curious to see, that the descriptions of magnificence, introduced in these tales, is even superior to all the pompous oriental fictions of the kind. [M]
19.   spear.] spear. Tell him of my deeds in war! Tell where his father fell! 1773
20.   ridgy] the 1773
21.   were] was 1763 1765
22.   gathers] settles 1773
23.   He] Fingal 1773
24.   is] is dwelling 1773
25.   Torcul-torno, according to tradition, was king of Crathlun, a district in Sweden. The river Lulan ran near the residence of Torcul-torno. There is a river in

Sweden, still called Lula, which is probably the same with Lulan. The war between Starno and Torcul-torno, which terminated in the death of the latter, had its rise at a hunting party. Starno being invited, in a friendly manner, by Torcul-torno, both kings, with their followers, went to the mountains of Stivamor, to hunt. A boar rushed from the wood before the kings, and Torcul-torno killed it. Starno thought this behaviour a breach upon the privilege of guests, who were always *honoured*, as tradition expresses it, *with the danger of the chace*. A quarrel arose, the kings came to battle, with all their attendants, and the party of Torcul-torno were totally defeated, and he himself slain. Starno pursued his victory, laid waste the district of Crathlun, and, coming to the residence of Torcul-torno, carried off, by force, Conban-carglas, the beautiful daughter of his enemy. Her he confined in a cave, near the palace of Gormal, where, on account of her cruel treatment, she became distracted.

The paragraph, just now before us, is the song of Conban-carglas, at the time she was discovered by Fingal. It is in Lyric measure, and set to music, which is wild and simple, and so inimitably suited to the situation of the unhappy lady, that few can hear it without tears. [M]

26.   locks!] locks! she said, 1773
27.   Conban-carglas!] Conban-cârgla! 1773
28.   poured] rolled 1763 1773
29.   on lonely Conban-carglas.] on thy lonely daughter. 1773
30.   at length,] in his blood, 1773
31.   the stream of winds.] the rushing winds. 1773
32.   on Conban-carglas.] on me in love. 1773
33.   By *the beam of youth*, it afterwards appears, that Conban-carglas means Swaran, the son of Starno, with whom, during her confinement, she had fallen in love. [M]
34.   cave.] cave. The son of Starno moves, in my sight. 1773
35.   in the soul of the daughter of Torcul-torno.] in my soul. 1773
36.   Daughter] Maid 1773
37.   Conban-carglas;] daughter of grief! 1773
38.   the] thy 1773
39.   daughter of Torcul-torno.] the terror of thy foes! 1773
40.   From this contrast, which Fingal draws, between his own nation, and the inhabitants of Scandinavia, we may learn, that the former were much less barbarous than the latter. This distinction is so much observed throughout the poems of Ossian, that there can be no doubt, that he followed the real manners of both nations in his own time. At the close of the speech of Fingal, there is a great part of the original lost. [M]
41.   wild, young light of Torcul-torno.] wild. We melt along the pleasing sound! 1773
42.   The sword of Fingal, so called from its maker, Luno of Lochlin. [M]
43.   The helmet of Swaran. The behaviour of Fingal is always consistent with that generosity of spirit which belongs to a hero. He takes no advantage of a foe disarmed. [M]
44.   Conban-carglas, from seeing the helmet of Swaran bloody in the hands of Fingal, conjectured, that that hero was killed.—A part of the original is lost. It appears, however, from the sequel of the poem, that the daughter of Torcul-torno did

not long survive her surprize, occasioned by the supposed death of her lover.—The description of the airy hall of Loda (which is supposed to be the same with that of Odin, the deity of Scandinavia) is more picturesque and descriptive, than any in the Edda, or other works of the northern Scalders. [M]

45. from the king.] From Fingal. 1773
46. of Conban-carglas!"] of the mournful maid!" 1773
47. *asterisks deleted* 1773
48. a crust of darkness.] a darkened orb. 1773
49. white-armed Conban-carglas.] Lulan's white-bosomed maid. 1773
50. *asterisks deleted* 1773

Cath-loda: Duan Second

1. In this short episode we have a very probable account given us, of the origin of monarchy in Caledonia. The *Caël*, or Gauls, who possessed the countries to the north of the Firth of Edinburgh, were, originally, a number of distinct tribes, or clans, each subject to its own chief, who was free and independent of any other power. When the Romans invaded them, the common danger might, perhaps, have induced those *reguli* to join together, but, as they were unwilling to yield to the command of one of their own number, their battles were ill-conducted, and, consequently, unsuccessful.—Trenmor was the first who represented to the chiefs, the bad consequences of carrying on their wars in this irregular manner, and advised, that they themselves should alternately lead in battle. They did so, but they were unsuccessful. When it came to Trenmor's turn, he totally defeated the enemy, by his superior valour and conduct, which gained him such an interest among the tribes, that he, and his family after him, were regarded as kings; or, to use the poet's expression, *the words of power rushed forth from Selma of kings.*—The regal authority, however, except in time of war, was but inconsiderable; for every chief, within his own district, was absolute and independent.—From the scene of the battle in this episode (which was in the valley of Crona, a little to the north of Agricola's wall) I should suppose that the enemies of the Caledonians were the Romans, or provincial Britons. [M]

2. In tradition, this Cromma-glas makes a great figure in that battle which Comhal lost, together with his life, to the tribe of Morni. I have just now, in my hands, an Irish composition, of a very modern date, as appears from the language, in which all the traditions, concerning that decisive engagement, are jumbled together. In justice to the merit of the poem, I should have here presented to the reader a translation of it, did not the bard mention some circumstances very ridiculous, and others altogether indecent. Morna, the wife of Comhal, had a principal hand in all the transactions previous to the defeat and death of her husband; she, to use the words of the bard, *who was the guiding star of the women of Erin.* The bard, it is to be hoped, misrepresented the ladies of his country, for Morna's behaviour was, according to him, so void of all decency and virtue, that it cannot be supposed, they had chosen her for their *guiding star.*——The poem consists of many stanzas. The language is figurative, and the numbers harmonious; but the piece is so full of anachronisms, and so unequal in its composition, that the author, most undoubtedly, was either mad, or drunk, when he wrote it.——It is worthy of being remarked, that Comhal is, in this poem, very often called, *Comhal na h'Albin,* or, *Comhal of*

Albion, which sufficiently demonstrates, that the allegations of Keating and O'Flaherty, concerning *Fion Mac-Comnal*, are but of late invention. [M]

3.   folded in thoughts.] lost in thought. 1773

4.   Crom-charn,] Crathmo, 1773

5.   at rocky Crathmo-craulo.] as he wanders in Crathmo's fields. 1773

6.   The family of Duth-maruno, it appears, came originally from Scandinavia, or, at least, from some of the northern isles, subject in chief, to the kings of Lochlin. The Highland senachies, who never missed to make their comments on and additions to, the works of Ossian, have given us a long list of the ancestors of Duth-maruno, and a particular account of their actions, many of which are of the marvellous kind. One of the tale-makers of the north has chosen for his hero, Starnmor, the father of Duth-maruno, and, considering the adventures thro' which he has led him, the piece is neither disagreeable, nor abounding with that kind of fiction, which shocks credibility. [M]

7.   An island of Scandinavia. [M] (*only*) 1773

8.   hissed,] whistled 1773

9.   bursted] broke 1773

10.   Crathmo-craulo's chief.] he that is laid so low. 1773

11.   This episode is, in the original, extremely beautiful. It is set to that wild kind of music, which some of the Highlanders distinguish, by the title of *Fón Oi-marra*, or, the *Song of mermaids*. Some part of the air is absolutely infernal, but there are many returns in the measure, which are inexpressibly wild and beautiful. From the genius of the music, I should think it came originally from Scandinavia, for the fictions delivered down concerning the *Oi-marra*, (who are reputed the authors of the music) exactly correspond with the notions of the northern nations, concerning their *diræ*, or, *goddesses of death.*—Of all the names in this episode, there is none of a Galic original, except Strina-dona, which signifies, the *strife of heroes*. [M]

12.   The *Cana* is a certain kind of grass, which grows plentifully in the heathy morasses of the north. Its stalk is of the reedy kind, and it carries a tuft of down, very much resembling cotton. It is excessively white, and, consequently, often introduced by the bards, in their similies concerning the beauty of women. [M]

13.   of Tormoth's isle.] of Tormoth wild. 1773

14.   Ul-lochlin, *the guide to Lochlin*; the name of a star. [M]

15.   The continuation of this episode is just now in my hands; but the language is so different from, and the ideas so unworthy of, Ossian, that I have rejected it, as an interpolation by a modern bard. [M]

The 1763 edition concludes this duan *with two lines of asterisks.*

Cath-loda: Duan Third

1.   The bards, who were always ready to supply what they thought deficient in the poems of Ossian, have inserted a great many incidents between the second and third *duän* of Cath-loda. Their interpolations are so easily distinguished from the genuine remains of Ossian, that it took me very little time to mark them out, and totally to reject them. If the modern Scotch and Irish bards have shewn any judgment, it is in ascribing their own compositions to names of antiquity, for, by that means, they themselves have escaped that contempt, which the authors of such futile performances must, necessarily, have met with, from people of true taste.—I was led into this observation, by an Irish poem, just now before me. It concerns a descent made

by Swaran, king of Lochlin, on Ireland, and is the work, says the traditional preface prefixed to it, of *Ossian Mac-Fion*. It however appears, from several pious ejaculations, that it was rather the composition of some good priest, in the fifteenth or sixteenth century, for he speaks, with great devotion, of pilgrimage, and more particularly, of the *blue-eyed daughters of the convent*. Religious, however, as this poet was, he was not altogether decent, in the scenes he introduces between Swaran and the wife of *Congcullion*, both of whom he represents as giants. It happening, unfortunately, that *Congcullion* was only of a moderate stature, his wife, without hesitation, preferred Swaran, as a more adequate match for her own gigantic size. From this fatal preference proceeded so much mischief, that the good poet altogether lost sight of his principal action, and he ends the piece, with an advice to men, in the choice of their wives, which, however good it may be, I shall leave concealed in the obscurity of the original. [M]

Laing (2:328, n. 3), quoting Macpherson as far as people of true taste—, *observes:* "The unexpected truth contained in this strange note, is too important to be suppressed." *Laing's comment may in its turn be considered to contain the tacit admission that he himself has been guilty of arbitrary suppression, particularly in the latter stages of his edition.*

2. The surly attitude of Starno and Swaran is well adapted to their fierce and uncomplying dispositions. Their characters, at first sight, seem little different; but, upon examination, we find, that the poet has dexterously distinguished between them. They were both dark, stubborn, haughty and reserved; but Starno was cunning, revengeful, and cruel, to the highest degree; the disposition of Swaran, though savage, was less bloody, and somewhat tinctured with generosity. It is doing injustice to Ossian, to say, that he has not a great variety of characters. [M]

3. Foinar-bragal.] Foina-brâgal. 1773

4. came to] rushed into 1773

5. stood Annir of lakes.] my father stood. 1773

6. Ossian is very partial to the fair sex. Even the daughter of the cruel Annir, the sister of the revengeful and bloody Starno, partakes not of those disagreeable characters so perculiar to her family. She is altogether tender and delicate. Homer, of all ancient poets, uses the sex with least ceremony. His cold contempt is even worse, than the downright abuse of the moderns; for to draw abuse implies the possession of some merit. [M]

7. Fingal, according to the custom of the Caledonian kings, had retired to a hill alone, as he himself was to resume the command of the army the next day. Starno might have some intelligence of the king's retiring, which occasions his request to Swaran, to stab him; as he foresaw, by his art of divination, that he could not overcome him in open battle. [M]

8. of Annir of Gormal, Swaran shall] of Annir, said Swaran, I shall 1773

9. the king of Gormal.] the king. 1773

Oina-morul

1. Fingal. [M] (*only*) 1765

2. Con-cathlin, *mild beam of the wave*. What star was so called of old is not easily ascertained. Some now distinguish the pole-star by that name. A song, which is still in repute, among the sea-faring part of the Highlanders, alludes to this passage of Ossian. The author commends the knowledge of Ossian in sea affairs, a

merit, which, perhaps, few of us moderns will allow him, or any in the age in which he lived.—One thing is certain, that the Caledonians often made their way thro' the dangerous and tempestuous seas of Scandinavia; which is more, perhaps, than the more polished nations, subsisting in those times, dared to venture.—In estimating the degree of knowledge of arts among the antients, we ought not to bring it into comparison with the improvements of modern times. Our advantages over them proceed more from accident, than any merit of ours. [M]

3.   Son] Descendant 1773

4.   There is a severe satire couched in this expression, against the guests of Mal-orchol. Had his feast been still spread, had joy continued in his hall, his former parasites would not have failed to resort to him. But as the time of festivity was past, their attendance also ceased. The sentiments of a certain old bard are agree-able to this observation. He, poetically, compares a great man to a fire kindled in a desert place. "Those that pay court to him, says he, are rolling large around him, like the smoke about the fire. This smoke gives the fire a great appearance at a distance, but it is but an empty vapour itself, and varying its form at every breeze. When the trunk, which fed the fire, is consumed, the smoke departs on all the winds. So the flatterers forsake their chief, when his power declines." I have chosen to give a paraphrase, rather than a translation, of this passage, as the original is verbose and frothy, notwithstanding of the sentimental merit of the author.—He was one of the less antient bards, and their compositions are not nervous enough to bear a literal translation. [M]

5.   like] *deleted* 1773

6.   the chief of Sar-dronlo.] Ton-thormod in fight. 1773

7.   in fight.] in war. 1773

8.   isle,] isle, I said, 1773

9.   arms] hands 1773

Colna-dona

1.   Toscar] Toscar, the son of Conloch and father of Malvina, 1773

2.   Colna-dona signifies *the love of heroes*. Col-amon, *narrow river*. Car-ul, *dark-eyed*. Col-amon, the residence of Car-ul, was in the neighbourhood of Agricola's wall, towards the south. Car-ul seems to have been of the race of those Britons, who are distinguished by the name of Maiatæ, by the writers of Rome. Maiatæ is derived from two Galic words, MOI, *a plain*, and AITICH, *inhabitants*; so that the significa-tion of Maiatæ is, *the inhabitants of the plain country*, a name given to the Britons, who were settled in the Lowlands, in contradistinction to the Caledonians, (i.e. CAEL-DON, *the Gauls of the hills*) who were possessed of the more mountainous division of North-Britain. [M]

The French were among a number of European nations who imagined they had a proprietary interest in Ossian. Such notes indicate why.

3.   Crona, *murmuring*, was the name of a small stream, which discharged itself in the river Carron. It is often mentioned by Ossian, and the scenes of many of his poems are on its banks.—The enemies, whom Fingal defeated here, are not men-tioned. They were, probably, the provincial Britons. That tract of country between the Firths of Forth and Clyde has been, thro' all antiquity, famous for battles and rencounters, between the different nations, who were possessed of North and South Britain. Stirling, a town situated there, derives its name from that very circum-

stance. It is a corruption of the Galic name, STRILA, i.e. *the hill, or rock, of contention.* [M]

4. The manners of the Britons and Caledonians were so similar, in the days of Ossian, that there can be no doubt, that they were originally the same people, and descended from those Gauls who first possessed themselves of South-Britain, and gradually migrated to the north. This hypothesis is more rational than the idle fables of ill-informed senachies, who bring the Caledonians from distant countries. The bare opinion of Tacitus, (which, by-the-bye, was only founded on a similarity of the personal figure of the Caledonians to the Germans of his own time) tho' it has staggered some learned men, is not sufficient to make us believe, that the antient inhabitants of North-Britain were a German colony. A discussion of a point like this might be curious, but could never be satisfactory. Periods so distant are so involved in obscurity, that nothing certain can be now advanced concerning them. The light which the Roman writers hold forth is too feeble to guide us to the truth, thro' the darkness which has surrounded it. [M]

5. trees with their leaves.] trees before him. 1763 branches before him. 1773
6. placed] kindled 1773
7. Here an episode is intirely lost; or, at least, is handed down so imperfectly, that it does not deserve a place in the poem. [M]
8. seized] seized with love 1773
9. heaved] rose 1763 1773
10. rising] trembling 1763 rising graceful 1773

A Specimen of the Original of Temora

1. *The* Specimen *is omitted from the revised edition of 1773. As to the status and quality of the Gaelic, the reader is referred Thomson, pp. 86 f. It is generally reckoned to be better than most of what was subsequently offered in the Gaelic Ossian of 1807 - particularly if Macpherson's kinsman, Lachlan Macpherson of Strathmashie (no mean poet in his own right), is thought to be the author. There is, however, no direct evidence that the text emanated from Strathmashie's pen, and it should not be forgotten that in 1763 James's Gaelic would still have been relatively fresh (the legend that his competence in his native tongue was deficient can be shown to rest on shaky foundations). What might perhaps speak in favour of someone else's authorship are the deviations from the English of 1763. Certainly, in the* Works *edition of 1765 Macpherson is at pains to harmonize the English with the Gaelic retrospectively, and this accounts for the large number of unique readings in the 1765 version of* 'Temora' VII *(in the 1773 edition, which does not include the* Specimen, *the original English is largely reinstated). It can probably be safely assumed that the* Specimen *was precisely that - Macpherson's thoughts would have turned to the production of a Gaelic "original" at a relatively early stage, and his phrasing here, in the* Advertisement, *suggests that what was put on display at his publisher's shop consisted, not of ancient manuscripts (and he did have some), but of a copy of a more or less complete Gaelic* 'Fingal', *concocted by Macpherson himself, with or without help from his friends. (For further speculations about these matters, see Gaskill,* 'What did James Macpherson really leave at his publisher's shop in 1762?'.) *When the* Specimen *appeared, the spelling of Scottish Gaelic had not yet stabilized. For the 1807 pseudo-originals the versions left behind by Macpherson on his death in 1796 were re-transcribed, using the conventions of the*

Gaelic Bible of 1767. And they appeared in Roman characters. - for a time Macpherson had seriously considered using Greek.

2.   *In the case of many elisions in this text, it is not always easy to determine whether a space is intended following the apostrophe. So with the particle* dh', *used to indicate a past tense before a verb beginning with a vowel. But the practice observed does appear to be inconsistent (in 1763 less so), and the safest course seemed to be to reproduce the text as (apparently) printed in 1765 - it was after all in this form that the ur-*Ossian *appeared to intrepid Germans such as Herder and Goethe who made their heroic attempts at translation, armed with an Irish-English dictionary and little else.*

3.   A dealra'] A dcalra' 1763 1765 (*also Laing*) - *misprint; corrected in 1807*

4.   English (p. 279): But when the third sound arose ... *The Gaelic omits the* But *and makes what follows a continuation of the effects of the second beating of the shield.*

5.   air an t'shluaigh,] air an l'shluaigh, 1763 1765 (*also Laing*) - *misprint; see second line of preceding stanza; corrected in 1807 to* air an t-sluagh

6.   am fionas] am fion as 1765 (*also Laing*) - *misprint, caused by defective type-setting in 1763*

7.   'S ám] 'Sám 1765 (*misprint*)

8.   a] á 1763

9.   illsich] ilsich 1763 (*although the 1765 version also has this spelling in the second stanza - modern Scots Gaelic:* illsich/islich = *lower, abase*)

10.   fein.] fein, 1765 (*misprint*)

11.   á nceo.] á neco. 1765 (*misprint -* an ceò = *the mist; fog.*)

12.   na] no 1765 (*misprint*)

13.   English (p. 283): The joy of grief belongs to Ossian, amidst his dark-brown years. *Here we have the first published (and perhaps none too successful) attempt to render the famous Ossianic* joy of grief *into Gaelic. According to Stern (p. 65), in the pseudo-originals of 1807 it is hardly ever translated the same twice.*

Blair's A Critical Dissertation on the Poems of Ossian

1.   *For the publication history of Blair's immensely influential* Dissertation, *see Jiriczek, 'Zur Bibliographie und Textgeschichte von Hugh Blair's* Critical Dissertation on the Poems of Ossian'; *also Steve Rizza, 'A Bulky and Foolish Treatise?'. The first edition appeared at the beginning of 1763 in identical format to* Fingal, *with which it could be bound if the reader so desired. The subsequent publication of* Temora *in March of that year meant that Blair's thoughts soon turned to the preparation of a new, revised edition. However, at the prompting of David Hume, it was felt advisable that this should contain convincing evidence as to the authenticity of the Ossianic poems. It was towards the gathering of such that Blair's energies were directed from autumn 1763, so that the expanded edition, complete with authenticating 'Appendix', did not in fact appear until the middle of 1765, shortly before the* Works of Ossian, *in whose second volume it is included (with page references to that edition). All subsequent (authorized) editions of* Ossian *published during Macpherson's lifetime, and most 19th-century ones, contain the* Dissertation *(though not the 'Appendix'); the page references are, however, omitted (latterly most of the notes as well), and the quotations from* Ossian, *which were in any case*

still based on the original editions, not that of 1765, are not adjusted to conform with the more radical textual revisions of 1773.

It is easy to underestimate the prestige which Hugh Blair enjoyed well into the nineteenth century, not just in Britain, but throughout Europe and beyond. As with Cesarotti, the unconditional public support of someone of this stature for the value of Macpherson's work has to be regarded as an extremely important factor in its reception. In addition to its historical significance, it should also be said that the Dissertation *provides us with literary exegesis of generally very high quality - Ossian has never been better served.*

2.   Olaus Wormius, in the appendix to his Treatise de Literatura Runica, has given a particular account of the Gothic poetry, commonly called Runic, from *Runes*, which signifies the Gothic letters. He informs us that there were no fewer than 136 different kinds of measure or verse used in their *Vyses*; and though we are accustomed to call rhyme a Gothic invention, he says expressly, that among all these measures, rhyme, or correspondence of final syllables, was never employed. He analyses the structure of one of these kinds of verse, that in which the poem of Lodbrog, afterwards quoted, is written; which exhibits a very singular species of harmony, if it can be allowed that name, depending neither upon rhyme nor upon metrical feet, or quantity of syllables, but chiefly upon the number of the syllables, and the disposition of the letters. In every stanza was an equal number of lines: in every line six syllables. In each distich, it was requisite that three words should begin with the same letter; two of the corresponding words placed in the first line of the distich, the third, in the second line. In each line were also required two syllables, but never the final ones, formed either of the same consonants, or same vowels. As an example of this measure, Olaus gives us these two Latin lines constructed exactly according to the above rules of Runic verse;

Christus caput nostrum/ Coronet te bonis.

The initial letters of Christus, Caput and Coronet, make the three corresponding letters of the distich. In the first line, the first syllables of Christus and of nostrum; in the second line, the *on* in coronet and in bonis make the requisite correspondence of syllables. Frequent inversions and transpositions were permitted in this poetry; which would naturally follow from such laborious attention to the collocation of words.

The curious on this subject may consult likewise Dr. Hick's Thesaurus Linguarum Septentrionalium; particularly the 23d chapter of his Grammatica Anglo Saxonica & Mæso Gothica; where they will find a full account of the structure of the Anglo-Saxon verse, which nearly resembled the Gothic. They will find also some specimens both of Gothic and Saxon poetry. An extract, which Dr. Hicks has given from the work of one of the Danish Scalders, entitled, Hervarer Saga, containing an evocation from the dead, may be found in the 6th volume of Miscellany Poems, published by Mr. Dryden. [B]

3.

1.

Pugnavimus Ensibus/ Haud post longum tempus/ Cum in Gotlandia accessimus/ Ad serpentis immensi necem/ Tunc impetravimus Thoram/ Ex hoc vocarunt me virum/ Quod serpentem transfodi/ Hirsutam braccam ob illam cedem/ Cuspide ictum intuli in colubrum/ Ferro lucidorum stipendiorum.

2.

Multum juvenis fui quando acquisivimus/ Orientem versus in Oreonico freto/ Vulnerum amnes avidæ feræ/ Et flavipedi avi/ Accepimus ibidem sonuerunt/ Ad sublimes galeas/ Dura ferra magnam escam/ Omnis erat oceanus vulnus/ Vadavit corvus in sanguine Cæsorum.

3.

Alte tulimus tunc lanceas/ Quando viginti annos numeravimus/ Et celebrem laudem comparavimus passim/ Vicimus octo barones/ In oriente ante Dimini portum/ Aquilæ impetravimus tunc sufficientem/ Hospitii sumptum in illa strage/ Sudor decidit in vulnerum/ Oceano perdid:ᵗ exercitus ætatem.

4.

Pugnæ facta copia/ Cum Helsingianos postulavimus/ Ad aulam Odini/ Naves direximus in ostium Vistulæ/ Mucro potuit tum mordere/ Omnis erat vulnus unda/ Terra rubefacta Calido/ Frendebat gladius in loricas/ Gladius findebat Clypeos.

5.

Memini neminem tunc fugisse/ Priusquam in navibus/ Heraudus in bello caderet/ Non findit navibus/ Alius baro præstantior/ Mare ad portum/ In navibus longis post illum/ Sic attulit princeps passim/ Alacre in bellum cor.

6.

Exercitus abjecit clypeos/ Cum hasta volavit/ Ardua ad virorum pectora/ Momordit Scarforum cautes/ Gladius in pugna/ Sanguineus erat Clypeus/ Antequam Rafno rex caderet/ Fluxit ex virorum capitibus/ Calidus in loricas sudor.

7.

Habere potuerunt tum corvi/ Ante Indirorum insulas/ Sufficientem prædam dilaniandam/ Acquisivimus feris carnivoris/ Plenum prandium unico actu/ Difficile erat unius facere mentionem/ Oriente sole/ Spicula vidi pungere/ Propulerunt arcus ex se ferra.

8.

Altum mugierunt enses/ Antequam in Laneo campo/ Eislinus rex cecidit/ Processimus auro ditati/ Ad terram prostratorum dimicandum/ Gladius secuit Clypeorum/ Picturas in galearum conventu/ Cervicum mustum ex vulneribus/ Diffusum per cerebrum fissum.

9.

Tenuimus Clypeos in sanguine/ Cum hastam unximus/ Ante Boring holmum/ Telorum nubes disrumpunt clypeum/ Extrusit arcus ex se metallum/ Volnir cecidit in conflictu/ Non erat illo rex major/ Cæsi dispersi late per littora/ Feræ amplectebantur escam.

10.

Pugna manifeste crescebat/ Antequam Freyr rex caderet/ In Flandrorum terra/ Cæpit cæruleus ad incidendum/ Sanguine illitus in auream/ Loricam in pugna/ Durus armorum mucro olim/ Virgo deploravit matutinam lanienam/ Multa præda dabatur feris.

11.

Centies centenos vidi jacere/ In navibus/ Ubi Ænglanes vocatur/ Navigavimus ad pugnam/ Per sex dies antequam exercitus caderet/ Transegimus mucronum missam/ In exortu solis/ Coactus est pro nostris gladiis/ Valdiofur in bello occumbere.

12.

Ruit pluvia sanguinis de gladiis/ Præceps in Bardafyrde/ Pallidum corpus pro accipitribus/ Murmuravit arcus ubi mucro/ Acriter mordebat Loricas/ In conflictu/ Odini Pileus Galea/ Cucurrit arcus ad vulnus/ Venenate acutus conspersus sudore sanguineo.

13.

Tenuimus magica scuta/ Alte in pugnæ ludo/ Ante Hiadningum sinum/ Videre licuit tum viros/ Qui gladiis lacerarunt Clypeos/ In gladiatorio murmure/ Galeæ attritæ virorum/ Erat sicut splendidam virginem/ In lecto juxta se collocare.

14.

Dura venit tempestas Clypeis/ Cadaver cecidit in terram/ In Nortumbria/ Erat circa matutinum tempus/ Hominibus necessum erat fugere/ Ex prælio ubi acute/ Cassidis campos mordebant gladii/ Erat hoc veluti Juvenem viduam/ In primaria sede osculari.

15.

Herthiofe evasit fortunatus/ In Australibus Orcadibus ipse/ Victoriæ in nostris hominibus/ Cogebatur in armorum nimbo/ Rogvaldus occumbere/ Iste venit summus super accipitres/ Luctus in gladiorum ludo/ Strenue jactabat concussor/ Galeæ sanguinis teli.

16.

Quilibet jacebat transversim supra alium/ Gaudebat pugna lætus/ Accipiter ob gladiorum ludum/ Non fecit aquilam aut aprum/ Qui Irlandiam gubernavit/ Conventus fiebat ferri & Clypei/ Marstanus rex jejunis/ Fiebat in vedræ sinu/ Præda data corvis.

17.

Bellatorem multum vidi cadere/ Mane ante machæram/ Virum in mucronum dissidio/ Filio meo incidit mature/ Gladius juxta cor/ Egillus fecit Agnerum spoliatum/ Impertertitum virum vita/ Sonuit lancea prope Hamdi/ Griseam loricam splendebant vexilla.

18.

Verborum tenaces vidi dissecare/ Haut minutim pro lupis/ Endili maris ensibus/ Erat per Hebdomadæ spacium/ Quasi mulieres vinum apportarent/ Rubefactæ erant naves/ Valde in strepitu armorum/ Scissa erat lorica/ In Scioldungorum prælio.

19.

Pulchricomum vidi crepusculascere/ Virginis amatorem circa matutinum/ Et confabulationis amicum viduarum/ Erat sicut calidum balneum/ Vinei vasis nympha portaret/ Nos in Ilæ freto/ Antiquam Orn rex caderet/ Sanguineum Clypeum vidi ruptum/ Hoc invertit virorum vitam.

20.

Egimus gladiorum ad cædem/ Ludum in Lindis insula/ Cum regibus tribus/ Pauci potuerunt inde lætari/ Cecidit multus in rictum ferarum/ Accipiter dilaniavit carnem cum lupo/ Ut satur inde discederet/ Hybernorum sanguis in oceanum/ Copiose decidit per mactationis tempus.

21.

Alte gladius mordebat Clypeos/ Tunc cum aurei coloris/ Hasta fricabat loricas/ Videre licuit in Onlugs insula/ Per secula multum post/ Ibi fuit ad gladiorum ludos/ Reges processerunt/ Rubicundum erat circa insulam/ Ar volans Draco vulnerum.

22.

Quid est viro forti morte certius/ Etsi ipse in armorum nimbo/ Adversus collocatus sit/ Sæpe deplorat ætatem/ Qui nunquam premitur/ Malum ferunt timidum incitare/ Aquilam ad gladiorum ludum/ Meticulosus venit nuspiam/ Cordi suo usui.

23.

Hoc numero æquum ut procedat/ In contactu gladiorum/ Juvenis unus contra alterum/ Non retrocedat vir a viro/ Hoc fuit viri fortis nobilitas diu/ Semper debet amoris amicus virginum/ Audax esse in fremitu armorum.

24.

Hoc videtur mihi re vera/ Quod fata sequimur/ Rarus transgreditur fata Parcarum/ Non destinavi Ellæ/ De vitæ exitu meæ/ Cum ego sanguinem semimortuus tegerem/ Et naves in aquas protrusi/ Passim impetravimus tum feris/ Escam in Scotiæ sinubus.

25.

Hoc ridere me facit semper/ Quod Balderi patris scamna/ Parata scio in aula/ Bibemus cerevisiam brevi/ Ex concavis crateribus craniorum/ Non gemit vir fortis contra mortem/ Magnifici in Odini domibus/ Non venio desperabundis/ Verbis ad Odini aulam.

26.

Hic vellent nunc omnes/ Filii Aslaugæ gladiis/ Amarum bellum excitare/ Si exacte scirent/ Calamitates nostras/ Quem non pauci angues/ Venenati me discerpunt/ Matrem accepi meis/ Filiis ita ut corda valeant.

27.

Valde inclinatur ad hæreditatem/ Crudele stat nocumentum a vipera/ Anguis inhabitat aulam cordis/ Speramus alterius ad Othini/ Virgam in Ellæ sanguine/ Filiis meis livescet/ Sua ira rubescet/ Non acres juvenes/ Sessionem tranquillam facient.

28.

Habeo quinquagies/ Prælia sub signis facta/ Ex belli invitatione & semel/ Minime putavi hominum/ Quod me futurus esset/ Juvenis didici mucronem rubefacere/ Alius rex præstantior/ Nos Asæ invitabunt/ Non est lugenda mors.

29.

Fert animus finire/ Invitant me Dysæ/ Quas ex Othini Aula/ Othinus mihi misit/ Lætus cerevisiam cum Asis/ In summa sede bibam/ Vitæ elapsæ sunt horæ/ Ridens moriar. [B]

Since they form an essential part of his argument, and may also be regarded as an important contemporary source of information on such matters, Blair's notes and their quotations have been preserved in full. They are, however, given exactly as printed and no attempt has been made to correct errors or check the accuracy of the references. For technical reasons it has, however, been necessary to sanitize the Greek. I am extremely grateful to Gordon Howie for his advice. Any remaining "gobbledegreek" is my responsibility (or Blair's).

4. This was the name of his enemy who had condemned him to death. [B]

5. Τρία φῦλα τῶν τιμωμένων διαφερόντως ἐστί. Βαρδοι τε καὶ οὐάτεις, καὶ Δρῦιδαι. Βαρδοι μὲν ὑμηταὶ καὶ ποιηταὶ. Strabo. lib. 4.; Εἰσὶ παρ' αὐτοῖς καὶ ποιηταὶ μελῶν, οὓς βαρδους ὀνομαζουσιν. οὗτοι δὲ μετ' ὀργάνων, ταῖς λύραις ὁμοίων, οὓς μὲν ὑμνοῦσι, οὓς δὲ βλασφημοῦσι. Diodor. Sicul. 1. 5.; Τὰ δὲ ἀκούσματα αὐτῶν εἰσιν οἱ καλούμενοι βαρδοι. ποιηταὶ δ' οὗτοι τυγχάνουσι μετ' ᾠδῆς ἐπαίνους λέγοντες. Posidonius ap. Athenæum. 1. 6. [B]

6.   Per hæc loca (speaking of Gaul) hominibus paulatim excultis, *viguere studia ladabilium doctrinarum*; inchoata per Bardos & Euhages & Druidas. Et Bardi quidem fortia virorum illustrium facta heroicis composita versibus cum dulcibus lyræ modulis cantitarunt. Euhages vero scrutantes seriem & sublimia naturæ pandere conabantur. Inter hos, Druidæ ingeniis celsiores, ut auctoritas Pythagoræ decrevit, sodalitiis adstricti consortiis, quæstionibus altarum occultarumque rerum erecti sunt; & despectantes humana pronuntiarunt animas immortales. Amm. Marcellinus, l. 15. cap. 9. [B]

7.   Vid. Cæsar de bello Gall. lib. 6. [B]

8.   *In the extended version of his* Dissertation *Blair's page references, given as footnotes, are to the edition of 1765, though the text of the quotations has not been updated. Here the page numbers are those of the present edition and are inserted in parentheses in the text (those in square brackets are editorial additions). Where Blair uses dashes to indicate omissions, they have been replaced by dots to avoid confusion with Macpherson's own dashes. Where the latter are omitted by Blair (and they usually are), they have not been reinstated here. In fact, apart from the insertion of the odd alternative or missing word in square brackets, none of his apparent deviations (from the originals of 1762/63) have been corrected, since some or even most are probably intentional. This seems particularly to be the case with the punctuation: commas are occasionally omitted, more often replaced by semi-colons; semi-colons and colons can be turned into full-stops. In this and other respects, for instance in the addition of exclamation marks, Blair curiously antici-pates Macpherson's own revisions of 1773. Although this may simply testify to a certain insouciance with regard to accurate quotation, it is likely that Blair thought he was rectifying some of his immediate source's idiosyncrasies - as a mere trans-lation there could be nothing sacrosanct about Macpherson's text (for which Blair himself had in any case played the role of midwife).*

9.   Surely among the wild Laplanders, if any where, barbarity is in its most perfect state. Yet their love songs which Scheffer has given us in his Lapponia, are a proof that natural tenderness of sentiment may be found in a country, into which the least glimmering of science has never penetrated. To most English readers these songs are well known by the elegant translations of them in the Spectator, $N^{\underline{o}}$. 366 and 406. I shall subjoin Scheffer's Latin version of one of them, which has the appearance of being strictly literal.

Sol, clarissimum emitte lumen in paludem Orra. Si enisus in summa picearum cacumina scirem me visurum Orra paludem, in ea eniterer, ut viderem inter quos amica, mea esset flores; omnes suscinderem frutices ibi enatos, omnes ramos præsecarem, hos virentes ramos. Cursum nubium essem secutus, quæ iter suum istituunt versus paludem Orra, si ad te volare possem alis, cornicum alis. Sed mihi desunt alæ, alæ querquedulæ, pedesque, anserum pedes plantæve bonæ, quæ deferre me valeant ad te. Satis expectasti diu; per tot dies, tot dies tuos optimos, oculis tuis jucundissimis, corde tuo amicissimo. Quod si longissime velles effugere, cito tamen te consequerer. Quid firmius validiusve esse potest quam contortinervi, catenæve ferreæ, quæ durissime ligant? Sic amor contorquet caput nostrum, mutat cogitationes & sententias. Puerorum voluntas, voluntas venti; juvenum cogitationes, longæ cogitationes. Quos si audirem omnes, a via, a via justa declinarem. Unum est consilium quod capiam; ita scio viam rectiorem me reperturum. Schefferi Lapponia, Cap. 25. [B]

As with the ubiquitous 'Regner Lodbrog', *references to the Lapp "juoiks", first popularized by Addison in the* Spectator *in 1712, were to become almost obligatory in primitivist discourse in the second half of the 18th century: Herder's - for Germany - seminal essay of 1773,* Über Oßian und die Lieder alter Völker' *(which is in some respects derivative of Blair almost to the point of plagiarism), includes a translation of this particular song. There is in fact a nice irony in its choice. Blair's source here is Scheffer's* Lapponia *of 1673. But Scheffer's source had been Olaus Sirma, the literate Lapp who had been collared by the author and enjoined to produce some of his native poetry in Swedish translation. The parallel with Macpherson is quite striking, particularly when one knows how the first Ossianic fragments were squeezed out of him by John Home and latterly Hugh Blair himself. Both Macpherson and Sirma were born into one culture, wholly or predominantly oral, and educated in another which was distinctly bookish. Both seem to have been extremely self-conscious about their origins, viewing them with a mixture of shame and pride, aware of a rich and vital literary tradition to which outsiders had no access, but fearful of exposing it to a polished people, lest it be ridiculed as barbarous. Though one should not perhaps press the parallel too far, it seems that both reacted in a similar fashion: they gave their audience what they thought it could take, carefully rationing what they saw as the rudeness of the original to acceptable doses and injecting a note of what Blair calls* "natural tenderness of sentiment."

10.   When Edward I. conquered Wales, he put to death all the Welch bards. This cruel policy plainly shews, how great an influence he imagined the songs of these bards to have over the minds of the people; and of what nature he judged that influence to be. The Welch bards were of the same Celtic race with the Scottish and Irish. [B]

11.   *No reference given. This is in fact a slightly adapted quotation from* 'Temora' III *- see above, p. 246 - and is added in the 1765 version of the* Dissertation.

12.   Their skill in navigation need not at all surprize us. Living in the western islands, along the coast, or in a country which is every where intersected with arms of the sea, one of the first objects of their attention, from the earliest time, must have been how to traverse the waters. Hence that knowledge of the stars, so necessary for guiding them by night, of which we find several traces in Ossian's works; particularly in the beautiful description of Cathmor's shield, in the 7th book of Temora. Among all the northern maritime nations, navigation was very early studied. Piratical incursions were the chief means they employed for acquiring booty; and were among the first exploits which distinguished them in the world. Even the savage Americans were at their first discovery found to possess the most surprizing skill and dexterity in navigating their immense lakes and rivers.

The description of Cuchullin's chariot, in the 1st book of Fingal, has been objected to by some, as representing greater magnificence than is consistent with the supposed poverty of that age. But this chariot is plainly only a horse-litter; and the gems mentioned in the description, are no other than the shining stones or pebbles, known to be frequently found along the western coast of Scotland. [B]

13.   *In fact:* deer and woods.

14.   *Macpherson:* The battle ceased along the field, for the bard had sung the song of peace.

15. *This quotation from* 'Oina-morul' - *see above p. 323 - replaces the one used in the first edition of the* Dissertation: "the light of his soul arose; the days of other years rose before him", *which I have been unable to trace.*

16. Iliad 16. 830, Il. 17. 127. [B]

17. When he commands his sons, after Swaran is taken prisoner, to "pursue the rest of Lochlin, over the heath of Lena; that no vessel may hereafter bound on the dark-rolling waves of Inistore;" he means not assuredly, as some have mis-represented him, to order a general slaughter of the foes, and to prevent their saving themselves by flight; but, like a wise general, he commands his chiefs to render the victory compleat, by a total rout of the enemy; that they might adventure no more for the future, to fit out any fleet against him or his allies. [B]
Cf. 'Fingal' V, *above, p. 92*

18. *A composite quotation: the first sentence (*They rest ... mortal men.*) is from* 'Fingal' II, *above, p. 66; the second (*Their songs ... worlds.*) from* 'The Six Bards', *appended to* 'Croma', *above, p. 190; the third is a generalisation, based on the appearance of Crugal's ghost in* 'Fingal' II, *above, p. 67:* He comes to the ear of rest, and raises his feeble voice. *In addition, Blair gives the following references: 114, 116, and 170.*

19. *Macpherson:* My hero saw in his rest a dark-red stream of fire coming down from the hill. *(p. 65) Whence it would seem that the vision occurs as a dream, one from which the* son *of battle is later said to wake.*

20. *Macpherson:* a chief that lately fell. He fell by the hand of Swaran,

21. Job iv. 13-17. [B]

22. Odyss. Lib. 11. [B]

23. *Slightly adapted quotation from Colma's lament in the* 'Songs of Selma'.

24. The scene of this encounter of Fingal with the spirit of Loda is laid in Inistore, or the islands of Orkney; and in the description of Fingal's landing there, it is said, p. [160]. "A rock bends along the coast with [all] its echoing wood. On the top is the circle of Loda, with [and] the mossy stone of power." In confirmation of Ossian's topography, it is proper to acquaint the reader that in these islands, as I have been well informed, there are many pillars, and circles of stones, still remaining, known by the name of the stones and circles of Loda, or Loden; to which some degree of superstitious regard is annexed to this day. These islands, until the year 1468, made a part of the Danish dominions. Their ancient language, of which there are yet some remains among the natives, is called the Norse; and is a dialect, not of the Celtic, but of the Scandinavian tongue. The manners and the superstitions of the inhabi-tants, are quite distinct from those of the Highlands and western isles of Scotland. Their ancient songs too, are of a different strain and character, turning upon magical incantations and evocations from the dead, which were the favourite subjects of the old Runic poetry. They have many traditions among them of wars in former times with the inhabitants of the western islands. [B]

25. *This passage, ending with* than to dwell on all his beauties., *p. 374, is added in 1765.*

26. *Literally, in fact only in* 'Temora' III and VIII - *see above, pp. 245, 288, 291.*

27. *See above,* 'Temora' VI, *p. 275 - the reading* tearful *is peculiar to the edition of 1765.*

28. *Adapted from* 'Temora' III, *above, p.246.*

29. *Blair's original reference* - vol. ii. p. 49 - *is inaccurate by 16 pages (it should be* vol. ii. 65*). Similarly the previous reference given (for* few are the marks of my sword ...*) is nine pages out (vol. ii. 30, instead of* vol. ii. 39*). The evident reason for this is that Blair wrote with the text of the 1763 quarto* Temora *in front of him and later neglected to update the page references here (subsequent ones are correct).*

30. *The last sentence quoted is an amalgam of two separated by a third in the original, and the order is reversed.*

31. *An example of Blair's "improvements". The original reads:* and strewed, with dead, the heath. *Nor did Blair apparently approve of the hyphen in* wide-spreading.

32. *Macpherson:* Shall Fingal take the sword of Luno? But what should become of thy fame, son of white-bosomed Clatho?

33. *The original edition here contains a brief passage on the '*Temora*' fragment, as initially published in* Fingal.

34. Vid. Huetius de origine fabularum Romanensium. [B]

35. *Macpherson (above, p. 189):* when their renown is heard! The feeble will not behold them in the hall; or smile at their trembling hands.

36. *No source given. It would not appear to be Classical Latin.*

37. *The* O *before* Toscar *is Blair's embellishment. For that he omits the epithet* car-borne *and transforms* Conloch *into* Comloch *(corrected here).*

38. *Paragraph added in 1765.*

39. *As Jiriczek points out (3:229), in Macpherson* Loda *refers to the cultic stone circles, or to Valhalla, but is never identified with Odin himself.*

40. See the rules of poetical description excellently illustrated by lord Kaims [*Kames = Henry Home*] in his Elements of Criticism, vol. iii. chap. 21. Of narration and description. [B]

41. *The reader may judge whether this is an improvement on:* Have not I seen the fallen Balclutha?

42. *Blair's original above is presumably a misprint, albeit an entertaining one.*

43. *Not so much the man as his hair.*

44. whilst *added by Blair.*

45. *See above, p. 62, note 101.*

46. Odyss. 11.211. Iliad 23.98. [B]

47. *Corrected from Blair's* breasts.

48. See Elements of Criticism, ch. 19. vol. 3. [B]

49. *Macpherson:* the darkened moon, the daughter of the starry skies, when she moves, a dun circle, through heaven.

50. *Blair's improvement on:* bright as the bow of heaven; as the moon on the western wave *(both '*Carric-thura*' and '*Fragment*' I), though the misspelt* Venvela *has been corrected here.*

51. There is a remarkable propriety in this comparison. It is intended to explain the effect of soft and mournful musick. Armin appears disturbed at a performance of this kind. Carmor says to him, "Why bursts the sigh of Armin? Is there a cause to mourn? The song comes with its musick to melt and please the ear. It is like soft mist, &c." that is, such mournful songs have a happy effect to soften the heart, and to improve it by tender emotions, as the moisture of the mist refreshes and nourishes the flowers; whilst the sadness they occasion is only transient, and soon dispelled by the succeeding occupations and amusements of life: "The sun returns in its strength, and the mist is gone." [B]

Armin may perhaps be forgiven for being disturbed at the prospect of his ear being melted, an indignity spared him by Macpherson.

52. old *added by Blair.*
53. by degrees *added by Blair in place of* slowly vanished *in the preceding (unquoted) clause.*
54. *The following passage, ending with* reedy pool, *is added in 1765.*
55. Iliad iv. 446. and Il. viii. 60. [B]
56. Iliad xiv. 393. [B]
57. Iliad iv. 275. [B]
58. *Blair's original reference is out by 100 pages: the quotation is from* 'The War of Inis-thona'.
59. Iliad, v. 522. [B]
60. *Again something of a paraphrase: the* slowly *is imported from the previous clause, and* having long *is in fact* long having.
61. *Blair reverses the order of the sentences.*
62. Iliad, xxii. 26. [B]
63. Iliad, xvii. 53. [B]
64. Iliad, xiii. 298. [B]
65. See Dr. Lowth de Sacra Poesi Hebræorum. [B]
66. Isaiah xvii. 13. [B]
67. *Blair has* Trathal, *and his original reference, as printed, is out by 200 pages.*
68. Numbers xiii. 32, 33. [B]
69. Milton's Lycidas. See Theocrit. Idyll. 1: Πᾶ ποκ' ἀρ ἦσθ' ὁκα Δάφνις ἐτάκετο; πᾶ ποκα, Νύμφαι, &c. And Virg. Eclog. 10: Quæ nemora, aut qui vos saltus habuere, puellæ, &c. [B]
70. The noted saying of Julius Cæsar, to the pilot in a storm; "Quid times? Cæsarem vehis;" is magnanimous and sublime. Lucan, not satisfied with this simple conciseness, resolved to amplify and improve the thought. Observe, how every time he twists it round, it departs farther from the sublime, till, at last, it ends in tumid declamation.

Sperne minas, inquit, Pelagi, ventoque furenti/ Trade sinum, Italiam, si cœlo auctore, recusas,/ Me, pete. Sola tibi causa hæc est justa timoris/ Vectorem non nosse tuum; quem numina nunquam/ Destituunt; de quo male tunc fortuna meretur,/ Cum post vota venit; medias perrumpe procellas/ Tutelâ secure meâ. Coeli iste fretique,/ Non puppis nostræ, labor est. Hanc Cæsare pressam/ A fluctu defendit onus./ ——Quid tantâ strage paratur,/ Ignoras? Quærit pelagi cælique tumultu/ Quid præstet fortuna mihi.—— PHARSAL. V. 578. [B]

71. *A composite quotation,* æstuat ... pudor *being from Virgil, Aeneid, 10.870 f., and* conscia virtus *from Aeneid, 5.455. (I am obliged to Roy Pinkerton for providing me with the references.)*
72. Ossian himself is poetically called the voice of Cona. [B]

Critical Dissertation: Appendix

1. *John Home.*
2. *The most urgent urging emanated from David Hume.*
3. *For the use made by Blair of Sir James Macdonald's testimony, and the latter's role in promoting Ossian in Paris in the mid-1760s (together with David Hume), see David Raynor, 'Ossian and Hume', pp. 155 f.*

Preface to *The Poems of Ossian* (1773)

1.   *For Macpherson's pre-Ossianic poetry, including the* Highlander *(1758), see* Laing, *2:445 ff.*
2.   The Gaëlic name of Scandinavia, or Scandinia. [M]
3.   The mountains of Sevo. [M]

INDEX and REGISTER
of names used by Macpherson in text and notes

between Culgorm and Suran-dronlo. 301-2, 307, 314-15, 533

Job - 367, 422, 445, 549
Judges - 442
Jura - Hebridean island; name of Fura in 'Fragment' XI. 22,
Juteland - 216, 516
Jutland - 421

Keating - Geoffrey Keating; Irish historian (1570-1644). 201, 211, 217, 220, 450, 525, 538
Keneth - 9th century king of Scotland; Keneth Mac-Alpin. See also Conad. 517-18, 523
Kenneth - see Keneth.
Kinfena[1] - father of the bard Carril; "Cean-feana, i.e. *the head of the people*". 54, 61, 236, 249, 423, 462, 491, 500
Kinfena[2] - father of the (Irish) Toscar[2]. 443
Kings - (Bible). 454
Kirmor - name of Carmor in 'Fragment' XI. 22

Lamdarg - "the chief of other times"; pre-sumably identical with Lamderg. 76
Lamderg - "chief of Cromla"; lover of Gel-chossa for whom he fights and kills Ullin[3], dying himself; "Lamh-dhearg, *bloody hand*". 31, 90, 93-5, 431-2
Lamgal - Colmal assumes the name of son of Lamgal when disguised as a young warrior. 172
Lamhor - ancient hero who reports the fall of Cuchullin to the sons of Usnoth in Tura; "Lamh-mhor, *mighty hand*". 144, 454
Lamor - son of Garmállon, father of Hidallan; chief of Balva; slaughters disgraced son. 111-12, 436
Lano - "lake in Scandinavia, remarkable for emitting a pestilential vapour in autumn". 57, 87, 112, 116-7, 124, 145, 348, 367, 440
Lánul - daughter of Cathmol; "Lánul, *full-eyed*". See Cathlin. 294-5, 530
Lanul[1] - see Lánul. 294
Lanul[2] - wife of Duth-maruno. 314
Lara - "the river Lara in the neighbourhood of Lego"; "Lara, a country in Connaught". 54, 75, 136-7, 144, 237, 240, 248, 274, 279, 331, 368, 381, 421, 449, 515
Larmon - "Larmon's grassy hill"; presumably in Morven. 323
Larnir - companion-in-arms of Calmar. 450
Larthmor - petty king of Berrathon; vassal of the kings of Lochlin; hospitable to Fingal; deposed and imprisoned by his son Uthal, liberated and restored by Ossian and

Toscar[1]. 194-7, 472
Lartho - hall of Dargo[3]. 174-5
Larthon - "of Lumon" (Inis-huna); husband of Flathal[1]; ancestor of Cathmor; "Lear-thon, *sea-wave*, the name of the chief of that colony of the Fir-bolg, which first migrated into Ireland". 210, 257, 278, 282-3, 337-40, 480, 499, 520-1, 530
Lathmon - son of Nuäth, brother of Oithóna, husband or lover of Cutha; son of British or Pictish prince; defeated once by Fingal, he invades Morven, is defeated by Ossian, but Gaul saves his life whereupon he is recon-ciled with Fingal. 176, 178, 180-5, 375, 407, 466-9
Lavath - name of river; in 'Temora' it is in Ireland, near the mountain of Crommal. 195, 287, 503
Lego - "A lake in Connaught, in which the river Lara emptied itself"; "Leigo, *the lake of disease*, probably so called on account of the morasses which surrounded it". See esp. the opening of 'Temora' VII (279). 56, 65, 82-3, 99, 135-8, 144, 154, 233, 237, 249, 278-9, 288, 295-6, 331, 355, 359, 367, 392, 439, 448-9, 481, 485, 515, 530
Lena - "the heath of Lena"; on the coast of Ulster, near the mountain of Cromla; scene of 'Fingal' and 'Temora' (where it tends to be called Moi-lena). 55-6, 60, 62, 65-6, 68, 75-7, 83-7, 92-5, 99, 101-2, 104, 145, 148-53, 246, 288, 292, 360, 362, 367, 419, 434, 455, 549
Leogaire - (Laeghaire) Irish king. 201, 210
Leth[1] - one of Lathmon's warriors; slain by Gaul. 179
Leth[2] - Morlo son of Leth is Gaul's compan-ion-in-arms on expedition to Tromáthon. 183, 185, 469
Lethmal[1] - father of Clono. 505
Lethmal[2] - "the gray-haired bard of Selma" accompanies the young Ossian to Berra-thon. 196
Livy - 417
Loch Eta - "an arm of the sea in Lorn" (Loch Etive). 451
Lochlin - "The Galic name of Scandinavia in general; in a more confined sense that of the peninsula of Jutland". 37, 419, 421, *et passim*
Lochlyn - "the name of Denmark in the Erse language". See Lochlin. 6, 14, 28
Lochy - river in Inverness-shire. See Lotha. 462
Loda[1] - "the circle of Loda is a place of wor-ship among the Scandinavians ... There are some ruins and circular pales of stone, remaining still in Orkney, and the islands of

CPSIA information can be obtained
at www.ICGtesting.com
Printed in the USA
JSHW060725170123
36336JS00004B/261